Microsoft

MICROSOFT® .NET AND J2EE INTEROPERABILITY TOOLKIT

Microsoft .net

Simon Guest

PUBLISHED BY
Microsoft Press
A Division of Microsoft Corporation
One Microsoft Way
Redmond, Washington 98052-6399

Library of Congress Cataloging-in-Publication Data
Guest, Simon, 1973-
Microsoft .NET and J2EE Interoperability Toolkit / Simon Guest.
p. cm.
Includes index.
ISBN 0-7356-1922-0
1. Microsoft .NET. 2. Java (Computer program language). I. Title.

QA76.76.M52G84 2003
005.2'76--dc21 2003052790

Printed and bound in the United States of America.

1 2 3 4 5 6 7 8 9 QWT 8 7 6 5 4 3

Distributed in Canada by H.B. Fenn and Company Ltd.

A CIP catalogue record for this book is available from the British Library.

Microsoft Press books are available through booksellers and distributors worldwide. For further information about international editions, contact your local Microsoft Corporation office or contact Microsoft Press International directly at fax (425) 936-7329. Visit our Web site at www.microsoft.com/mspress. Send comments to *mspinput@microsoft.com*.

Acquisitions Editor: Anne Hamilton
Project Editor: Devon Musgrave
Technical Editor: Robert Brunner
Copyeditor: Michelle Goodman
Principal Desktop Publisher: Kerri DeVault
Interior Artist: Joel Panchot
Interior Graphic Designer: James D. Kramer
Cover Designer: Methodologie, Inc.

Body Part No. X09-71488

To Mako

Contents at a Glance

Table of Contents

Acknowledgments

Writing this book has been quite the adventure. Fortunately for me, this has been an adventure that I haven't had to endure alone. I'd like to spend a minute recognizing all the people that have helped make this book complete.

First, I'd like to thank Scott Kerfoot and Steven Ramirez, as they were the first people to get my material in front of an audience and they provided valuable feedback. And for extolling the virtues of turning my content into a written book (or at least planting the idea in my head), I'd like to extend a special thank you to Dan Begallie.

As I was writing this book, I often called on people for information or ideas. For offering solutions and extending support when needed, I would like to thank Keith Ballinger, Dino Chiesa, Fred Chong, Wayne Citrin, Manish Godse, David Hill, Joe Klug, John Nolte, Doug Purdy, Thomas Rizzo, Arvindra Sehmi, Gerry Shaw, and Hervey Wilson. Additional thanks must go to Adam Denning and Sanjay Parthasarathy for support (and continued publicity!) of the contents of the book.

Special thanks is also due to two companies that I worked closely with to produce the technical content of many chapters—Intrinsyc and The Mind Electric (TME), both of which offer invaluable products that make interoperability between the Java and Microsoft .NET platforms a reality today. At Intrinsyc, my extended thanks go to Roy Lim, Kerry Lynn, Damian Mehers, and Mike Preradovic. At TME, I would like to personally thank Graham Glass, Wes Moulder, Christopher St. John, and Bruce Sundquist.

Making sense of and providing feedback for my chapters was the "enviable" task of the reviewers who kindly donated their time to review each chapter. For this, I would like to thank Gianpaolo Carraro, Mark Demers, John deVadoss, Graham Glass, Shelby Goerlitz, Kevin Hammond, Kristopher Johnson, Doron Juster, Chris Kurt, Damian Mehers, Andy Milligan, Mark Piller, Matt Powell, Harris Reynolds, Bob Schmidt, Christopher St. John, Brenton Webster, David Weller, and Joe Yong. Many of these people went out of their way to provide feedback that ultimately had an incredible impact on the content.

Taking my ramblings and producing the book you see in front of you has been the responsibility of the fine people at Microsoft Press. It is this team that inarguably adds the professionalism and quality to each Microsoft Press title. For this, my heartfelt thanks go to Robert Brunner, my technical editor (and mentor) during the whole project. Despite dealing with sample code that rarely compiled, products that would not install, and machines that would not work, Robert persevered and delivered feedback that really made the book what it is today. For the content editing, I would like to thank Michelle Goodman. Michelle has a rare talent for taking the manuscript I delivered and making it read like a book. For keeping us all on track (and at times, sane), I'd like to recognize Devon Musgrave. On numerous occasions, Devon was the "point man" for making those "cut or keep" decisions. In addition, I must also include Anne Hamilton for taking the book idea on and managing the relationships, as well as Heather Freck, Matt Carter, Robert Lyon, Tess McMillan, Roger LeBlanc, and Joel Panchot for their continued involvement.

I would like to thank my family and friends, especially Mom and Ian, for their advice, support, and confidence with both the project and my move to the United States. A final and special mention goes to my wife Mako, who—despite the long nights and missed weekends—provided her love, support, and trust throughout. This wouldn't have been possible without you!

Introduction

During the past two years, I have presented on the subject of interoperability between Microsoft .NET and Sun's J2EE at a number of conferences, customer meetings, and internal seminars. The majority of the presentations I've given have concentrated on the key takeaways and elements presented in this book. I decided to write this book because I wanted to share this information with a wider audience. My rationale and support for interoperability has evolved over time based on my experience, my work on development projects, and most importantly, customer feedback.

When the Microsoft .NET Framework was first released, I spent a lot of time looking at migration strategies and how customers could move existing applications based on the J2EE platform to the .NET platform. I soon adopted the view that we should concentrate on developing a broad strategy for migrating from J2EE, starting with examining common code patterns in a J2EE application. I had a background in designing applications for the J2EE platform, and I discussed with peers and customers how particular J2EE components could map well to their .NET equivalents. I then began writing some prototype code for identifying these patterns in J2EE and for using refactoring processes to migrate them to .NET.

The work went well. I delivered a number of prototypes that took raw Java source code from J2EE applications and reconstructed .NET components with a relatively high degree of accuracy. With the help of a newly released product—Microsoft Visual J# .NET, which enables existing Microsoft Visual Studio .NET users to develop solutions using the Java language syntax on .NET—I created a number of key presentations and roadmaps.

I delivered one of my main presentations on the topic to the Southern California Architect Council in April 2002. This council is a group of top CTOs and CIOs from leading blue-chip enterprises in Southern California. The group gathers every quarter to discuss the direction and strategies for their adoption of Microsoft technology and products. I polished my "migration roadmap" presentation with some stunning (if I do say so myself) demos. Some of these demos showed samples first running under J2EE, and then running under .NET after a few clicks of the mouse. I eagerly imagined the jaw-dropping gasps and wide-eyed stares my presentation was sure to elicit from the audience members, whom I knew were running their solutions on existing implementations of J2EE.

Part of the process of presenting to such a select audience involves screening the slides with the organizers of the event. I forwarded my slide deck to a couple of colleagues from the Southern California Microsoft office for review and awaited their feedback. Their feedback was brutally honest. It went something like this:

"Simon, the migration message that you have for moving from J2EE to .NET is great. We think you have some excellent points, a great message, and some awesome demos."

I was beginning to enjoy the feedback…

"There's just one problem. Our customers aren't interested."

I was in shock. How could they not be interested? Did the customers invited to this event not care about .NET? Maybe they weren't J2EE adopters after all? Was I speaking to the right audience here?

I soon learned that the real reason wasn't that these customers weren't interested in .NET or that they weren't running any J2EE applications. It was that migration wasn't an option for them at that time. They didn't want to hear the "rip and replace" story from Microsoft, or anyone else—regardless of how accurate or technically astute that rip-and-replace story was. The facts showed that many of these CTOs and CIOs had already invested in J2EE. This commitment ranged from purchasing application servers from various J2EE vendors to building and training their own communities of developers and deploying production code. These executives weren't interested in entertaining a roadmap to migrate all their existing code to .NET just for the sake of moving to a new platform in the short term.

I still had some time before the presentation to absorb this feedback from my reviewers. Drawing on the energy and enthusiasm that I'd put into my migration strategy, I developed content based on interoperability—namely on strategies that would allow an application written for .NET to interoperate with an existing J2EE-based application. Given that migration often begins with interoperability, I was also able to recycle many parts of my original presentation.

The presentation, although not as rehearsed as I would've liked, went very well.

Defining Interoperability

What does the term *interoperability* really mean? What does it mean to "interoperate" or be "interoperable" when designing solutions? A number of definitions are available depending on whom you speak to or where you search.

Some define interoperability in terms of relationships; others have a much more specific view based on the technology that they're describing.

To define this term, I use a three-part explanation: one formal, one pictorial, and one comparative. The first part of the definition, the formal part, is derived from the ISO Information Technology Vocabulary and looks like this:

Interoperability enables communication, data exchange, or program execution among various systems in a way that requires the user to have little or no awareness of the underlying operations of those systems.

I find the final part of this definition the most pertinent: *in a way that requires the user to have little or no awareness of the underlying operations of those systems.* To me, this is the ultimate goal of building a solution today. Interoperability is about connecting and building applications that work with each other to such an extent that the presentation to the user is seamless.

One analogy for this leads to my second definition of interoperability—the pictorial representation. When describing interoperability, I always make reference to a popular lake-dwelling species, the duck. If you've seen a duck swimming across a lake, you might have noticed that the top half of the duck looks very serene. The duck appears to glide across the lake with little to no effort. Despite this calm exterior, you know that underneath, the duck's legs are frantically kicking in all directions to get to the other side of the lake. Such is the way of interoperability. A well-designed solution that interoperates among many diverse systems should appear "calm and serene" to the user—the user should have no awareness that a click of a button or a switch of a page might create many calls to various systems throughout the enterprise, somewhat akin to the frantically kicking legs of our feathered friend.

The third part of this interoperability definition draws upon the previous two but offers a slightly different slant. *Migration, portability,* and *interoperability* are three terms used in many situations when dealing with developing applications to work in a cross-platform environment. These three terms can have different meanings to different people. When dealing with projects that require one or all of these characteristics, keep in mind the following comparison:

Imagine two components. They can be business components, Web pages, classes—anything at all. Imagine that one of the components has been written for the .NET platform and the other has been written for the J2EE environment.

If you convert it or rewrite one of the components (using either an automatic process or a manual one) so that it now runs on the other platform, this is known as *migration*. If you move one of the components to a different vendor but keep it on the same platform, this is known as *portability*. If, however, you leave each of the components on its own native platform but enable communication and data exchange between the .NET and J2EE platforms, this is *interoperability*.

You might find your own definition of interoperability, one that better applies to the systems you use today, or you might find an alternative way to describe it. Either way, I hope my three-part definition helps illuminate the key messages put forth in this book.

Interoperability vs. Migration

So what did I learn from my experience at the Architect Council? Did I learn that no one cares about migration and any attempt to migrate from J2EE to .NET will be futile? Absolutely not.

A huge opportunity does exist in the migration space. Customers do have code that can benefit from running on the .NET Framework, and some of this code already exists within J2EE applications today. Migration for many customers will happen over time. At the time of this writing, for many customers, interoperability is more important than migration.

Interoperability vs. Portability

As I mentioned in the last part of the interoperability definition, portability is the notion of running a single component or piece of code on platforms based on multiple implementations from various vendors. For the J2EE space, this is an easier concept to digest. I can, for instance, take a component written to the J2EE specification and, in theory, run it on either Application Server A or Application Server B based on my strategy with (or like or dislike of) the application server vendor at that particular time. In addition, Application Server A might be written for the Microsoft Windows platform, and Application Server B might be written for UNIX.

Because versions of .NET aren't developed by multiple vendors or for multiple operating systems, portability does not apply to a .NET application today. The point of this book isn't to detail (or argue about) the suitability of either the Java or .NET platform for developing applications. This book only succeeds if it promotes interoperability between the two platforms. Many arguments exist for and against portability and realizing portability in the enterprise. Some developers see portability as key for maintaining a vendor-neutral approach, and others are doubtful that portability will ever be realized—citing that the application-server vendor market becomes more fragmented with vendor-specific extensions each day.

I prefer to leave the argument about portability to other programming books and resources. This book is mainly concerned with showing you how to achieve interoperability. In my opinion, designing solutions that achieve interoperability allows a lot more flexibility for the enterprise than portability alone.

The Benefits of Interoperability

Many customers whom I've spoken with want to be confident that there's a good strategy for developing solutions using the .NET Framework that interoperate with heterogeneous systems. This is the real concept driving this book.

As a systems designer, architect, developer, or user, why should you be interested in interoperability? What does interoperability give you that replacing and recycling technology doesn't? I see four clear advantages:

- **Reuse of existing systems** Most established companies have a number of legacy systems. By the term *legacy*, I mean technology that's not being actively developed upon today. For example, a system located in the data center that's still in production but no longer offers a strategic advantage to the company is a legacy system. A plan to move these systems to a new platform might be a longer-term strategy. A solution that has the ability to interoperate with these systems has the potential to extend the life of these systems and more importantly, the knowledge of the developers who work with them.
- **Delivery based on technical merit** Designing an architecture that can enable interoperability promotes the selection of platforms based on technical merit. One could argue that every platform and technology—whether it's .NET, J2EE, or anything else—has its own merits for deployment. This could be maturity, reliability, scalability, security, technical advancement, and so forth. An approach to developing applications and services that have the ability to interoperate with one another allows platforms to be selected based on their merit and applicability to the job, allowing greater choice regardless of the vendor.
- **Pilot for adoption** When organizations want to deploy a new technology such as the .NET Framework, it's rare that they simply rip and replace an entire application or system. In many cases, a replacement is normally triggered by a pilot, or proof-of-concept, project. Such a pilot tends to be a short-term project with an aim to

prove that the technology can work well with existing systems and applications. The ability for this pilot or proof-of-concept project to interoperate with existing production systems is imperative, and in many cases, can often determine its success.

- **Migrations** Even if a system will be replaced or updated, it's rare to find a case where this can be done with a single "flick of a switch"—many migrations have to be well planned and carefully executed, and often involve moving an application a few parts at a time. This way of dividing a system for migration purposes often creates a demand for interoperability (because some parts that have been migrated still might need to communicate with others that have not).

If interoperability helps enable these tasks, it might ultimately result in savings in developer time and resources. For example, you might increase the shelf life of existing applications and systems, maximize current developer skills, and provide agility by creating proof-of-concept projects and carefully planned migrations.

The History of Interoperability

Is the ability for systems to interoperate new? Well, yes and no.

Interoperability in its most general form has been around for years—it started when the first computers started communicating via a network. If you look at some of the early protocol definitions in the 1970s and earlier, you'll find concrete examples of two systems "interoperating" over a network.

If, on the other hand, you look at the history for interoperability between pre-.NET Microsoft technology and Java (for example, connecting a COM object to a JavaBean), you'll find that relatively few options existed until recently. During the past couple of years, a number of options to connect the two platforms have emerged. These have included custom socket classes, custom implementations of Java RPC specifications (some deriving from standards such as Remote Method Invocation, or RMI), and a number of basic interoperability scenarios via HTTP.

The problem with these options is that although they're technically sound and suited to the task, they were never built on standards. For example, a developer might have created a custom protocol based on network sockets (which both a COM-based and standalone Java application could support). This implementation might have signed and encrypted data across the network between the two platforms and been very successful at the task it was designed to perform. However, if the developer then wanted to connect this system to another system that a third party had created (which again might implement a similar set of security functionality), chances are that unless the two developers had worked together on both the projects, the systems wouldn't interoperate.

This is probably the most fundamental difference in interoperability during the past few years and how products that enable interoperability continue to evolve today. It's no longer a question of *if* you can achieve interoperability—it's a question of *how* you achieve interoperability. Existing and emerging standards bodies will play an increasingly important role as these products mature during the next few years. The later chapters in this book should highlight how important this standardization is.

Who Should Read This Book

Interoperability is a broad subject that covers many technologies, platforms, and, ultimately, roles within an organization. Interoperability can be as important a goal for a company's CIO as it can for a new developer on any team.

With this in mind, I've tried to structure the book to appeal to as many readers as possible. The first few chapters of the book concentrate on the business aspects and fundamentals of interoperability. This discussion includes scenarios that might require interoperability, the reasoning behind these interoperability needs from a business perspective, and some core technology choices. As we move through the chapters, we'll start to look at some of the technical options and products that can be used to address these initial business scenarios in an environment with both .NET and J2EE. Again, the book initially presents these technical options with a wider audience in mind and then drills down to cover the requirements for implementing these options and products in your own environment. The later sections draw on some of my personal ideas and the new XML Web services specifications—and show implementations of these on both the .NET and J2EE platforms. Although the fundamental concepts are clearly explained, this code will appeal to readers with a more technical background.

So who should read this book? Anybody who believes that both the .NET and J2EE platforms are immutable will find information that can help them realize a solution.

The Structure of the Book

With the book's broad audience in mind, I'd like to summarize the structure of this book as a whole:

- **Refreshing some .NET and J2EE fundamentals** Targeting the readers of a book on interoperability between two technologies is difficult. Many of the chapters will appeal to two distinct audiences: readers with a J2EE background who are now learning how to build solutions that interoperate with .NET, and readers who have followed a more traditional Microsoft approach over the years and are now looking to integrate with existing J2EE implementations. (Many readers of course will have skills in both these areas.)

  To ensure that readers from both backgrounds have sufficient knowledge of each other, Part I, "Getting Started," will explore some fundamentals of both technologies. This section will cover Microsoft .NET from a Java perspective and J2EE from a Microsoft perspective, hopefully providing enough terminology to clarify the structure and technical elements of the book for both audiences.

- **Outlining business requirements for interoperability** Architects and developers usually don't design solutions that interoperate for no reason. More often than not, an application that has the capability to interoperate with another application is driven by one or more business requirements. For example, suppose Application A needs to interoperate with Application B due to specific business needs or use cases. In Part I of the book, we'll look at three common business-requirement scenarios, the requirements for interoperability, and the business benefits that enabling those scenarios would yield. Part I concludes by introducing some of the technical challenges of exchanging data between .NET and Java.

- **Exploring technologies for interoperability** For the developer, a key goal of reading this book is to get to the meat of the information. Given each scenario and business requirement outlined in Part I, we'll discuss which interoperability technologies apply and how you can realistically use them. Many technical options are available for creating a solution that can bridge both the .NET and J2EE platforms. This book will examine two architectures, identify the scenarios in which they fit best, and see where the technology really applies. Part II, "Interoperability Technologies: Point to Point," will look at point-to-point interoperability and cover options for connectivity. Part III, "Interoperability Technologies: Resource Tier" addresses interoperability at the resource tier and discusses how .NET and J2EE can interoperate in a reliable, asynchronous way.

- **Advanced interoperability** At the time of this writing, I still had not found many books, white papers, and resources that cover .NET-to-J2EE interoperability. One of the reasons for this lack of material is that the ability to interoperate among so many systems has changed and evolved so rapidly during such a short period of time. As a result, few people have managed to capture all the options and information concisely.

  The latest evolvement in interoperability technology is what I refer to as *advanced interoperability*. We'll cover this in Part IV of the book, aptly named "Advanced Interoperability." I wanted to cover this subject in the book because we're at a point in time where advanced interoperability is a reality in many areas of implementation. The focus of this section isn't to tell you (as a developer or solutions architect) what interoperability solutions can be performed, but to actually show them in action. This part of the book will include many code samples and guides for putting these technology options into practice.

  To me, advanced interoperability is about *what happens next*, after the communication channels between .NET and J2EE have been opened. In many cases, just getting the two systems to communicate and exchange data over a common protocol is an achievement in itself, but this alone doesn't lead to creating business applications and services that are reliable, secure, and production-worthy. We need to broaden our thinking to include the services and features that are required to build a business-ready solution.

Goals and Objectives of the Book

I thought it important to share my overall goals for delivering the material:

- **Thoroughly cover the topic area** In each section of the book, my first goal is to thoroughly cover the topic area. When describing technical options, especially those for connectivity, the book will try to show as many permutations as possible. I think it's important to show interoperability at work in environments where many readers might be using technology in a variety of scenarios.

- **Maintain a neutral stance on .NET vs. J2EE** As mentioned earlier, the goal of this book is not to serve as a showdown between the two technologies. Instead, all the chapters remain as neutral as possible, concentrating on interoperability, not comparison.

- **Provide sample code** As you start to explore the book, you'll see that many of the chapters have been written to take advantage of the sample code on the accompanying CD. Because interoperability encompasses such a broad area, I believe it's important to not only describe how interoperability works, but also provide samples where appropriate.

Feedback

In addition to writing this book, I wanted to provide a forum where readers can share experiences in creating interoperable solutions, submit ideas and thoughts on the book's content, and download updated sample code that didn't make it onto the accompanying CD.

To facilitate this, I've set up a Web log where I will post various comments, ideas, and updates on the topic. You can access this Web log at *http://www.simonguest.com*.

Microsoft Press Support Information

Every effort has been made to ensure the accuracy of this book and the contents of the companion CD. Microsoft Press provides corrections for books and companion content through the World Wide Web at

http://www.microsoft.com/mspress/support/

To connect directly to the Microsoft Press Knowledge Base and enter a query regarding a question or issue that you may have, go to

http://www.microsoft.com/mspress/support/search.asp

If you have comments, questions, or ideas regarding this book or its companion CD, or questions that are not answered by querying the Knowledge Base, please send them to Microsoft Press via e-mail to

mspinput@microsoft.com

or via postal mail to

Microsoft Press
Attn: Microsoft .NET and J2EE Interoperability Toolkit Editor
One Microsoft Way
Redmond, WA 98052-6399

Please note that product support is not offered through the above addresses.

Part I

Getting Started

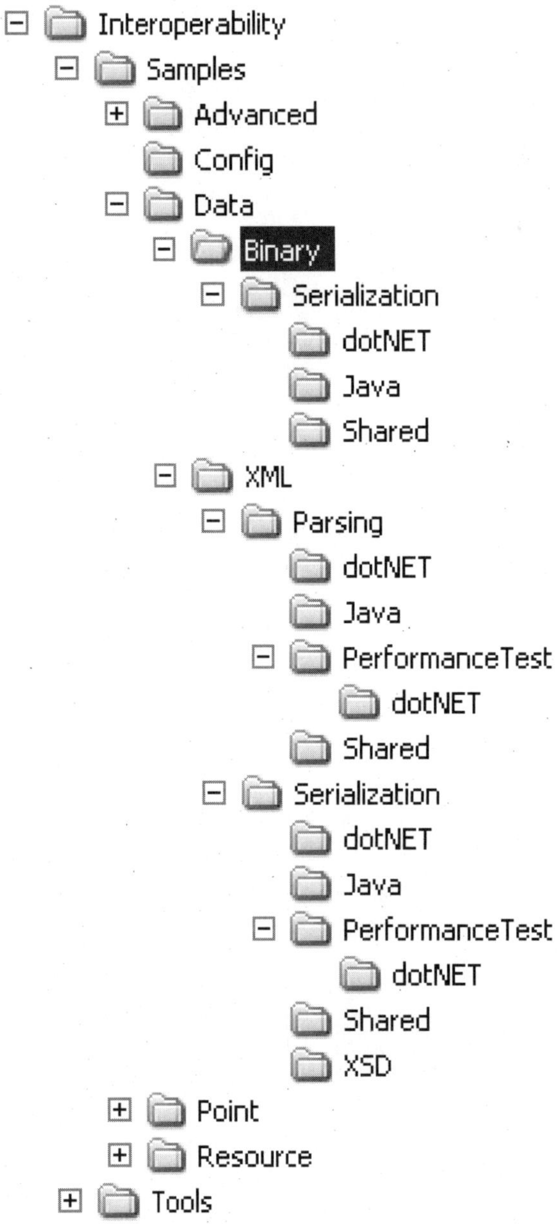

```
Interoperability
  Samples
    Advanced
    Config
    Data
      Binary
        Serialization
          dotNET
          Java
          Shared
      XML
        Parsing
          dotNET
          Java
          PerformanceTest
            dotNET
          Shared
        Serialization
          dotNET
          Java
          PerformanceTest
            dotNET
          Shared
          XSD
    Point
    Resource
  Tools
```

1

Microsoft .NET and J2EE Fundamentals

As mentioned in the Introduction, this book will appeal to two audiences. The first of these is developers who have a background in either Java, the Java 2 Enterprise Edition (J2EE) platform, or both, and want to develop solutions that interoperate with Microsoft .NET. The second audience is developers who are accustomed to working with Microsoft .NET (and probably have a Microsoft Windows DNA background) and want to build solutions that interoperate with existing Java or J2EE implementations. In addition, many developers reading this book will have some exposure to both platforms.

This chapter offers two sections that serve as a primer to the terminology and technical details used in the book. One section covers terminology for Microsoft .NET and is specifically targeted at existing Java and J2EE developers. The other covers Java and J2EE technology for developers more accustomed to Microsoft products.

These two sections provide a view of the technology of each platform that will appeal to developers working on the other platform—ideally using familiar terms and language. I thought providing these sections would be more helpful to you than simply posting a glossary of terms at the end of the book. Use these sections as either a walk-through or a reference when you encounter an unfamiliar term in the book. These two sections won't drill too deeply into any particular element of either platform, nor will they cover topics that will be explained in more detail in later chapters. Moreover, these sections aren't meant to be a showdown between the two platforms.

Later in this chapter, you'll find a table that provides a mapping between .NET Framework technologies and their Java counterparts. I use this table as a resource in presentations I make within the developer community to help clarify the terms and APIs developers might encounter on both platforms when designing solutions that must interoperate between them.

Microsoft .NET Fundamentals for Java/J2EE Developers

The .NET Framework is Microsoft's initiative to deliver a new way of building and deploying applications and services. As .NET becomes accepted in the programming community, this vision is starting to encompass many products, ideas, and other services.

For the Java developer, the .NET Framework really does promote interoperability. The foundations of .NET have been built from the ground up, with standards such as HTTP and XML embedded within the classes of the framework itself. Java developers who have tried to create a Java-to-COM interface or call an existing Win32 API by using Java Native Interface (JNI) often will welcome the implementation of these standards with open arms.

The .NET Framework is the platform that contains the classes, APIs, and tools on which .NET applications can be built. Although I usually shy away from direct comparisons because they tend to draw out the religious side of developers, it is possible to compare some elements of the .NET Framework to the corresponding Java counterpart, although they sometimes work in very different ways. The .NET Framework is required to build and run any .NET application and is available today as a download via Windows Update—a system from which the Microsoft Windows operating system can download new patches and drivers—or directly from the Microsoft .NET Web site (*http://www.microsoft.com/net*).

At the core of the .NET Framework lies the common language runtime (CLR). Some roles of the CLR can be likened to those of the Java Virtual Machine (JVM). The CLR is responsible for the many tasks that are involved in running and hosting .NET applications.

The CLR can work with only one type of code: Intermediate Language (IL). This code also is known as Microsoft Intermediate Language (MSIL) and often is referred to as *managed code*. The CLR contains a just-in-time (JIT) compiler to compile the IL into native code. (This is currently x86 code for the Windows operating system.) Managed code running in the CLR is inherently type safe and provides support for garbage collection—terms that should be familiar to Java developers with a C/C++ background. In addition, the CLR runs managed code applications in the context of application domains, which allows multiple applications to run within a single process on the machine.

Because IL is a pseudo–machine language code, writing in IL isn't an intuitive experience for most developers. To write to the .NET Framework, you'll need to choose one or more languages. These languages include Microsoft Visual Basic .NET, C#, J#, Managed C++ from Microsoft, and third-party languages such as Perl, Python, Eiffel, and COBOL. Each of these languages compiles down to IL and is then compiled again by the CLR when the application is run. In this book, I'll use C#. This is purely a personal preference; any of the previously mentioned languages would be suitable. Feel free to convert any of the C# sample code in this book to the language of your choice.

Building a .NET Application

You can access the compiler of choice installed within the .NET Framework in one of two ways. Each of the compilers can be called from the command line, and they are normally located in the Microsoft.NET\Framework\v1.1.4322 subdirectory (for version 1.1 of the .NET Framework) of your Windows installation directory. (From now on, I'll refer to this as C:\WINDOWS, which is the installation directory for Microsoft Windows XP.) The executable for the C# compiler is CSC.EXE, and the compiler for Visual Basic .NET is VBC.EXE; both are located in this directory.

Alternatively, you can build applications by using Microsoft Visual Studio .NET, Microsoft's integrated development environment (IDE) for the .NET Framework. As with many IDEs for the Java platform, Visual Studio .NET provides the developer with a comprehensive set of tools to enable productivity. The majority of the code in this book is built and run using the command-line compiler (making it easy to switch between the Java compiler and the C# compiler to build and run the samples), while Visual Studio .NET is used when it offers additional functionality.

When you successfully compile an application by using either the command-line compiler or Visual Studio .NET, one or more assemblies are produced. An *assembly* is the module that's designed to be executed by the CLR. Assemblies usually take the form of an .EXE or .DLL file and can be examined by using the MSIL Disassembler tool that comes with the .NET Framework. Every assembly contains metadata that describes it, including the Windows Portable Executable Header, dependencies on other assemblies, and version information. Java has no direct equivalent of an assembly. However, Java developers can think of an assembly as a Java Archive (JAR) file that contains a number of classes that can store additional metadata and has the ability to make cross-references to other JAR files without referencing a *CLASSPATH*.

Locating and Sharing Other Assemblies

Assemblies have the ability to make cross-references to other assemblies with information stored in metadata, but this still doesn't solve the problem of dynamic binding or locating an assembly when an application is running. Instead of using an environment variable in these scenarios, the .NET Framework uses a global assembly cache (GAC), a machine-specific store that contains assemblies to be shared between applications. Assemblies stored within the GAC can be found in the C:\WINDOWS\ASSEMBLY directory and can be added or removed by using the GACUTIL tool.

In addition, the GAC can hold multiple versions of the same assembly. (Recall how the version number was stored in the metadata of the assembly itself.) Using this metadata, applications that reference an assembly in the GAC can ask for a specific version at run time.

Attributes

Attributes are a key element of the CLR. They're important to understand because they do not appear in the current version of the Java 2 platform, yet they're common in many of the .NET samples in this book.

Attributes are keywords that utilize a tag syntax within a source code file. They can be used to annotate classes, types, fields, and methods at design time to specify runtime information and behavior. The attribute information is saved within the metadata of an assembly. Attributes can be widely found in many of the namespaces in the .NET Framework. You also can create custom attributes for your applications.

The *WebMethod* attribute is a good example of an attribute in action. *WebMethod* is used to indicate that a method within a class is callable as an XML Web service, which we'll look at in more detail starting in Chapter 5, "Connectivity with XML Web Services, Part 1." Prefixing the *WebMethod* tag at the start of the method automatically instructs the compiler to generate the additional information required to expose the method as a Web service:

```
[WebMethod]
public String HelloWorld()
{
    …
}
```

Attributes can also accept parameters in a way similar to a constructor invocation. For example:

```
[WebMethod(Namespace="http://www.microsoft.com/interoperability")]
```

This line of code will assign the namespace property of the *WebMethod* attribute to the URL that was passed.

For developers with an understanding of J2EE, some functionality that attributes provide can be achieved using the configuration settings found within deployment descriptors.

Because attributes are CLR specific, they're supported in all CLR-compliant languages, including C#, Visual Basic .NET, and J#. The way in which the tags are prefixed, however, differs slightly with each language's syntax.

Creating Applications for the Web

.NET applications that are designed for the Web are built using ASP.NET, which is Microsoft's next-generation development of Active Server Pages (ASP). Although not strictly tied to a Web server, Microsoft Internet Information Services (IIS) is typically used as the foundation for hosting ASP.NET-based applications.

To developers with a background in JavaServer Pages (JSP), ASP.NET is more than a .NET equivalent. Within the .NET Framework, ASP.NET contains certain features (such as code-behind and event-driven Web controls) that to achieve similar functionality in J2EE would require both JSP v1.2 and additional tools.

Because of their graphical nature, pages that make up ASP.NET applications are normally developed using Visual Studio .NET. Another alternative for developing ASP.NET solutions is to use the Web Matrix IDE. This IDE is best suited for developers who want to build visual applications but don't require the power of Visual Studio .NET. You can use any language the CLR supports to create ASP.NET Web applications.

Hosting Components

For better or for worse, the .NET Framework and the Windows platform have no direct equivalent to Enterprise Java Beans (EJBs). However, because hosting components is key for many enterprise applications, three alternatives to sharing a component with multiple clients exist:

- **Run as a Windows Service** Windows Services (also known as NT Services) are system-level processes that run on the machine independent of the user who is logged in. Typical services include functions of the operating system, schedulers, virus scanners, database engines, and network components. Using templates supplied with Visual Studio .NET, it is possible to take a .NET assembly and run it as a service; however, the assembly will need to handle its own networking if it will be called remotely. This capability can be useful for applications that must be active for the lifetime of the machine.

- **Host through IIS** Building a custom framework to host assemblies can be relatively complex. This process can include creating custom network sockets and listeners, caching, performing connection pooling for multiple clients, and so on. Many of these features are also found in products that host Web applications, such as IIS. One way of hosting an assembly is to take advantage of these features. IIS allows an assembly to be deployed and will handle incoming connections, protocols, pooling, and security via a configuration file located with the assembly.
- **Use Component Services** Although hosting an assembly via IIS provides an easy and convenient way of sharing components, certain functionality that exists in EJBs might be required. This functionality can include recycling, state, transactions, method-level security, logging, impersonation, and message queue support. You can achieve this functionality with a .NET assembly by using Component Services. Also known as COM+ Services, Component Services enable you to apply this functionality to hosted components through either an administration tool or the use of attributes. I'm frequently asked whether a Microsoft equivalent of Container Managed Persistence (CMP) EJBs exists—in other words, whether the ability to provide object–to–relational database mapping exists. As of this writing, this capability does not exist within the .NET Framework; however, a number of third-party implementations are available. In addition, Visual Studio .NET contains many tools that can auto-generate SQL statements and that even allow database tables to be dragged and dropped into the IDE itself.

Where's the Application Server?

Because I came from a J2EE background, this was certainly one of my first questions when learning .NET. Although I had done some COM programming, I was used to the concept of building and deploying for an application server that ran independent of the operating system.

As explained earlier, all the functionality found in a commercial J2EE application server (such as security, messaging, transactions, and logging) can be found in Windows and can be accessed by the classes in the .NET Framework. However, in contrast with a typical J2EE application server, this .NET functionality tends to be distributed across various parts of the operating system rather than being stored in one place. Many of these distributed parts have their own interface, configuration, and store; as a J2EE developer, you'll find that learning where this application server functionality lies is one of the challenges of learning about .NET. A lot of this design stems from historical reasons (providing backward compatibility with existing Win32 APIs and Windows DNA applications) and the way that the components have evolved over the years.

Throughout this book, I'll address these parts of the Windows application server as they relate to the interoperability areas being covered. Because many Java developers will have little knowledge of these components, I'll make these explanations and instructions clear and precise.

References and Resources

I have found the following list of references and resources useful for introducing Microsoft .NET and various elements of the framework.

Microsoft .NET Product Page

Go to *http://www.microsoft.com/net* to download the .NET Framework SDK and find links to .NET-related information and products.

GotDotNet Community

GotDotNet at *http://www.gotdotnet.com* is a community resource that contains sample downloads, tools, forums, links, and guides for the .NET Framework and related technologies.

ASP.NET Community

The *http://www.asp.net* site contains a collection of tools, community resources, samples, and tutorials specifically for ASP.NET application development. A rich component library is also available for building and extending your own ASP.NET applications.

Windows Forms Community

The *http://www.windowsforms.net* site is similar in nature to *http://www.asp.net* but is focused solely on Windows Forms development using Microsoft .NET.

Java and J2EE Fundamentals for Microsoft .NET Developers

This section of the chapter provides a brief overview of Java and J2EE for developers who have a background in Microsoft products. This section assumes that such developers have a typical Windows DNA architecture background and have had limited exposure to the Java platform.

Java, which is developed by Sun Microsystems, is both a platform and a programming language. The Java platform can be categorized in three editions: Java 2 Standard Edition (J2SE), Java 2 Enterprise Edition (J2EE), and Java 2

Micro Edition (J2ME). When I use the term *Java* in this book, I'm mainly referring to the functionality available in J2SE. When referring to the Enterprise Edition specifically, I'll use the acronym J2EE.

The Java platform shares much of the vision and underpinnings of .NET, ranging from the language itself to the wide use of the term *Java* and the number of products that have names prefixed with a *J* to indicate their adoption of Java. Microsoft developers will find many concepts in both Java and J2EE familiar, which is good news when it comes to developing interoperable solutions.

Three key factors differentiate Java from .NET. First, the Java platform targets multiple operating systems, meaning that applications written in Java can be executed on Windows, flavors of UNIX, Mac OS, and others. Today, applications written for Microsoft .NET will run only on Windows and on FreeBSD (via an academic port of the .NET Framework called Rotor). The second difference comes down to the programming language. Applications for the Java platform can only be written using the Java programming language. By contrast, .NET supports multiple programming languages on top of one common language runtime. The third difference is in the way that applications are compiled and executed. With Microsoft .NET, the IL is compiled to native machine-level code by the JIT compiler within the CLR. With Java, the Java source gets compiled to Java bytecode. The Java bytecode is then interpreted rather than compiled by the Java Virtual Machine (JVM), although newer versions of the compiler are starting to implement JIT by default.

The Java platform consists of the JVM and the Java API. The JVM shares some similarities with the CLR, but its main role is to translate the Java bytecode into instructions the native platform can understand and execute.

J2EE is a set of specifications that build on the J2SE platform to deliver a framework for creating and hosting enterprise-level applications. At the time of this writing, J2EE 1.3 has been released and J2EE 1.4 is in draft.

In essence, the J2EE framework comprises many parts that have evolved over the past few years. These technologies include JavaServer Pages (JSP), Server Side APIs (Java Servlets), Enterprise Java Beans (EJBs), Java Naming and Directory Interface (JNDI), Java Message Service (JMS), Java Transaction API (JTA), and many more. Many of these technologies have equivalent mappings to either namespaces within the .NET Framework or to components and elements of Microsoft Windows. For example, similar functionality offered by the JMS API can be found in the *System.Messaging* namespace in the .NET Framework.

As with the Java 2 SDK Standard Edition, Sun licenses the J2EE specification to vendors who want to create and resell application servers, branded with the J2EE logo via a compatibility test suite. At the time of this writing, these vendors include Sun (offering its ONE application server), IBM (WebSphere), BEA

(WebLogic), and others. In addition, open-source implementations are now also available, with JBoss heading the pack.

Building a Java Application

The latest version of the Java 2 SDK Standard Edition is 1.4.1. The Java 2 SDK can be downloaded from Sun's Java software site (*http://java.sun.com*). It has also been licensed to other vendors who have produced their own versions. As with the J2EE application servers, these vendors include IBM, BEA, and a number of open-source implementations.

The Java 2 SDK contains the APIs and libraries for creating the source, as well as the compiler and binaries for executing these applications. The bin directory of the SDK contains JAVAC.EXE, which is used to compile Java source code (*.java files) into Java bytecode (*.class files).

One main difference with the Java compiler is that each class in Java will generate a separate .class file, whereas in .NET, an assembly can contain multiple classes. Because many applications often contain multiple .class files, the distribution and execution of Java applications tends to rely on Java Archive (JAR) files. In their simplest form, JAR files are collections of compiled Java classes; however, JAR files can contain files of any type, and they have a directory structure. You can use a tool named JAR.EXE, also found in the bin directory of the SDK, to add, list, or extract .class files from a JAR file.

Because classes and JAR files aren't recognized by the file system as executables, to execute a class file (either a standalone .class file or one embedded within a JAR file), you must use the JAVA.EXE tool.

Locating and Sharing Other Classes

The Java platform doesn't have an equivalent to the GAC in the .NET Framework, but many applications still need to cross-reference and share other classes. To do this, an environment variable named *CLASSPATH* is used to set a path for all classes that are required for executing an application.

By default, the *CLASSPATH* variable needs to include the main JAR file (tools.jar for v1.4.1) within the Java 2 SDK and a reference to the current directory (which is notated by a period). Any other JAR files required to execute an application are then added to the *CLASSPATH* just before the application is run.

For example, if you're developing an application that contains calls to a third-party library, you can adjust your *CLASSPATH* to include the required JAR just before compiling. This can be done using the MS-DOS *SET* command from the command line:

```
SET CLASSPATH = %CLASSPATH%;C:\THIRDPARTY\OTHER.JAR
```

This will append the OTHER.JAR file in the C:\THIRDPARTY directory to the existing *CLASSPATH*.

In addition, both JAVAC.EXE (the compiler) and JAVA.EXE (the tool to execute Java classes) accept a *–classpath* parameter for including the *CLASSPATH* variable when they're run. Many Java IDEs will also allow the *CLASSPATH* variable to be set within their environment.

If you receive a *ClassNotFoundException* when executing your Java application, check your *CLASSPATH* environment variable to ensure that all the required libraries are included on the path. In most instances, not having all the required libraries will be the reason why the Java Virtual Machine threw the *ClassNotFoundException*. This is especially true for J2EE environments where some application servers require references to many libraries in order to run.

Other Environment Variables

Environment variables tend to be used much more for developing Java applications than for developing applications in Microsoft .NET. Because Java applications can be developed to run on multiple operating systems, using environment variables offers a common denominator for setting and controlling the configuration.

Many other tools for the Java platform require other environment variables to be set in order to run correctly. These can include *JAVA_HOME*, which specifies the location of the Java SDK, and product-specific variables such as *ANT_HOME* and *ELECTRIC_HOME*.

Java IDEs

As with .NET, the Java compiler can be accessed from the command line to build applications, as you saw a moment ago. In addition, a number of Java IDEs are available from multiple vendors. The combination of multiple application servers and IDEs has produced a number of add-ins that allow deployment and control of the J2EE application from within the IDE itself. For example, you might use a BEA WebLogic add-in for Borland JBuilder to deploy a Web application back to WebLogic.

Given the diversity of both the application server and IDE market, the samples in this book have been designed to be compiled and executed from the command line alone, and all of them have been designed to work with any application server that implements the J2EE 1.3 specification. Before you run any of the samples, I recommend that you include the bin directory of the Java 2 SDK in your System Path (*PATH)* variable. (See the "Setting Environment Variables" section toward the end of this chapter for further information.) Including this directory in the System Path will allow you to run the tools in the directory without having to specify the directory name each time.

If you are familiar with Microsoft tools and are looking to view and develop the Java sample code without having to install a second IDE, you can edit all the code using Visual Studio .NET and the Microsoft Visual J# add-in, which is available from MSDN. (Visual J# enables you to develop .NET applications using the Java language syntax.) Using J# for your editing purposes will provide syntax highlighting and IntelliSense for API calls made in versions of the Java SDK earlier than v1.1.4. To build the application, however, you'll need to use the JAVAC.EXE compiler from the command line to run the application in a JVM.

Creating Applications for the Web

JavaServer Pages, or JSP, is part of the J2EE specification and is a server-side technology for the development of Web applications on the Java platform. JSP technology is based on dynamically compiled .jsp pages and Java Servlets, which is a Java interface that provides server-side processing for Web-based applications. When a presentation tier is said to be *based on JSP*, the implication is that it's a mixture of JSP pages and Servlets. The terminology in this book makes this implication too.

Many technology options are available for hosting both JSP and Servlets. These options can range from free lightweight engines such as Apache Tomcat to the fully supported, vendor-based J2EE servers mentioned earlier.

Typically, JSP pages and Servlets are developed using one of the many IDEs available for Java, some of which include the ability to graphically develop pages and controls on the fly. A number of freeware and shareware independent JSP editors also exist that can be used to write and test pages. Many of these editors can be found and downloaded after a simple search on the Web.

The scripting elements within both JSP pages and Servlets are created using the Java programming language. At the time of this writing, the latest version of the Java Servlet API is v2.3, and the latest version of the JavaServer Pages specification is v1.2.

Hosting Components

The key part of the J2EE specification is Enterprise Java Beans (EJBs). EJBs provide the framework for hosting components in a distributed enterprise environment. As with Component Services, the functionality provided by EJBs can include recycling, state, transactions, method-level security, logging, impersonation, and message queue support.

Without delving into the full specification, I can simply say that the most important thing for a Microsoft developer is to understand the two types of

EJBs: Session Beans and Entity Beans. Session Beans are typically used to host business logic, and Entity Beans are used to map data from database tables to objects.

Each type of bean has two subtypes. Session Beans can be either *stateful* or *stateless*—meaning that the state of a Session Bean can be tied to the client for the lifetime of the object. Entity Beans can be managed either by the container (known as *Container Managed Persistence*, or *CMP*) or by the bean itself (known as *Bean Managed Persistence*, or *BMP*). The management of the bean dictates how the code to access the database will be managed. With CMP, the container manages the mapping between fields in the bean and fields in the database. (An application server can contain many containers to host different beans.) A mapping file is used to configure this relationship. With BMP, the process of supplying the code to access the database is left to the developer. The EJB interfaces provide methods for loading, storing, removing, and so on. The developer is then free to supply the code as required.

So, why do EJBs have both CMP and BMP? Each has its own advantages. CMP tends to be easier to configure and maintain because no database code has to be written. The notion of mapping objects to databases, however, can come at a price: decreased performance. With BMP, the performance of the bean is directly related to the performance of the underlying database code that is written. Plus, the developer gets a lot more flexibility with BMP. For example, you could create a BMP EJB that maps against a Lightweight Directory Access Protocol (LDAP) directory or another source that doesn't use a database.

Building and Deploying to a J2EE Application Server

Building an application to run on a J2EE application server can involve a number of steps to ensure that all the required components are deployed correctly. In addition to JAR files that contain a number of Java class files, the J2EE specification defines Web Archive (WAR) files, which are essentially JAR files that contain a predefined structure for Web applications, and Enterprise Archive (EAR) files, which can contain WAR files, JAR files containing EJBs, and other content.

The settings for a J2EE deployment are configured via prespecified XML files known as *deployment descriptors*. Deployment descriptors are used to instruct the application server how to run the application by configuring services such as security, transactions, and logging. These files can contain settings similar to those found in Component Services. Although J2EE deployment descriptor settings are part of the J2EE specification, some descriptor files are specific to the application server vendor.

References and Resources

I've found the following collection of references and resources useful for introducing the Java language and various elements of the platform.

Sun Java Product Page

At *http://java.sun.com*, you can download the Java 2 SDK and find other links to Java-related information and products.

ServerSide.com Community

The *http://www.theserverside.com* site is one of the most popular Java and J2EE community resources on the Web. Included on the site are news, design patterns, reviews, and discussions around Java and J2EE technologies.

JSP and Struts

At *http://jakarta.apache.org/struts*, learn how to extend JSP and implement a Model-View-Controller (MVC) approach using Apache Struts, an open-source framework for building Web applications.

AWT and SWING

Use *http://java.sun.com/products/jdk/awt/* as a starting place to find additional information about AWT and SWING, the Java UI libraries.

Microsoft.NET and J2EE Technology Map

Table 1-1 shows a technology map between the .NET Framework and the J2EE specification. This table is meant to be used for looking up the corresponding product or feature set on the other platform. Use the table to understand the fundamentals described in this book, not to compare and contrast the two technologies. Also be aware that many of the rows in this table do not represent one-to-one mappings. For example, MSMQ is a product, whereas JMS is an API.

Table 1-1 Microsoft .NET and J2EE Technology Map

Service or Feature	Microsoft .NET (Product or Framework Class)	J2EE (API or Vendor Product)
Client-side GUI/forms	WinForms	AWT/SWING
Web GUI	ASP.NET	JSP
Web scripting	ISAPI, *HttpHandler*, *HttpModule*	Servlet, Filter
Web application hosting	Internet Information Services (IIS)	Multiple possibilities, including Apache Tomcat, and vendor-specific servers

Table 1-1 Microsoft .NET and J2EE Technology Map

Service or Feature	Microsoft .NET (Product or Framework Class)	J2EE (API or Vendor Product)
Server-side business logic component	Serviced Component (COM+)	Session Bean
Server-side data component	Serviced Component (COM+) with Database Logic	Bean Managed Persistence (BMP) Bean
Server-side data component	Third-Party Solution	Container Managed Persistence (CMP) Bean
Directory access	ADSI (via LDAP)	JNDI (via LDAP)
Remote invocation	.NET Remoting	RMI-IIOP
Data access	ADO.NET	JDBC, SQL/J
Messaging	MSMQ	JMS
Transactions	COM+/DTC	JTA

Running the Sample Code in This Book

Many chapters in the book contain sample code. All the samples referenced in the text are also included on the CD that accompanies the book. The requirements for running the samples are as follows.

Operating Systems

I've assumed that you'll use a Windows operating system to run the code samples in this book, ideally either Microsoft Windows XP or Microsoft Windows 2003. For certain server-specific samples, Microsoft Windows 2003 will be required.

.NET Environment

All the .NET code samples are written to work on version 1.1 of the Microsoft .NET Framework (v1.1.4322). The Microsoft .NET download site (found at *http://www.microsoft.com/net*) offers two download options: the .NET Framework Redistributable or the .NET Framework SDK.

If you plan to use Visual Studio .NET, the .NET Framework SDK is automatically installed as part of the product and will not require downloading separately. If you do not plan to use the IDE, you should download and install the .NET Framework SDK. The SDK contains a number of command-line utilities that will be used throughout many of the chapters.

Many of the code samples also require ASP.NET. Although Web pages and controls are not shown in every chapter, the underlying mechanisms to host Web services rely on ASP.NET. Before running any of these samples, you need to ensure that IIS and ASP.NET are both correctly installed and that security is correctly configured. The next three sections will take you through this process.

Installing ASP.NET on Windows Server 2003

Windows Server 2003 allows servers running the operating system to be assigned roles. For example, certain servers within a data center could be designated as File and Print servers, whereas others could be designated as Web or Application servers. Servers are installed with different software components based on their assigned role.

To allow many of the samples found within this book to work correctly with Windows Server 2003, you'll need to configure the server to have the role of an application server. Configuring the server for this role will install the required software (FrontPage Server Extensions and ASP.NET) for the samples.

To assign the role of your server, open the Configure Your Server Wizard. This wizard can be launched by selecting it from the Start\Program Files\Administrative Tools menu. After the wizard is launched and detects your network settings, a list of available roles will be displayed, as shown in Figure 1-1.

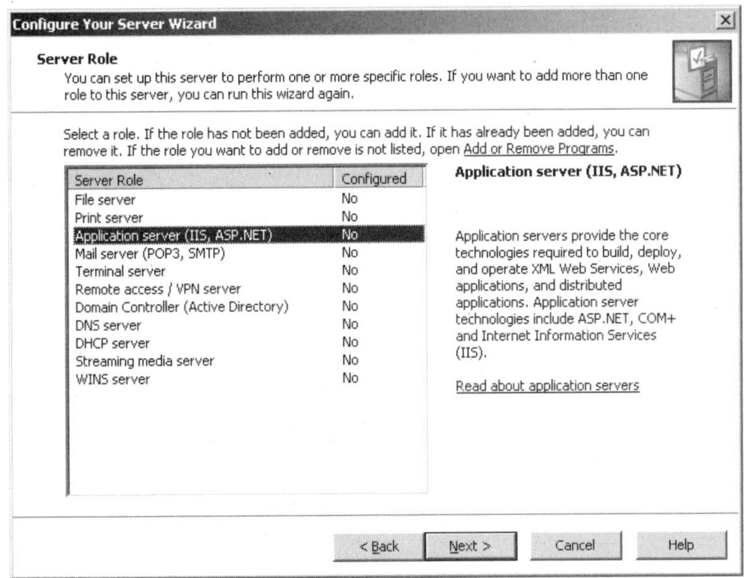

Figure 1-1 Configuring the Server Role in Windows Server 2003.

Select the Application Server role as highlighted in the figure, and click the Next button. As displayed in Figure 1-2, check both the FrontPage Server Extensions option and the Enable ASP.NET option. ASP.NET is used to serve all the .NET Web services that are shown in this book. FrontPage Server Extensions is used to provide access to Web sites from a number of Microsoft applications, including Visual Studio .NET 2003.

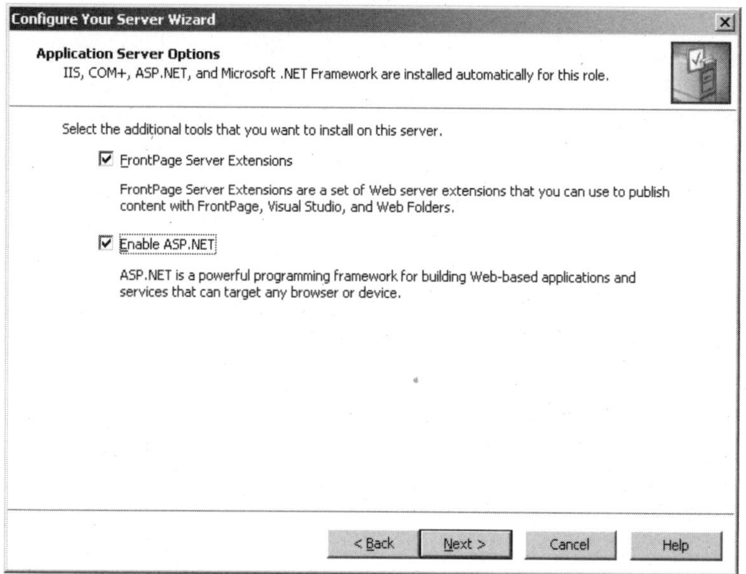

Figure 1-2 Enabling FrontPage Server Extensions and ASP.NET in Windows Server 2003.

Click the Next button to confirm these choices, and complete the wizard to install the necessary components. During this installation, you might be prompted for the Windows Server 2003 CD or network location.

Installing ASP.NET on Windows XP Professional

Installation of ASP.NET for Windows XP Professional is done using the Add Or Remove Programs control panel. Within the control panel, select Add/Remove Windows Components and ensure that Internet Information Services is installed. (The common files and FrontPage extensions are required.) Installing the Microsoft .NET Framework SDK will include all the required ASP.NET options.

Configuring ASP.NET Security

Some of the ASP.NET samples that will be demonstrated write to the event log, which requires additional privileges not normally required by applications that use ASP.NET. To enable these samples to work correctly, you'll need to adjust the ASP.NET security settings.

> **Warning** Changing the ASP.NET security settings could provide rogue programs with the ability to access and alter nearly all resources on the computer. It is *highly* recommended that these modifications be done only for the purposes of running this book's sample code and that you consult the following articles to correctly set up the security of a deployed application: *http://www.microsoft.com/technet/treeview/default.asp?url=/technet/prodtechnol/windowsserver2003/proddocs/server/aaconprocessmodelelement.asp* and *http://www.microsoft.com/technet/treeview/default.asp?url=/technet/prodtechnol/windowsserver2003/proddocs/server/aaconconfiguringaspnetprocessidentity.asp.*

For the security settings, we are going to adjust the ASPNET account (that is, the account the ASP.NET process uses) to run under the context of the local system account. These instructions apply to both Windows Server 2003 and Windows XP Professional.

To do this, edit the machine.config file in the C:\Windows\Microsoft.NET\Framework\v1.1.4322\CONFIG directory. This directory might be different depending on your exact installation setup of Microsoft Windows. Within this file, search for a section called *processModel*. The section should start like this:

```
<processModel
    enable="true"
    timeout="Infinite"
    idleTimeout="Infinite"
    shutdownTimeout="0:00:05"
    requestLimit="Infinite"
    requestQueueLimit="5000"
    restartQueueLimit="10"
    memoryLimit="60"
⋮
```

Change the *userName* attribute to **SYSTEM**:

```
userName="SYSTEM"
```

Also, ensure that the password is set to *AutoGenerate*. Save and close the file.

For Windows 2003 only, one additional step is required. The same configuration change needs to be made to the application pool. Launch Internet Information Services Manager from the Start/Programs/Administrative Tools menu. Expand the Application Pools tree, and right-click the DefaultAppPool. Select Properties, and click the Identity tab. Set the security account for this pool as Predefined and Local System. Confirm the security warning, and close the dialog box.

After you have made these security adjustments, launch a command prompt window and type **iisreset**. This will stop and start the IIS services to ensure that the adjusted security configuration is applied.

Java/J2EE Environment

This book does not include a version of the JVM with the sample code on the companion CD. Nor does it include a version of any J2EE application server. The intent was to ensure that all the code samples are as vendor neutral and application server neutral as possible because it would be impossible to anticipate which environment each reader of the book would use.

For testing purposes, the scripts supplied with the samples are configured to deploy the sample code to a local instance of JBoss version 3.0.7. As mentioned previously, JBoss is an open-source J2EE application server that can be downloaded from *http://www.jboss.org*. When downloading, make sure that you select the version that includes JBossWeb.

All code samples have been written for and tested against a JVM based on the Java 2 SDK 1.4.1 specification and the J2EE 1.3 specification.

Microsoft Products

The following Microsoft products are referenced in the code samples throughout the book.

Microsoft SQL Server 2000

Chapter 7, "Creating a Shared Database," Chapter 11, "Asynchronous Interoperability, Part 4: BizTalk Server," and Chapter 12, "Presentation Tier Interoperability," all make use of Microsoft SQL Server 2000 to cover certain interoperability elements. Although using most vendor databases with these samples is entirely possible, the drivers referenced and some of the stored procedures written are specific to SQL Server.

Downloading an evaluation Microsoft SQL Server 2000 is not included on the accompanying sample code CD. If you do not currently have an instance of SQL Server that can be used for these samples, you might want to take a look at *http://www.microsoft.com/sql*. At the time of this writing, a 120-day trial version of SQL Server 2000 can be downloaded from *http://www.microsoft.com/sql/evaluation/trial/*.

Microsoft SQL Server 2000 Driver for JDBC

To allow connectivity to Microsoft SQL Server 2000 from the Java environment, we'll be using the Microsoft SQL Server 2000 Driver for JDBC. This driver allows the Java Clients in the samples to access an instance of SQL Server 2000, and it's used in Chapter 7 and Chapter 12.

Downloading The Microsoft SQL Server 2000 Driver for JDBC can be downloaded from the Microsoft SQL Server MSDN downloads at *http://msdn.microsoft.com/downloads/list/sqlserver.asp*. The sample code that uses this JDBC driver has been tested with the SP1 (Service Pack 1) release.

Microsoft Host Integration Server 2000

Chapter 10, "Asynchronous Interoperability, Part 3: Bridging with Host Integration Server," shows how components within Microsoft Host Integration Server can be used to bridge Microsoft MSMQ and the IBM WebSphere MQ product.

Downloading an evaluation Microsoft Host Integration Server 2000 is not included on the sample code CD. Product information and licensing is available from *http://www.microsoft.com/hiserver*. If you do not already have Microsoft Host Integration Server 2000, a 120-day trial can be downloaded from *http://www.microsoft.com/hiserver/evaluation/trial/default.asp*.

Microsoft BizTalk Server 2004 Beta 1

To utilize a broker-based solution, as described in Chapter 11, we'll use a prerelease copy of Microsoft BizTalk Server 2004. BizTalk Server includes many features that include message transformation, support for legacy adapters, and orchestration. Running the sample code in Chapter 11 will require Visual Studio .NET 2003.

Downloading the beta At the time of this writing, Beta 1 is going through release. To download the latest trial edition of the software, go to *http://www.microsoft.com/biztalk/evaluation/trial/default.asp*. Although the sample code in this book is based upon Beta 1 code, you should always use the latest version of the product.

Microsoft Web Services Enhancements 1.0

We'll use Microsoft Web Services Enhancements (WSE) 1.0 for the advanced interoperability samples in Part IV of this book. WSE 1.0 provides a number of libraries to extend the functionality of the Web Services classes in .NET, based on the new specifications.

Downloading WSE 1.0 is a free download from MSDN and can be found at *http://www.microsoft.com/webservices*. In addition to downloading this version, installation of SP1 (Service Pack 1) from the same location is highly recommended.

Third-Party Products

It would be impossible to write a book on interoperability between the .NET and Java platforms without using resources from third-party companies because so many connectors and implementations we'll be working with aren't part of either framework. The following third-party products, some of which are included on the companion CD, are referenced in the book.

TME GLUE 4.0.1 and Electric XML

Chapter 3, "Exchanging Data Between .NET and Java," looks at data exchange between .NET and J2EE. One fundamental demonstration of this exchange uses XML serialization to pass data between the two platforms as XML documents.

To achieve XML serialization for the Java sample code, we'll use the XML classes that are available from a third party known as The Mind Electric (TME) and can be found at *http://www.themindelectric.com*. This implementation, known as TME Electric XML and which is part of the TME GLUE 4.0.1 product, was found the most compatible with the samples presented in this book.

As we'll discuss in Chapter 5, Web services today are more of a vendor-specific approach than an integral part of the current J2SE and J2EE specifications. As a result, to develop Web services for the Java platform, you must choose a third-party implementation.

As with the classes we'll use later in the book to demonstrate XML serialization, I've chosen to standardize on GLUE, also from The Mind Electric. I'll discuss my reasoning behind this selection and offer an objective look at the Web services standards in the Java platform in Chapter 5.

What Is The Mind Electric?

The Mind Electric (TME) is a leading pioneer and provider of Web Services Infrastructure Solutions. TME's mission is to fundamentally simplify the creation, deployment, management, and orchestration of next-generation distributed applications. Its first product, TME GLUE, is the leading independent Java Web Services platform and has been branded the "Turbo Pascal of Web Services" by Forrester Research. The company's second product, TME GLUE Web Services Fabric (code-named GAIA), is intended for enterprises that wish to deploy production-grade service-oriented architectures (SOA) and provides critical features such as service registration, dynamic discovery, management, failover, distributed security, and XML message processing.

TME GLUE Web Services Fabric plugs natively into any .NET or J2EE server or can be hosted standalone. Its decentralized architecture provides scalability and reliability; servers self-assemble using their unique GAIA technology to form a smart Web services fabric that self-heals if servers become temporarily disconnected. The more servers that are added, the more powerful the fabric becomes.

Licensing Although TME GLUE 4.0.1 is installed with the sample code, you will need to download an evaluation license from The Mind Electric. For using the sample code within this book, a license is available that will allow all the features to be used within a 60-minute period. A license can be downloaded from *http://www.themindelectric.com/books*. From this link, select the option for this book, and a license file will be sent to you via e-mail.

Once it is received, install the license file by copying it to the C:\Interoperability\Tools\Glue\lib directory. Using a command prompt, navigate to this directory and run the following command to add the license file to the libraries:

```
jar -uvf glue-all.jar glue-license.xml
```

Additional information about installing the license and more options for the commercial product can be found at *http://www.themindelectric.com*.

Intrinsyc Ja.NET 1.4

Microsoft does not create an implementation of .NET Remoting for Java, which is discussed in Chapter 4, "Connectivity with .NET Remoting." However, the specification is available, and as a result, a number of third-party implementations have begun to appear. The implementation used for the samples in Chapter 4 and Chapter 7 is Intrinsyc Ja.NET, which is installed with the sample code.

What Is Intrinsyc?

Intrinsyc (*http://www.intrinsyc.com*) is a global leader in providing unique, cost-effective software and hardware solutions that enable companies to create, network, and manage a wide range of specialized, intelligent devices. Intrinsyc's products and services include its flagship Ja.NET enterprise application integration product, through which the .NET Framework can seamlessly interoperate with the Java and J2EE platforms.

Licensing At the time of this writing, Intrinsyc Ja.NET provided the best implementation for the samples for using the .NET Remoting stack with Java that I wanted to show in this book. Not only does the product support the .NET Remoting stack, but it also supports enterprise application technology on both .NET and J2EE. For example, Ja.NET calls components hosted as EJBs or through Component Services.

As with GLUE 4.0.1, although Ja.NET is installed as part of the sample code, a separate license file has to be requested from Intrinsyc. To request this file, go to *http://support.intrinsyc.com/book/* and supply your name, e-mail address, and company name in order to request a license. Once you receive the license e-mail, copy the janet_license.xml file attachment to the C:\Interoperability\Tools\Ja.NET\lib directory. Configuration of the license is performed when the tools are run and will be covered with the sample code shown in Chapter 5.

IBM WebSphere MQ

In Chapter 9, "Asynchronous Interoperability, Part 2: WebSphere MQ," and Chapter 10, we'll look at using a Message Queue to achieve interoperability at the resource tier. IBM WebSphere MQ (formerly known as MQ Series) has been adopted by many enterprises. Throughout Part III, "Interoperability Technologies: Resource Tier," we'll show code examples that use both WebSphere MQ and Microsoft Message Queuing (MSMQ).

Downloading an evaluation IBM WebSphere MQ is not supplied on the accompanying CD. For those who do not own the product but who want to run the sample code, a 90-day evaluation version is available at *http://www.ibm.com/mqseries*.

Installing the Sample Code

Install the sample code from the accompanying CD, which will auto-run when inserted. All the code examples and the required third-party libraries (described earlier) are installed in a C:\Interoperability directory. Although this can be changed during setup, to simplify the process of following along with the samples as you read the book, it is recommended you accept the default location for this directory.

Make sure that the Microsoft .NET Framework 1.1 is present prior to installing the sample code. Doing this, and rebooting after the sample code has been installed, will ensure a correct installation.

Building and Running the Sample Code

Everyone has a different setup and environment, and if the sample code does not run, it's difficult from where I sit to predict where the errors might lie. However, I can offer several tips that might help you get all the samples working.

Building the Source with Ant and NAnt

Ant is one of the common build tools used for deploying applications in the J2EE environment. Its popularity is largely due to the way it can be extended with XML files and calls to regular Java classes to perform complex builds. With each sample in this book, I've included an appropriate build.xml file that can be used with Ant 1.5.1 or later to compile. Obviously, the Java source also can be loaded and compiled in an IDE.

I have chosen the .NET equivalent of Ant (known as NAnt) for building the .NET samples that are to be run from the command line. For each sample, a default.build file contains the build instructions for NAnt 0.7.9 or later.

The Ant and NAnt build tools are installed automatically with the sample code. For more information about the build tools, consult *http://ant.apache.org* and *http://nant.sourceforge.net*.

Common Script Functions

Launching Ant or NAnt from the command line is performed by typing **ant** or **nant** from within the directory that contains the build file. By default, using these commands without any parameters will compile the source code in that directory. In a number of the samples, the following parameters can be used to specify targets within the build files for certain operations:

- **ant clean** or **nant clean** is typically used to remove the compiled classes associated with a build.

- **ant run** or **nant run** can be used with samples that can be executed directly from the command line. These are normally samples that do not require any additional infrastructure or deployment to run.
- **ant package** is used for J2EE samples that require building into a J2EE package. For example, this could include the creation of a JAR, WAR, or EAR file that is to be deployed to a J2EE application server.
- **ant deploy** is used for J2EE samples that require deployment to a J2EE application server; it performs the copy from the source directory to the application server. In the samples, this deploy script is configured to deploy to a local instance of JBoss 3.0.7.
- **ant undeploy** is used to remove a deployment from a J2EE application server.

Configuration Directory

Many of the samples and build scripts rely on information from other software installations for proper execution. For example, building the sample code for the WebSphere MQ client requires access to the JAR files that are supplied with the WebSphere MQ product. Because it's not possible to second-guess where these files might be located on your machine, properties files are used by both the Ant and NAnt scripts to determine these file locations.

These property files can be found in the C:\Interoperability\Samples \Config directory. For example, the settings to indicate where the WebSphere MQ libraries are located can be found in the webspheremq.properties file. Properties files are also used by some of the NAnt scripts. It's important to make necessary adjustments to these property files to reflect your own configuration. This will ensure that the build process of the sample code is successful.

Running the Code on Multiple Machines

The majority of the code samples have been designed to run on a single machine. Doing so allows you to fully examine the processes and messages that are passed between the .NET and J2EE environments without the complications of adding networking issues. It's fair to say that because teaching you to achieve interoperability is the goal of this book, the book's code examples will work perfectly well when distributed to a number of machines. Doing so, however, might require some slight modifications of configuration files to reference multiple machines on the network instead of just referencing the local machine. These modifications will be referenced where necessary.

All the samples in the book assume that IIS is configured for *localhost* on port 80 and that J2EE Web applications (regardless of the server or vendor) run on port 8080 on the same machine. When you run the code samples while following this book, I recommend using these configurations. Once they are working, you can change these settings and the appropriate configuration files as required.

Setting Environment Variables

Because many of the code samples can be run from the command line, you must ensure that you've correctly set the environment variables. On a machine running the Windows operating system, you can specify this configuration in the System control panel, under the Advanced tab. The recommendations are as follows:

C# sample code

- Ensure that the System Path contains an entry to the directory containing the C# compiler (CSC.EXE). This compiler is normally found in the C:\WINDOWS\Microsoft.NET\Framework\v1.1.4322 directory for v1.1 of the .NET Framework.
- Ensure that the System Path also contains an entry for the bin directory of the NAnt installation (for example, C:\Interoperability\Tools\NAnt\bin). This will allow the NAnt executable to be run from the command line.
- Ensure that the System Path contains an entry for the bin directory of the Framework SDK. This will allow many of the command-line tools to be run from a command prompt. If you have installed Visual Studio .NET 2003 in the default location, this should be C:\Program Files\Microsoft Visual Studio .NET 2003\SDK\v1.1\Bin. If you are using the .NET Framework SDK 1.1 alone, this will be C:\Program Files\Microsoft.NET\FrameworkSDK\Bin.

Java sample code

- Ensure that the System Path contains an entry to the directory containing the Java compiler (JAVAC.EXE) and the executable to run Java applications (JAVA.EXE). These two programs are located in the bin directory of the J2SE SDK.
- Ensure that the System Path also contains an entry for the bin directory of the Ant installation (for example, C:\Interoperability\Tools\Ant\bin). This will allow the Ant executable to be run from the command line.
- Set the *JAVA_HOME* environment variable to the root of the J2SE SDK installation. This is normally performed with the installation of the J2SE SDK, and is required by Ant.

- Ensure that the *CLASSPATH* environment variable contains an entry to %*JAVA_HOME*%\lib\tools.jar, where %*JAVA_HOME*% is the previous environment variable.
- The *CLASSPATH* environment variable should also be modified to include the required JAR files for the sample code to compile and run. This is especially important when running sample code that includes code for third-party tools, such as Ja.NET and GLUE. A number of these JAR files will be added to the default path by the sample code installer. It is worth double-checking these values before compiling any of the samples.

Running the Setup Validation Tool

As the majority of the examples shown within this book contain dependencies on numerous installations, environment variables, and other settings, the sample code also ships with a setup validation tool. This tool can be used to verify which products have been installed and configured, and potentially highlight any problems that may prevent the samples from running correctly.

The tool, called SETUPVALIDATOR.EXE, can be found in the C:\Interoperability\Tools\Setup directory. Running the tool from the command line will display potential problems and also record these to a SetupValidator.log file in the same directory. In the case where problems are found, the tool will offer suggestions or recommendations to allow them to be corrected.

Summary

This chapter presented two angles for learning some of the fundamentals of this book. The first was an overview of the Microsoft .NET Framework for Java and J2EE developers; the second covered Java and J2EE for developers who come from a Microsoft programming background.

Consider these fundamentals a steppingstone for the rest of the book, rather than an exhaustive description of the way each of the two platforms and development environments works. The resources listed throughout this chapter will help if you want to research the topic further.

Now that we've covered the terminology and technology required to start our journey into .NET and J2EE interoperability, let's look at interoperability scenarios and requirements in Chapter 2, "Business Requirements for Interoperability."

2

Business Requirements for Interoperability

The objective of this chapter is to introduce the concept of business requirements for interoperability and explain the role that these requirements play in helping you select a correct design and choose technical options when building a solution. The term *business requirements for interoperability* refers to business drivers, needs, or requirements that compel you to create a solution that benefits from being written partly for the Microsoft .NET Framework and partly for the Java2 Enterprise Edition (J2EE) framework. These solutions either can be created anew or can exist within the enterprise already.

We'll work with three common requirements throughout this chapter and look at the two architectural concepts that are derived from them. The three requirements we will look at are interoperability at the presentation tier, reuse of business tier components, and business tier resource sharing. The two architectural concepts that we'll be deriving from these and using throughout the book are point-to-point interoperability and resource tier interoperability. You might have your own requirements, scenarios, or ideas—maybe from projects you've been involved with or interoperability use cases you've come across. The requirements and scenarios presented in this chapter are based on my own experience with customers. My goal in presenting them is to capture some of the fundamental designs that drive interoperability with .NET and J2EE in business software solutions today.

Technology-Aligned Development

Before we look at some requirements, I want to introduce the term *technology-aligned development*. For the past few years, development of applications at a particular company has tended to be aligned to a particular platform or technology. For example, in one of my previous positions, I consulted for a company that used J2EE technology for all its applications and services. The organization standardized on this single technology, mandated by the CIO, and chose a preferred vendor to supply the application server that the company used.

The mindset of the architects and developers who worked for this company was *aligned* with the technology decisions that had been made, hence the term *technology-aligned development*. For example, when the business had a new requirement for an application, the architects and developers were already thinking in terms of the preferred technology. If the application would be hosted on the Web, discussions were immediately started about the best way of using JavaServer Pages (JSP), Java tag libraries, and Servlets to construct and present this experience to the user. This Web-based front end naturally had to call business tier, or middle tier, components. Therefore, these discussions led to the J2EE-specific components that would reside at the business tier, how they would be invoked, and the required protocols. Because J2EE-specific components often have to work with persistent data, the conversation turned to J2EE-specific ways of accessing databases.

The choices made for architecting the system at that time were largely based on the platform and technology the company had standardized upon. Such companywide decisions are in no way specific to J2EE—many Microsoft-based projects have taken the same route. As applications take on a more loosely coupled and service-oriented approach, the ability to create solutions that are independent of the technology is becoming much more important for organizations—even more so as applications and processes run across organizations via partnerships, mergers, or acquisitions. It might be possible to dictate your organization's strategy for technology development; however, choosing a technology for outside companies that you work with or might become part of requires a more heterogeneous approach.

Figure 2-1 shows the technology-aligned development paradigm. The figure shows some system building blocks we'll use in our requirements and the diagrams throughout this book. Excluding the client making the request, the figure depicts three tiers. The *presentation tier* contains the technology required to host Web-based applications. For the J2EE platform, this will likely be a combination of JSPs and Servlets, hosted on a J2EE application server or a Web server such as Apache Tomcat. For .NET, this is ASP.NET hosted via Microsoft Internet Information Server (IIS), which we briefly covered in Chapter 1, "Microsoft .NET and J2EE Fundamentals."

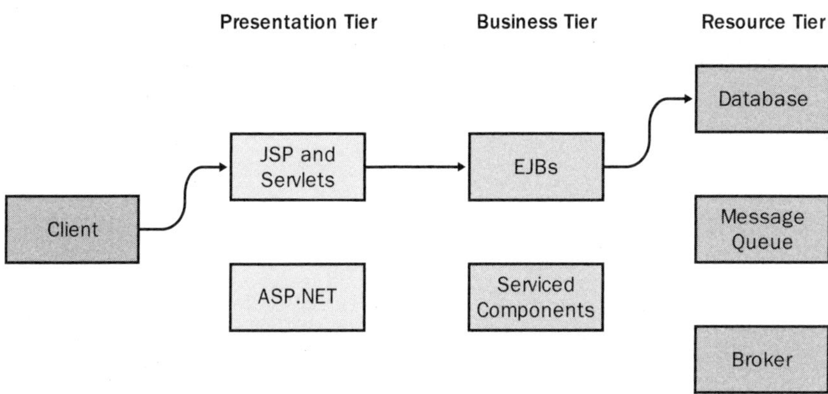

Figure 2-1 Technology-aligned development for a J2EE-specific application or service.

For the *business tier* (or *middle tier*), Figure 2-1 shows a number of Enterprise Java Beans (EJBs) for the J2EE platform and Serviced Components for .NET. For both J2EE and .NET, we could have used ways of hosting the components other than the ones shown in the figure, but these fit the scenarios described in this book and map well to many applications that are in production today.

Finally, to the right, the figure shows the *resource tier*. The resource tier contains a number of systems and services that tend to be shared resources within an application. Such resources can include databases, message queues, and brokers, all of which we'll cover in Part III.

As mentioned previously, the concept of technology-aligned development isn't exclusive to any platform. Figure 2-2 shows the same approach taken in a Microsoft-centric world. The arrows in the figure show a Microsoft Web-based application calling the ASP.NET tier, which references business tier Serviced Components that persist data in a database.

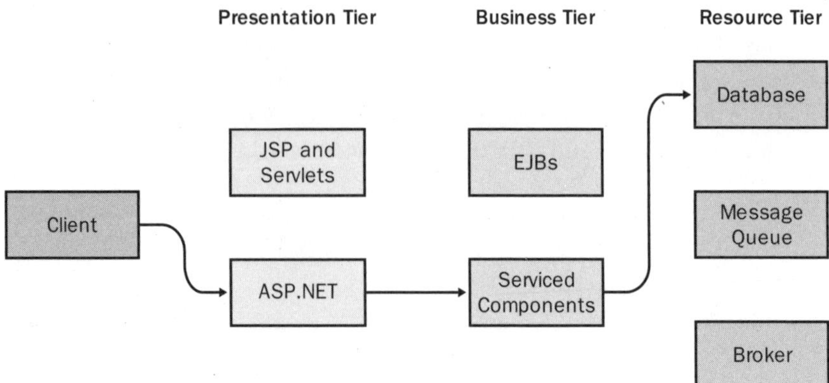

Figure 2-2 Technology-aligned development for a .NET-specific application or service.

Now that we have some nomenclature for the tiers, let's look at the requirements and business drivers for enabling interoperability in your solutions.

Three Common Requirements

For each of the requirements described in the following sections, I'll point out the requirement's business driver (that is, the fundamental reason for requiring interoperability in the solution) and business benefits. I'll also offer examples where appropriate. The purpose of this chapter isn't to provide solutions for these requirements—it's to make sure you understand when they might arise and the reasoning behind them. These requirements and examples are the ones we'll use throughout the book.

Interoperability at the Presentation Tier

Business requirement: *To replace or extend an existing presentation tier by using the technology of a different platform, or to integrate an application written to a different platform with an existing presentation tier.*

Business benefits: *Allows selection of the presentation tier based on the best overall user experience, regardless of technology.*

On a couple of occasions, I've been asked this question: "If you had five minutes with a team of developers proficient in J2EE and wanted to highlight a single advantage of using .NET, what would it be?" This is a tough question to answer, but if I had to pick only one piece of the .NET Framework, I'd have to say designing Web applications using ASP.NET. Don't get me wrong, some great innovations have been made in JSP technology and the frameworks that support this technology. Personally, I am a fan of Apache Struts and the concepts and ideas it employs. But when it comes to developing pages, I find that the current version of JSP (v1.2) can be likened to Microsoft's previous platform, Active Server Pages (ASP), leaving ASP.NET in a class of its own.

Many organizations that share my view have already recognized an opportunity to use ASP.NET for creating a new user experience, portal, or other user interface via the Web. Leveraging ASP.NET for this purpose can range from creating an ASP.NET page that needs to be integrated into an existing JSP framework to replacing the entire JSP portal over time. In either case, the interoperability requirement between the presentation and business tiers in an application remains the same.

This chapter's introduction described how interoperability, not migration, is the relevant issue today—and this requirement fits well here. Many organizations looking to write a new version of an application already have the core infrastructure in place and working. However, for now, such organizations might not want to replace all the components just to deliver a new or updated user experience.

Introducing ASP.NET into an organization to extend or replace the existing JSP user interface that implements the presentation tier for a J2EE application has an interoperability requirement that follows a pattern similar to the one shown in Figure 2-3.

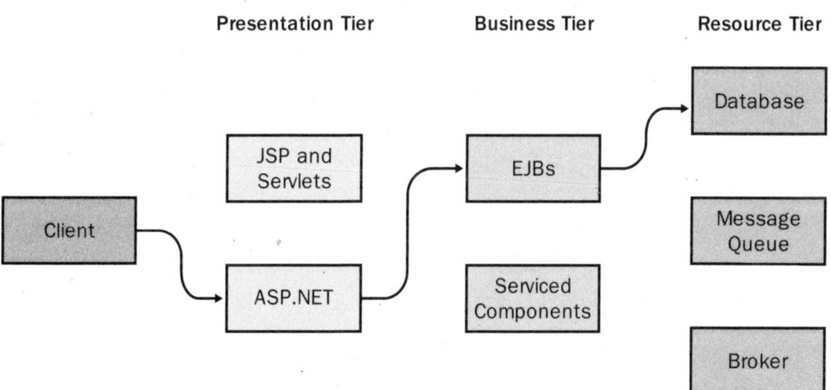

Figure 2-3 Replacing the JSP and Servlets presentation tier with one created in ASP.NET.

This sets in stone our first requirement and poses our first interoperability question: how does a typical ASP.NET presentation tier (a page, component, or replacement for a JSP equivalent) interoperate with a typical J2EE middle tier?

The reverse scenario is also very real. Imagine a business scenario in which an organization wants to adopt a third-party solution that runs on the .NET Framework in the business tier. This organization might have invested a lot of resources and development time in creating a Web experience by using JSP and probably won't want to force its users to relearn a new interface to work with the .NET services. In this case, the scenario shown in Figure 2-4 might work well, where the existing J2EE/JSP–based Web user interface is preserved but the new third-party service in .NET can still be utilized.

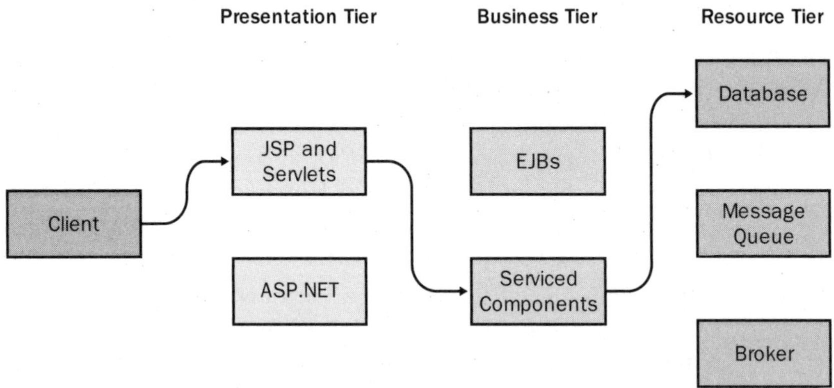

Figure 2-4 Utilizing a .NET application or service within an existing J2EE infrastructure.

For both topologies, our first requirement for the presentation tier (as a client) is to call the business tier from the other platform. Herein lies our first interoperability challenge.

Reuse of Business Tier Components

Business requirement: *To create or integrate applications and services that have the ability to reuse exposed business tier components from an existing application or service.*

Business benefits: *Saves developer time and resources by utilizing components that already exist today, reducing the time required to deliver a solution.*

The previous requirement focused on replacing all or parts of the presentation tier with a new solution. The business driver behind this decision might be to leverage some advantages of the other presentation tier, adding new functionality that isn't available, a new look and feel for the portal, or a mix of these. Our second requirement, the reuse of business tier components, takes a look at the interoperability requirements for a solution based on a scenario similar to the one described in the next paragraph.

Imagine an organization that has a number of applications and services already deployed using the J2EE platform. The organization wants to undertake a proof-of-concept project to create a new application or service in .NET, as shown in Figure 2-5.

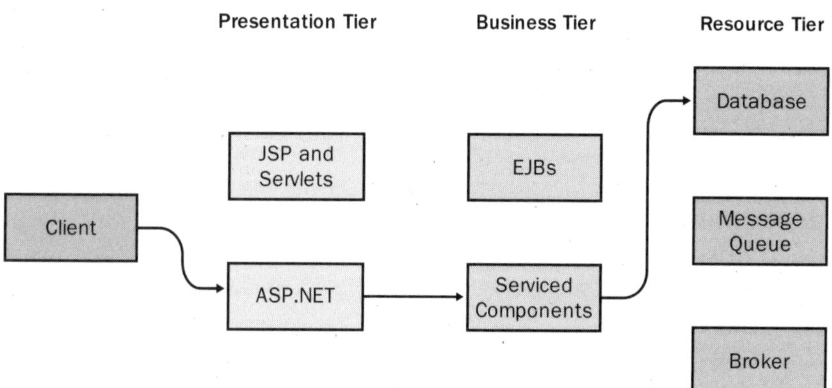

Figure 2-5 A new application or service based on the .NET platform.

To decrease time to market for developing its new .NET proof of concept, the organization has concluded that it could reuse some of the components that already exist in its J2EE implementations. For example, a set of security services (to allow authentication with other systems) might have already been created on the J2EE platform. These services have been proven in previous applications, and it seems unreasonable to expect the developers to spend time reinventing the wheel in order to use new technology.

Because the J2EE specification has evolved over a longer period of time than .NET, this type of interoperability requirement is realistic for many organizations that begin developing with .NET. Some organizations decide that certain business tier components in .NET will call business tier components in J2EE, which necessitates interoperability between the two business tiers, as shown in Figure 2-6.

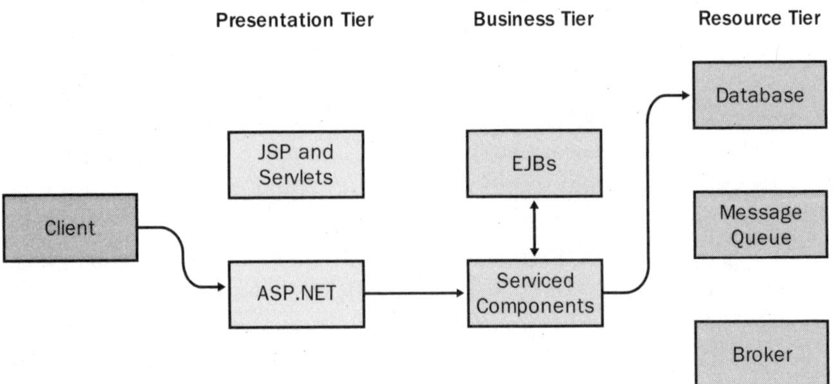

Figure 2-6 Interoperability from reusing existing business tier components within a new .NET application.

The components that are called could return data from another source such as a message queue, so the J2EE business tier components could have their own access to the resource tier as well as to the new application. To reuse the business tier components from the J2EE platform, the .NET components need to communicate between the two tiers. This requirement, to reuse existing business tier components, defines our second interoperability scenario.

You might be wondering what the difference is in selecting a solution for this requirement and selecting one for our first requirement—interoperability at the presentation tier—given that it's just a different tier calling the business tier. Although the solutions and options to connect the two tiers are similar, components at the business tier tend to be used in different ways than components and pages at the presentation tier, which affects how we make the solution interoperable. The following sections describe some of these differences.

Security Issues

Many business tier components that are called from the presentation tier are usually called with the credentials of the signed-in user. In our first requirement, the authentication and authorization for calling the component at the business tier will likely be driven by the presentation tier. The credentials used to log on to the presentation tier can be passed to the business tier component to help achieve this. If we compare this with our earlier interoperability scenario in which a business tier component is invoked from within the same business tier, authentication is still an important part of the solution but will likely be performed using different credentials than those of the original signed-in user.

Again, this example will vary among different situations. The point is that it's likely that the security model for calling middle tier components from the presentation tier will be different from the security model for calling them from the corresponding middle tier. If the security model differs, this affects how you design a solution that can interoperate between the two platforms.

Transactional Issues

Components called from the corresponding business tier are much more likely to be part of a transaction (a coordinated set of processes) than those called from the presentation tier. Typically, a call from the presentation tier will be a one-off call driven by user input. For example, a presentation tier call to the business tier might be interpreted like this: "This is what the user asked for. Do something with it, and give me the result in a format I can understand."

In comparison, a call from the corresponding middle tier might be involved in a much larger transaction. The business tier component could be part of a complex system and might be subject to rollback—in other words, if other parts of the transaction fail, this component must undo its actions. Additionally, the component might also be run synchronously with other components. As mentioned, the way a component interacts with a transaction can affect the choices and design for interoperability.

Performance Issues

If you design a solution in which the presentation tier calls a business tier component on a different platform, you'll still expect a reasonable level of performance from the application. This is especially true for a presentation tier component because any performance-related delay could ultimately affect the user, leaving the user with the equivalent of the spinning hourglass.

Business tier components might also be subject to reasonable performance expectations. However, if a component is executed as part of a long-running asynchronous transaction, a performance degradation might not have a significant impact on the end user.

In general, interactions between components within the business tier are more coarsely grained and more loosely coupled than the interaction between components from the presentation tier and components from the business tier.

Business Tier Resource Sharing

Business requirement: *To create or integrate an application or service that has the ability to access data from an existing application or service.*

Business benefits: *Allows applications to share existing resources, thus avoiding the creation of duplicate points of data or multiple stores.*

As with the second interoperability requirement, the third requirement assumes that a new application is being created. But instead of connecting J2EE and .NET components directly, interoperability is performed by sharing resources.

Imagine the following example: an organization has developed a public stock-trading application by using J2EE technology as shown in Figure 2-7. The application allows online users to trade and manage their stock portfolios via the Web.

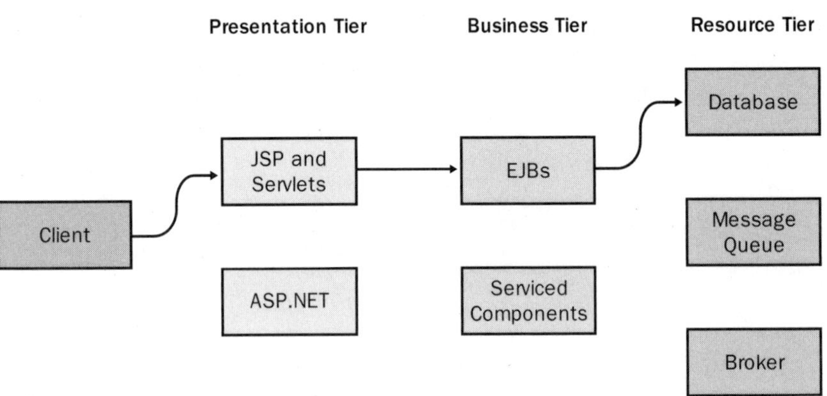

Figure 2-7 An application written for the J2EE platform.

Now suppose the organization wants to provide some new functionality, such as portfolio recommendations, and wants to deliver this information via a new interface. These new recommendations could be sent to a user via a cell phone or PDA. The organization chooses to develop the interface and business components on .NET, and the new recommendations will be accessed by the client as shown in Figure 2-8.

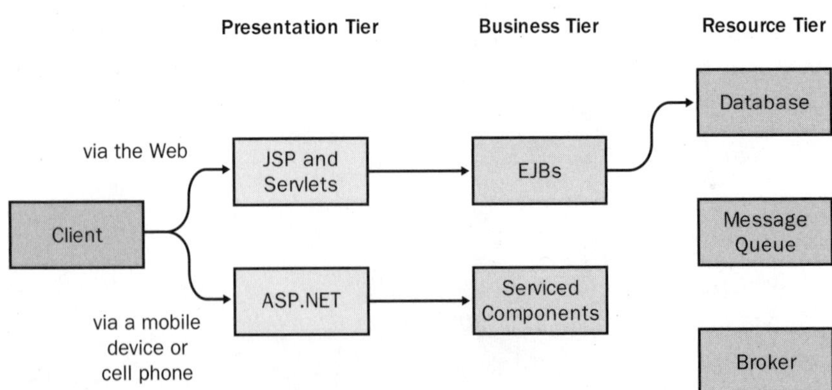

Figure 2-8 Introduction of a new .NET application with different presentation and business tiers.

Unlike the second interoperability scenario, the functionality of this new application hasn't been implemented in J2EE. The EJBs and other J2EE components at the business tier don't apply to the business logic of the new .NET application; therefore, it doesn't make sense to reuse those components.

The data, however, is still valid in this requirement. All the account and portfolio data resides in a single database. To avoid duplicating that data, we need to access the tables and records from the business tier of our new application, as shown in Figure 2-9.

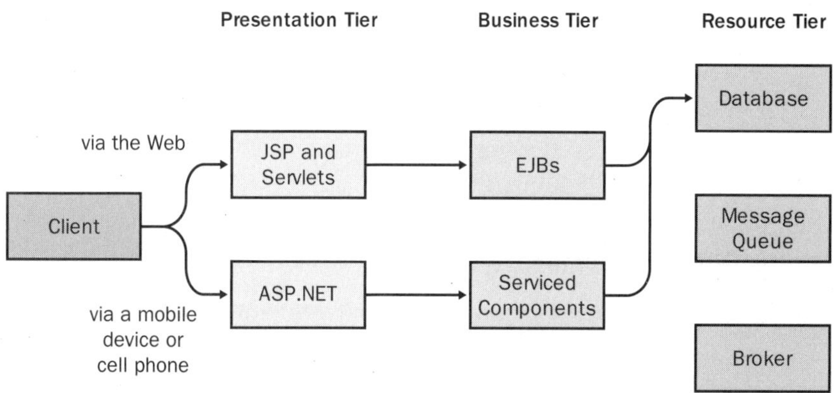

Figure 2-9 Both applications share the data at the resource tier.

You might also have a requirement to access other areas of the resource tier. The database might be used to store and access account records, and for committing trades, a message queue might be used to execute orders in a timely fashion. To implement this performance boost for our new application, we might also want to provide interoperability for the message queue, as shown in Figure 2-10. The same interoperability technique can be applied to any other technology at the same tier.

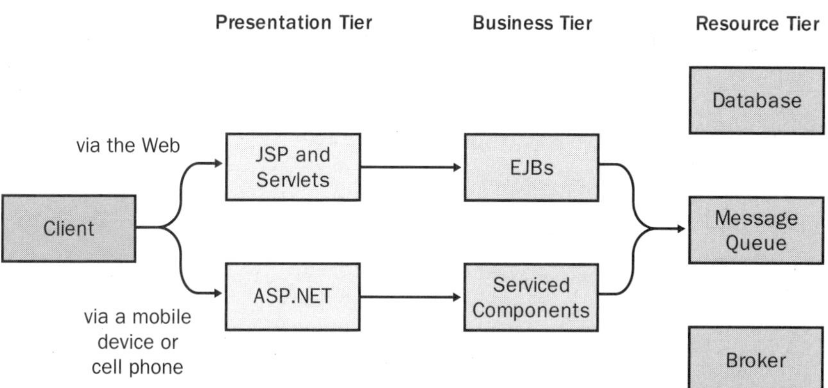

Figure 2-10 Both applications share a message queue at the resource tier.

Many variations and permutations can be applied to each of these requirements, but these three main requirements drive a significant portion of the solutions that we'll discover, work with, and expand upon in this book.

Interoperability Concepts

The three common requirements that drive interoperability outlined in this chapter allow us to introduce two concepts that will help you select the correct technology for developing solutions. These technology options will make up Parts II and III of the book.

After working through the requirements, you might have guessed that the two interoperability concepts that can be derived from them are *point-to-point interoperability* and *resource tier interoperability*. Let's define these terms before we start looking at technical options.

Point-to-Point Interoperability

Point-to-point interoperability covers the main points of connecting components discussed in this book. These points of interoperability are the .NET presentation tier to the J2EE business tier, the J2EE presentation tier to the .NET business tier, and the .NET business tier to the J2EE business tier and vice versa. These lines of connectivity are shown in Figure 2-11.

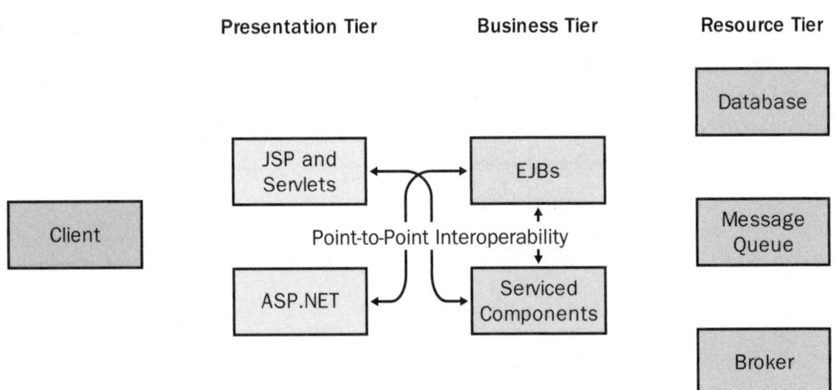

Figure 2-11 Point-to-point interoperability between a .NET application and a J2EE application.

As you'll see when we start exploring the technical options for point-to-point interoperability in Part II, "Interoperability Technologies: Point to Point," the connectivity tends to be between two single points and, although it's not exclusively the case, it's often a synchronous call—in other words, the calling component waits for a response from the other system. The point-to-point interoperability options we'll cover are .NET Remoting and XML Web services.

Resource Tier Interoperability

Resource tier interoperability covers the other connectivity points outlined in our requirements. These points connect the two platforms' business tiers to each of the resource tiers, as well as to the database, the message queue, and the broker, as shown in Figure 2-12.

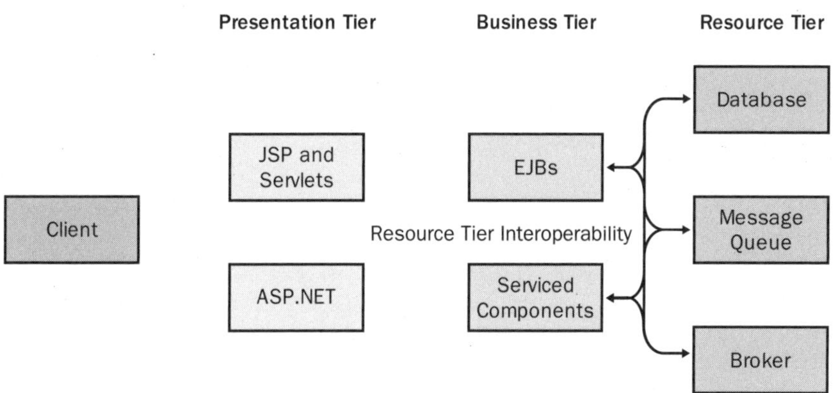

Figure 2-12 Resource tier interoperability between a .NET and J2EE application.

When we cover the technical options for resource tier interoperability in Part III, "Interoperability Technologies: Resource Tier," these calls tend to be arbitrated (handled by the third party in the resource tier) and mostly asynchronous (meaning that data is sent to the resource tier without the expectation of an immediate reply). These options will include a shared database, message queue, and broker.

Summary

This chapter covered three basic requirements that drive interoperability in solutions today: interoperability at the presentation tier, reuse of business tier components, and business tier resource sharing. These requirements are based on three particular scenarios, and many variations might be applied to make them fit your own situation.

In addition to covering these requirements, we introduced two new terms: *point-to-point interoperability* and *resource tier interoperability*. These two concepts stem from the architecture in the three scenarios just mentioned and will help us categorize the technology choices presented throughout the book.

Before we look at these technology options, we'll discuss exchanging data between .NET and J2EE. This will give you the foundation to understand some of the most common elements of interoperability, regardless of the technical solution you select.

3

Exchanging Data Between .NET and Java

Before you consider which technical options apply to creating solutions that can interoperate between Microsoft .NET and Java 2 Enterprise Edition (J2EE)—or buy products for creating such solutions—it is vital that you first consider how data will be passed between the tiers outlined in Chapter 2, "Business Requirements for Interoperability," and what types of data you'll likely encounter. With any of the requirements presented in the previous chapter, data will always need to pass between at least some of the tiers on different platforms.

For example, the first scenario presented in Chapter 2 had a business requirement for a new presentation tier in Microsoft ASP.NET that called a business tier written for J2EE, as shown in Figure 3-1.

Imagine that an Enterprise Java Bean (EJB) in the J2EE business tier exposes a method that will be called by the ASP.NET tier. In a production system, the data returned by the EJB could be relatively *complex* and probably goes beyond the prototypical "Hello World" example. (Data types will be defined shortly.)

When various vendor implementations of Java Web services were released, many came with interoperability samples to show how they could interoperate with .NET. When run, these samples passed a "Hello World" string or another primitive data type between code written in both Java and .NET.

Although this was impressive in sales presentations, very few production systems simply pass "Hello World" between tiers, and in such cases, the data tends to be much more complex. When customers used these early implementations to try building robust systems, many found it impossible to pass the types of data that they wanted to.

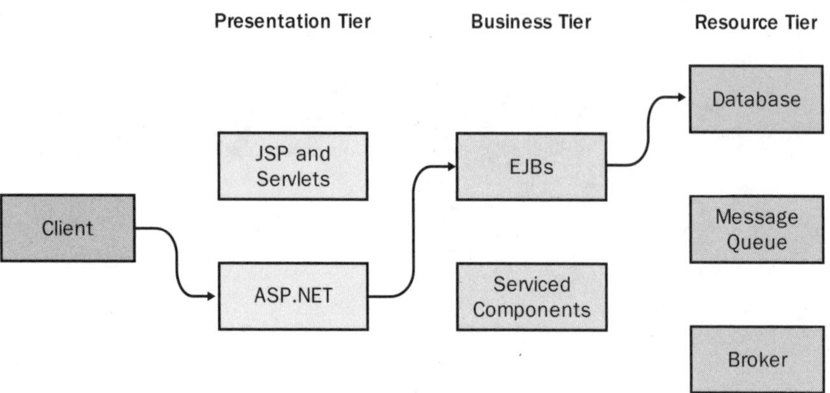

Figure 3-1 Requirement for a new ASP.NET presentation tier for an existing J2EE application.

As you look at some of the options for achieving interoperability in this chapter—options that are not necessarily specific to Web services—you'll find that things have progressed considerably since the days of those early implementations. You'll also find that with the technical options covered in this chapter, exchanging complex data between .NET and J2EE has become more of a reality. However, some caveats for exchanging data between the two platforms still exist, which makes data exchange one of the major challenges of achieving interoperability.

Data Exchange Challenges

Three immediate data exchange challenges exist when connecting any two disparate platforms, all of which revolve around type compatibility. These challenges are primitive data type mappings, nonexistent data types, and complex data types, and they all can hinder the flow of data between the two platforms.

> **Note** What is a primitive data type? In this context, a primitive data type is data based on the underlying type system of either .NET or Java—for example, a string, an integer, a double, and so forth.

These three challenges can be defined as follows:

- **Primitive data type mappings** The string data type exists in both the common language runtime (CLR) and Java. But does this mean that the *java.lang.String* class in Java is the same as the *System.String* class in the CLR? If you create your own interoperability sample that exposes types of *java.lang.String*, how do you map these types to the equivalent types in .NET?
- **Nonexistent data types** Assuming that you've defined mappings for primitive data types (strings, integers, and so forth), what do you do about data types on one platform that don't exist on the other? Many data types in the CLR don't exist in Java and vice versa. For example, you might not find an appropriate counterpart for the *System.Collections.Specialized.HybridDictionary* type in Java. So how would you expose data of this type?
- **Complex data types** Many applications expose complex data types—custom data types that are made up of primitive data types. An example of this data type is a stock record that contains the company name, current share price, and previous share price. In addition, complex data types can be nested. For instance, imagine a shopping cart that contains multiple *Item* data types. In this cart, the *Item* type might also be a complex data type. The challenge lies in exposing the structure of this complex data type so that it can be consumed by a component on another platform.

Fortunately, a number of options discussed throughout this chapter can be used to help exchange data types between applications in .NET and J2EE and vice versa.

Our Sample Scenario

Before we look at these options in detail, let's use the business requirements discussed at the beginning of this chapter. Figure 3-2 repeats Figure 3-1 for simplicity's sake.

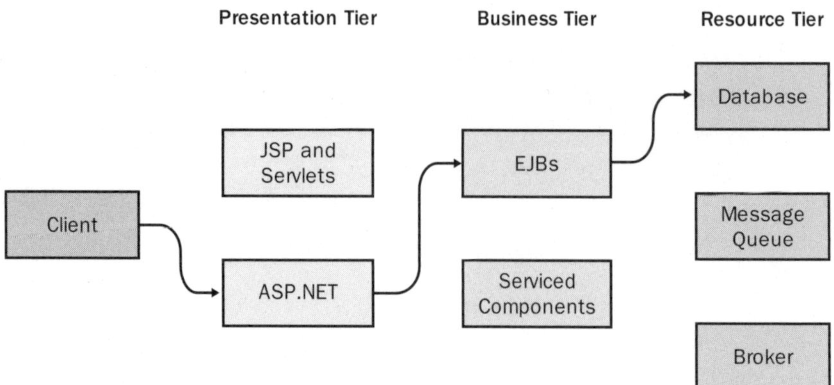

Figure 3-2 Requirement for a new ASP.NET presentation tier for an existing J2EE application.

Imagine that the application depicted in Figure 3-2 is a stock-trading Web site. Until now, the application has been based entirely on J2EE technology, but with the release of ASP.NET, the company that operates the site decided that there could be potential for improving the user experience.

In this example, a development team was assigned the task of creating a new look and feel for the site by using ASP.NET, but the challenge of connecting the new portal to the existing EJB infrastructure remains. To start, let's look at the types of data that are potentially exposed by the EJBs that will be called.

Our example application passes stock information to the user from a database populated by another system, or in the language of Chapter 2, from the business tier to the presentation tier. This information might be recommendations for purchases or sales or might simply be a quote for the user's current portfolio. In all these cases, a *stock data type* is used, as shown in Table 3-1.

Table 3-1 Our Sample's Stock Data Type

Data Field	Type	Example
Ticker	string	FTHC
Name	string	Fourth Coffee
Price	double	3.02
Previous	double	3.23
Volume	integer	1330

The stock type defines five elements: a ticker symbol to uniquely identify the stock, the name of the stock, the current trading price, the previous trading price at the last close, and the volume (in thousands) of this stock that's been traded since the last close. This basic example gives us a realistic data type to work with. As you can see, the Ticker and Name fields are both strings, the Price and Previous fields are doubles, and the Volume field is an integer.

Now that we have defined the complex type that we need to pass from an EJB to a calling ASP.NET page, let's look at the two available methods of data exchange we can use to do this: *binary serialization* and *XML serialization*. Given that both involve serialization, let's also define the term.

What Is Serialization?

Serialization is the process by which an object or class can be encoded into a form that can be persisted and/or transported. This can prove useful in many scenarios because it allows complex data types to be encoded, saved, transferred, and decoded, potentially by a different process.

As mentioned, two general types of serialization exist: binary serialization and XML serialization. In binary serialization, a data type is serialized into a stream of bytes. In XML serialization, a data type is serialized into an XML document. The resulting binary stream or XML document can then be stored in memory or a file, or it can be passed across the network as required.

For binary serialization in both the CLR and Java, any type that will be serialized must be appropriately modified. In the CLR, this is done by either annotating the type with the *[Serializable]* attribute or implementing the *ISerializable* interface. In Java, a class must implement the *java.lang.Serializable* interface in order to be serialized.

For XML serialization, the rules are slightly different. Data types in .NET don't necessarily have to be labeled with an attribute, although it's still a good idea. Also, a .NET data type must have a valid default public constructor. (We'll look at this concept in more detail when we examine the sample code in the "Using XML Serialization" section.)

The process of restoring a serialized object to its original form is known as *deserialization*. The rule of thumb is that objects must be deserialized into the same type that they were serialized from. For example, if I serialize a *myStock* data type into a stream of bytes or an XML document, I need to deserialize it into the same data type—I can't deserialize it into a type of *yourStock*.

> **Note** A few exceptions to the rule of deserialization exist. For binary serialization, these include writing your own custom serializer and using a process in Java known as *evolution*, which allows versioning of serialized objects. For XML serialization, you can use XML Schema to define a new type for a document, provided you adhere to the data transformation rules defined by the W3C in the XML Schema recommendation.

Let's look at both binary and XML serialization in action.

Using Binary Serialization

Time for some good news and bad news. First, the good news: both Java 2 Standard Edition (J2SE) v1.4 and Microsoft .NET Framework version 1.0 ship with a binary serializer that can convert any data type that's marked as serializable into a stream of bytes. The classes to perform this serialization are similar and relatively simple.

Now for the bad news: the formats that these binary serializers write are incompatible. This means that if I use the Java binary serializer to serialize an object to a file, the format of this file won't make any sense to the binary serializer that ships with the .NET Framework, and vice versa.

Running the Sample Code

To prove this, let's look at the first example of the book. After installing the samples from the companion CD, you'll find this example in the C:\Interoperability\Samples\Data\Binary\Serialization installation subdirectory. This directory contains three subdirectories: dotNET, Java, and Shared. The dotNET directory contains an example of serializing a CLR type by using C#, and the Java directory contains the equivalent for the Java platform. The Shared directory is an empty directory that output can be written to and read from.

Navigate to the dotNET directory first, and build the sample. (Refer to the "Running the Sample Code in This Book" section in Chapter 1, "Microsoft .NET and J2EE Fundamentals," for instructions on how to do this.) The sample contains three parts: Stock.dll, which contains the data type to be used; Writer.exe, which creates a new *Stock* object and serializes it to a file, and Reader.exe, which does the reverse.

To test the sample, run Writer, supplying the parameter of a file to write the serialized stream of bytes to:

```
Writer ..\Shared\stock.bin
```

If serialization is successful, the following message will be displayed:

```
..\Shared\stock.bin was created successfully.
```

If you want, you can take a look at the stock.bin file in Microsoft Notepad or another text editor. You'll notice that the file contains a binary representation of a stock (that of course will be unreadable).

To deserialize this file, run Reader. Again, supply the parameter for the file that was written:

```
Reader ..\Shared\stock.bin
```

If deserialization was successful, the sample will display the data held in the stock:

```
Stock Information:
------------------
Ticker:   FTHC
Name:     Fourth Coffee
Price:    3.02
Previous: 3.12
Volume:   25
```

Now let's look at the same example in Java. The Java subdirectory has a similar setup. Once compiled, Stock.class contains the data type definition, Writer.class contains the method to serialize the object to a file, and Reader.class contains the code to deserialize the object. Running both the Java Writer and Reader examples, which can easily be done by executing **ant reader** and **ant writer** from the command prompt should yield similar results to those produced by the .NET sample code.

How the Sample Code Works

The sample code works relatively simply. First, the sample in .NET contains the definition for a stock based on our sample scenario:

```
using System;

namespace Binary
{
    [Serializable]
    public class Stock
    {
```

```
            public String Ticker="";
            public String Name="";
            public double Price=0;
            public double Previous=0;
            public int Volume=0;
        }
}
```

This type definition is relatively simple and is marked with the *Serializable* attribute. To create an object of this type and write it to a file, you use *BinaryFormatter*, which is part of the *System.Runtime.Serialization.Formatters.Binary* namespace. Combined with a *FileStream*, the binary formatter can serialize the object with the following code:

```
IFormatter formatter = new BinaryFormatter();
Stream fs = new FileStream(binFile, FileMode.Create);
formatter.Serialize(fs,FTHC);
fs.Close();
```

The reader uses exactly the same approach, but in reverse. Here, the *BinaryFormatter* is still used, but the *Deserialize* method is called to convert the binary file into the required object:

```
IFormatter formatter = new BinaryFormatter();
Stream fs = new FileStream(binFile, FileMode.Open);
Stock incomingStock = (Stock)formatter.Deserialize(fs);
fs.Close();
```

The Java sample works in a similar way, using standard Java classes. Again, a class is defined for the stock type that's marked as being serializable:

```
public class Stock implements java.io.Serializable
{
    public String Ticker;
    public String Name;
    public double Price;
    public double Previous;
    public int Volume;
}
```

To write the object to a binary file, the *java.io.ObjectOutputStream* class is used. The *writeObject* method takes the object and outputs a stream, which is then written to a file:

```
fs = new FileOutputStream(binFile);
os = new ObjectOutputStream(fs);
os.writeObject(FTHC);
os.close();
```

For reading, you use a similar approach, but the corresponding class is named *ObjectInputStream*:

```
fs = new FileInputStream(binFile);
is = new ObjectInputStream(fs);
incomingStock = (Stock)is.readObject();
is.close();
```

In this example, we have similar .NET and Java classes being used to serialize and deserialize an object into a binary format.

Breaking the Sample Code

The beginning of this section mentioned that the binary serializers in both the CLR and Java were not compatible. We can prove this by rerunning the sample code, except this time, we'll write and read the data type using code from the different platforms. (It's a little ironic that the first sample in a book covering interoperability is designed to not work, but it's a good test all the same.)

To run the code, return to the dotNET subdirectory in C:\Interoperability\Samples\Data\Binary\Serialization. Rerun the .Net writer sample, passing a location of a file within the Shared subdirectory:

```
Writer ..\Shared\stock.bin
```

Now navigate to the Java subdirectory and rerun the Java reader sample, using the same location of this file. Instead of the data type being deserialized, an exception is thrown:

```
java.io.StreamCorruptedException: invalid stream header
```

According to the Java deserializer, this is not a valid byte stream, and for this demonstration, it's correct. We can observe the same behavior if we switch the writer to Java and the reader to .NET. From the Java subdirectory, rerun the writer to overwrite the shared file. Once done, return to the dotNET directory and run Reader. The exception shown here is a *SerializationException*:

```
System.Runtime.Serialization.SerializationException:
BinaryFormatter Version incompatibility.
Expected Version 1.0.  Received Version 1801678708.2084051481.
```

Again, the .NET sample cannot interpret the stream of bytes that's been written by the Java serializer and cannot reconstruct the object.

Can Binary Serialization Ever Be Used for Interoperability?

In short, yes. The principles of serialization, however, state that the serialization and deserialization of any object must be performed with the same formatter. The format that takes the data type and creates a stream of bytes must match the format that takes the bytes and reconstructs the object.

Although the default binary serializers in the CLR and Java aren't compatible and wouldn't serve as a good example of interoperability, a number of ways to achieve this interoperability do exist. For instance, you can use a custom serializer that shares the same formatting options for both the CLR and Java. Alternatively, the binary formatter within the .NET Framework can be licensed, allowing third parties to create their own implementations. One good example of this is using binary serialization in conjunction with .NET Remoting, which we'll explore in some detail in Chapter 4, "Connectivity with .NET Remoting." In Chapter 4, we'll use a third-party product, Ja.NET from Intrinsyc, which relies on a version of the CLR binary serializer created for Java.

Using XML Serialization

Now that we've taken a look at the principles of serialization with regard to binary formatting, let's look at our second option, which takes the same approach but uses XML.

In its simplest form, XML is a markup language for documents that contain structured data. The key tenet of XML is that it can be used to describe any data in a human-readable, structured form. Structured information can contain both content (such as words, pictures, annotations, and inserts) as well as information that defines the content.

This book does not cover the basics of XML; I'm assuming that you already understand some of the principles of this markup language. For additional information on creating XML documents, see one of the many articles and resources that have been written about this topic, including *XML Programming* (Microsoft Press, 2002).

To discover how XML documents can aid data exchange between applications and services in .NET and Java, let's look at a sample based on our earlier stock data type:

```
<?xml version="1.0"?>
<Stock>
    <Ticker>CONT</Ticker>
    <Name>Contoso</Name>
    <Price>12.45</Price>
```

```
    <Previous>12.23</Previous>
    <Volume>23</Volume>
</Stock>
```

One of the key observations about this document and XML in general is that—unlike the output from the binary serializer—the data is not bound to any platform. Because of the nature of XML, this *Stock* record can be read by .NET, Java, and even humans. The use of XML in this form doesn't restrict the data from being transferred between platforms, which is crucial when using XML to achieve interoperability between .NET and Java.

One limitation of this XML document is that currently it holds only one *Stock* record. (*Stock* is the root element of our XML document.) Because our examples will show multiple *Stock* items being stored in XML, let's also define a root element named *Stocks*. This type can be used to hold one or more stocks:

```
<?xml version="1.0"?>
<Stocks>
    <Stock>
        <Ticker>CONT</Ticker>
        <Name>Contoso</Name>
        <Price>12.45</Price>
        <Previous>12.23</Previous>
        <Volume>23</Volume>
    </Stock>
</Stocks>
```

As this document shows, the *Stock* type becomes a subelement within *Stocks*. This allows you to hold more than one stock in the XML document. For example, the following code adds a second *Stock* to the document:

```
<?xml version="1.0"?>
<Stocks>
    <Stock>
        <Ticker>CONT</Ticker>
        <Name>Contoso</Name>
        <Price>12.45</Price>
        <Previous>12.23</Previous>
        <Volume>23</Volume>
    </Stock>
    <Stock>
        <Ticker>FTHC</Ticker>
        <Name>Fourth Coffee</Name>
        <Price>3.44</Price>
        <Previous>3.52</Previous>
        <Volume>16</Volume>
    </Stock>
 </Stocks>
```

XML Parsing

Before we look at XML serialization, let's examine *XML parsing*, a technique for reading and editing XML documents on either .NET or Java. XML parsers for both platforms are now mature and stable, and many examples are available that demonstrate using these parsers for reading and writing XML data.

Generally, two types of parsers can be used for reading and writing XML data: Document Object Model (DOM) parsers and Simple API for XML (SAX) parsers. DOM XML parsers read the whole document into memory and offer a flexible and easy way to traverse the document hierarchy. These parsers tend to be easy to use, yet they aren't recommended for large XML documents. This is because the entire document needs to be loaded into memory each time, which can impact performance. On the other hand, SAX parsers use streams to read portions of the XML file as needed. This parsing method is much more memory efficient, which increases performance. Yet many SAX parsers lack the ease and flexibility of their DOM equivalents. For example, SAX parsers cannot traverse backward through an XML file.

To parse XML in .NET using DOM, you can use the *XmlDocument* and *XmlElement* classes from the *System.Xml* namespace. These classes provide methods that allow you to traverse an XML document and add or modify its elements.

To parse XML in Java, we'll use packages and classes from Electric XML to achieve a result very similar to that obtained by parsing XML in .NET. (For details on Electric XML, see the "Running the Sample Code in This Book" section in Chapter 1.) The Electric XML *Document* and *Element* classes will allow us to parse an XML document.

Running the Sample Code

To see how to use XML parsing to read and write a shared XML document, we'll look at two samples, one for .NET and the other for Java. Each version of the sample code reads and writes a shared stock.xml file from a location specified by a passed parameter, which is very similar to the binary serialization sample shown earlier. A summary of the information in the XML file is displayed, and a new *Stock* record is written to the file.

The sample code for this interoperability example can be found in the C:\Interoperability\Samples\Data\XML\Parsing directory. It shows how to pass a *Stock* record as an XML document between .NET and Java. This example is the first technical option for doing so covered in the book, and it demonstrates basic usage of the DOM parser for both platforms.

The sample code directory contains four directories: dotNET, Java, Shared, and PerformanceTest. The first three subdirectories contain the sample code and map to the previous example, while the last subdirectory, PerformanceTest, will be discussed later in the "Introducing the Interoperability Performance Tests" section in this chapter. The sample code can be compiled and executed using the run target with the provided NAnt and Ant scripts in the dotNET and Java directories, respectively. Be sure to run the .NET and Java samples in sequence to see how they are both able to read and write data in the same file.

The .NET sample code Stepping through the main elements of the .NET sample code, you can see how generic XML parsing works as part of the .NET Framework. First, you declare a *using* statement for the *System.Xml* namespace:

```
using System.Xml;
```

This namespace contains all the classes required to perform XML parsing. After reading the arguments to obtain the name of the XML file, the next step is to load that file from disk. This is performed with the *Load* method from the *XmlDocument* class:

```
XmlDocument doc = new XmlDocument();
doc.Load(xmlFile);
```

Now the XML is in a DOM structure that you can read and manipulate. Next, your need to iterate through all the *Stock* records within the document. This will yield an *XmlNodeList* containing each of the companies to extract more data from. To do so, use the *GetElementsByTagName* method on the *XmlDocument*:

```
XmlNodeList allStocks = doc.GetElementsByTagName("Stock");
```

Once all the *Stock* records are contained in an *XmlNodeList*, you can step through the list to extract the finer details, such as the ticker symbol, price, and other values stored:

```
Console.WriteLine("There are "+allStocks.Count
    +" Stocks in this document");
for (int f=0; f<allStocks.Count; f++)
{
    Console.WriteLine("Stock Found:");
     foreach (XmlElement n in allStocks.Item(f))
     {
        Console.WriteLine("The value of "+n.Name+" is "
         +n.ChildNodes[0].Value);
    }
}
```

All in all, this is a relatively simple piece of code for walking through a nested piece of XML in a document. The next step is to create a new stock based on the XML structure we've been using and write it to the *XmlDocument*. To create the new stock, first create each of the *Stock* element's child elements (*Ticker*, *Price*, and so on). After these elements are created, create the *Stock* element itself and add all the child elements to it:

```
XmlElement newTicker = doc.CreateElement("Ticker");
newTicker.InnerText = "NWND";
XmlElement newName = doc.CreateElement("Name");
newName.InnerText = "Northwind Traders";
XmlElement newPrice = doc.CreateElement("Price");
newPrice.InnerText = "20.33";
XmlElement newPrevious = doc.CreateElement("Previous");
newPrevious.InnerText = "20.00";
XmlElement newVolume = doc.CreateElement("Volume");
newVolume.InnerText = "34";

XmlElement newStock = doc.CreateElement("Stock");
newStock.AppendChild(newTicker);
newStock.AppendChild(newName);
newStock.AppendChild(newPrice);
newStock.AppendChild(newPrevious);
newStock.AppendChild(newVolume);
```

You now have a fully formed stock—in this case, for the Northwind Traders company. To complete the update, you need to write the *Stock* to the *XmlDocument* and output the file to disk:

```
XmlNodeList root = doc.GetElementsByTagName("Stocks");
root.Item(0).AppendChild(newStock);

XmlTextWriter tw
    = new XmlTextWriter(xmlFile,System.Text.Encoding.ASCII);
doc.WriteTo(tw);
tw.Close();

doc.Save(Console.Out);
```

As this code shows, you obtain the *Stock* element's parent by searching for the *Stocks* tag, and you add the new *Stock* node as a child of this element. The final stage is to save the document to both the XML file that was passed as a parameter and to the console for display.

The Java sample code Stepping through the Java sample code, you'll see that the calls made to the Electric XML *Document* and *Element* classes are similar to the methods we used for .NET. The main class starts by importing the *electric.xml* and *java.io* packages for reading and writing the document:

```
import java.io.File;
import electric.xml.*;
```

Again, after accepting the parameter required for the file location, a new XML document is created and loaded with the XML data from the stock.xml file. A *NodeList* of type *electric.xml.NodeList* is created with the company records that are read from the XML file:

```
Document document = new Document(new File(xmlFile));
NodeList allStocks
    = (NodeList)document.getElementsByTagName("Stock");
```

Once this is complete, you can iterate through the *Stock* records, displaying the data for each:

```
for (int f=0; f<allStocks.size(); f++)
{
    System.out.println("Stock Found:");
    NodeList stockInfo
        = (NodeList)allStocks.item(f).getChildNodes();

    for (int g=0; g<stockInfo.size(); g++)
    {
        System.out.println("The value of "
            +stockInfo.item(g).getNodeName()+" is "
            +((Element)stockInfo.item(g)).getText());
    }
}
```

Finally, as with the .NET version of this code, we create a new *Stock* record that will be written back to the XML document. In this case, we've chosen Fourth Coffee:

```
Element newTicker = (Element)document.createElement("Ticker");
newTicker.setText("FTHC");
Element newName = (Element)document.createElement("Name");
newName.setText("Fourth Coffee");
Element newPrice = (Element)document.createElement("Price");
newPrice.setText("4.67");
Element newPrevious = (Element)document.createElement("Previous");
newPrevious.setText("4.88");
Element newVolume = (Element)document.createElement("Volume");
newVolume.setText("56");

Element newStock = (Element)document.createElement("Stock");
newStock.appendChild(newTicker);
newStock.appendChild(newName);
```

```
newStock.appendChild(newPrice);
newStock.appendChild(newPrevious);
newStock.appendChild(newVolume);
```

Once the new stock is created, add it to the *Stocks* element in the document and save the file:

```
NodeList root = (NodeList)document.getElementsByTagName("Stocks");
root.item(0).appendChild(newStock);

document.write(new File(xmlFile));
document.write(System.out);
```

More Efficient Parsing

This simple example shows XML parsing for both .NET and Java, using relatively similar methods and classes. You probably noticed that this wasn't the most efficient way of parsing the document, despite using similar code for both versions.

The .NET Framework and Electric XML libraries have more efficient ways of parsing. The examples shown here are designed to just illustrate the basics of parsing a document using similar code; they do not demonstrate a best-practices approach to working with XML.

Limitations of Parsing XML

In addition to making the code more efficient, we could expand this sample code in many ways to offer additional functionality. For example, we could use network sockets on both the .NET and Java sample applications to pass the XML document between the two platforms (as opposed to writing to a shared file), or we could even store the XML document on an HTTP resource to allow sharing among multiple machines across the Internet.

XML parsing for data exchange does have its limitations, however. Using the parsing methods described in this section can work well for accessing and reading distinct data elements from documents. But when it comes to working with the data in an XML document, the commands to perform operations can quickly become verbose and unwieldy for developers.

For example, if you want to perform some business logic or calculations on the company data read in the previous sample, you have no natural way of using the parser to map objects within the XML document to classes created in either .NET or Java. For a more flexible approach, you need a way to map data stored in an XML document to objects and classes that you define and that work within your application. As previously mentioned, this mapping, or binding, is commonly known as XML serialization.

XML serialization takes document creation to a new level. It shields the developer from much of the underlying XML parsing and allows her to concentrate on developing the application and data types. This doesn't mean that all the XML parsing tools and classes are removed from the process—they are still very present. However, XML serialization offers a layer of abstraction that simplifies the process of converting an object from one platform into an XML document that can be easily read by another platform.

XML Serialization for the .NET Platform

The .NET Framework contains classes and APIs to perform XML serialization. The *System.Xml.Serialization.XmlSerializer* class allows types within the .NET Framework to be serialized to an XML document and allows XML documents to be converted back into the relevant types. (As mentioned earlier, this process is known as deserialization.)

Serializing an Object to XML

Within the *XmlSerializer* class, serialization is performed as follows:

```
XmlSerializer mySerializer = new XmlSerializer(typeof(myType));
mySerializer.Serialize(myStream, myType)
```

The *Serialize* method of an *XmlSerializer* object takes the object passed as the second parameter and serializes that object to an XML document. If the serialization is successful, the serialized object is written to a stream, which can be an in-memory stream, a file, or a network socket.

Deserializing an Object from XML

The *Deserialize* method works in exactly the opposite way:

```
XmlSerializer mySerializer = new XmlSerializer(typeof(myType));
Object myType = mySerializer.Deserialize(myStream);
```

The XML document is passed to the serializer as a stream, the document is read and deserialized, and if the deserialization is successful, an object is returned. As shown in the following code, the *Deserialize* method returns an object with a type of *System.Object*, thus the returned value must be cast appropriately before being assigned to the target type:

```
Stocks myStocks = (Stocks)mySerializer.Deserialize(myStream);
```

The descriptions of the previous two examples use the wording *if the serialization is successful* and *if the deserialization is successful* because sometimes serialization and deserialization fail. This can happen for a number of reasons.

One of the main reasons for this failure is that the incoming XML document isn't well-formed. For example, the document might contain fields that the serializer isn't expecting, or it might not include the correct namespaces or types. Conversely, some objects can't be correctly serialized to XML at all. These include objects in the .NET Framework that implement *IDictionary*. In addition, for objects to be serialized, their class must be declared *public* and have a valid no-argument constructor.

In many of the cases just mentioned, trying to serialize an object will cause the *XmlSerializer* to throw a *System.InvalidOperationException*, indicating that the application had trouble serializing the object or type to an XML document.

XML Serialization for the Java Platform

A number of XML Serializers available for the Java platform use Java classes to generate XML documents. As with the parsing example shown earlier in this section, we'll use the libraries contained in Electric XML to illustrate this.

Serializing an Object to XML

The Electric XML serializer is invoked by first declaring a new object of type *electric.xml.io.IWriter*:

```
IWriter writer = new LiteralWriter(namespace, classname);
```

LiteralWriter accepts two parameters. The first defines the XML namespace for the document; the second defines the name of the class.

You can use two types of *IWriter* for serialization, *EncodedWriter* and *LiteralWriter*. The *EncodedWriter* class employs an encoding scheme that's used by the majority of the SOAP community for sending RPC-style data between endpoints. We'll investigate this in Chapter 6, "Connectivity with XML Web Services, Part 2," when we cover passing types between platforms by using XML Web services. The *LiteralWriter* class (as well as the *LiteralReader* class) provides a direct mapping between Java objects and XML elements. In general, *LiteralWriter* is not as advanced as *EncodedWriter*, but it offers a great introduction to serialization because it uses the encoding style used by the *XmlSerializer* in .NET.

Once *IWriter* is created, you can use write methods within the class to populate data. To write generic objects, you can use the *writeObject* method:

```
writer.writeObject(myObject);
```

After objects have been written to *IWriter*, extract the XML document by calling the *getDocument* method on the *IWriter* object itself:

```
electric.xml.Document document = writer.getDocument();
```

As shown, the *getDocument* method returns an XML document of type *electric.xml.Document*. From here, you can pass the document to a memory stream, network, or file by using the *Document.write* method on the XML document that's returned.

Deserializing an Object from XML

Deserializing an object by using Electric XML requires the opposite set of commands. First, the XML document is read into a new instance of a *LiteralReader*:

```
IReader reader = new LiteralReader(document);
```

To deserialize the object from XML into its native form, you use the *readObject* method:

```
Stocks myStocks = (Stocks)reader.readObject(Stocks.class);
```

As you can see, the *IWriter* and *IReader* implementations within Electric XML complement the similar serialization functions found in .NET.

What About JAXB?

You might be wondering why Java Architecture for XML Binding (JAXB) hasn't been mentioned yet. JAXB is a specification along with a reference implementation that provides an API and tools to automate the mapping between Java objects and XML documents, in much the same way as the serialization techniques discussed in this chapter.

Although JAXB has been in development for some time, at the time of this writing, the product was still in a beta release phase. Rather than using sample code that might change before the final release of JAXB, I've based the code in this book on the Electric XML serializer.

Despite this, testing of the early JAXB implementation against the *XmlSerializer* in .NET was performed. You can see how the JAXB parser is used by first creating an instance of *JAXBContext*:

```
JAXBContext jc = JAXBContext.newInstance("com.test.Package");
```

From this context, you can derive either a *Marshaller* (to serialize the data) or an *Unmarshaller* (for deserialization). The *Unmarshaller* takes an input stream parameter from which the XML document is read and returns an object that can be cast into the type that's required:

```
Unmarshaller u = jc.createUnmarshaller();
Stocks myStocks = (Stocks)u.unmarshal(new
    FileInputStream("stock.xml"));
```

The *Marshaller* works in exactly the opposite way—an object is passed with an output stream for the resulting XML document:

```
Marshaller m = jc.createMarshaller();
m.marshal(myStocks, System.out);
```

> **More Info** Additional information regarding the JAXB implementation can be found via the Java Community Process at *http://www.jcp.org/en/jsr/detail?id=31*.

Using XML Serialization and Ensuring Type Compatibility

We've looked at some basic commands for serializing to and deserializing from XML by using classes from both the .NET Framework and Electric XML. However, one question remains: How do we ensure that the XML document that's created by using serialization in either .NET or Java is compatible with the other platform? As mentioned, binary formatters exist in both .NET and Java, but neither platform can read a binary serialized file from the other platform because of serialization incompatibilities. To ensure that a document you produce is compatible with both platforms, you can use XML Schema.

Introducing XML Schema

The easiest way to explain XML Schema is to show how it applies to the previous example. Let's expand upon the XML document that was discussed toward the start of this section, on page 52:

```
<?xml version="1.0"?>
<Portfolio>
    <Stocks>
        <Stock>
            <Ticker>CONT</Ticker>
            <Name>Contoso</Name>
            <Price>12.45</Price>
            <Previous>12.23</Previous>
            <Volume>23</Volume>
      </Stock>
    </Stocks>
</Portfolio>
```

Notice how we've modified the XML document by adding a root element named *Portfolio*. Doing this allows the flexibility for the portfolio to hold other items in the future (bonds, mutual funds, and cash, for example).

As you saw earlier, within this portfolio, this document uses XML to describe a single *Stock* and the elements or values within it. If you pass this XML document between .NET and J2EE, you'll have two potential problems.

First, you have to determine what *Price* is. Looking at the value of 12.45, you can guess that it might be a double or float. But it could be a string value as well. The XML document doesn't describe the type of the data that it holds.

Second, the document describes a type named *Stock*. Application A might use this definition for a *Stock* item, but application B might have its own definition. Nothing is differentiating the XML document named Stock from another document with the same name.

These problems can be overcome by using XML Schema (as well as XML namespaces). XML Schema allows you to create and use an XML Schema Definition (XSD) document to define types and constraints for each element within the document. By using XML Schema with XML namespaces, you can distinguish a *Stock* type from another data type with the same name or structure.

What Is an XSD?

XSDs are XML documents with a predefined structure. The elements and nodes within these documents are used to describe data types and elements for another document. Let's use the XSD for our *Portfolio* and *Stock* data types as an example:

```
<?xml version="1.0" encoding="utf-8" ?>
<xs:schema elementFormDefault="qualified"
    xmlns:xs="http://www.w3.org/2001/XMLSchema">
    <xs:complexType name="Portfolio">
        <xs:sequence>
            <xs:element minOccurs="0" maxOccurs="1"
                name="Stocks" type="ArrayOfStock" />
        </xs:sequence>
    </xs:complexType>
    <xs:complexType name="ArrayOfStock">
        <xs:sequence>
            <xs:element name="Stock" type="Stock"
                maxOccurs="unbounded" minOccurs="0" />
        </xs:sequence>
    </xs:complexType>
    <xs:complexType name="Stock">
```

```
        <xs:sequence>
            <xs:element name="Ticker" type="xs:string" />
            <xs:element name="Name" type="xs:string" />
            <xs:element name="Price" type="xs:float" />
            <xs:element name="Previous" type="xs:float" />
            <xs:element name="Volume" type="xs:int" />
        </xs:sequence>
    </xs:complexType>
    <xs:element name="Portfolio" type="Portfolio"></xs:element>
</xs:schema>
```

Let's examine how the structure is defined in this XSD. First, the XSD defines a common namespace (http://www.w3.org/2001/XMLSchema). This namespace allows elements used within the document (for example, *xs:complexType*) to be uniquely declared within an XML document even when other elements with the same name but a different namespace are also used.

The first definition in this XSD is of the *Portfolio*:

```
<xs:complexType name="Portfolio">
    <xs:sequence>
        <xs:element minOccurs="0" maxOccurs="1"
            name="Stocks" type="ArrayOfStock" />
    </xs:sequence>
</xs:complexType>
```

This complex type entry defines *Portfolio* and indicates that it includes either zero or a single array of *Stock* objects—in other words, *Portfolio* could contain no *Stock* objects or could contain a group of *Stock* objects. The definition for this array is as follows:

```
<xs:complexType name="ArrayOfStock">
    <xs:sequence>
        <xs:element name="Stock" type="Stock"
            maxOccurs="unbounded" minOccurs="0" />
    </xs:sequence>
</xs:complexType>
```

The *ArrayOfStock* type defines the array needed. As just shown, this array will contain anywhere from zero to an infinite (unbounded) number of *Stock* objects:

```
<xs:complexType name="Stock">
    <xs:sequence>
        <xs:element name="Ticker" type="xs:string" />
        <xs:element name="Name" type="xs:string" />
        <xs:element name="Price" type="xs:float" />
        <xs:element name="Previous" type="xs:float" />
        <xs:element name="Volume" type="xs:int" />
```

```
    </xs:sequence>
</xs:complexType>
```

After the *Portfolio* and *ArrayOfStock* are defined, you define the *Stock* element itself. Each field within the *Stock* is written as a separate element. Each element name is defined as well as a standard basic type.

Finally, the XSD contains a top-level element: *Portfolio*. This is because the XSD tool in the .NET Framework that we'll use shortly requires a top-level element for the document in order to automatically generate a data type.

```
<xs:element name="Portfolio" type="Portfolio"></xs:element>
```

Creating an XSD

As a developer, how do you go about creating the XSD document? Because the XSD is in XML format, you of course can use any text editor. However, to make things easier, you should use a tool that provides a graphical representation of the schema and helps create a useful XSD document. One such tool is Microsoft Visual Studio .NET. You can use the integrated development environment (IDE) to switch between a graphical representation of the schema (which tends to be easier to work with when defining data types) and the actual XSD document.

To create an XSD document using Visual Studio .NET, launch the IDE and create a new project, as shown in Figure 3-3. The type, language, and location of the project aren't important at this stage because you won't compile the project. To demonstrate this process, I'll create a C# project in my C:\Temp directory.

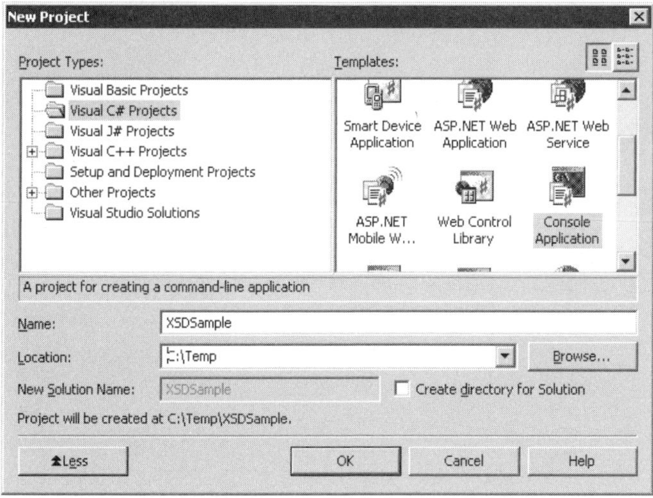

Figure 3-3 Creating a new project in Visual Studio .NET.

After the solution has been created, right-click the project—in my demonstration this is XSDSample—in Solution Explorer (the pane toward the top right of the IDE), and then select Add New Item. Alternatively, you can select Add New Item from the Project menu. This will bring up the Add New Item dialog box, shown in Figure 3-4.

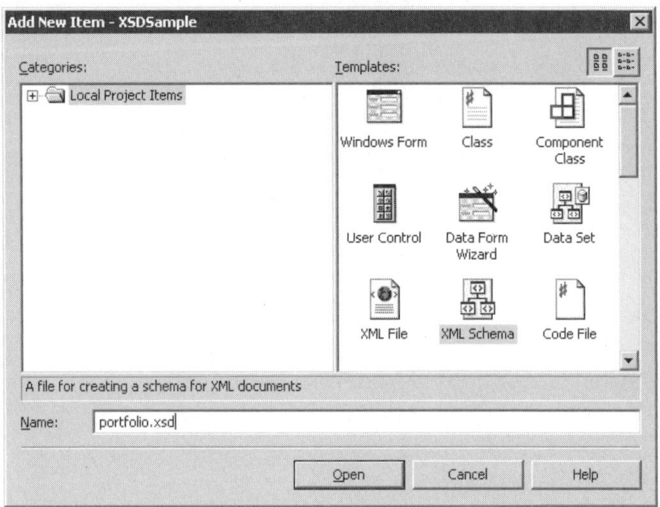

Figure 3-4 Adding an XML Schema to a project in Visual Studio .NET.

A list of new items is displayed. Because you're creating a new XSD, select XML Schema from the list of available items and name the XSD portfolio.xsd. As shown in Figure 3-5, the new XSD will be created as part of the solution and will be opened graphically within the IDE.

Figure 3-5 The new XSD document in Visual Studio .NET.

At the moment, it doesn't look like much. And of course, we don't have any types or elements defined within the document. Let's start creating some types for the XSD. We'll start with the *Stock* type.

In the main window in the IDE, with the portfolio.xsd file displayed in the designer surface window, right-click Add/New complexType. Name the type **Stock**, and within the complex type, define the fields shown in Table 3-2.

Table 3-2 The *Stock* fields

Data Field	Type
Ticker	string
Name	string
Price	float
Previous	float
Volume	int

Once complete, the type should look similar to the one shown in Figure 3-6.

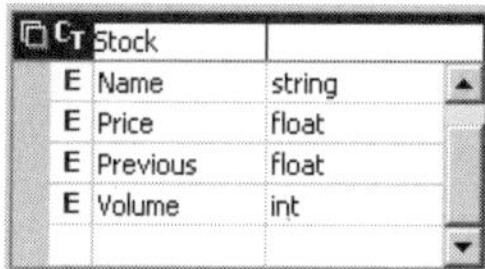

Figure 3-6 The *Stock* type in the XSD.

One nice feature of using the XSD designer in Visual Studio .NET is having the ability to switch between this graphical view of the schema and the actual XSD document, as depicted in Figure 3-7. To do this, either click the XML icon at the bottom of the designer surface or right-click the main window and select View XML Source.

Figure 3-7 shows the schema displayed in its native XML format. As you can see, by defining the graphical view of the *Stock* type, we've created the required XSD elements within the document. To add more data types, either click the Schema icon at the bottom of the main window or right-click the designer surface again and select View Schema.

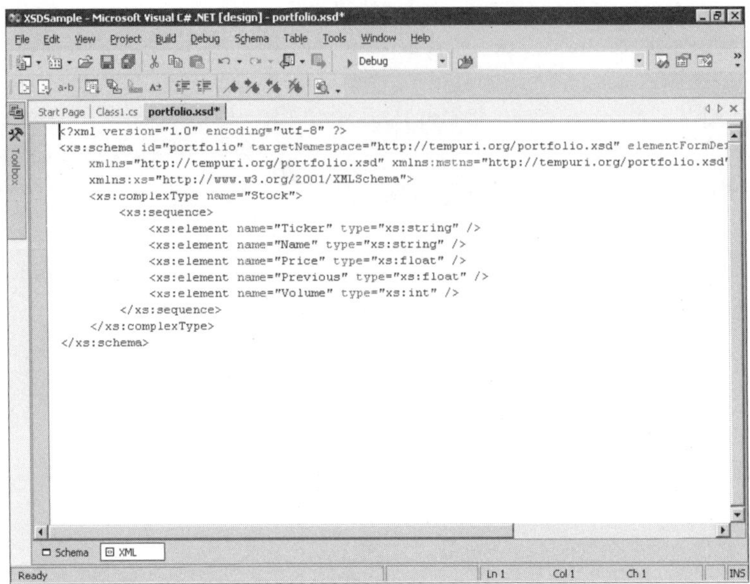

Figure 3-7 Viewing the XSD document in Visual Studio .NET.

Add a new complexType named **ArrayOfStock**. This type will have one child element named **Stocks**, that has a data type of *Stock*. As you add this type, the XSD designer automatically displays a graphical hierarchy of the relationship between the *ArrayOfStock* and *Stocks* types, as Figure 3-8 shows.

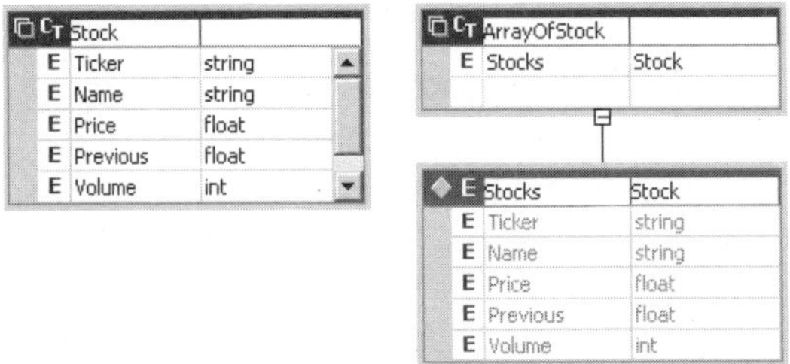

Figure 3-8 Adding the *ArrayOfStock* data type to the XSD document.

As discussed earlier, the array will have between zero and an infinite number of *Stock* items. To configure this, select the Stocks element that is connected to the ArrayOfStock element, and in the Properties window (toward the bottom right of the IDE), locate the minOccurs and maxOccurs fields.

Enter **0** for the minOccurs property, and **unbounded** for the maxOccurs property, as shown in Figure 3-9. This will allow an unbounded (infinite) number of stocks to be contained in the array.

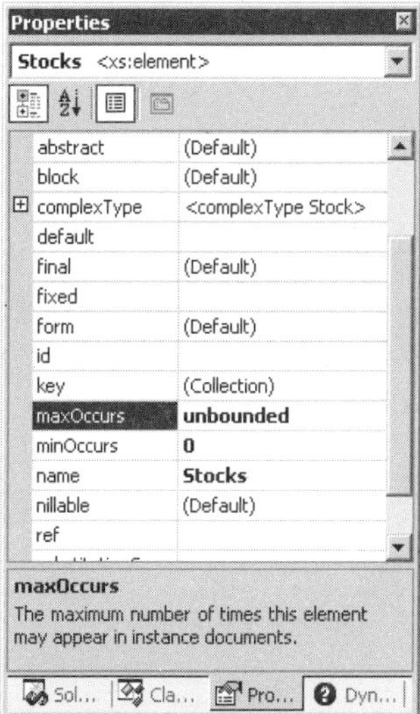

Figure 3-9 Setting the properties for the array type.

Now that you have defined the stock and a stock array, you need to define the *Portfolio* type itself. To do this, add a new complexType named **Portfolio**, as shown in Figure 3-10. This type will contain one element named **Stocks**, and that element's type will be **ArrayOfStock**.

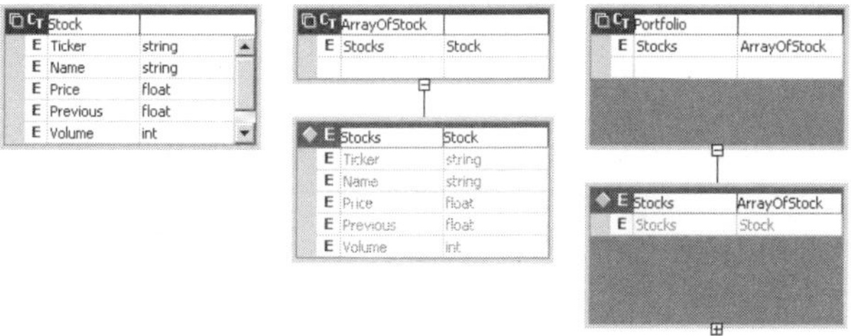

Figure 3-10 Adding the *Portfolio* type to the schema.

You might be wondering why we have to define the *ArrayOfStock* type—and why we just don't define *Portfolio* as having an unbounded number of *Stock* elements instead. We define this *ArrayOfStock* type to produce the *Stocks* element within the *Portfolio* element. As mentioned earlier, this categorization allows for other types to be added to the portfolio in the future.

The final step for defining types is to create a top-level element within the document. This will define *Portfolio* as the top-level object. To do this, right-click the main window and select Add/New Element.

Give the new element the name **Portfolio** and a type of Portfolio, as shown in Figure 3-11. Ensure that this type is not contained within parentheses because this will create a second XML element.

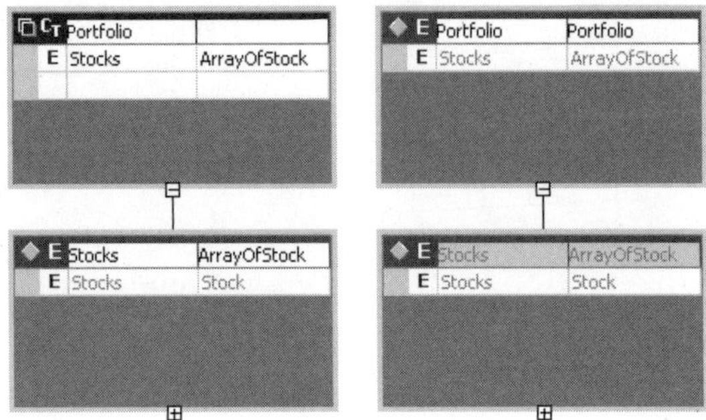

Figure 3-11 Completing the schema.

The XSD is almost complete now. The final step is to set a namespace to uniquely identify the XSD as yours so that if anyone else generates the same schema, you can differentiate between the types.

To set the namespace, click the main part of the window, and in the Properties window, locate the *targetNamespace* property. The default namespace is currently set to http://tempuri.org/portfolio.xsd. Change this to **http://www.microsoft.com/interoperability/package/**.

Now save the document. Congratulations! You've completed an XSD that you'll use to allow XML serialization to exchange types between .NET and J2EE.

Generating Types from an XSD

We now have an XSD that defines a portfolio containing stocks. You might be wondering what benefits we gained by creating the XSD first and whether it would have been easier to just create the classes from scratch in .NET and Java. Although it might have been easier to craft something as simple as this stock type just by writing the class, by using an XSD, you guarantee that you build data types and a schema in a format that's common to both platforms. This is especially important for solutions that use more complex types.

Now that we have an XSD, let's use it to generate some classes for both platforms. We'll do this from a command prompt, so ensure that the portfolio.xsd file is saved in Visual Studio .NET. At a command prompt, navigate to the directory containing the portfolio.xsd file, as it was saved by the IDE. In the sample created earlier, this directory is C:\Temp\XSDSample.

If you chose not to create the sample, or want to compare the XSD file with the one generated in our sample, a correct XSD can be found in the C:\Interoperability\Samples\Data\XML\Serialization\XSD directory.

Next we'll run two tools that generate classes based on our new XSD: XSD.EXE, which generates types for .NET, and schema2java, which generates types for Java.

Generating a class in .NET from the XSD XSD.EXE is a command-prompt tool that ships with the .NET Framework SDK. If you have Visual Studio .NET installed, this tool should be run from the Visual Studio .NET Command Prompt (found in the Microsoft Visual Studio .NET 2003/Visual Studio .NET Tools' Program Group). If you don't have Visual Studio .NET, this tool can be run directly from the .NET Framework directory.

XSD.EXE is a tool that can be used to generate either classes or data sets from XSD documents and to generate XSD documents from existing classes. For a full list of arguments, type **XSD /?** at the command-prompt window.

For this sample, we'll generate classes from the portfolio.xsd file that we created. To do that, run the following command from the directory that contains this portfolio.xsd file:

```
XSD /c portfolio.xsd
```

If all is successful, you'll get the following output:

```
Microsoft (R) Xml Schemas/DataTypes support utility
[Microsoft (R) .NET Framework, Version 1.1.4322.573]
Copyright (C) Microsoft Corporation 1998-2002. All rights reserved.

Writing file 'C:\temp\XSDSample\portfolio.cs'.
```

The XSD tool has taken the XSD and generated the required classes. The output for this has been stored in portfolio.cs. Open this file now in Visual Studio .NET:

```
//------------------------------------------------------------------
// <autogenerated>
//     This code was generated by a tool.
//     Runtime Version: 1.1.4322.342
//
//     Changes to this file may cause incorrect behavior and will
//     be lost if the code is regenerated.
// </autogenerated>
//------------------------------------------------------------------
```

```
//
// This source code was auto-generated by xsd, Version=1.1.4322.342.
//
using System.Xml.Serialization;

/// <remarks/>
[System.Xml.Serialization.XmlTypeAttribute(
    Namespace="http://www.microsoft.com/interoperabililty/package/")]
[System.Xml.Serialization.XmlRootAttribute(
    Namespace="http://www.microsoft.com/interoperabililty/package/",
    IsNullable=false)]
public class Portfolio {

    /// <remarks/>
    [System.Xml.Serialization.XmlArrayItemAttribute(
        "Stocks", IsNullable=false)]
    public Stock[] Stocks;
}

/// <remarks/>
[System.Xml.Serialization.XmlTypeAttribute(
    Namespace="http://www.microsoft.com/interoperabililty/package/")]
public class Stock {

    /// <remarks/>
    public string Ticker;

    /// <remarks/>
    public string Name;

    /// <remarks/>
    public System.Single Price;

    /// <remarks/>
    public System.Single Previous;

    /// <remarks/>
    public int Volume;
}
```

As you can see, this file contains two classes. (The classes are written using C#, which is the default for the XSD tool, although other languages can be specified with the appropriate command-line parameters.) The *Stock* class contains the required elements for the stock type, and the *Portfolio* class contains an array of *Stock* objects. In addition, where applicable, the tool has used the

XmlRoot and *XmlType* attributes to annotate the classes with the defined namespace.

Generating a class in Java from the XSD Let's now perform the same process to generate code that can be used for the Java platform. To perform a similar function to the one performed by the XSD tool in .NET, you can use a tool named schema2java, which ships with Electric XML. The schema2java tool can be found in the bin directory of the C:\Interoperability\Tools\Glue installation.

If this bin directory is in your system *PATH*, you can run this tool in the directory containing the target XSD document:

```
schema2java portfolio.xsd
```

If all is successful, the following files will be created:

```
write file Stock.java
write file Portfolio.java
write file portfolio.map
```

Portfolio.java contains the generated Java class:

```
public class Portfolio implements java.io.Serializable
{
    public Stock[] Stocks;
   }
```

And similarly, Stock.java contains the definition for the *Stock* class:

```
public class Stock implements java.io.Serializable
{
    public String Ticker;
    public String Name;
    public float Price;
    public float Previous;
    public int Volume;
}
```

Notice how both classes look similar to the ones generated for C# by the XSD.EXE tool; however, they're specific to Java. The third file is a mapping file, specific to Electric XML, and is not required by our sample code.

We now have the classes required for both .NET and Java, based on the common XSD that we defined. Now let's use XML serialization to pass data between the .NET and Java platforms.

Using the Generated Classes with XML Serialization

The sample code for testing XML serialization can be found in the C:\Interoperability\Samples\Data\XML\Serialization directory. This directory already contains classes that were generated from an XSD. On the other hand, you can also use the classes that were created in the previous subsection.

The .NET example code uses the *Portfolio* class to create a portfolio containing two companies that are prepopulated with sample information. This *Portfolio* object is then serialized to the XML file whose name was passed as a parameter. After this serialization is complete, the .NET example code prompts the user to run the Java version while it pauses.

The Java sample code deserializes the XML data into the Java-specific data types that were created from the XSD. After the objects are deserialized, the prices for the companies stored within the portfolio are updated. The updated objects are then reserialized back into the XML file. After the Java sample has completed, the .NET sample can be resumed in order to read in the new values.

Running the sample code To run the code, compile both the .NET and Java samples within the dotNET and Java subdirectories of the Serialization directory. To run the samples after compiling the code, open two command-prompt windows. This example requires the code in .NET to be run simultaneously with the code in Java, and using two command-prompt windows will help you see both processes in action. To execute the .NET sample, enter the following at the command line:

```
SimpleSerializer ..\shared\portfolio.xml
```

When prompted, switch to the second command-prompt window and run the Java sample code, which can easily be done using the run target with the provided Ant script.

The .NET sample code Stepping through the listing for the sample code (SimpleSerializer.cs) will show us how to first initialize the sample company data by using the *SampleData* method:

```
private static Portfolio SampleData()
{
    Stock NWND = new Stock();
    Stock CONT = new Stock();

    NWND.Ticker = "NWND";
    NWND.Name = "Northwind Traders";
    NWND.Price = 50.12;
    NWND.Volume = 123;

    CONT.Ticker = "CONT";
    CONT.Name = "Contoso";
    CONT.Price = 12.45;
    CONT.Volume = 23;
```

```
    Stock[] myStocks = new Stock[]{NWND,CONT};

    Portfolio myStocks = new Portfolio();
    myStocks.Stocks = myStocks;

    return myStocks;
}
```

After calling the *SampleData* method, you have an object (a complex data type) of type *Portfolio* named *myStocks*. This object contains the two companies that you'll serialize to XML and pass to the sample code in Java. The next task is to serialize the object. The following code achieves this:

```
XmlSerializer sz = new XmlSerializer(typeof(Portfolio));

System.IO.FileStream fs =
    System.IO.File.Open(xmlFile,System.IO.FileMode.Create);

Console.WriteLine("Serializing portfolio to the XML file...");
sz.Serialize(fs,myStocks);
fs.Close();
```

The first thing this code does is create a new instance of the serializer. To initialize the serializer, the code passes to it the type of the object to serialize. The sample uses *typeof(Portfolio)* to indicate that you'll be serializing an object of type *Portfolio*. After the serializer has been initialized, create a new *FileStream* with a path to the file, as specified in the parameters that were passed to run the example code. Upon closer examination, you can see that the serialization occurs in the following line:

```
sz.Serialize(fs,myStocks);
```

The code passes the *FileStream* (*fs*) for the new file created and the object to be serialized. (Earlier, we created the *myStocks* object in the code from the sample data.) After the serialization is complete, the *FileStream* is closed and the user is prompted to press a key to indicate that serialization is complete.

The XML file that's generated at this point should look similar to the following. You can view this file by opening it in Microsoft Internet Explorer, Visual Studio .NET, Microsoft Notepad, or your favorite XML editor.

```
<?xml version="1.0"?>
<Portfolio xmlns:xsd="http://www.w3.org/2001/XMLSchema"
    xmlns:xsi="http://www.w3.org/2001/XMLSchema-instance"
    xmlns="http://www.microsoft.com/interoperabililty/package/">
    <Stocks>
```

```
        <Stock>
            <Ticker>NWND</Ticker>
            <Name>Northwind Traders</Name>
            <Price>50.12</Price>
            <Previous>0</Previous>
            <Volume>123</Volume>
        </Stock>
        <Stock>
            <Ticker>CONT</Ticker>
            <Name>Contoso</Name>
            <Price>12.45</Price>
            <Previous>0</Previous>
            <Volume>23</Volume>
        </Stock>
    </Stocks>
</Portfolio>
```

The Java sample code The XML document contains the two stocks that are defined in the portfolio and the data that you set for each of the stocks.

As you saw, the sample updates the prices for the two companies in the portfolio, serializes the objects into the XML file, and then rereads the file in .NET to check that the changes have been applied and that the objects can still be deserialized successfully.

If we look through the *SimpleSerializer* class in Java, we can see that before the objects are read, we configure a number of Electric XML settings. These settings ensure that the decoding and encoding of the XML document is compatible with the *XmlSerializer* in .NET.

```
ArrayTypeFactory.setDefaultArrayType(
    "electric.xml.io.array.LiteralArrayType");
LiteralWriter.setWriteTypes(false);
SchemaProperties.setNamespaces(NAMESPACE_PREFIX);
```

These settings ensure the XML document is configured to contain elements that are literal types (and not encoded with the SOAP formatter). The final line also sets the namespace correctly (to http://www.microsoft.com/interoperability/) so that it matches the namespace used by the types in .NET.

After the objects are deserialized, two companies in the portfolio are updated with the following code:

```
myStocks.Stocks[0].Previous = myStocks.Stocks[0].Price;
myStocks.Stocks [0].Price += 1.20;
myStocks.Stocks [1].Previous = myStocks.Stocks[1].Price;
myStocks.Stocks [1].Price -= 0.50;
```

To write the updated object back to the XML file, use the following lines of code:

```
IWriter writer = new LiteralWriter(NAMESPACE_PREFIX+"package/",
    Strings.getLocalJavaName(Portfolio.class.getName()));

writer.writeObject(myStocks);
document = writer.getDocument();
document.write(new File(xmlFile));
```

Here, a new instance of *IWriter* is created, with the correct XML namespace and the name of the class that will be written to the XML document. (Again, we'll use *LiteralWriter* to ensure compatibility with the XML serializer in .NET.) The *writeObject* method is used to serialize the object to the *electric.xml.Document* object. This document is then written back to the portfolio.xml file that was read earlier.

Starting with a Class

The previous example of creating an XSD first and then generating the required .NET and Java classes from it is great for ensuring data compatibility between the two platforms; however, it does assume that you're creating both sides of the application anew.

Some of the business requirements covered in Chapter 2 presented scenarios that involved creating solutions that interoperate with *existing* systems. Chances are these existing systems already have had their data types defined—and it's probable that no good justification for developing a new schema to replace them exists.

Generating an XSD from an existing class in Java The good news is that you can still use the XSD tools to generate documents from data types that already exist—you just have to use these tools in a slightly different way. For example, imagine that you have an existing data type already defined in Java and that you need to create an equivalent data type in .NET. Ideally, you'll want to do this by using an XSD.

Earlier we used the schema2java tool in Electric XML to generate a Java class from a defined XSD. Fortunately, a tool named java2schema performs exactly the opposite function. Using java2schema, you can reference an existing Java class and generate an XSD from there. Note that the existing Java class has to be a compiled class, not source code.

Before we look at the sample, we need to make some global modifications to the Electric XML implementation. These modifications are required to correctly configure the tools that will generate the XML and XSD from the Java classes.

To make these modifications, first navigate to the C:\Interoperability\Tools\Glue\lib directory. This directory contains all the classes for the

GLUE and Electric XML libraries. From this directory, extract the default configuration file, using the following command:

```
jar -xvf glue-all.jar glue-default-config.xml
```

This will extract the glue-default-config.xml file from the JAR file. Overwrite this XML file with the version contained in the C:\Interoperability\Samples\Data\XML\Serialization\XSD directory. This new version contains changes for the *namespacePrefix*, *writeTypesForLiteral*, and *defaultArrayType* settings so that they are compatible with .NET.

To replace the file and update the JAR file, run the following command:

```
jar -uvf glue-all.jar glue-default-config.xml
```

The modifications to the JAR file are now complete. To see how we can now generate the XSD from the Java class, navigate to the C:\Interoperability\Samples\Data\XML\Serialization\Java directory. After you compile and run the previous sample, this directory will contain two class files: Portfolio.class and Stock.class.

From this directory, run the following command:

```
java2schema Portfolio
```

The tool will read the class files (using a process known as *reflection*) and will generate the required XSDs from the data types it finds.

> **Tip** What is reflection? At run time, reflection allows an application to examine a class as well as that class's methods, declarations, properties, and fields. Reflection functionality is provided by a set of APIs that exist in both .NET and Java.

The output should be similar to the following:

```
write file Portfolio.xsd
write file ArrayOfStock.xsd
write file Stock.xsd
write file Portfolio.map
```

Notice that the java2schema tool has created a single XSD for each type. Although this is technically valid, you'll need to combine these files to get them into a format you can use with .NET. (The XSD.EXE tool can handle multiple XSDs, but not when the target namespace is the same in each XSD.)

To combine the files, open Stock.xsd and ArrayOfStock.xsd in a text editor. Cut out the complex type definitions between the *<xsd:complexType>* tags in each of the XSDs and paste them into the portfolio.xsd file. (Placing these definitions after the definition for the *Portfolio* element, but still within the *<xsd:schema>* element, is fine.)

Remember how we needed a top-level element for the XSD tool in our previous sample? You need to create such an element again because the java2schema tool does not automatically generate this element. Insert the following line of code:

```
<xsd:element name="Portfolio" type="n2:Portfolio"/>
```

between the *<xsd:schema>* tags in the document. Save the new portfolio.xsd document.

You now have a valid portfolio.xsd document that can be used with the XSD tool to generate a .NET class. As you did in the previous example, run the XSD command to generate the required classes:

```
XSD /c portfolio.xsd
```

This will generate the portfolio.cs class, which can be examined and compiled.

Generating an XSD from an existing class in .NET To complete the picture, let's look at how to generate an XSD from an existing .NET class. Again, this is useful when existing classes have already been defined in .NET and you need to generate compatible classes in Java.

As you did in the previous Java example, navigate to the directory that contains the compiled code from the previous sample (C:\Interoperability\Samples\Data\XML\Serialization\dotNET). In this directory, you'll find an assembly named SimpleSerializer.exe. This assembly not only holds the main class for the sample code, but it also contains the data types.

To generate an XSD from these classes, run the XSD tool. Use the */c* switch again, but this time, supply the executable as the parameter:

```
XSD /c SimpleSerializer.exe /type:Portfolio
```

The */type* parameter is used for specifying the types to generate a schema for. Because a .NET assembly can hold multiple types, this parameter is used to ensure that you select the correct type. If all is successful, you'll get the following output:

```
Writing file
"C:\Interoperability\Samples\Data\XML\Serialization\dotNET\schema0.xsd".
```

Unlike the java2schema tool, the XSD tool places the complete schema within Schema0.xsd. You can reuse the Electric XML tool to generate a Java class from the XSD file:

```
schema2java schema0.xsd
```

> **Warning** On some machines on which I used the XSD.EXE tool, I noticed that the file was encoded with a character set that had a nasty habit of inserting a few rogue characters at the front of the file. If you get an *electric.xml.ParseException: java.io.IOException: expected '=', got 'v',* exception when using the schema2java tool on an XSD that has been generated by the XSD.EXE tool, open the XSD document in a text editor and resave it to delete all characters before the opening <?xml...> tag.

Upon successfully creating the classes required for Java, you'll see the following output:

```
write file Portfolio.java
write file Stock.java
write file schema0.map
```

These files can then be used in new Java applications.

XSD in the Real World

In this section, we've uncovered the notion of using an XSD to define data that needs to be exchanged between the .NET and Java platforms. First we created our own XSD. Then we generated classes for both Java and .NET, compiled and ran the serialization sample, and from these classes, regenerated the XSD to close the loop.

Using an XSD to create the schema first and then generate classes certainly isn't without its pitfalls. You saw this in the example where we had to make slight adjustments to accommodate each tool. That said, using XSDs to generate types is a very powerful technique. Not only do XSDs go a long way in guaranteeing that the types you create have a reproducible version on the other platform, but XSDs also lie at the foundation of the Web Services Description Language (WSDL), which we'll cover in Chapter 5, "Connectivity with XML Web Services, Part 1." Knowing how XSDs work and how the underlying technology uses XSDs is a great step toward understanding how data types are transported via Web services.

XSD Type Mapping

To help summarize this discussion on XSDs, Table 3-3 shows the mappings between XSDs, .NET, and Electric XML. This table can be useful when working with XSDs to ensure that the basic types are what you expect. We'll use similar tables throughout the book as we look at other technologies.

Table 3-3 Mappings Between XML Data Types and Data Types in .NET and Electric XML

XML Data Type	.NET Data Type	Electric XML Data Type
AnyUri	*String*	*java.net.URL*
base64Binary	*Byte[]*	*Byte[]*
Boolean	*Boolean*	*boolean*
Byte	*SByte*	*byte*
DateTime	*DateTime*	*date*
Decimal	*Decimal*	*BigDecimal*
Double	*Double*	*Double*
Float	*Single*	*float*
HexBinary	*Byte[]*	*electric.Util.Hex*
Int	*Int32*	*int*
Long	*Int64*	*int*
NegativeInteger	*String*	*int*
nonNegativeInteger	*String*	*int*
nonPositiveInteger	*String*	*int*
Short	*Int16*	*short*
UnsignedInt	*UInt32*	*int*

Introducing the Interoperability Performance Tests

Before concluding the chapter, I want to introduce the interoperability performance tests, a common thread in many chapters in this book. One of the primary aims of this book is to show a broad range of technology options that span the .NET and J2EE platforms. I'm frequently asked questions such as, "How does option x perform?" and "When it comes to performance, how does using option x compare with using option y?" Giving an exact answer to such questions is difficult because the performance of any solution can depend on a variety of factors. These factors can include the passing of data between platforms, network latency, machine speed, processor utilization, application tuning, and vendor selection. This book aims to illuminate the differences among these solutions by including sample interoperability code and descriptions that you can modify for your own programming environment.

To further this goal, many interoperability samples in this book include a modified sample that allows you to run a simple performance test. This modified sample resides in the same structure as the sample code, under a PerformanceTest subdirectory. The parsing and serialization samples presented in this chapter include performance tests.

How Do the Tests Work?

Most of the interoperability performance tests work by simply repeating the same instructions for a number of iterations and then calculating the average time taken to complete one iteration. For example, to execute the performance test version of the parsing sample code presented in this chapter, run the following from the command line:

```
SimpleParser ..\..\Shared\portfolio.xml 1000
```

This instructs the program to run the simple parser code 1000 times and report on the average time taken to process each request.

> **Note** As many of the tests read, modify, and write the same file many times per second, it is recommended that any antivirus software be disabled. This will prevent the shared file from being locked as the test is running, and the results reported will be more accurate.

How Do You Ensure Accuracy of the Tests?

Most of the tests in the book complete very quickly. To ensure accurate results, use a Win32 API named *QueryPerformanceCounter*. *QueryPerformanceCounter* obtains the current reading of the system's high-performance counter and samples at a frequency based on the CPU cycles of the machine. By measuring the number of cycles that occur between two points in time and then dividing that number by the frequency of the counter, you can obtain very accurate readings (in most cases, to a fraction of a millisecond [ms]).

The *QueryPerformanceCounter* implementation is in the Counter.cs class, which is included in all the performance test samples in this book. The API exposes two methods that are used frequently throughout the tests: *Value* and *TimeElapsed*. The *Value* method returns a *long* value of the cycles that have elapsed since a specific point in time. By calling the *Value* method twice (once when the test begins, and again when it's complete), you can calculate the number of counter cycles that have passed. The *TimeElapsed* method of the Counter.cs class takes these two *long* values and returns a value in milliseconds (of type *float*).

Why Not Use *System.DateTime* and *System.TimeSpan*?

In a word: accuracy. In similar tests, *System.DateTime* and *System.TimeSpan*—two packages included in the .NET Framework to measure time—are accurate only within about 10 milliseconds. This is perfectly acceptable for most general-use applications, but in our tests, the serialization of objects and XML normally falls within the 10-millisecond range. Rather than guess or aggregate an average, we can use the *QueryPerformanceCounter* API to obtain a more accurate representation of how much time has elapsed.

Why Are All the Performance Tests in .NET and Not Java?

All the performance tests are in .NET mainly for consistency reasons and immediate access to the *QueryPerformanceCounter* Win32 API. The aim of this book is to encourage the selection of the correct interoperability solution for a specific scenario, not to serve as a showdown between .NET and Java. The performance tests should be used to measure a delta between various interoperability solutions (for example, serialization commands vs. parsing commands), not the platforms themselves.

Interoperability Performance Test—XML Parsing

The performance test can be found in the following directory:

```
C:\Interoperability\Samples\Data\XML\Parsing\PerformanceTest\dotNET
```

After compilation, run the following command to execute the test:

```
SimpleParser ..\..\Shared\stock-stress.xml 1000
```

The performance test measures the time required to read each of the 20 records in the XML file and append a record to the end of the file. (Incidentally, the stock-stress.xml file is similar to the stock.xml file that was used in the previous example, but it contains a few more companies for test purposes.)

On my development machine (a modest machine with a Pentium 4, 1.6 GHz processor), this test takes about 4.1 ms to complete a single parsing of the document. Again, this figure should be used to determine the difference between the interoperability options presented throughout the book, not the performance of a particular machine.

Interoperability Performance Test—XML Serialization

The performance test can be found in the dotNET subdirectory of the following directory:

```
C:\Interoperability\Samples\Data\XML\Serialization\PerformanceTest
```

After compilation, run the following command to execute the test:

```
SimpleSerializer ..\..\Shared\portfolio-stress.xml 1000
```

The performance test measures the time required to serialize and deserialize a portfolio of 20 records in the XML file. (The portfolio-stress.xml file that's created is similar to the portfolio.xml file that was used in an earlier example, but it contains a few more stocks for test purposes.)

In my tests, this test takes about 3.6 ms to complete. Again, these tests are most beneficial when customized to your own environment. That said, my results show that serialization of this particular file offers a slight performance increase over regular parsing. For additional results, you might want to add more companies and data to the serialization test.

Data Exchange Recommendations

The start of this chapter outlined three challenges to cross-platform data exchange: primitive data type mappings, nonexistent data types, and complex data types. Primitive data type mappings present the challenge of mapping types from one platform to equal types on the other. If the data type doesn't exist on one platform, there is a second challenge—that is, to convert it to a type that does exist on the other platform. Finally, when we deal with complex data types, we must ensure that they are sent using a structure and format that can be understood by both platforms.

To wrap up this chapter, here are three recommendations for meeting these challenges and successfully exchanging data between .NET and Java:

1. **Use XSD to define common types.** As the second half of the chapter illustrated, XSD can be used to define shared types, which—with the right tools—can be used to generate platform-specific code. Some organizations set up an "XSD repository" for their development teams. This is a great idea and gives developers a central resource for examining and maintaining data types that are common throughout the business.
2. **Avoid exposing elements that are not contained in XSD.** As the start of the chapter implied, some data types exist on one platform but don't exist on the other. When defining types that will be exchanged between .NET and Java, stick to the types that are published in XSD.
3. **Use test harnesses to verify data types before writing your application.** When it comes to creating solutions that need to interoperate between .NET and J2EE, start with the data types: determine which types need to be sent and the format for doing so. Once the data types have been defined, it's always useful to create a *test harness*. A test harness is a simple program that demonstrates the exchange of the data—similar to the samples presented in this chapter. You can use this test harness to prove that the data exchange will succeed, before you make any investment in creating the user interface or other elements of the application.

Summary

This chapter offered a high-level overview of exchanging data between .NET and Java. We looked at two technologies for performing this exchange: binary serialization and XML serialization. In its raw form in the .NET Framework and in Java, binary serialization doesn't make for a good interoperability story, but the concepts still apply, given the right set of third-party tools. The chapter's examination of using XML for data exchange started with a quick example of using XML parsing to exchange data between the two platforms. The discussion then concentrated on using XML serialization and creating data types that map to a standard XSD document for each platform.

This concludes Part I of the book, "Getting Started," which detailed the fundamentals, the business requirements, and the exchange of data as a way of introducing interoperability concepts. Part II, "Interoperability Technologies: Point to Point," will cover point-to-point interoperability. Chapter 4 begins the part by expanding on the concept of binary serialization introduced in this chapter and investigating how .NET Remoting can be used to communicate between the two platforms.

Part II

Interoperability Technologies: Point to Point

- Interoperability
  - Samples
    - Advanced
    - Config
    - Data
    - Point
      - Remoting
        - dotNETToEJB
        - dotNETToJava
        - JavaToComponentServices
        - JavaTodotNET
        - JavaToIIS
        - PerformanceTest
        - Utils
      - WebServices
        - Async
        - dotNET
        - dotNETComponentServices
        - Java
        - JavaEJB
        - PerformanceTest
        - Solution
        - UDDI
    - Resource
  - Tools

4

Connectivity with .NET Remoting

Microsoft .NET Remoting is a framework that can be used to enable components and objects to communicate and transfer data within a distributed architecture. In some contexts, .NET Remoting is referred to as the "next version of DCOM." Although this is slightly biased, I do agree that .NET Remoting solves many problems that DCOM and similar technologies didn't address. For developers working with Java 2 Enterprise Edition (J2EE) technology, .NET Remoting can in some circumstances be considered the .NET parallel to Remote Method Invocation (RMI) and Remote Method Invocation over Internet Inter-ORB Protocol (RMI-IIOP).

The foundation of .NET Remoting is encapsulated by the concepts of *channels* and *formatters*. Channels are used for passing information between remote components. Two of the default channels of .NET Remoting are TCP and HTTP. Formatters are used to convert an object from one platform into a format that another platform can understand. The Microsoft .NET Framework ships with two types of default formatters: binary formatters and SOAP formatters. Chapter 3, "Exchanging Data Between .NET and Java," covered binary formatters in its investigation of how binary serialization works. The SOAP formatter can be used with the serialization classes in the .NET Framework.

Note SOAP is a three-part definition that specifies an XML structure for the framework of a message (known as a *SOAP Envelope*). The three parts, which are all placed inside the *SOAP Body*, include the data types defined using XML Schema Definition (XSD), a convention for representing remote procedure calls (RPCs), and the data that's returned from those calls. Additional information on the SOAP specification can be found at *http://www.w3.org/TR/SOAP/*.

.NET Remoting channels and formatters are used in combination to define how communication between two systems will be established. For example, Figure 4-1 shows point-to-point communications between a potential ASP.NET page and a business-tier component in .NET. If this communication will be established by using .NET Remoting, the channel can be either HTTP or TCP and the formatters can be either binary or SOAP.

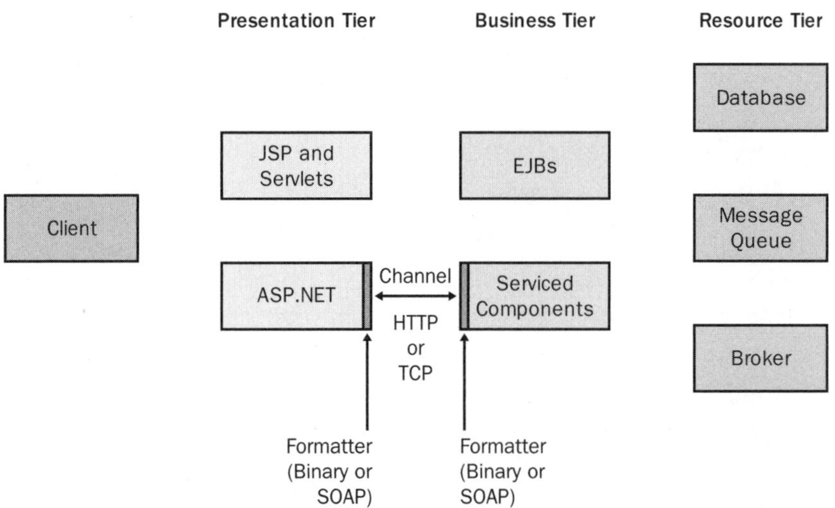

Figure 4-1 .NET Remoting using channels and formatters.

Advantages of Using .NET Remoting

.NET Remoting is not only about intersystem communications. It also can be used for interprocess communications. .NET Remoting can be configured to communicate and exchange data between two or more components in separate application domains on .NET—all on the same machine. This is useful for creating systems that are local today but might need to be adapted for a more distributed deployment tomorrow.

Furthermore, .NET Remoting supports both *pass-by-value* and *pass-by-reference* implementations for remote data. To define these terms, let's return to our previous example. Remember in the "Interoperability at the Presentation Tier" section of Chapter 2, "Business Requirements for Interoperability," how the ASP.NET page called the business-tier component, which in turn returned a set of data? With .NET Remoting, you have two ways of passing this data back to the calling component. First, you can pass all the data back to the caller, which is known as *passing by value*. Alternatively, you can pass only a pointer to the data, which is known as *passing by reference*.

When you use pass by reference, the data will remain in state on the server, and the client will use a reference to that data when required. One advantage of passing by reference is that if the data is large or if operations are better suited to run on a remote system, network latency isn't an issue. The client can still use and reference the object, even though it's contained within the boundaries of the server. Figure 4-2 shows how you would pass data by reference using our previous example.

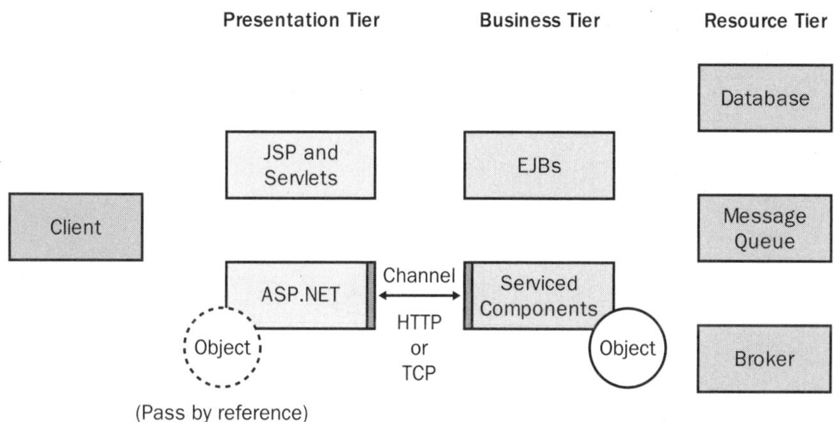

Figure 4-2 Passing by reference with .NET Remoting.

Comparing .NET Remoting to XML Web Services

I'm frequently asked the question, "How does .NET Remoting compare with Web services—aren't they the same technology?" .NET Remoting complements Web services—it doesn't compete with them. It's true that some pieces of the technology stacks naturally overlap with each other—for instance, in their ability to send SOAP-formatted messages over an HTTP channel, which both technologies do equally well. However, both technologies offer distinct areas of functionality.

First, .NET Remoting supports a TCP channel and a binary formatter. Removing the need for HTTP headers and selecting a raw formatter improves the performance in most cases. Therefore, if you need to pass multiple requests (for example, thousands of requests per second) across a communication channel, using .NET Remoting with a binary formatter in combination with a TCP channel might give you better performance than using a Web service implementation.

Second, as mentioned, .NET Remoting supports passing by value and passing by reference. You can still pass by value and pass by reference using a Web service, but passing by reference is more difficult to implement. Moreover, storing session state with Web services can be troublesome in some applications, which also can make working with events and callbacks more difficult.

On the other hand, you could argue that the Web services space has more momentum. Many providers that haven't adopted an architecture similar to .NET Remoting have instead selected Web services as their primary transport technology. For solutions that need to dynamically interoperate with other systems using Web services, adopting a pure Web services strategy can be an advantage.

Before you select one of these two communications technologies, look at what each can do and how each can provide solutions for your applications. Select a technology based on its merit, and feel free to use both .NET Remoting and Web services when they complement each other.

Developing an Application That Uses .NET Remoting

When developing an application that uses .NET Remoting, three steps are required to get the communication up and running:

1. **Create the server component** The server component will offer a number of methods that can be called (by reference) and some type of data that will be passed to and returned by these methods (by value). Classes on the server component must implement the *MarshalByRefObject* interface to allow communication via .NET Remoting. Any data to be passed by value must also be serializable.

2. **Create the client** The client application calling the server component doesn't need to implement any additional interfaces to enable

.NET Remoting, but it does need a reference to the server component assembly or the interface itself. This reference is used to interrogate the methods and data types that are exposed by the server component.

3. **Configure the Remoting.Config file** You have two options for configuring a system that uses .NET Remoting. The configuration—which includes the reference to the remote systems, channels, and formatters that will be used—can be stored either in the code or in a configuration file that's accessed at run time.

One advantage of storing the configuration in a configuration file is that the values in the configuration file can be changed without recompiling the application. This means that if the configuration of distributed components in a production environment change or if another channel is required (for example, because of the implementation of a firewall), you can make these configurations on the fly. Storing the configuration in code still works, but it means that any changes will require the component to be recompiled and potentially redeployed.

Fortunately, in .NET, the structure of the remoting.config file is fairly simple. Here's a sample:

```
<configuration>
    <system.runtime.remoting>
        <application>
            <client url="tcp://localhost:8888/URL">
                <activated type="Namespace.Class, AssemblyName"/>
            </client>
        </application>
    </system.runtime.remoting>
</configuration>
```

In addition to recognizing that the file is written in XML, you can see that the main configuration lies within the *<client>* element tags in the file. The attribute in the *<client>* element specifies the URL for the endpoint of the server component, and within the server component, the activated types are specified. These are the classes to be called by reference.

.NET Remoting Samples

So far, we've talked about .NET Remoting in the context of the .NET Framework as a whole. Because our focus is interoperability, let's look at how to use .NET Remoting to enable connectivity between .NET and J2EE.

Introducing Intrinsyc's Ja.NET

As mentioned in Chapter 1, "Microsoft .NET and J2EE Fundamentals," the book's sample code uses a product named Ja.NET from Intrinsyc. Ja.NET provides a two-way implementation of the .NET Remoting stack for Java. By using Ja.NET, we can generate Java proxies that have the ability to expose or consume components using the .NET Remoting protocol. Figure 4-3 shows an example of this, a JavaServer Pages (JSP) page consuming a .NET Serviced Component.

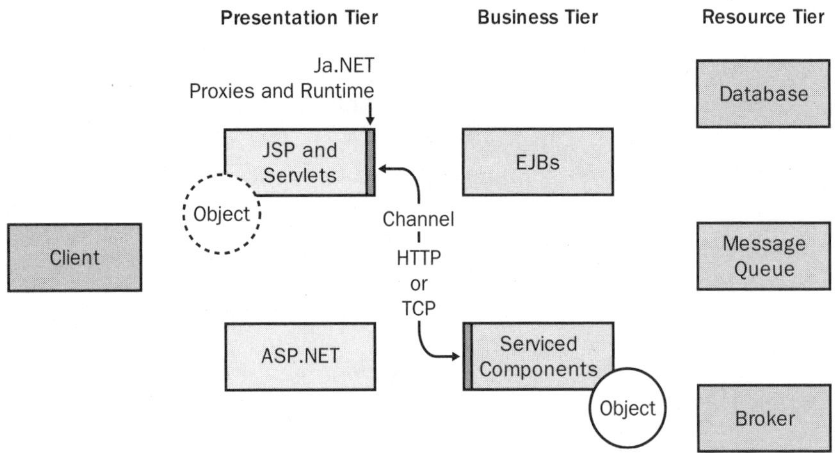

Figure 4-3 Using Ja.NET to call a remote .NET server object.

In addition, the Ja.NET tools can expand upon this functionality by hosting the generated Java proxies within a Web Archive (WAR) file to enable access to Enterprise Javabeans (EJBs) from .NET—again, with all the communications based on .NET Remoting.

This chapter will cover five technical scenarios using .NET Remoting and the Ja.NET product, showing sample code for each. These scenarios range from a simple .NET component calling a simple Java component via .NET Remoting to a look at accessing components hosted in an EJB container and Component Services in Microsoft Windows Server 2003 to provide automatic transaction, security, and life-cycle management.

Ja.NET Tools

Six main parts make up the Ja.NET toolset. They are:

- **GenService** Used by the GenNet and GenJava tools (discussed next) to provide access to .NET assemblies for development. This tool is required only to generate the proxies, and installation isn't required to put the code into production.

- **GenNet** Used to generate .NET proxies to access Java classes via the Ja.NET runtime.
- **GenJava** Used to generate Java proxies to access .NET assemblies via the Ja.NET runtime.
- **Janetor** Used to view and modify Ja.NET runtime configuration settings. This includes licensing for the Ja.NET product, as well as locally shared and remotely accessed objects.
- **Ja.NET TCP server** Used to provide standalone hosting via the Ja.NET runtime for Java classes that aren't hosted on a J2EE server. This tool is included in the Ja.NET runtime.
- **Ja.NET runtime** The main collection of classes (located in the janet.jar file) required to host the other tools in this list.

Ja.NET Installation

All the Ja.NET libraries, documentation, and tools are installed with the main installation via the accompanying CD. All these files are located in the C:\Interoperability\Tools\Ja.NET directory.

In addition to installing this directory, before running any of the samples, you'll need to install GenService as a Windows service. To install this tool, navigate to the C:\Interoperability\Tools\Ja.NET\Install directory and run the GenServiceSetup.msi file that's located in this directory.

Run through the wizard, accepting the defaults. For additional information, consult the documentation in C:\Interoperability\Tools\Ja.NET\doc. The GenService is required for all the samples listed in this chapter.

The Sample Code

The *Stock* and *Portfolio* sample types have undergone a slight face-lift since the last set of samples in Chapter 3. Previously, we had a *Stock* object that contained some fields to represent a stock ticker and a *Portfolio* object that contained an array of stocks, *Stock[]*.

The examples in this chapter replace the *Portfolio* object with the *ArrayList* object. (The .NET examples use a type named *System.Collections.ArrayList*, and the Java examples use a type named *java.util.ArrayList*.) The *ArrayList* objects provide some additional functionality over a regular array, including the ability to more easily add and remove members. Using this data type highlights how well the Ja.NET product converts objects between the two platforms.

The new *Stock* object in this chapter's samples now looks like this:

```
namespace SimpleRemoting
{
    [Serializable()]
    public class Stock
    {
        public String Ticker="";
        public String Name="";
        public double Price;
        public double Previous;
        public int Volume;

    }
}
```

Any functions that return more than one *Stock* object will return them in an *ArrayList* (for either platform).

Java Client to .NET Remoted Object

The first sample shows a simple Java client consuming a server component hosted on .NET. This sample shows a simple two-way communication between the Java and .NET platforms. This sample code, which can be found in the C:\Interoperability\Samples\Point\Remoting\JavaTodotNet directory, is shown in Figure 4-4.

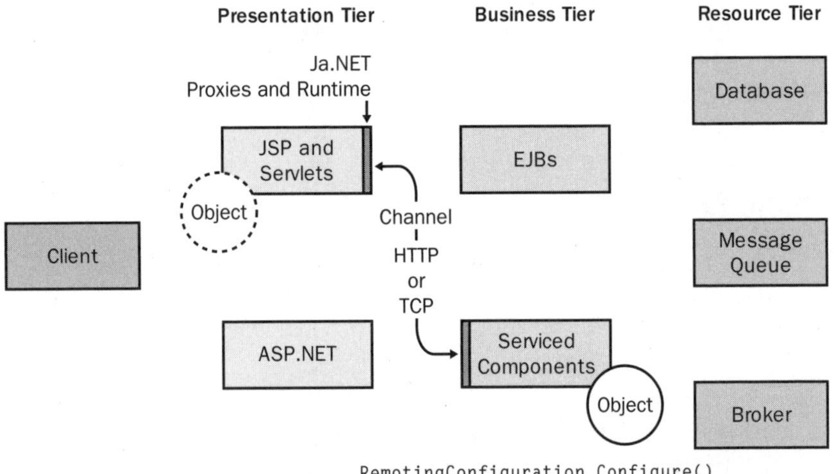

Figure 4-4 A Java client calling a .NET remoted object.

As shown in the figure, the Java client will directly call the .NET server application using .NET Remoting. Although Figure 4-4 shows the sample code running as both presentation-tier and business-tier components, the first two samples in this chapter will be run from the command prompt.

The .NET Server Sample Code

Take a look at the .NET code first, located in the Server subdirectory. You'll see two source files there. The first, DataTypes.cs, contains the new *Stock* class definition. The second, RemotingServer.cs, contains three classes.

The first class (*SampleData*) creates five sample stocks. (Imagine that these stocks are recommendations from an online stock broker.) *SampleData* then adds these sample stocks to an *ArrayList* and returns the result:

```
public class SampleData : MarshalByRefObject
{
    public ArrayList getRecommendations()
    {
        Stock NWND = new Stock();
        Stock CONT = new Stock();
        Stock FTHC = new Stock();
        Stock ASKI = new Stock();
        Stock WOOD = new Stock();

        NWND.Ticker = 'NWND";
        NWND.Name = 'Northwind Traders";
        NWND.Price = 50.12;
        NWND.Previous = 51.00;
        NWND.Volume = 123;
        // This is repeated for 4 other stocks

        ArrayList myStocks = new ArrayList();

        myStocks.Add(NWND);
        myStocks.Add(CONT);
        myStocks.Add(FTHC);
        myStocks.Add(ASKI);
        myStocks.Add(WOOD);

           myStocks.TrimToSize();

           // return the sample data
        return myStocks;
    }
}
```

Note that the *SampleData* class extends the *MarshalByRefObject* base class. *MarshalByRefObject* is used to enable access to objects across application domain boundaries in .NET. As we'll discuss later in the section, generating the automatic proxies for .NET using the tools that are supplied with Ja.NET is dependent on this base class being referenced. Only classes that derive from this class or classes that are tagged as being serializable have proxies generated for them by the GenJava tool.

The second class in the RemotingServer.cs file is named *StockServer*. This sample class is used to simulate the functionality of the server application:

```
public class StockServer : MarshalByRefObject
{
    public bool BuyStocks(Stock stockToBuy, int quantity)
    {
        // Display to the console
        Console.WriteLine("Incoming request to purchase "
            +quantity+" common shares of "+stockToBuy.Name
            +" ("+stockToBuy.Ticker+")");

        // do the real work here!...

        // Assume that the trade was committed
        return true;
    }
}
```

This code contains a single method named *BuyStocks*, which simulates a stock purchase, taking a *Stock* object and a quantity as two parameters. Once the method is called, it simply writes the result to the console. However, it's possible to imagine how, in a production system, this method could potentially commit a trade purchase on behalf of the user. Again, this class implements *MarshalByRefObject*, which indicates that we'll be exposing the method via .NET Remoting and passing this object to a Java client by reference (not by value).

The third class in the .NET Remoting sample is the main class. This class is used solely to host the server components within a console application:

```
public class RemotingServer
{
    [STAThread]
    static void Main(string[] args)
    {
        RemotingConfiguration.Configure('remoting.config');
        Console.WriteLine('.NET Remoting Server Sample is '
            +"ready to process messages');
        Console.WriteLine('Enter to Exit');
```

```
            Console.In.Read();
        }
    }
```

The key line of code in this file is the *RemotingConfiguration.Configure* entry. This line instructs the remoting components to initialize with the values and settings found in the configuration file (remoting.config). These remoting components are valid for the lifetime of the application that they're configured within. We prevent the application from terminating by calling the *Console.In.Read* method, which pauses until the user presses the Enter key. If we hadn't prevented the application from terminating, the remoted components would immediately be lost when the main class completed.

As you've probably guessed, the final piece of the puzzle for the .NET server side is the configuration file. The configuration file for this sample, remoting.config, can be found in the same directory and contains the remoting instructions for hosting the components:

```
<configuration>
    <system.runtime.remoting>
        <application>
            <service>
                <activated type="SimpleRemoting.SampleData,Server"/>
                <activated type="SimpleRemoting.StockServer,Server"/>
            </service>
            <channels>
                <channel port="5656" ref="tcp">
                    <serverProviders>
                        <formatter ref="binary"
                            typeFilterLevel="Full"/>
                        <formatter ref="soap"
                            typeFilterLevel="Full"/>
                    </serverProviders>
                </channel>
            </channels>
        </application>
    </system.runtime.remoting>
</configuration>
```

The remoting.config file has two important elements. The first is the *<activated>* elements within the *<service>* element. These elements define which components are to be hosted and take this format: Namespace.Class, Assembly.

In this case, the namespace is *SimpleRemoting*, the class names are *SampleData* and *StockServer*, and the final assembly will be named Server.exe. Therefore, we have the values to create these entries. The channel is also defined in the remoting.config file within the *<channel>* element. For this sample, we've selected the TCP channel and will use IP port 5656.

> **Warning** You must ensure the validity of the remoting.config file—not only for this sample, but for all applications and solutions that you write using .NET Remoting. One simple error within the remoting.config file could mean that components you thought were being hosted are not. Also, no validation occurs when the remoting.config file is loaded, so incorrect entries are rarely detected.

Before we look at the Java side of things, let's compile the .NET server source code, which is done by running NAnt from the command prompt in the sample directory (C:\Interoperability\Samples\Point\Remoting\JavaTodotNET\Server). The output will be a Server.exe executable file.

At this point, we'll also run the server code. Execute the server file that was generated by the build. To confirm that the server is running, the following message should be displayed:

```
.NET Remoting Server Sample is ready to process messages
Enter to Exit
```

Because this code must run simultaneously with the Java sample that you'll see next, you should keep this process running in a separate command-prompt window. We did something similar with the *SimpleSerializer* sample that we ran in Chapter 3.

> **Tip** If you enter **start server** from the command prompt instead of **server**, the process will automatically be launched in a separate console window.

The Java Client Sample Code

Change to the directory containing the Java sample code, which can be found in C:\Interoperability\Samples\Point\Remoting\JavaTodotNet\Client. This directory contains only one class, Client.java, which contains the code to call the server component:

```
import SimpleRemoting.*;

public class Client
{
    public static void main(String[] args)
    {
```

```
        try
        {
            // Create the new remote object
            SampleData sd = new SampleData();

            // Create the portfolio as an ArrayList
            java.util.ArrayList myStocks =
                new java.util.ArrayList(sd.getRecommendations());

            // Display the header information...
            System.out.println("There are "+myStocks.size()
                +" stocks recommended for purchase.");

            // Display the detailed stock information...
            for (int f=0; f<myStocks.size(); f++)
            {
                Stock currentStock = (Stock)myStocks.get(f);
                System.out.println("-----------");
                System.out.println("Ticker:     "
                    +currentStock.Ticker);
                System.out.println("Name:       "
                    +currentStock.Name);
                System.out.println("Price:      "
                    +currentStock.Price);
                System.out.println("Previous:   "
                    +currentStock.Previous);
                System.out.println("Volume:     "
                    +currentStock.Volume);
            }

            // Puchase the stocks for one of the stocks
            Stock stockToBuy = (Stock)myStocks.get(1);

            // Make request to purchase
            StockServer ss = new StockServer();
            // buy a 100 of the second stock in the recommendations
            boolean successfulTrade = ss.BuyStocks(stockToBuy,100);
            // Display confirmation
            System.out.println("\nThe purchase "
                +(successfulTrade ? "completed" : "failed"));
        }
        catch (Exception e)
        {
            e.printStackTrace(System.out);
        }
    }
}
```

The client code is relatively simple. First, a new reference to the *SampleData* component is made and the *getRecommendations* method from this class is called, which returns a list of *Stock* objects contained within an *ArrayList*. The returned information is displayed on the screen, after which a new reference to *StockServer* is created, and then the *BuyStocks* method is called. The code passes a *Stock* in the returned recommendations as the first parameter and a quantity to purchase as the second parameter.

Looking through the code and the directory, you might have noticed something fundamental missing. Although we have the correct class and method names for the remote object within the client code, we don't reference the Ja.NET libraries directly and we don't have any other classes in the Java samples directory. To create this link between the Java client code and the .NET server components, we need to run two of the Ja.NET tools.

The first tool needed is GenJava, which generates the required Java proxies from a .NET assembly. From the command prompt, run **genjava**. The GenJava tool will be displayed, as shown in Figure 4-5.

> **Note** GenJava is one of five batch files that can found in the C:\Interoperability\Samples\Point\Remoting\Utils directory. This directory should be added to your system *PATH* as part of the sample code installation. You should verify this setting, as we'll be using the batch-file versions of other tools within this chapter.

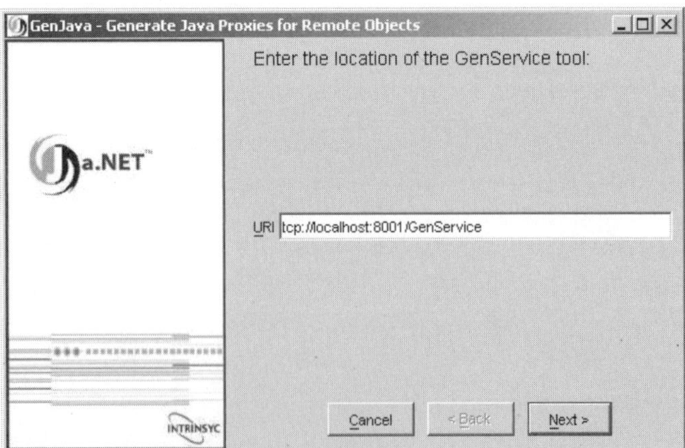

Figure 4-5 The GenJava wizard.

The first step in the GenJava wizard is to locate the GenService tool. The GenService was the Windows service that we installed earlier in the chapter. Enter **tcp://localhost:8001/GenService** as the URL. Note that I'm using the same machine to host the .NET component; therefore, the URL is *tcp://localhost:8001/GenService*. If your GenService tool is installed on another machine, you'll need to change localhost to the name of that particular machine. Once you've entered this information, click the Next button.

The second step of the wizard, shown in Figure 4-6, sets the location of the .NET assembly and the output directory for the Java proxies. The GenJava tool reads the .NET assembly by using a process known as *reflection*. This process allows the tool to interrogate the methods and fields that are required to create a valid Java proxy file. Enter the following location for the .NET assembly created in the previous step (keeping in mind that your directories might differ slightly if you installed the sample code to a different location):

C:\Interoperability\Samples\Point\Remoting\JavaTodotNET\Server\Server.exe

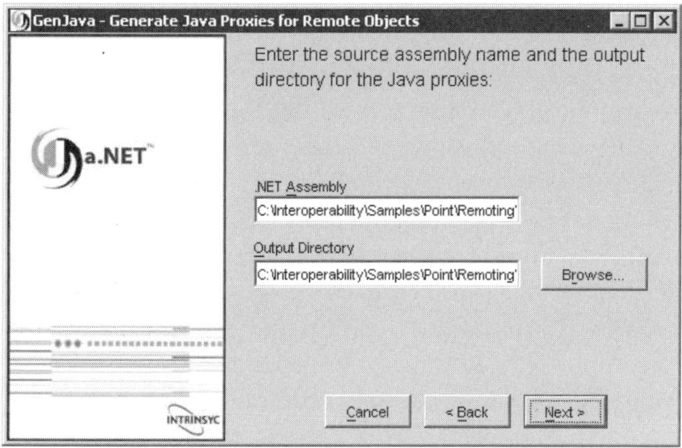

Figure 4-6 Setting the location and output directory.

For the Java output, we'll create the proxy code in the same directory as the client class, so enter the following location for the Output Directory: **C:\Interoperability\Samples\Point\Remoting\JavaTodotNET\Client**. Upon clicking the Next button, the Java proxies will be created in the Client directory and the wizard will display the confirmation, as shown in Figure 4-7.

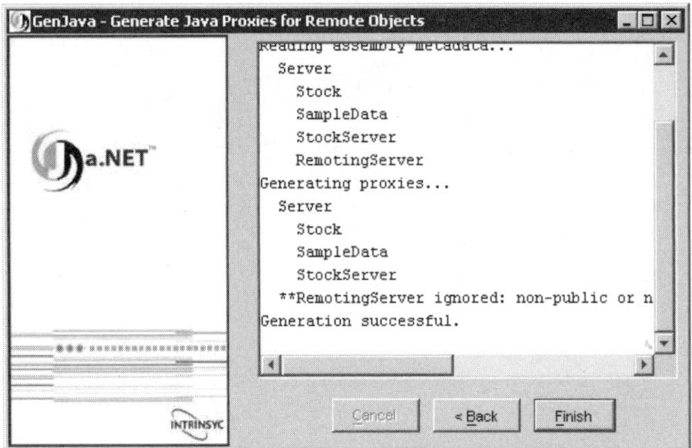

Figure 4-7 A successful generation of the proxies.

Click the Finish button. Now we can investigate exactly what's been created by the tool. First, the Client directory contains a genjava.xml file. This XML file contains the wizard settings that you've just used. Upon rerunning the GenJava tool, this file will be used to prepopulate the wizard with the choices that were made earlier to prevent you from having to re-enter all the data.

In addition to this XML file, a new subdirectory named SimpleRemoting was created. (This is the namespace of the .NET server component.) This directory contains three Java proxies representing the classes that were read from the .NET assembly: Stock.java (the *Stock* type), SampleData.java (a reference to the sample data object with the recommendations), and StockServer.java (a reference to the class that has the *buyStocks* method). Feel free to examine these generated proxies. This chapter won't cover the internals of these proxies because they contain only automatically generated code; however, the proxies offer insight into the workings of some of the Ja.NET classes.

You now have created the Java proxies, which contain the classes that were referenced in the Client.java file. The next step for getting the Java sample code running is to execute a second tool from the Ja.NET application, named Janetor. Janetor configures the client side and licensing for the Ja.NET proxy and must be run to complete the configuration. To run the tool, type **janetor** at the command prompt. (Again, ensure that your system *PATH* contains an entry for C:\Interoperability\Samples\Point\Remoting\Utils.)

After the Janetor tool has launched, as shown in Figure 4-8, the first step is to set the licensing correctly. To do this, place the janet_license.xml file that was sent to you by Intrinsyc (discussed in Chapter 1) in the C:\Interoperability\Tools\Ja.NET\lib directory. If your license file is installed elsewhere, right-click the Licensing entry and select Install License to open the Select A Ja.NET License file dialog box. Once you have selected your janet_license.xml file, click Open to return to the Janetor main window.

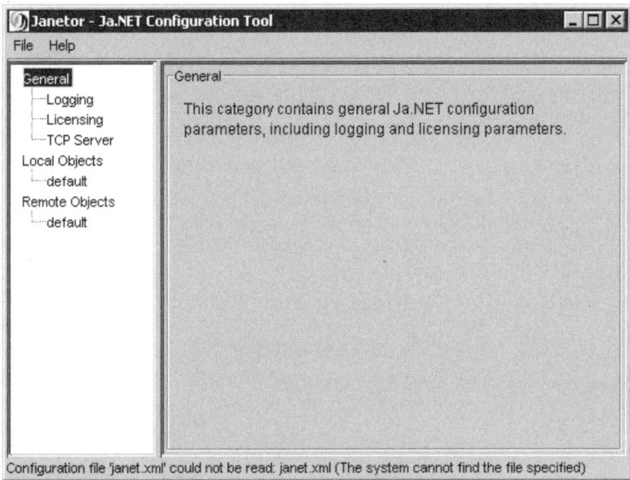

Figure 4-8 Using the Janetor configuration tool.

Next, click the default entry within the Remote Objects option. The dialog box shown in Figure 4-9 should appear.

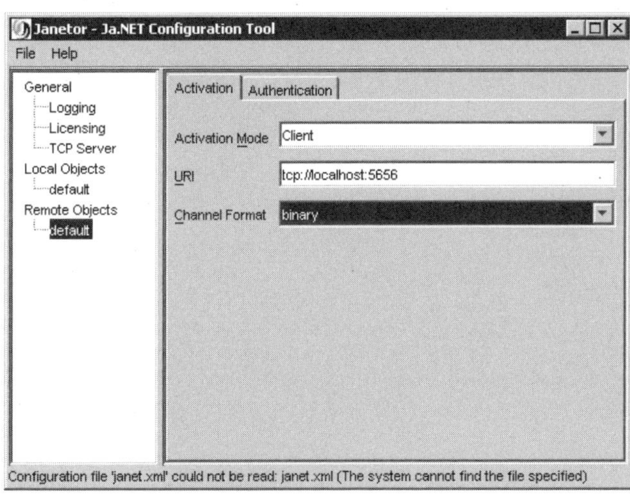

Figure 4-9 Configuring the activation mode, URI, and channel format.

You need to enter the Uniform Resource Indicator (URI) for the remotely hosted component and the channel format. In the remoting.config file that we used earlier in the .NET sample code, we configured the server to communicate on port 5656. Because we're also using the TCP channel on the same machine, our URI will be **tcp://localhost:5656**.

The channel format is the option that determines which formatter to use and by default is either binary or SOAP. This option is always configured on the client, and there's no need to change anything in the remoting.config file on the server. For this test, select the binary channel format option.

Save the settings, and exit the Janetor tool. Now you're ready to build and test the Java client. The Janetor tool saves its configuration in a janet.xml file, again located in the Client directory.

Build and run the client sample code, using the run target with Ant. If all is successful, this is the output you should see:

```
There are 5 stocks recommended for purchase.
-----------
Ticker:      NWND
Name:        Northwind Traders
Price:       50.12
Previous:    51.0
Volume:      123
-----------
Ticker:      CONT
Name:        Contoso
Price:       12.45
Previous:    12.01
Volume:      33
-----------
Ticker:      FTHC
Name:        Fourth Coffee
Price:       3.45
Previous:    3.6
Volume:      6
-----------
Ticker:      ASKI
Name:        Alpine Ski House
Price:       32.45
Previous:    32.09
Volume:      45
```

```
-----------
Ticker:      WOOD
Name:        Woodgrove Bank
Price:       14.45
Previous:    14.45
Volume:      50

The purchase completed
```

The Java client sample code will report back the five stock recommendations that were retrieved from the .NET server component. Toward the bottom of the recommendations listing, you should see a message that indicates that your purchase was made successfully.

If you switch to the .NET server component (which is running as Server.exe in a separate command-prompt window), you should see that it has received the incoming request from the Java client to purchase the stocks:

```
Incoming request to purchase 100 common shares of
Fourth Coffee (FTHC)
```

So, what's happening under the covers here? The Client.java code makes two calls: one to display the recommendations, and the other to make the purchase. What's actually called is the Java proxy code that was generated by the GenJava tool we ran earlier. This proxy code is receiving the request and formatting a .NET Remoting call to the .NET server component, based on the channel and formatting parameters you entered in Janetor. Replies and return data are then passed back to the original Client.java class.

Before we move on to the sample that shows the .Net to Java version, let's look at the exception that occurs when the .NET server component isn't running. To test this, stop the Server.exe server component by pressing the Enter key in the appropriate command-prompt window. Rerun the client to execute the Java client sample code. You should observe the following exception:

```
com.intrinsyc.janet.RemoteException: Connection refused: connect
```

This exception indicates that the Java proxy could not establish communication by using the .NET Remoting protocol. If you're building code based on Ja.NET in your production application, it's recommended you trap for this exception to help detect when server failures occur or when the server component isn't available.

.NET Client to Java Object Hosted by Ja.NET TCP Server

The previous example generated Java proxies to access a .NET component via .NET Remoting. In this next example, we'll switch the roles so that the client is now .NET and the server object is hosted in Java. However, as Figure 4-10 shows, we'll still use .NET Remoting to access the remote object, and we'll have access to the same sets of parameters as in the previous example.

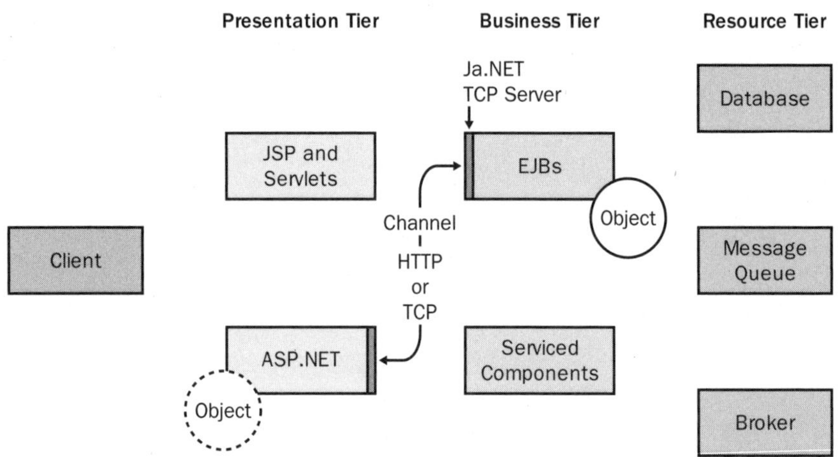

Figure 4-10 .NET client calling a Java object hosted by Ja.NET TCP server.

The Java Server Sample Code

The sample code for this second option is located in the C:\Interoperability\Samples\Point\Remoting\dotNETToJava directory. The Server subdirectory contains the three classes that will form the Java server component: Stock.java is the Java equivalent of the *Stock* object, SampleData.java returns the same five sample stocks (recommendations) as the .NET example, and StockServer.java contains a method named *sellStocks* that will be used the same way as the *BuyStocks* method was used in the previous example. Compile these classes in this directory before continuing, by running Ant.

Once you've compiled these Java classes, you need to run three Ja.NET tools in order to configure a .NET client that can consume them. The first tool, GenNet, is used to generate a .NET assembly that's referenced to create the client. Figure 4-11 shows this tool. To run the GenNet tool, enter **gennet** at the command prompt.

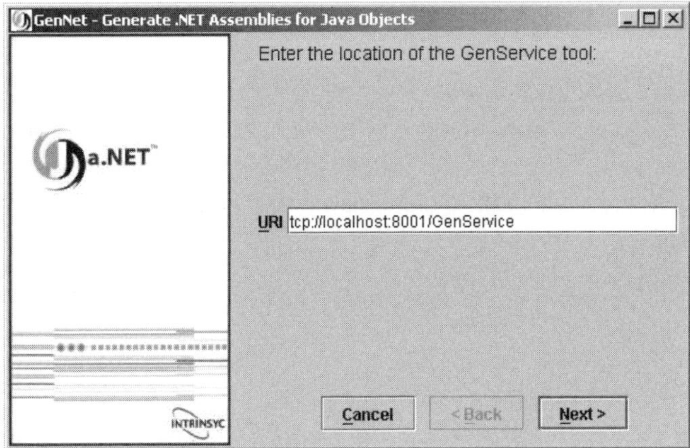

Figure 4-11 The GenNet tool.

As with the GenJava tool, the first stage of the GenNet wizard asks for the location of the GenService service. As with our previous example, this location is **tcp://localhost:8001/GenService**. The next stage of the wizard is to tell the GenNet tool the Java classes that it must generate .NET proxies for, as shown in Figure 4-12.

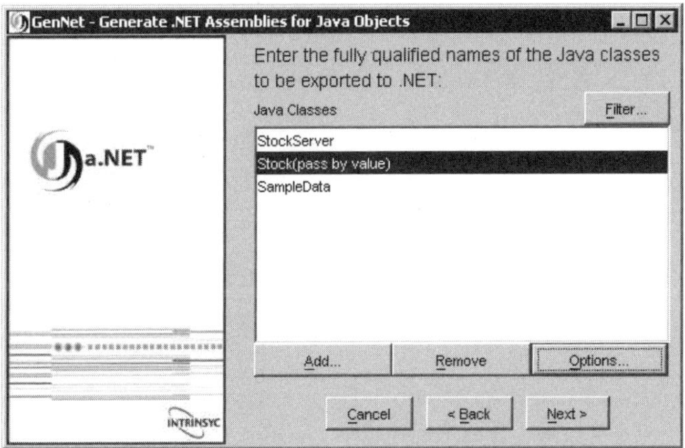

Figure 4-12 Adding classes to generate .NET proxies.

Click the Add button in the wizard. Enter the name of each Java class: **StockServer**, **Stock**, and **SampleData**.

> **Tip** Because *Stock* is a valid class, the Add Java Class dialog box has a tendency to auto-detect the class name when you enter it. For this same reason, the dialog box tends to lose focus when you enter the *StockServer* class name. If this happens, simply click the text field where you are entering the class name and finish entering the remainder of the class name.

Before clicking the Next button, highlight the *Stock* class and click the Options button. Select the Pass By Value check box, and click OK. Unlike the *StockServer* and *SampleData* classes, the *Stock* class is one that we need to pass by value between the client and server.

Once the classes have been defined (as shown in Figure 4-12), click the Next button to proceed. Now tell the GenNet wizard how the tool should name the generated .NET assembly and where to place it, as shown in Figure 4-13.

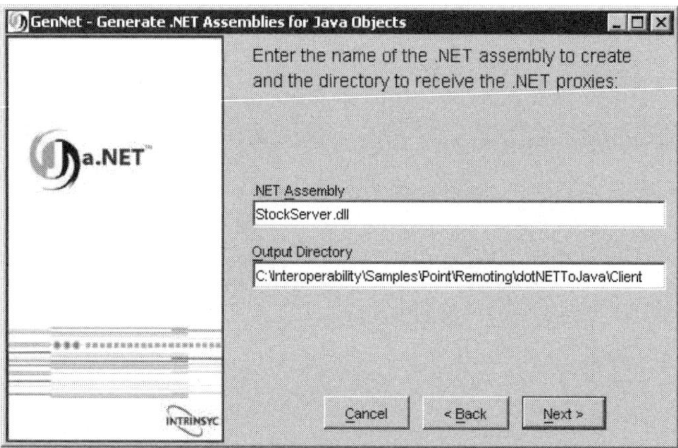

Figure 4-13 Entering the name and output directory for the .NET proxies.

As shown in Figure 4-13, name the assembly **StockServer.dll** and set the Output directory to **C:\Interoperability\Samples\Point\Remoting\dotNETToJava\Client**. This will generate the DLL in the same directory as the client.

Click the Next button to complete the wizard. The GenNet tool will generate the client proxy that you need, yielding a similar output to that shown in Figure 4-14. Click on the Finish button to close the GenNet tool.

The second tool you need to run is Janetor. In the previous sample, we ran the Janetor tool to configure the name of the machine and port to be used for the remote location of the server component. In this example, we'll use the same tool to configure the local hosting of this Java component. To run the Janetor tool, enter **janetor** at a command prompt.

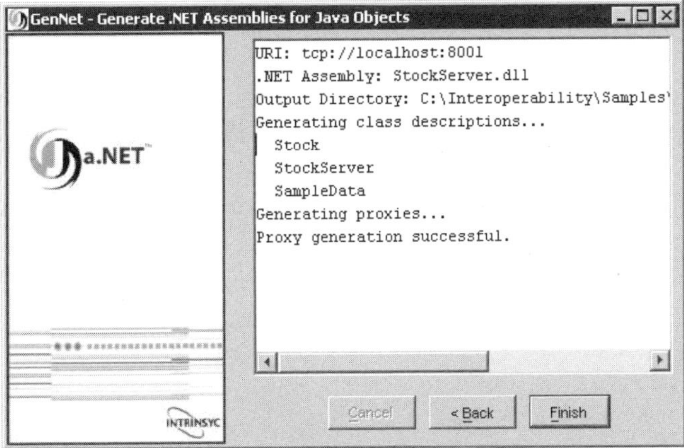

Figure 4-14 Successful generation of the .NET proxies.

As in the previous example, ensure that the licensing is correctly configured. To configure the server component, click the Default option in the Local Objects part of the tree, as shown in Figure 4-15. For the component, set the activation mode to Client, the URI to **tcp://localhost:8888/StockServer**, and the assembly name to **StockServer**. In the previous example, we configured the port number as 5656. The choice for this is entirely yours, but for this example, I've chosen a different port to ensure that no clashes occur.

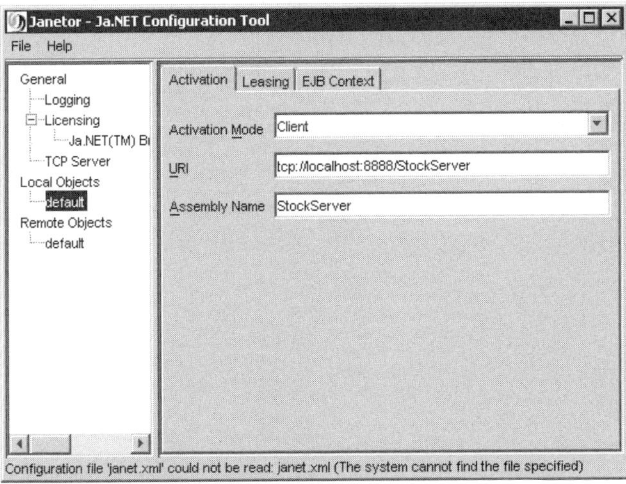

Figure 4-15 Setting the activation mode, URI, and assembly name.

Once this is set, save the configuration and exit the tool. The Java server component is ready to be hosted. In the previous example, we used the *Remoting.Configure* command from the .NET Remoting namespace to instruct the .NET server component to start listening for requests. Because we don't have access to the .NET Remoting classes in Java, we need to use an alternate method to host the component.

Fortunately, the Ja.NET tool comes with a TCP server that allows the component to be hosted. The TCP server creates a layer between the Java classes and the .NET Remoting channel, using the configuration information set with the Janetor tool to listen on a particular interface and port. To run the Ja.NET TCP server from the command prompt, type **start janetserver**. (As in the earlier example, this points to a batch file in the Utils directory.) This will launch the Ja.NET TCP server in a second command-prompt window, which is similar to the way we hosted the previous .NET component.

The .NET Client Sample Code

Navigate to the C:\Interoperability\Samples\Point\Remoting\dotNETToJava\Client directory. StockServer.dll is the assembly that was automatically generated by the GenNet tool in the previous step. To generate this assembly, the tool also created Client.cs, SampleData.cs, and StockData.cs. Although you can look in these files to see the code that was generated, a more interesting approach is to examine the assembly itself.

The .NET Framework SDK ships with a tool called ILDASM.EXE. ILDASM, which stands for *Intermediate Language Disassembler*, is a great tool to investigate assemblies within .NET. (Intermediate Language, or IL, is the language used for .NET assemblies just before they are compiled into native code.) Launch the tool by running **ildasm** from a command prompt. When the tool is launched, open the StockServer.dll assembly from within the Client directory of the sample.

You can see exactly what the assembly contains by using the ILDASM tool to expand through the types and methods, as shown in Figure 4-16. Remember that this assembly was automatically generated by the GenNet tool. Using ILDASM to interrogate the assembly is a great way to verify that the expected types and methods are available before you start coding the client. Everything in Figure 4-16 looks as expected, so we can continue building the client code.

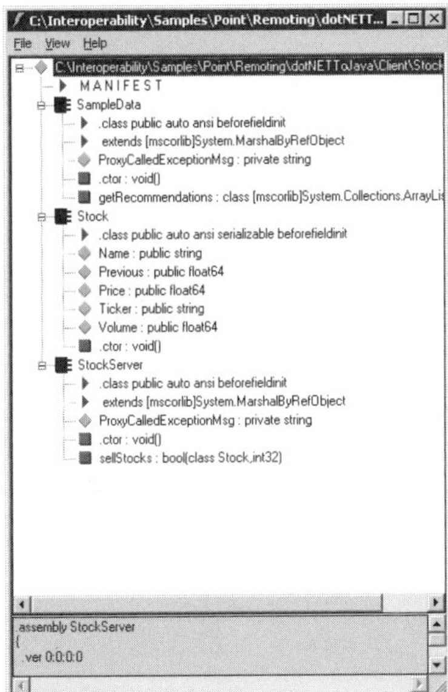

Figure 4-16 Using ILDASM to investigate the contents of the generated assembly.

The .NET client is located in Client.cs and looks very similar to the Client.java file we used in the previous example. Compile this now, using NAnt, to build the required client files.

Finally, before running the client, let's look at the remoting.config file that the .NET client will use. The configuration file, which follows, is located in the same directory:

```
<configuration>
    <system.runtime.remoting>
        <application>
            <client url="tcp://localhost:8888/StockServer">
                <activated type="StockServer, StockServer"/>
                <activated type="SampleData, StockServer"/>
            </client>
        </application>
    </system.runtime.remoting>
</configuration>
```

As you can see, the client URL matches the URI that we set in the Janetor tool. If you changed the port number in the last step of the previous example, be sure to change it to the same port number here as well. You need to include only the activated types that you call by reference: *StockServer* and *SampleData*. The *Stock* type returned is implicit to the call and does not need to be stated.

Run the client by executing Client.exe, ensuring that the Ja.NET TCP server is still running in a second command-prompt window. If all is successful, the client should list the five stock recommendations, as in the previous example. However, this time, the client will make a call to sell some stocks for the Java server component. This should be confirmed in the Ja.NET TCP server command prompt, with the following message:

```
Incoming request to sell 250 common shares of Fourth Coffee (FTHC)
```

To conclude this sample, let's take a look at the exception that's generated if the Ja.NET TCP server isn't running. (Performing this test is also a great way to prove that the communication really is happening!) Stop the Ja.NET TCP server by pressing Ctrl+C in the command prompt window in which the server is running, and rerun the .NET Client. You should observe a stack trace similar to the following:

```
System.Net.Sockets.SocketException: No connection could be made
because the target machine actively refused it
```

When designing a more production-worthy version of this code, you can trap the *SocketException* and report a potential "Server is offline" message to the user.

Building Production Code

The previous two samples demonstrated how, in both .NET and Java, you can create a server component that can be called by the other platform by using the .NET Remoting protocol to communicate. In each of the samples, the server side had to listen for incoming requests in a second command-prompt window.

Although this procedure is adequate for showing the samples in action, it doesn't lend itself toward a production-worthy solution. For example, in a production system, you don't want to have to ensure that all servers sharing these components are logged in and running this pseudo–server application from a command prompt. What happens if a user logs off the machine? What if a reboot happens? How do you scale this solution to offer the component to potentially hundreds of calling clients, supporting life cycle, security, and transactions?

The remainder of this chapter covers three additional samples and shows how to host these types of server components by using more production-worthy techniques in conjunction with the .NET Remoting protocol. First, we'll look at hosting the .NET server component within Microsoft Internet Information Server (IIS). IIS provides a proven, HTTP-based framework that can be leveraged to host such components to the respective Java client. Second, we'll reverse the situation, hosting the Java server component code within two EJBs—one Session-based and one Entity-based. You'll see how to use the Janetor tool to create an abstracted Web-based layer to allow these EJBs to be called from your .NET client.

Finally, we'll conclude by examining a late-breaking sample of a .NET component hosted through Component Services (using Microsoft Windows Server 2003) and called by a Java client. A new release of Component Services in Windows Server 2003 provides additional functionality for creating enterprise components and automatically generating a *SOAP virtual root* that can be consumed by the Ja.NET proxies.

Java Client to .NET Remoted Object, Hosted by IIS

Before we look at this particular sample, let's discuss some advantages of hosting the server component in IIS over using a sample standalone application. Figure 4-17 shows a server component hosted by IIS.

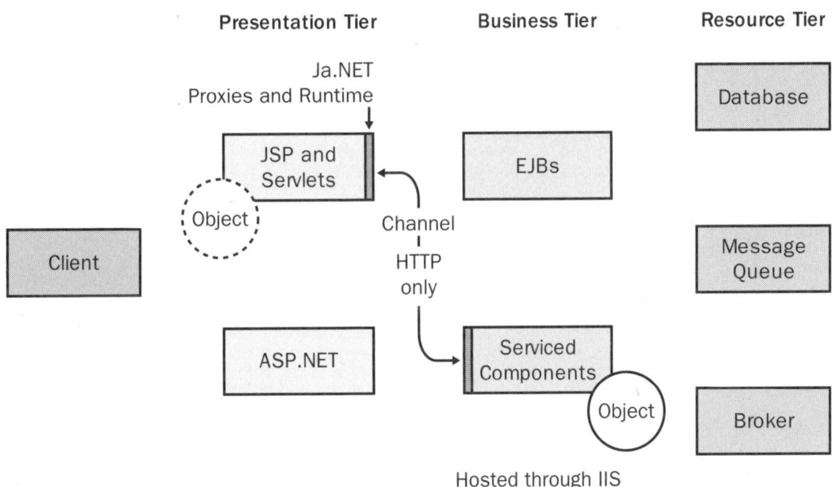

Figure 4-17 Java client calling a .NET server component, hosted by IIS.

With a little work, we could have used the examples in the previous section to move the .NET Remoting server component into a Windows service, which could be a viable option to hosting the server component in IIS. Although this would increase the stability of the component, it wouldn't automatically provide for the following:

- **Security** By hosting the server component within IIS, we can use the authentication mechanisms that are provided as part of the Web server. The process of locking down the server component with a username and password is the same as that of locking down an HTML page.
- **Isolation** IIS provides a number of pooling options that allow pages (and this component) to be pooled based on load and priority. Objects that run can be either executed as part of the IIS process or isolated within a separate process, thus protecting the Web server in case of a fault with the component.
- **Logging** Any logging mechanism (to a file or database) that's currently configured within IIS can now be applied to calls to the hosted server component.

The .NET Server Sample Code

The sample that demonstrates hosting the IIS server component is located in the C:\Interoperability\Samples\Point\Remoting\JavaToIIS directory. As with the Java-to-.NET example in the previous section, the Server subdirectory contains the classes for the server component. However, to host this component using IIS instead of the default .NET Remoting server method, you need to make a few changes. As the sample is also using IIS, you should ensure that you have followed the "Installing ASP.NET on Windows Server 2003" or "Installing ASP.NET on Windows XP Professional" and "Configuring ASP.NET Security" sections in Chapter 1.

First, there is no remoting.config file, and instead the settings are now present in web.config, which is the default configuration file for ASP.NET applications. In the web.config file, the reference to the port and channel have been removed. This is because HTTP is the only channel that IIS can host, and the port will be derived from the IIS settings.

```
<configuration>
    <system.runtime.remoting>
        <application>
            <service>
                <activated type="SimpleRemoting.SampleData,Server"/>
```

```
            <activated type="SimpleRemoting.StockServer,Server"/>
         </service>
      </application>
   </system.runtime.remoting>
</configuration>
```

In addition, the sample now has a bin directory. This directory is used to store the .NET assembly for the IIS virtual directory.

This sample also makes a couple of changes in the RemotingServer.cs class file. A *Main* method no longer exists. This is because the assembly generated is a DLL, not an executable. Recall that the *Main* method was used only to set up the .NET Remoting server configuration in the previous Java-to-.NET example. This is no longer required.

In addition, the previous example wrote the incoming purchases and sales by calling the *Console.WriteLine* method. When the component is hosted via IIS, however, we no longer have access to the *Console* object. To record the purchase, the component now writes to the Windows Event Log by using the following code:

```
EventLog ev = new EventLog("application",".",
    "Ja.NET Interoperability Sample");
ev.WriteEntry("Incoming request to purchase "+quantity+
    " common shares of "+stockToBuy.Name+" ("
    +stockToBuy.Ticker+")");
```

Compile the server code within this directory using NAnt. This will generate the required DLL in the bin directory for IIS. Once this has completed, you need to set up the IIS Virtual Directory. To do so, launch IIS by selecting the Start/Programs/Administrative Tools/Internet Information Services (IIS) Manager program menu item.

> **Tip** You can also run IIS by going to the Start menu, selecting Run, and typing **INETMGR**.

Within the Internet Information Services (IIS) Manager tool, navigate to and right-click the Default Web Site entry. From the drop-down menu, select New and then select Virtual Directory. The Virtual Directory Creation wizard will be opened, as shown in Figure 4-18.

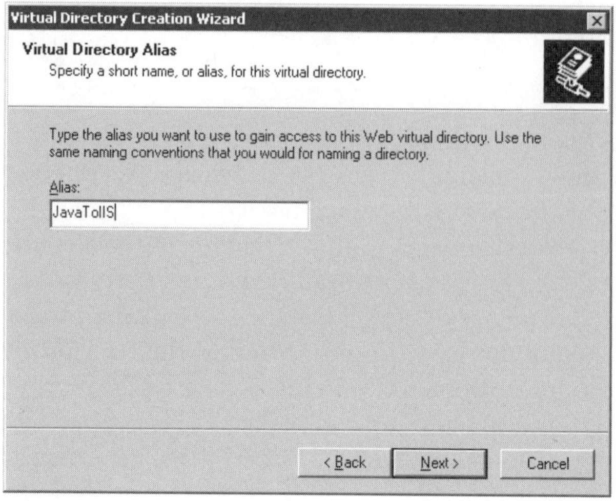

Figure 4-18 Creating an IIS Virtual Directory.

The alias for this sample's virtual directory will be **JavaToIIS**. (Note that virtual directories in IIS are case sensitive.) For the directory containing the content, point to our sample Server directory, **C:\Interoperability\Samples\Point\Remoting\JavaToIIS\Server**, as shown in Figure 4-19.

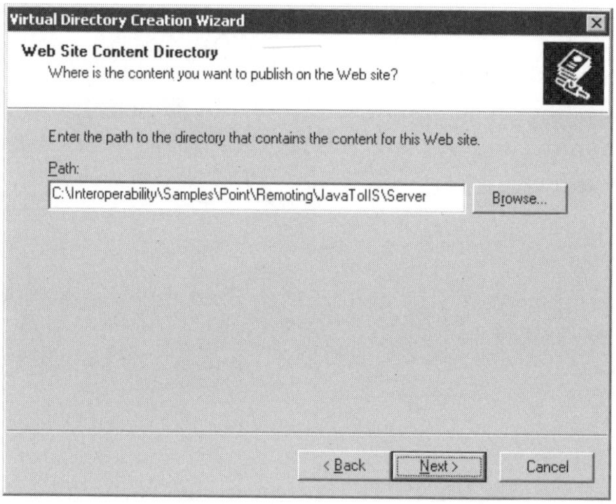

Figure 4-19 Setting the directory location for the virtual directory.

Complete the wizard by selecting the defaults for the remainder of the options. The .NET server component in IIS is now configured and ready to be called.

The Java Client Sample Code

With the server component now hosted through IIS, the configuration of the Java calling client is relatively straightforward. In the Client directory, run the GenJava tool. For the URI, enter **tcp://localhost:8001/GenService**. For the .NET Assembly, enter **C:\Interoperability\Samples\Point\Remoting\JavaToIIS\Server\bin\server.dll**, and for the Output Directory, enter **C:\Interoperability\Samples\Point\Remoting\JavaToIIS\Client**. (We've actually hardly changed the assembly, but we still need to generate the proxy files for the Java client.)

Navigate to the C:\Interoperability\Samples\Point\Remoting\JavaToIIS\Client directory. The client code for Client.java is the same as the code for the previous Java client connecting to a .NET server example.

In the client directory, run the Janetor tool, but this time, select the default option under the Remote Objects node in the tree, as shown in Figure 4-20.

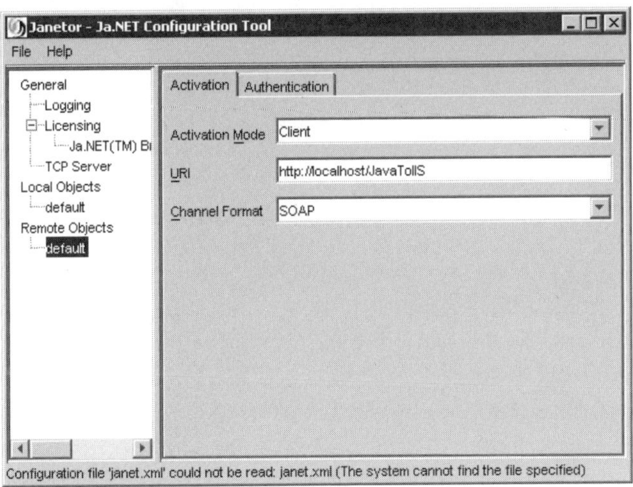

Figure 4-20 Setting the activation mode, URI, and channel format for the client.

With the activation mode set to Client, set the URI to the root of the IIS virtual directory. (In this sample, this is **http://localhost/JavaToIIS**.) Also, select either SOAP or Binary for the channel format—both work with IIS.

Notice the Authentication tab on the remote object activation panel, shown in Figure 4-21. This is a useful option because it allows you to configure authentication on the IIS Web server if required. (For example, these authentication credentials could come from an Active Directory directory service store.) The Authentication tab then lets you apply this authentication to the component that you remotely host.

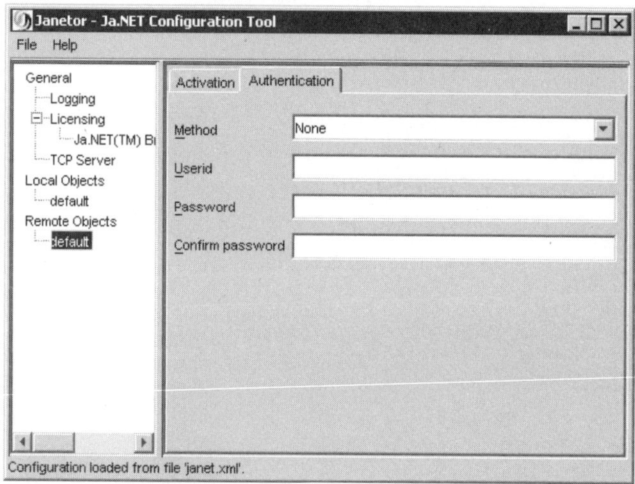

Figure 4-21 Using the Authentication tab to set credentials for the exposed component.

The Authentication tab supports Basic and Digest authentication, which both can be selected in IIS. In addition, this authentication information can be set programmatically.

Save the configuration, compile the sample, and run the client side of the code. After the call is made, the client object will call the remote server object as in the previous sample and will display the results and confirmation of the purchase to the console.

To validate this sample, go to the Event Viewer. (If you're running this demo across multiple machines, use the Event Viewer on the machine that the IIS Server is running on.) You can run the Event Viewer by selecting either Start/Programs/Administrative Tools/Event Viewer or Start/Run and entering **EVENTVWR** at the command prompt.

Within the Event Viewer, navigate to the Application Log File. If the sample code ran successfully, the remote server component should have written an entry into the Event Log to confirm the purchase, as shown in Figure 4-22.

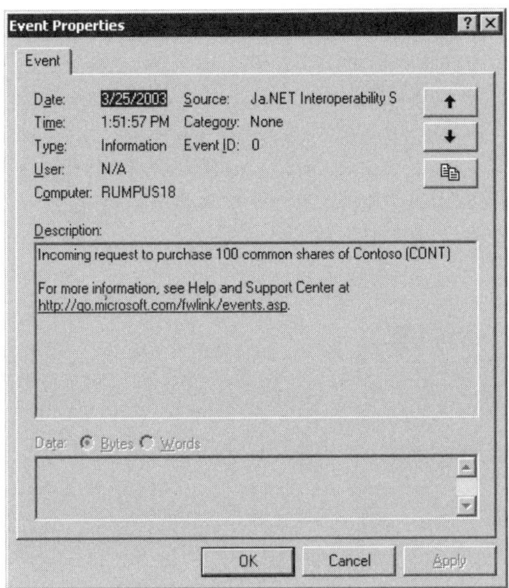

Figure 4-22 An event written to the Windows Event Log.

If you open and look at this event, you'll see a similar message to the one that was written to the console in previous examples.

Analyzing the Samples with the SOAP Trace Utility

The skeptic in me always likes to validate the data sent for each of these samples, especially when running the demos on the same machine. When running the demos on the same machine, it's easy to lose your appreciation for the type of data that's sent between processes.

One way of analyzing this communication is with the SOAP Trace Utility that's packaged as part of the Microsoft SOAP Toolkit version 3.0. The toolkit, which is designed to support SOAP for existing Microsoft Windows DNA architectures, can be downloaded from *http://msdn.microsoft.com*. The easiest method to find the SOAP toolkit is to search the MSDN Web site for "SOAP Toolkit".

The SOAP Trace Utility works by listening on one designated IP port and forwarding the data to another. As this tool intercepts and forwards the requests and responses, it logs the output of the message headers, body, and content. This is a great way to see both the size and type of data as they are transmitted along the wire.

Rerunning the current IIS sample, you can use the SOAP Trace Utility to view the data that's being passed. Once installed, the Trace Utility is available from the Start/Programs/Microsoft SOAP Toolkit Version 3 Program menu. To try this, configure the SOAP Trace Utility to create a new formatted trace, by selecting New/Formatted Trace from the File menu and setting the Local port to **8080**, the Destination host to **localhost**, and the Destination port to **80**, as shown in Figure 4-23.

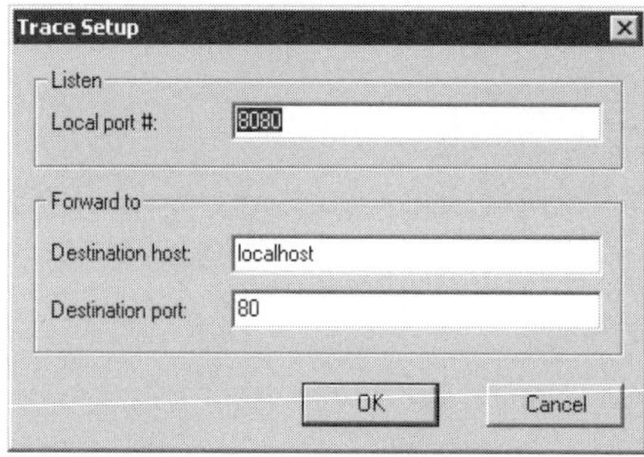

Figure 4-23 Setting the ports in the SOAP Trace Utility.

Now, return to the C:\Interoperability\Samples\Point\Remoting\Java-ToIIS\Client directory and rerun the Janetor tool. In the default node of Remote Objects, set the port so that the URL is **http://localhost:8080/JavaToIIS**, as shown in Figure 4-24. This will configure the Java client to communicate with the server component on port 8080, sending the request through the SOAP Trace Utility.

Save the configuration, and rerun the sample. You don't need to regenerate the proxies or recompile the code because the Janet.xml file is read dynamically by the Ja.NET libraries.

Once the demo has run, switch back to the active SOAP Trace Utility. An entry for the previous message, shown in Figure 4-25, will have been recorded. Expand the entry to inspect the contents of the message.

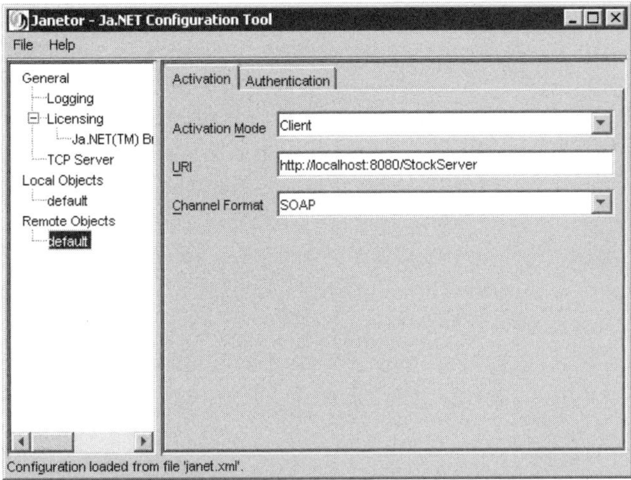

Figure 4-24 Setting the activation mode, URI, and channel format.

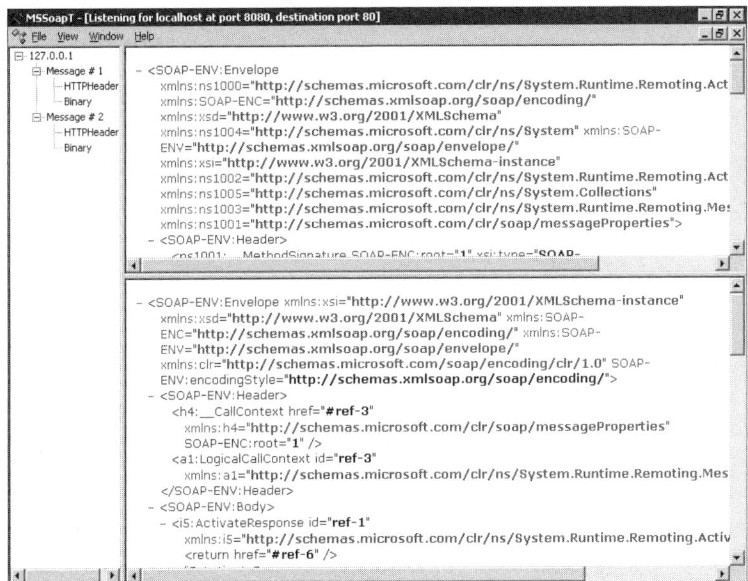

Figure 4-25 Examining the output from the SOAP Trace Utility.

You should see two messages displayed in the utility: the call to the *SampleData* and the call to the *StockServer* (which calls the *purchaseStock* method).

Click the first message to display the SOAP envelope, header, and body for the message. The top window shows the request from the client, and the bottom window displays the response from the server. From here, you can interrogate the types and content that make up the two messages. You can view the content of the SOAP message by clicking on the Binary node. By clicking the HTTPHeaders node in the tree, you can see that the size of the message (its content length) is 2553 bytes for the client request and 3038 bytes for the reply. These values might differ slightly based on your environment.

Now, clear the window in the SOAP Trace Utility and return to the client code (without closing the SOAP Trace Utility). Rerun the Janetor tool. This time, in the Remote Object defaults, select Binary for the channel format. Run the Client again, and return to the SOAP Trace Utility to view the generated output, as shown in Figure 4-26.

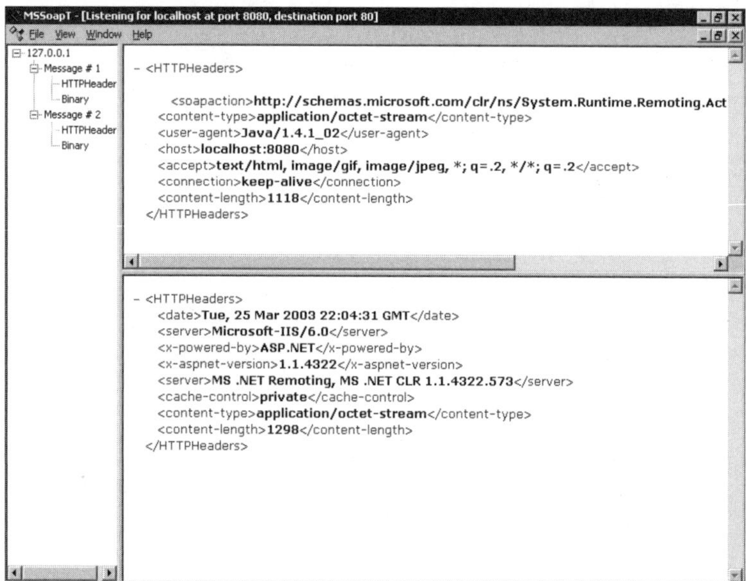

Figure 4-26 Examining the output from the SOAP Trace Utility.

Using binary format changes the output in a number of ways. First, when you click the Message node, you can't see any output. The only way to view the binary output is to click the Binary node. Second, the content length for the two calls is significantly smaller than the SOAP output. The content length is 1395 bytes for the first request and 1298 bytes for the reply. Although this is only a simple example based on the sample code, using the SOAP Trace Utility in conjunction with the Janetor tool options illustrates how you can obtain valuable insight into the data passed with calls using .NET Remoting.

.NET Client to EJB, Hosted by J2EE Application Server

Now that we've spent some time looking at a Java client calling a .NET component hosted in IIS, let's look at a scenario in which the server component is hosted on the J2EE platform, using both Session and Entity EJBs. Figure 4-27 depicts such a scenario.

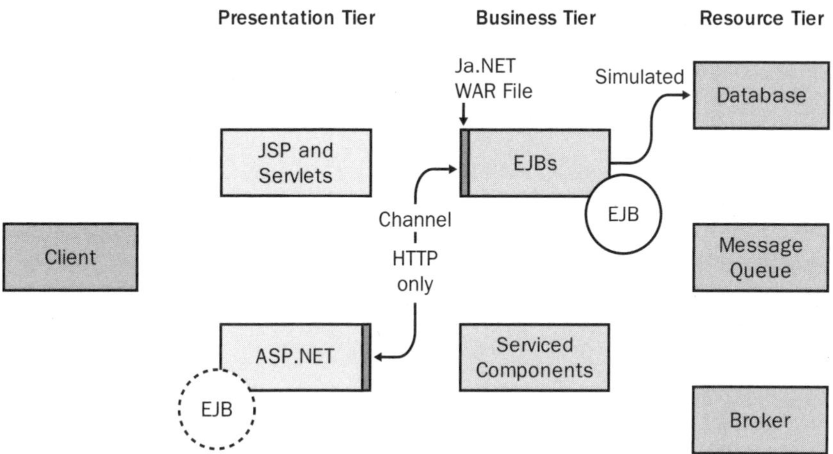

Figure 4-27 .NET client to EJB, hosted by J2EE application server—with simulated database access.

To show this example, we'll use the *Stock* object from earlier samples in this chapter to create a Stock Entity Bean. The bean, which uses Bean Managed Persistence (BMP), contains the same fields as the original *Stock* object and simulates calls to the database within the *ejbLoad* and *ejbFindByPrimaryKey* methods. You can easily extend this example to make the appropriate database calls if you want.

The *StockServer* code is now running in the context of a Session Bean. This bean exposes a method to accept only the ticker symbol for a particular stock and then does an internal Java Naming and Directory Interface (JNDI) lookup for the Stock Entity Bean. As with many J2EE architectures and best practices, the Entity Bean is never passed back to the calling application. (I share the view that Entity Bean data should always be hidden behind a Session Bean interface for both security and maintainability reasons.)

The Java EJB Sample Code

The EJB sample code for this example can be found in the C:\Interoperability\Samples\Point\Remoting\dotNETToEJB\Server directory. The package name for the samples is *com.microsoft.samples.ejb*. The SessionBean.java class contains the main methods for the Session Bean exposing the *sellStocks* method. This method is invoked by passing a ticker (of type *java.lang.String*, which is set to be the primary key type for the Stock Bean) and a quantity for the number of shares to sell.

The Session Bean first tries to get the home interface for the Stock Bean with a simple context lookup:

```
StockHome newStockHome;

try
{
    InitialContext newContext = new InitialContext();
    Object ref = newContext.lookup("StockBean");
    newStockHome = (StockHome)PortableRemoteObject.narrow(ref,
        StockHome.class);
}
catch (Exception e)
{
    throw new EJBException(e);
}
```

After this lookup is performed, the *Stock* object is created, and a *findByPrimaryKey* method is called to pass in the value of the ticker. If you look in the StockBean.java class, you'll see a simple *if...then* statement used to return the values that simulate a lookup in the database. When the Stock Bean is returned, you write the sell stock request to *STDOUT*, which on most J2EE application servers gets translated to the EJB console window.

```
Stock newStock;

try
{
    newStock = newStockHome.findByPrimaryKey(ticker);
}
catch (Exception e2)
{
    throw new StockNotFoundException();
}

System.out.println("Incoming request to sell "+quantity
    +" common shares of "+newStock.getName()+" ("
    +newStock.getTicker()+")");

// do the real work here!
```

```
// Assume that the trade was committed
return true;
```

Before building the EJB package, it is important to ensure that the relevant J2EE libraries are available to the GenNet tool, by being in the *CLASSPATH*. This varies from application server to application server. For using the sample code with JBoss, the jboss-j2ee.jar (found in the jboss\server\default\lib directory) should be used.

Once this is set, use the supplied Ant build script to compile the EJB package. Upon a successful compilation, a SampleEJB.jar file will be created in the Deploy subdirectory in C:\Interoperability\Samples\Point\Remoting\dotNET-ToEJB\Server.

You now have a JAR file that can be deployed to the application server. Before we actually deploy the server component, let's create the required proxy for the .NET client. To create the proxy from the classes for the EJB, navigate to the Classes directory, C:\Interoperability\Samples\Point\Remoting\dotNET-ToEJB\Server\Classes. This directory contains the compiled classes from the Session Bean and the Entity Bean and will be used to generate the proxy. Run the GenNet tool from within this directory.

Again, enter the URI for the GenService tool (**tcp://localhost:8001/Gen-Service**), and enter the following two required classes, which the code will generate:

com.microsoft.samples.ejb.StockSessionBean

com.microsoft.samples.ejb.StockSessionHome

The GenNet wizard should show these classes, as Figure 4-28 depicts.

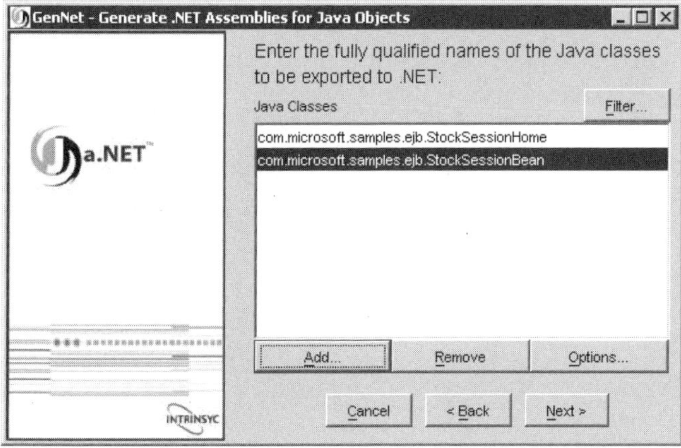

Figure 4-28 Setting the Java classes for the exposed EJB.

Once you've completed this step, click Next to proceed. To generate the .NET proxy, name the assembly **SampleEJB.dll**, and this time, save all the classes into a References subdirectory for the client. Set the output directory to **C:\Interoperability\Samples\Point\Remoting\dotNETToEJB\Client\References**, as shown in Figure 4-29.

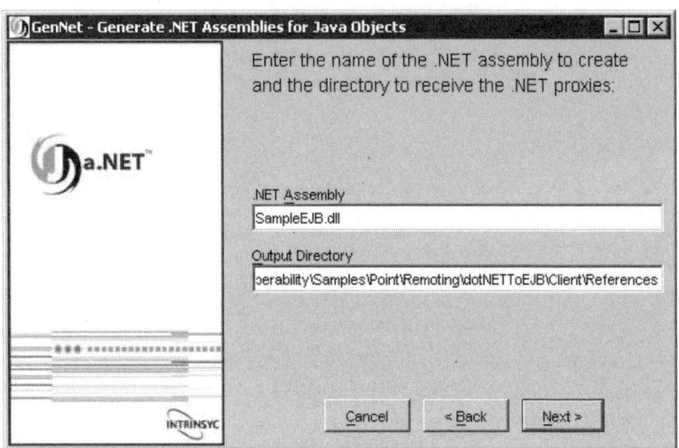

Figure 4-29 Setting the assembly and output directory for the .NET client proxies.

You need to use a second subdirectory because generating the .NET proxy can require a lot of classes. Generating this proxy in a subdirectory allows for a cleaner client solution. A neat way of cleaning up this generation is to use the Filter button in the previous wizard step. (Use the Back button to see this.) From there, you can filter out classes that aren't required for the .NET assembly, such as the *java.io* classes the tool detects.

To complete the generation of the .NET proxy, click the Next button and then click the Finish button once all the required proxy classes have been generated.

The final step you'll perform with the Java server code is to run the Janetor tool again to configure the settings. This time, part of the configuration involves creating a WAR file that can be used to expose the EJBs to the .NET Remoting client.

To perform this step, run janetor from the C:\Interoperability\Samples\Point\Remoting\dotNETToEJB\Server directory. Click the default node in the Local Objects tree, as shown in Figure 4-30.

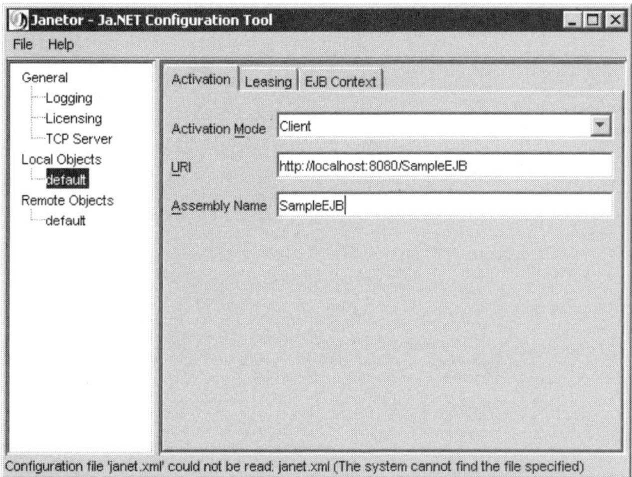

Figure 4-30 Setting the activation mode, URI, and assembly name for the client.

Now set the activation mode to **Client**, the URI to **http://localhost:8080/SampleEJB**, and the assembly name to **SampleEJB**. This configures the endpoint for the server component. Now click the EJB Context tab in the wizard, shown in Figure 4-31.

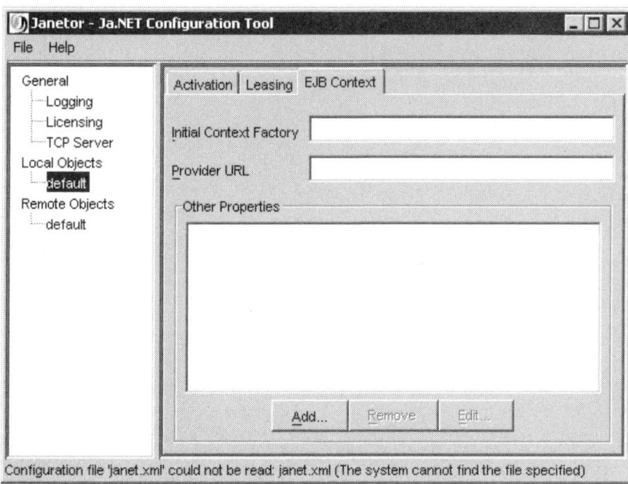

Figure 4-31 Setting the EJB context to expose the EJBs via a Ja.NET WAR file.

Now you need to enter the Initial Context Factory and Provider URL to enable EJB lookups in the server. This class and URL will be specific to the J2EE application vendor you choose, so you should check with the documentation that accompanies your server to see which class and URL to use.

For the sake of this example, you can use Table 4-1 as a guide to the defaults for a number of J2EE application servers. With the exception of JBoss 3.0.7, this information has not been tested with the sample code, and any settings in the documentation or notes that are supplied with your J2EE application server should always supersede this information.

Table 4-1 Context Factory Settings for J2EE Application Servers

J2EE Application Server	Initial Context Factory	Provider URL
JBoss 3.0.7	**org.jnp.interfaces.NamingContextFactory**	**localhost:1099**
BEA WebLogic	**weblogic.jndi.WLInitialContextFactory**	**t3://localhost:7001**
IBM WebSphere	Not required	Not required
Oracle 9i	Not required	Not required
Borland Enterprise Server	**com.imprise.j2ee.jndi.CtxFactory**	Not required

Once you've configured this information, save the configuration but do not close the Janetor wizard yet. Once the file is saved, select the Export Web Application Archive option from the File menu, shown in Figure 4-32.

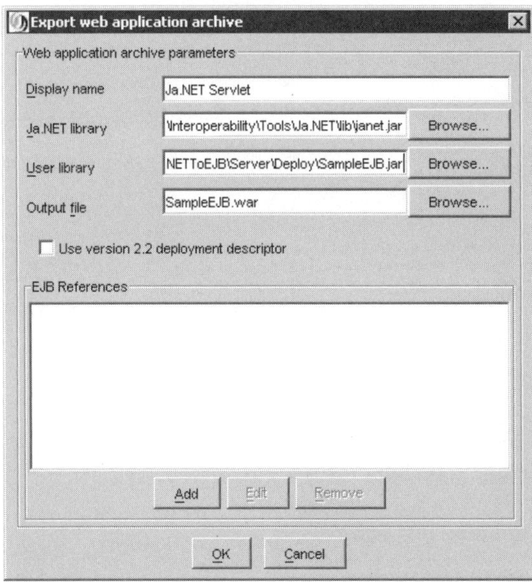

Figure 4-32 Configuring the Web application archive to be exported.

The Export Web Application Archive dialog box has a number of options that you need to configure. First, enter the location of the Ja.NET library. This is required for packaging in the WAR file that's created and is normally **C:\Interoperability\Tools\Ja.NET\lib\janet.jar**.

You then need to reference the user library, which is the JAR file that was created by the initial Ant build script (via **C:\Interoperability\Samples\Point\Remoting\dotNETToEJB\Server\Deploy\SampleEJB.jar**) and then specify the output file, which is the name of the WAR file to be generated by the tool (**Deploy\SampleEJB.war**). After entering this information, click the OK button. A SampleEJB WAR file will now be created in the Deploy subdirectory. Close the Janetor wizard.

You've now completed all the steps required to share the EJBs with a .NET Remoting client. To complete the deployment, deploy the SampleEJB.jar file (in the Deploy directory), and deploy the SampleEJB.war file that was created by Janetor to the application server. The deploy target can be used with the provided Ant script to deploy both the JAR and WAR file to a JBoss J2EE server. As mentioned earlier, follow the deployment instructions that are specific to the J2EE application server that you're using. Once deployed, start the application server to allow the .NET sample client to call the exposed EJB component.

The .NET Client Sample Code

You configure the .NET client to call the deployed EJB in largely the same way as you did in the previous code. The remoting.config file (which can be found in the C:\Interoperability\Samples\Point\Remoting\dotNETToEJB\Client directory) references the URL, type, and assembly name configured in the previous steps:

```
<client url="http://localhost:8080/SampleEJB">
    <activated type=
        "com.microsoft.samples.ejb.StockSessionBean, SampleEJB"/>
</client>
```

Build and run the client from this directory using NAnt. The .NET client will call the deployed Stock Session EJB via the Ja.NET Servlet that's been deployed to the application server as part of the WAR file that was generated. This Session Bean in turn calls the Stock Entity Bean to perform the simulated stock sale. With luck, the following message will be displayed in the console window of the J2EE application server:

```
Incoming request to sell 200 common shares of Woodgrove Bank(WOOD)
```

Notice also how in the J2EE application server console the EJB methods (for example, *ejbLoad* and *ejbStore*) are displayed, showing activation of the bean.

Java Client to .NET Object, Hosted by Component Services

The final example in this section—which rounds out the chapter by showing the many permutations of using .NET Remoting for interoperability—depicts a component hosted within Component Services running on either Microsoft Windows XP Professional SP1 or Microsoft Windows Server 2003. This example will use Windows Server 2003.

Component Services has evolved somewhat during the past few years and through the past few generations of Microsoft server products. It began life as Microsoft Transaction Services (MTS) in Microsoft Windows NT 4.0 and expanded into COM+ Services with Microsoft Windows 2000. Component Services is now a highly integrated part of Windows Server 2003.

As Chapter 1 discussed, today Component Services allows a .NET assembly to be deployed and configured in a way that supports integrated security, transactions, pooling, and activation. All this configuration can be performed through the Component Services user interface, which can be accessed from the Administrative Tools program menu, or programmatically by applying attributes to the .NET component source code.

In this example, we'll look at a feature of Component Services known as *SOAP activation*. SOAP activation enables the developer to deploy a component within Component Services (known as a *Serviced Component*) and then automatically create a SOAP endpoint for consumption by a client using .NET Remoting. This example will demonstrate how to deploy a component, configure the SOAP activation, and consume that component from a Java client (with the proxies generated by the Ja.NET tool), as shown in Figure 4-33.

All the sample code for this example is located in the C:\Interoperability\Samples\Point\Remoting\JavaToComponentServices directory.

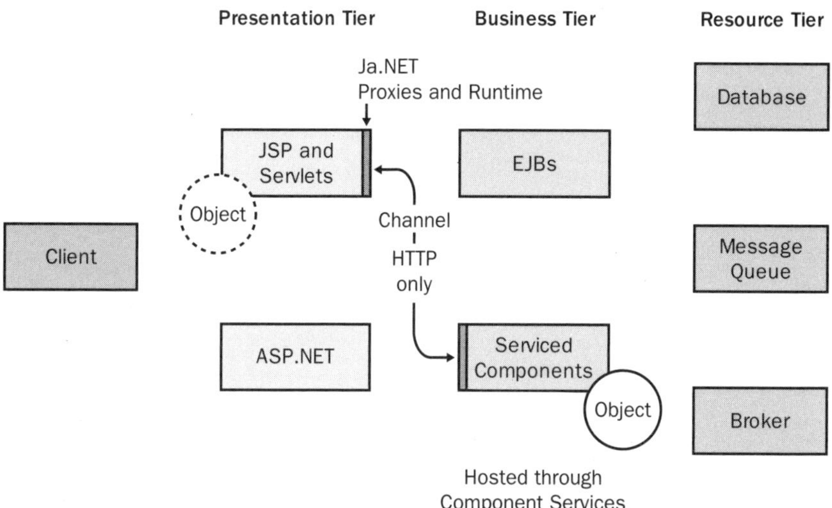

Figure 4-33 Java client to .NET object, hosted by Component Services on Windows Server 2003.

The .NET Serviced Component Sample Code

Let's first look at the code that makes up the component we'll deploy. To do this, open the RemotingServer.cs class, which is located in the Server directory. First, you can see that the class imports the *System.EnterpriseServices* namespace. This namespace contains all the interfaces, classes, and attributes used to deploy a component within Component Services. Also, the beginning of the class contains some assembly attributes:

```
[assembly: ApplicationName("StockServer")]
[assembly: AssemblyKeyFile("StockServer.snk")]

[assembly: ApplicationAccessControl(
    Value=false,Authentication=AuthenticationOption.None)]
[assembly: ApplicationActivation(
    ActivationOption.Server, SoapVRoot="StockServer")]
```

The first attribute specifies the name of the application that will be deployed within Component Services. The second attribute references a key file that will be used to create a strongly named assembly.

> **Note** What is a strongly named assembly? .NET assemblies must be deployed into the global assembly cache (GAC) so that they can be accessed by many processes (including system processes such as Component Services). The GAC is a machine-based store that's responsible for centralizing and sharing these version-specific assemblies. To be installed into the GAC, an assembly must be strongly named. To strongly name an assembly, the assembly must be signed with a key. This key either can be specific to the developer or autogenerated by the system. Once the assembly is signed by this key, the assembly will remain unique within the GAC regardless of other assemblies that might have the same name or that might expose the same methods.

The *ApplicationAccessControl* attribute turns the security authorization level off and sets the authentication option to *None*. This negates the requirement to install a certificate or set up a Secure Sockets Layer (SSL) context to call our component. (Of course, this default option is still available if you want to investigate it further.) The *ApplicationActivation* attribute automatically configures the component to run as a server component—meaning that the component is allocated a dedicated server process for activation—and defines a SOAP virtual root called StockServer.

Also, notice how each class inherits from *ServicedComponent*:

```
public class SampleData : ServicedComponent
{

}
```

This signifies to Component Services that the component will be exposed as a hosted component. This inheritance of *ServicedComponent* replaces the *MarshalByRefObject* used in the previous samples and will be detected by the Ja.NET tools when generating the required proxies.

Build the code in the C:\Interoperability\Samples\Point\Remoting\Java TodotNETServer\Server directory, using NAnt. The build creates two things: a StockServer.dll file that can be hosted through Component Services and an

Invoker.exe file that's used to deploy the component. The Invoker.exe file is created within the Invoker subdirectory.

After the build has completed, use the invoke target with the provided NAnt script to launch the invoker. If you plan to run the component on a second machine, you'll need to copy the contents of this directory to that machine and run it there. The invoker batch file that is called deploys the assembly to Component Services so that you can configure it via the administration interface.

The invoke script also automatically runs a utility named GACUTIL, which is used to place a copy of the StockServer.dll into the GAC. If installation into the GAC is successful, the invoke script should report this final message:

```
Assembly successfully added to the cache
```

If the GACUTIL does not work, check that the directory holding gacutil.exe is in the System Path.

> **Note** In certain rare cases, you might get a *System.Runtime.InteropServices.COMException* exception when you run the NAnt script with the invoke target, indicating that the server process must be run under a different identity. In this case, the StockServer component will be deployed, but it needs to be configured to be able to run properly. Open the Properties window for the StockServer component within Component Services (the steps necessary to do this are detailed below), and select the Identity Tab. Change the settings to make the StockServer component run using the Local Service account, and click OK. Now rerun the invoke batch file to complete the StockServer component installation.

To check that all this completed successfully, go to Start/Programs/Administrative Tools/Component Services on the machine that the component was deployed on. Drill down through the Component Services, Computers, My Computer, and COM+ Applications folders until you reach the StockServer application folder, as shown in Figure 4-34.

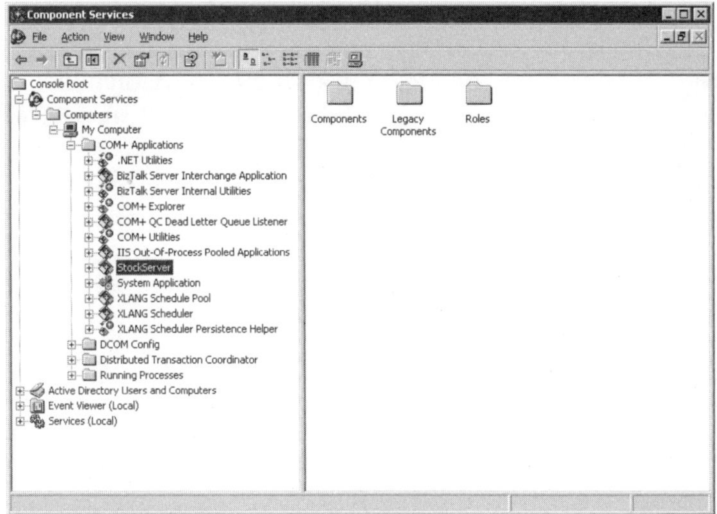

Figure 4-34 Using the Component Services administration tool to examine the deployed component.

To view properties on the application, simply right-click the StockServer node and select Properties to display a properties window. The properties that are available allow the component to be configured for services that are supported under Component Services.

Because we're interested in activating the component via SOAP, click the Activation tab, as shown in Figure 4-35. As you can see, the attributes used on the class define that the component will run as a server application. Furthermore, SOAP activation is enabled using a SOAP VRoot of StockServer.

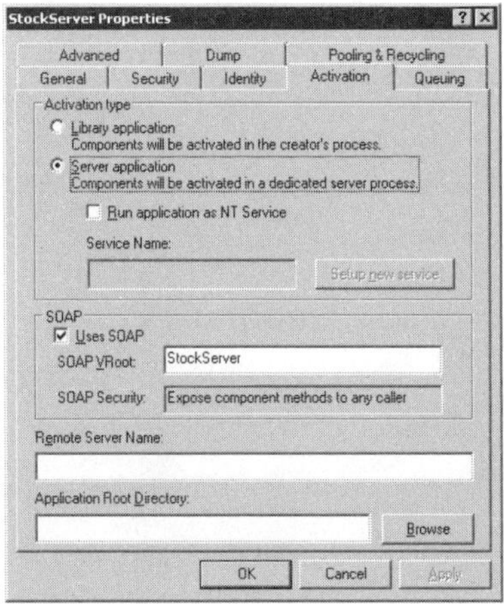

Figure 4-35 Using the Component Services administration tool to examine the deployed component.

Close this properties window. Before building the client, you can test the component by browsing to *http://localhost/StockServer*. (Replace *localhost* with the name of the machine on which you're running the component.) Figure 4-36 shows the Web page that should appear.

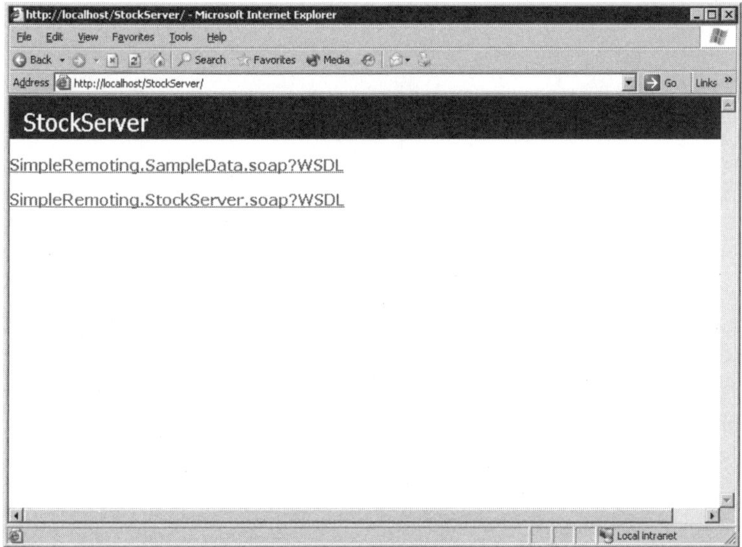

Figure 4-36 Using Microsoft Internet Explorer to test the SOAP VRoot.

One new feature of Windows Server 2003 provides a Web interface for the components that are exposed. Viewing this Web page means that the components have been successfully deployed.

The SOAP root—and location of the files—for the StockServer component is by default set to C:\WINDOWS\System32\Com\SoapVRoots\StockServer on the machine on which the component is deployed. Before running the Java client, one remaining configuration item is to make a security change to allow the stock type to be passed by value. A restricted security setting in the .NET Framework 1.1 prevents these types from being passed automatically.

To make this change, edit the web.config file in the newly created SOAP root (C:\WINDOWS\System32\Com\SoapVRoots\StockServer). Within the channels section of the file, replace *<channel ref="http server" />* with the following text:

```
<channel ref="http server">
    <serverProviders>
        <formatter ref="binary" typeFilterLevel="Full"/>
    </serverProviders>
</channel>
```

This will set the filter level for the binary formatter such that the stock data type can be serialized without raising a security exception. Additional information about the workings of this security model can be found by searching for "Automatic Deserialization in .NET Remoting" on *http://msdn.microsoft.com*.

The Java Client Sample Code

Now that you have the .NET server component completed, it's time to configure the Java client. To do so, navigate to the C:\Interoperability\Samples\Point\Remoting\JavaTodotNETServer\Client directory. From there, you need to run the GenJava utility to create the Java proxies for the component deployed in Component Services.

Run the GenJava tool, enter the URL for the GenService tool (**tcp://localhost:8001/GenService**), and point the .NET assembly to the location of the StockServer DLL that's created in the server directory (**C:\Interoperability\Samples\Point\Remoting\JavaToComponentServices\Server\StockServer.dll**). For the Output Directory, enter **.** (a period) for the current directory. Figure 4-37 shows the dialog box used to make these settings.

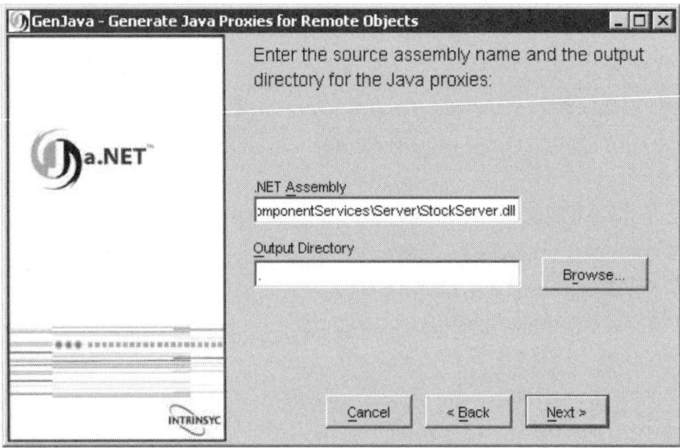

Figure 4-37 Setting the .NET assembly and output directory for the Java proxies.

Click Next and then Finish to generate the required proxies. From the client directory, the final step is to configure the URL and ports.

Run the Janetor tool, and select the default node under the Remote Object tree, as shown in Figure 4-38.

Table 4-3 Ja.NET Collection Mappings Between Java and .NET

.NET Collection Class	Java Collection Class
System.Collections.Ilist	*java.util.ArrayList*
System.Collections.Ilist	*Java.util.LinkedList*
System.Collections.Ilist	*Java.util.Vector*

Table 4-4 Ja.NET Collection Mappings Between .NET and Java

.NET Collection Class	Java Collection Class
System.Collections.ArrayList	*java.util.List*

Events and Exceptions

Before ending this chapter on using .NET Remoting to achieve interoperability between the .NET and Java platforms, let's examine two additional points that relate to the other examples in the book.

Events

.NET Remoting and the Ja.NET tool support the notion of events—something that our samples did not show but that can be easily demonstrated. The Ja.NET tool has the ability to map events that extend *java.util.EventListener* to system events in .NET. One advantage of using the .NET Remoting protocol this way is that the server component has the ability to "call back" to the client using this event model. This can be especially useful in situations where asynchronous operations or long-running transactions are required.

Exception Handling

In a couple of samples in this chapter, an exception was thrown and reported back (hopefully, on purpose). Be aware that exceptions are handled using the Ja.NET tool but that specific exceptions do get mapped accordingly. The rules of exception handling are generally as follows:

- Any exception that occurs in a Java server gets mapped to *System.Runtime.Remoting.RemotingException* in .NET.
- Any exception that occurs in a .NET server gets mapped to *com.intrinsyc.janet.RemoteException* in Java.

In the majority of cases, the original exception message is embedded in the text produced from these exceptions. Therefore, when handling exceptions, you can trap this single exception and then search through the text of the inner exception if additional information is required.

Additional Java Support for .NET Remoting

For the sample code in this chapter, we've used Intrinsyc's Ja.NET software to enable Java classes and J2EE components to interoperate with .NET applications and services. In addition to Ja.NET, a similar third-party product named JNBridgePro also exists.

JNBridgePro promotes itself as a Java/.NET interoperability tool that enables Java code to fully participate in the cross-language development capabilities of Microsoft .NET while maintaining Java's cross-platform portability and conformance to Java standards. There are two versions of JNBridgePro. JNBridgePro SE supports J2SE, and JNBridgePro EE supports J2EE and the leading J2EE application servers, allowing .NET code to access J2EE components, including EJBs and JNDI.

JNBridgePro is built on top of .NET remoting and encapsulates most of the details of remoting so that the calls between .NET and Java appear to be "local" calls, not remoting calls. JNBridgePro allows custom exceptions to be thrown from Java to .NET and supports accessing any and all public members of Java classes: both static and instance members, and both methods and fields. Like Intrinsyc's Ja.NET, both HTTP/SOAP and TCP/binary communications channels are supported.

> **More Info** Additional information and an evaluation copy can be found at *http://www.jnbridge.com.*

.NET Remoting and CORBA Interoperability

In this chapter, we have seen elements of how .NET Remoting can be implemented on both .NET and J2EE, using the native support in the .NET Framework and Intrinsyc's Ja.NET for Java. As mentioned in the chapter's introduction, .NET Remoting was designed to be an extensible framework that can be expanded to include new functionality. By developing new channels, it's possible to use .NET Remoting to connect to other technologies and systems.

One example of such a new development is the enabling of .NET Remoting with CORBA. Using .NET Remoting to connect to existing CORBA implementations offers some interesting interoperability scenarios.

> **Note** *CORBA* stands for Common Object Request Broker Architecture, a standard developed by the Object Management Group (OMG), *http://www.omg.org*. In addition to being used in standalone applications and many network devices, CORBA is the middleware technology that underpins J2EE. All J2EE application servers implement RMI-IIOP, and IIOP is based on the CORBA specification. For verticals, based on my experience, I've found CORBA to have a high penetration in both financial and telecom marketplaces.

While it's too early to write about a released product, one of the ongoing projects in this area is called Remoting.Corba (*http://remoting-corba.sourceforge.net/*). This is an open-source project being run by an independent developer named Kristopher Johnson. Although the project is in its early stages, it's easy to see the areas that it could address.

Remoting.Corba uses a custom channel in .NET Remoting to communicate with a CORBA 2.6–compatible Object Request Broker (ORB). The channel works like a regular .NET Remoting channel, except that the URL is a standard CORBA IOR string as opposed to a regular tcp:// or http:// URL. An IOR (Interoperable Object Reference) is a bundle of data used to connect to the server and object and is automatically generated by the CORBA server. The goal is not to create a complete ORB for .NET, but merely to use .NET Remoting as a channel for accessing components hosted in existing ORBs. Although this is the case, Remoting.Corba can also act as both a CORBA client and server.

The first stage for using Remoting.Corba is to take the CORBA IDL and generate an interface in .NET. Today, this has to be created by hand, because there is no C# IDL compiler. An example IDL could be as follows:

```
// CORBA IDL
interface Echo
{
    typedef sequence<Object> List;
    List echo_list (in string message);
    string echo_string (in string message);
    oneway void shutdown ();
};
```

Using this IDL, the following interface would need to be created for .NET (using C#):

```
// C#
interface Echo
{
    string echo_string(string message);
    [OneWay] void shutdown();
}
```

Within the .NET client project, the channel is created by importing a Remoting.Corba DLL and registered using the following command:

```
ChannelServices.RegisterChannel(new IiopClientChannel());
```

An activator is used to create a new reference to the remote CORBA component. Once the reference to the object has been created, methods can then be called based on the interface definition.

There are of course some limitations with the version (1.3) as it exists today. This includes a few limitations for type mappings, no security support, and no IDL compiler, but as the development evolves this looks like a very promising project.

> **More Info** For a more complete tutorial on how Remoting.Corba can work with the sample interfaces and classes shown here, visit *http://kristopherjohnson.net/cgi-bin/rc/wiki.pl?Tutorials/Echo_Client.*

Summary

This chapter showed how you can use the .NET Remoting protocol, especially by using the Ja.NET tool, to generate the required Java proxies in order to bridge the gap between .NET and J2EE. This chapter presented five permutations of interoperability by using .NET Remoting, ranging from hosting simple components to managing component hosting within an EJB container on a J2EE application server or using Component Services within Windows Server 2003.

Thinking back to the discussion in Chapter 2 on business requirements for interoperability between the Java and .NET platforms, you can see how .NET

Remoting can allow for point-to-point connectivity for the first two scenarios presented in that chapter.

The concepts presented in this chapter will be referenced throughout the remainder of this book. The samples presented in the coming chapters, which feature a variety of scenarios, are flexible enough to allow you to expand them for your own solutions. In Chapter 5, "Connectivity with XML Web Services, Part 1," we'll continue to discuss point-to-point interoperability and we'll look at a second technology option: XML Web services.

5

Connectivity with XML Web Services, Part 1

Although we touched on XML Web services briefly in Chapter 3, "Exchanging Data Between .NET and Java," given the amount of media coverage Web services get, you might be surprised to have reached this point in the book without seeing more coverage of interoperability using Web services. The earlier chapters didn't cover Web services more extensively because I wanted to give you as much detail about the foundation of interoperability before covering the technology.

This chapter and Chapter 6, "Connectivity with XML Web Services, Part 2," will cover some of the basics of using Web services for both the Microsoft .NET and Java platforms. Both chapters will use the last set of samples presented in Chapter 4, "Connectivity with .NET Remoting," and will cover the samples' implications for interoperability where appropriate. These chapters aren't intended to be a full-fledged guide to implementing the Web services technology. Rather than covering each and every part of the specification, the samples presented will give you enough information so that you can run them and learn how to achieve interoperability.

The topic of Web services spans a broad range of subjects. As a result, we'll cover Web services in two parts. Part 1 (this chapter) will introduce the concepts of Web services, cover a little history, explain the landscape of both .NET and Java, and present a set of simple examples to show connectivity between the two platforms. Part 2 (Chapter 6) will expand upon these samples, showing how they can be extended and covering some areas that can impact interoperability in production environments.

What Is an XML Web Service?

Component-based programming is a widely accepted practice used to help develop distributed systems. As these systems become more complex, distributing an application across a number of remote machines becomes an attractive option. During the past few years, a number of technologies have emerged to help build these types of distributed systems within the enterprise:

- **Distributed Component Object Model (DCOM)** Microsoft's approach to allow components written to the COM specification to be distributed and called on remote machines.
- **Common Object Request Broker Architecture (CORBA)** A specification released by the Object Management Group (OMG) to unify distributed system technology across a number of vendors.
- **Java Remote Method Invocation (RMI)** Formed part of the Java v1.1.x core specification. Allows components written in Java to be distributed to remote machines and processes.

The release of these standards allowed a large number of enterprises to benefit from developing distributed applications that spanned many processes, machines, and servers. But in general, the concept of distributed computing rarely left the data center—and if it did, it tended to stay within the boundaries of the organization as a whole.

A large portion of this was due to the technology itself. Early releases of the technology didn't lend themselves well to working with multiple organizations across the Internet. This was largely due to the ports and protocols to which these organizations were bound. As organizations joined the race to get online and security became a more controlled issue, many developers and architects found themselves restricted to using only ports 80 and 443—the ports for HTTP and HTTPS, respectively. Existing applications that used distributed components and were destined to reside in the perimeter network (also known as DMZ, demilitarized zone, and screened subnet) of an extranet were difficult to deploy and maintain or were generally unstable.

Microsoft and Sun Microsystems made attempts at fixing some of these problems by releasing versions of their respective component technologies that passed only HTTP requests and responses across the wire. Microsoft released COM Internet Services (CIS), which tunneled an existing DCOM solution across port 80. The Java specification grew to include RMI over Internet Inter-Orb Protocol (IIOP) to tie in the RMI specification with CORBA. Unfortunately, for various reasons, neither platform fully convinced enterprise architects to run a distributed architecture across the Internet.

Given the history of the products that were already available, Web services were not a new, groundbreaking concept. The introduction and formalization of Web services had more to do with applying the existing technologies and lessons learned to a set of new standards.

To be accepted, Web services must address these three key issues:

- **Internet standards** The lowest common denominator for intercommunication with most organizations is HTTP and HTTPS. This is mainly because of firewall restrictions that have been applied and the fact that these protocols tend to be used to promote an organization through a Web site. HTTP and HTTPS must be the initial underlying protocols for Web services to succeed, but the technology should be flexible enough to allow any transport protocol to be used.
- **Type definitions** Data types that were exposed by Web services must use strongly typed XML. A type that's exposed by using one Web service must be understood and consumed regardless of the underlying language or platform.
- **Multiple language, platform, and vendor support** Web services must not be tied to a particular platform, language, or vendor. This is necessary to allow one consumer of Web services to work on a different platform and in a different language from another Web services consumer.

So, that's a little history, but you're probably still wondering what makes up a Web service. In other words, how can you define a Web service based on the technology that it uses? Five components make up the definition of a Web service, as shown in Figure 5-1.

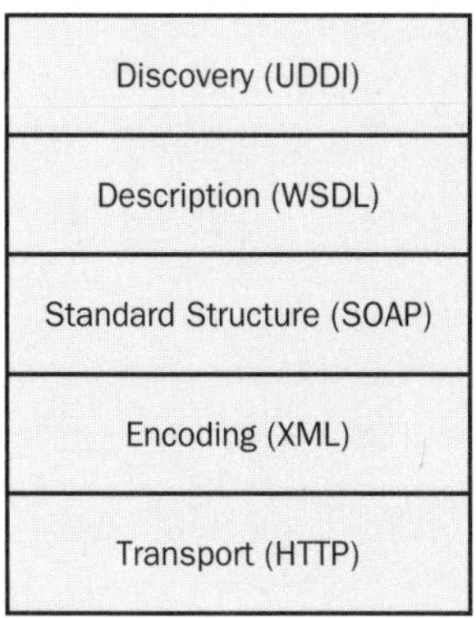

Figure 5-1 The five components of a Web service.

Let's examine these components:

- **Transport (HTTP)** For any distributed component architecture to work, the two machines (sender and receiver) must agree on a transport. As mentioned previously, in many organizations, HTTP tends to be a standard that's widely accepted as a gateway through the firewall. However, this doesn't mean that Web services are tied to HTTP. Web services can potentially run on Simple Mail Transfer Protocol (SMTP), Sequenced Packet Exchange (SPX), NetBIOS Extended User Interface (NetBEUI), and even a custom sockets implementation if needed. For now, the generally accepted transport is HTTP (with HTTPS for secure connections), but the transport protocol independence of the Web service specifications means that the dominance of HTTP could change sometime in the future without requiring a rewrite of the specification.
- **Encoding (XML)** Regardless of the transport used to carry it, the message must be correctly formatted as a valid XML document. We touched on this a little in Chapter 3, where XML was used in a number of ways to exchange data between .NET and Java. The result was that both platforms knew how to parse and interpret the XML standard. The same is true of using Web services.
- **Standard Structure (SOAP)** XML defines how the message is encoded but doesn't dictate the structure or format of the document. With XML, you're free to choose your own element and attribute names, types, and labels, but for true interoperability, both platforms need to know what to send and what to expect. SOAP is a three-part definition that specifies an XML structure for the framework of a message (known as a *SOAP envelope*), the data types that are defined, and a convention for representing RPCs and the data returned from them (all of which are placed in a SOAP body).
- **Description (WSDL)** Suppose you create a component for a distributed architecture. So far, we know that XML and SOAP can be used to correctly construct a message that can be understood by different platforms. However, we lack a way to describe which services exist (can be consumed) on the remote system. You need a contract or complete description that says these are the components being exposed and gives the names, data types (using XML Schema Definition), methods, and parameters required to call them. This contract is known as a Web Services Description Language (WSDL) document

and is normally one of the first points of contact to determine how a Web service will be called.

- **Discovery (UDDI)** This is the last of the five pieces of the Web services puzzle. The first four pieces enable you to create self-described services using SOAP and XML over an agreed-upon transport, but the invocation of these services still requires you to know the exact location, or URL. For example, suppose you know that a remote system exposes a Web service. To call that Web service, you'd use the exact URL (such as *http://server1/services/WebService1.asmx*). But how do you get that URL? Just as the phone book uses telephone numbers, we need a way of associating something a little more descriptive with the previous URL—for example, the name Woodgrove's Stock Quote Web service. Universal Description, Discovery, and Integration (UDDI) provides us this functionality. Again, by using an agreed-upon message format, you can issue requests to a UDDI server to locate the exact URL for a published Web service.

Now that I've given you the basics of Web services—and possibly a refresher in some terminology that you already might have known—let's dive deeper into the topic of interoperability using Web services.

> **More Info** For further reading on what Web services are comprised of, see Scott Short's book, *Building XML Web Services for the Microsoft .NET Platform* (Microsoft Press, 2002).

The Web Services Landscape

Before you see some samples, I want to describe today's Web services landscape (actually, the landscape in existence at the time of this writing). This should highlight the organizations that are helping to develop and promote Web services as a standard. This description isn't meant to be a comparison of vendors—the frequency with which new product releases reach the market often means that the information becomes quickly out of date. Instead, use the list to gain an understanding of the commitment many vendors have to Web services technology as a whole.

- **Microsoft** Microsoft's public embracement of Web services coincided with the release of .NET. The main integration of Web services can be found in the Microsoft .NET Framework, designer support in Microsoft Visual Studio .NET, server support in a number of .NET server products, and additional support in desktop applications such as Microsoft Office XP. In December 2002, Microsoft released version 1.0 of Microsoft Web Services Enhancements (WSE), which includes support for a number of the latest Web services specifications. (We'll cover these specifications in Part IV of the book, "Advanced Interoperability.") UDDI services can be found as an integral part of Microsoft Windows Server 2003.

- **Apache** The Apache Software Foundation provides support for a community of open-source projects, the majority of which are written in Java. These have included Tomcat and Struts. Within the Apache Web Services Project, Axis (the successor to Apache SOAP) can be used as a framework to build Web services.
- **IBM** IBM was one of the first organizations to wrap a number of value-added services around the Apache Axis implementation. Its offering, IBM Web Services Toolkit (WSTK) provides support for creating Web services for Apache Tomcat and IBM WebSphere server products. In addition, IBM also has its own public UDDI registry and server product.
- **The Mind Electric (TME)** TME has a vendor-neutral approach to delivering Web services for the Java platform. TME's Web services product, GLUE, allows the creation and hosting of Web services either through a standalone hosting environment or by creating a deployment compatible with most Java 2 Enterprise Edition (J2EE) application servers. TME also packages a UDDI server with its offering.
- **Systinet** Systinet WASP is another good example of a third-party Web services toolkit that provides support for both C/C++ and Java environments. As with GLUE, WASP includes a number of add-ins to compliment and extend existing integrated development environments (IDEs). Systinet also offers a UDDI server.

In addition to these toolkits, a number of J2EE application server vendors are integrating Web services into their platform. An extensive list of J2EE application servers, with appropriate links for more information, can be found at *http://www.theserverside.com/reviews/matrix.jsp.*

Web Services and the J2EE Specification

You might be wondering whether and how Web services are used within the J2EE specification. An API for Web services doesn't exist within the J2EE 1.3 specification. As a result, there currently is no *javax.webservices* package that can be imported and used as part of the Java syntax language.

At the time of this writing, however, support does exist for a number of underlying APIs used to create Web services on the Java platform, known as the Java APIs for XML (JAX) pack. This pack, in turn, is used by a number of vendors for their toolkits. Chapter 3 already mentioned one of the APIs: Java Architecture for XML Binding (JAXB). Here's a list of the JAX pack members:

- **Java API for XML Processing (JAXP)** Contains implementations of Document Object Model (DOM), Simple API for XML (SAX), and XML Stylesheet Language Transformations (XLST) for manipulating and working with XML documents.
- **Java API for XML Binding (JAXB)** Binds an XML document to an object graph. This is based on the same serialization principles covered in Chapter 3.
- **Java API for XML Registries (JAXR)** Abstracts a number of registries, namely UDDI and Electronic Business XML (ebXML), that can contain descriptions for Web services.
- **Java API for XML Messaging (JAXM)** Specifies an abstraction of the SOAP message infrastructure.
- **Java API for XML-based RPC (JAX-RPC)** This specification is similar to JAXM but focuses on RPC-style calls, whereas JAXM is intended for both RPC-style and document-style formatting.

The JAX pack provides the underpinnings of Web services for the Java platform but can be lacking in the level of its implementation. To help address this, in February 2003, Sun Microsystems announced that the next version of the J2EE specification (v1.4, due for release in the summer of 2003) will fully support Basic Profile 1.0, one of the first guidelines released from a body named the Web Services Interoperability Organization (WS-I).

The Web Services Interoperability Organization (WS-I)

With so many vendors committed to and enthused by Web services technology, some direction is needed to ensure interoperability between all the flavors and standards of Web services. The Web Services Interoperability Organization (*http://www.ws-i.org*) is an open-industry effort to drive Web services interoperability across platforms, toolkits, applications, and vendors. The community that makes up WS-I today comprises approximately 170 vendors (including Microsoft, Sun, and IBM), systems integrators, enterprise customers, and others with a sincere interest in ensuring that Web services remain interoperable.

Deliverables

The organization's charter is to target developers to ensure that Web services and the underlying protocols conform to a published and agreed-upon set of standards and guidelines. To enable this, WS-I is tasked with providing the following:

- **Profiles** Sets of specifications that define technology standards.
- **Samples** Sets of samples to show interoperability concepts and demonstrate the features of the profiles.
- **Implementation guidelines** Show a best-practices approach to design solutions that require interoperability with Web services.
- **Tools** A sniffer and analyzer to monitor and log interactions with Web services, including identifying errors and warnings for implementations that do not meet the profiles guidelines.

Basic Profile 1.0

One of the first deliverables from the WS-I was the Basic Profile version 1.0, which is published via the WS-I Web site. A *profile* is a named group of version-specific Web services specifications. Basic Profile 1.0 outlines recommendations for how these Web services specifications should be used together to achieve consistency within each implementation and, therefore, to promote interoperability. The four building blocks that make up the Basic Profile are messaging, description, discovery, and security. This covers XML 1.0, XSD 1.0, SOAP 1.1, WSDL 1.1, UDDI 2.0, and the use of HTTP and HTTPS.

Do We Need Another .org?

One of the important things to recognize with the WS-I is the strong relationship it has with the Organization for the Advancement of Structured Information Standards (OASIS) and other standards organizations. As proof of this, each of the four specifications that make up the Basic Profile come from and are controlled by other organizations. This demonstrates that the role of the WS-I isn't to serve as just another governing standards body but to embrace the relationships and ensure consistency among other organizations.

Joining the WS-I

WS-I membership is open to any individual or business that wants to make a contribution in supporting Web services interoperability. To join the organization, you must pay an annual fee and participate in a number of working groups. Membership checklists and instructions can be found on the WS-I Web site.

Web Services Toolkit Selection

In the samples in this chapter and throughout the rest of the book, we'll use GLUE 4.0.1 Professional from The Mind Electric. GLUE is based on the standards and specifications of the WS-I Basic Profile.

Given the current plans for J2EE v1.4 and the contents of a number of books on the topic, you might be wondering why I chose to use GLUE for the book's samples instead of relying on the existing Java Specification Requests (JSRs), JAX packs, and draft. The reasons are fourfold:

- This book's aim is to demonstrate how to use Web services to achieve interoperability between .NET and Java—not how to build Web services for either .NET or J2EE. That said, GLUE delivers an implementation of Web services for the Java platform without the necessity of explaining the underlying required APIs. Because GLUE is based on the WS-I Basic Profile, it should align well when implementations of J2EE v1.4 are available.
- Both the Electric XML and GLUE libraries are vendor neutral. The samples in this book should work on any J2EE application server, regardless of the vendor. Because I cannot predict which application server each reader will use, I thought it important to create code samples that could be run by anyone.
- The XML formatting, Schema, and serialization implementations used by GLUE for Web services are provided by the same libraries as the XML classes that are discussed in Chapter 3. Thus, there will be parity between the .NET and Java implementations.
- The Mind Electric was one of the first adopters of the latest Web services specifications, adopting these specifications as part of their toolkit offerings. This is important in the context of this book because in Part IV, "Advanced Interoperability," you'll see actual implementations of these specifications in the samples.

Configuring GLUE

GLUE is installed in the C:\Interoperability\Tools\Glue directory as part of the samples installation. This directory contains a full implementation of GLUE 4.0 Professional, including required libraries, binaries, and documentation.

Configuration of GLUE is performed by using a config.xml file. The location of this file is determined as follows:

1. If the *electric.config* environment variable is set, the configuration file is loaded from the specified path.
2. If this environment variable is not set, the *CLASSPATH* is searched for a suitable config.xml file that can be used.
3. If no config.xml file is found, the default-config.xml file (which is included as part of the glue-all.jar file) is used.

Most of the samples in this chapter and Chapter 6 apply configuration settings in GLUE by using statements within the code. This allows you to see what settings are required for a new installation of the product. In a production environment, it's recommended that you apply configuration settings by using an XML file as described earlier. You saw an example of this in the "Generating an XSD from an Existing Class in Java" section in Chapter 3.

Creating Web Services

If you look back at the business requirements addressed in Chapter 2, "Business Requirements for Interoperability," you can start to see where Web services can be used to achieve interoperability. Chapter 2 ended with the concept of point-to-point interoperability. Figure 5-2 illustrates this concept.

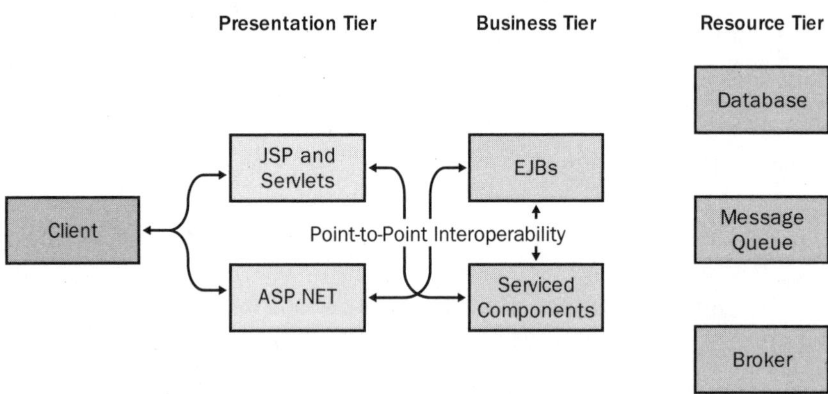

Figure 5-2 Point-to-point interoperability.

As with the .NET Remoting examples in Chapter 4, Web services can be used to meet a requirement to communicate between the presentation tier and the business tier shown in Figure 5-2. This communication can be presentation-based content (such as ASP.NET and JavaServer Pages) calling some business-tier logic (such as hosted classes, Enterprise JavaBeans, and serviced components), or it can be business-tier components calling other business-tier components.

In addition, Web services can extend to the client itself. Many nonbrowser clients (such as a Windows Forms client on the .NET Framework or Microsoft Office installed with the Web Services Toolkit) have the ability to call Web services. All the samples in this chapter will examine communication between a client and a Web service, addressing both the .NET and Java technologies. Figure 5-3 shows this extended model.

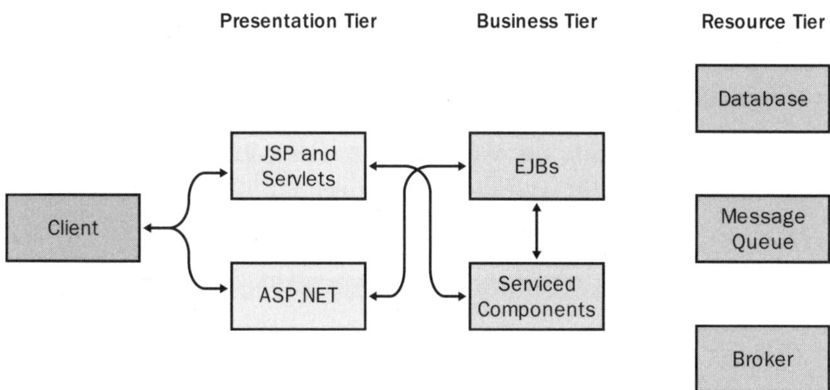

Figure 5-3 Extending point-to-point interoperability to the client.

As Figures 5-2 and 5-3 show, the concepts of "client" and "service" can relate to two situations: one where the client is the presentation tier and the service resides on the business tier, and another where the client is the client software employed by the user and the service is hosted via the presentation tier. All the samples shown in this chapter are perfectly applicable to both situations.

Creating a Web Service in .NET

Web services are an integral part of the .NET Framework and Microsoft's .NET strategy as a whole. As a result, the process of creating a Web service using .NET integrates with both the development tools and the hosting environment provided by the .NET Framework. For example, Visual Studio .NET includes functionality to allow the direct reference of Web services and the creation of proxies without the developer having to run external tools or be involved with the potential complexities of WSDL. Likewise, a new Web service can be created directly from the IDE, which in turn will configure the underlying Internet Information Services (IIS) implementation.

For these samples, we'll show two ways of creating and hosting the .NET Web service. Option 1 will show how Visual Studio .NET can be used to create a Web service from scratch. For developers who haven't used Visual Studio .NET yet, I recommend following this section. For developers who are already familiar with creating a Web service in Visual Studio .NET, or for those who aren't using the IDE during the course of this book, Option 2 shows how to compile and host the same pregenerated sample Web service.

Regardless of which option you choose, you should ensure that you have followed the "Installing ASP.NET" and "Configuring ASP.NET Security" sections in Chapter 1, "Microsoft .NET and J2EE Fundamentals." This will ensure that the installation and security settings for underlying products are configured correctly for this sample code.

Option 1: Creating the Web Service Using Visual Studio .NET

To start, launch the Visual Studio .NET application and create a new project. A dialog box will appear, as shown in Figure 5-4.

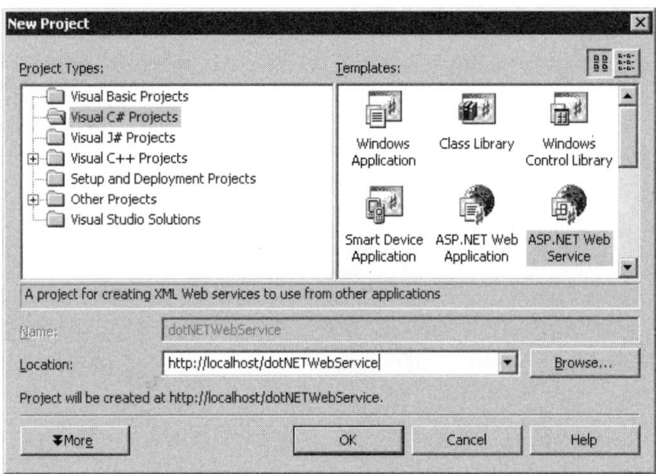

Figure 5-4 Creating a new ASP.NET Web service in Visual Studio .NET.

Select Visual C# Projects, and click the ASP.NET Web Service icon to select the project type. In the Location text box, enter the URL of this test service: **http://localhost/dotNETWebService**. Click the OK button to create the new project.

The project that is created should look similar to the one shown in Figure 5-5. Typically, a default Web service gives you several files automatically generated within the solution—as shown in Solution Explorer, to the upper right of the IDE window.

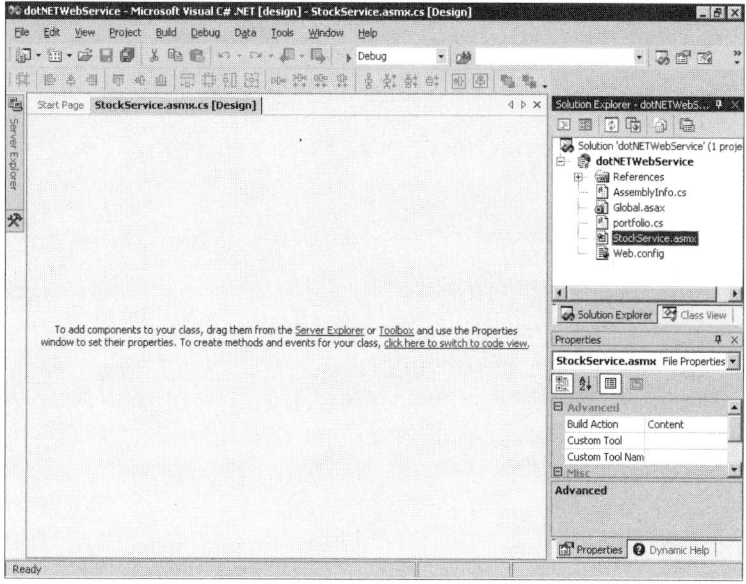

Figure 5-5 A new Web service in Visual Studio .NET.

The main file that we're interested in is Service1.asmx because it contains the exposed classes for the Web service. Notice that in the main window, you have the option to either drag components from Server Explorer or the Toolbox or switch to code view. Visually dragging components (such as timers, processes, database connections and tables, and stored procedures) from the IDE is a powerful way of dynamically creating code. For now though, let's switch to code view to look at the Web service code that's been generated for us.

You should see a class that looks similar to the following:

```
public class Service1 : System.Web.Services.WebService
{
```

```
        public Service1()
        {
        // CODEGEN: This call is required by the
        // ASP.NET Web Services Designer
        InitializeComponent();
    }

        #region Component Designer generated code
            ...
        #endregion

        // WEB SERVICE EXAMPLE
        // The HelloWorld() example service returns the string
        // Hello World. To build, uncomment the following lines
        // then save and build the project
        // To test this web service, press F5

//          [WebMethod]
//          public string HelloWorld()
//          {
//              return "Hello World";
//          }
    }
```

This class, *Service1*, implements *System.Web.Services.WebService.* Within this class is a constructor, some component designer–generated code (typically used to describe the layout of any visual components that have been dragged to the editor window), and a sample *WebMethod* that's commented out.

To get the interoperability sample up and running quickly, we'll remove the default class that's been created for us and use two classes from the samples directory. These classes take the stock recommendations and purchase examples from Chapter 4 and expose them by using Web services.

To replace this default class, go to Solution Explorer in the IDE, right-click the Service1.asmx file, and select Delete. This will remove the class from your project. To add the sample classes, right-click the dotNETWebService project and then select Add and Add Existing Item. Browse to the C:\Interoperability\Samples\Point\WebServices\dotNET\WebService.IDE directory and select the Portfolio.cs and the StockService.asmx file in this directory. When you add these files, ensure that you select StockService.asmx and not StockService.asmx.cs (because this gets added automatically). You might need to change the filter on the Add Existing Item dialog box to ensure that the correct files are selectable.

Once this is done, open the StockService.asmx file in Solution Explorer and view the code, as depicted in Figure 5-6.

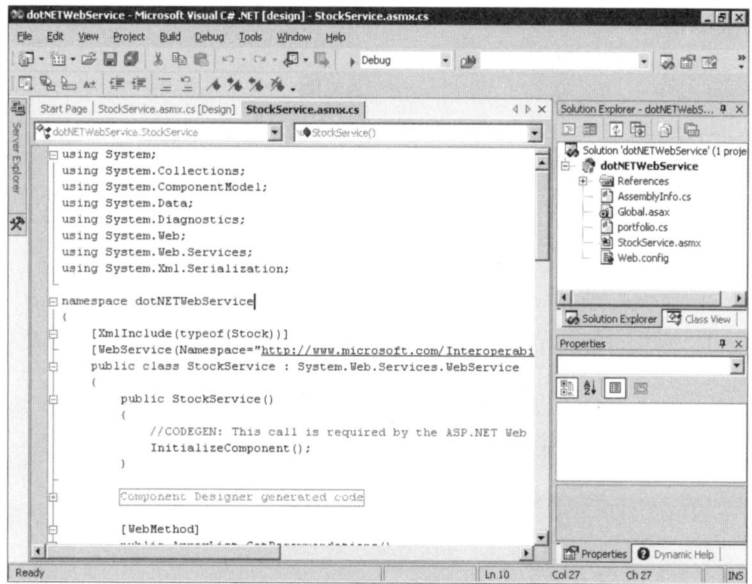

Figure 5-6 Viewing the StockService.asmx file in Visual Studio .NET.

As with the automatically generated class we removed, the *StockService* class implements the *System.Web.Services.WebService* interface but also includes a namespace attribute (set to *http://www.microsoft.com/interoperability*). This is used to uniquely identify any types and methods that are exposed via this Web service. For example, two Web services that both expose a *Stock* object can be made unique by setting a separate namespace for each. If no namespace is set for a Web services project, *http://tempuri.org* is used.

You might also notice a second attribute named *XMLInclude*. This is used to expose the *Stock* data type in the WSDL document. We'll expand on this as we move through the sample.

Within the code itself, the *GetRecommendations* and *BuyStocks* methods are both annotated with a *[WebMethod]* declaration. This attribute is used to expose these methods as Web services.

Before this Web service can be used, it must be compiled. This can be done within the IDE by selecting Build Solution from the Build menu.

Option 2: Creating the Web Service Using the NAnt Script

Creating the Web service using the supplied NAnt script involves first compiling the sample code, and then using the Internet Information Services administration tool to create a virtual directory for the Web service.

The files for the prebuilt Web service can be found in the C:\Interoperability\Samples\Point\WebServices\dotNET\WebService.Nant directory. Using a command prompt, navigate to this directory and run the NAnt build script by typing **nant**.

The files that make up the Web service will be compiled, and a DLL will be created in a bin subdirectory.

Next, launch IIS by selecting the program from Start\Programs\Administrative Tools. Drill down through the computer entry and the Web Sites folder, and right-click Default Web Site. Select New\Virtual Directory from the menu. This will display the Virtual Directory Creation Wizard. Navigate through the wizard and for the Virtual Directory Alias, enter **dotNETWebService**, as shown in Figure 5-7. Note that the alias is case sensitive.

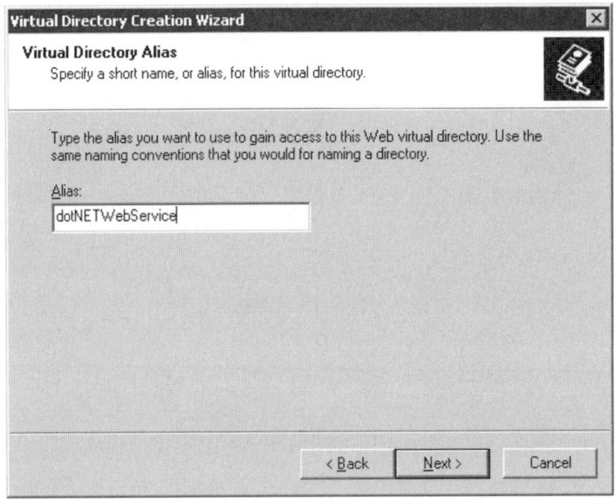

Figure 5-7 Creating a new virtual directory in IIS.

Click the Next button to proceed, and for the directory, enter the location of the prebuilt Web service sample files. If you accept the defaults during installation, this will be C:\Interoperability\Samples\Point\WebServices\dotNET\WebService.Nant, as shown in Figure 5-8.

Click the Next button and accept the rest of the defaults to complete the wizard. The sample code has now been compiled, a virtual directory in IIS has been created, and the .NET Web service is ready to be tested.

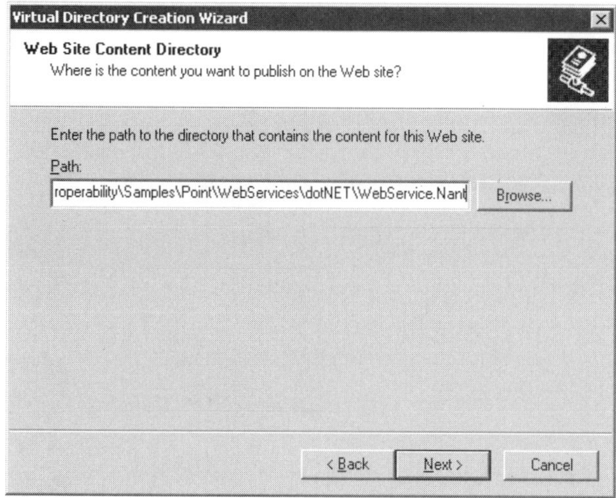

Figure 5-8 Setting the Web site content directory for the .NET Web service.

Testing the .NET Web Service

Regardless of whether the Web service was created using the IDE or built using the NAnt script, we can test it by opening a new browser window to *http://localhost/dotNETWebService/StockService.asmx*. The default presentation interface, shown in Figure 5-9, is automatically generated from the underlying Web service files in a similar way that an interface was created for components by using .NET Remoting and hosted through Component Services on Windows Server 2003.

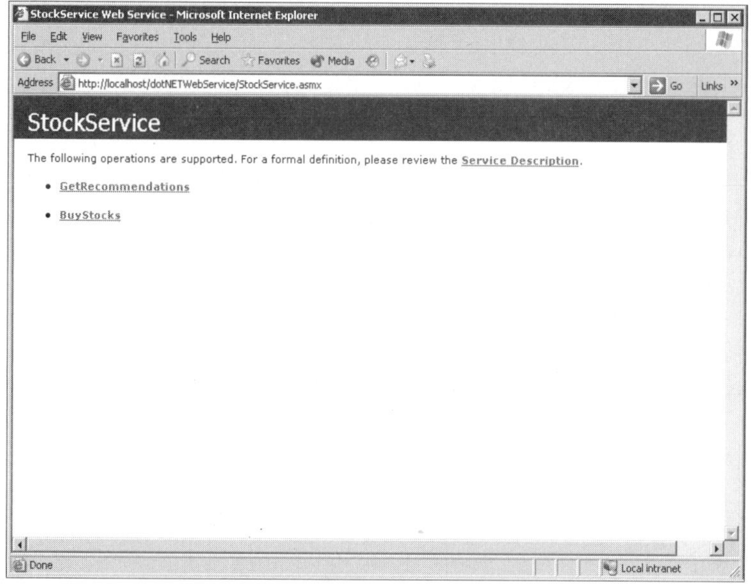

Figure 5-9 The Web service presentation interface.

Click the GetRecommendations link to display the description for the method, and then click the Invoke button. This will execute the *GetRecommendations* method of the Web service, returning the XML that will be passed back to the calling client, as shown in Figure 5-10.

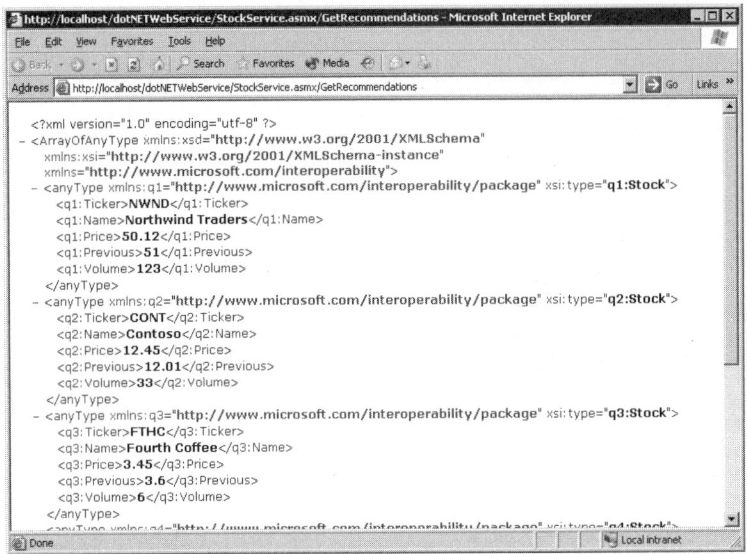

Figure 5-10 Viewing the XML output from the invoked Web service.

As you can see, the *ArrayList* containing the stock information is returned by serializing into XML. Notice that all the types in the XML document use XML Schema Definition (XSD), as noted by the *XMLSchema* declaration toward the top of the document.

This browser-based interface for consuming Web services is a useful feature to test exposed methods and view the XML result without having to build a client. However, the client that you will eventually build must use an exposed WSDL document to call these methods. To view the WSDL that's used in this sample, type **?WSDL** at the end of the Web service URL, like this: **http://localhost/dotNETWebService/StockService.asmx?WSDL**.

Figure 5-11 shows the WSDL contract, which is a lot more descriptive than the previous user interface. As mentioned earlier, this is the contract that the client will use to understand which methods and types the Web service exposes.

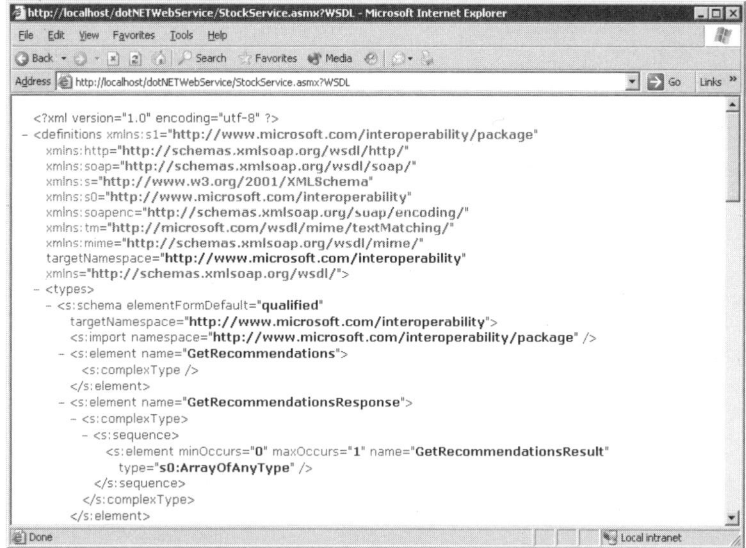

Figure 5-11 Viewing the WSDL document in Microsoft Internet Explorer.

Consuming the .NET Web Service Using a .NET Client

The sample .NET Web service is now up and running. The first client that we'll look at is a .NET client to consume this Web service. As with creating the Web service itself, you again have two options for building this client. Developers who haven't used Visual Studio .NET but want to see how Web services are consumed within a project should follow Option 1. For developers who are familiar with how Visual Studio .NET works, a NAnt script has been created to automatically generate a client, which is outlined in Option 2.

Option 1: Creating the .NET Client Using Visual Studio .NET

As we did when creating the Web service itself, let's first look at how to consume Web services by using the Visual Studio .NET IDE. In the samples directory, open the dotNETClient.sln Visual Studio .NET solution file from the C:\Interoperability\Samples\Point\WebServices\dotNET\dotNETClient.IDE directory. As you can see in Figure 5-12, the solution contains one main class, Client.cs. This class calls the expected methods to get the stock recommendations and make a sample stock purchase, as before.

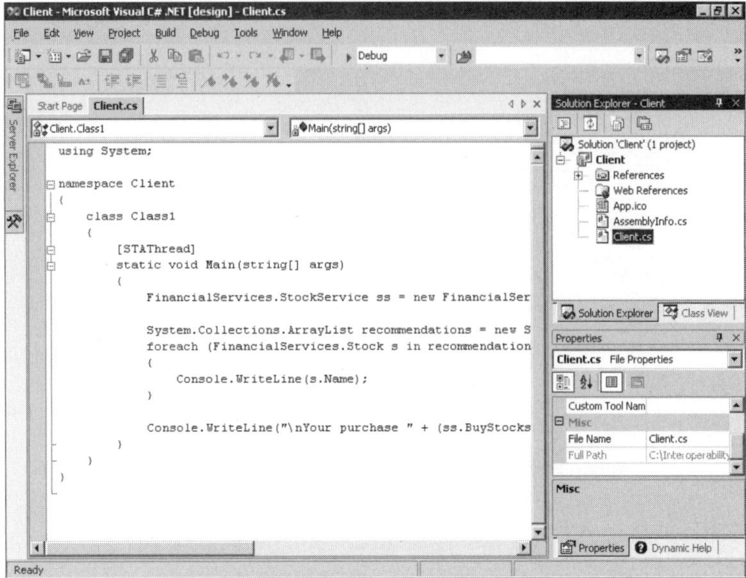

Figure 5-12 Working with the .NET client in Visual Studio .NET.

To complete this sample, we need to add a reference to the Web service created in the last step. To do this, right-click the Web References folder in Solution Explorer and select the Add Web Reference option. Figure 5-13 shows the dialog box that appears. This dialog box enables you to view the WSDL contract for the Web service that you want to consume.

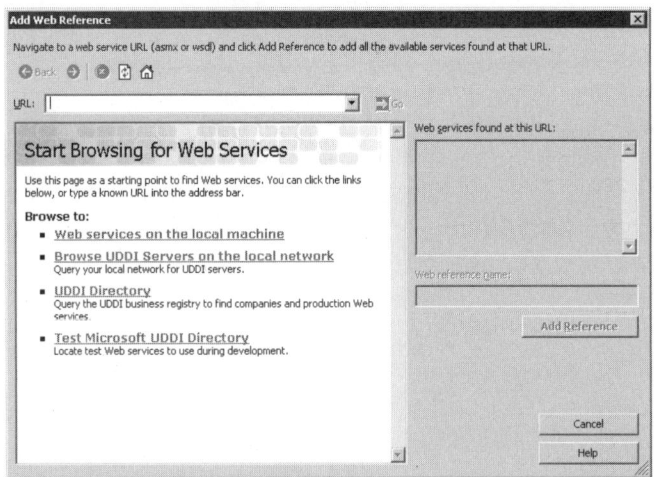

Figure 5-13 Browsing for Web services within Visual Studio .NET.

In this dialog box, enter the URL of the WSDL you used earlier when viewing the document via Internet Explorer (**http://localhost/dotNETWebService/StockService.asmx?WSDL**) and click the Go button. Figure 5-14 shows the dialog box that will appear. Behind the scenes, Visual Studio .NET downloads the WSDL contract and displays the services that it finds published. A description is also given for each method in the service, which matches the sample code you saw.

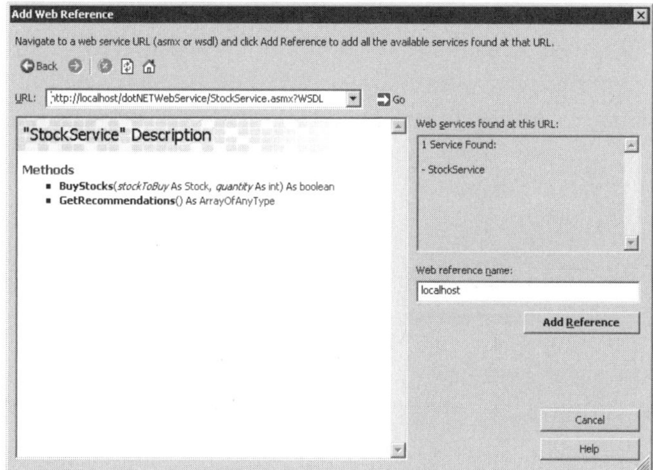

Figure 5-14 Viewing the StockService Web reference.

In the Web reference name field, type **FinancialServices**. This is the name of the namespace that will be used for the proxy files that will be automatically generated. To select this service and return to the main editor window, click the Add Reference button. Within Solution Explorer, you now have a reference to the Web service, labeled *FinancialServices.*

To complete the sample, compile the client and run it. If all executes successfully, the output should display in a console window:

```
Northwind Traders
Contoso
Fourth Coffee
Alpine Ski
Woodgrove Bank

Your purchase completed

Press ENTER to continue.
```

As with the examples in previous chapters, this client sample lists the stock recommendations and makes a sample stock purchase. The Web service *BuyStocks* method writes the trade into the Windows Application Log, which can be examined to ensure that the Web service was called correctly.

Option 2: Creating the .NET Client Using the NAnt Script

To create the .NET client using the NAnt script, navigate to the C:\Interoperability\Samples\Point\WebServices\dotNET\dotNETClient.Nant directory. From the command line, type **nant run** to build and run the sample code.

The NAnt script performs two operations. The first is to generate the Web service proxy file by using a tool named WSDL.EXE. We'll cover this shortly, in the "Consuming the Java Web Service Using a .NET Client" section. The second operation is to run the client executable. Upon a successful build, the list of returned stocks will be displayed:

```
Northwind Traders
Contoso
Fourth Coffee
Alpine Ski
Woodgrove Bank

Your purchase completed
```

This client lists the stock recommendations and makes a sample stock purchase. In addition, the Web service *BuyStocks* method writes the trade into the Windows Application Log, which can be examined to ensure that the Web service was called correctly.

Consuming the .NET Web Service Using a Java Client

As mentioned earlier, we'll explore the Java samples by using GLUE 4.0.1 Professional. To allow the tools to be run from the command line, your system *PATH* was updated to include the C:\Interoperability\Tools\Glue\bin directory when the sample code was installed. Before compiling and running the Java sample code here, it's recommended to confirm this setting.

To prepare to build the Java client sample, from a command prompt, navigate to the C:\Interoperability\Samples\Point\WebServices\dotNET\JavaClient directory. The first thing you need to do is build the proxy files for the .NET Web service. This procedure, although run from the command line, is similar to the Add Web Reference operation in Visual Studio .NET.

Note What are proxy files? GLUE and Visual Studio .NET interrogate the WSDL contract when generating the proxy files to see which methods and types are exposed by the Web service. An interface (also known as a *proxy*) is then built based on the exposed methods and types, which can then be referenced by the client code. This gives the developer of the client a natural way to program against the Web service as though it were a local object or class. When the term *proxy* (or *Web service proxy*) is used in this book, it refers to these automatically generated files.

To generate the proxies using GLUE, you'll use a tool named wsdl2java. As the name suggests, the tool takes a WSDL file and generates the required Java classes. To use wsdl2java in this sample, run the following command from the JavaClient directory:

wsdl2java http://localhost/dotNETWebService/StockService.asmx?WSDL

Alternatively, you can also use the WSDL target with the provided Ant script, which performs the same task.

This generates the same files and is used by the overall build process when compiling the client. The output of both command-line instructions displays the four files that are created:

```
write file IStockServiceSoap.java
write file StockServiceHelper.java
write file Stock.java
write file StockService.map
```

The Stock.java class is the representation of the *Stock* object, which is similar to its .NET equivalent. In addition, notice that this class looks very similar to the Stock.java file that was created when you generated classes from the XSD document in Chapter 3. If we go back and look at the WSDL that's exposed by the .NET Web service, you'll notice a schema definition for the *Stock* class:

```
<s:schema elementFormDefault="qualified" targetNamespace=
    "http://www.microsoft.com/interoperability/package">
    <s:complexType name="Stock">
        <s:sequence>
```

```
                <s:element minOccurs="0" maxOccurs="1"
                    name="Ticker" type="s:string" />
                <s:element minOccurs="0" maxOccurs="1"
                    name="Name" type="s:string" />
                <s:element minOccurs="1" maxOccurs="1"
                    name="Price" type="s:float" />
                <s:element minOccurs="1" maxOccurs="1"
                    name="Previous" type="s:float" />
                <s:element minOccurs="1" maxOccurs="1"
                    name="Volume" type="s:int" />
            </s:sequence>
        </s:complexType>
</s:schema>
```

The wsdl2java tool uses the same principles to extract this XSD type from the WSDL and generate the required Java class.

The IStockServiceSoap.java file is an interface that exposes the methods that you'll call in the Java client. StockServiceHelper.java is used to bind the URL that you called to the interface itself. The map file is generated in case you want to use these types with other Web services in the environment.

Now that you have the proxy files, let's look at the Client.java class, which is the actual code you'll run. First, you have the required imports for the class:

```
import java.util.ArrayList;
import java.util.Arrays;
```

The *ArrayList* and the *Arrays* class handle the response returned from the Web service itself.

In the main class of the code, you can see that the first task is to handle the binding, which you perform with the following line of code:

```
IStockServiceSoap FinancialServices = StockServiceHelper.bind();
```

After the binding is created, you call the *GetRecommendations* method from the Web service. You should already be familiar with this method if you examined the .NET client.

```
ArrayList recommendations =
    new ArrayList(Arrays.asList(
        FinancialServices.GetRecommendations()));
```

Note that the return type of the *GetRecommendations* method is an array of objects (*Object[]*). This brings us back to the familiar problem of type mapping between .NET and Java. There is no natural equivalent in XSD to *ArrayLists* in either .NET or Java. Objects of type *ArrayList* that are published get exposed as type *Object[]*. The .NET or Java client has to make the necessary provisions to convert the *Object[]* type to the correct *ArrayList*.

In the .NET client example, this was handled by passing the *Object[]* type as a constructor to the *ArrayList*, which is a feature of that collection object:

```
ArrayList recommendations =
    new ArrayList(FinancialServices.GetRecommendations);
```

In Java, you use the *Arrays.asList* method to convert between object arrays (*Object[]*) and *ArrayLists*:

```
ArrayList recommendations =
    new ArrayList(Arrays.asList(
        FinanicalServices.GetRecommendations()));
```

In both examples, we could have worked with the *Object[]* types throughout the sample, but converting them allows us to take advantage of a more functional set of classes. The remainder of the code displays the stock recommendations and makes the stock purchase, as with the other samples that we've looked at:

```
for (int f=0; f<recommendations.size(); f++)
{
    System.out.println(((Stock)recommendations.get(f)).Name);
}
System.out.println("\nThe purchase "+
    (FinancialServices.BuyStocks((Stock)recommendations.get(2),295)
        ? "completed" : "failed"));
```

As with the .NET sample code, you need to cast each element of the stock recommendations array into an object of type *Stock*.

Build and run the code by entering **ant run** at a command prompt within the Java client directory. This will re-create the proxy files, and you'll see a similar output to that of the .NET sample:

```
Northwind Traders
Contoso
Fourth Coffee
Alpine Ski
Woodgrove Bank

The purchase completed
```

You've now seen how to create a Web service by using Visual Studio .NET and then consume that service with a client written in both.NET and Java. Now let's look at the reverse—creating the Web service in Java and creating two similar clients.

Creating a Web Service in Java

To host Web services for Java, GLUE can be run by using one of two modes: *standalone* or *hosted*. In standalone mode, GLUE uses its own application server to take the Java classes and to handle the creation of WSDL and the incoming HTTP requests from clients. This gives you a clean and easy approach to hosting Web services, especially for this sample code. Hosted mode, which we'll look at in more detail in Chapter 6, allows the classes to be hosted in a third-party J2EE application server.

Hosting a Web service in GLUE using the standalone mode approach is usually a two-step process. First, you need to create and compile the classes to be hosted. Second, you write a class that configures the hosting based on the GLUE libraries.

To do this, navigate to the Java Web service sample in C:\Interoperability\Samples\Point\WebServices\Java\WebService. In this directory, three classes will make up the Web service. Stock.java is the stock object that's passed between the Web service and the client. StockService.java contains the *GetRecommendations* and *SellStocks* methods that we've been using. Publish.java, the class that configures the hosting of the Web service, is worth taking a look at before we run the sample:

```
import electric.registry.Registry;
import electric.server.http.HTTP;

public class Publish
{
    public static void main( String[] args ) throws Exception
    {
        HTTP.startup("http://localhost:8004/JavaWebService");
        Registry.publish("StockService", new StockService());
    }
}
```

As you can see, the required packages are imported, and then two lines make up the actual class. The *HTTP.startup* method is used to configure the root of the Web service. And the *Registry.Publish* method is used to publish the *StockService* class under a path of the same name.

If you build and run this class, which can be done by entering **start ant run** at a command prompt, you can see the service in action. Compile and run the sample in this directory.

As the message implies, the GLUE HTTP server is now listening on port 8004. As with the Visual Studio .NET example, you can test this before consuming the Web service with a client application, by looking at the WSDL that's exposed. Within Internet Explorer, navigate to **http://localhost:8004/JavaWebService/StockService.wsdl**, as shown in Figure 5-15.

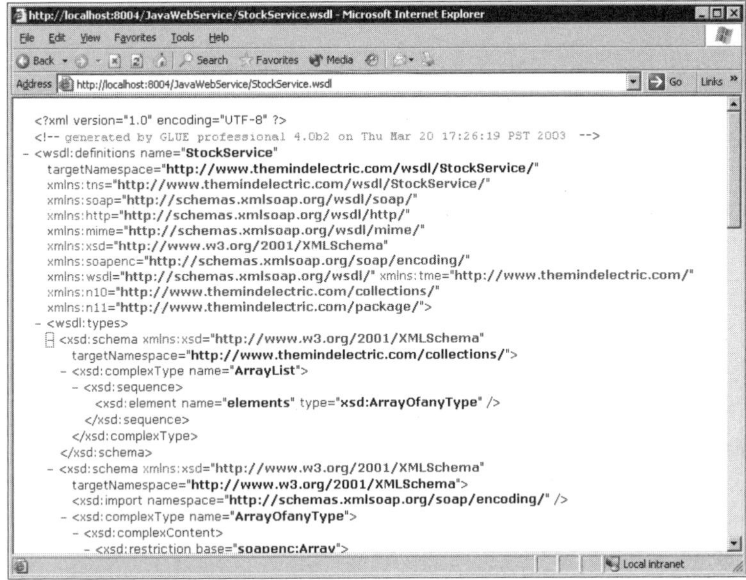

Figure 5-15 Viewing the WSDL document generated by GLUE.

You now have the WSDL that describes the Web service exposed by the GLUE HTTP server. When navigating through the WSDL, you might notice that some of the namespaces and types are slightly different than the one created in .NET, but both platforms essentially expose the same types and methods.

Consuming the Java Web Service Using a Java Client

For the Java Web service, we'll use both a Java and a .NET client to show how this WSDL is consumed by the two platforms. We'll first look at the Java client sample code, which can be found in the C:\Interoperability\Samples\Point\WebServices\Java\JavaClient directory.

As expected, the client is very similar to the one that called the .NET Web service in the previous example—with the exception that the URL is different and the method is *SellStocks*, not *BuyStocks* (currently the primary difference between the two). If you want to examine the proxy files for the client, you can again run the wsdl2java tool, this time with the URL of the Java Web service hosted through GLUE:

wsdl2java http://localhost:8004/JavaWebService/StockService.wsdl

You can also use the WSDL target with the provided Ant script to generate these proxy files. Now build and run the sample by entering **ant run** at a command prompt to display the expected recommendations and sell stocks result.

Consuming the Java Web Service Using a .NET Client

To conclude the chapter's introductory Web service interoperability samples, let's consume the Java Web service hosted by using GLUE with a .NET client. Instead of creating the Web reference using Visual Studio .NET, as we did in the first option of the previous .NET client example, we'll use a command-line tool named WSDL.EXE to create the proxy file.

Navigate to the sample code in the C:\Interoperability\Samples\Point\WebServices\Java\dotNETClient directory. The Client.cs class in this directory is of course very similar to the code that you viewed in Visual Studio .NET earlier. Here, we'll use the WSDL.EXE, a command-line tool, to generate the proxy or Web reference. WSDL.EXE is a tool that accompanies the .NET Framework as part of the SDK. To run WSDL.EXE from the command prompt, pass it the URL of the WSDL for the Java Web service:

wsdl http://localhost:8004/JavaWebService/StockService.wsdl /out:FinancialServices.cs /namespace:FinancialServices

This same effect can be achieved by using the WSDL target with the included NAnt script. Notice that the code also passes an */out* parameter to the tool, which specifies the name of the file that's generated, and a */namespace* parameter, which creates a namespace for the service class. The WSDL tool generates a FinancialServices.cs class, which upon closer inspection is actually the same as the class generated by the Visual Studio .NET Add Web Reference option—both classes use the same APIs to generate the code.

When running the WSDL tool, you might notice the following warning:

```
Warning: one or more optional WSDL extension elements were ignored.
Warnings were encountered. Review generated source comments for more details.
```

GLUE 4.0.1 uses a WSDL extension element to offer some optimizations for Java clients. Because these do not get interpreted by the tool, the warnings are displayed and commented in the generated proxy file.

> **Tip** When should you use WSDL.EXE and when should you use Visual Studio .NET? If using both WSDL.EXE and Visual Studio .NET produces the same proxy file, what's the reasoning behind using one over the other? The proxy file that WSDL.EXE creates is *static*—meaning that unless you run the WSDL.EXE tool again, this file will never be overwritten. Although the same process is used for the proxy file in Visual Studio .NET, it tends to be a little more *dynamic*—in theory, the proxy file can be updated on the fly as the IDE sees fit. If you plan to make any modifications to the proxy file (such as adding authentication or modifying the methods), using WSDL.EXE is the best approach because you can guarantee that the file will remain under your control.

Within the client class itself, notice how the object array (*Object[]*) is exposed by using the GLUE Web service and subsequently converted to a *System.Collections.ArrayList*:

```
System.Collections.ArrayList recommendations =
    new System.Collection s.ArrayList(
        ss.GetRecommendations().elements);
```

Using the standard mapping within GLUE, if you expose a return type of *java.util.ArrayList*, the type gets mapped to an *ArrayList* of the class that you're calling. (For this example, this is *FinancialServices.ArrayList*.) The custom *ArrayList* class implements a field named *elements*, which returns the list as type *Object[]*. To convert this *elements* method to a *System.Collections.ArrayList* type, call it as part of the constructor, as shown in the previous code.

To conclude this set of samples, compile and run this sample, which can be done by entering **nant run** at a command prompt, to show the .NET client calling the Java Web service.

Summary

This chapter presented an introduction to Web services, examined the commercial landscape of Web services, discussed the WS-I, and introduced a set of Web service samples that demonstrated basic connectivity between the .NET and Java platforms.

In Chapter 6, you'll see more advanced samples of Web services, including some of the elements that are required to deliver interoperability in a production environment and the use of UDDI to provide a central registry for these Web service elements.

6

Connectivity with XML Web Services, Part 2

Chapter 5, "Connectivity with XML Web Services, Part 1," demonstrated how to create an XML Web service using both the Microsoft .NET Framework and GLUE for Java. For each of the Web services created in Chapter 5, you saw a client written in both .NET and Java, looked at how proxy files were generated, and saw some of the compensations that had to be made in order to return data in the correct format and type.

We'll now look at some common challenges that affect interoperability with Web services, especially in a production environment. As we did with the .NET Remoting samples in Chapter 4, "Connectivity with .NET Remoting," we'll look at the requirements of hosting these components using different containers—for example, Enterprise JavaBeans (EJBs)—and some of the authentication and exception issues that can arise. To conclude this topic, I'll introduce recommendations for designing solutions that require interoperability using Web services.

Exposing EJBs by Using Web Services

For a look at a more realistic Java environment, we'll use the same EJB deployment (a stateless session and bean-managed entity) that was used in Chapter 4—only this time, we'll expose the components as Web services. Figure 6-1 illustrates this.

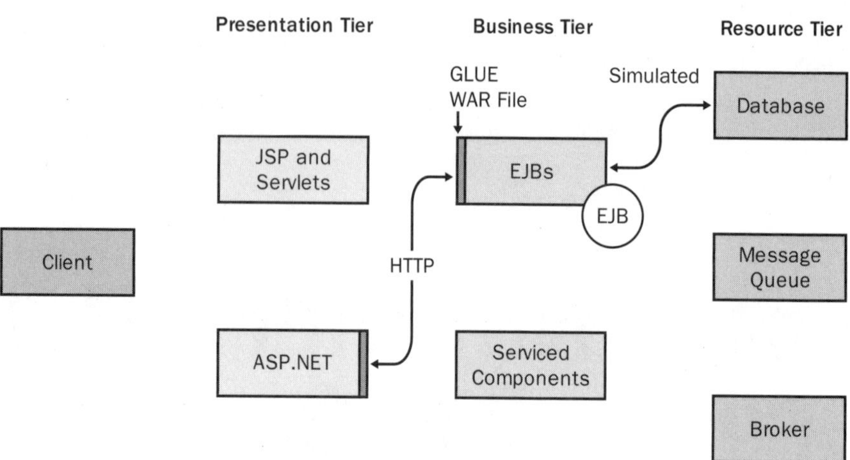

Figure 6-1 Using GLUE for EJB deployment.

Publishing the Sample EJBs

The EJBs that we'll use contain both a stateless Session Bean and an Entity Bean in order to simulate the "sell stocks" method. All incoming requests are written to the console for demonstration purposes. For further details on how the EJBs work in the sample, refer to the ".NET Client to EJB, Hosted by J2EE Application Server" section in Chapter 4.

The sample code to show this is located in the C:\Interoperability\Samples\Point\WebServices\JavaEJB\StockServiceEJB subdirectory of your sample code installation. Build the source in this directory by running **ant package** in this directory at a command prompt. This will produce a SampleEJB.jar file in the Deploy subdirectory. Deploy this Java Archive (JAR) file to the Java 2 Enterprise Edition (J2EE) application server that you're using. If you're using JBoss 3.0.7, simply run **ant deploy**, which will copy the SampleEJB.jar file to the server\default\deploy directory and the required GLUE libraries to the server\default\lib directory of your JBoss installation.

In Chapter 4, to expose the EJBs using .NET Remoting, we ran a third-party tool to create a *wrapper*, or *listener*, that would accept incoming .NET Remoting calls and perform the necessary calls in order to invoke the EJBs. Using the GLUE toolkit, we now perform a very similar operation. We create a Web Archive (WAR) file that holds the configuration information for our EJBs, and this exposes the required Web services interfaces to the client.

To create this WAR file, navigate to the C:\Interoperability\Samples\Point\WebServices\JavaEJB directory, and run the following command:

```
newapp GlueStockService
```

The newapp command-line tool in GLUE is used to create a new application structure (a set of directories) that can be deployed to a J2EE application server. When this command is run, a directory named GlueStockService is created that contains a single subdirectory named WEB-INF. Within this subdirectory are additional subdirectories (classes, lib, maps, security, and services), some of which will look familiar to anyone who has seen the structure of a WAR file.

After running this command, navigate to the WEB-INF\services directory within the GlueStockService directory. In this directory, using an editor of your choice, create a new file named StockService.xml. This is the service deployment descriptor that will be used to configure which EJBs are mapped to the service.

Create the following XML structure within this file. (Instead of typing this code, you can copy it from the C:\Interoperability\Samples\Point\Web-Services\JavaEJB\Templates directory.)

```
<?xml version="1.0"?>
<service>
    <constructor>
        <class>
            electric.service.ejb.StatelessSessionBeanService
        </class>
        <args>
            <contextFactory>
                org.jnp.interfaces.NamingContextFactory
            </contextFactory>
            <url>localhost:1099</url>
            <jndiName>StockSession</jndiName>
            <homeInterfaceName>
                com.microsoft.samples.ejb.StockSessionHome
            </homeInterfaceName>
        </args>
    </constructor>
</service>
```

This deployment descriptor has five key elements that perform the mapping between the EJBs and the Web services that will be exposed by GLUE:

- ***class*** Determines which class from the GLUE toolkit should be used to expose the EJB. The *electric.service.ejb.StatelessSessionBean-Service* element is used for Session Beans and shouldn't need to be changed unless the documentation suggests otherwise.
- ***contextFactory* and *url*** Both are specific to the J2EE application server that you're using. Recall how in the .NET Remoting sample in Chapter 4, we also had to specify the context factory and URL. The

settings shown in the previous XML document are valid for a JBoss 3.0.7 implementation, although the GLUE documentation offers default settings for J2EE application servers from Sun Microsystems (ONE), BEA (WebLogic), and IBM (WebSphere).

- ***jndiName*** The Java Naming and Directory Interface (JNDI) name of the exposed Session Bean.
- ***homeInterfaceName*** The name of the home interface for the Session Bean.

If you're using an application server other than JBoss 3.0.7, supply the context factory and URL settings suitable for your application server and save the file. (Table 4-1 in Chapter 4 lists some other J2EE application servers.)

To complete the deployment, you simply package the directory structure into a WAR file and deploy it to the J2EE application server. To do this, navigate to the C:\Interoperability\Samples\Point\WebServices\JavaEJB\GlueStockService directory and run the following command:

```
jar -cvf GlueStockService.war .\
```

This will create a WAR file in the current directory. Deploy this WAR file to publish the EJBs, and expose the interfaces using Web services. To deploy to JBoss 3.0.7, you can use the deploy-warfile target with the Ant build script in the JavaEJB\StockServiceEJB directory. This will copy the WAR file to the server\default\deploy directory of your JBoss installation. For other application servers, you should follow the deployment instructions that were used for deploying the previous JAR file.

Testing the Deployment

To test that the deployment was successful, the J2EE application server must be started (or restarted if it was already running). You can now navigate to the URL of the exposed Web Services Description Language (WSDL) file: *http://localhost:8080/GlueStockService/services/StockService.wsdl*. If the deployment was successful, the generated WSDL for the *StockSession* Session Bean will be displayed.

Consuming the Exposed EJB by Using a .NET Client

The consumption of the exposed Session Bean with a .NET client is straightforward and similar to the consumption of a standalone Java Web service. The client sample code, which can be found in the C:\Interoperability\Samples\Point\WebServices\JavaEJB\dotNETClient directory, uses a proxy class that was generated with the WSDL.EXE tool using the exposed WSDL. The client simply creates a new instance of the *StockService* (which is the exposed Session Bean) and calls the *sellStocks* method:

```
StockService ss = new StockService();
Console.WriteLine(ss.sellStocks("CONT", 100));
```

To test the .NET client, compile and run using the run target with the provided NAnt script. If the simulated sale was successful, the following message is displayed in the console window of the J2EE application server:

```
Incoming request to sell 100 common shares of Contoso (CONT)
```

As with the EJB sample shown in Chapter 4, the J2EE console also displays how the bean is activated and loaded.

Consuming the Exposed EJB by Using a Java Client

To test consuming the EJB by using Web services from the Java platform, use the sample code in C:\Interoperability\Samples\Point\WebServices\Java-EJB\JavaClient. As with the .NET code, this sample relies on a preconfigured proxy class that was generated using the wsdl2java tool, which we covered in Chapter 5. The client binds to the Web service and calls the *sellStocks* method of the EJB. This is done with a *StockSessionHelper*, a class that's automatically created with the wsdl2java tool. This class has a private field for the target URL and a *bind* method which loads all the required registry classes from the GLUE libraries.

```
IStockSession ss = StockSessionHelper.bind();
System.out.println(ss.sellStocks("FTHC",200));
```

Execute the Java sample by using the run target with the provided Ant script. Again, if the simulated sale was successful, this is displayed in the console window of the J2EE application server:

```
Incoming request to sell 200 common shares of Fourth Coffee
 (FTHC)
```

Interoperability Advantages of Consuming EJBs via Web Services

In this section, we have looked at a process in which a collection of EJBs (in this case, an Entity Bean fronted by a Session Bean) can be exposed by using Web services. The result, especially in the context of interoperability, is that we can use this process to consume any exposed EJB by using any client that supports Web services.

This technique is obviously of great advantage to clients built on the .NET Framework because it allows EJB methods to be called from .NET without relying on any custom client implementations or connectors. In addition, this technique can offer a layer of abstraction and simplicity for Java clients. The proxy class that's generated from the WSDL provides for a clean and formalized way of calling EJBs from a Java client without having to rely on any JNDI lookups, the creation of a home interface, and so on.

In essence, exposing EJBs by using Web services moves a Java-centric technology to a more loosely coupled model, which has a significant impact on and benefits for both Java and non-Java consumers.

Exposing Serviced Components by Using Web Services

In the .NET Remoting samples in Chapter 4, we exposed a .NET component and through Component Services, consuming it in Java with Intrinsyc's Ja.NET. We can now do the same with Web services. To expose the serviced components via Web services, however, we'll create an additional layer to enable them to be called from a suitable client.

Can't You Just Use SOAP Activation?

SOAP activation in Component Services for Microsoft Windows Server 2003 can be used to expose a Serviced Component to either .NET or Java. SOAP activation is the option in which a SOAP endpoint is automatically generated and hosted through Microsoft Internet Information Services (IIS) for deployed components.

Given that this SOAP endpoint could be accessed by using HTTP via a WSDL document that's created for you, it begs the question of whether the endpoint could be classified as a Web service (and whether you could just use the sample client created in the previous section in order to consume it). Unfortunately, the answer is "not always."

Although SOAP, HTTP, and WSDL were used to construct the endpoint, the WSDL generated by using the SOAP activation option is not XML Schema Definition (XSD) compliant. In essence, the WSDL that's generated by using SOAP activation contains data types that are specific to .NET Remoting (and not based on XSD). As a result, the types exposed have the potential to be consumed by using either a .NET client or a Java client that understands .NET Remoting (for example, with Ja.NET installed). But in most cases, a Web services implementation that doesn't understand the .NET Remoting data types cannot access the service. To overcome this, you'll now see how to publish the components in the same way as before, and how a small layer can be used to accept incoming Web service requests and pass them on to the hosted components.

Publishing the Serviced Components

The samples that you'll reuse are located in the C:\Interoperability\Samples\Point\WebServices\dotNETComponentServices\Server directory. These samples expose the same methods used in the .NET Remoting example in Chapter 4, but they don't publish a SOAP VRoot (the SOAP endpoint). In addition, the name of the component is changed slightly to allow the .NET Remoting and Web service components to run side by side.

As before, the sample code shows an implementation of the *GetRecommendations* and *BuyStocks* methods that are hosted by Component Services. To build and deploy the server component, run the NAnt script in the Server directory by using the invoke target. This will build the StockServer DLL file, create an Invoker subdirectory, and install the component. Running NAnt on its own will build the component but not install it. This can be useful for deploying to other machines. For additional information on building the server component, refer to the "Java Client to .NET Object, Hosted by Component Services" section in Chapter 4.

> **Note** In certain rare cases, you might get a *System.Runtime.InteropServices.COMException* exception when the invoke.bat file is executed (which implicitly occurs when the invoke target is used with the provided NAnt script). As was the case in Chapter 4, the StockServerWS component will be deployed, but it needs to be configured to run under a different identity in order to run properly. Open the Properties window for the StockServerWS component within Component Services, and select the Identity tab. Select This User, enter account credentials for a valid user account, and click OK. Now rerun the NAnt script with the invoke target to complete the StockServerWS component installation.

The layer that allows these components to be exposed by using Web services can be found in the C:\Interoperability\Samples\Point\WebServices\dotNETComponentServices\WebService directory. To configure the Web services layer, build the sample code and create a virtual root in IIS that points to this directory. (This was shown in the scripted .NET Web service at the start of Chapter 5.) To run the Web services sample side by side with the .NET Remoting sample, use the alias StockServerWS. (The .NET Remoting sample used StockServer.)

Once the virtual directory has been created, browse to *http://localhost/StockServerWS/StockService.asmx?WSDL*. This will show the WSDL document for the Web service.

How Does the Web Service Wrapper Work?

Essentially, the Web service wrapper is simply a class that's hosted through Microsoft ASP.NET as a Web service and that exposes the same methods as the original component.

Looking at the main Web service class, StockService.asmx.cs, you can see how the Web service exposes these methods. First, two instances of the *SampleData* and *StockServerWS* classes are created when the Web service is invoked:

```
private SampleData _servicedComponentSampleData
    = new SampleData();
private StockServerWS _servicedComponentBuyStocks
    = new StockServerWS();
```

After this, the methods from each of the classes are exposed as a Web method:

```
[WebMethod]
public ArrayList getRecommendations()
{
    return _servicedComponentSampleData.getRecommendations();
}

[WebMethod]
public bool BuyStocks(Stock stock, int quantity)
{
    return _servicedComponentBuyStocks.BuyStocks(stock, quantity);
}
```

As this code demonstrates, although Component Services do not facilitate exposing components as Basic Profile–compliant Web services, it's easy to generate a wrapper that can expose components this way.

Consuming the Exposed Component

You consume the serviced component via this Web service in the same way as shown in the earlier basic samples, including the sample that consumed the EJB via Web services. Two clients (one for .NET and one for Java) located in the dotNETClient and JavaClient subdirectories of C:\Interoperability\Samples\Point\WebServices\dotNETComponentServices will demonstrate this.

Build and run the clients to test consuming the Serviced Component using Web services. To prove that the component is being invoked and managed by Component Services, you can use the Component Services administration tool to observe the life cycle of the component.

To do this, launch the Component Services administration tool from Start Menu/Programs/Administrative Tools/Component Services. Navigate through the Component Services hierarchy in order to open a folder named Running Processes, as shown in Figure 6-2. Before you execute the client, this folder will contain no existing processes (with the exception of some systems and any other applications that you've installed). Run either of the clients and observe how the StockServerWS component is invoked. The figure shows how the component exposed by the Web service layer is listed under the running processes.

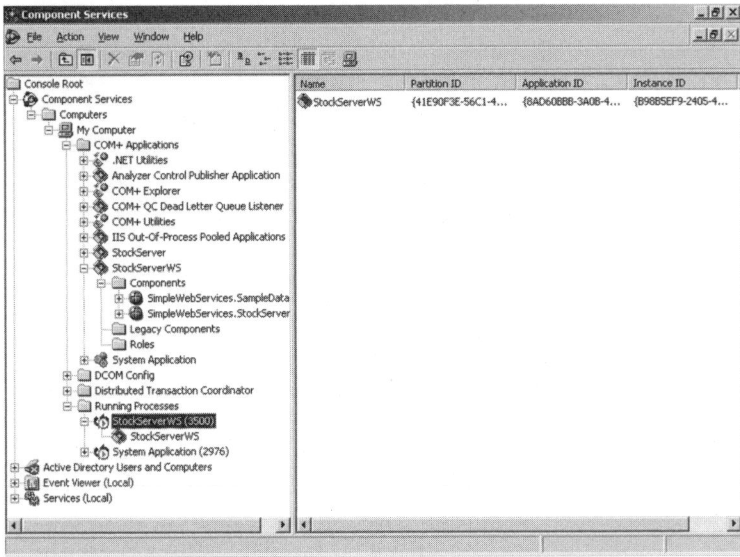

Figure 6-2 Using the Component Services administration tool.

Web Services Authentication and Authorization

In the sample code presented so far, you've used Web services to enable connectivity between a service that was published in either .NET or Java, and you then saw how clients could consume that service.

However, if you used these samples in a production environment, you'd probably need to think about some kind of authentication. Chances are, unless you were making a public Web service, you'd want to know who was using the service and for what purpose. Ideally, you need to authenticate each of the clients that are consuming Web services and configure authorization to allow access only to certain individuals and/or groups.

One of the easiest ways of doing this is to take advantage of the underlying transport that Web services rely on. In all the samples that you've seen, HTTP has been the transport used to communicate between the client and server components. HTTP has a framework that allows usernames, passwords, and domains to be used for authenticating the connection. Web services published using either .NET or GLUE can take advantage of HTTP authentication.

Enabling Authentication and Authorization for the .NET Web Service

By viewing the properties in IIS for a .NET Web service, you can see how this type of authentication can be applied. Figure 6-3 shows the properties dialog box of the virtual directory used for the .NET Web service that was built and hosted in Chapter 5. (You can reach this properties dialog box by launching Internet Information Services Manager, navigating through the Web Sites tree to the dotNETWebService directory, and then right-clicking and selecting the Properties option.)

If you didn't create the dotNETWebService Web service in the previous chapter, I recommend that you do this now because in this section we'll apply security settings based on that example. Use the instructions in the "Creating the Web Service Using the NAnt Script" section of the previous chapter to do this.

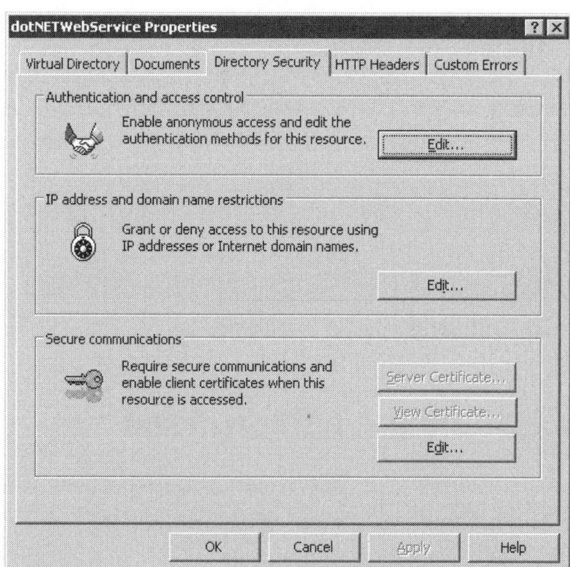

Figure 6-3 Setting the authentication properties for a virtual directory in IIS.

Within the authentication dialog box, you can set the authentication methods for the directory, specify restrictions based on IP address or domain name, and secure the virtual directory by using Secure Sockets Layer (SSL). Here, we'll change the authentication method and controls for the current directory in order to show how this affects both .NET and Java calling clients.

Clicking the Edit button in the Authentication And Access Control panel (which is named Anonymous Access And Authentication Control in Microsoft Windows XP Professional) shows the authentication mechanisms that are in place for the directory. By default, as shown in Figure 6-4, the directory is configured for anonymous access—which allows anyone to call the Web service without being challenged for credentials. The Anonymous Access option links to an account that's automatically created on the system when IIS is installed. (The account used by default will be *IUSR_MACHINENAME*, where *MACHINENAME* is the host name of the server.) Any operation that's performed by the Web service runs under the context of this user account.

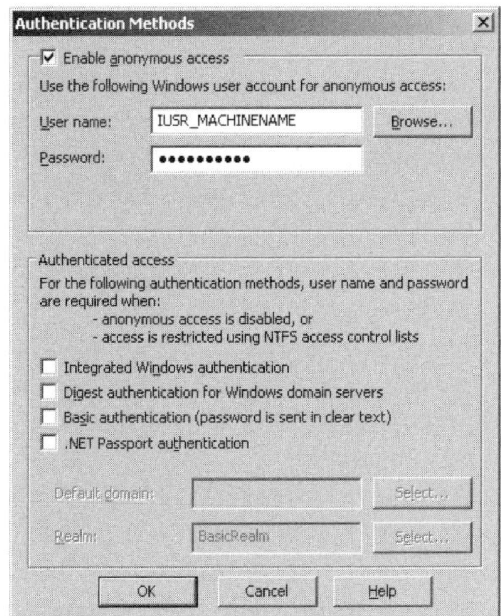

Figure 6-4 Editing the authentication methods for a virtual directory.

Now let's assume that to use the sample code into a production environment, we'll want to restrict the Web service to authenticated clients. To do this, you have a number of ways of securing the virtual directory, including these:

- **Integrated Windows authentication** Can be used to validate the access against a local Windows store and works well if no suitable access to a Windows domain exists.

- **Digest authentication** An authentication method that's compatible for Windows servers participating in an Active Directory setup.
- **Basic authentication** As the name suggests, this is the most basic form of authentication and one in which the username and password are passed in clear text.
- **.NET Passport authentication** Allows users to use existing Passport accounts to authenticate against resources on the server. This option isn't available for the Windows XP Professional operating system.

For additional information on these types of authentication, consult the documentation that accompanies your installation of IIS. If the Help files are installed, this can normally be accessed by navigating to *http://localhost/iishelp*.

Authentication Against LDAP Directories

I'm frequently asked how to authenticate against an existing Lightweight Directory Access Protocol (LDAP) directory. From my experience working with customer projects, I've found that native LDAP directories (such as Sun ONE Directory Server) tend to be more common in environments that have applications based on J2EE. The authentication options exposed via the IIS authentication console do not natively support a type of connection to a native LDAP store.

Although a number of third-party implementations can be used to get around this, one successful way to solve this is with the inclusion of a standalone Active Directory server. Active Directory supports LDAP v3.0. As a result, one of the options of integrating an Active Directory domain into an existing environment can be to use LDAP replication methods to take data from one LDAP directory into Active Directory.

As shown in Figure 6-5, this can be a read-only copy of the existing directory, but once the replication is complete, IIS can integrate with the Active Directory server, recognizing the directory as a valid domain.

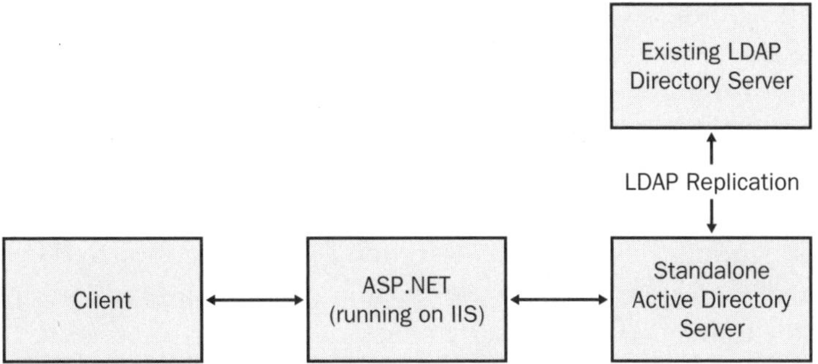

Figure 6-5 Transferring data from an LDAP directory to an Active Directory using LDAP replication methods.

Let's now take a look at what's required to secure a Web service hosted in NET. In the properties dialog box of the dotNETWebService virtual directory, disable anonymous authentication and enable basic authentication, as shown in Figure 6-6. In addition, set the realm to **BasicRealm**. This will be required when you test the Java client. Accept the warning that indicates that passwords will be sent as clear text, and click OK to commit the change.

Authentication Methods

Enable anonymous access

Use the following Windows user account for anonymous access:

User name: Browse...

Password:

Authenticated access

For the following authentication methods, user name and password are required when:
- anonymous access is disabled, or
- access is restricted using NTFS access control lists

Integrated Windows authentication

Digest authentication for Windows domain servers

Basic authentication (password is sent in clear text)

.NET Passport authentication

Default domain: Select...

Realm: BasicRealm Select...

OK Cancel Help

Figure 6-6 Adjusting the authentication methods for the virtual directory.

Setting these credentials for each of the clients allows them to access the Web service, based on having an account either on the local machine or possibly in a directory.

To further refine the security settings, you might want to select certain individuals or groups within your organization who will be either granted or denied access. To configure this, edit the web.config file for the Web service. This configuration file supports a section for authorization and enables you to allow or deny users based on username or group. This authorization typically maps to the local users on a machine or to an active directory within the enterprise.

```
<system.web>
    <authorization>
        <allow users="Administrator"/>
        <allow users="MYDOMAIN\Simon"/>
        <deny roles="MYDOMAIN\PublicUsers"/>
    </authorization>
</system.web>
```

Feel free to adjust any of these settings to test various authorization scenarios applicable to your own environment. When testing the sample code, however, the default settings are fine.

Rebuilding the Clients

To test that the Web service is secure—so that it will allow only authenticated clients to connect—you can now run the existing .NET and Java clients to see how this configuration affects them.

Before you do this, however, consider how this will affect the build processes. In Chapter 5, both the .NET and Java clients used an Ant/NAnt script to compile the code and to run the WSDL tools in order to generate the proxy. Because you've applied security at the transport level, this can cause problems. And because the Web services have been secured at the transport level, it's no longer possible to view the WSDL contract without supplying some form of credentials. The WSDL is critical in generating the proxy files for the client; therefore, you must supply valid credentials to the build scripts.

To do this, edit the default.build file in the C:\Interoperability\Samples\Point\WebServices\dotNET\dotNETClient.Nant directory (for the .NET client) and the build.xml file in the C:\Interoperability\Samples\Point\WebServices\dotNET\JavaClient directory (for the Java client). For each of the build scripts, locate the username, password, and domain properties toward the top of the build file:

```
<property name="Username" value="Username"/>
<property name="Password" value="Password"/>
<property name="Domain" value="Domain"/>
```

For each of these settings, set the values to the credentials of a user who'll be able to call the Web service—for example, a user in the domain or a user in a group (if authorization was applied in the web.config file). If no domain is present in your environment, you should use the machine name instead for the *Domain* property.

> **Note** The NAnt/Ant build files are valid XML documents. Therefore, if you have a password that includes one of the five XML entity characters (', ", <, >, and &), you must replace the entity character with the corresponding XML entity reference; otherwise, the build script will not parse correctly.

Once applied, save the build scripts and rebuild both the clients to ensure that the proxy files are created successfully.

Testing Unauthorized Clients

Making the modification to the build script will allow the WSDL tools to generate the proxy, but when the clients run, you should still experience what happens when an unauthenticated Web services client tries to connect.

To test this, from a command prompt, navigate to the directory that contains the .NET client (C:\Interoperability\Samples\Point\WebServices\dotNET\dotNETClient.Nant). From there, run the client. An exception should be raised:

```
Unhandled Exception: System.Net.WebException: The request
failed with HTTP status 401: Unauthorized.
```

If you're testing this using Windows XP Professional, you'll see an exception of the same type, although the text will be slightly different. Second, try the same thing by launching the Java client in the C:\Interoperability\Samples\Point\WebServices\dotNET\JavaClient directory. You'll see an exception similar to the following:

```
Exception in thread "main" electric.registry.RegistryException:
could not bind to path:
http://localhost/dotNETWebService/StockService.asmx?WSDL
```

Now that you've secured the .NET Web service, both the .NET client and the Java client fail to authenticate because they are not passing any authentication details to the .NET Web service. This failure appears as a different exception type for each of the two platforms.

We need to apply some settings so that both clients are able to authenticate. But before we do that, let's look at securing a Java Web service.

> **Note** You might have tried accessing the published WSDL of the .NET Web service (*http://localhost/dotNETWebService/StockService.asmx?WSDL*) through Microsoft Internet Explorer instead of via our two clients. If you did this, you no doubt noticed that you were prompted for credentials within the browser.

Enabling Authentication and Authorization for the Java Web Service

You of course can configure similar authentication and authorization requirements for the Java Web service. Because you don't rely on an underlying Web server or administration tool when using GLUE, configuration is performed via a configuration file or in the class that publishes the Web service. The rest of this section outlines the basic principles involved. In practice, however, be sure to consult the GLUE documentation for the complete details.

In GLUE, both authentication and authorization of Web services are performed by selecting one of three realms: *Basic Realm*, *ACLRealm*, or *JAASRealm*. A Basic Realm is simply the place where the username, password, and domain are stored in memory. All information stored in a Basic Realm is lost after the realm is destroyed. An ACLRealm allows authentication information to be stored in an XML file, local to the application itself. This access control list (ACL) XML file takes on the following format:

```
<acl>
    <!--list of user/password/role entries-->
    <user>
        <name>admin</name>
        <password>changeme</password>
        <role>administrator</role>
    </user>
</acl>
```

Notice how the name, password, and an optional role are used with the file to provide credentials at run time. An ACLRealm can hold 0 or more role entries for each user.

The final realm, JAASRealm, allows authentication against any implementation of the Java Authentication and Authorization Service (JAAS) standard login module (*javax.security.auth.LoginModule*). Many JAAS modules are available for enterprise directories, including LDAP and Active Directory. Using a third-party JAAS module, you can enable authentication based on the same directory as the one used in the .NET sample shown earlier.

The easiest realm to configure is the ACLRealm, and it is also the default. The authentication section in the config.xml file declares an ACLRealm named *acl*. This realm specifies an acl.xml file that is loaded from the WEB-INF\security directory of a deployed application:

```
<realm>
    <constructor>
        <class>electric.security.acl.ACLRealm</class>
        <args>
            <name>acl</name>
            <!-- path can be relative to WEB-INF\ or absolute -->
            <path>security\acl.xml</path>
        </args>
    </constructor>
</realm>
```

Once a realm has been decided upon, the process of actually locking down the Web service is configured either through modification of the config.xml file or by using a number of runtime APIs when the Web service is published. This process of locking down the Web service is performed by using what's known as a *guard*.

Within the service descriptor, the guard is configured by setting the *<authenticate/>* element and uses the *<role>* element to specify the roles that are allowed to access the service. (Recall how a number of roles can be configured in the acl.xml file.)

To enable the guard as part of the runtime APIs, a guard property can be set as part of the HTTP context. (As you'll see shortly, enabling the guard in this manner uses the same process as the client in order to set the username and password.)

```
httpContext.setProperty("guard", new Role("administrators"));
```

Now that you've seen how Web services can be configured to prevent unauthorized access, let's examine how to add authentication credentials to both the .NET and Java clients (to allow them to call the Web service again).

Configuring Credentials for the .NET Client

In .NET, you can add manual credentials as part of the Web service call by setting the *Credentials* property in the Web service declaration. For example:

```
FinancialServices.StockService ss
    = new FinancialServices.StockService();
ss.Credentials
    = new System.Net.NetworkCredential("Username", "Password", "Domain");
```

You set the credentials to a new instance of *System.Net.NetworkCredential* and pass the username, password, and domain name that you want to use. (The domain name is optional for accounts that are on the same machine.)

Besides specifying the credentials manually, by configuring integrated authentication (in addition to the basic authentication option within IIS), you have the option of using *default credentials*—that is, instructing the .NET client to use the credentials of the user who is currently logged on to the Windows operating system. After setting integrated authentication within the properties of a virtual directory in IIS, you can specify this with the following code:

```
FinancialServices.StockService ss
    = new FinancialServices.StockService();
ss.Credentials = System.Net.CredentialCache.DefaultCredentials;
```

This can be particularly useful for .NET Windows Forms and console applications because it allows authentication to be passed through, based on the credentials of the logged-on user.

For applications that require interoperability between .NET and Java, however, be aware that using integrated authentication and the default credentials just shown will work only for a .NET client calling a .NET Web service. Because this is the case, it can be worth setting both basic and integrated authentication options within the virtual directory properties in IIS to allow for a potential mix of .NET and Java clients.

Configuring Credentials for the Java Client

Using GLUE, authentication details are passed from the Java client to the .NET Web service via a similar method. First, a new context is created, the credentials are applied, and this context is passed as a parameter to the *bind* method:

```
import electric.util.Context;
...
Context context = new Context();
context.setProperty("authUser", "domain\\username");
context.setProperty("authPassword", "password");

String url
    = "http://localhost/dotNETWebService/StockService.asmx?WSDL";
IStockServiceSoap FinancialServices
    = (IStockServiceSoap)Registry.bind(url,
        IStockServiceSoap.class, context);
```

The domain, username, and password are set within the *authUser* and *authPassword* fields of the context. This context is then passed to the *Registry.bind* method.

This section has shown how HTTP authentication can be applied to a Web service and how .NET and Java clients can use basic authentication in order to access these Web services. For the .NET client, we were also able to use the credentials of the logged-on user when accessing a .NET Web service.

HTTP authentication for Web services is certainly not without its problems. First, the username and password are passed in clear text between the client and the service—meaning that anyone with access to a network analyzer could potentially pick up the credentials on the wire. This can be overcome by using HTTPS instead, but doing so offers only point-to-point security for Web services.

In Chapter 13, "Web Services Interoperability, Part 1: Security," we'll look at how a new specification known as WS-Security can be used to secure a Web service at a message level (as opposed to the transport level).

Web Service Exception Handling

In most applications, exceptions tend to be either application-based (for instance, no cash is left in an ATM machine, so you can't withdraw any money) or infrastructure-based (for instance, someone has accidentally tripped over a power cable in the data center). Exceptions in Web services follow a similar pattern. Exceptions can be thrown as part of the Web service (for example, you cannot place an order because the markets are not open) or if the service cannot be activated (for example, the particular machine cannot connect to the server).

Understanding how these exceptions are trapped and caught in the context of interoperability between .NET and Java is very useful: it can help determine the appropriate course of action within an application, especially when writing a client on one of the two platforms in order to access a Web service published on the other. Using the previous samples, this section formalizes exception handling—showing which exceptions can be thrown, given a number of circumstances on both the Java and .NET platforms.

Web Service URL Not Available

This is an infrastructure-specific exception. It can occur when no part of the Web service is available but when the machine can be accessed (for instance, when trying to view the service with a browser prompts an HTTP 404—Not Found error).

.NET Client to Unavailable Java Web Service

When this exception occurs, the .NET client reports a *System.Net.WebException*:

```
System.Net.WebException - The underlying connection was
closed: Unable to connect to the remote server.
```

The *System.Net.WebException* inherits from *System.Exception*, so all the general *Exception* fields (*Message*, *InnerException*, and so on) are available. *System.Net.WebException* also contains properties for *Response* and *Status*, which will provide additional information about the reason for the exception.

Java Client to Unavailable .NET Web Service

When this exception occurs, the Java client reports an *electric.registry.RegistryException* to indicate that the .NET Web service could not be reached:

```
Exception in thread "main" electric.registry.RegistryException:
could not bind to path:
http://localhost/dotNETWebService/StockService.asmx?WSDL
```

The *electric.registry.RegistryException* defines a *getClause* method that returns the underlying *Exception* that can be used to indicate the reason for failure. In this example of the machine being unavailable, the underlying exception is one of *java.rmi.ConnectionException*.

Web Service Method Not Available

The second type of exception we'll examine is specific to the Web service itself. In this exception, the WSDL contract is available, but the Web service method that is exposed no longer exists. An example of this occurs when the client has been built based upon methods exposed by an old version of a WSDL document. The exposed methods have changed and are no longer available for the client to consume.

.NET Client to Unavailable Java Web Service Method

The .NET client throws a *System.InvalidOperationException* exception, indicating that it was expecting some kind of XML document but that it received something different (probably the HTTP 404—Not Found error page):

```
System.InvalidOperationException: Client found response
content type of '', but expected 'text/xml'.
```

Java Client to Unavailable .NET Web Service Method

The GLUE toolkit throws an exception of type *electric.util.WrappedException*:

```
Exception in thread "main"
electric.util.WrappedException: java.lang.NoSuchMethodException: BuyStocks
```

This exception defines a *getException* method, which returns a more specific exception to trap. In this instance, a *java.lang.NoSuchMethodException* indicates that the method is no longer part of the WSDL contract.

Security-Specific Exceptions

You saw this type of exception come up in the previous section, "Web Services Authentication and Authorization." Assuming that the Web service is functional, you can still receive an exception if the HTTP authentication credentials that you supply are not sufficient to access the service.

Unauthorized .NET Client to Java Web Service

The .NET client throws a *System.Net.WebException*, indicating that the status is Access Denied:

```
System.Net.WebException: The request failed with HTTP
status 401: Unauthorized.
```

Unauthorized Java Client to .NET Web Service

For the Java client, a *RegistryException* is thrown, indicating that the client could not bind to the service:

```
Exception in thread "main" electric.registry.RegistryException:
could not bind to path:
http://localhost/dotNETWebService/StockService.asmx?WSDL
```

Application-Specific Exceptions

The final type of exception we'll discuss is an application-specific exception that has been thrown as part of the Web service code. Application-specific exceptions differ from infrastructure-based exceptions in that they tie in more tightly to the SOAP specification. As you've seen with data types so far in the book, exceptions that mean something in .NET don't necessarily map to exceptions that occur in Java. (After all, an exception on either platform is still a data type, so the same rules apply.) A *StockNotFoundException* thrown from a .NET Web service doesn't mean anything to a Java client. Even if you could map exceptions between the two platforms, it would be an exhaustive process.

How SOAP Defines Exceptions

To help overcome this (and to help with non-.NET and non-Java Web service consumers), SOAP defines an element known as a *SOAP Fault*. This fault element defines four subelements:

- ***faultcode*** A code that indicates the type of the fault.

- ***faultstring*** Some human-readable description of the fault.
- ***faultactor*** Because SOAP messages can be carried among a number of nodes in a delivery path, this is an optional field to specify where the fault occurred.
- ***detail*** An XML document describing the detail of the fault.

This SOAP Fault element maps to each platform in one of the two ways discussed next.

Both the .NET Framework and GLUE map user-thrown exceptions to SOAP exceptions as described in the following sections.

.NET Client Connecting to a Java Web Service Method that Throws an Exception

For the .NET client, an application exception is caught as a *System.Web.Services.Protocols.SoapException*:

```
System.Web.Services.Protocols.SoapException: Sorry, Stock Service
is Unavailable
```

The *SoapException* class is the exception that implements the details of the SOAP Fault. From properties within *SOAPException*, you can investigate the *Message*, *Code*, *Actor*, and *Detail* from the SOAP Fault specification. Likewise, if you know that the code will throw such an exception, you might want to throw a custom exception that implements *SOAPException* in order to prepopulate these details.

This exception can actually be demonstrated with one of the samples shown earlier. The sample code that exposed an EJB by using Web services made a simulated call to find a stock based on the ticker that was passed. If the stock ticker was not found, the method on the Session Bean threw a *StockNotFoundException*, a custom exception that was part of the sample.

This exception can be caught in .NET as a *SoapException*. If you look back at the sample code for the .NET client that calls this exposed EJB (in the C:\Interoperability\Samples\Point\WebServices\JavaEJB\dotNETClient directory), this exception is shown with the following *try/catch* block:

```
try
{
    FinancialServices.StockService ss =
        new FinancialServices.StockService();
    Console.WriteLine("\nYour sale "
        +((ss.sellStocks("CONT",100))? "completed" : "failed"));
}
catch(SoapException se)
```

```
{
    Console.WriteLine(se.Detail.InnerText);
}
```

The detail for the exception (part of the SOAP Fault definition) is returned as an XML element and can be examined as shown in the *catch* block of the code. To test this, revisit the EJB sample at the start of this chapter and change the stock ticker in the client from "CONT" to a ticker that will not be recognized by the EJB (for example, "COHO").

```
Stock was not found
    at com.microsoft.samples.ejb.StockSessionBean.sellStocks
    (Unknown Source)
    at java.lang.reflect.Method.invoke(Native Method)
    (…rest of the exception follows…)
```

This shows that the message thrown by the original exception ("Stock was not found") is passed as part of the *SoapException* that's caught on the client. Although application-specific exception types are not communicated by Web services, following this practice of wrapping Web service invocations in a *try/catch* block can prove a useful way to trap these types of exceptions and return a suitable result to the end user.

Java Client Connecting to a .NET Web Service Method that Throws an Exception

For the Java client, *electric.util.WrappedException* is caught for each application-specific exception:

```
Exception in thread "main" electric.util.WrappedException:
SOAPException( Server: System.Web.Services.Protocols.SoapException:
Server was unable to process request. ---> System.Exception:
Sorry, Stock Service is Unavailable
```

The *WrappedException* contains an exception of type *electric.soap.SOAPException*. This *SOAPException* contains methods (*getSOAPCode*, *getSOAPActor*, and *getSOAPDetail*) that can be used to further interrogate the SOAP-specific details of the exception, similar to the way the previous .NET exception type worked.

Exception Conclusion

Overall, these examples give a basic insight into how exceptions can be handled and caught when using Web services that bridge .NET and J2EE. As a general recommendation, I suggest that anyone writing a client to consume a Web service be aware of the types of exceptions that can be thrown (both infrastructure and application) and know how to deal with them to give the best overall experience and information to the user.

Using UDDI

As described in Chapter 5, Universal Description, Discovery, and Integration (UDDI) is an accepted industry specification for publishing and locating Web services. Using UDDI, organizations can publish business contact information, services, and interfaces through a common directory—which can either be located in a public UDDI directory or internally hosted via an intranet.

In simple terms, UDDI can be thought of as a phone directory or Domain Name System (DNS) for Web services. As you've seen in the examples in this chapter, to call a Web service, the client relies on knowing a particular URL. For example:

http://server/dotNETWebService/StockService.asmx

One problem with this is the URL doesn't naturally describe the service or reveal anything about the business that's hosting the service. Judging from the name of this example, you can tell that it might have something to do with stocks, but you can't gather much additional information. For instance, what company offers this service? Is this service hosted in a location near you? Another problem with URLs is their transient nature. A URL endpoint can change from month to month. You need a way to uniquely identify services, a way that is independent of the nonstatic and nondeterministic URL.

The UDDI directory allows these URLs (known in the directory as *access points*) to be associated with services (which provide additional information about the functionality offered) and businesses themselves. The business information can hold a point of contact, information about the type of business, and categorization to allow flexibility for searches.

Interoperability Benefits of Using UDDI

UDDI expands the possibilities when developing solutions that have a requirement to interoperate by giving .NET or Java clients (or any client that supports Web services) the ability to perform dynamic lookups for available services—some of which can be hosted on the same platform as the client.

For interoperability between .NET and J2EE, using UDDI offers the following benefits:

- **Common Web service publication** Using UDDI gives a universal view of Web services regardless of whether they were created or hosted using .NET, Java, or any other platform or language.

- **Dynamic configuration** The UDDI registry can be accessed by developers and administrators who want to search and publish new Web services. It can also be accessed programmatically in client applications. These client applications, which can be written in either .NET or Java, can use UDDI to dynamically configure a Web service proxy without relying on a hard-coded URL. This can also include the dynamic rebinding of URLs. If multiple access points for a service exist and the chosen access point fails to respond, the client can requery UDDI to find another compatible service instance from the same provider.
- **Web service reuse** Within an organization that has many development units, it's possible to create multiple Web services that perform the same function. Using UDDI allows developers to browse through a list of available Web services—which can be .NET or Java based—in order to enable reuse and prevent the duplication of a service.
- **Location-specific Web services** Using categories in UDDI, a location can be assigned to an individual Web service. This Web service can then be replicated throughout the organization, but the location category can help local clients find the closest version of the Web service in order to aid in performance.

UDDI Registries

The UDDI directory is referred to as a *registry*. Currently, four nodes make up a public registry named the UDDI Business Registry (UBR). For more details, see *http://www.uddi.org/find.html*. Public UDDI entries are replicated between each of these four nodes.

This registry allows any developer, team, or organization to publish location information for services that are publicly available. In addition, Microsoft, IBM, and SAP host a test version of the registry in order to allow developers to test registration and publication of services before moving into production.

These registries work well for organizations that want to write and publish Web services that will be available publicly, but UDDI also offers a lot of advantages for internal use. Configuring a UDDI registry internally can be a great idea because it creates a single point of administration for Web services within a company. UDDI running internally can provide many benefits to applications that rely on Web services today.

A number of product offerings are available to enable you to run an internal UDDI registry:

- **Microsoft** UDDI is available as a core service within Microsoft Windows Server 2003.

- **IBM** IBM has a UDDI registry as part of its WebSphere product offering, based on DB2.
- **The Mind Electric (TME)** GLUE from The Mind Electric is packaged with a UDDI server.

Many other vendors have implementations of UDDI as well. When choosing a vendor, it's a good idea to always ensure that the offering is compliant with the latest version of UDDI and that the vendor participates in the UDDI specification process and the UBR (because of its extensive interoperability test suites). The version of UDDI that we'll discuss here is v2.0.

To demonstrate the samples presented in this book, I'll use UDDI Services in Windows Server 2003. However, the sample code will work perfectly well with any UDDI v2.0–compliant registry.

Using UDDI Services in Windows Server 2003

As mentioned, UDDI is a core service in Windows 2003. As with other application server–specific services, UDDI is installed through the Add/Remove Programs component of the Windows Control Panel. To install UDDI Services for Windows Server 2003, from the Windows control panel, select Add/Remove Windows Components from the Add/Remove Components. Within that list, check the UDDI Services box, as shown in Figure 6-7.

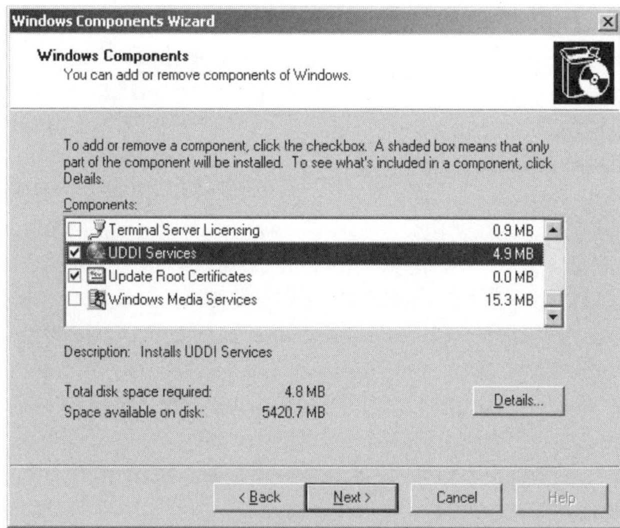

Figure 6-7 Selecting UDDI Services to install on Windows Server 2003.

The UDDI registry can use an instance of either Microsoft SQL Server 2000 Desktop Engine (MSDE) or Microsoft SQL Server 2000 installed on the same machine. Use the next page of the wizard to configure this for your own environment. For production environments, where performance is key, I recommend using SQL Server to take advantage of functionality that's shipped with the product. For small-scale usage and running the samples in this chapter, however, MSDE will work fine.

After selecting the database location, follow the wizard to the next step, which asks whether SSL is required for publishing and administration of the site. Again, for production implementations of UDDI, the recommended choice is to require SSL because without it, user credentials will be passed across the network in clear text. For the purpose of these samples, however, you do not need SSL. Figure 6-8 shows this selection of SSL encryption.

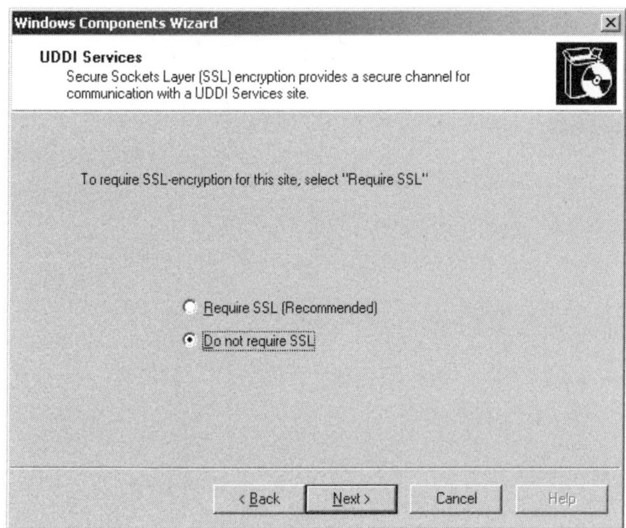

Figure 6-8 Selecting SSL encryption for the UDDI Services site.

Proceed through the wizard. In the next step, the wizard prompts for a location to install the database files, the default of which is C:\Inetpub\uddi\data. Accept this default.

In the next step of the wizard, use the Network Service account to configure the UDDI Service, unless there's a preference to use another account to start the service.

The penultimate step of the wizard is to provide a site name for the UDDI site, as shown in Figure 6-9. This name won't be used programmatically in these samples; instead, it's used as a friendly name for the site.

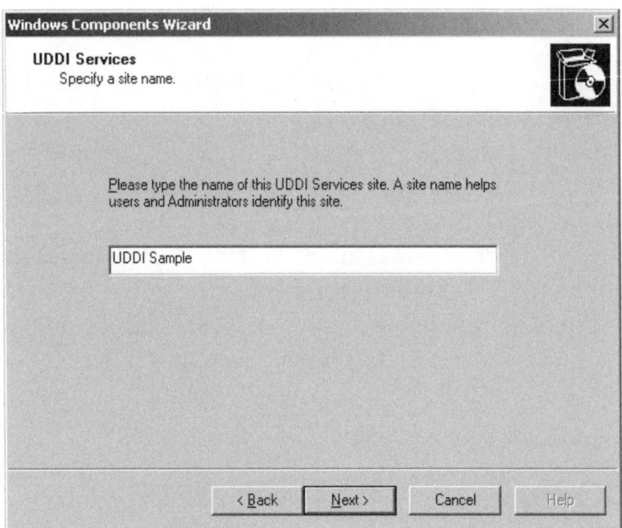

Figure 6-9 Specifying a site name for the UDDI Services site.

The final step of the wizard is to select whether the UDDI Server will use self-registration to document the available interfaces. This is required for at least one of the servers in a multi-instance UDDI site. For this sample, ensure that the check box is checked, as shown in Figure 6-10, and continue.

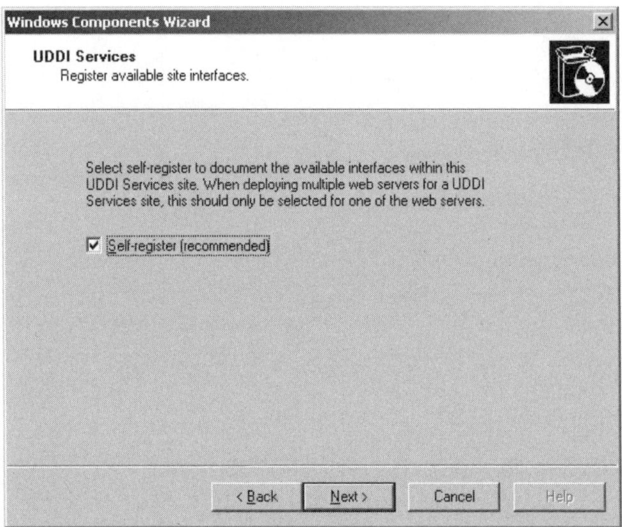

Figure 6-10 Setting self-registration for UDDI Services.

The wizard will now complete, and all required files will be installed. After this, the UDDI Services for the Windows Server 2003 installation is complete.

Microsoft UDDI SDK

To complement the UDDI Services for Windows Server 2003, a UDDI SDK is available. This SDK contains the required .NET libraries to allow you to develop clients that can make UDDI-specific calls. It's available as part of the Platform SDK (now known as the Microsoft Windows Software Development Kit) and can be downloaded from *http://www.microsoft.com/msdownload/platformsdk/sdkupdate/default.htm*.

To download the SDK on Windows Server 2003, be sure to set your security settings correctly within Internet Explorer. The SDK is updated using an ActiveX control, which must be downloaded. As a result, Internet Explorer must be configured to allow the download of ActiveX controls. You might also need to disable the Internet Explorer enhanced security configuration for the purpose of the download. Once the SDK has been installed, you can revert the browser to a more secure setting.

When installing the SDK, I recommend selecting the Core SDK. For the Core SDK option, ensure that the Build Environment is selected. This will install components to C:\Program Files\Microsoft SDK. After installation has completed, you need to register the UDDI components by running C:\Program Files\Microsoft SDK\Bin\UddiSdkRegister.exe.

One of the tools included with the SDK is the UDDI Publish Wizard. This wizard can be used to publish any Web service (based on either .NET or Java) to any UDDI v2.0–compliant registry.

After UDDI Services for Windows Server 2003 has been installed, you can use the publishing wizard to publish this chapter's previous samples in the registry. To perform this after the SDK has been installed and registered, start the wizard by selecting UDDI Publish Wizard from the Microsoft Visual Studio .NET 2003 Tools program menu or by running C:\Program Files\Microsoft SDK\Bin\UddiPublishWizard.exe. The wizard will be launched, as shown in Figure 6-11.

To publish the Web service, we'll need to provide information about the location of the UDDI registry, a name, a description, an access point, and WSDL for the service. Click the Next button to proceed.

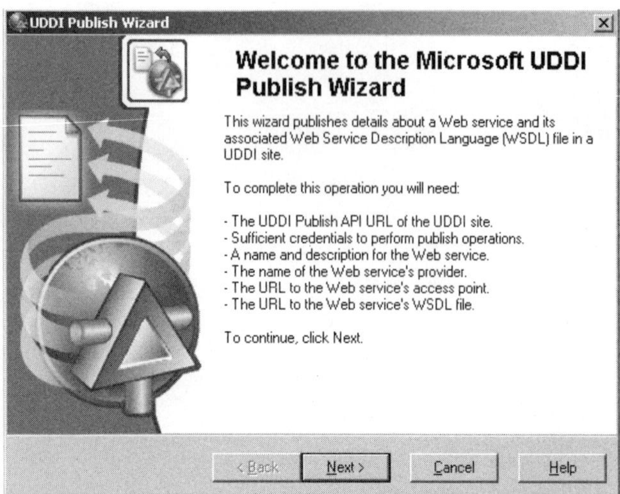

Figure 6-11 The Microsoft UDDI Publish Wizard.

The publishing wizard needs to communicate with the UDDI server to publish the required services. To authenticate against the UDDI server, the wizard offers two options: Windows Integrated Authentication and UDDI Authentication.

If you're using UDDI Services for Windows Server 2003, which we set up in the last section, you can use Windows Integrated Authentication. To run this sample with another UDDI server, you will need to select UDDI authentication and present the required credentials. Once this is done, click the Next button to proceed.

The wizard now prompts for the location of the UDDI registry that you want to publish the service to, as shown in Figure 6-12. Two options are presented: you can either use a UDDI registry that's exposed via Active Directory or specify the URL of the UDDI registry. To locate the UDDI registry installed on the same machine, use the following URL: *http://localhost/uddi/publish.asmx*.

If you're using UDDI Services for Windows Server 2003 on a different server, simply replace *localhost* with the name of the machine that you're using. If you're using a different implementation of a UDDI registry, consult the documentation for the publishing URL you should use.

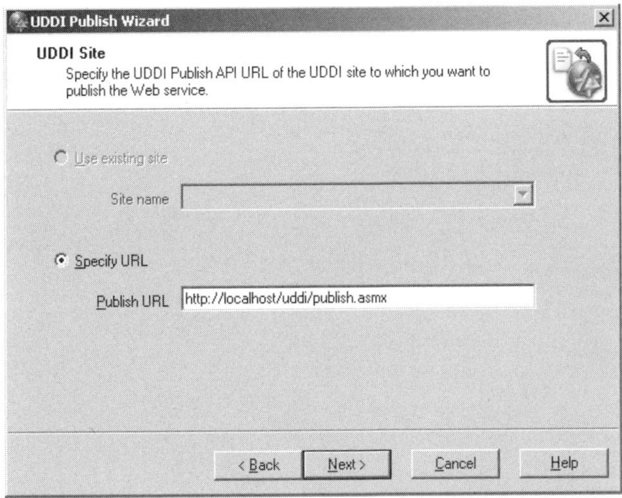

Figure 6-12 Specifying a publishing URL for the UDDI site.

The next stage of the wizard is to either select or create a new provider (or business) to publish the Web service under. Because this is a new installation of UDDI, there aren't any existing providers, so we'll create our own. Given that we've been dealing with fictitious stock-trading Web services in this chapter, the provider will have the following characteristics:

- **Provider name Woodgrove Bank**
- **Provider description We supply the best stock-trading Web services on the planet!**

Figure 6-13 shows this provider name and description. You of course are free to choose your own business name and description if you don't care for these.

> **Tip** The Categorize button, shown in Figure 6-13, appears a number of times throughout the wizard and allows categories to be assigned to providers and services. For implementations of UDDI Services for Windows Server 2003, this button can be used to label the provider in order to provide faster and easier search capabilities.
>
> For example, you might want to use the Categorize button to assign a location category. Suppose that you want to replicate a number of Web services throughout your organization—maybe for each remote office. In this example, based on the location category, UDDI can be used to return the access point for a Web service that's local to the calling client.

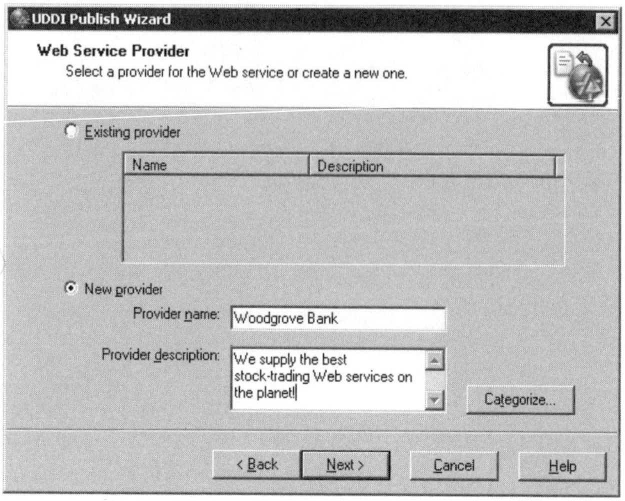

Figure 6-13 Setting the name for the new provider, Woodgrove Bank.

Once you've entered the provider name and description, click the Next button. It's now time to enter details for the Web service itself. For this example, we'll publish the Web services already presented in this chapter. In the UDDI registry, we'll enter two Web services—the service to buy stocks, which is hosted on the .NET Framework, and the service to sell stocks, which is hosted on the Java platform.

We'll enter the information for the .NET Web service first, as shown in Figure 6-14.

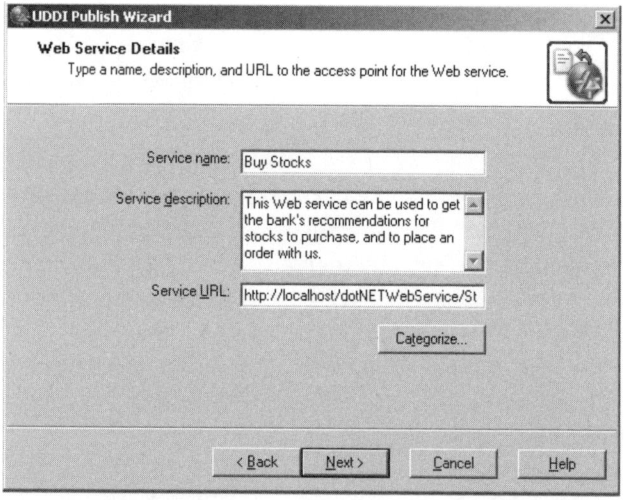

Figure 6-14 Creating a new service to purchase stocks.

Enter the following information:

- **Service name Buy Stocks**
- **Service description This Web service can be used to get the bank's recommendations for stocks to purchase and to place an order with us.**
- **Service URL http://localhost/dotNETWebService/StockService.asmx**

Again, alternate names and descriptions can be chosen. The service URL is the URL of the .NET Web service that was created in Chapter 5 and is the one we've been working with throughout this chapter. Notice how this URL (also known as the *access point*) is indeed the point where the service is accessed and is not the published WSDL document. Ideally, you should replace *localhost* with the name of the machine that offers the Web service.

Click the Next button to continue through the wizard. The next stage, shown in Figure 6-15, is where you supply the interface definition—the location and description of the WSDL document.

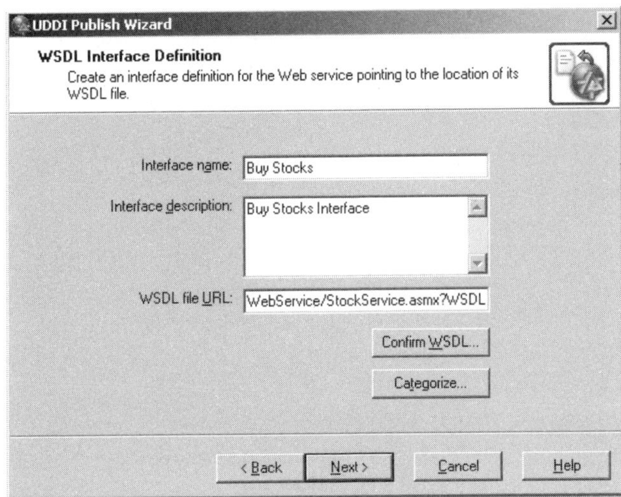

Figure 6-15 Setting the interface description and WSDL file URL.

For this sample, use the following details:

- **Interface name Buy Stocks**
- **Interface description Buy Stocks Interface**
- **WSDL file URL http://localhost/dotNETWebService/StockService.asmx?WSDL**

Notice the Confirm WSDL button in the wizard. This will launch the WSDL file in a separate Internet Explorer window in order to confirm that this is the correct location.

Click the Next button to continue. You've now supplied enough information to the wizard to publish the Web service. This information is summarized in the final dialog box. After reviewing this information, click the Publish button. If publishing is successful, the wizard will complete.

You've completed the Web service that allows you to buy stocks published in the UDDI registry. Before running the sample code, rerun the publishing wizard, but this time supply the details for the Sell Stocks Web service, which was hosted using GLUE.

As you run through the wizard for a second time, you'll notice that many of the fields and setting are now completed, and when it comes to selecting a provider, the one you entered in the previous step—Woodgrove Bank—should be available for selection, as Figure 6-16 shows.

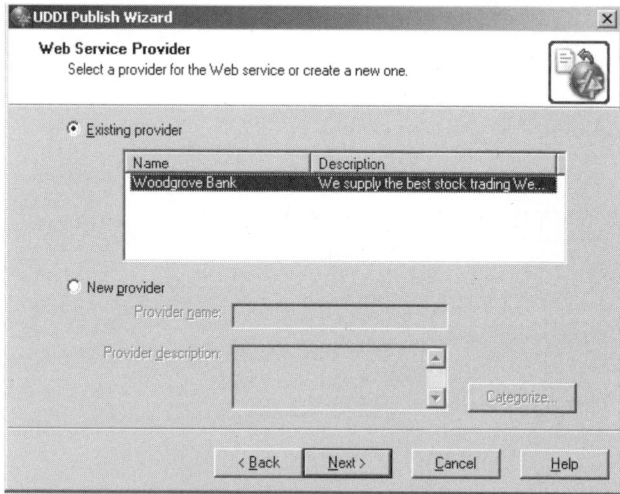

Figure 6-16 Selecting the existing provider.

For the service to work with the previous sample in Java, use the settings shown in the following list and Figure 6-17:

- **Service name Sell Stocks**
- **Service description This Web service can be used to get the bank's recommendations for stocks to get rid of and to place an order with us.**
- **Service URL http://localhost:8004/JavaWebService/StockService**

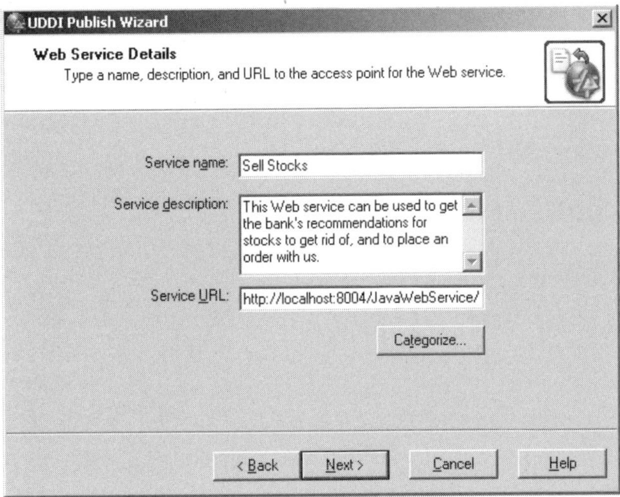

Figure 6-17 Entering the Web service details for the Sell Stocks service.

For the interface definition, use the setting shown in the following list and Figure 6-18:

- **Interface name Sell Stocks**
- **Interface description Sell Stocks Interface**
- **WSDL file URL http://localhost:8004/JavaWebService/StockService.wsdl**

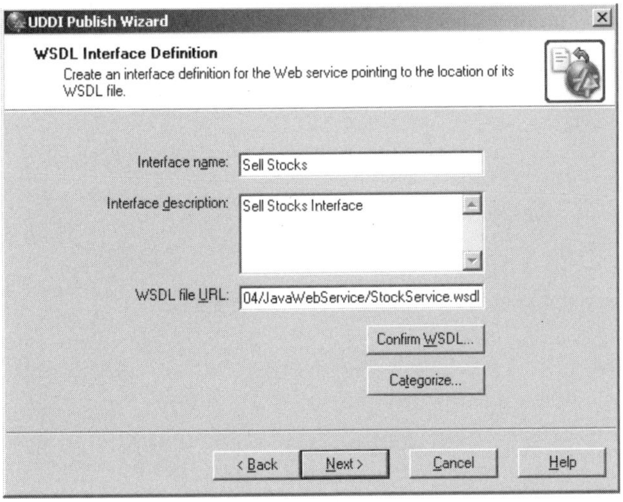

Figure 6-18 Interface definition for the Sell Stocks service.

Once this is complete, the two Web services will be published in the UDDI registry.

Next let's look at how this works under the covers. After that, we'll see how to create clients in both .NET and Java to use UDDI to get a reference to the published services.

Exploring the UDDI Registry

You've now seen how the UDDI Publish Wizard can be used to publish a Web service into the UDDI registry. This interface offers a great way to publish Web services, but it's also important to know what's being created under the covers. When it comes to using the SDK to program against the UDDI registry, you should know how providers and services are structured.

In addition to the wizard, UDDI Services has its own Web-based interface—for both publishing and exploring the directory. This interface can be accessed by browsing to *http://localhost/uddi* (you can replace *localhost* with the machine name of your UDDI server), as shown in Figure 6-19.

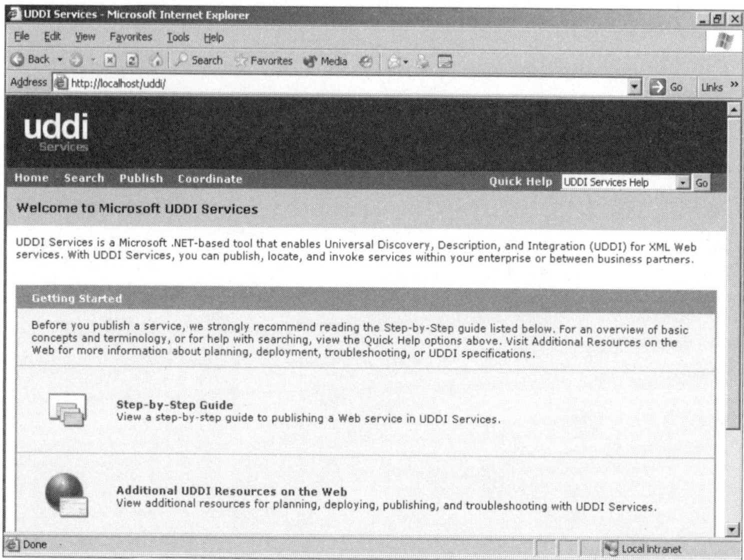

Figure 6-19 Using the Web user interface for UDDI Services.

After running the UDDI Publish Wizard, you can use this interface to discover exactly what has been created. To locate your provider, click on the Search option at the top of the page, and in the screen that follows, select the Providers tab. As shown in Figure 6-20, enter the name of the provider that you want to locate (in this case, **Woodgrove**).

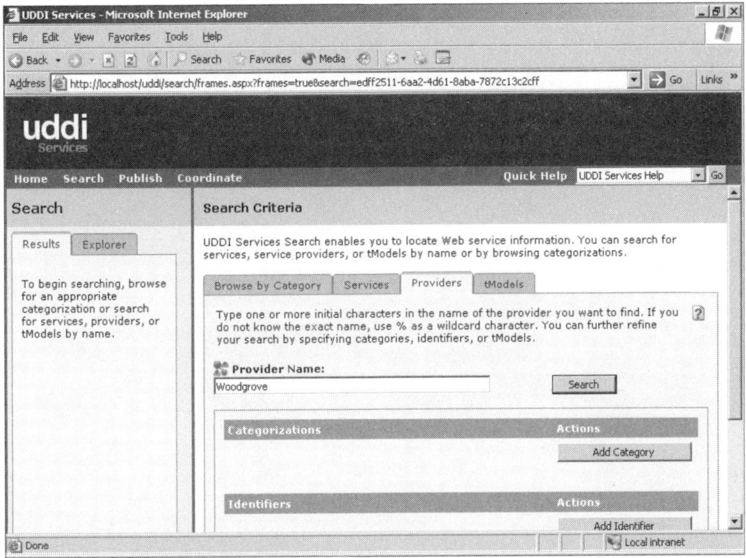

Figure 6-20 Entering the provider name for searches.

Enter all or part of the provider name, as was created using the publishing wizard. Click the Search button to locate that provider. The results from the search are displayed in the left-hand panel. As you can see in Figure 6-21, we've managed to locate our provider, Woodgrove Bank.

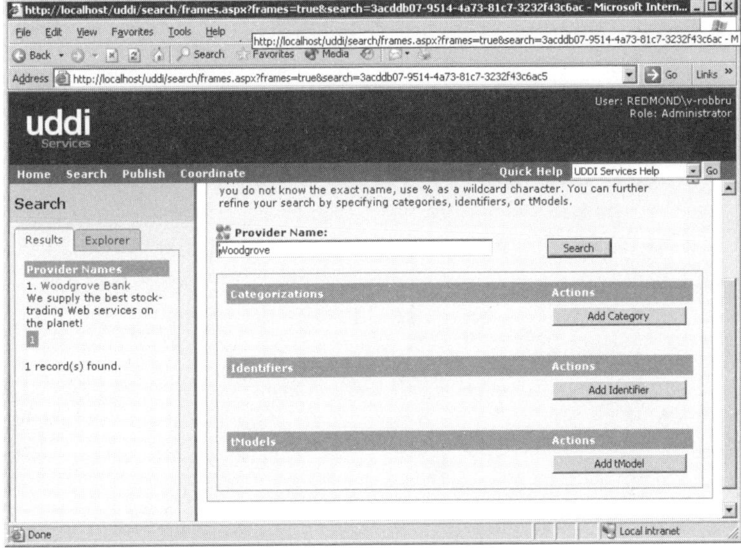

Figure 6-21 Search results from UDDI Services.

Click the provider name in the search window. This will display the root of the provider and list all the services that the provider offers.

Figure 6-22 shows how once the Woodgrove Bank provider is selected, you can investigate the details associated with the business. As the owner of the service, you can also modify any of the information (such as name, description, categories, and so on).

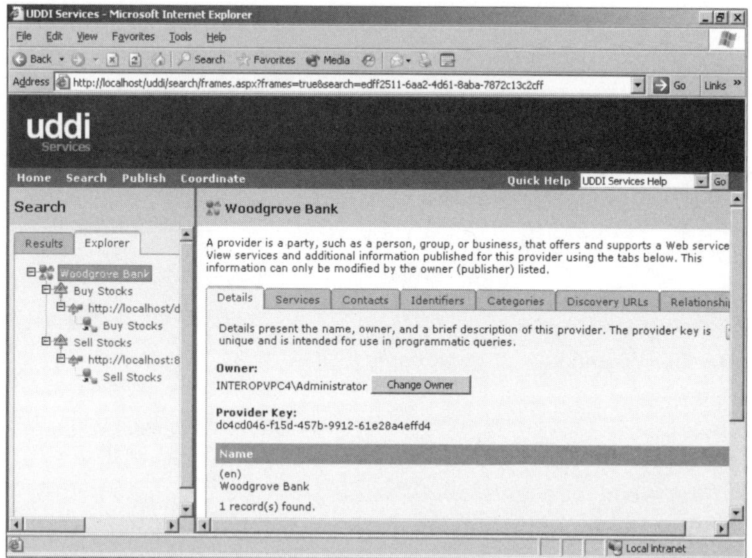

Figure 6-22 Browsing services available from a provider.

Within the explorer tree, located underneath the Woodgrove Bank provider, are our two services: Buy Stocks and Sell Stocks. Listed underneath the services are the access point and interface information required for each, as shown in Figure 6-23. The URL that's displayed directly underneath the service is known as a *binding*. This binding contains the access point (the URL that you must call to invoke the Web service) and the interface information.

The binding represents the connection between the access point (the URL) and the interface (the WSDL file that describes the service). Figure 6-24 shows this information.

You might be wondering why the service doesn't just list the access point and the WSDL as one piece of information. This information is listed separately to allow multiple instances of the same service to be deployed by using the same interface definition. For example, if you want to offer the Buy Stocks and Sell Stocks services at multiple locations or across a number of servers in a group, you can create additional services but still use the same interface for each.

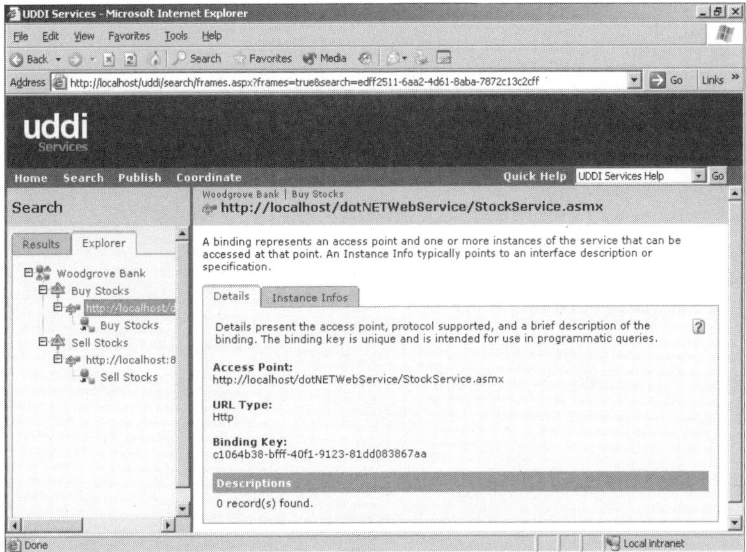

Figure 6-23 Navigating to the binding of a provider.

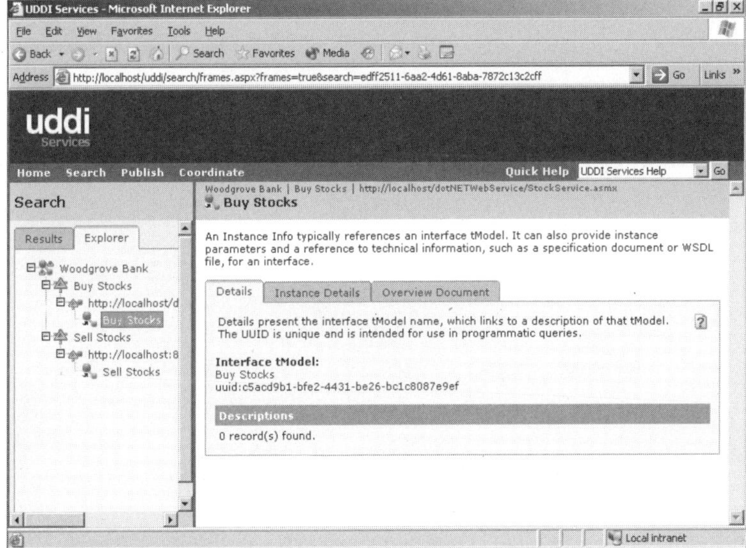

Figure 6-24 Viewing details of the service.

Finally, let's look at the interface. In UDDI terminology, this interface is also known as the *tModel* (Technical Model). You see this term used when you create your clients.

You might also notice how every object within the registry has a unique ID (UUID). For identification purposes, tModels are prefixed with the text *uuid* before the UUID. For example, the tModel in Figure 6-24 has a UUID of uuid:c5acd9b1-bfe2-4431-be26-bc1c8087e9ef. The one that's created in your directory will have a different identifier. This is a unique way of referencing any object within the registry and can be used by clients to quickly access exact parts of the registry without having to perform a full search.

Consuming by Using a .NET Client

By now you have a good understanding of how to publish to a UDDI registry and use the Web user interface that comes with UDDI Services for Windows Server 2003 to search and edit information within the UDDI registry.

Now let's look at how to build a .NET client to perform a search against the registry and invoke a Web service based on the results returned. The sample located in the C:\Interoperability\Samples\Point\WebServices\UDDI\dotNET directory contains a simple client that accesses the registry that we configured earlier. The client code demonstrates some of the UDDI SDK for .NET calls that are used to access the information.

First, the client imports the required namespaces for the UDDI SDK:

```
using Microsoft.Uddi;
using Microsoft.Uddi.Businesses;
using Microsoft.Uddi.Services;
```

These namespaces are provided as part of the Microsoft.Uddi.DLL file that is included with the SDK installation. After the imports, the first action for the client is to create a new *UDDIConnection*:

```
UddiConnection uc = new UddiConnection(_uddiUrl);
```

The URL supplied is the inquiry URL of the registry. In this case, the URL is *http://localhost/uddi/inquire.asmx*. (Notice how this inquiry URL is a Web service; we'll cover this shortly.)

The next step is to run a search against the directory for providers that match by name:

```
FindBusiness fbs = new FindBusiness(_provider);
BusinessList allBusinesses = fbs.Send(uc);
BusinessInfo myProvider = allBusinesses.BusinessInfos[0];
```

The search is conducted by using the *FindBusiness* class, with the name of the provider (Woodgrove Bank) passed in the constructor. The *Send* method is used to execute the search, and the result is a list of businesses that match (similar to the list of providers yielded when we performed the same process via the administration interface). From this list of businesses, we extract the information (as a *BusinessInfo* type) for the first business returned.

The *BusinessInfo* type contains a business key. This is the unique identifier for this particular business and is used for additional searches because it provides an unambiguous way of representing the business:

```
FindService fs = new FindService();
fs.BusinessKey = myProvider.BusinessKey;
ServiceList ProviderServices = fs.Send(uc);
```

When you next search for services offered by this business, you provide the business key just shown. This returns a list of services (as a *ServiceList*), which you can then iterate through. To complete the sample, display the information for each of the services:

```
for (int f=0; f<ProviderServices.ServiceInfos.Count; f++)
{
    Console.WriteLine("\nService found:  "
        +ProviderServices.ServiceInfos[f].Names[0].Text);

    // Get the service detail in order to get the access point
    GetServiceDetail gsd = new GetServiceDetail(
        ProviderServices.ServiceInfos[f].ServiceKey);
    ServiceDetail sd = gsd.Send(uc);

    // list the default access point and interface.
    // Assuming that a single one exists for each.
    Console.WriteLine("Access point:  "+sd.BusinessServices[0].
        BindingTemplates[0].AccessPoint.Text);

    String tModelKey = sd.BusinessServices[0].BindingTemplates[0].
        TModelInstanceInfos[0].TModelKey;

    GetTModelDetail gtm = new GetTModelDetail(tModelKey);
    TModelDetail tmd = gtm.Send(uc);
    TModel tModel = tmd.TModels[0];

    Console.WriteLine("Interface: "+tModel.OverviewDoc.OverviewUrl);

}
```

Notice that this code assumes a single access point and a single overview document (which contains the interface WSDL). This is obviously based on the entries defined earlier in the UDDI registry and is simplified to demonstrate the API. For a true browser experience, you could expand the registry tree to list all the available access points and tModels for each service that was found.

Compile the code. Because the sample depends on the UDDI SDK, a reference to the DLL is used. This can be found in the C:\Interoperability\Samples\

Config\uddi.nant.properties file. The default setting for this file assumes that the Platform SDK is installed in C:\Program Files\Microsoft SDK\Bin. If this isn't the case for your machine, you should edit as appropriate.

> **Note** The UDDI components will work only with version 1.1 of the .NET Framework. If you receive an exception when running the client indicating that this could be a problem, ensure that the system *PATH* includes an entry to version 1.1 of the .NET Framework (C:\Windows\Microsoft.NET\Framework\v1.1.4322) rather than an entry for the 1.0 release (C:\Windows\Microsoft.NET\Framework\v1.1.3705).

If you now run this client code, you should get the following result:

```
Creating a new connection to the UDDI service at:  http://localhost/uddi/
inquire.asmx

Trying to find Woodgrove Bank...
Finding services offered by Woodgrove Bank...
2 services were found

Service found:  Buy Stocks
Access point:  http://localhost/dotNETWebService/StockService.asmx
Interface:  http://localhost/dotNETWebService/StockService.asmx?WSDL

Service found:  Sell Stocks
Access point:  http://localhost:8004/JavaWebService/StockService
Interface:  http://localhost:8004/JavaWebService/StockService.wsdl
```

As this code shows, the client sample has created a new connection to the UDDI registry and performed a search on the businesses within the registry based on the URL supplied. The sample then lists the two services that are published, with their corresponding access points and interface URLs.

Consuming by Using a Java Client

Using the GLUE toolkit, you can perform exactly the same operation in Java. Located in the C:\Interoperability\Samples\Point\WebServices\UDDI\Java directory is the sample code that does this.

The imports required for the UDDI client are as follows:

```
import electric.util.Context;
import electric.uddi.*;
import electric.uddi.client.*;
```

The UDDI-specific classes are located in the *electric.uddi* and *electric.uddi.client* packages. In this example, *electric.util.Context* is used to set the credentials for the UDDI server:

```
Context context = new Context();
context.setProperty("authUser","DOMAIN\\Username");
context.setProperty("authPassword","password");

UDDIClient uc = new
    UDDIClient("http://localhost/uddi/inquire.asmx",context);
```

A new context is created to hold the username and password. This context uses exactly the same calls that were shown in the "Web Services Authentication and Authorization" section, where we looked at authentication from the Java client. Before compiling the client, edit the Client.java file and replace the authentication details with suitable credentials for your own machine. If you're not running within a domain, use the machine name instead.

> **Tip** You might be wondering why the Java client requires credentials while the .NET client did not. Implicitly, the UDDI SDK for .NET uses the default credentials of the locally logged-on user. This is the same as using the *DefaultCredentials* API you saw earlier in the "Web Services Authentication and Authorization" section of this chapter. This, of course, can be overridden by a username and password, if required.

Looking back at our Java client, the UDDI client is created, with the URL of the UDDI inquiry Web service:

```
FindBusinesses fb = new FindBusinesses();
fb.setNames(new Name[]{new Name(_provider)});
BusinessInfos allBusinesses = uc.findBusinesses(fb);
BusinessInfo myProvider = allBusinesses.list[0];
```

To find businesses (providers), the *FindBusinesses* class is used. Here, you set the search criteria as the name of the provider that you're looking for and instruct the UDDI client to find any matching records. Select the first record from the results that are returned (because you have only a single provider in your test registry), which is of type *BusinessInfo*:

```
FindServices fs = new FindServices();
fs.setBusinessKey(myProvider.getBusinessKey());
ServiceInfos providerServices = uc.findServices(fs);
```

The *BusinessInfo* type is the object that you'll derive the business key from as you did with the .NET version of the code. The business key is then used to perform a second search for all matching services that belong to that business. GLUE returns this information as an array of *ServiceInfos*:

```
for (int f=0; f<providerServices.list.length; f++)
{
    System.out.println("\nService Found: "
        +providerServices.list[f].getName());

    Service service
        = uc.getService(providerServices.list[f].getServiceKey());

    System.out.println("Access point:  "
        +service.getBindings()[0].getAccessPoint().getAddress());

    String tModelKey =service.getBindings()[0].
        getTModelInstances()[0].getTModelKey();
    TModel tModel=uc.getTModel(tModelKey);
    System.out.println("Interface: "
        +tModel.getOverview().getOverviewURL());
}
```

The final step is to iterate through the *ServiceInfos* that were returned and make a final call via the client to retrieve the service information for each *ServiceInfo*. (This is done by using the *getService* method to return a service.) From the service, you can drill down into both the default access point and the tModel instances to get both the endpoint for the service and the WSDL location itself.

Compiling and running this code should produce the following output:

```
Trying to find Woodgrove Bank...
Finding services offered by Woodgrove Bank...
2 services were found...

Service Found: Buy Stocks
Access point:  http://localhost/dotNETWebService/StockService.asmx
Interface:  http://localhost/dotNETWebService/StockService.asmx?WSDL

Service Found: Sell Stocks
Access point:  http://localhost:8004/JavaWebService/StockService
Interface:  http://localhost:8004/JavaWebService/StockService.wsdl
```

The UDDI Clients—Under the Covers

While explaining how the samples worked, I mentioned that under the covers, the UDDI client was simply a Web service itself. You saw how the following piece of code from the .NET sample was used to find all businesses that matched a particular search string:

```
FindBusiness fbs = new FindBusiness(_provider);
BusinessList allBusinesses = fbs.Send(uc);
BusinessInfo myProvider = allBusinesses.BusinessInfos[0];
```

Under the covers, the *fbs.Send* method is actually constructing a SOAP request to pass to the UDDI registry. If you were to investigate this request—you can call *fbs.ToString* to do so—you'd see something similar to the following:

```
<?xml version="1.0" encoding="utf-8"?>
<find_business
    xmlns:xsd=http://www.w3.org/2001/XMLSchema
    xmlns:xsi="http://www.w3.org/2001/XMLSchema-instance"
    generic="2.0" maxRows="1000" xmlns="urn:uddi-org:api_v2">
    <name>Woodgrove Bank</name>
</find_business>
```

What we have here is the body of a SOAP request for *find_business*, a standard of version 2.0 of the UDDI specification that's used to instruct the UDDI server to carry out the search. The same is also true for messages returned from the UDDI server to the client. The representation for the reply in this case might look like this:

```
<?xml version="1.0" encoding="utf-8"?>
<businessList
    xmlns:xsd="http://www.w3.org/2001/XMLSchema"
    xmlns:xsi="http://www.w3.org/2001/XMLSchema-instance"
    generic="2.0" operator="UDDI Sample"
    truncated="false" xmlns="urn:uddi-org:api_v2">
    <businessInfos>
        <businessInfo
            businessKey="a35de1c2-5f5e-42f5-bcd3-6ff0bcfe46ff">
            <name xml:lang="en">Woodgrove Bank</name>
            <description xml:lang="en">
                We supply the best stock trading Web Services
                on the planet!
            </description>
            <serviceInfos>
...
            </serviceInfos>
        </businessInfo>
    </businessInfos>
</businessList>
```

Here you can see the message returned. (You can also try this by using *allBusinesses.ToString* method from the previous example.) Notice how the *business-*

Infos element contains the description of the provider and the *serviceInfo* elements that have the service keys that will be used to look up further information.

With the layer of abstraction that both the UDDI SDK for .NET and the GLUE UDDI client libraries offer, it's rare to have to deal with the SOAP requests themselves, unless you're either replacing or extending some of the implementation. On the other hand, an appreciation of the structure of the messages that travel back and forth between a UDDI client and server is always extremely useful when troubleshooting problems.

Other UDDI APIs

Both the UDDI SDK for .NET and the GLUE UDDI client libraries contain additional APIs to perform the following tasks:

- Publishing a new business, service, binding, or tModel.
- Updating an existing business, service, binding, or tModel.
- Publishing assertions between two businesses. (An *assertion* is a parent-child relationship between two business entities.)

We won't look at these APIs in this chapter because they don't offer any additional support for interoperability between .NET and Java. For further information, I recommend reading the documentation that comes with each API.

Can UDDI Be Used for .NET Remoting?

By default, UDDI is used for description and discovery of Web services. In a number of interoperability projects that I've worked on, however, customers have asked whether UDDI can also be used as a lookup service for .NET Remoting endpoints. Recall in Chapter 4 how a client using .NET Remoting also uses a URL to establish the communication with the server—for example, *tcp://localhost:5656*.

Technically speaking, because this is simply a URL, there's nothing to stop this information from being stored in a UDDI directory as an alternate access point for a service. A provider and a service can be created, and the access point can be set to the URL endpoint of the .NET Remoting service. The same UDDI calls can be made from the .NET Remoting client in order to obtain this access point and then configure the URL on the fly by using the *System.Runtime.Remoting* namespace and APIs instead of storing the information in a configuration file.

From a standards perspective, however, there's no recommended way or best practices for storing .NET Remoting access points in UDDI. Because of this, internal UDDI registries that facilitate lookups of .NET Remoting calls are certainly feasible, but unless the UDDI standard encompasses this technology, this probably won't be consistently or widely used in a public registry.

Best Practices

In following the samples in this chapter, you've encountered a number of new technical terms and concepts. This is compounded by a structure in UDDI that allows maximum flexibility for storing information about providers and services.

To help further understand how UDDI works—and more importantly, how UDDI should be used with WSDL described services—a best practices white paper is available at *http://www.uddi.org*. This white paper outlines best practices for constructing and working with entities in the UDDI registry.

Pulling It All Together—Web Services Interoperability

So far, we've concentrated on some key aspects of Web services and seen how they can be implemented on both the .NET and Java platforms. To conclude the chapter's technical discussion, this section will pull together all the topics covered so far and show an extended example that builds upon what you've learned.

Figure 6-25 shows the two Web services that we've used throughout this chapter: the Buy Stocks Web service, based on the .NET platform, and the Sell Stocks Web service, based on the Java platform and using GLUE. These two services will play a key role in the chapter's final sample. To further illustrate interoperability between the .NET and Java platforms, we'll see a client that acts as a façade to these two Web services. This façade is based on ASP.NET and presents a Web-based UI representation of the two services.

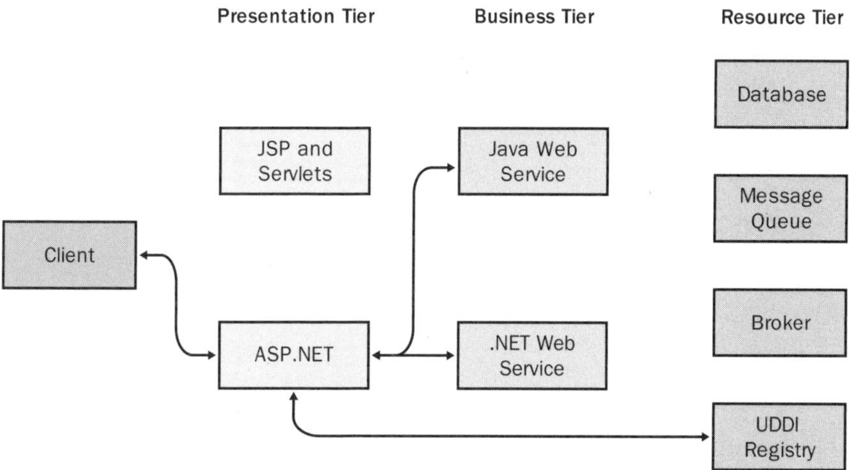

Figure 6-25 Scenario for the final sample.

The ASP.NET interface will touch on a number of points that have been introduced in the past few sections, including calling services from both .NET and Java; maintaining data type fidelity between the two platforms; and handling exceptions, authentication, and UDDI. In addition, as we step through the solution, I'll point out additional best practices and patterns that apply.

To install and run the solution, you'll need to have built the .NET and Java Web services in Chapter 5 and configured UDDI as described in the previous section.

Installing the Solution

The sample solution is located in the C:\Interoperability\Samples\Point\WebServices\Solution directory. To install the sample, first compile the code, and then within IIS Manager, create a new virtual directory that points to this folder. To create this virtual directory, follow the same directions that you used to create the sample .NET Web service at the start of Chapter 5. For this to run correctly, the alias for the virtual directory needs to be **WebServiceSample**.

After the virtual directory has been created, you need to set the IIS virtual directory security correctly in order to allow access to the UDDI registry. The UDDI registry that was configured in the previous section is, by default, set to allow Windows authentication. In order to pass the credentials to the UDDI registry, set the authentication mode for the WebServiceSample virtual directory to Integrated Authentication and remove Anonymous Access. You can set this by right-clicking the virtual directory, selecting Properties, and navigating to the Directory Security tab. This was covered earlier in this chapter in the "Web Services Authentication and Authorization" section. In addition, if you followed the samples in this section, you might want to check the security settings on the dotNETWebService virtual directory. Ensure that anonymous access is enabled.

The solution is now correctly installed and configured. To ensure that the sample can be run, start the Java Sell Stocks Web service by entering **start ant run** at a command prompt in the C:\Interoperability\Samples\Point\WebService\Java\WebService directory (which was shown at the end of Chapter 5).

Running the Solution

After installing and configuring the solution, browse to *http://localhost/WebServiceSample*. This will display the home page for the solution, which Figure 6-26 shows.

The home page introduces the sample and presents two options to the user: Buy Stocks and Sell Stocks. In addition, the user is asked for the UDDI inquiry URL, which is prepopulated for a local instance of UDDI Services for Windows Server 2003.

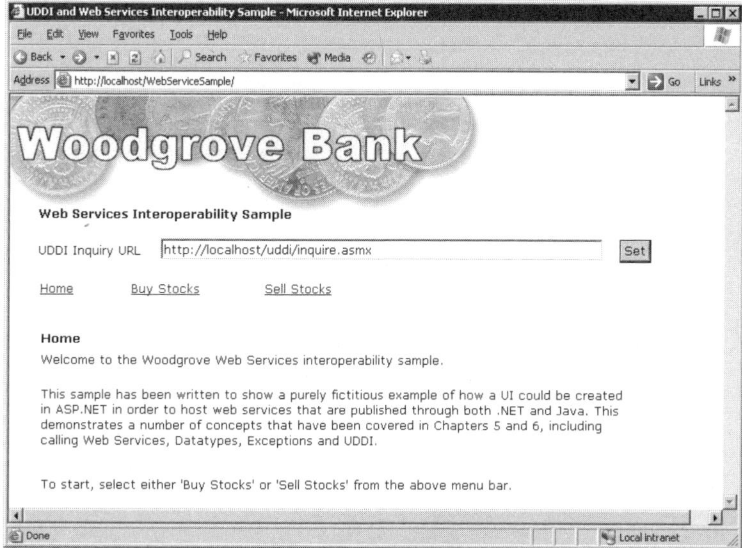

Figure 6-26 The home page of the Woodgrove Bank sample.

Modify the UDDI inquiry URL as required for your own environment (for example, set the server to something other than localhost), and click the Buy Stocks option. The page used to buy stocks will be displayed, as shown in Figure 6-27.

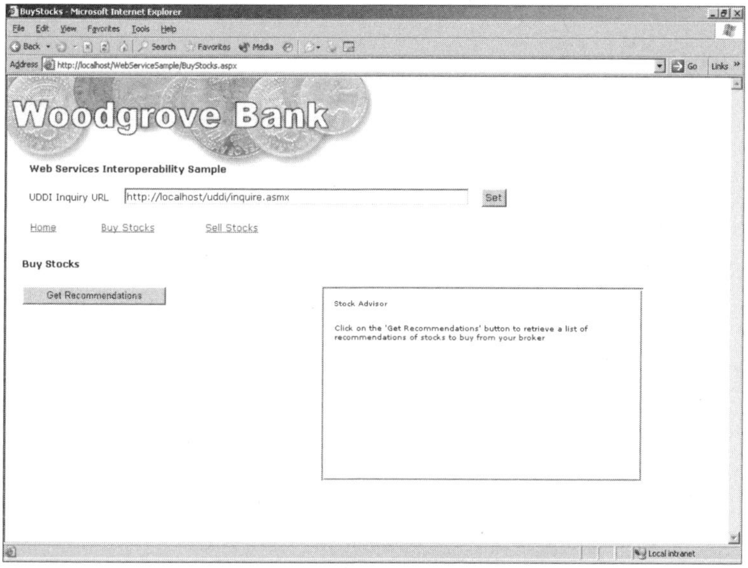

Figure 6-27 The Buy Stocks page and the UDDI inquiry URL.

Recall how in the chapter's earlier samples the Buy Stocks and Sell Stocks Web services contained two methods each—one to get the list of recommendations, and the second to execute the actual order. In essence, ASP.NET is just a graphical representation of this.

On the Buy Stocks page, click the Get Recommendations button. In order to make this call, the ASP.NET page first makes a request to the UDDI server. By default, the ASP.NET page knows nothing about the location of the Buy Stocks Web service and relies on the UDDI directory for access point information. If you have a debug tracer attached to the ASP.NET process, it's possible to view the progress of the UDDI call.

Once the UDDI access point has been returned, ASP.NET UI then makes a call to the Buy Stocks Web service (which also is hosted via ASP.NET) and displays the list of recommendations as they're returned. Figure 6-28 illustrates this.

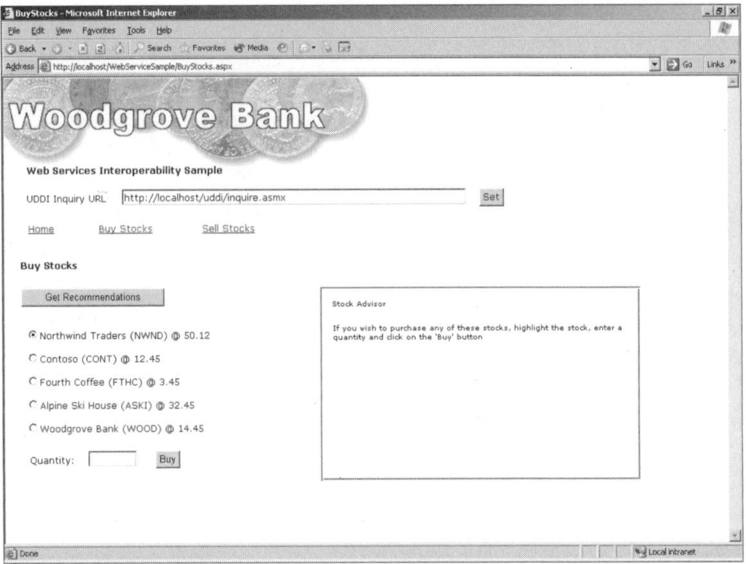

Figure 6-28 List of recommendations returned by the Buy Stocks .NET Web service.

Select one of the recommendations, enter a valid quantity, and click the Buy button. Again, this will make another call to UDDI and return the address for the Web service. Then the *BuyStocks* method will be invoked.

> **Tip** In a production system, you'd probably consider caching the access point returned by the UDDI server, especially if you have an environment in which the Web service endpoints remain fairly static. Making a call to a UDDI server for each Web service request clearly has an impact on performance.

If all is successful, the ASP.NET page will report that the order was placed, presenting a confirmation in the Stock Advisor window, as shown in Figure 6-29.

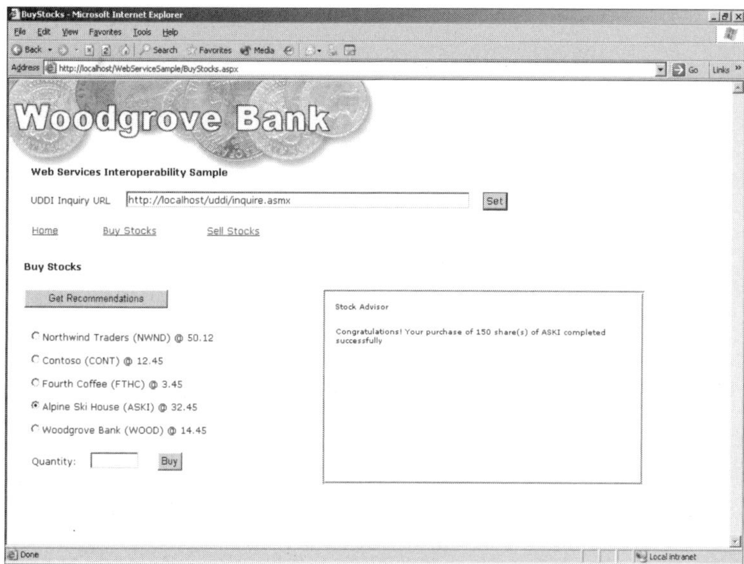

Figure 6-29 Selecting a stock to purchase.

To confirm this, recall how the .NET Web service shown earlier in this chapter writes all incoming orders to the Windows Event Log. If you check the application log, you should see an entry similar to the one shown in Figure 6-30.

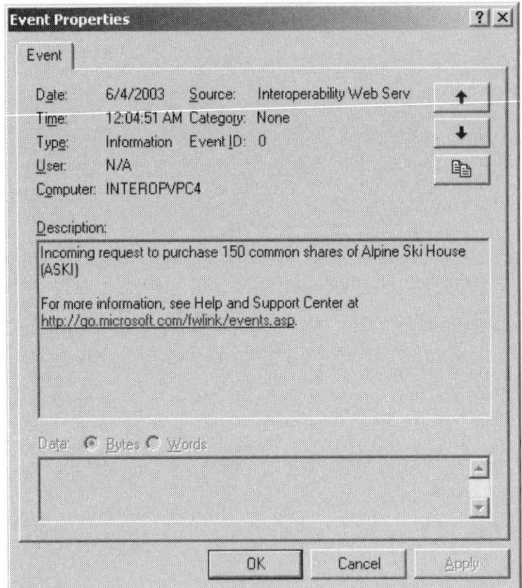

Figure 6-30 Viewing the purchase in the Windows Event Log.

Now let's look at how the call to the corresponding Java Web service is invoked. From the Web page, click the Sell Stocks button.

Again, click the Get Recommendations button. (See Figure 6-31.) This process uses the same code underneath but asks the UDDI server for the address of the Sell Stocks Web service, which will be resolved to our Java Web service.

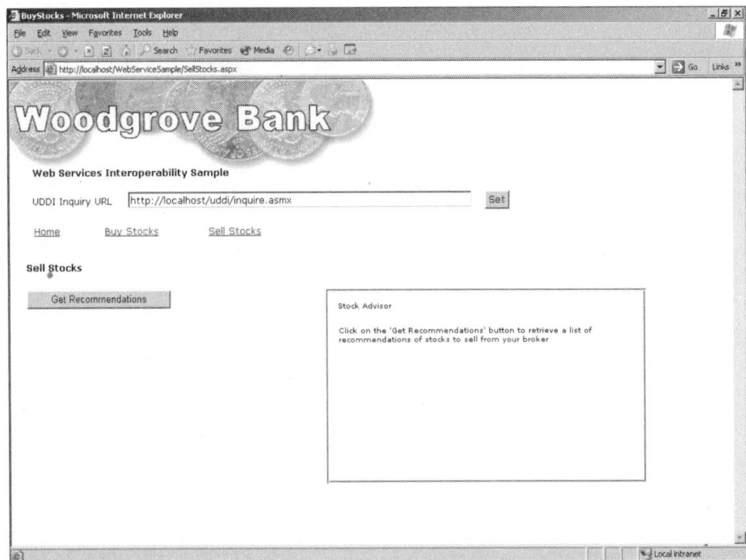

Figure 6-31 Selecting the recommendations for stocks to sell.

As before, select a stock (this time to sell) and enter a quantity. If successful, the screen should display a confirmation message, as shown in Figure 6-32. If you look at the Java Web service as it's running in the background, you should see this message in the console window:

```
Incoming request to sell 50 common shares of Wingtip Toys (WING)
```

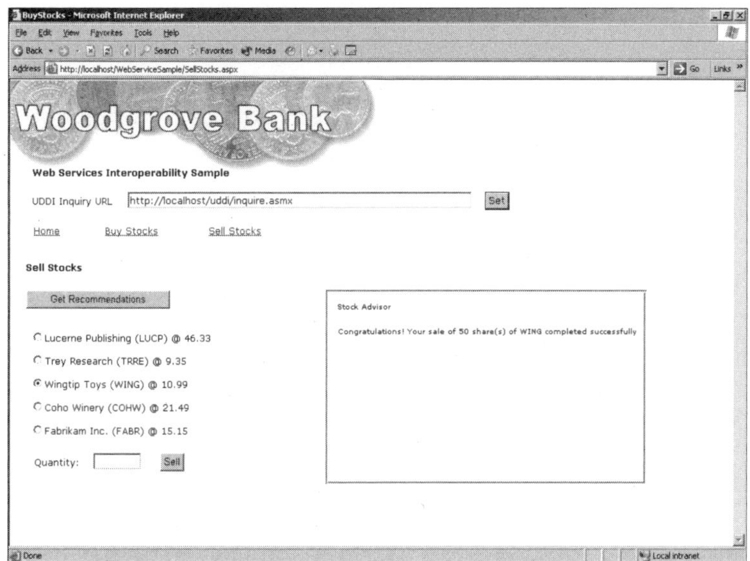

Figure 6-32 Selecting and processing a stock to sell, using the Java Web service.

Although this is a basic solution, it shows a clean example of how you can abstract two Web services—one from .NET and the other from Java—and present them through a unified interface. By using a common interface and Web services to achieve interoperability between the two platform, you have the potential to build a unified interface for any number of disparate services. One advantage of doing this is that the user doesn't know whether the underlying connection is a Web service hosted in .NET or one hosted in Java. This comes back to some of the fundamentals outlined earlier in the book: the goal of interoperability is to present a user experience that doesn't necessarily expose the underlying number of disparate systems.

How the Solution Works

The project structure is relatively simple, and in looking through the code, you can see the approach that's been taken. The solution itself—examined either from the command line or through Visual Studio .NET—comprises a number of base pages: Default.aspx, BuyStocks.aspx, SellStocks.aspx, and Header.ascx. Header.ascx is an ASP.NET Web user control and is responsible for displaying a consistent banner at the top of each page you saw.

In addition to these pages, there are five subfolders:

- **Images** Contains the JPEG image for the screen.
- **Datatypes** Contains the shared stock type by using exactly the same schema as defined in Chapter 3, "Exchanging Data Between .NET and Java," where we looked at XSD and data types.
- **UDDI** Contains a *UDDILookup* class that contains the commands for looking up an access point based on a service name.
- **Proxies** Contains the proxies to call the Web services themselves.
- **Agents** Acts as a layer between the pages and the proxies and is used to abstract the Web service proxy code away from the actual calling page, which we'll cover shortly.

Now that we have an overview of the solution, let's look at what happens when a user launches the sample and makes a request to either buy or sell some stocks.

Open the BuyStocks.aspx page. This page displays the controls required for buying a stock. Locate the *BuyStockRecommendationsButton_Click* method. This method is executed when the user clicks the Get Recommendations button.

```
BuyStocksAgent agent
    = new BuyStocksAgent(((String)Session["InquiryURL"]));
ArrayList recommendations = agent.GetRecommendations();
```

After the button is clicked, a new instance of the *BuyStocksAgent* is created, which is passed the *InquiryURL*, which is the UDDI URL that's configured in the header of the page and stored in the ASP.NET session state. As you can see, the agent exposes a method named *GetRecommendations*.

Follow the code to the BuyStocksAgent.cs class. Here is the code that makes up the agent:

```
dotNETStockService ss = new dotNETStockService();
ss.Url = _accessPointURL;
return new ArrayList(ss.GetRecommendations());
```

You can see how a new instance of the .NET Web service is created. Just before it's invoked, the URL is set. (The access point URL is obtained via UDDI in the constructor of the agent.) The *UDDILookup* class that's used to do this is based on the same sample code shown earlier. The agent then calls the "real" *GetRecommendations* method from the Web service.

> **Note** Why do we use the agent layer? The agent service is a pattern that I like to adopt when creating solutions that invoke Web services. In essence, it's a layer that separates the underlying proxy for the Web service from the calling code. Separating this underlying proxy yields a number of advantages when calling Web services in general. We'll cover this momentarily, in the next section.

Finally, let's take a look at the proxy files that are used to call the Web service. Both files (dotNETStockService.cs and JavaStockService.cs) have been generated by using the WSDL.EXE tool. After they were generated, we made some modifications manually to get them to work neatly in the solution.

First, we added the *WebServiceSample* namespace to each file. (By default, WSDL.EXE doesn't add a namespace.) Second, we stripped out the definition for *Stock* from each file. This is really important. When WSDL.EXE was used to generate the proxy file, a stock type was also created (because it's exposed in the WSDL from the Web services). Unfortunately, as you create proxies for different platforms, you end up with multiple copies of the same type defined in the solution. To resolve this, you can rely on our standard definition for *Stock* (which is defined in portfolio.cs) and delete the definitions that are auto-generated by the tool. Because we're using a single version of the type definition, it's important to ensure that this type is attributed with a namespace that's shared by both Web services.

Finally, the proxy that's generated for the Java Web service contains a type named *ArrayList*, which is created and exposed by GLUE. To avoid confusion between this *ArrayList* and the *ArrayList* in the *System.Collections* namespace, this was renamed to *GlueArrayList* throughout the proxy file.

Hopefully, this extended sample pulls together some of the concepts we've addressed in the book so far. Feel free to step through this example in more detail to reaffirm some of the options and recommendations presented.

Recommendations for Web Services Interoperability

A large part of achieving interoperability today by using Web services depends on how well the WSDL and SOAP specifications have been interpreted from one vendor to another. For example, if I use vendor A's Web service stack and expose a Web service that has a stock data type exposed, vendor B's Web service stack needs to know exactly how to map that data type; otherwise, there may very well be problems.

To help mitigate these types of problems, I always make the following recommendations when designing solutions that need to interoperate between the .NET and Java platforms via Web services.

Define Data Types First

About six months ago, I worked on a project for a large financial customer. The concept that they were looking to develop involved moving a large amount of Customer Relationship Management (CRM) data from one system to another—using Web services as the transport. The data types were quite complex, and given our previous experience with sending this type of data over a Web service, the development team decided that our process must mitigate the risks that could arise.

One of the first things that we did was sit down with the business analysts. (The analysts were responsible for driving the flow and requirements of the application, without wanting to know about the technical elements.) By "sit down," I do not mean to imply that this was a leisurely chat: we spent about a third of the project designing a data model from the ground up, building complex data types, fields, properties, methods, sequences, and database mappings.

Once we had an accurate representation of the data by using the Unified Modeling Language (UML), we created the actual classes for the objects—and created simple test harnesses to send them back and forth by using Web services. (In fact, these test harnesses were similar to the samples that you've been working with in this chapter.)

The key message here is that before any of the UI or underlying infrastructure for the application was written, we already knew what would (and what would not) work with using Web services as the underlying transport in our distributed approach. In the end, we did have to make some minor changes based on the choice to use Web services. These mostly involved choosing XSD-compliant data types. But we gained a tremendous advantage by making these changes early on in the project, as opposed to having to factor them in later on. This also gave us a great opportunity to run some performance tests on the data (because we had some skeptics in the group who'd labeled Web services as too slow).

To summarize, if you plan to send complex types back and forth over Web services, design them before any code is written. Build the complex data types first, build a test harness to prove that they work, and then work on designing a great application around them.

Keep Data Types Simple and Based on XSD

In general, the simpler the data type, the more chance it has in being successfully used in conjunction with Web services. As your data types become more complex, one simple rule to adhere to is to stick with XSD.

In Chapter 3, you saw how to define data types from XSD documents and vice versa—and how to use a tool such as Visual Studio .NET to create XSD documents. Keeping data types that are exposed via Web services in line with an XSD model will help interoperability by ensuring compatibility between different versions of Web services toolkits.

In many cases, I also recommend that data types are removed from the underlying proxy file and stored in a location that's central to the solution. If the data types have been automatically generated from the XSD document, this is an easy approach to adopt and is one that you saw in the previous section's extended sample. Doing this not only can help separate data types used throughout the application from the proxies, but also is useful when both the .NET and Java environments need to agree on a single XML namespace for all types.

Keep Compliant with WS-I Basic Profile 1.0

To achieve interoperability with Web services, I recommend keeping up to date with the latest publications and guidance from the Web Services Interoperability Organization (WS-I). This advice is best used when considering solutions from multiple vendors that might claim to be Web services compatible. Use the Basic Profile as a guide to selecting these vendors and keeping up to date with new profile releases from the WS-I.

Standardize on a Document/Literal Style

This is something that we haven't covered specifically in this chapter so far, but it's worth mentioning. SOAP structure and encoding standards is a subject that has been under debate in the Web services community for some time, and it relates to the way that SOAP messages are structured in Web service requests.

Let me explain. There are two ways to structure a SOAP request: by using Document style or RPC style. Initially, when SOAP was first released, it supported only RPC style. The SOAP 1.0 specification was the first iteration to introduce support for both styles.

RPC style dictates that the SOAP body must contain a method name and a set of parameters. This style is tightly coupled to the service and driven by the interface itself. Here's an example:

```
<SOAP-ENV:Envelope...>
    <SOAP-ENV:Body>
        <m:BuyStocks xmlns:m="someURL">
            <Ticker>COHO</Ticker>
        </m:BuyStocks>
    </SOAP-ENV:Body>
</SOAP-ENV:Envelope>
```

By Document style, we mean that the request to call the method and its associated parameters are passed in the format of a document. This provides for a much more loosely coupled approach to passing calls and parameters to a Web service. The structure can look much more like this:

```
<SOAP-ENV:Envelope ...>
    <SOAP-ENV:Body>
        <BuyStocks Ticker="COHO"/>
    </SOAP-ENV:Body>
</SOAP-ENV:Envelope>
```

Another element of the style and format (which can constitute a larger problem) is the encoding method used. Two types of encoding exist: Literal and SOAP. Literal is the encoding method that conforms to a particular XML Schema. SOAP encoding uses XML Schema data types to encode the data, but the document itself doesn't conform to any schema. The result is that with SOAP encoding, you can't validate against a schema—which can affect transformations (using Extensible Stylesheet Language Transformations, or XSLT) and serialization to and from objects.

The .NET Framework and most of the Java Web service implementations found today support both RPC and Document style structures. One challenge that you might face is that in .NET, the default is Document style, whereas many of the Java toolkits standardize on RPC. The sample code throughout this book uses a mix based on which style generates the best results for interoperability.

When defining a Web service strategy that incorporates both .NET and J2EE, you should always try to standardize or at least head toward all services using a Document/Literal style. In addition, the WS-I Basic Profile 1.0 standard promotes the use of Document/Literal style (and actively disallows RPC/Encoding).

Ensure the Latest Version of Java Web Services Distribution

If you haven't already, you could soon be in a position where you want to develop a solution or application that needs to interoperate between the .NET and Java platform. At the time of this writing—as mentioned in Chapter 5—no formal specification for deploying and building Web services on the Java platform exists. As a result, you might encounter vendors who will provide you with this functionality before it becomes part of the specification.

Regardless of the vendor that you choose for your Java Web services stack, I recommend always making sure that you use the latest version of the distribution. Because specifications evolve so rapidly, tools in the XML-based Web services realm also move at a lightning-fast pace. Keeping up with the latest version (even a point release) will ensure that your solution not only works with the latest specifications, but also helps enable reliable and consistent interoperability.

Allow Abstraction with an Agent-Service Pattern

In the final Web services sample in this chapter, you saw how an agent-service pattern was used to provide a layer of abstraction between the business logic (which in our case was the calling ASP.NET page) and the proxy file used to call the Web service itself.

Performing this abstraction gave you the option of adding more functionality to the Web service call without having to modify the caller logic. For example, in our example scenario, the agent was purely responsible for working out the URL from the UDDI registry. If you didn't have this agent layer, you'd have to do this work as part of the calling ASP.NET page, which in turn could have polluted your calling code. In addition, when you consider adding other functionality in the future (for example, authentication or clustering between a number of services), it's the additional agent layer that promotes a cleaner solution.

Use UDDI for the Discovery of Web Services

My final recommendation is to use UDDI for the discovery of Web services. In a situation where multiple Web services are distributed throughout an organization, the presence of a UDDI registry can help provide a central repository to services written for both .NET and J2EE.

When selecting a UDDI registry for internal use, also consider how that registry will be located by clients. Having an unstable location for the UDDI registry can prove as troublesome for clients as having no registry at all. To help with this, look at how the UDDI registry will integrate with any directory solution that's currently implemented. For example, UDDI Services for Windows Server 2003 has the ability to publish its location via Active Directory. By using this publication, clients can use a direct method to query for registered UDDI servers.

Interoperability Performance Test

We'll conclude this chapter with an interoperability performance test that follows the same format as the previous ones in the book. This test can be found in the C:\Interoperability\Samples\Point\WebServices\PerformanceTest directory and can be used to measure the response time between a .NET client and a Java Web service, by using the samples provided throughout this chapter. The Web service can be run by entering **start ant run** within the Server subdirectory. To build the client, run **nant run** from the Client subdirectory. This test assumes the client and server are on the same machine but can easily be distributed by modifying the URL in the FinancialServices.cs proxy file.

For those interested in the performance differences between using .NET Remoting and Web services for a solution that requires interoperability, I recommend using this performance test's sample code and comparing it with its counterpart in Chapter 4. Another way to extend these tests is to use XSD, as shown in Chapter 3, to rerun the tests with data types that more accurately represent your own environment. The results can help you judge the potential performance of using custom data types over Web services.

For these particular tests on my development machine, I've seen an average of 12.9 ms to download the five stock recommendations, and 14.1 ms to call and commit the sale command. This compares with 4.6 ms and 8.1 ms when running the .NET Remoting samples on the same setup.

Again, using this code and modifying it for your own controlled environment will be the best performance guide between the two solutions.

Summary

This chapter and Chapter 5 offered an introduction to how Web services can be used to achieve interoperability between .NET and J2EE. In these chapters, we covered Web service technology, vendor support, introductory samples, some of the recommendations for using Web services in a production environment, basic security, exceptions, UDDI, and using all these together in a single solution.

Still, we've covered only a small set of Web service functionality that's available in both .NET and GLUE, specifically focusing on the areas that are pertinent to interoperability. As you start to explore Web services in more detail, I encourage you to examine areas that we haven't touched upon in order to help you deploy a production-worthy solution.

Finally, I recommend revisiting Chapter 2, "Business Requirements for Interoperability," and reviewing the requirements and scenarios in order to see how Web services can help you address point-to-point interoperability. For the scenarios that demanded connectivity between two distinct points (for example, when the presentation tier calls the business tier), Web services can be used to provide a compelling solution. In addition, if these points of connectivity are ever extended to third parties or other systems, using Web services can provide the most compatible way of extending interoperability.

Part III

Interoperability Technologies: Resource Tier

- Interoperability
  - Samples
    - Advanced
    - Config
    - Data
    - Point
    - Resource
      - BizTalk
        - Deployment
        - Project
        - WebServices
      - Database
        - DAO
        - Simple
        - SQL
        - UpdateDAO
      - MSMQ
        - Simple
        - Transactional
        - WebServiceAPI
      - MSMQBridge
        - dotNET
        - Java
      - WMQ
        - GlueJMS
        - JMS
        - MDB
        - Scripts
        - Simple
  - Tools

7

Creating a Shared Database

At the resource tier, creating a shared database between the Microsoft .NET Framework and Java 2 Enterprise Edition (J2EE) can be one of the simplest yet most effective ways of achieving interoperability between the two platforms. Database connectivity lies at the core of both .NET and J2EE, and with data access drivers available for each, it's relatively easy to create applications that share fields, records, and tables among both platforms.

Chapter 2, "Business Requirements for Interoperability," introduced the common scenario of business tier resource sharing. That chapter featured an example that built an application in .NET that shared the same data as an application that already existed in J2EE.

In previous projects I've worked on, I've observed how certain functionality has been added to an existing application where a requirement to keep the same data but use technology from a different platform was made. For example, with a reporting application, the reporting software is written for a different platform than the original application.

In this chapter, we'll look at data access in the context of both .NET and J2EE and explore two connectivity options. To enable this connectivity, we'll explore accessing Microsoft SQL Server 2000 from J2EE by using JDBC and from

.NET by using Microsoft ADO.NET. To run the samples, you'll need a local installation of Microsoft SQL Server 2000. Service Pack 3 is recommended.

Although both samples presented in this chapter are based on the connection and sharing of data based on Microsoft SQL Server, these samples certainly aren't limited to products from a single vendor. Both JDBC and ADO.NET drivers are available for a number of database providers—hence the term *open data access*, which you'll see throughout this chapter. The chapter will provide an introduction to JDBC and ADO.NET, but because the topic of accessing databases has been widely covered in other programming books and documentation, we'll stick to the context of using a shared database.

To conclude the chapter, we'll look at using a data access pattern that can be applied to both .NET and J2EE and cover the advantages of doing so.

Open Data Access

As mentioned in Chapter 1, "Microsoft .NET and J2EE Fundamentals," database connectivity APIs are core packages for both .NET and J2EE. The J2EE 1.3 specification promotes the use of JDBC to provide database access. For .NET, ADO.NET is used.

To recap, JDBC is an API that allows Java applications to access fields, records, tables, and stored procedures from any database for which a JDBC driver exists. Although JDBC 3.0 is in its final release, we'll use JDBC 2.0 calls for the chapter's examples. Many vendors have produced JDBC-compatible drivers for a number of popular databases. These include Microsoft SQL Server, many versions of the Oracle database, and the IBM DB2 database.

ADO.NET is the next stage in the evolution of Microsoft's data access strategy—with an emphasis on providing database access and connectivity for the .NET Framework. In addition to simple database connectivity, ADO.NET has a strong relationship with XML (to enable persistence and transport) and introduces the concept of a *DataSet*, allowing a disconnected view of data.

ADO.NET uses *managed providers* to connect to a database. Managed providers are database drivers that expose APIs by using classes that are based on managed code (which is Microsoft Intermediate Language, or MSIL, under the covers). Today, managed providers exist for SQL Server, Oracle 8i, and DB2. In addition, an ADO.NET managed provider can be used to access other drivers that are based on either OLEDB or ODBC.

Creating a Sample Database Table

To see examples of how to connect to a shared database, we'll use a table that simulates incoming orders for the stock-trading scenario that we've used in previous chapters. To keep things simple, the database defines a single table named ORDERTBL, which has the schema shown in Table 7-1.

Table 7-1 Schema for the ORDERTBL Database Table

Column Name	SQL Data Type
ID	*BIGINT*
TYPE	*CHAR(1)*
ACCOUNT_ID	*BIGINT*
TICKER	*CHAR(6)*
QTY	*INT*
PRICE	*MONEY*

In this example, ID correlates to the ID of the order. TYPE indicates whether the item is a purchase (indicated by a *P*) or a sale (indicated by an *S*). ACCOUNT_ID is an account number for the trade. TICKER is the ticker symbol of the stock. QTY is the amount bought or sold. PRICE is the price of the stock at the time of the trade. Based on the examples you've seen so far in the book, imagine how a table of this type could be used to store records of stock trades.

To create this shared database and table, run the SQL script (dbscript.sql) located in the C:\Interoperability\Samples\Resource\Database\SQL directory. With Microsoft SQL Server 2000 installed, this script can be processed by loading and executing this file within the Query Analyzer, which can be accessed from the Microsoft SQL Server program group.

> **Tip** During SQL Server installation, it's important to ensure that the SQL Server And Windows authentication mode is selected in the properties dialog box of the SQL Server instance, as shown in Figure 7-1. If the authentication mode is set to Windows Only, a JDBC application won't be able to connect to the database. This is because the Java Virtual Machine, or JVM, doesn't have access to the Windows authentication credentials stored on the machine.

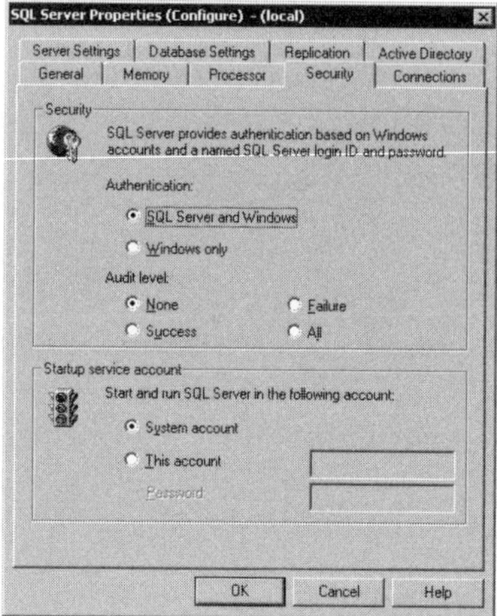

Figure 7-1 Configuring the SQL Server security properties.

Running this script will create a new database named SharedDB, which has a table named ORDERTBL, the result of which is shown in Figure 7-2. A few sample records have also been included. The script also creates a test user account named testuser. This account is given a default password of Strong-Password and ownership rights of the SharedDB database. This user account is used by the client sample code in this chapter.

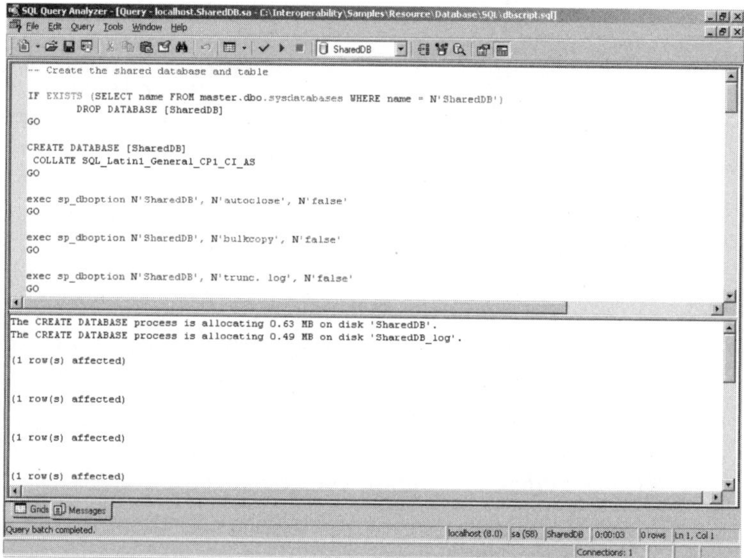

Figure 7-2 Processing the dbscript.sql in Query Analyzer.

Connecting to Microsoft SQL Server 2000 Using JDBC

To allow Microsoft SQL Server 2000 to be accessed from a Java application, a number of JDBC drivers are available. Some of these are free, some are commercial, and in the past some have even been packaged with a number of J2EE application servers.

Microsoft's offering is a JDBC driver that's available as a free download through the Microsoft Developer Network (MSDN). The driver is a Type 4 JDBC driver.

> **Note** JDBC drivers are categorized into four types. Type 1 and Type 2 drivers require native code to be installed on the client machine. Type 3 drivers do not require native code but require additional security to work over the Internet. Type 4 drivers are preferred because they use the native protocol to access the database without requiring any additional installation.

Downloading and Installing the Driver

The Microsoft SQL Server 2000 Driver for JDBC (Service Pack 1) can be downloaded by navigating to *http://msdn.microsoft.com/downloads/list/sqlserver.asp* and selecting the appropriate product.

The installation for the Microsoft Windows operating system is a simple SETUP.EXE. A TAR package is also available for running it on UNIX systems.

Simple JDBC Access

Once the installation has completed, three Java Archive (JAR) files can be found in the C:\Program Files\Microsoft SQL Server 2000 Driver for JDBC\lib directory. These three JAR files contain the required libraries to connect to an instance of Microsoft SQL Server 2000 by using JDBC.

To see the JDBC driver in action, look at the sample located in the C:\Interoperability\Samples\Resource\Database\Simple\JDBC directory. Stepping through this sample (Client.java), you can examine how the driver works. Because the driver is based on JDBC, you need to import classes from the existing *java.sql.** packages:

```
import java.sql.Connection;
import java.sql.DriverManager;
import java.sql.ResultSet;
import java.sql.Statement;
```

After the declaration for your main class, you need to load the SQL Server 2000 Driver for JDBC by using the class loader. This ensures that the driver is loaded for the following JDBC calls:

```
Class.forName("com.microsoft.jdbc.sqlserver.SQLServerDriver");
```

If you plan to use this sample code with an alternative JDBC driver and/or database, this line will need to reference the driver that you want to use.

Once the class is loaded, a connection string is built to specify how to connect to your database. This connection string will determine the parameters to use to find and connect to the instance of SQL Server. The format of a default connection string follows, and the list explains the different components in the string.

```
jdbc:microsoft:sqlserver://server:port;DatabaseName=db
```

- ***server*** The machine name where SQL is installed.
- ***port*** The IP port that the driver should use to connect with SQL Server. If defaults have been accepted during the SQL Server installation, this port should be 1433.
- ***db*** The name of the database to access.

The username and password that should be used to access the server and the database are supplied separately when the database connection is created.

This sample uses a connection string that connects to a local instance of SQL Server 2000, via a user named *testuser* and a password of *StrongPassword*. The *DriverManager.getConnection* method is used to create the connection:

```
Connection conn = DriverManager.getConnection("jdbc:microsoft:"
    +"sqlserver://localhost:1433;DatabaseName=SharedDB",
    "testuser","StrongPassword");
```

After the connection to the database has been successfully established, a *SELECT* statement is issued to the SQL Server instance:

```
Statement stmt = conn.createStatement();
ResultSet rs = stmt.executeQuery("SELECT * FROM ORDERTBL");
```

This query requests all records from the order table. The query will execute and an object of type *java.sql.ResultSet* is returned. You can then iterate through the *ResultSet* to display the data from the query.

```
while (rs.next())
{
    System.out.println(rs.getString("ID")
        +"\t"+rs.getString("TYPE")
```

```
        +"\t"+rs.getString("ACCOUNT_ID")
        +"\t"+rs.getString("TICKER")
        +"\t"+rs.getString("QTY")
        +"\t"+rs.getString("PRICE"));
}
```

This code displays the values for each of the six columns defined within the table, simply by using the *getString* method from the *ResultSet*. (We'll perform more complex calls later in the chapter.) To complete this JDBC sample, we wrap the code in a *try...catch* block. Some of the JDBC calls throw explicit exceptions that are caught by trapping for a general exception.

Build and run the code by entering **ant run** at a command prompt in the Simple\JDBC directory. As you saw, this sample accesses the Microsoft SQL Server 2000 Driver for JDBC at run time. The build script assumes the libraries (JAR files) are located in the default installation directory (C:\Program Files\Microsoft SQL Server 2000 Driver for JDBC\lib). If this isn't the case, you should modify the C:\Interoperability\Samples\Config\sqljdbc.properties file to reflect the correct directory.

Upon successfully calling the database, a list of records will be returned:

```
1000    P       47238   CONT    400     12.7700
1001    P       93083   CONT    200     12.7800
1002    S       39223   NWND    1000    50.1200
1003    P       29080   WOOD    150     14.4500
1004    S       37973   FTHC    10000   3.4500
1005    P       32279   WOOD    800     14.7900
1006    P       38084   LUCP    5000    46.4400
1007    S       39397   COHO    200     21.6000
1008    S       71129   FABR    950     15.1100
1009    P       38293   TRRE    250     9.3500
1010    P       38293   COHO    250     21.5800
```

Connecting to Microsoft SQL Server 2000 Using ADO.NET

Now that we've looked at how the JDBC driver can be used to access the sample database and display some simple records, let's look at the same functionality using ADO.NET.

Simple ADO.NET Access

Again, with the JDBC driver, the best way to show simple access to a database by using ADO.NET is with a sample. The code from the previous sample, but this time using ADO.NET rather than JDBC, can be found in the C:\Interoperability\Samples\Resource\Database\Simple\ADO.NET directory.

Most of the APIs required to access the SQL Managed Provider for ADO.NET reside within the *System.Data.Sql* namespace. This namespace is imported at the start of the sample:

```
using System.Data.SqlClient;
```

The connection to the database is defined by using the *SqlConnection* class. A connection string is built that includes the machine, username, password, and database information. This is similar to how the JDBC connection string was built, but it uses different parameters. The connection is opened with the *Open* method:

```
SqlConnection conn
    = new SqlConnection("Data Source=localhost; User ID=testuser; "
        + "Password=StrongPassword; Initial Catalog=SharedDB");
conn.Open();
```

To issue a command to the database, a *SqlCommand* is constructed that contains the select statement that will be executed. The results from the select statement will be returned as a *SqlDataReader* object:

```
SqlCommand cmd = new SqlCommand("SELECT * FROM ORDERTBL", conn);
SqlDataReader reader = cmd.ExecuteReader();
```

As you did with the Java *ResultSet*, to extract the fields from this reader, you index them with the *GetValue* method. This will return the values in a format that will allow them to be written to the console:

```
while (reader.Read())
{
    Console.WriteLine(reader.GetValue(0)+"\t"
        +reader.GetValue(1)+"\t"
        +reader.GetValue(2)+"\t"
        +reader.GetValue(3)+"\t"
        +reader.GetValue(4)+"\t"
        +reader.GetValue(5));
}
```

As you continue to look at other samples in this chapter, you'll see how to use the actual types of the fields instead of getting a default value from them.

Build and run the ADO.NET code by entering **nant run** at a command prompt in the Simple\ADO.NET directory. Upon successfully calling the database, a list of records matching the ones that were observed with the JDBC sample will be returned.

Using JDBC and ADO.NET to Share Data

So far, you've seen how JDBC and ADO.NET can be used to perform simple database access from Java and .NET, respectively. From here, it should be clear how both drivers could point to the same instance of a database and be used to insert, update, and delete records, thus enabling data to be shared between the two platforms, as shown in Figure 7-3.

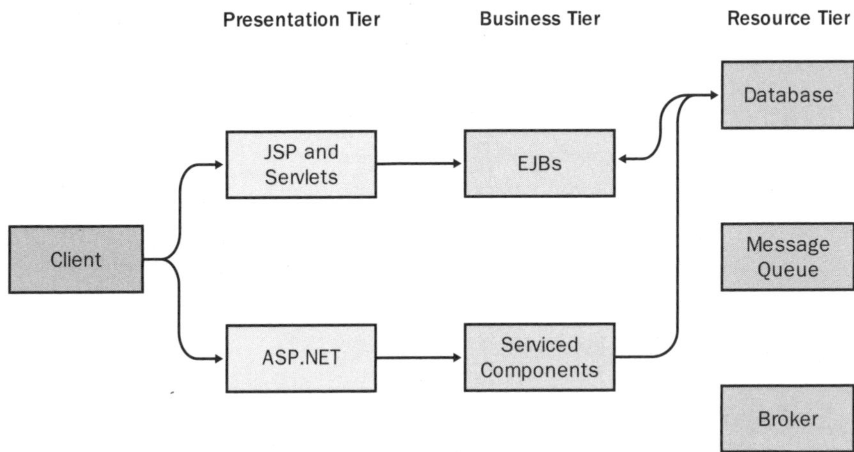

Figure 7-3 Creating a database that's shared between .NET and J2EE.

To show a particular implementation of this, we'll work with a design pattern known as the Data Access Object (DAO). This is also known as the Data Access Component (DAC) or Data Access Layer Component (DALC).

> **More Info** The DAO pattern was first introduced by Erich Gamma, Richard Helm, Ralph Johnson, and John Vlissides, affectionately referred to as the Gang of Four. You can learn more about this and other design patterns in *Design Patterns* (Addison-Wesley, 1995).

The DAO Pattern

In its simplest form, the DAO is used to separate database access code (such as the samples you just saw) from business logic. The DAO is very similar to the agent-service pattern discussed in Chapter 6, "Connectivity with XML Web Services, Part 2," except that instead of abstracting a Web service proxy, you abstract code that makes direct calls to the database.

If you look at this pictorially, in Figure 7-4, you can see how the DAO layer resides directly between the database layer and the business logic layer.

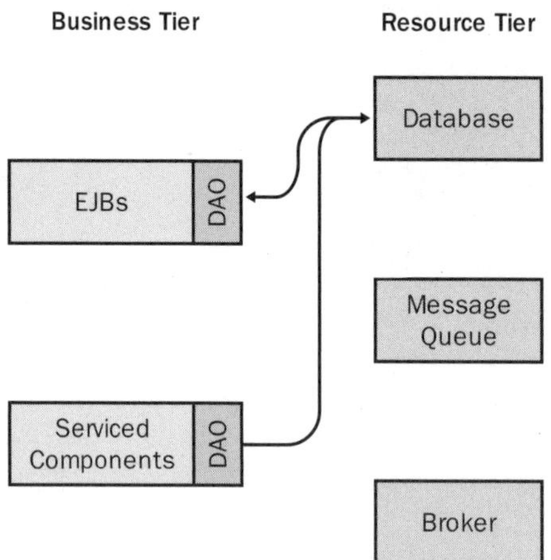

Figure 7-4 Use of the DAO pattern in a shared database environment.

In general, a DAO is used to provide CRUD-type functionality for abstracting a database from business logic. CRUD is an acronym commonly used in the database world that stands for:

- Creating new records in the database
- Reading records from the database (and returning them as data types used by the business logic)
- Updating records in the database (by using updated data types that are used by the business logic)
- Deleting records in the database

In the chapter's samples, you'll see examples of creating and reading these records by using both the Java and .NET platforms. By examining the code, it will be possible to see how update and delete methods can be introduced.

The sample code for the DAO can be found in the C:\Interoperability\Samples\Resource\Database\DAO directory. Two versions, one for

ADO.NET and one for JDBC, can be found there. Both of the samples define a data type named *StockRecord*, which contains elements that match the fields of the order table, and a class for the DAO itself, named *StockRecordDAO*. The *StockRecordDAO* class is responsible for maintaining the connection to the database and for exposing the database connection through a series of methods to perform the creates and updates. These methods include the following:

- *GetStockRecord(long ID)*
- *GetStockRecords(long accountID)*
- *GetStockRecords(String type, long accountID)*
- *GetStockRecords(String type, String ticker)*
- *GetStockRecords(long accountID, String ticker)*
- *GetStockRecords(String type, long accountID, String ticker)*
- *GetAllStockRecords()*
- *AddStockRecord(StockRecord record)*

When a method is invoked, the DAO constructs the correct *SELECT* statement, executing the query against the database and returning the result either as a *StockRecord* (for single records returned) or an *ArrayList* that contains one or more *StockRecords*.

Compile both the ADO.NET and JDBC samples, using either NAnt or Ant depending on the programming language selected. The DAO is invoked by a *Client* class that simulates some simple business logic to read and add a record from the database:

```
Reading a single record with ID=1000:  CONT
There are 2 records with ID = 38293
Adding a record...
```

Each time you run the sample, it displays the ticker of an individual record and adds a new record to the table. By running both samples multiple times, you can observe how new records are created by both the ADO.NET and JDBC sample.

Notice that the client code is very similar for both .NET and Java, whereas the platform-specific code (the database access) is abstracted in the DAO layer. For developers using both platforms, this abstraction is one of the benefits for using a consistent DAO.

Interoperability Benefits

What benefit does a shared DAO pattern yield when you're developing solutions that require interoperability between .NET and J2EE? In terms of direct database access, the calls to the database will be the same regardless of whether a pattern is used. Therefore, the main advantages are twofold.

First, developing data access based on a shared DAO gives you a common frame of reference for accessing data on either platform. If you were to follow a similar pattern to the one shown in the previous sample, writing business logic for either .NET or J2EE would allow for a consistent feel regardless of the platform used to access the data.

Second, as with the agent-service pattern you saw in Chapter 6, the DAO pattern has the ability to provide additional logic and functionality for accessing databases. For example, a DAO could include code that provides the following:

- A level of caching between the business logic and the database. Records that were recently accessed could be returned from a cache to increase performance.
- Management for security (authentication and authorization) for connecting to the database.
- Handling for transactional and locking issues.
- Data paging to allow pages (or blocks) of data to be returned for large data sets.

Based on this list, a DAO pattern that's used by both the .NET and J2EE platforms also allows for some other interesting notification options in a shared database. Imagine a configuration in which business components from both .NET and J2EE access a shared database by using the DAO pattern, as Figure 7-4 depicted.

Using this setup, it might be desirable to find out when either of the platforms has updated a particular record in a database. For example, if a component on one of the platforms has made an update, a component on the other platform might want to reload that data to either perform some function or keep the cache current.

Using this DAO pattern, you have the potential to extend the DAO layer on both .NET and Java in order to provide some notification from each platform to the other. For example, you could use either .NET Remoting or Web services to pass an update message between the two DAO layers, as shown in Figure 7-5.

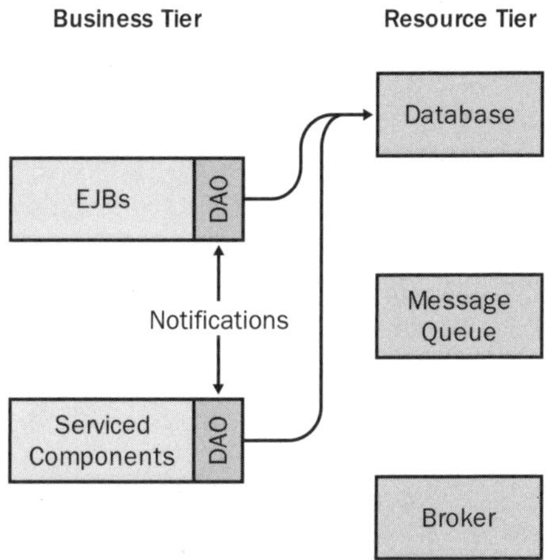

Figure 7-5 A DAO implementation with notifications between the .NET and J2EE tiers.

Doing this can eliminate the need for each of the platforms to constantly "poll" records in the database for changes—which can be common in situations where a shared database setup is required.

Extending the DAO to Include an Update Operation

The final sample in this chapter will demonstrate how the DAO can be extended to include such an update operation. This sample can be found in the C:\Interoperability\Samples\Resource\Database\UpdateDAO directory and is based upon a particular customer requirement that I encountered recently.

The sample shows a small .NET application based on Windows Forms that's used to monitor the order table in the database. The forms-based application allows the user to view the current records populated in this table and uses methods exposed from the same DAO pattern shown in the previous discussion. The second half of the sample shows a Java client that also accesses the database by using the DAO pattern and adds a new record when run.

The update operation is performed by using .NET Remoting between the Java client and the Windows Forms application. The Windows Forms application exposes a server-side component that can be called by using .NET Remoting. After the Java DAO successfully adds a new record to the database, it uses a .NET Remoting call to inform the Windows Forms application that it should refresh its view of the database. Figure 7-6 illustrates this.

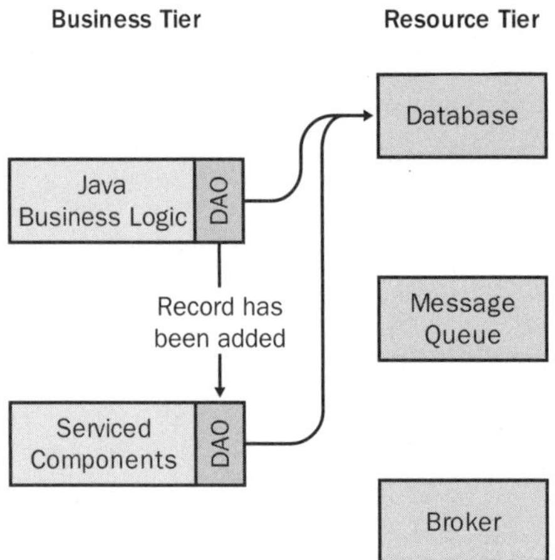

Figure 7-6 The DAO being used to notify the Windows Forms application of a new addition to the database.

The server-side component of the Windows Forms application that's exposed is attached to an event in code. When an incoming call is made by the Java DAO, the event triggers a refresh of the screen.

To see this in action, compile both the ADO.NET and JDBC portions of the UpdateDAO sample code. Because the JDBC code uses Intrinsyc Ja.NET to perform .NET Remoting, you might want to refer to Chapter 4, "Connectivity with .NET Remoting," for further details. All the required proxies have been generated as part of the sample, but the licensing will need configuring by using the janetor tool.

Within the ADO.NET sample directory, compile and run the Windows Forms code by using **nant run**. The form that's displayed shows a simple summary of each record within the order table, as depicted in Figure 7-7. To scroll through the records, use the navigation control to view a particular record number.

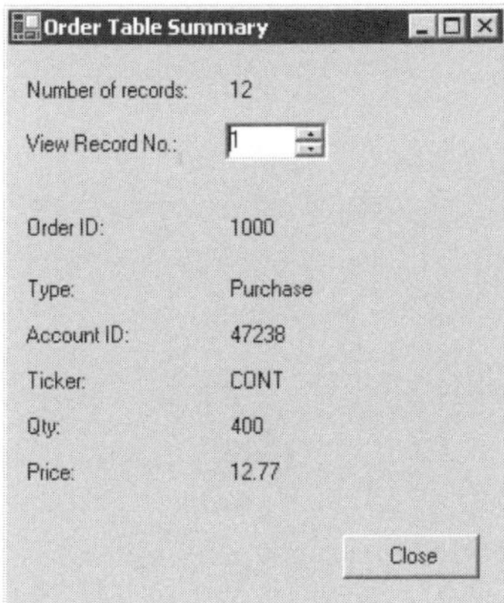

Figure 7-7 The .NET sample client, showing a Windows Form with a record summary.

Now switch to the JDBC sample in the UpdateDAO directory. Run the Client application. This will use the DAO layer to add a new record to the database, indicated by the following output:

```
Adding a record...
```

Once this operation is complete, switch back to the Windows Forms application. You should notice that the number of records has been incremented automatically, as shown in Figure 7-8. Navigating to the last record will show the details of the record that was added by the Java DAO layer.

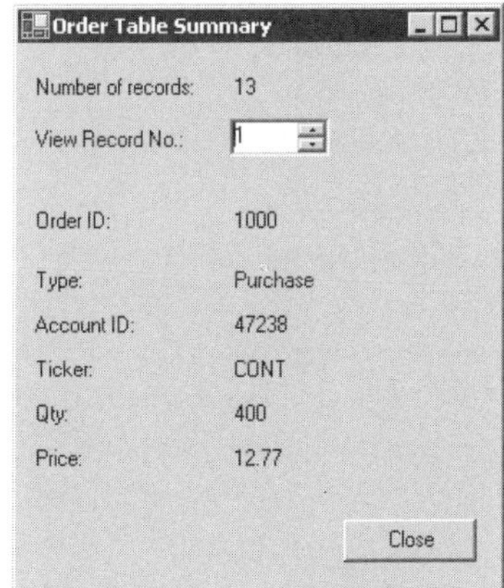

Figure 7-8 The .NET sample client, showing an updated number of records.

In addition, the following line can be uncommented in the SummaryForm.cs class:

```
MessageBox.Show("The Java client has added a record to the order"
    +" table.  Click on OK to refresh.");
```

This will display a message each time the database is updated by the Java DAO layer.

How the Update Operation Works

To allow the Java DAO layer to inform of a database update, the Windows Forms application exposes a *NotificationRemoting* object. When called, this object calls a *NotificationFactory* in order to obtain a singleton reference to a notification object. In .NET Remoting terms, a *singleton* is a static instance of an object that can be shared across processes. Because the same reference of a notification object is required for both the Java and ADO.NET DAO layer, a singleton provides a single point where update events can be shared.

When the notification object is called, it creates a new event that's handled by the ADO.NET DAO layer. The DAO layer in turn reexposes a new event that can be consumed by the business logic of the application. This setup is shown in Figure 7-9.

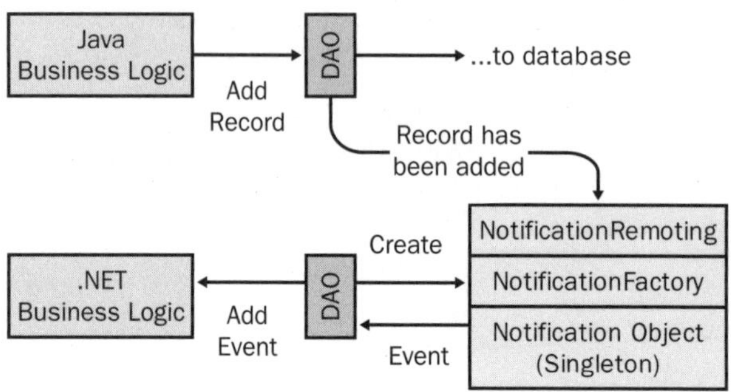

Figure 7-9 The updated operation for the two DAO layers.

Because all the notification and access logic is abstracted by the DAO layer, the business logic code simply has to take action on the update event. The Windows Forms application includes a line to register the event handler from the DAO layer:

```
dao.Updated += new UpdateEventHandler(dao_Updated);
```

The *dao_Updated* method contains the code that updates the screen.

This sample shows a simple notification process between the DAO layers on the Java and .NET platforms. To extend this concept, imagine how the DAO layer could pass additional information with the update to further optimize the sample. For example, the DAO layer could pass information on which record was affected by the update.

Summary

This chapter introduced the concept of creating a shared database to provide interoperability between the .NET and J2EE platforms. In addition to covering the open access drivers that are available for both platforms, we looked at how the DAO pattern can be used to provide a unified way of accessing a database that's shared between the two platforms. You also saw how this data sharing can be extended by providing a level of notification between the two platforms, using some point-to-point interoperability concepts.

It's important to realize that we've only scratched the surface of the capabilities of both ADO.NET and JDBC. The aim of this chapter was to introduce a simple approach to the topic and show interoperability between the .NET and Java platforms when both are accessing a shared database. This approach of course can be expanded to include the more advanced features of database connectivity for both platforms.

Next we'll look at how message queue technologies can be used to provide interoperability at the resource tier—effectively extending the updates/ notifications that you saw in the DAO pattern and formalizing a process of sending asynchronous messages between .NET and J2EE.

8

Asynchronous Interoperability, Part 1: Introduction and MSMQ

At the end of Chapter 7, "Creating a Shared Database," you saw an example of how a Data Access Object (DAO) class in Java can send a message to a DAO class in .NET to indicate that an operation on the database has been completed. In the sample, this message notified the .NET application to refresh the display in order to show the new record that had been added.

This type of communication and all the samples shown in Part II of the book, "Interoperability Technologies: Point to Point," depict types of calls between the .NET and Java platforms that are synchronous in nature. This means that the calling application waits for an acceptance or result from the receiving application before continuing and that the receiving application must be available to receive the message as it's being sent.

Although synchronous calling helped illustrate interoperability between the two platforms in the preceding chapters, many situations require an asynchronous approach. An example of this occurs when the receiver isn't available to immediately process the incoming message. This might be due to some planned or unplanned offline operation, or it might be due to the receiver being too saturated to immediately deal with the incoming request.

Another example of asynchronous calling occurs when the request takes a long time to process before an answer is returned to the client. This is known as a *long-running process*. For example, imagine a loan application process in which credit details for the applicant have to be collected from various sources before an acceptance can be returned. This credit check might take seconds, minutes, hours, or even days to complete. In either case, the calling application probably doesn't need to wait for the result—and can instead work on submitting more loan applications.

In a system that has a mix of processes running on .NET and J2EE, such situations demand a level of asynchronous interoperability between the two platforms. The term *asynchronous* tends to be overloaded: many definitions and interpretations of the word exist. In this chapter, we'll look at two types of asynchronous examples: *nonblocking asynchronous calls* and *fire-and-forget asynchronous calls*.

In a nonblocking asynchronous call, the asynchronous style of the request is handled by the client. The actual call is synchronous in nature, but the client handles the call in another thread or process (giving the impression that the call is asynchronous).

In a fire-and-forget asynchronous call, the asynchronous nature of the call is handled by the architecture of the system. The client sends a message, and at some point in the future, is able to view the status of the message and/or receive the result.

Let's start by looking at asynchronous-supported calls in XML Web services (which will demonstrate nonblocking calls in action). We'll then continue to explore fire-and-forget asynchronous interoperability by using the Microsoft Message Queuing product, MSMQ.

Asynchronous Calls Using Web Services

In the samples shown in Chapter 5, "Connectivity with XML Web Services, Part 1," and Chapter 6, "Connectivity with XML Web Services, Part 2," some of the .NET proxy code that was generated contains some asynchronous style calls. For example, by using either Microsoft Visual Studio .NET or the WSDL tool, if a method named *GetRecommendations* is exposed by the Web service, two methods named *BeginGetRecommendations* and *EndGetRecommendations* are created in the proxy file. These methods give the .NET client the ability to make asynchronous types of calls by using Web services.

The Sample Code

A sample has been created to best demonstrate this asynchronous callback using Web services. This sample code can be found in the C:\Interoperability\Samples\Point\WebServices\Async directory. This directory contains two subdirectories. One contains the Java Web service (JavaWebService) that will be called; the other contains the .NET client code (dotNETClient).

The Java Web service code is exactly the same as the sample shown in Chapter 5. As with the sample in Chapter 5, the Java Web service code in this chapter implements two methods: *GetRecommendations* and *SellStocks*. The *GetRecommendations* method performs the same operation of returning some sample stock recommendations, but in this chapter's code, we'll introduce a small delay before the method returns. To do this, a private method named *simulateDelay* is used. This method simulates the type of delay a production system might experience (for example, if operating under a heavy load).

The .NET client is a small application built using Windows Forms. This small sample allows you to select whether to call the Java-based Web service by using a standard method call (as you saw in Chapters 5 and 6) or by using an asynchronous callback. When the Web service is called, the user can observe the effect it has on the calling application.

To test, build both the Java Web service and the .NET client by using the supplied scripts. Run the Java Web service so that it's waiting for requests from the client. To do this, enter **start ant run** from a command prompt in the JavaWebService subdirectory. When this is done, run the .NET sample client by entering **nant run** from a command prompt in the dotNETClient directory.

The .NET client shows the two available options for calling the Java Web service, as depicted in Figure 8-1. Ensure that the No Callback option is checked and click the Call Web Service button.

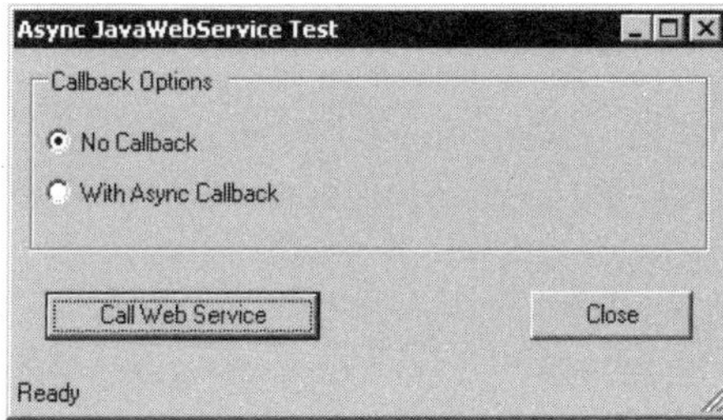

Figure 8-1 The asynchronous .NET Windows Forms sample.

The status bar will change to indicate that the Web service is being called. After a preset amount of time (10,000 milliseconds, which is determined by the *simulateDelay* call in the Java Web service), the result will be returned to the client, as shown in Figure 8-2.

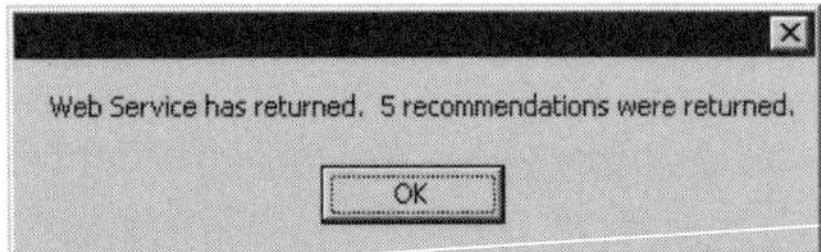

Figure 8-2 The result, returned back to the client.

The key observation from this demo is that although the Web service is being called, the .NET client is essentially "frozen." Rerun the same test, but this time try moving or closing the window while the Web service is being called. You should find that this isn't possible—and that the client appears to "hang" until the result is returned. This happens because the call to the Web service is a blocking call, made via the same thread as the client itself. Until the Web service is returned, the application cannot continue.

Return to the sample, and this time select the With Async Callback option, as shown in Figure 8-3. Click the Call Web Service button, as you did before.

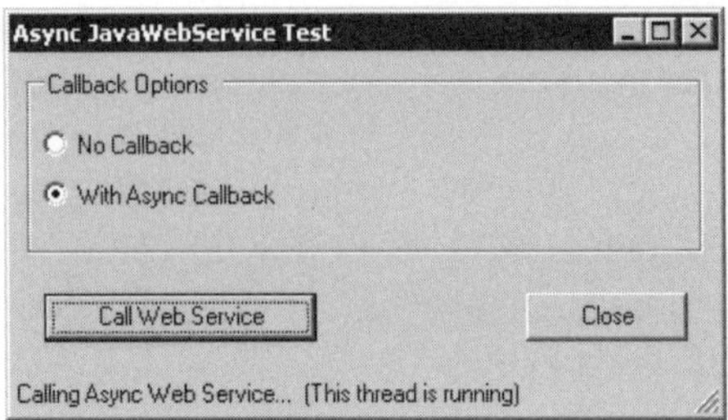

Figure 8-3 The Windows Forms client running asynchronously.

As with the previous test, the client makes the call to the Web service, which will return a value after some time. This time, however, observe how the client application is much more usable. The window can be moved around the screen and even closed while the Web service is being called. Once the Web service returns a value, a message similar to that with the previous test is displayed, indicating the number of recommendations.

In the second example, the call to the Web service is handled by a different thread (which is nonblocking) than the one that controls the update of the window. When this second thread receives a result from the Web service, a callback is raised. This callback runs the code to display the result onscreen.

This type of threading operation isn't something new with Web services or interoperability. Multithreaded Microsoft Windows clients have been around for some time. The point is that the code required to implement this threading and callback is automatically generated and handled by the proxy file—leaving very little for the developer to do in order to achieve this asynchronous approach.

How the Callback Works

Looking through the sample code, you can see how this callback mechanism works. The form itself (AsyncForm.cs) implements a method named *button1_Click*, which is called when the user clicks the Call Web Service button. This method verifies which of the check boxes are selected. If the No Callback check box is selected, the Web service is called by using a regular approach:

```
service.GetRecommendations();
```

On the other hand, if the Async Callback check box is selected, a slightly different approach is taken. First, callback and state objects are defined:

```
AsyncCallback callback = new AsyncCallback(this.ShowResults);
Object state = new Object();
```

The *AsyncCallback* class is a delegate (think of this as a pointer to a method) from the *System* namespace. This delegate specifies which method will be called when the callback occurs. In this case, the method to be called is named *ShowResults*. The state isn't used in the sample, but it's there to access the last parameter of the call if required at some point in the future.

The final step in calling the Web service is to make the call and update the status bar:

```
service.BeginGetRecommendations(callback,state);
statusBar1.Text
    = "Calling Async Web Service...  (This thread is running)";
```

Notice how the call is made to the *BeginGetRecommendations* method (and how the callback and state are passed). This method now completes, and the user is returned to the form and can interact with controls as usual.

When the Web service call completes, the callback executes the *ShowResults* method:

```
private void ShowResults(IAsyncResult result)
{
    ArrayList recommendations = new
        ArrayList(service.EndGetRecommendations(result).elements);
    MessageBox.Show("Web Service has returned.  "
        +recommendations.Count+" recommendations were returned.");
    statusBar1.Text = "Ready";
}
```

The incoming callback provides a parameter of type *IAsyncResult*. This parameter is used with the corresponding *EndGetRecommendations* method to obtain the result from the Web service proxy. Once this is done, the message and status bar can be displayed as appropriate.

Applicability of Callbacks in Client Applications

In the previous example, you saw how the Web service proxy generation for a .NET client allows calls to be made in an asynchronous fashion with little effort. This type of call works equally well with any Web service, and many of the Web services toolkits for Java support this type of operation. (If these toolkits don't support this type of operation, you can easily program the operation manually.)

Although this section has illustrated the concept of callbacks, the benefits of using this technique apply only in synchronous-style operations. For example, using the callback mechanism is helpful for allowing the user to perform another operation while a call to a Web service is made (as you saw in the sample), but the call to the Web service is still synchronous. It must still complete while the client is open and connected to the Web service. The client cannot go offline or disconnect from the network. Doing so would break the Web service call, and the callback would never be returned.

In addition, this type of callback is dependent on how long the Web service takes to complete. A client will benefit if the Web service takes a few seconds or minutes to return—but this wait will lose its appeal if the Web service takes a week to return the required data.

Given these scenarios, we have to look beyond nonblocking callbacks and investigate other types of asynchronous communication—especially those that focus on interoperability between the .NET and Java platforms. In particular, fire-and-forget asynchronous communication fits the bill. The first fire-and-forget technology that we'll look at is Microsoft Message Queuing (MSMQ).

Using MSMQ

MSMQ allows applications that might run at different times to communicate with each other via one or more centrally located queues. Applications use these queues to send and receive messages. These messages can contain most types of data (such as simple primitive data types and complex data types).

MSMQ 1.0 was introduced as part of the option pack with Microsoft Windows NT 4.0. The release of version 2.0 coincided with the release of Microsoft Windows 2000, and as a result, developers were able to take advantage of more integrated features. This included the ability to leverage COM+ transactions, alignment with the Windows security model, and clustering.

The latest version, MSMQ 3.0, is now shipped with Microsoft Windows XP Professional and Microsoft Windows Server 2003. It boasts all the features of 2.0 and includes HTTP as an optional transport, SOAP Reliable Messaging Protocol (SRMP) support, multicast options, triggers, and a number of management and deployment upgrades. Additional details on MSMQ can be found at *http://www.microsoft.com/windows2000/technologies/communications/msmq/default.asp*.

For the samples in this chapter, we'll look at this latest version of MSMQ, shipped with Windows Server 2003, and investigate the options for connecting to queues by using both .NET and Java clients. The samples will also work for users who are working with Windows XP Professional. This is the first technical option we'll examine in the book to provide asynchronous interoperability between the Java and .NET platforms.

Installing MSMQ on Windows Server 2003

Installation of MSMQ on Windows Server 2003 follows a similar pattern to installing UDDI Services—MSMQ is installed via the Add/Remove Windows Components portion of Add Or Remove Programs in the Control Panel. The required components can be found in the Application Server section, under a category named Message Queuing, as shown in Figure 8-4.

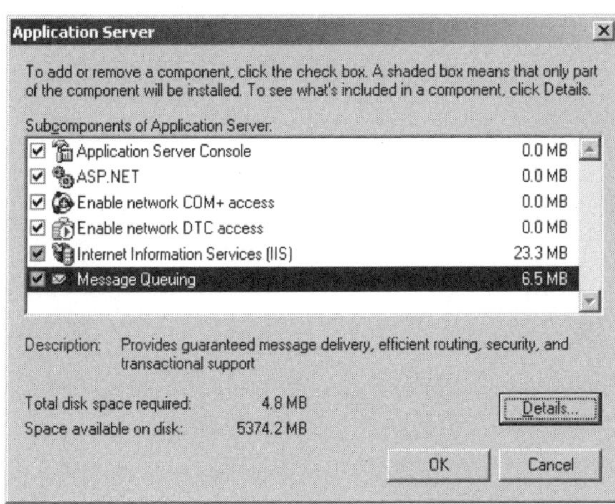

Figure 8-4 Installing MSMQ on Windows Server 2003.

Within this category, you have a number of additional options, as shown in Figure 8-5.

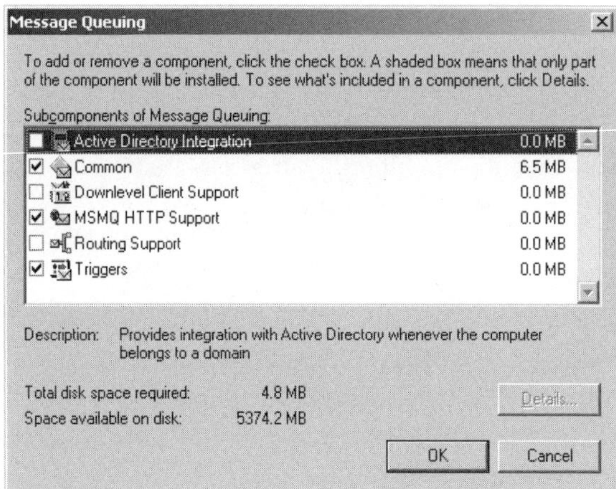

Figure 8-5 Options for installing MSMQ on Windows Server 2003.

Feel free to select any of these options (in addition to the required Common option) if you plan to experiment further with the MSMQ product set. Completing the Add/Remove Windows Components wizard will install MSMQ on the machine.

Administration of MSMQ is performed by using the Computer Management console, found in Start/Program Files/Administrative Tools. This is shown in Figure 8-6. When using Windows Server 2003, another route for accessing the same tree is through the Application Server administration console.

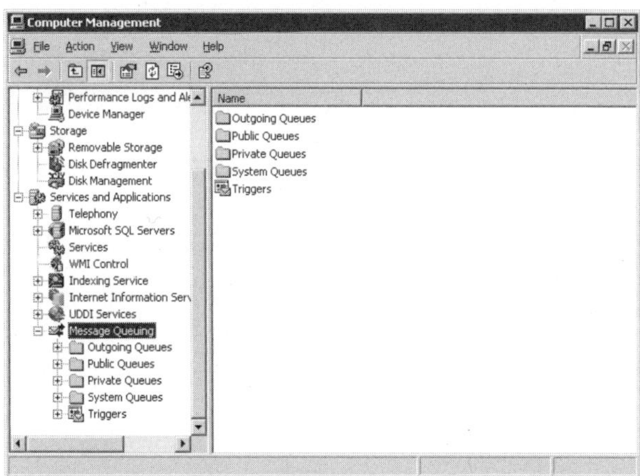

Figure 8-6 Administering MSMQ through the Computer Management interface.

This tool is used to configure systemwide settings, such as events, services, and storage. The Services And Applications tree contains an option for Message Queuing, as shown in Figure 8-6. This option contains a number of subfolders:

- **Outgoing Queues** Used for outgoing messages, normally for routing purposes.
- **Private Queues** You can create, manage, and programmatically send messages to the queues contained in this folder. We'll use these queues throughout the samples in this section.
- **Public Queues** Used for creating, managing, and programmatically sending messages to queues that will be made public to other users and computers. This option will be available if the server resides within an instance of Microsoft Active Directory directory service.
- **System Queues** Contains system-level queues—for examples, dead-letter queues, which store messages that couldn't reach their destination.
- **Message Queuing Triggers** Used to configure triggers and rules that can specify actions that occur when messages of a certain type are sent to a queue. This option will be available if MSMQ Triggers was selected at install time.

For these samples, we'll use a number of private queues. Right-click the Private Queues folder and select New. Create a queue named **stockpurchases**, as shown in Figure 8-7. (Casing doesn't matter for queue names.) This queue will be used to accept messages for incoming stock purchases from the fictitious set of examples that we've been working with. The queue shouldn't be labeled as transactional at this stage.

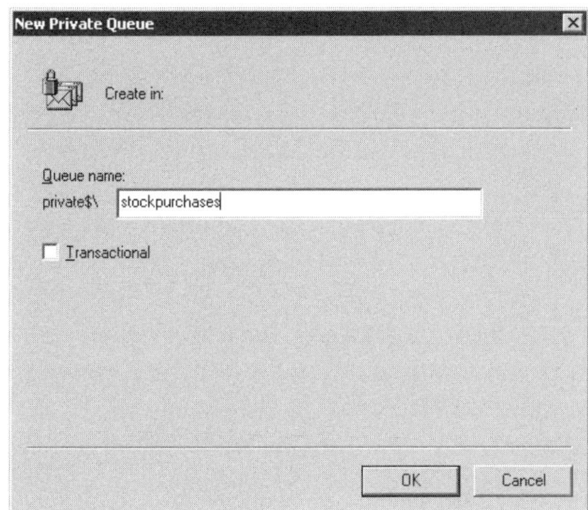

Figure 8-7 Creating a new, nontransactional queue in MSMQ.

Click OK to create the queue, which will now appear in the Private Queues folder. Using the same process, create a second queue, named **stocksales**. Again, this queue shouldn't be labeled as transactional. When complete, you should have two entries in the Private Queues folder, as shown in Figure 8-8.

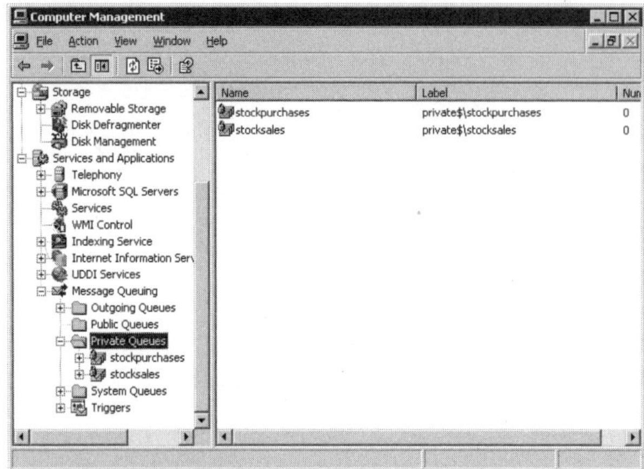

Figure 8-8 Viewing the queues in the MSMQ administration interface.

Now that you've installed the MSMQ components for Windows Server 2003 and created two queues to represent incoming stock purchases and sales from potential clients, let's look at how to access the queues programmatically.

Simple Message Queue Operations in .NET

Accessing MSMQ in .NET is performed by using the *System.Messaging* namespace. This namespace allows individual queues to be accessed, messages to be composed and retrieved, and a number of other message queue–related functions.

To show how classes and methods within this namespace can be used to access the two queues configured in the last section, refer to the sample code found in the C:\Interoperability\Samples\Resource\MSMQ\Simple directory. The main class (Client.cs) shows a series of calls used to place a message on each of the queues, a pause to allow the queues to be examined, and then a retrieval of each of the messages from the queues.

The sample code works by first opening the message queues that were previously set up. Two queues, *purchasesMQ* and *salesMQ*, are referenced:

```
MessageQueue purchasesMQ
    = new MessageQueue(@".\private$\stockpurchases");
MessageQueue salesMQ
    = new MessageQueue(@".\private$\stocksales");
```

After these queues are opened, the formatter for each of the queues is set. MSMQ has two ways of formatting messages placed in the queue, either by using an XML or Binary formatter. This is similar to the serialization techniques that you saw earlier in the book.

```
purchasesMQ.Formatter
    = new XmlMessageFormatter(new System.Type[]{typeof(String)});
salesMQ.Formatter
    = new XmlMessageFormatter(new System.Type[]{typeof(String)});
```

Here, we use the *XmlMessageFormatter* to specify that messages placed in the queue will be serialized with the XML formatter. Because messages of type *String* will be used, you specify this type as a parameter for the formatter.

Next, two messages (one for each queue) are created. These messages are of type *System.Messaging.Message*. After their creation, the *Send* method places the messages in the queue:

```
Message purchase
    = new Message("This could be a message to purchase stocks!");
purchase.Label = "StockPurchase";
Message sale
    = new Message("This could be a message to sell some stocks!");
sale.Label = "StockSale";
purchasesMQ.Send(purchase);
salesMQ.Send(sale);
```

After this is complete, the sample displays a message and prompts for a key to be pressed:

```
Console.WriteLine("Messages have been sent.  Check queues, "
    +"and hit enter to retrieve...");
Console.In.Read();
```

Build the sample code using the provided NAnt script. Type **client** at the command prompt to run the client. When prompted to check the queues, reopen the Computer Management console and navigate to the two private queues that were created earlier.

At this point, expand the two queues and open the Queue Messages folder, as shown in Figure 8-9. Observe how the messages currently in the queue are displayed. Double-clicking the messages in this administration tool displays further details about each message.

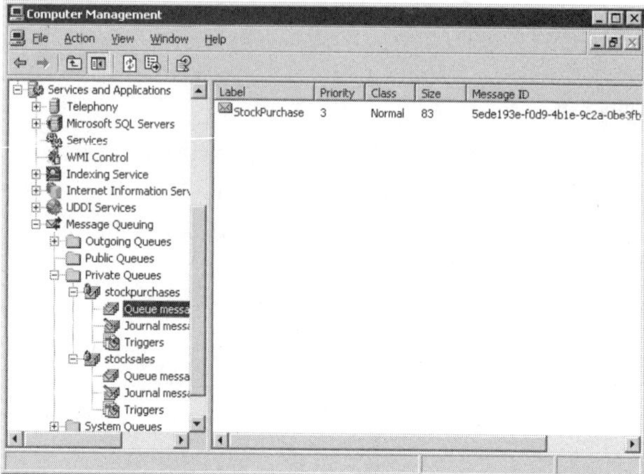

Figure 8-9 A new stock purchase shown in the MSMQ queue.

Navigating to the Body tab in the properties window shows the contents of the message, as serialized by the XML formatter that we configured earlier. (For those security-aware developers in the group, MSMQ does support levels of encryption to prevent this, if desired.) Figure 8-10 depicts the contents of this message.

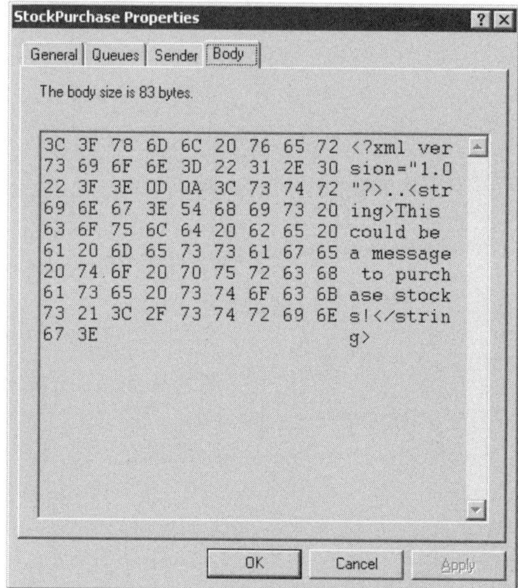

Figure 8-10 The body of the stock purchase message.

Now that you've observed how messages are placed in the queue, return to the running sample application and press Enter in order to continue the process.

To complete the sample, the *Receive* method from the *MessageQueue* class is used to read the message from the queue. Once read, the body element of the message is displayed:

```
Message incomingPurchase = purchasesMQ.Receive();
Console.WriteLine("Purchase Message received: "
    +(String)incomingPurchase.Body);

Message incomingSale = salesMQ.Receive();
Console.WriteLine("Sale Message received: "
    +(String)incomingSale.Body);
```

MSMQ supports two modes of reading messages from the queue. The *Receive* method returns the first message from the queue and removes that message from the queue. In the event that the message needs to be read but not removed from the queue (for example, to determine whether the message is meant for a particular process), the *Peek* method can be used. *Peek* returns a *System.Messaging.Message* object but leaves the message in the queue.

Java Interoperability Options with MSMQ

So far, you've seen how MSMQ can be called by using a .NET client in order to send and retrieve messages from a queue. In terms of interoperability, what options are available for applications and services that are written using the Java platform?

Microsoft does not publish an MSMQ client for Java. You need to explore other strategies to allow Java clients to send and receive messages from MSMQ.

Based on the experience of customers who've dealt with this situation, enabling Java to interoperate with MSMQ is generally a tough area and one that hasn't been addressed very well by Microsoft or any third-party vendor. With this in mind, let's look at the options that do exist.

Using a JMS Provider for MSMQ

JMS, the Java Message Service API, forms part of the J2EE specification. It is an API that's designed to provide an abstraction layer for a number of message queuing products and is something that we'll look at more closely in Chapter 9, "Asynchronous Interoperability, Part 2: WebSphere MQ."

Although JMS might one day be a suitable solution to access MSMQ from Java (as outlined in Figure 8-11), at the time of this writing no JMS providers exist for MSMQ. A third-party company named SpiritSoft (*http://www.spiritsoft.com*)

has been looking at developing a JMS driver to complement their messaging product set.

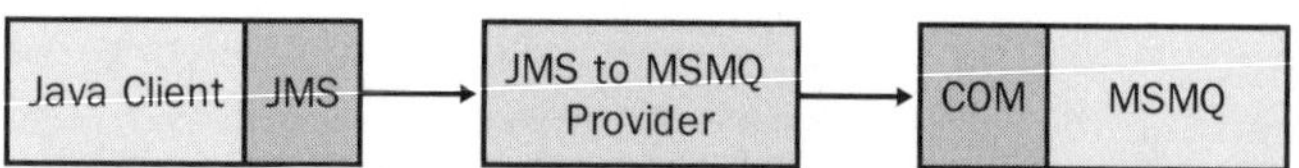

Figure 8-11 How a JMS provider for MSMQ would be used.

Looking back at some of the projects that I've been involved with, I have an idea why no JMS driver for MSMQ exists today. Although JMS is the messaging API for Java, it doesn't offer or dictate any underlying messaging product. Therefore, an organization that wants to use JMS in its applications has to couple this choice with the selection of a message queue provider. As a result, most—if not all—organizations that write against the JMS API already have a message queue within the enterprise. Because a message queue is already in place, there's little to no need to replace it with another (such as MSMQ).

Personally, I'd welcome a JMS provider for MSMQ. A number of customers that I've spoken to agree, especially the ones undertaking projects that require this interoperability between MSMQ and J2EE.

Using SRMP on HTTP

Version 3.0 of MSMQ, shipped with both Windows XP and Windows Server 2003, contains support for SOAP Reliable Messaging Protocol (SRMP). When released, SRMP was a Microsoft standard to extend SOAP with a number of headers, allowing a number of quality of service (QoS) attributes.

SRMP runs on top of HTTP and allows messages sent in the format to be based on concepts such as lifetime (the expiration of a message), durability, and delivery and commitment receipts.

Although SRMP was introduced in MSMQ 3.0, no implementations in Java have been reported. If one were to be created or to exist, the topology of a Java client calling MSMQ via this method would look similar to Figure 8-12.

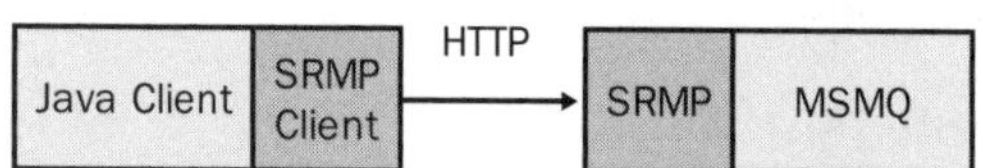

Figure 8-12 How a potential HTTP SRMP client for MSMQ would be used.

Given that this looks like a good way to allow Java clients to access MSMQ by using both HTTP and a reliable SOAP mechanism, you might be wondering why SRMP on HTTP hasn't been more widely adopted. I believe this is due to the standard being overtaken by a number of initiatives that are more closely aligned with Web services. We'll take a look at one of these initiatives, Web Services Reliable Messaging Protocol (WS-ReliableMessaging), toward the end of this chapter.

SRMP on HTTP is certainly supported in MSMQ 3.0, and a number of samples are available on the Microsoft Developer Network (MSDN) to show how this can be used from COM-based applications.

Using a Java-to-COM Bridge

As you've seen, the first two options for Java interoperability with MSMQ are technically possible but do not yet have any implementations. This third option is the first that has been implemented.

Although Microsoft does not support a native Java client from MSMQ, support is available for existing COM-based clients. These can include C/C++ and Microsoft Visual Basic applications based on the Win32 platform. A COM API is available to allow these types of clients to call MSMQ.

In addition, a number of third-party companies have released bridges that allow Java clients to call COM-based APIs. Put the two together, and it's possible for a Java client to call MSMQ by using COM, as shown in Figure 8-13.

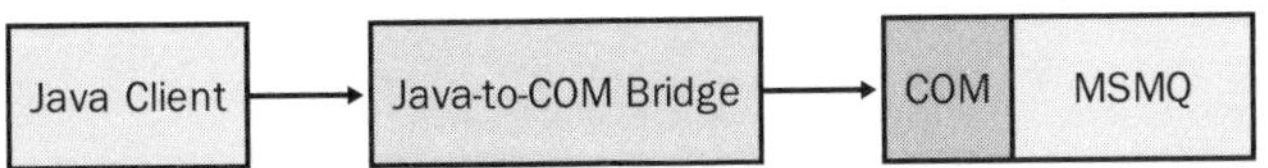

Figure 8-13 How a Java-to-COM bridge can be used to access MSMQ from a Java client.

One company that makes a Java-to-COM bridge is Intrinsyc. We used their Java-to-.NET product, Ja.NET, in Chapter 4, "Connectivity with .NET Remoting." Intrinsyc's Java-to-COM bridge is called J-Integra, which is available from the company's Web site (*http://www.intrinsyc.com*). In addition, Intrinsyc has a white paper showing how the J-Integra product can be used to make MSMQ calls from Java. This can be found at *http://www.intrinsyc.com/support/j-integra/doc/servlet_com/ServletToMsmqExample.html*.

Benefits and shortfalls of this approach Using a Java-to-COM bridge can provide a good way to call MSMQ libraries from Java. Although this uses a bridging concept, the MSMQ COM libraries are quite extensive and will provide a rich interface to MSMQ without the need to create an additional wrapper or interface.

A disadvantage of using this approach is that the Java client must be based on the Windows operating system (to use the Java-to-COM bridge), and the COM libraries for MSMQ must also be installed. This is in addition to any bridging software installed on the client, and therefore, this technique cannot be used for Java clients based on other operating systems (for example, UNIX and Linux).

In addition, if this technique will be used over a network, the transport used will be Distributed Component Object Model (DCOM), over a custom TCP socket. As we discussed in our coverage of Web services in Chapter 5, DCOM isn't well-suited for publishing and accessing services over the Internet.

In addition to the COM bridge, an alternative was available in the days of Microsoft Visual J++: using JActiveX to wrap Microsoft ActiveX MSMQ libraries. This approach shares a similar set of benefits and shortfalls to the COM approach.

Creating a Web Service Interface

The final option for accessing MSMQ from Java is the one that we'll expand on during the remainder of the chapter. In the example code, we'll create and use an interface for MSMQ based on Web services, as shown in Figure 8-14.

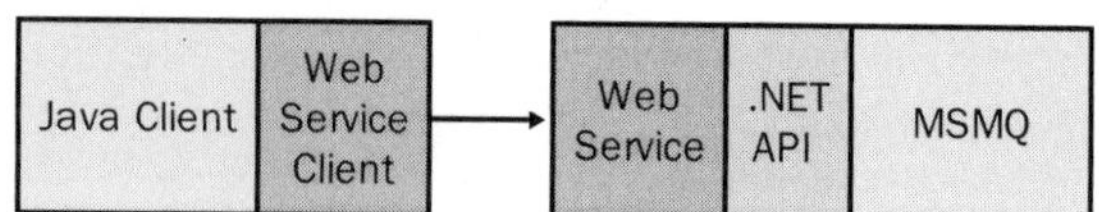

Figure 8-14 Accessing MSMQ using a custom Web service API.

Taking this approach offers some interesting concepts, which we'll discuss in this chapter, as well as a foundation based on some of the interoperability principles that you saw in earlier chapters.

Creating a Web Service Interface for MSMQ

The Web service interface that we'll use can be found in the C:\Interoperability\Samples\Resource\MSMQ\WebServiceAPI directory. Its subdirectories include the Web service itself (SimpleWebService) plus a number of clients, found under the SimpleClients subdirectory.

Open the Service1.asmx.cs file from the SimpleWebService directory. This class contains the main methods for the Web service API that exposes the MSMQ methods. The service class exposes a number of methods as Web services via the *WebMethod* attribute:

```
public void Send(String queuePath, MSMQInterop.Message message)

public bool IsQueueEmpty(String queuePath)
```

```
public bool IsMessageWaiting(String queuePath,
    String label, long timeout)

public MSMQInterop.Message Peek(String queuePath, long timeout)

public MSMQInterop.Message Receive(String queuePath, long timeout)
```

The *Send*, *Peek*, and *Receive* methods should look familiar from the overview of MSMQ in the previous section. *IsQueueEmpty* and *IsMessageWaiting* are helper methods. They use the *Peek* method to help simplify a couple of operations.

Looking at the method signatures in this code, you'll notice that when a message is either passed to or returned from the Web service, a type named *MSMQInterop.Message* is used. Given the Microsoft .NET Framework support for MSMQ, you might wonder why we didn't just expose the default *System.Messaging.Message* class instead.

Because *System.Messaging.Message* implements the *System.ComponentModel.Component.Site* interface, it can't be serialized via a Web service. This is a classic example of a non–XSD compliant data type that can't be passed over a Web service and something that we covered extensively in Chapter 3, "Exchanging Data Between .NET and Java." If we had exposed these types via the Web service, an error similar to the one shown in Figure 8-15 would have occurred.

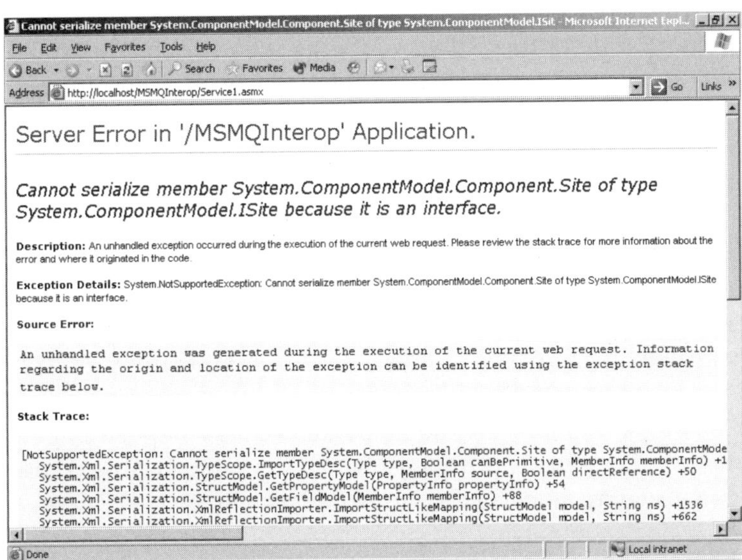

Figure 8-15 Error when trying to expose a *System.Messaging.Message* through Web services.

To overcome this, a new type named *MSMQInterop.Message* has been defined. The XML Schema Definition (XSD) document is provided in the Message.xsd file, which was created by hand by using the techniques described in Chapter 3. All classes that use this message type have been generated from this XSD file.

In addition, the Web service code contains two private methods:

```
private MSMQInterop.Message
    convertToInteropMessage(System.Messaging.Message message)
```

and

```
private System.Messaging.Message
    convertToMSMQMessage(MSMQInterop.Message message)
```

These methods are used to convert between the two types (the XSD type and the native *System.Messaging.Message* type). This allows the Web service interface to expose types of *MSMQInterop.Message* and convert them to *System.Messaging.Message* when placing them in the queue. The opposite is true when messages are retrieved from the queue.

Notice that in these methods, you're mapping only two of the elements (body and label) within the message itself. In a production-type system, you'd probably need to offer a richer set of attributes to handle messages of different types.

Configuring and Setting Security for the Web Service Interface

To run the sample client code and show the Web service interface in action, build the code in the SimpleWebService directory by using the provided NAnt script. Once complete, you need to create a new Internet Information Services (IIS) virtual directory to host the Web service. To do this, launch IIS from Start\Programs\Administrative tools. Navigate through the tree, and right-click Default Web Site. From here, select New/Virtual Directory. Ensure that the alias of the virtual directory is **MSMQInterop** and that the directory points to the **C:\Interoperability\Samples\Resource\MSMQ\WebServiceAPI\SimpleWebService** directory. For additional information on this process, revisit Chapter 5, where we first created a virtual directory for a Web service.

In addition to creating the virtual directory, you need to correctly set the security for the Web service interface. Access to queues in MSMQ follows the Windows security model, and as a result, any new queues that are created have permissions that are assigned to the creator by default.

To achieve this, you need to ensure that the Web service interface is running under the context of the same user (in other words, the logged-on user). To do this, you need to configure a couple of settings on the Web service.

The first setting is to ensure that the Web service deals with incoming security credentials and disables anonymous access. In order to do this, you need to configure the security on the virtual directory. This was covered in some detail in Chapter 6.

Within IIS, open the Properties window for the MSMQInterop virtual directory, navigate to the Directory Security tab and edit the authentication and access controls. Within this dialog box, ensure that Anonymous Access is disabled and both Integrated Windows Authentication (for the .NET client) and Basic Authentication (for the Java client) are enabled, as shown in Figure 8-16.

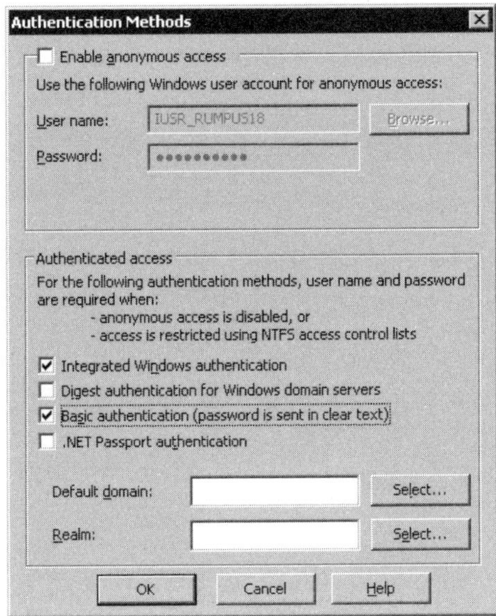

Figure 8-16 Configuring the MSMQInterop virtual directory for authentication.

Save these settings to apply the first security change to the Web service.

The second security setting involves setting an impersonation level for the Web service. Although the previous setting configured the Web service to use secure credentials, you need to ensure that any operation performed by the Web service (for example, adding messages to an MSMQ queue) is done under the context of the calling user.

To do this, you create an *impersonate* setting in the web.config file. This has already been done in the web.config file that's included in the samples. Open this file, and locate the following entry:

```
<identity impersonate="true"/>
```

This setting allows the Web service to correctly impersonate the calling user.

With this configured, the Web service interface for MSMQ is ready to be tested by your clients. Browsing to *http://localhost/MSMQInterop/Service1.asmx* will display the Web service access page, as shown in Figure 8-17.

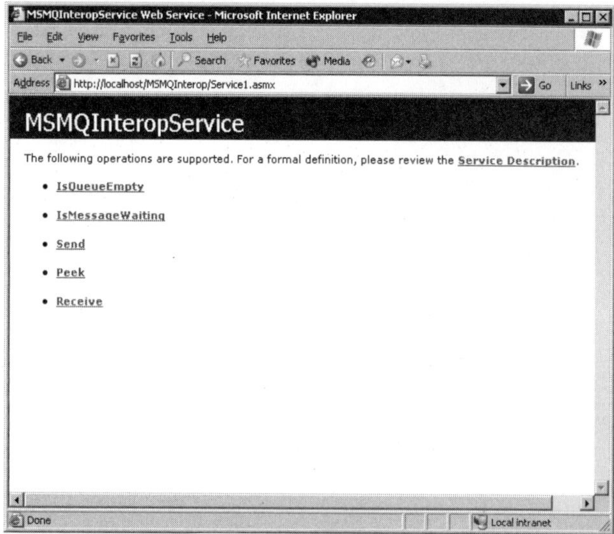

Figure 8-17 The deployed MSMQInterop Web service.

These are the Web service methods that we'll consume by clients in both .NET and Java.

Client Access to the MSMQ Web Service Interface

To show how this MSMQ Web service interface can be utilized from either a .NET or Java client, let's look at the sample code that accesses each, located in the C:\Interoperability\Samples\Resource\MSMQ\WebServiceAPI\SimpleClients directory. This directory contains two subdirectories for each type of client.

Each of the samples shown selects a queue to send messages to and receive messages from. The .NET sample code sends a message on the stock purchase queue and receives any incoming messages from the stock sales queue. The Java client does the opposite, sending a message to the stock sales queue and receiving all incoming messages from the stock purchase queue. Both use the Web service interface to access MSMQ. Figure 8-18 illustrates this.

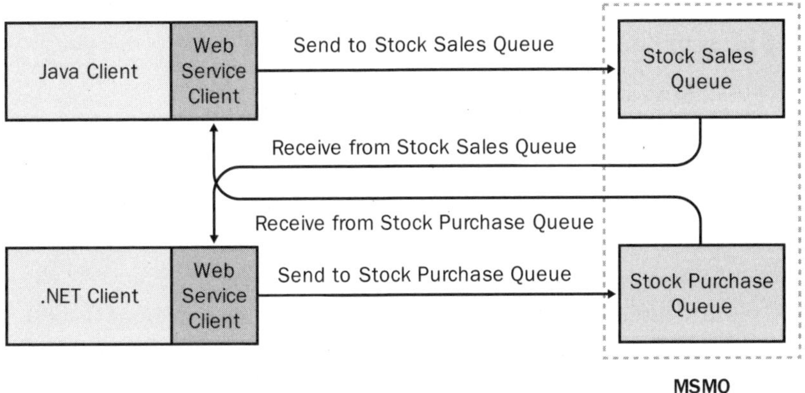

Figure 8-18 Client and queue configuration in the first sample.

At this point, the messages that will be used with the queues are simple text messages.

Accessing the MSMQ Web Service Interface with a .NET Client

The .NET client (the code for which can be found in the Client.cs file in the dotNETClient subdirectory) works by first defining the paths of the two queues.

```
String purchaseQueuePath = @".\private$\stockpurchases";
String saleQueuePath = @".\private$\stocksales";
```

After these declarations follows the definition for the MSMQInterop Web service itself. This definition is stored in the proxy file, MSMQInteropService.cs. It was generated by using the WSDL.EXE tool from the command line.

```
MSMQInteropService msmqAPI = new MSMQInteropService();
msmqAPI.Credentials
    = System.Net.CredentialCache.DefaultCredentials;
```

Notice how the credentials are set to use the default credentials of the logged-on user. The next step is to create the message to be sent to the purchase queue. A new message of type *MSMQInterop.Message* is created and populated with some values.

As with the Web service, the message class (Message.cs) has been created by using the XSD.EXE tool that was discussed in Chapter 3. This ensures that you have a compatible data type to exchange between the client and Web service.

```
MSMQInterop.Message message = new MSMQInterop.Message();
message.Label = "Stock Purchase";
message.Body = "Imagine this is a stock purchase sent at "
    +System.DateTime.Now.ToString();
```

Using this message, the *Send* method from the Web service is then called to send the message to the purchase queue:

```
msmqAPI.Send(purchaseQueuePath,message);
```

At this point, the message is sent to the purchase queue. Notice how the *Send* method returns *void* (nothing). You might imagine a scenario in which an ID or "receipt" is returned to the caller. We'll look at how to take advantage of this in a moment, when we extend the sample and discuss using a Java client to access an MSMQ Web service interface.

In the final piece of the sample code, the *IsQueueEmpty* method is used to see whether the sales message queue contains any messages for retrieval. If it does, each message is extracted in turn and displayed on the screen:

```
if (msmqAPI.IsQueueEmpty(saleQueuePath))
{
    Console.WriteLine("There are no messages on the "
        +"Stock Sale Queue.");
}
else
{
    while (!msmqAPI.IsQueueEmpty(saleQueuePath))
    {
        MSMQInterop.Message incomingMessage
            = msmqAPI.Receive(saleQueuePath,0);
        Console.WriteLine("Message Received...  "
            +incomingMessage.Label+": "+incomingMessage.Body);
    }
}
```

Compile and run the code to test. Upon running, the .NET client sample should display text similar to the following:

```
Sending a message to the Stock Purchase Queue...
There are no messages on the Stock Sale Queue.
```

This indicates that the message was successfully sent to the purchase queue and that there were no messages for retrieval from the sales queue.

Accessing the MSMQ Web Service Interface with a Java Client

Now let's look at the Java client. As with many of the samples shown so far in the book, a lot of the .NET and Java client code tends to be similar, and this sample is no exception.

As with the .NET sample, define the queue paths at the start of the class (Client.java in the JavaClient subdirectory), define the URL of the Web service, and set the security for accessing the .NET Web service:

```
String purchaseQueuePath = ".\\private$\\stockpurchases";
```

```
String saleQueuePath = ".\\private$\\stocksales";
String url = "http://localhost/MSMQInterop/Service1.asmx?WSDL";
Context context = new Context();
context.setProperty("authUser","domain\\user");
context.setProperty("authPassword","password");
```

With the Java client, you need to specify a username and password to authenticate with the Web service. (Again, this was the primary reason that basic authentication security had to be applied on the Web service.) To get this sample working, replace the *domain\\user* and *password* settings with credentials that work in your own environment. These credentials will need read and write access to the MSMQ queues.

As with the .NET client, the Java client calls the Web service, constructs a new message type (again generated from that XSD), sends the message to the sales queue, and retrieves any messages that are within the purchases queue:

```
IMSMQInteropServiceSoap msmqAPI
    = (IMSMQInteropServiceSoap) Registry.bind(url,
        IMSMQInteropServiceSoap.class,context);

Message message = new Message();
message.Label = "Stock Sale";
message.Body = "Imagine this is a stock sale sent at "
    +Calendar.getInstance().getTime().toString();

System.out.println("Sending a message to the Stock Sale Queue...");
msmqAPI.Send(saleQueuePath,message);

if (msmqAPI.IsQueueEmpty(purchaseQueuePath))
{
    System.out.println("There are no messages on the "
        +"stock purchase queue.");
}
else
{
    while (!msmqAPI.IsQueueEmpty(purchaseQueuePath))
    {
        Message incomingMessage
            = msmqAPI.Receive(purchaseQueuePath,0);
        System.out.println("Message Received...  "
            +incomingMessage.Label+": "+incomingMessage.Body);
        }
}
```

After the username and password fields have been adjusted to reflect your own settings, build and run the Java client code. Observe that the Java client sends a message to the sales queue and retrieves the last message that was sent to the purchase queue by the .NET client we recently ran:

```
Sending a message to the Stock Sale Queue...
Message Received...  Stock Purchase: Imagine this is a
stock purchase sent at 3/17/2003 9:56:56 PM
```

Notice how the incoming message is a stock purchase and contains the time that it was sent by the .NET client.

To complete the sample, return to the .NET sample code and rerun the client. Again, you'll see that the .NET client sends a new purchase message to the purchase queue, but this time, the last sale message will be retrieved:

```
Sending a message to the Stock Purchase Queue...
Message Received...  Stock Sale: Imagine this is a stock
sale sent at 3/17/2003 10:09:38 PM
```

Extending the Sample

In the previous sample, you saw how a potential Web service interface for MSMQ can enable messages to be sent to and from different queues, by using either a .NET client or a Java client.

Although this demonstrates how a Web service can act as a façade to an MSMQ interface, you might want to expand the sample in a number of ways:

- **Change the interfaces to be more representative of the business processes** The Web service interfaces that we have been using mimic the MSMQ interfaces. These include calls for sending and receiving messages, supplying the path each time. Although this is technically correct, the premise behind Web services is to generally offer business-type services that others can consume—not strict APIs.
- **Change the security model** The previous samples used and relied on the security of the transport itself—providing the username and password as part of the call and then having the Web service impersonate the client based on these credentials. Again, although this is technically accurate, in a production system, you might want to think about authenticating against another system—one that's not necessarily dependent on the Windows domain model.
- **Pass across a "real type"** Until now, we've exchanged fictitious messages about purchases and sales of stocks. However, we need to use a complex type that will more accurately describe the data moving between the Java and .NET platforms via MSMQ.

To demonstrate the items in this list, look at the sample code in the C:\Interoperability\Samples\Resource\MSMQ\WebServiceAPI directory. In addition to the previously discussed Simple Web service example, this directory contains two subdirectories, ExtendedWebService (which is the Web service that supports the items in this list) and ExtendedClients.

If you first look at the methods exposed by the Web service (Service1.asmx.cs), you can see some of the main differences between this sample and the previous one. Instead of exposing Web service APIs that mimic the send and receive APIs of MSMQ, these methods are much more aligned to the task at hand:

```
public String CreateStockPurchase(StockRecord record,
    Credentials creds)
public String CreateStockSale(StockRecord record,
    Credentials creds)
public StockRecord GetNextStockPurchase(Credentials creds)
public StockRecord GetNextStockSale(Credentials creds)
```

The code contains two methods that allow new stock purchases and sales to be created, and two other methods that allow the stock purchases and sales to be retrieved from the queue. Notice that each of the methods requests a parameter for credentials. This again differs from the previous example. Here, you forward the security details with the method of the Web service, instead of relying on the authentication mechanisms of the underlying transport (HTTP).

To simulate the other authentication model, the Web service has a class named *Authenticator*. This class accepts credentials and returns a Boolean value based on their validity. You can imagine how in a production system, this class can be used to call some external or shared authentication mechanism.

Finally, notice how all the methods used to create new sales or purchases accept a record of type *StockRecord*. Within the class, an XML serialization process is used to serialize this *StockRecord* class to an XML document. The XML document then makes up the body of the MSMQ message. This message uses the same serialization techniques discussed in Chapter 3.

To configure the Web service, build the code in the C:\Interoperability\Samples\Resource\MSMQ\WebServiceAPI\ExtendedWebService directory. Create a new IIS virtual directory with an alias of **MSMQInteropExt** that points to the sample code. This virtual directory can be set up for anonymous access, which is the default setting.

Because the authentication provided by HTTP and IIS isn't being used in this sample, you might need to set the appropriate permissions in the two queues. This is required because the account that the Web service is running under needs write permission to these queues. If you followed the "Configuring ASP.NET Security" section in Chapter 1, "Microsoft .NET and J2EE Fundamentals," you don't need to do anything because the process is running under the context of the SYSTEM account.

Note If ASP.NET is running under an alternative or restricted account (which would be recommended for production purposes), you'll need to apply the appropriate permissions for the queues. To do this, open the Computer Management console and locate the purchase and sales queues. In turn, right-click each of these, select the Properties menu item, and navigate to the Security tab, as shown in Figure 8-19.

Next, add and grant full permission to the queues for the account that ASP.NET is running under. (You might have to explicitly add this user account to the list of users.) The default for this will be ASPNET. If you're running the ASP.NET process under another account, select that account.

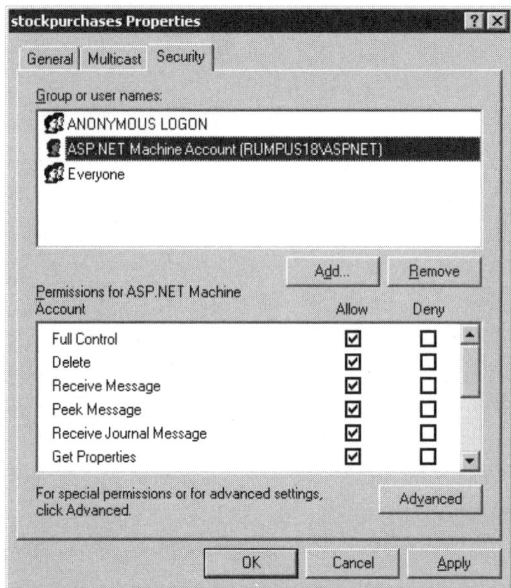

Figure 8-19 Enabling the ASP.NET account to access the queues in the extended sample.

Browse to *http://localhost/MSMQInteropExt/Service1.asmx* to validate that the new sample Web service is running, as shown in Figure 8-20.

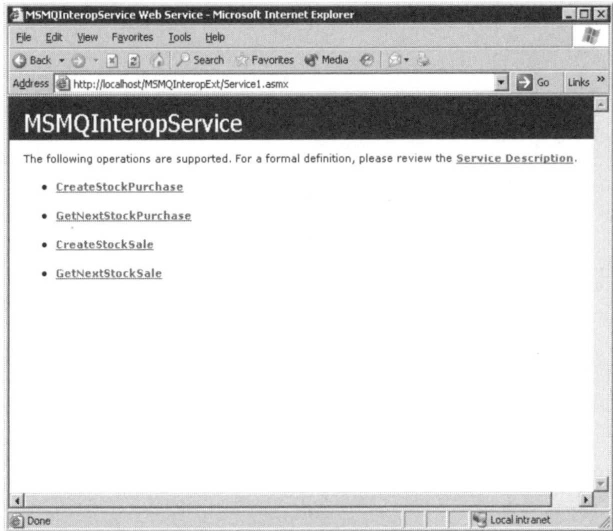

Figure 8-20 The deployed Web service, MSMQInteropExt.

Accessing the Extended Sample with a .NET Client

To show the extended sample in action, two slightly different clients have been created. The .NET client acts as a stock trade monitor, listening for stock records that are placed in the queues. The Java client actively places such records in the queues.

The .NET sample client, which can be found in the C:\Interoperability\Samples\Resource\MSMQ\WebServiceAPI\ExtendedClients\dotNETClient directory, runs as a Windows Forms application. Build the sample in this directory by using NAnt, and type **client** from the command prompt to launch the application. The application shown in Figure 8-21 will be displayed.

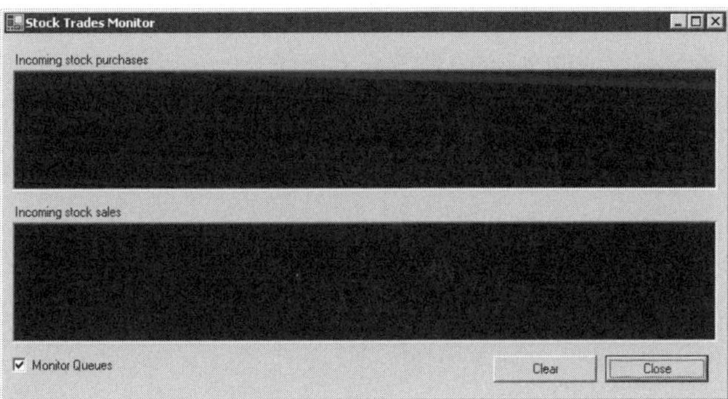

Figure 8-21 The Windows Forms sample application, which monitors the stock purchases and sales.

The sample client displays the two queues (purchases and sales) and has a check box to stop and start monitoring of the queues. This monitoring is performed by using a polling approach, where the *GetNextStockPurchase* and *GetNextStockSale* methods of the Web service are called by using two separate threads within the application (to prevent the application from being blocked by the calls). If nothing is available from either of the queues, the thread sleeps for a predetermined amount of time and retries the operation when that time frame has elapsed. Once an item is discovered in the queue, the appropriate thread will raise an event that's caught by the form itself.

Looking through the code, you'll also notice the agent-service pattern that was discussed in Chapter 6. This pattern (which can be found in StockMonitorAgent.cs) is used to abstract the underlying Web service proxy class and manages the passing of the authentication credentials.

Accessing the Extended Sample with a Java Client

Now that we have the Web service deployed and the .NET Windows Forms client listening for incoming messages, let's generate some sample stock sales and purchases by using the Java client. The Java client sample, found in the JavaClient subdirectory, contains the Web service proxy files to consume the extended Web service. Within the code (Client.java), a new sample stock sale and purchase is created and sent to the Web service.

You might notice that the new Web service calls return a string, shown in the following code:

```
String purchaseReceipt = qs.CreateStockPurchase(purchase,creds);
```

When the Web service writes the stock record to the queue in MSMQ, the ID of the MSMQ message is returned to the client. This ID is a globally unique identifier (GUID) followed by a sequence number and is automatically generated by the MSMQ API.

Compile and run the Java client code. Upon successful completion, the client displays the confirmation of the two actions—your receipt strings will be different:

```
Purchase entered successfully.
    Receipt is: 5ede193e-f0d9-4b1e-9c2a-0be3fb1cd6ff\12
Sale entered successfully.
    Receipt is: 5ede193e-f0d9-4b1e-9c2a-0be3fb1cd6ff\13
```

If you now switch to the .NET Windows Forms client (or open the client, if it's not already running), you should see the two entries recorded, as shown in Figure 8-22.

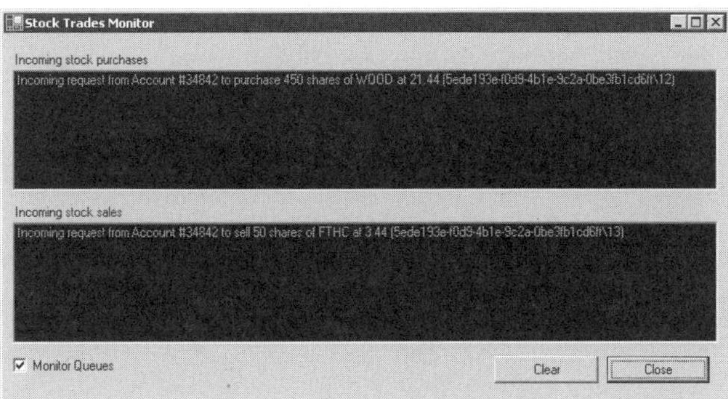

Figure 8-22 The .NET stock monitor, asynchronously receiving incoming records from the Java client.

The clear difference between this demo and the last notification demo in Chapter 7 (where the Java DAO updated the .NET equivalent) is the asynchronous nature of the call. In the Chapter 7 example, in which the .NET client was notified by the DAO of an update to the database, the .NET client had to be online to respond. Here, you can close or disable the monitoring in the .NET client and rerun the Java client, and the message will still reach the .NET client when it's reopened.

Web Service Interface to MSMQ—What You Lose

In this chapter, you've seen how to build a Web service interface for MSMQ and send both simple and serialized messages between the .NET and Java platforms. Although this provides a neat way of exchanging asynchronous messages between the two platforms via the Web Services model, for a number of reasons, this approach certainly isn't nirvana for enterprise messaging. Certain features included in MSMQ are difficult to replicate with an additional Web services interface layer. These features include reliable messaging, transactions, and true callback.

Reliable Messaging

Reliable messaging is the art of sending a message and ensuring that it either reaches its destination or doesn't—and knowing which of these states occurred.

One of the problems with trying to guarantee reliable messaging by using Web services is the transport itself, HTTP. HTTP was designed to run primarily as an Internet-based protocol—the Internet being a network of potentially slow and unreliable connections. As a result, many implementations and providers of the HTTP protocol contain a certain element of "retry" logic. For example, if you've ever had a bad connection to the Internet over a dial-up line, you might have noticed that some pages and images appear to pause when downloading. In a lot of these cases, this ability to continue without immediately throwing an error is the result of an intentional design choice of the HTTP protocol itself.

Based on this, using HTTP for reliable messaging can have some consequences. For example, using the previous stock-trading scenario, imagine this example: Alice, a user of your system, uses the Web service interface API for MSMQ sample demonstrated throughout this section to place an order to buy stock. The order is for $1 million worth of shares. In her share-dealing client software, Alice enters the details of the trade and presses the Commit button.

Alice's client software constructs a Web service request, similar to the Java client request presented earlier, and submits the message to the Web service interface, as shown in Figure 8-23.

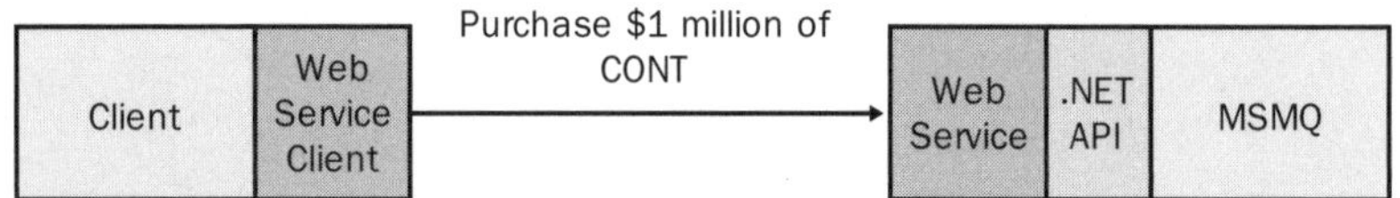

Figure 8-23 A request from Alice to purchase $1 million worth of shares.

The message successfully reaches the Web service. To confirm that the Web service request was accepted, the Web service sends an HTTP 200 ACCEPT message to the client. This is default behavior of the HTTP protocol. Imagine, however, that at this point in time, a temporary network failure occurs. The HTTP 200 ACCEPT message is never returned to Alice's client, as shown in Figure 8-24.

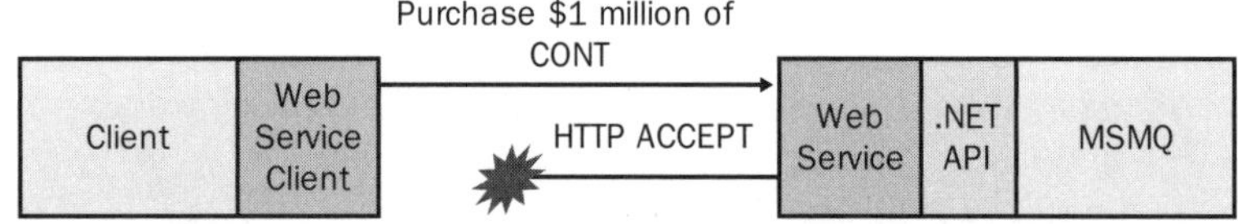

Figure 8-24 The acknowledgment for the purchase never reaches Alice.

As mentioned, Alice's Web service client never receives the HTTP 200 ACCEPT message from the Web Service. Thinking that a network error has occurred, the client automatically resends the Web service request (to purchase the order of $1 million worth of shares). It could be either a feature of the HTTP provider on the client or something in Alice's client software that resends the request.

Now that network connectivity has been restored, the message reaches the destination and an HTTP 200 ACCEPT message is successfully returned to the client. The problem here is that the Web service has received two messages requesting a $1 million order for Alice, whereas Alice (and her client software) believes that only one order has been placed! Subsequently, $2 million is withdrawn from Alice's account, as Figure 8-25 depicts.

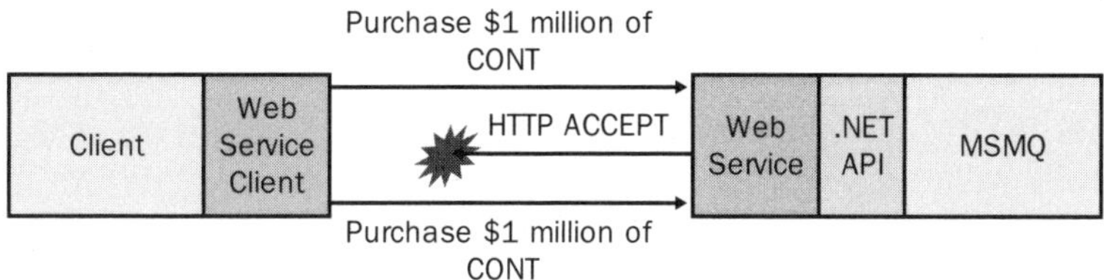

Figure 8-25 Thinking that the send failed, Alice's client software resends the purchase.

Preventing this type of situation from occurring when using HTTP requires a solution that uses messages classified as *idempotent*. Idempotent is defined as something that's unchanged when multiplied by itself.

In this example, because HTTP is the transport of choice, you have to use a solution that uses idempotent messages. That way, regardless of how many times the Web service receives the $1 million order message from Alice, the system will have to recognize that just a single order was placed. This can be achieved by using a unique message ID that's generated by the client. Imagine if when Alice places her order, the client passes a unique ID with her request, as shown in Figure 8-26. Business logic on the server can determine whether the message ID has already been received and can ignore or process it accordingly.

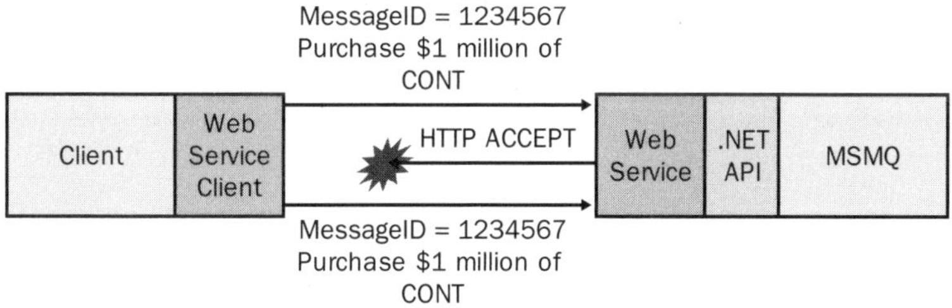

Figure 8-26 Alice adds unique message IDs to help avoid duplication.

> **More Info** This discussion has merely presented an introduction to dealing with idempotent messages and reliable messaging in general. For additional information and research on this and other elements of autonomous computing, I recommend starting with this webcast on the topic, given by Microsoft Architect Pat Helland: *http://www.microsoft.com/usa/Webcasts/ondemand/892.asp*.

Looking ahead to WS-Reliable Messaging Today's Web services offer a great way to achieve interoperability between points in a distributed architecture. I hope that the samples and chapters you've seen so far have illustrated this. Interoperability using Web services is really about connectivity—the ability to connect one client, application, or service to another.

As we've delved deeper into Web services, it's become clear that the Web services stack lacks certain functionality—which I define as application-specific interoperability. As you've seen in this section, reliable messaging is one of these limitations.

A number of members of the Web Services Interoperability Organization (WS-I) are developing specifications to overcome some of these shortfalls. (I call these the *WS-* specifications* because they all begin with this prefix.) At the time of this writing, many of these specifications are still in draft, but we are now seeing some actual implementations being released.

One of these specifications, *WS-Reliable Messaging*, was coauthored by Microsoft, IBM, BEA, and TIBCO. The specification itself defines a modular mechanism for implementing reliable messaging over Web services. It defines a protocol that identifies, tracks, and manages a message between two points. This is performed by a number of defined SOAP headers and bindings.

This specification, which can be found at *http://msdn.microsoft.com/webservices/default.aspx?pull=/library/en-us/dnglobspec/html/ws-reliablemessaging.asp*, demonstrates some of the work that's being addressed in this area.

Transactions

In addition to reliable messaging, enterprise message queues are renowned for their transactional qualities—in other words, their ability to send messages to multiple queues as part of a single transaction. As with reliable messaging, transactions are difficult to incorporate into the Web services model.

Again, this is best described with a small example. Suppose that after spending so much money on her stock shares, Alice decides that she needs to move money from her checking account into her share-dealing cash account. Moving this money from her checking account to her share-dealing account is a transaction. The debit from Alice's checking account and the credit to her share-dealing account must complete—or both must fail—for the transaction to be valid.

Alice wouldn't want to debit the money from her checking account if, for some reason, it could not be placed into her share-dealing account. Likewise, the bank will want to ensure that the checking account is properly debited the amount of the funds moved to the share-dealing account. Both sides of the operation must succeed for the transaction to be valid.

MSMQ 3.0 supports the ability to create transactional message queues to handle situations similar to this example. Recall how at the start of the chapter, in Figure 8-7, we had the option of specifying whether a queue was transactional.

To see these types of transactions in action, create two new private queues using the Computer Management console. Name them **checkingaccount** and **shareaccount**, and mark them both as transactional, using the check box shown in Figure 8-27.

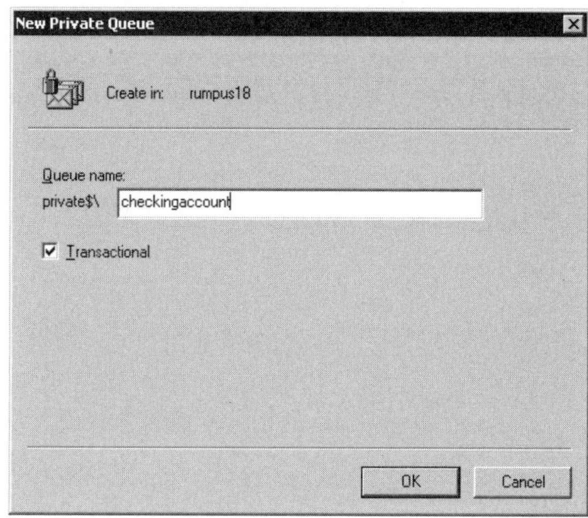

Figure 8-27 Creating a transactional queue in MSMQ.

Once done, look at the sample code located in the C:\Interoperability\Samples\Resource\MSMQ\Transactional directory. This sample code in Client.cs creates two messages as part of a transaction: one to the checking account (to instruct the debit), and one to the sales account (to inform it of a credit).

The transaction is managed by a class in the *System.Messaging* namespace named *MessageQueueTransaction*, defined by the following piece of code:

```
MessageQueueTransaction mqt = new MessageQueueTransaction();
```

As part of a *try...catch* block, the transaction is started. The various send methods used to send the messages to MSMQ include the reference to the previous *MessageQueueTransaction*. Notice how the debit message is sent to the checking account and the credit message is sent to the share-dealing account.

```
try
    // Start the transaction
    mqt.Begin();

    // Send the messages
    checkingMQ.Send(debit,mqt);
    shareMQ.Send(credit,mqt);

    // Nothing went wrong - commit the transaction
    mqt.Commit();
    Console.WriteLine("The transaction completed successfully.");
}
```

If nothing goes wrong with the transaction, both messages are placed in the queue by using the *Commit* method. If, however, something does fail, this is caught in the *catch* block of the code:

```
catch (Exception e)
{
    Console.WriteLine("An exception occured as part of the "
        +"transaction. "+e.ToString());
    Console.WriteLine("Aborting the transaction...");
    mqt.Abort();
}
```

The exception is reported to the user, and the *Abort* method is used to stop the transaction. If the transaction is aborted, no messages will be written to either queue.

Now compile and run the code. If all is successful, the transaction will complete and two messages (one per queue) will be available in the transactional versions of the queues that were just created. Note that you might need to refresh the queue for the message to be displayed.

Now we'll make the transaction fail. Purge the two queues by right-clicking Queue Messages and selecting All Tasks/Purge. Step back into the code, and locate the following line:

```
MessageQueue shareMQ = new MessageQueue(@".\private$\shareaccount");
```

Change the path of the share-dealing account queue to something that doesn't exist (for example, *".\private$\doesnotexist")*. Recompile and rerun the sample.

The message to debit the checking account will succeed. The message to credit the share-dealing account, however, fails (because no queue with that name is found). This error is caught in the *catch* block of the code. Because all these operations form part of a transaction, everything is aborted (including the previous debit from the checking account). The result is the following exception and abort message from the client:

```
An exception occurred as part of the transaction.
System.Messaging.MessageQueueException:
Queue is not registered in the DS.
    at System.Messaging.MessageQueue.ResolveFormatNameFromQueuePath(
    String queuePath, Boolean throwException)
    at System.Messaging.MessageQueue.get_FormatName()
    at System.Messaging.MessageQueue.SendInternal(Object obj,
    MessageQueueTransaction internalTransaction,
    MessageQueueTransactionType transactionType)
    at System.Messaging.MessageQueue.Send(Object obj,
    MessageQueueTransaction transaction)
    at dotNET.Client.Main(String[] args)
Aborting the transaction...
```

In addition, nothing will be written to either of the transactional queues.

So how does this all relate to the MSMQ Web service API that we created? And why is it difficult to create a transactional call using the Web service API? To achieve the results from the previous example, you need to create the transaction, send the messages, and then either commit or abort. This process requires a number of actions, whereas the Web service API is only capable of dealing with a single action at a time. The Web service is stateless, which means that no affinity is held between the client and the service. The Web service takes a single action (for example, sending a message to a certain queue), acts upon it, and is then complete.

To perform a transaction, you need to perform a number of related actions. To do this, you need to create some session state on the Web service. This state would hold the number of requests as they're received and then process them as part of a transaction that runs on the Web service, as shown in Figure 8-28.

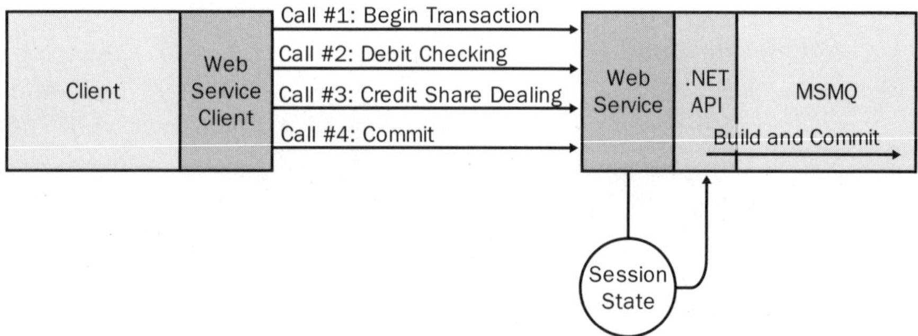

Figure 8-28 Dealing with transactional state using Web services.

Storing state with a Web service is technically possible, but a number of valid arguments against doing so exist. These include

- **Jeopardizing the ability to scale** Multiple instances of Web services running with state can cause heavy load.
- **Possible denial-of-service attacks** Multiple Web services are called; all create and hold state, using valuable memory and resources.
- **Failover** What happens when a Web service fails halfway through creating a transaction?

Looking ahead to WS-Transaction In addition to WS-Reliable Messaging, another specification that addresses some of the application interoperability challenges of Web services is WS-Transaction. The latest version of this specification, which can be found at *http://msdn.microsoft.com/webservices/understanding/gxa/default.aspx?pull=/library/en-us/dnglobspec/html/ws-transaction.asp*, defines both atomic transactions and business activities.

An atomic transaction is typically short lived and is used to identify an operation that must exhibit ACID (atomic, consistent, isolated, and durable) attributes. In an atomic transaction, all operations either complete successfully or are rolled back in the event of an error or exception. The previous example demonstrated an atomic transaction. A business activity is a long-running transaction that involves compensations. Business activities are typically used in situations where atomic transactions do not apply.

For example, let's reexamine Alice's bank balance. The reliable messaging discussion mentioned that Alice's bank balance had been withdrawn twice by accident—as a result of the Web service receiving the message a second time.

If this had been the case, Alice would have contacted her bank to have the error fixed. Once realizing that they were at fault, it's likely that the bank wouldn't have scrubbed the withdrawal from Alice's records (because this could cause inconsistencies with statements issued). Instead, they would have recredited her account with the $1 million to correct the error. This type of transaction rollback (or abort) is known as a *compensating transaction* and is well defined in the scope of a business activity.

I recommend reading through the current WS-Transaction specification. This will give you an appreciation of the topic, the problems you face when making transactions, and the work that's being done to improve the use of transactions in Web services.

True Callback

The final area that isn't truly addressed by the MSMQ Web service wrapper has to do with true callback. You might have noticed that in all the samples shown in this chapter, receiving a message is always controlled by the client. It's the responsibility of the client to "poll" the message queue and see whether a message is waiting.

As a developer, there are certain actions you can take to make this polling a little more asynchronous. This includes using the *AsyncCallback* methods investigated at the start of the chapter. In addition to this type of callback being valid for Web services, it's supported in the *System.Messaging* class through the *BeginReceive* and *EndReceives* methods of the *MessageQueue* class.

But is this true callback? Technically, it isn't. Although the callback is made through a second thread to prevent blocking of the client, this callback is still a request-response type of operation and has to utilize the polling approach as before. This is similar to how the previous MSMQ transaction example worked and is shown in Figure 8-29.

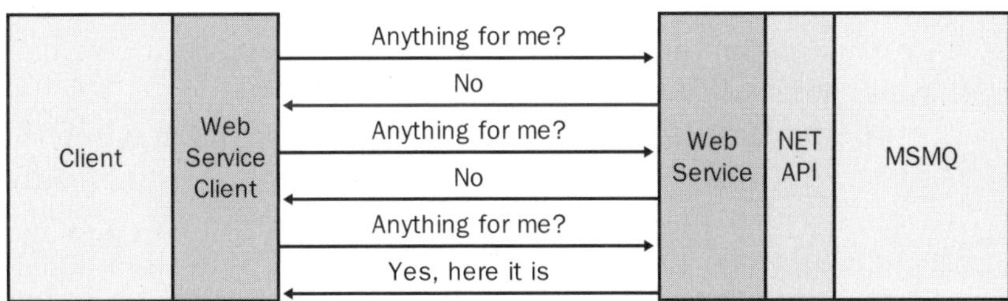

Figure 8-29 Web services polling approach used in the previous MSMQ transaction example.

In this case, the client is still polling, which generates additional (and arguably unnecessary) network traffic. A more ideal solution to enable a *true callback* is for the queue to notify the client when a message is ready to be collected, as shown in Figure 8-30.

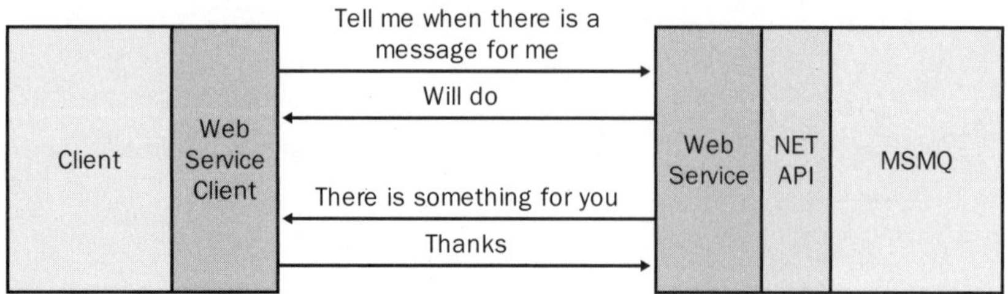

Figure 8-30 What's required for a true callback notification.

Generally in message queue technology, true callback can be achieved by giving the queue a callback location when connecting or sending a message. The queue registers the client and sends notifications directly when messages that match certain criteria enter the queue. Another option is to use a multicast protocol—based on User Datagram Protocol (UDP)—to widely distribute the notification to any client that happens to be listening. To facilitate this, MSMQ 3.0 supports the Pragmatic General Multicast (PGM) "reliable multicast" protocol.

Unfortunately, this is difficult, if not nearly impossible, with Web services today. The underlying reason is again that Web services are based on HTTP, request-response interactions. Callback notifications using these methods with just a regular Web services client is impossible. This is because the Web services client can only issue requests and waits for a response to these requests—and therefore, has no ability to independently "listen" for incoming messages. Of course, it's possible to set up a Web services server component on the client itself (to listen for incoming requests), but then you face potential issues with firewalls and Network Address Translation (NAT).

The underlying problem is that today Web services rely on the HTTP request-response communication model. As the development community moves forward with new implementations of Web services, I think we'll start to see the Web services stack decoupled from the transport. Once this becomes an accepted practice, true callback in asynchronous Web services applications will be more of a reality.

Summary

This chapter introduced the concept of asynchronous interoperability. We started by looking at the concepts of callbacks that are available when generating .NET Web service client proxy files and then looked at the Microsoft Message Queuing product, MSMQ. We also discussed what options are available for Java clients that have a requirement to interoperate with such a queue.

The next chapter will focus on the Java side of enterprise messaging. We'll examine IBM's WebSphere MQ product and the JMS specification and assess the options that are available for achieving interoperability between .NET and J2EE.

9

Asynchronous Interoperability, Part 2: WebSphere MQ

In the previous chapter, we covered how Microsoft Message Queuing (MSMQ) 3.0 can be used to provide some level of asynchronous interoperability between .NET and J2EE. By using a custom API with XML Web services, we exposed some simple endpoints for sending messages to and retrieving them from an instance of MSMQ. We then looked at what this means in a production environment.

In this chapter, we'll look at IBM's message queue solution, WebSphere MQ. Throughout the chapter, we'll examine the support IBM has for both Java and .NET. In particular, we'll look at the Java Message Service (JMS) specification and see an example of how a Message Driven Bean (MDB) in J2EE can be modified to call a .NET Web service upon activation. The chapter concludes by discussing how mixing SOAP and the WebSphere MQ product can offer future options to achieve interoperability.

IBM WebSphere MQ

IBM's WebSphere MQ was more commonly known until recently as MQSeries; the name change applied with version 5.3 of the product. Throughout the chapter, we'll look at WebSphere MQ 5.3, covering the details of the product and then using it to provide interoperability between .NET and J2EE.

WebSphere MQ has evolved dramatically since it was first used as a message queuing product for IBM mainframes, and it is supported on more than 35 platforms today. More recently, IBM's focus has been to offer message queue integration for Java. This includes a full library for Java and support for the JMS specification.

Given the goal of demonstrating interoperability between .NET and J2EE, you might wonder why I chose the WebSphere MQ product for this chapter rather than a similar product from another vendor. My main reason for selecting WebSphere MQ is its position in the enterprise market. Three out of four businesses that use message queue implementations use WebSphere MQ (including MQSeries), and two-thirds of the top 100 North American and European banks use WebSphere MQ (source: *http://www.ibm.com/mqseries*). Given this reach, I felt it was important to show options for how .NET, J2EE, and WebSphere MQ itself can interoperate in these types of enterprise environments.

Downloading and Installing

To allow evaluation of the product, IBM has a 90-day trial version of WebSphere MQ 5.3. This can be downloaded from *http://www.ibm.com/mqseries* and is supported on Microsoft Windows, AIX, Linux, Sun Solaris, and a number of other operating systems.

If you already have a copy of WebSphere MQ 5.3 and are familiar with the setup of the product, you can skip this section. This chapter's sample code, however, does assume that you're running WebSphere MQ on either Microsoft Windows XP Professional or Microsoft Windows Server 2003.

Once you've downloaded the evaluation version of the product, you must follow a number of steps to get an instance of WebSphere MQ up and running. The installation of WebSphere MQ is performed via a series of wizards, the first screen of which is shown in Figure 9-1.

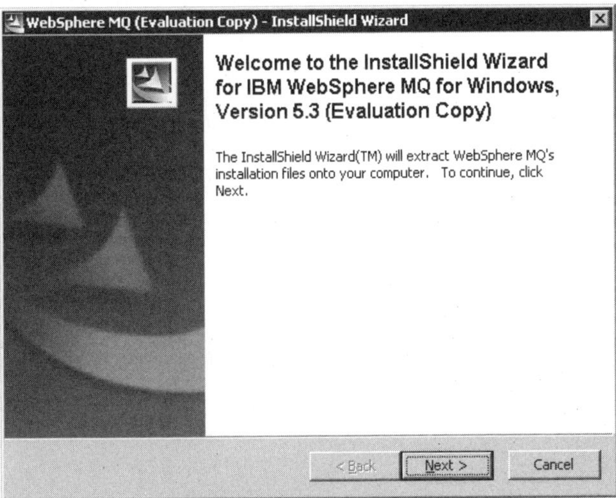

Figure 9-1 Starting the evaluation installation of WebSphere MQ 5.3.

The first wizard prompts for a location to which you'll extract all the files required for installation. After the files are copied to this directory, a second installation wizard will be launched. After a short video (which can be skipped), the installation launchpad will be displayed. Within the launchpad, check that the machine onto which you're installing WebSphere MQ has the correct prerequisites. These include a recent copy of a Java Virtual Machine (JVM)—essentially, 1.3 or higher—and a number of Windows components that are used by some of the administration tools. If you're using the Sun Java 2 Standard Edition (J2SE) 1.4.1, you might find that the launchpad doesn't recognize that the JVM has been installed. Despite this, when you run the sample code in this book, you should be able to proceed and ignore the warning messages.

In addition, WebSphere MQ will require details for the account to use for running the WebSphere MQ Windows Service. As the prompts suggest, it's advisable to check with your system administrator to find out the exact details here. These details are confirmed later in the installation process.

After validating the options in the launchpad, the final wizard (which installs the software) will be run. Read and accept the license agreement, and select a Custom installation. This will allow the selection of components that you'll need for the chapter's examples. Choose an installation location for the program, data, and log files; it's assumed for the examples that WebSphere MQ is installed in the default location.

> **Tip** When installing WebSphere MQ 5.3, if you do have an existing installation of MQSeries 5.2 on your machine, you might be prompted to upgrade. In all situations, I recommend following the custom option to ensure all the required components are installed.

Select all the available options, as shown in Figure 9-2.

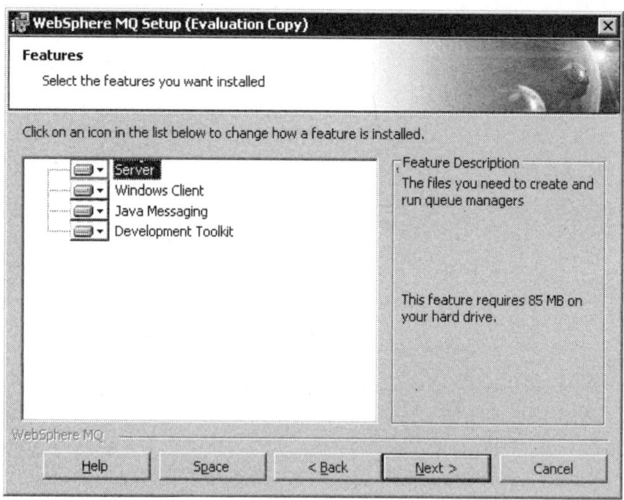

Figure 9-2 Selecting all the installation options for WebSphere MQ.

Confirm the installation details in the next screen, and complete the wizard. WebSphere MQ is now installed.

After the installation has completed, a preparation wizard will be launched to allow you to prepare WebSphere MQ. This is used to configure network account information and verify the setup of the product. Within this wizard, either select Yes and enter the account details that you'll use for the WebSphere MQ service, or select No to configure the service to run as the SYSTEM account. Once given this information, the service will be configured and started.

After the Prepare WebSphere MQ Wizard has completed, you'll be presented with a list of next-step options. Clear all the options—because we'll explore the tools together throughout this chapter—and complete the installation.

Important As with ASP.NET security, although using the SYSTEM account allows the samples in this book to work, this is not recommended in a production environment. Instead, you should create a dedicated user account and assign that account the minimal amount of privileges required. If you do plan to use the SYSTEM account, you should consult the WebSphere MQ documentation for security guidelines.

Configuring WebSphere MQ

After a successful installation, launch the WebSphere MQ Explorer. The Explorer can be found in the IBM WebSphere MQ Programs folder and is the main administration console for creating new queues and queue managers. As with the MSMQ administration tool, the WebSphere MQ administration tool runs as a Microsoft Management Console (MMC) snap-in. Figure 9-3 shows this tool.

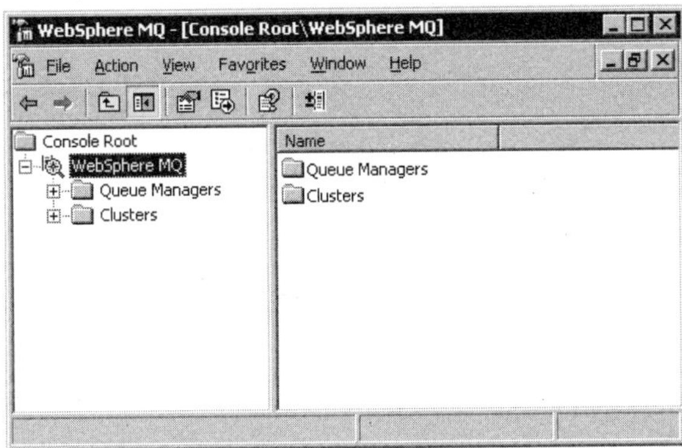

Figure 9-3 The WebSphere MQ Explorer administration tool.

Your first task is to create a queue manager. Within WebSphere MQ, it's possible to logically group queues together under a queue manager. This queue manager allows resources and system options to be shared among the queues that are contained within WebSphere MQ.

To create a queue manager, right-click the Queue Managers folder in the left-hand pane and select the New/Queue Manager option. Create a queue manager named **STQM** (which stands for STock Queue Manager). This name and its casing are important for the samples that we'll run in this chapter. Also, it's important to make this the default queue manager, as shown in Figure 9-4. You don't need to specify a Default Transmission or Dead Letter Queue.

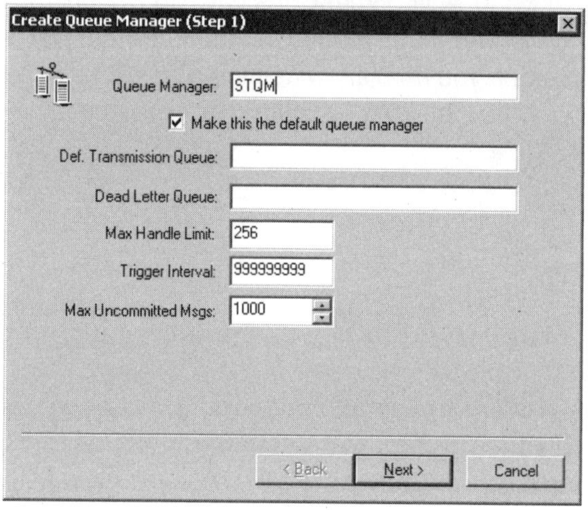

Figure 9-4 Creating a new queue manager and making it the default.

Accept the logging defaults in the next screen as part of step 2, shown in Figure 9-5, and, in step 3, ensure that the queue manager will be started once this creation step has been completed.

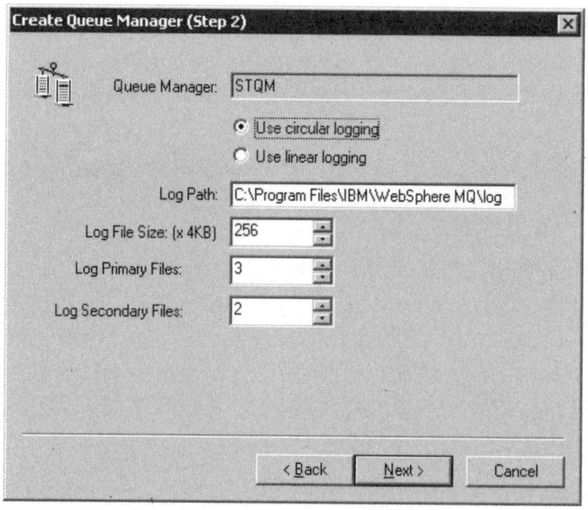

Figure 9-5 Setting the logging options for the queue manager.

Accept the defaults for the next screen, as shown in Figure 9-6. This configures the TCP/IP port settings for incoming connections. Port 1414 should be used for compatibility with the sample code.

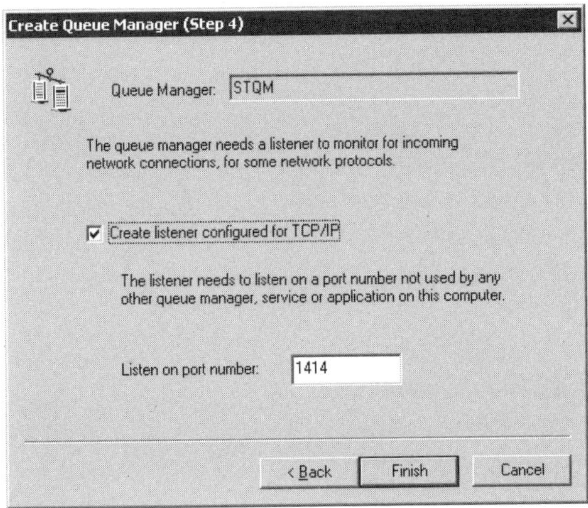

Figure 9-6 Creating a TCP/IP listener for the queue manager.

The queue manager is now created. Returning to the MMC administration tool, you should see the default queue manager, STQM (shown in Figure 9-7).

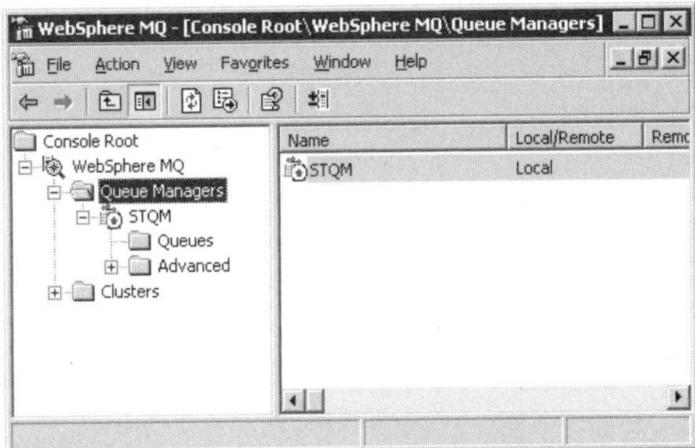

Figure 9-7 Viewing the new queue manager in WebSphere MQ Explorer.

You'll find a folder named Queues under the STQM option in the tool. This folder is currently empty but will contain queues as you start to define them.

Note Although the Queues folder is currently empty, creating the queue manager also created some system queues. These can be examined by right-clicking the Queues folder and selecting the View/Show System Objects option.

To create a new queue, right-click the Queues folder and select New/Local Queue. To show the samples using the same theme, let's create two new local queues, **LOCAL.STOCKPURCHASES** and **LOCAL.STOCKSALES**. For each of these queues, enter the queue name and queue description, as shown in Figure 9-8.

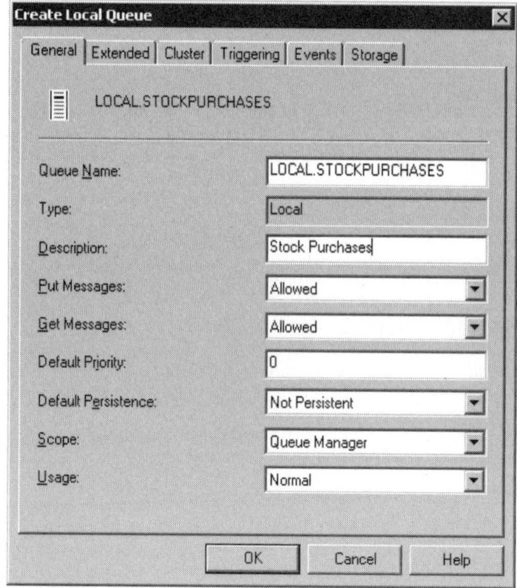

Figure 9-8 Creating a new queue named LOCAL.STOCKPURCHASES.

Ensure that the LOCAL.STOCKPURCHASES and LOCAL.STOCKSALES queue names contain no spaces. Feel free to browse through the options available for the local queue, but accept the defaults. Once complete, the two queues will be visible in the Queues folder of the queue manager, as Figure 9-9 depicts.

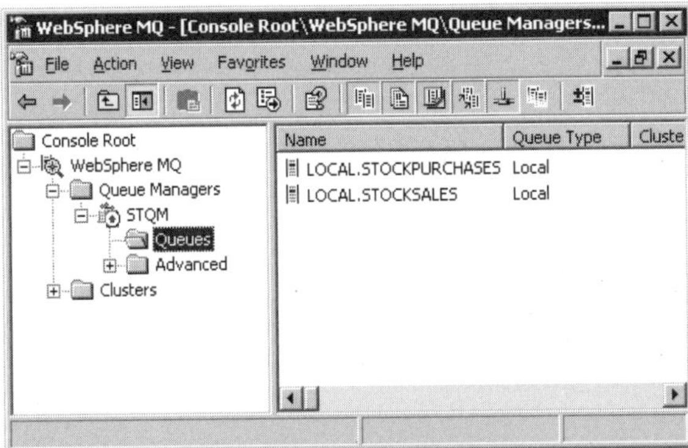

Figure 9-9 Viewing these queues in the WebSphere MQ Explorer.

> **Tip** You might be wondering why we're using uppercase names for the queue manager and queues. WebSphere MQ (and previous implementations of MQSeries) have a history of support for connecting to mainframes. Providing this support constrains the names that can be used. For example, a Multiple Virtual Storage (MVS) system connecting to WebSphere MQ has a limit of four characters that can be used for the queue manager. If we had chosen DefaultQueueManager as the name, connecting to MVS at some point in the future might have not been possible. (And renaming queue managers shouldn't be taken lightly—renaming means that all queues need to be re-created.) In addition, general guidelines and experience dictate that we should follow a naming convention similar to that of other system queues that we'll work with throughout the chapter.

You now have your two queues created. The WebSphere MQ administration tool allows you to list any messages in the queues by double-clicking these items and supports placing a test message on the queue. To do this, right-click one of the queues and select Put Test Message. Enter some text in the window that appears, as shown in Figure 9-10, and press OK to submit the message to the queue.

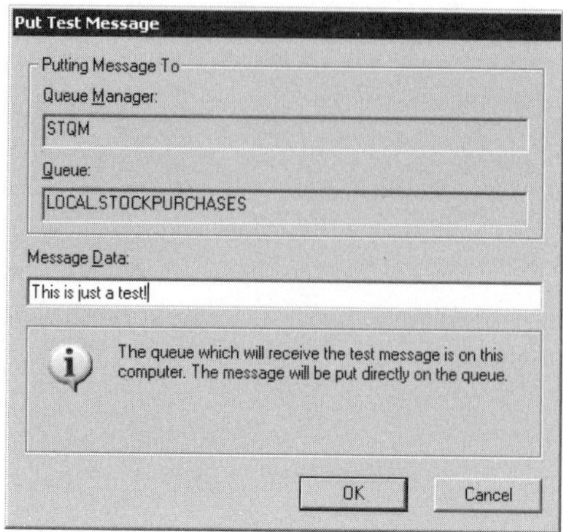

Figure 9-10 Creating and sending a test message for one of the queues.

To clear the messages in a queue, right-click the queue and select the All Tasks/Clear Messages option. We'll now continue the installation and configuration by installing publish/subscribe support for the queues.

Installing Publish/Subscribe Support for WebSphere MQ

Publish/subscribe systems consist of producers of information (known as *publishers*) which is sent to or collected by consumers (known as *subscribers*). The publish/subscribe concept is also frequently known as *pub/sub*.

In WebSphere MQ, pub/sub is enabled by installing the MA0C SupportPac from IBM. This SupportPac, which can be downloaded from *http://www.ibm.com/software/ts/mqseries/txppacs/ma0c.html*, allows WebSphere MQ 5.3 to control the underlying queues required for pub/sub functionality. It's required for the samples presented in this chapter.

> **Note** What is a SupportPac? SupportPac is the IBM term for software that provides fixes or extends the functionality of an existing application. IBM offers four categories of SupportPacs. Category 1 applies to fee-based support. Category 2 includes freeware (and unsupported) fixes and additions. Category 3 is considered a product extension, and Category 4 is used for contributions from third parties.

Download the SupportPac (ma0c_ntmq53.exe) from this site and run it. Follow the simple setup program and ensure that the installation directory matches that of the previous WebSphere MQ installation. Although it's not required, I do recommend a reboot of the machine after installation has completed. This will help ensure that all environment variables are set correctly.

After the reboot and when the WebSphere MQ Service has successfully initialized (indicated by a green, upward-facing arrow in the System Tray), run the following command from the bin directory of the WebSphere MQ installation (default is C:\Program Files\IBM\WebSphere MQ\bin):

```
strmqbrk -m STQM
```

This command will configure our default queue manager (STQM) to handle pub/sub messages. After running the command, the following confirmation message is displayed:

```
MQSeries Publish/Subscribe broker started for queue manager STQM.
```

Note that the MQSeries Publish/Subscribe broker will need to be rerun after every reboot. With this in mind, you might want to add the command to a startup script or menu item.

Now navigate to the C:\Program Files\IBM\WebSphere MQ\Java\bin directory. From here, run the following command, exactly as shown:

```
..\..\bin\runmqsc.exe STQM < MQJMS_PSQ.mqsc
```

This will execute a WebSphere MQ script that sets up the queues required for supporting the pub/sub mechanism in JMS. We'll cover this topic later in this chapter, but it's advisable to run this command at this stage.

If successful, the following message should be displayed at the end of the script:

```
8 MQSC commands read.
No commands have a syntax error.
All valid MQSC commands were processed.
```

The required pub/sub functionality has now been installed for WebSphere MQ.

You can validate this installation by running a predefined verification script supplied with WebSphere MQ. Within the same directory (C:\Program Files\IBM\WebSphere MQ\Java\bin), run the PSIVTRun batch file with the following parameters:

```
psivtrun -nojndi -m STQM
```

This script will create a connection, factory, session, and topic and will add a message to test the pub/sub elements. You don't need to be concerned about these terms now—you need only know that a successful verification will be shown with a series of messages similar to the following:

```
Creating a Connection
Creating a TopicConnectionFactory
Creating a Session
Creating a Topic
Creating a TopicPublisher
Creating a TopicSubscriber
Creating a TextMessage
Adding text
Publishing the message to topic://MQJMS/PSIVT/Information
Waiting for a message to arrive [5 secs max]...

Got message:
JMS Message class: jms_text
  JMSType:         null
…
  JMSXDeliveryCount:1
A simple text message from the MQJMSPSIVT program
Reply string equals original string
Closing TopicSubscriber
Closing TopicPublisher
Closing Session
Closing Connection
PSIVT finished
```

In the event that this isn't successful, WebSphere MQ should produce a reason code (for example, 2085). Running the command-line tool MQRC with the code will give some detail about the error. For example:

```
C:\Program Files\IBM\WebSphere MQ\Java\bin>mqrc 2085
0x00000825  MQRC_UNKNOWN_OBJECT_NAME
```

This error can then be traced and resolved by using the IBM WebSphere MQ documentation.

Congratulations, you have successfully installed WebSphere MQ. We can now investigate the libraries supplied by IBM, explore the chapter's sample code, look at the options available when using the product to pass messages, and achieve interoperability between the .NET and platforms.

WebSphere MQ Support for Java

IBM provides two sets of libraries that can be used with a Java environment. The first is an IBM-provided (vendor-specific) implementation. All the classes in these libraries fall within the *com.ibm.mq.** package. The second is a JMS implementation of these libraries (which can be found in *javax.jms.**).

We'll start by looking at the IBM-provided libraries that can be accessed from a Java client because these map well to the classes that IBM also supplies for .NET.

To best demonstrate this Java library support, a sample has been created in the C:\Interoperability\Samples\Resource\WMQ\Simple\Java directory. This sample, shown in Figure 9-11, is similar to the MSMQ example illustrated in Figure 8-18 (on page 279), where a test message is written to the stock purchases queue and a message is read from the stock sales queue, if available.

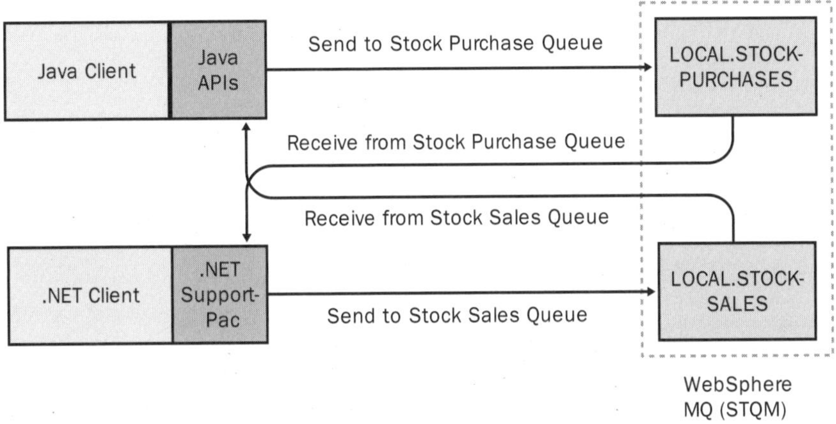

Figure 9-11 Configuration for the supplied WebSphere MQ sample code.

The sample (Client.java) starts by first setting some variables that we'll use to access the WebSphere MQ implementation:

```
String qmName = "STQM";
String purchasesQName = "LOCAL.STOCKPURCHASES";
String salesQName = "LOCAL.STOCKSALES";
```

These include the name of the queue manager and the two local queues that were defined.

Next, in the boundary of a *try...catch* block, the queue manager is opened:

```
MQQueueManager qmgr;
qmgr = new MQQueueManager(qmName);
```

This uses the *MQQueueManager* class within the *com.ibm.mq* package. In order to open queues within the queue manager, you need to first specify how the queues should be opened—for example, whether a queue should be opened for reading messages, writing messages, or both. With the IBM libraries, the process of stating how to open a queue is done by passing specific constants as parameters when opening the queue.

For this example, you'll write to the stock purchases queue and read from the stock sales queue. The options required are as follows:

```
int purchasesOptions
    = MQC.MQOO_OUTPUT | MQC.MQOO_FAIL_IF_QUIESCING;
int salesOptions
    = MQC.MQOO_INPUT_AS_Q_DEF | MQC.MQOO_FAIL_IF_QUIESCING;
```

The *MQC.MQOO_FAIL_IF_QUIESCING* option will cause the sample to throw an exception if the queue or queue manager is in the process of shutting down when the call is made. In order to open the queues, these options are passed with the queue name. First, the purchases queue is opened:

```
MQQueue purchaseQ
    = qmgr.accessQueue(purchasesQName,purchasesOptions);
```

Once the queue is opened, a new message is created and placed on the queue. Part of this message creation process involves setting the encoding and character set:

```
MQMessage msg = new MQMessage();
msg.writeString("This is a test purchase!");
msg.characterSet = 1208;
purchaseQ.put(msg);
purchaseQ.close();
```

> **Tip** To ensure compatibility between the Java and .NET samples, I recommend a character set of 1208 (which is UTF-8 encoding). This might change based on your environment and depending on the type of data that's being passed across the queue. A full list of supported character sets can be found at *http://www.ibm.com/software/ts/mqseries/library/manualsa/csqzaw05/csqzaw0521.htm#TBLCSQ77T8.*

Now that you've placed the message on the queue, you need to open the sales queue to see whether any messages are waiting. The queue is opened with the options previously set:

```
MQQueue salesQ = qmgr.accessQueue(salesQName,salesOptions);
```

To retrieve a message, a new blank message is created. The *get* method from the queue is used to retrieve the message—placing the data into the message that was created:

```
MQMessage incomingMessage = new MQMessage();
salesQ.get(incomingMessage);
```

If a message to be retrieved from the sales queue exists, the details (in this case, just the text of the message) are displayed to the console:

```
System.out.println("Message:  "+incomingMessage.readString(
    incomingMessage.getMessageLength()));
```

If no message is waiting to be collected, an exception of type *com.ibm.mq.MQException* will be raised. One of the fields of *MQException* is a reason code—which is returned from WebSphere MQ to indicate what the problem is. Within the *catch* block of the sample, you check for reason code 2033 (no messages are in the queue) and display a suitable message based on this result:

```
if (mqe.reasonCode == 2033)
{
    System.out.println("There are no messages awaiting collection");
}
else
{
    mqe.printStackTrace();
}
```

The sales queue is closed, and the queue manager is then disconnected.

Build and run the sample code using the provided Ant script. Type **ant run** from a command prompt in the C:\Interoperability\Samples\Resource\WMQ\Simple\Java directory. When both the purchases and sales queues are empty, the following should be observed:

```
Test message has been placed on the purchase queue.
MQJE001: Completion Code 2, Reason 2033
There are no messages awaiting collection.
```

You've seen how the IBM libraries allow connectivity to an instance of WebSphere MQ from a Java application or service. Now let's look at the support available for .NET.

WebSphere MQ Support for .NET

To support .NET, IBM released a SupportPac in February 2003. This SupportPac (MA7P) is based upon an extended proof-of-concept written by a former IBM engineer in 2002.

At the time of this writing, this SupportPac is classed as Level 2. This means that IBM doesn't explicitly offer support for it. Although this classification might restrict organizations from using the SupportPac within production environments, the SupportPac is well suited for the sample code shown in this section.

To download the MA7P SupportPac, go to *http://www.ibm.com/software/integration/support/supportpacs/individual/ma7p.html*. Download and run the MA7P.MSI installer. Accept the defaults, which state that additional files will be installed to the C:\Program Files\IBM\WebSphere MQ\Tools\dotnet directory.

> **Note** At the end of the installation process, the MA7P SupportPac installer might issue a warning that it was unable to add the AMQMDNET.DLL to the global cache. This can easily be corrected by executing the following command from within the C:\Program Files\IBM\WebSphere MQ\bin directory:
>
> ```
> gacutil -i amqmdnet.dll
> ```

The MA7P SupportPac installs a AMQMDNET.DLL in the bin directory of the WebSphere installation. This DLL provides a set of classes that can be used with any .NET application. Although the classes are exposed as managed classes (using Intermediate Language, or IL), under the covers, the classes make PInvoke calls to other MQ client DLLs. This is important because any application that uses these classes will have a dependency on the WebSphere MQ client (or at least the underlying DLLs) installed on each machine.

> **Tip** What is PInvoke? PInvoke provides a direct way for managed code in .NET to call direct methods and functions in a Win32 DLL. Although this avoids using methods such as COM to achieve interoperability, managed code support (for example, garbage collection) isn't provided for these types of calls.

The classes that the AMQMDNET.DLL exposes are remarkably similar to the classes exposed in the Java environment. If, as a developer, you're either porting code between Java and .NET, or writing clients for each platform by using these classes, these matching APIs could be advantageous.

To complement the Java sample and to show these classes being used by a .NET client, a sample is included in the C:\Interoperability\Samples\Resource\WMQ\Simple\dotNET directory.

The client works in almost the exact same way as the Java classes. The classes exposed by AMQMDNET.DLL fall under the package *IBM.WMQ*, which is referenced at the top of the class:

```
using IBM.WMQ;
```

Each of the classes and methods exposed by the *IBM.WMQ* namespace uses the same names as the Java classes:

```
MQQueueManager qmgr;
qmgr = new MQQueueManager(qmName);
int salesOptions
    = MQC.MQOO_OUTPUT | MQC.MQOO_FAIL_IF_QUIESCING;
int purchasesOptions
    = MQC.MQOO_INPUT_AS_Q_DEF |   MQC.MQOO_FAIL_IF_QUIESCING;
```

Build and run the .NET sample code using the provided NAnt script (enter **nant run** at a command prompt). The script makes reference to the required AMQMDNET.DLL library for compiling. The location of this DLL is defined in C:\Interoperability\Samples\Config\webspheremq.nant.properties. If WebSphere MQ is installed in a location other than the default or if you have problems compiling, you should check the properties of this file.

Because the Java client sample has previously been run, you should observe the following output:

```
Test message has been placed on the sales queue.
Message:  This is a test purchase!
```

The .NET client has placed a test message on the sales queue and picked up the message that the Java client placed on the purchases queue. If you now return to the Java client and rerun it, you should observe a similar behavior:

```
Test message has been placed on the purchase queue.
Message:  This is a test sale!
```

While running these samples, you can use the IBM WebSphere MQ Explorer to view the messages as they're placed on the queue by each of the clients. As with the MSMQ examples earlier in the section, the administration tool lets you investigate the data of the message, as shown in Figure 9-12.

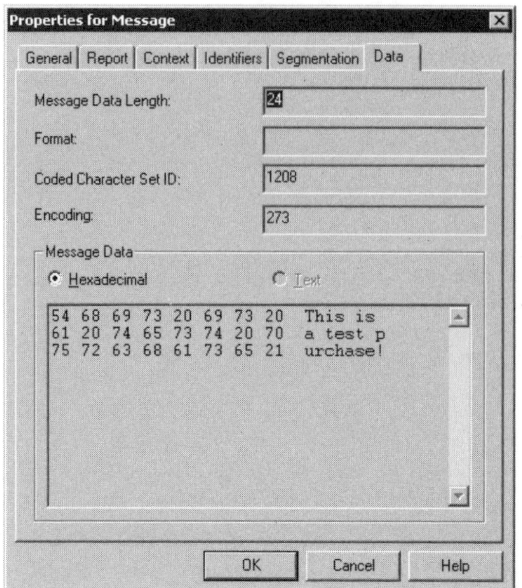

Figure 9-12 Viewing the message in WebSphere MQ Explorer.

This will become more useful as we continue to look at different message types in the following sections. As you can see in the figure, the text is passed between the Java and .NET clients in a "raw" format (meaning that it's not serialized or packaged in any way). The raw format that composes the message is literally a stream of bytes.

Differences Between the Java and .NET Classes

You saw earlier how to use the MA7P SupportPac to create a simple client application in .NET that has the ability to put messages to and get messages from an instance of WebSphere MQ. Creating the .NET client required classes and methods that were almost identical to their Java equivalents, allowing simple messages to easily be exchanged between them.

Unfortunately, not all the methods available in the Java classes are replicated in .NET. Today the MA7P SupportPac remains a subset of the classes that can be found in Java.

Looking through the documentation that accompanies the SupportPac, you can see that the following list of classes are available in Java but aren't present in the .NET version:

- *MQChannelExit*
- *MQDistributionList*

- *MQDistributionListItem*
- *MQMessageTracker*
- *MQPoolServices*
- *MQPoolServicesEvent*
- *MQPoolServicesEventListener*
- *MQPoolToken*
- *MQProcess*
- *MQSimpleConnectionManager*
- *MQReceiveExit*
- *MQSendExit*
- *MQManagedConnection*
- *MQManagedConnectionFactory*
- *MQManagedConnectionMetaData*

So, what is lost today with using the .NET MA7P SupportPac? *MQDistributionList* and *MessageTracker* are used by clients that need to send a single message to multiple queues. The *MQPool* classes are used for setting up a connection pool—the .NET version supports only individual connection types. The *ManagedConnection* classes are supersets of existing connection classes and are used to provide additional data about the connection type.

Introduction to JMS

One of the first things to understand about Java Messaging Service, or JMS, is that it's a specification—not a product. When laterally comparing the message queue products from various platforms, this is easily forgotten. Sun Microsystems defines the JMS specification and API as part of the J2EE specification (*http://java.sun.com/products/jms/index.html*), but it's left to third-party vendors to actually provide the implementation.

The first draft of the JMS specification was released in 1998 and was intended to unify all the message queue vendors at that time, who were starting to introduce their own Java libraries to the market. The goal of the JMS specification was to ensure a standard, programmatic interface for messaging.

Many message queue vendors (those with a Java background) write JMS providers for their products. By doing so, they provide the "glue" between the JMS API and the message queue product itself. For example, IBM's model looks similar to Figure 9-13.

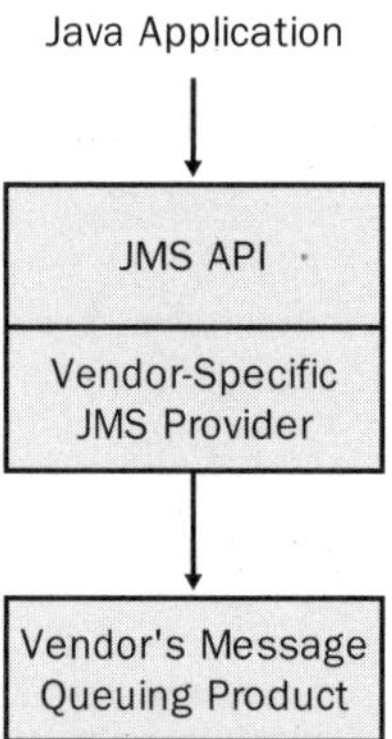

Figure 9-13 A typical JMS model showing the specification and vendor integration.

The theory is that the JMS API can be used to switch vendors and provide portability, although the specification doesn't dictate this.

JMS Message Types and Concepts

JMS defines two types of messaging concepts: queue-based messaging and publish/subscribe. Queue-based messaging is where the JMS sender and receiver both agree on a predefined queue. A JMS object of type *javax.jms.Queue* is used to define a preexisting queue that's used to handle asynchronous messages. For example, a client will send a message to Queue1 and a receiver will receive the message from the same queue. This is very similar to the MSMQ model you saw in Chapter 8, "Asynchronous Interoperability, Part 1: Introduction and MSMQ."

Publish/subscribe (also known as pub/sub, as noted earlier) is a slightly different model. Here, queues are categorized as topics (*javax.jms.Topic* is used). An application using JMS either can be a publisher or subscriber to a particular topic. As a publisher, the application is responsible for publishing new messages to the topic. A subscriber receives these messages if it is subscribed to that particular topic. Multiple subscribers can receive the same message for each topic, and options defined within the JMS specification control how durable the message is (whether the message is available after the time of publication).

Most message queue vendors that support pub/sub control the management of topics automatically. Because topics can be created and modified dynamically by clients, a fixed queue or service isn't always possible. The MA0C publish/subscribe SupportPac used by WebSphere MQ takes control of topic management by using predefined system queues and channels.

JMS supports five types of messages:

- ***javax.jms.TextMessage*** Used for simple string messages.
- ***javax.jms.BytesMessage*** Used for sending raw bytes as messages.
- ***javax.jms.ObjectMessage*** Used to send a serializable Java object as a message.
- ***javax.jms.MapMessage*** Used to send a message that can support name/value pairs (similar to a hash table).
- ***javax.jms.StreamMessage*** Used to support the same types as *MapMessage*, but where the contents of the message need to be sent in order.

All of these message types implement the *javax.jms.Message* interface. We'll look at *MapMessage* and *BytesMessage* in more detail in the samples in this section.

> **More Info** For additional information and research on JMS, you'll find a wealth of books and resources on the topic. For an enterprise perspective, I recommend Shaun Terry's *Enterprise JMS Programming* (John Wiley & Sons, 2002).

JMS, WebSphere MQ, and Interoperability

Although not mandatory, the JMS specification—and resources authoritative on the topic—recommend using the Java Naming and Directory Interface (JNDI) to register objects in JMS. Accessing WebSphere MQ queues and topics by using JMS requires a registration process to create references to these objects in JNDI. Client access via JMS in the samples presented in this section must be performed by looking at queues and topics that are registered using JNDI. Figure 9-14 illustrates this.

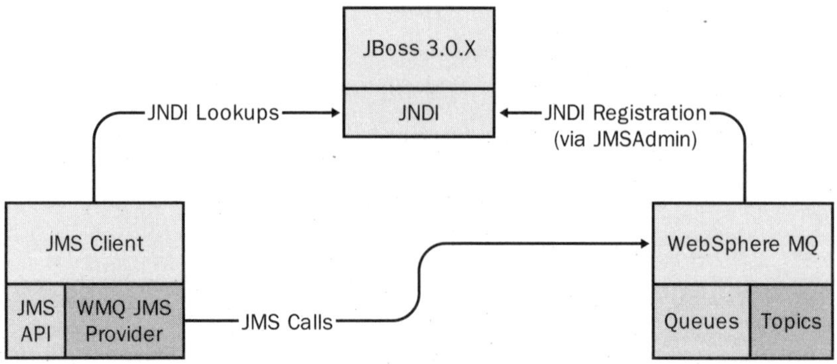

Figure 9-14 Setup required for the sample code to show a JMS client accessing WebSphere MQ.

As shown in Figure 9-14, an instance of JNDI must be available to register the WebSphere MQ queues and topics and to provide lookup capability for clients that want to access these resources. This setup tends be unique for each type of J2EE application server.

This chapter and its samples will show how this can be achieved by using JBoss 3.0.7. All the samples that use JBoss assume that the application server is installed locally, to a directory of C:\JBoss. If this isn't the case, you can modify the jboss.properties and ejbdeploy.properties files in the C:\Interoperability\Samples\Config directory to suit your own environment.

Using JMSAdmin to Configure JNDI

To start configuring the JNDI context shown in Figure 9-14, we'll look at a tool named JMSAdmin. JMSAdmin is supplied with WebSphere MQ and enables the registration of WebSphere MQ–specific objects (for example, queues, topics, and factories) in a JNDI instance. The JMSAdmin tool can be found in the C:\Program Files\IBM\Websphere MQ\Java\bin directory (assuming defaults were accepted during installation).

To connect to an application server, the tool uses settings that are stored in a configuration file in this directory, named JMSAdmin.config. This file specifies how the tool should connect, libraries that are required for connection, security information, and other details. To aid deploying to an instance of JBoss 3.0.7, a preconfigured Ant script has been supplied, which overwrites the default configuration with settings explicit to JBoss. This script (with some other supporting files) can be found in the C:\Interoperability\Samples\Resource\WMQ\Scripts directory. Run the provided Ant script with the deploy target from this directory. This will copy these files to the appropriate WebSphere MQ directory.

To access the application server, the JMSAdmin tool will use the following settings in the JMSAdmin.config file:

```
INITIAL_CONTEXT_FACTORY: org.jnp.interfaces.NamingContextFactory
PROVIDER_URL: jnp://localhost:1099
```

These provide an initial context factory, which can be used to allow the JNDI tree to be traversed. If the JBoss implementation is on a different machine than the instance of WebSphere MQ, you'll need to change the *PROVIDER_URL* to reflect the relevant location.

You'll configure the JMS entries in JNDI by using a script. This will ensure accuracy for the remaining samples in this section and prevent a lot of retyping. This script is copied to the C:\Program Files\IBM\WebSphere MQ\Java\bin directory as part of the previous Ant deployment and is named JMSScript.txt. Open this file in Microsoft Notepad or another text editor.

This script defines a number of objects that will be created in JMS. These objects will be used by the JMS sample code in the remainder of this chapter. Moving through the file, the following is defined:

```
DEFINE QCF(StockQCF) QMGR(STQM) TRAN(CLIENT) HOST(LOCALHOST)
PORT(1414)
DEFINE TCF(StockTCF) QMGR(STQM) TRAN(CLIENT) HOST(LOCALHOST)
PORT(1414)
```

QCF stands for *QueueConnectionFactory*. The *QCF* object in this script will link an instance of *javax.jms.QueueConnectionFactory* with the instance of the queue manager in WebSphere MQ. *TCF* stands for *TopicConnectionFactory* and will do the same for a pub/sub model. If you're running JBoss on a different machine to WebSphere MQ, you'll need to replace the *HOST* value with the name of the machine running WebSphere MQ.

After the *QCF* and *TCF* have been defined, the context is changed into a JNDI directory named *queue*. (This is where JBoss stores references to queues.) Within the script, you create two new queues. (These are queue objects within JMS that will point to the queues that you previously created in the WebSphere MQ administration console.)

```
CHANGE CTX(queue)
DEFINE Q(StockPurchasesQueue) QMGR(STQM) QUEUE(LOCAL.STOCKPURCHASES)
DEFINE Q(StockSalesQueue) QMGR(STQM) QUEUE(LOCAL.STOCKSALES)
```

Notice how the *QMGR* and *QUEUE* properties of the definition match the details on the WebSphere MQ implementation. Next, two topics are defined in a JNDI directory named topic. The two topics are *HotStocks* and *NotSoHotStocks*—think of these as news feeds based on the recommendations example you've seen throughout the book. Once these are defined, the script ends.

```
CHANGE CTX(=UP)
CHANGE CTX(topic)
DEFINE T(HotStocks)
DEFINE T(NotSoHotStocks)
END
```

Before running the JMSAdmin tool, ensure that jnpserver.jar, jboss-common.jar, and log4j.jar are in the *CLASSPATH*. To aid this, a batch file named setenv.bat can be run. This file was copied to the WebSphere MQ directory when the Ant script was previously run with the deploy target. You might need to edit this batch file to reflect settings suitable for your environment.

Start the JBoss server and run the JMSAdmin tool, passing the script file as a parameter. The following command should be run:

```
jmsadmin -t -v < jmsscript.txt
```

This will take the line entries in the script and create the required JMS objects in JNDI. The JMSAdmin tool won't display these commands as it processes them. If you're not using JBoss, you might have to adjust the JMS script to include the creation of queue and topic contexts. These are noted as comments in the JMSScript.txt file, but you should also consult the documentation for your application server.

JNDI is now configured with JMS-aware objects that reference our implementation of WebSphere MQ.

Persistent and Nonpersistent JNDI with JMSAdmin

When using the JMSAdmin script, be aware of the persistence of the objects that are created. By default, using *org.jnp.interfaces.NamingContextFactory* generates "administered" objects in JMS. This means that when the JBoss server is restarted, this information is lost and the script has to be rerun. This can be useful in a test environment, where different permutations of queues and topics are being used, but it's not suitable for more stable environments.

All the sample code used in this chapter will use this nonpersistent mode. One option for making this code persistent is to use Sun's File System context service provider classes (*com.sun.jndi.fscontext.RefFSContextFactory*). To use these classes with the chapter's samples, uncomment the relevant lines within the jmsadmin.config file, rerun the jmsadmin script, and in the sample code, adjust the *InitialContext* calls to use this provider library and URL instead. I recommend following all the examples through once before making any persistent changes to JNDI stores.

Using JMS to Access WebSphere MQ Queues

With JNDI configured, let's look at some sample client code that uses the JMS libraries to access WebSphere MQ. The sample code can be found in the C:\Interoperability\Samples\Resource\WMQ\JMS\Queue directory. The client (Client.java) works by first importing the required JMS and JNDI libraries:

```
import javax.jms.*;
import javax.naming.Context;
import javax.naming.InitialContext;
import javax.naming.NamingException;
```

The first thing for the *main* method is to create the context for JNDI, which is done with the following code:

```
Hashtable ht = new Hashtable();
ht.put(Context.INITIAL_CONTEXT_FACTORY,
    "org.jnp.interfaces.NamingContextFactory");
ht.put(Context.PROVIDER_URL,"jnp://localhost:1099");
Context context = new InitialContext(ht);
```

Notice how the *INITIAL_CONTEXT_FACTORY* and *PROVIDER_URL* settings match the library and URL used by the JMSAdmin tool. To start using the defined queues, you must first access the *QueueConnectionFactory*. This was one of the first items created by our JMSAdmin script.

```
QueueConnectionFactory qcf
    = (QueueConnectionFactory)context.lookup("StockQCF");
QueueConnection qc = qcf.createQueueConnection();
QueueSession qs
    = qc.createQueueSession(false,Session.AUTO_ACKNOWLEDGE);
```

After this, define the two queues that you'll use in the sample. Both the purchases and sales queues are prefixed with the JNDI queue path that was defined earlier.

```
Queue purchasesQ
    = (Queue)context.lookup("queue/StockPurchasesQueue");
Queue salesQ = (Queue)context.lookup("queue/StockSalesQueue");
```

To send a message, create a sender from the *QueueSession*, create the message to be sent, and call the *send* method. Notice that you're creating a message of type *javax.jms.MapMessage*.

```
QueueSender sender = qs.createSender(purchasesQ);
sender.setDeliveryMode(DeliveryMode.PERSISTENT);
MapMessage msg = qs.createMapMessage();
msg.setString("Body","This is a test JMS Stock purchase");
sender.send(msg);
```

To receive incoming messages, you perform a similar process, but you use a *QueueReceiver*. A new *QueueReceiver* is created that points to the sales queue object in JNDI. You then use the *receive* method to collect the first message from the queue, waiting for 10 seconds before timing out.

```
QueueReceiver receiver = qs.createReceiver(salesQ);
qc.start();  // required for receiving messages

try
{
    //wait for 10 secs, blocking thread
    Message incomingMsg = (Message)receiver.receive(10000);

    if (incomingMsg instanceof MapMessage)
    {
        System.out.println("JMS Map Message received:  Body="
            +((MapMessage)incomingMsg).getString("Body"));
     }
```

If a message is available on the queue and is of type *MapMessage*, it's retrieved and the *Body* string of the message is displayed.

Ensure that the purchases and sales queues are clear of messages by using the WebSphere Explorer administration tool. Build and run the code using the provided Ant script. (You'll return to the rest of the code sample soon.) The JMS sample will place a JMS *MapMessage* on the queue, wait for 10 seconds, and then time out (because there's no message waiting to be collected):

```
Sending a test message to the stock purchase queue.
Complete
```

From within the WebSphere MQ Explorer administration console, open the message that has been placed on the queue. You can see the contents of the JMS message by selecting the Data tab in the message itself, as shown in Figure 9-15. You have some header information, followed by a JMS message, the elements of which are described in XML. The elements of the *MapMessage* will follow this JMS header.

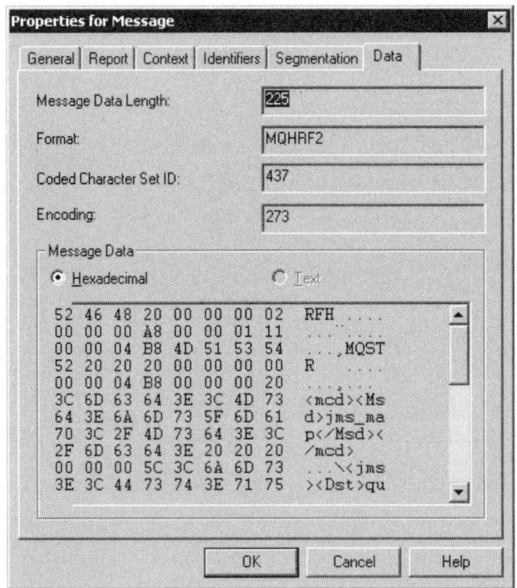

Figure 9-15 A JMS message, as shown in WebSphere MQ Explorer.

Given that you can now send JMS messages to WebSphere MQ, how feasible is it to interoperate with the WebSphere MQ classes for .NET?

Using the MA7P to Send a Message to a JMS Listener

As we've discussed, the JMS libraries aren't supported by or provided for .NET. However, as you saw earlier, you can still use the MA7P SupportPac to send and receive messages via a queue. With a little work on the Java client, you can determine this message type, and based upon that message type, you can take an alternate course of action for messages from .NET clients.

Reopen the sample code in the C:\Interoperability\Samples\Resource\WMQ\Simple\dotNET\Client directory. This sample showed using the IBM WebSphere MQ classes for .NET to access the queue. Run the sample code. You should observe output similar to the following. First of all, the client writes a message to the sales queue, which is successful.

```
Test message has been placed on the sales queue.
```

Next, the MA7P client tries to read the JMS message as a series of bytes. (Recall how the WebSphere MQ libraries treated each message as a stream of bytes.) Although the output contains the valid data of the JMS message, the .NET client can do very little with this. The .NET client doesn't have an understanding of the JMS schema or header in order to process the message in full.

```
Message:  (leading binary characters)
<mcd><Msd>jms_map</Msd></mcd>    \
<jms>
    <Dst>queue://STQM/LOCAL.STOCKPURCHASES</Dst>
    <Tms>1049751767987</Tms>
    <Dlv>2</Dlv>
</jms>
<map><Body>This is a test JMS Stock purchase</Body></map>
```

Now return to the Java client in the C:\Interoperability\Samples\Resource\WMQ\JMS\Queue directory. Rerun the sample code from here using the Ant script. You'll observe that a JMS message is again placed on the purchase queue, but this time, the .NET message that's been waiting on the sales queue is picked up. The client reports the following:

```
Bytes Message received.  Message details:
JMS Message class: jms_bytes
  JMSType:         null
...
  JMS_IBM_PutDate:20030407
Integer encoding: 2, Floating point encoding 512
5468697320697320612074657374207361 6c6521

Message = This is a test sale!
Complete
```

The Java JMS client has successfully picked up the message from the .NET client by using the MA7P SupportPac. If you examine the second half of the Java client code, you can see how this works. The incoming message is received using the *receive* method from the *receiver* object:

```
Message incomingMsg = (Message)receiver.receive(10000);
```

After a message has been detected, a test is performed to see what type of message you're dealing with. Here, you test for *MapMessage* (which is the JMS map message you've been dealing with) and a *BytesMessage*:

```
if (incomingMsg instanceof MapMessage)
{. . .}

if (incomingMsg instanceof BytesMessage)
{. . .}
```

Using this test, you can see whether the incoming message has been generated by a regular JMS client or by a client using the IBM WebSphere MQ libraries (including the .NET libraries). If *BytesMessage* objects are also being sent by JMS clients in the enterprise, you can test some of the properties of the message to determine its origin.

So what does this all mean? Using what you've learned in the previous sample, clients in .NET can send messages to clients using JMS. Although this could be useful in a number of cases, it doesn't guarantee interoperability between the two platforms. In essence, I've found the following to be true: Using the methods described earlier, JMS clients can receive messages from the .NET client, providing that the message is cast to a *javax.jms.BytesMessage*. However, this doesn't work the other way. If a JMS client writes a message (of type *javax.jms.BytesMessage* or any other JMS type) to the queue without recognizing and decoupling the JMS header, it's still very difficult to read the message using the .NET client.

Using JMS Pub/Sub to Access WebSphere MQ Topics

Unfortunately, other aspects of JMS also provide for interoperability problems with .NET. One such aspect is using publish/subscribe (pub/sub) features. As you saw earlier, JMS supports a feature known as pub/sub, which enables clients, applications, and services to register to either publish or subscribe to a number of topics. For example, a topic named "Hot Stocks" could be created, and this topic could be used to list all the recommendations or tips to buy a particular stock. In JMS, a client would subscribe to this topic, meaning that it would receive any messages destined for this topic. Likewise, some server process (such as a stock-trading analyst) could act as a publisher. This analyst would publish the recommendations picked up by all the subscribers, as shown in Figure 9-16.

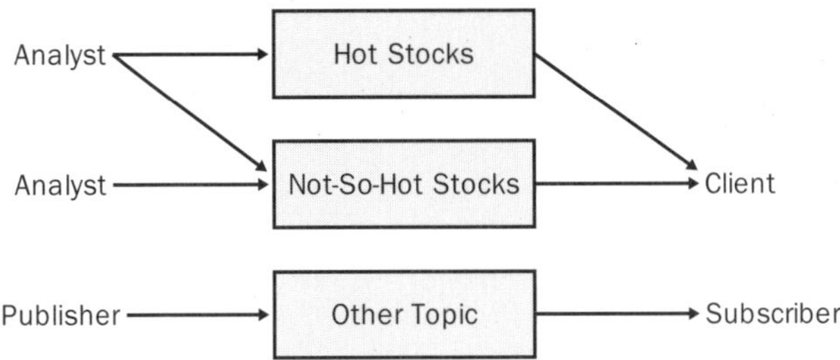

Figure 9-16 A pub/sub model showing publishers, topics, and subscribers.

Although we won't show it explicitly here, sample code demonstrating this publish and subscribe model can be found in the C:\Interoperability\Samples\Resource\WMQ\JMS\PubSub directory.

Because the pub/sub topics tend to be fluid (in other words, anyone can create a topic on the fly), WebSphere MQ doesn't automatically associate one queue per topic. Doing so might cause some restrictions on the number of topics allowed. Instead, the MA0C SupportPac (installed earlier) configures a number of channels and system queues to automatically handle the number of incoming requests.

Herein lies the problem of interoperability between JMS pub/sub topics and .NET clients. Today, the MA7P SupportPac doesn't provide support for accessing topics. Also, because the queues for each topic are handled by WebSphere MQ as system objects, a .NET client can do little to nothing to access the queues. Even if you use the *MQQueueManager* class, there's no way to associate a connection to a queue with a topic. This means that JMS topics, publishers, and subscribers remain solely for use by JMS clients. Interoperability using direct, client-access communication is very difficult to achieve.

Topic-Driven Interoperability with Message Driven Beans

Fortunately, you can apply some techniques to enable a .NET client to subscribe to a JMS topic. One such technique is to use Message Driven Beans, or MDBs. Enterprise JavaBeans (EJB) 2.0, a key component of Sun's J2EE v1.3 specification, introduced the concept of the Message Driven Bean. An MDB is an Enterprise JavaBean that derives from *javax.ejb.MessageDrivenBean* and is activated based upon a message being delivered to a JMS queue or topic.

For an MDB to be hosted using a J2EE application server, it must contain a deployment descriptor. This descriptor specifies the destination queue or topic that it should be invoked upon and any message filtering that should be applied. (For example, you might invoke the bean only for messages that start with *xyz*.) In addition to being based upon a topic in JNDI, a number of providers are required to link the MDB and container with the underlying JMS implementation, as shown in Figure 9-17.

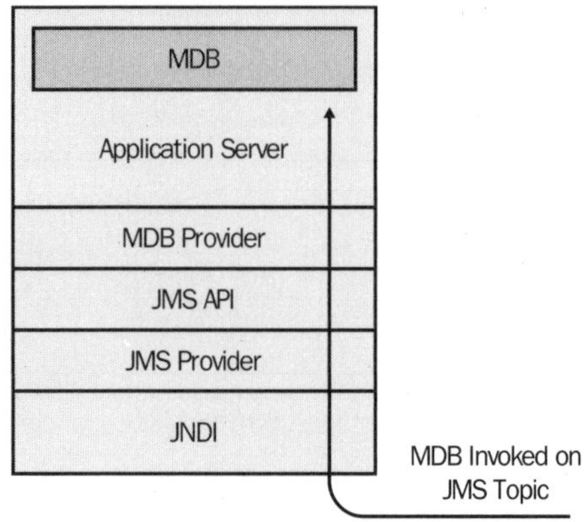

Figure 9-17 An EJB 2.0 MDB component, invoked by a JMS topic.

Once an appropriate message is received on the queue or topic, the container (application server) will run some EJB-specific methods (*ejbCreate* and *setMessageDrivenContext*) to invoke the MDB. Because MDBs are managed by the container, threading support is implicit. This means that multiple MDBs can be instantiated as needed to handle multiple messages in parallel as they're received. This pooling is normally configurable within the application server.

Each MDB must contain an *onMessage* method. This method is the first business logic method of the bean to be invoked and contains a parameter of the message that was received from the queue:

```
public void onMessage(Message msg)
```

Once it has this method, the MDB can process the request as it sees fit. This can include forwarding the message, invoking other beans, calling a Web service, writing to a database, and so on.

You now have the opportunity to take what you've learned about interoperability and apply it to this component. Because the MDB is invoked based on a message arriving for a particular topic, you can make a Web service call from the JMS MDB to a Web service in .NET. For example, you can activate a Stock MDB based on the *HotStocks* topic registered in JNDI.

Once activated, logic in the bean can determine the next course of action and whether a component running in .NET (via a Web service) should be notified, as shown in Figure 9-18.

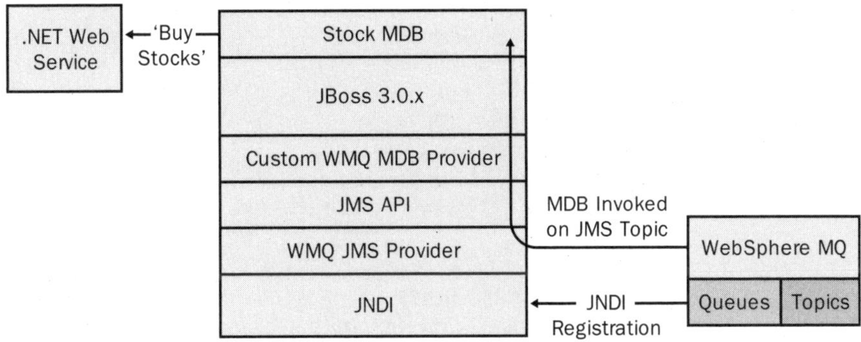

Figure 9-18 An EJB 2.0 MDB component, invoked by a JMS topic and calling a .NET Web service.

Sample code for this example is included in the C:\Interoperability\Samples\Resource\WMQ\MDB directory. Because we're using JBoss to show these samples, you need to perform some additional configuration to get the sample working.

Configuring MDB for JBoss and WebSphere MQ

JBoss ships with its own message queuing architecture, known as JBossMQ. This allows for an implementation of JMS that's based on a message queue internal to the JBoss product. Today, providing MDB support for connecting to other JMS providers through JBoss is possible, but it involves some extra work.

If you plan to run this sample code on another application server (for example, IBM's WebSphere Application Server), I recommend that you follow the instructions that accompany your application server. In addition, this approach is merely intended to demonstrate the samples in action; it's not supported and hasn't been tested for a production environment.

To start, you need to compile and install a WebSphere MQ provider for JBoss. This provides the necessary class for your MDB to access WebSphere MQ. The provider can be found in the C:\Interoperability\Samples\Resource\WMQ\MDB\JBoss directory, under the package *org.jboss.jms.jndi*. This class extends *AbstractJMSProviderAdapter* and contains the necessary code to return an initial context to the MDB:

```
public class WebsphereMQProvider extends AbstractJMSProviderAdapter
{
    public WebsphereMQProvider()
    {
    }

    public Context getInitialContext() throws NamingException
    {
        Hashtable ht = new Hashtable();
        ht.put(Context.INITIAL_CONTEXT_FACTORY,
            "org.jnp.interfaces.NamingContextFactory");
        ht.put(Context.PROVIDER_URL,"jnp://localhost:1099");
        return new InitialContext(ht);
    }
}
```

> **Note** If you're using a persistent JNDI store (as described earlier in the "Persistent and Nonpersistent JNDI with JMSAdmin" sidebar), you'll need to change the *INITIAL_CONTEXT_FACTORY* and *PROVIDER_URL* to match the *FSContext* settings used in the jmsadmin.config file.

Compile this class using the provided Ant script, and ensure that the JBoss server isn't running. When the Ant script is run with the deploy target, these classes will automatically be merged into the jboss.jar file, which can be found in the server\default\deploy directory of the JBoss server. A backup of the jboss.jar file will be made, named jboss.backup.

You now need to adjust some of the JBoss configuration settings to include a reference to this provider. Preconfigured files are supplied in the C:\Interoperability\Samples\Resource\WMQ\MDB\JBoss\Config directory for this purpose. Two files (jboss-service.xml and standardjboss.xml) are located in the conf subdirectory. One additional file (jms-service.xml) is located in the deploy subdirectory. These files need to be copied to the JBoss installation to activate the WebSphere MQ provider that has been installed.

To copy these files to a local instance of JBoss, use the supplied Ant script in this directory with the deploy target. The existing configuration files in the JBoss directory will be backed up (using the same name, appended with a .bak extension). If you've made any manual alterations to any of these files, you might need to merge the changes with the new files that are copied. In addition, the Ant script will copy some required WebSphere and GLUE libraries to the JBoss installation.

The modifications to standardjboss.xml replace the JMS Provider Adapter

```
<JMSProviderAdapterJNDI>DefaultJMSProvider</JMSProviderAdapterJNDI>
```

with this one:

```
<JMSProviderAdapterJNDI>WebsphereMQProvider</JMSProviderAdapterJNDI>
```

For the jboss-service.xml, the default JBossMQ provider is replaced with the custom one in the *jboss.ejb:service=EJBDeployer MBean* section:

```
<depends>jboss.mq:service=JMSProviderLoader,
    name=JBossMQProvider</depends>

<depends>jboss.mq:service=JMSProviderLoader,
    name=WebsphereMQProvider</depends>
```

You'll find a final modification in the jms-service.xml file. The JMS provider loader is again replaced with the sample WebSphere MQ one:

```
<mbean code="org.jboss.jms.jndi.JMSProviderLoader" name
    ="jboss.mq:service=JMSProviderLoader,name=MQSeriesProvider">
    <attribute name="ProviderName">DefaultJMSProvider</attribute>
    <attribute name="ProviderAdapterClass">
        org.jboss.jms.jndi.JBossMQProvider
    </attribute>
    <attribute name="QueueFactoryRef">
        java:/XAConnectionFactory</attribute>
    <attribute name="TopicFactoryRef">
```

```
        java:/XAConnectionFactory</attribute>
</mbean>

<mbean code="org.jboss.jms.jndi.JMSProviderLoader" name
    ="jboss.mq:service=JMSProviderLoader,name=WebsphereMQProvider">
    <attribute name="ProviderName">WebsphereMQProvider</attribute>
    <attribute name="ProviderAdapterClass">
        org.jboss.jms.jndi.WebsphereMQProvider
    </attribute>
    <attribute name="QueueFactoryRef">StockQCF</attribute>
    <attribute name="TopicFactoryRef">StockTCF</attribute>
</mbean>
```

With the new configuration files in place, go ahead and start JBoss.

> **Important** If you're using nonpersistent JNDI (*org.jnp.interfaces.NamingContextFactory*), remember to rerun the previous JMSAdmin script to repopulate the JNDI tree once the server has started. This is extremely important because without this you'll receive an exception when the bean is deployed.

Deploying the MDB

To deploy the MDB, first build the code using Ant in the C:\Interoperability\Samples\Resource\WMQ\MDB\Bean directory. Next, use the deploy target with the provided Ant script to deploy the bean to the JBoss server. If the bean was successfully deployed, you should observe the following output on the JBoss console:

```
INFO  [EjbModule] Creating
INFO  [EjbModule] Deploying StockMDB
INFO  [JMSContainerInvoker] Creating
INFO  [JMSContainerInvoker] Created
INFO  [EjbModule] Created
INFO  [EjbModule] Starting
INFO  [JMSContainerInvoker] Starting
INFO  [DLQHandler] Creating
INFO  [DLQHandler] Created
INFO  [DLQHandler] Starting
INFO  [DLQHandler] Started
INFO  [JMSContainerInvoker] Started
INFO  [EjbModule] Started
INFO  [MainDeployer] Deployed package:
    file:/C:/jboss/server/default/deploy/StockMDB.jar
```

Configuring the .NET Web Service

The MDB will call a .NET Web service that we covered in Chapter 5, "Connectivity with XML Web Services, Part 1." In Chapter 5, you saw how to set up a Web service in .NET that illustrated many of that chapter's examples. This MDB code in this chapter will also use that Web service. If you haven't already, follow the setup instructions in the "Option 2: Creating the Web Service Using the NAnt Script" section (beginning on page 162) of Chapter 5 for configuring and deploying the Web service.

The Web service will be hosted at *http://localhost/dotNETWebService/StockService.asmx*, which is called by this MDB. Be sure to validate this URL in Microsoft Internet Explorer before running the sample.

Running the Sample

To test the sample, you'll use a client that publishes two messages to the *HotStocks* topic: a recommendation for a purchase, and a recommendation for a sale. This in turn will invoke the MDB that has just been deployed. The MDB will look at the message and determine whether it's a recommendation for a purchase or a sale. If it's a recommendation for a purchase, invoke the .NET Web service to purchase that particular stock.

Build and run the client using Ant, which can be found in the C:\Interoperability\Samples\Resource\WMQ\MDB\Client directory. You should see that the client generates the two messages, publishes them to the *HotStocks* JMS topic, and returns a confirmation:

```
Hot stock news for CONT and WING has been published to
topic/HotStocks
```

This invokes the MDB, which will report output to the JBoss console that's similar to the following. Notice that each message invokes a separate MDB—both of which run in a multithreaded model. Bear this in mind when debugging the sample code. First, the bean was created:

```
INFO  [StockMDB] ctor called
INFO  [StockMDB] setMessageDrivenContext called
INFO  [StockMDB] ejbCreate called
```

A message was then received by the bean. This message was the client's request to sell some stocks, identified by the action string:

```
INFO  [StockMDB] A message has been received by StockMDB
INFO  [StockMDB] MapMessage action String = sell
INFO  [StockMDB] This is a request to sell some stocks.
INFO  [StockMDB] This will be invoked locally...
```

The second message is then processed. This time, the request to purchase some stocks was issued:

```
INFO  [StockMDB] A message has been received by StockMDB
INFO  [StockMDB] MapMessage action String = buy
INFO  [StockMDB] This is a request to buy some stocks.
INFO  [StockMDB] Invoking .NET Web Service to buy 500 of these...!
INFO  [StockAgent] ctor called
INFO  [StockAgent] Reading the mappings for the StockService
INFO  [StockAgent] Stock agent is binding to the .NET Web Service
INFO  [StockAgent] Calling Buy Stocks method
INFO  [StockMDB] Remote .NET Web Service purchase was successful
```

The latter half of this log shows the interaction with the .NET Web service. Here, a new message has been received, with an action (recommendation) to buy. The *StockMDB* realizes that this needs to be a call to the .NET Web service and invokes a *StockAgent* to handle the request. The *StockAgent* in turn uses the GLUE 4.0.1 libraries to make the Web service request from within the bean. Recall how in Chapter 5 the default .NET Web service wrote an entry into the event log when a request to purchase stocks was received.

If you now look at the event viewer, you'll see an entry for the purchase request from the MDB, as shown in Figure 9-19. This indicates that the .NET Web service successfully received and was able to work with the incoming request from the MDB.

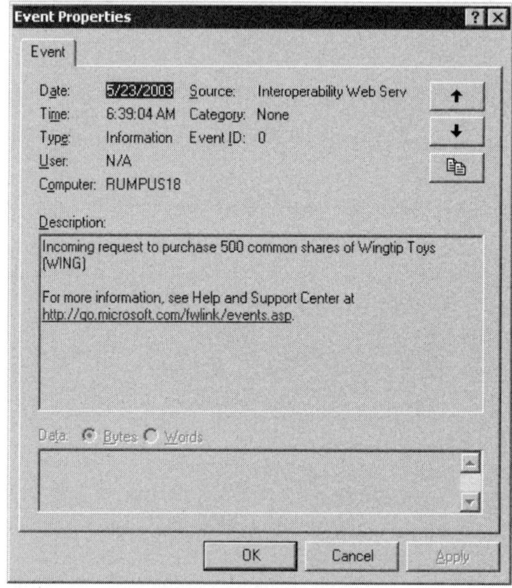

Figure 9-19 The .NET Web service confirms the purchase via the event log.

Key Elements of the Sample

In this section, you've seen how, with a little work, an MDB that's subscribing to a JMS topic—which would normally be isolated from the .NET world—can be made to forward incoming publications to Web services or any other listening service in .NET.

This approach suits organizations that have existing implementations of JMS MDBs and want to further extend this pub/sub model into .NET. As with the simple stock trade example, you can imagine how the MDB could be used to determine whether local processing should occur in the J2EE environment or whether the request should be extended to .NET. In addition, imagine a scenario in which this approach was combined with Universal Description, Discovery, and Integration (UDDI) to provide automatic lookups for the .NET Web services without having to hard-code the details in the bean. We covered UDDI in Chapter 6, "Connectivity with XML Web Services, Part 2."

In addition to using Web services as the transport, nothing is stopping you from using the Ja.NET libraries covered in Chapter 4, "Connectivity with .NET Remoting." The MDB would become the .NET Remoting client and could call a remote object running in .NET to pass across the message.

Most of the functionality of this sample can be found within the code of the MDB class. The MDB is deployed by using two deployment descriptors: ejb-jar.xml (which contains generic MDB configuration) and jboss.xml (which contains JBoss-related configuration).

The ejb-jar.xml deployment descriptor specifies the name, class, acknowledgment mode, and subscription durability of the bean itself. Notice that the destination type is a *javax.jms.Topic*; we also could have used a *javax.jms.Queue* type.

```
<message-driven>
    <ejb-name>StockMDB</ejb-name>
    <ejb-class>StockMDB</ejb-class>
    <transaction-type>Container</transaction-type>
    <acknowledge-mode>Auto-acknowledge</acknowledge-mode>
    <message-driven-destination>
        <destination-type>javax.jms.Topic</destination-type>
        <subscription-durability>
            NonDurable
        </subscription-durability>
    </message-driven-destination>
</message-driven>
```

The jboss.xml deployment descriptor contains JBoss-specific configuration. This links the name of the MDB to the destination JNDI topic that's created with the JMSAdmin script:

```
<enterprise-beans>
    <message-driven>
        <ejb-name>StockMDB</ejb-name>
        <destination-jndi-name>
            topic/HotStocks
        </destination-jndi-name>
        <xa-connection>false</xa-connection>
    </message-driven>
</enterprise-beans>
```

The code for the bean can be found in the StockMDB.java file. The MDB is invoked by the J2EE container with a call to the *onMessage* method. The container automatically passes a parameter of type *javax.jms.Message*.

```
public void onMessage(Message msg)
```

If the message is of type *javax.jms.MapMessage*, the action field is tested. This tells the bean whether the operation should be a sale or purchase.

```
String action = ((MapMessage)msg).getString("action");
```

If the action is indeed a purchase, a stock agent (following the agent-service pattern outlined in Chapter 6) is called:

```
StockAgent agent = new StockAgent();
Stock stockToBuy = convertToStock(((MapMessage)msg));

boolean result = agent.buyStocks(stockToBuy,STOCK_MDB_DEFAULT_QTY);
logger.info("Remote .NET Web Service purchase was "
    +(result? "successful" : "unsuccessful"));
```

This stock agent constructs a request to the .NET Web service much in the same way that the samples in Chapter 6 depicted. One important point about this agent example (which differs from the previous samples in this chapter) is the way that types in the Web service are mapped.

In previous samples in the book, when we ran the GLUE client against a .NET Web service, the types were based upon a map file. This map file was automatically generated by the WSDL2JAVA tool used to build the Java class. We still have a map file in the MDB version, but because we're never sure of the current path (because the bean is hosted in an application server), we need to explicitly load the file. The following command performs this:

```
Mappings.readMappings("StockService.map");
```

Once you've completed testing this sample code, be sure to undeploy this Web application. This can easily be done by running the Ant script with the undeploy target from the C:\Interoperability\Samples\Resource\WMQ\MDB\Bean directory.

SOAP Support for WebSphere MQ

The previous sections showed what's required to make existing JMS components and objects interoperate with .NET. Let's now look at the possible future for interoperability with WebSphere MQ. After reading the chapter, you'll no doubt agree that although today's developers can achieve tactical .NET and J2EE interoperability solutions with WebSphere MQ, one could make an argument for a more strategic approach.

Let's examine two options that promote the use of SOAP over WebSphere MQ. The first option is to use the product that we've used for Web services throughout the book, GLUE. This approach is similar to the MDB sample. The second option is to use another SupportPac from IBM, MA0R. This SupportPac shows a technical preview of using SOAP to host Web services by using both .NET and Apache Axis.

SOAP/JMS Support in GLUE

If you've been looking through the GLUE documentation that accompanies the libraries on the companion CD, you might have noticed that GLUE 4.0.1 shows support for JMS. This support allows the use of GLUE to create synchronous and asynchronous SOAP messages over JMS and provides integration with the J2EE Reference Implementation.

In short, this allows a message queue (such as WebSphere MQ) to be placed between a GLUE client and Web service by using the JMS API and the underlying provider transport instead of HTTP. Figure 9-20 illustrates this best. In the figure, the logical applications created by GLUE (*Service1* and *Service2*) are hosted using a system queue in WebSphere MQ.

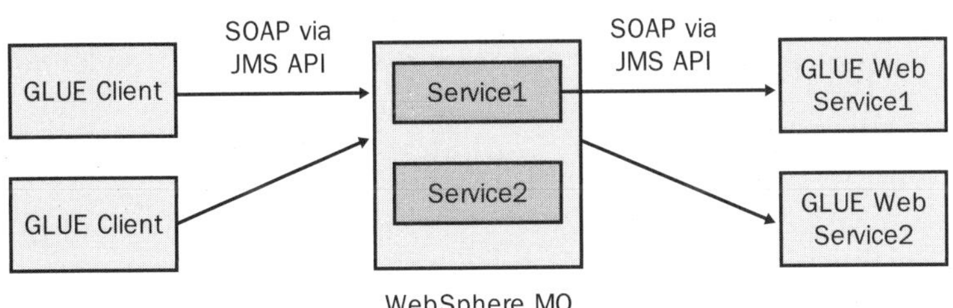

Figure 9-20 JMS support in GLUE and interoperability with WebSphere MQ.

In addition to WebSphere MQ, out of the box, GLUE supports adapters for other message queuing software, including SonicMQ, TIBCO, and SwiftMQ. By providing adapters that contain specific information about the queuing product itself, GLUE is able to connect without needing to know any additional configuration information.

Running the Sample Code

To show how GLUE works with JMS, let's look at the sample code, located in the C:\Interoperability\Samples\Resource\WMQ\GlueJMS directory. Using the same scenario as the earlier MDB sample, the sample code works by using JMS to listen for incoming messages and then making a Web service call to .NET. Because we're using the SYSTEM queues and calling JMS without referencing JNDI and/or JBoss, the setup is that shown in Figure 9-21. Notice how the calls between the GLUE client and Web service are asynchronous (taking advantage of the queue) and how the .NET Web service call uses a request/response mechanism.

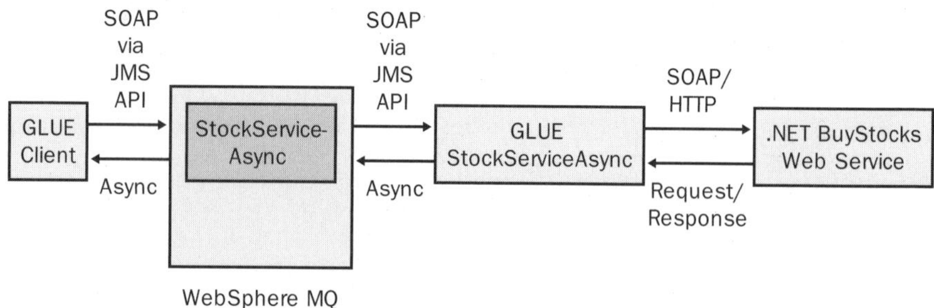

Figure 9-21 Asynchronous call styles between the services using GLUE's support for JMS.

The GLUE server side of the sample is contained within the Server subdirectory. Build and run the sample code in a separate command prompt window; this can easily be done by entering **start ant run** at the command prompt.

```
using MQSeries JMS provider
```

One of the nice features of GLUE is that it automatically detects which message queue libraries are in the *CLASSPATH* without forcing a developer to supply configuration information. Because the MQSeries libraries are in the *CLASSPATH* here, the provider is automatically loaded.

After the server is running in a separate window, navigate to the client directory. Then build and run the client sample, using the provided Ant script with the run target. The sample will create two stock recommendations (one sale and one purchase) and will use the GLUE JMS provider to make an asynchronous call. The client makes the call and waits for 10 seconds:

```
Waiting for 10 seconds...
```

While the client is waiting, switch to the server process. The *StockServerAsync* class uses the same agent and logic as the MDB example presented earlier in this chapter. Once the client has decided whether a stock should be purchased, the appropriate call is made to the .NET Web service. On the other hand, we simulate the Java Web service because the sell operation is handled locally:

```
Reading the mappings for the StockService
Stock agent is binding to the .NET Web Service
This will be handled locally...
Calling Buy Stocks method
```

After the 10 seconds elapse, the client reconnects and checks the asynchronous response for the two calls. Based on the result from the call, the client can determine whether the recommendation invoked a call to the .NET Web service:

```
Checking for the result...
The async purchase of Lucerne Publishing was made with the
.NET Web Service call
The async sale of Coho Winery was not made with the
.NET Web Service call
```

You can see that the purchase was indeed forwarded to the .NET Web service, whereas the sale was handled locally by GLUE.

Key Elements of the GLUE Sample

If you've used any of the GLUE sample code in the earlier chapters, you'll have noticed that the following line is used to publish a Web service by using the HTTP transport:

```
HTTP.startup("http://localhost:8004/JavaWebService");
Registry.Publish("StockService", new StockService());
```

Within GLUE, the mechanism used to publish the service via JMS is very similar:

```
JMS.startup("jms:///StockServiceAsync");
Registry.publish("StockServiceAsync",new StockServiceAsync());
```

This can be very useful for the Web services that need to be published via both HTTP and JMS because it gives developer a similar set of interfaces to use.

The GLUE client follows a similar pattern. In the sample, the following URL is used to bind to the Web service exposed by JMS:

```
jms:///StockService/StockServiceAsync.wsdl
```

Notice how the URL doesn't contain a *hostname*. Because GLUE support for JMS is for local clients only, no concept of a remote call exists and no hostname is required. To get the asynchronous callback working, the client defines and uses a class of type *electric.util.async.Async*:

```
Async asyncBuy = new Async();
```

This *Async* object is passed as part of the method call:

```
ss.AddRecommendation(LUCP,"buy",asyncBuy);
```

The client can now leave and potentially run other tasks while this message is dealt with on the server side. To check the status of the call, the *Async* object is used again—this time calling the *getResponse* method:

```
boolean buyResult
    = ((Boolean)asyncBuy.getResponse()).booleanValue();
```

The result from the asynchronous call is cast correctly and is returned to the client.

SOAP/JMS Messages and Interoperability with .NET

Apart from the different programming model, one thing that differentiates this sample from the MDB sample shown earlier is the message format on the wire. The GLUE JMS provider sends the message between the client and the server as a JMS *BytesMessage*. (You saw this earlier in the chapter in the discussion of message types.) The content of the message is actually a SOAP message.

You can see this by examining the SYSTEM.DEFAULT.LOCAL.QUEUE queue, until the queue is cleared. (You can see system queues in WebSphere MQ Explorer by right-clicking the Queues folder and selecting View/Show System Objects.)

The message, which can be viewed from the Data tab of the message's Properties window, contains the header information and JMS message payload shown earlier:

```
52 46 48 20 00 00 00 02  RFH ....
00 00 00 AC 00 00 01 11  ..."....
00 00 04 B8 20 20 20 20  ...,
20 20 20 20 00 00 00 00      ....
00 00 04 B8 00 00 00 20  ...,...
3C 6D 63 64 3E 3C 4D 73  <mcd><Ms
64 3E 6A 6D 73 5F 62 79  d>jms_by
```

```
74 65 73 3C 2F 4D 73 64  tes</Msd
3E 3C 2F 6D 63 64 3E 20  ></mcd>
00 00 00 60 3C 6A 6D 73  ...`<jms
3E 3C 44 73 74 3E 71 75  ><Dst>qu
65 75 65 3A 2F 2F 2F 53  eue:///S
59 53 54 45 4D 2E 44 45  YSTEM.DE
46 41 55 4C 54 2E 4C 4F  FAULT.LO
43 41 4C 2E 51 55 45 55  CAL.QUEU
45 3C 2F 44 73 74 3E 3C  E</Dst><
54 6D 73 3E 31 30 34 39  Tms>1049
39 32 32 39 30 34 31 39  92290419
36 3C 2F 54 6D 73 3E 3C  6</Tms><
44 6C 76 3E 32 3C 2F 44  Dlv>2</D
6C 76 3E 3C 2F 6A 6D 73  lv></jms
3E 20 20 20 3C           >
```

After this header, however, you can actually see the SOAP message, as shown next. This message is the *false* value returned from the GLUE Web service presented earlier.

```
               3F 78 6D     <?xm
6C 20 76 65 72 73 69 6F  l versio
6E 3D 27 31 2E 30 27 20  n='1.0'
65 6E 63 6F 64 69 6E 67  encoding
3D 27 55 54 46 2D 38 27  ='UTF-8'
3F 3E 0D 0A 3C 73 6F 61  ?>..<soa
70 3A 45 6E 76 65 6C 6F  p:Envelo
70 65 20 78 6D 6C 6E 73  pe xmlns
3A 78 73 69 3D 27 68 74  :xsi='ht
74 70 3A 2F 2F 77 77 77  tp://www
2E 77 33 2E 6F 72 67 2F  .w3.org/
32 30 30 31 2F 58 4D 4C  2001/XML
53 63 68 65 6D 61 2D 69  Schema-i
6E 73 74 61 6E 63 65 27  nstance'
20 78 6D 6C 6E 73 3A 78   xmlns:x
73 64 3D 27 68 74 74 70  sd='http
3A 2F 2F 77 77 77 2E 77  ://www.w
33 2E 6F 72 67 2F 32 30  3.org/20
30 31 2F 58 4D 4C 53 63  01/XMLSc
68 65 6D 61 27 20 78 6D  hema' xm
6C 6E 73 3A 73 6F 61 70  lns:soap
3D 27 68 74 74 70 3A 2F  ='http:/
2F 73 63 68 65 6D 61 73  /schemas
2E 78 6D 6C 73 6F 61 70  .xmlsoap
2E 6F 72 67 2F 73 6F 61  .org/soa
70 2F 65 6E 76 65 6C 6F  p/envelo
70 65 2F 27 20 78 6D 6C  pe/' xml
6E 73 3A 73 6F 61 70 65  ns:soape
```

```
6E 63 3D 27 68 74 74 70  nc='http
3A 2F 2F 73 63 68 65 6D  ://schem
61 73 2E 78 6D 6C 73 6F  as.xmlso
61 70 2E 6F 72 67 2F 73  ap.org/s
6F 61 70 2F 65 6E 63 6F  oap/enco
64 69 6E 67 2F 27 3E 3C  ding/'><
73 6F 61 70 3A 42 6F 64  soap:Bod
79 20 73 6F 61 70 3A 65  y soap:e
6E 63 6F 64 69 6E 67 53  ncodingS
74 79 6C 65 3D 27 68 74  tyle='ht
74 70 3A 2F 2F 73 63 68  tp://sch
65 6D 61 73 2E 78 6D 6C  emas.xml
73 6F 61 70 2E 6F 72 67  soap.org
2F 73 6F 61 70 2F 65 6E  /soap/en
63 6F 64 69 6E 67 2F 27  coding/'
20 78 6D 6C 6E 73 3A 73   xmlns:s
6F 61 70 3D 27 68 74 74  oap='htt
70 3A 2F 2F 73 63 68 65  p://sche
6D 61 73 2E 78 6D 6C 73  mas.xmls
6F 61 70 2E 6F 72 67 2F  oap.org/
73 6F 61 70 2F 65 6E 76  soap/env
65 6C 6F 70 65 2F 27 3E  elope/'>
3C 6F 62 6A 65 63 74 20  <object
78 6D 6C 6E 73 3A 78 73  xmlns:xs
69 3D 27 68 74 74 70 3A  i='http:
2F 2F 77 77 77 2E 77 33  //www.w3
2E 6F 72 67 2F 32 30 30  .org/200
31 2F 58 4D 4C 53 63 68  1/XMLSch
65 6D 61 2D 69 6E 73 74  ema-inst
61 6E 63 65 27 20 78 6D  ance' xm
6C 6E 73 3A 78 73 64 3D  lns:xsd=
27 68 74 74 70 3A 2F 2F  'http://
77 77 77 2E 77 33 2E 6F  www.w3.o
72 67 2F 32 30 30 31 2F  rg/2001/
58 4D 4C 53 63 68 65 6D  XMLSchem
61 27 20 78 73 69 3A 74  a' xsi:t
79 70 65 3D 27 73 6F 61  ype='soa
70 65 6E 63 3A 62 6F 6F  penc:boo
6C 65 61 6E 27 3E 66 61  lean'>fa
6C 73 65 3C 2F 6F 62 6A  lse</obj
65 63 74 3E 3C 2F 73 6F  ect></so
61 70 3A 42 6F 64 79 3E  ap:Body>
3C 2F 73 6F 61 70 3A 45  </soap:E
6E 76 65 6C 6F 70 65 3E  nvelope>
```

This message has some interesting possibilities for interoperability with .NET. Recall how the MA7P SupportPac (the .NET classes) used bytes messages without the JMS header when they wrote to the queue. In theory, you could build a .NET client that uses the MA7P SupportPac today, accepts these types of incoming messages, strips off the JMS header section, and deserializes the SOAP envelope into a request it can understand. This could work equally well with requests coming from .NET.

I haven't seen this technique tested, but it's worth contemplating for projects that require this level of custom interoperability. For such interoperability to be a success, you'd have to ensure that the JMS header information is correctly understood and translated (which might take some testing with multiple vendor implementations). However, this method does offer some interesting possibilities for achieving SOAP-based interoperability by using JMS.

IBM SupportPac MA0R

IBM released SupportPac MA0R around the same time that it released its MA7P SupportPac (the WebSphere MQ classes for .NET presented earlier in the chapter). SupportPac MA0R is titled SOAP Support for WebSphere MQ, and is a technical preview of what later releases of the product might bring.

The goal of SupportPac MA0R is to show how SOAP endpoints can be used with WebSphere MQ to provide reliable messaging between Web service–style clients and the queue itself. To overcome the reliability issues of HTTP that were discussed in Chapter 8, MA0R is designed to use HTTPR, which is IBM's draft specification for Reliable HTTP.

To set up the endpoints, MA0R uses a MQSOAPHost process. This allows Web services written to both the Java (Apache Axis implementation) and .NET specifications to be hosted independently. Web services clients that want to use this service can do so by specifying a WebSphere MQ–specific URI naming scheme, an example of which could be:

```
this.Url = "wmq:SOAP.StockQuoteDotNet@MQSOAP.DEMO.QM?"
    +"connectQueueManager=MQSOAP.DEMO.QM";
```

This naming scheme, and of course SOAP/HTTPR, are independent of the platform—meaning that both Java and .NET Web service clients can interoperate with the respective services hosted on the other platform.

At the time of this writing, MA0R can be downloaded from the IBM Web site, at *http://www.ibm.com/software/integration/support/supportpacs/individual/ma0r.html*. Although it wasn't possible to include any MA0R sample code in this book, it will be interesting to see how this SupportPac evolves in the near future.

Summary

This concludes the discussion of interoperability with IBM WebSphere MQ and JMS. In this chapter, we've examined the IBM product, looked at the default libraries that are available for Java, and seen how a recent SupportPac can be used to help provide connection for .NET clients.

The chapter introduced JMS and then presented some of the complexities of sharing a WebSphere MQ queue with both a JMS client and a .NET client. Continuing with the publish/subscribe features of JMS, the chapter examined a sample MDB (or Message Driven Bean), how that bean could subscribe to a JMS topic, and how it could call a .NET Web service based upon the operations of the bean. The chapter concluded by looking at the JMS support available with GLUE and a brief introduction to the MA0R SupportPac.

The goal of this chapter and Chapter 8 was to concentrate on direct access to each of the queuing products (MSMQ and WebSphere MQ) and examine the alternatives and options that exist for both platforms. In Chapter 10 and Chapter 11 ("Asynchronous Interoperability, Part 3: Bridging with Host Integration Server" and "Asynchronous Interoperability, Part 4: BizTalk Server"), we'll implement a bridge between the two queues by using both Microsoft Host Integration Server 2000 and Microsoft BizTalk Server 2004 Beta 1, and you'll see what each product can offer. In Chapter 11, our discussion of asynchronous interoperability will conclude by relating the contents of all four chapters on the topic back to the resource tier goals outlined in Chapter 2, "Business Requirements for Interoperability."

10

Asynchronous Interoperability, Part 3: Bridging with Host Integration Server

In the previous two chapters, we looked at Microsoft Message Queuing (MSMQ) and WebSphere MQ—with the goal of connecting both Java and Microsoft .NET clients to pass messages and to achieve interoperability between the two. Some of the approaches we used highlighted the challenge in connecting a Java client to MSMQ and in connecting a .NET client to WebSphere MQ directly. Although both can be done, as you saw, each approach has a number of drawbacks. For example, you could lose reliability or transactional support, or you might have access to only a subset of the required libraries.

In this chapter, we'll allow the clients to use their native message queue implementations (the *System.Messaging* namespace for the .NET client, and IBM's Java libraries for the WebSphere MQ client) and introduce a bridge that will connect the two queues together. The bridge that we'll examine is the MSMQ-MQSeries bridge, which is shipped as a component of Microsoft Host Integration Server 2000, a member of Microsoft's family of server products that evolved from a previous release named Microsoft SNA Server. Host Integration Server 2000 is designed to enable organizations to connect to existing infrastructure—typically, host-based mainframe systems.

Included with Host Integration Server 2000 is mainframe terminal emulation (3270 and 5250 clients), the ability to access and print files on a host system, functionality to allow two-phase commit transactions between platforms, the ability to provide a single logon for hosted environments (by using the credentials from Microsoft Windows), and the ability to create a bridge between MSMQ and MQSeries—which is the component that this chapter will cover. For more information on the details of the product itself, consult *http://www.microsoft.com/hiserver.*

MSMQ-MQSeries Bridge

The bridge that's supplied with Host Integration Server 2000 provides a mechanism that allows messages to be picked up from an MSMQ queue and delivered to a WebSphere MQ (MQSeries) queue and vice versa. In this chapter, we'll look at the architecture required for using the bridge, the installation of the bridge itself, and the running of test clients to observe how the bridge passes messages between the .NET and Java platforms. The test client samples you'll see in this chapter are based on the examples presented in Chapter 8, "Asynchronous Interoperability, Part 1: Introduction and MSMQ," and Chapter 9, "Asynchronous Interoperability, Part 2: WebSphere MQ."

> **Note** As discussed in Chapter 9, IBM changed the name of its queuing product from MQSeries to WebSphere MQ fairly recently. Although it uses the product's older name, the MSMQ-MQSeries bridge component within Host Integration Server remains compatible with IBM's queuing product. This chapter will refer to the bridge as the MSMQ-MQSeries bridge but refer to the queuing product as WebSphere MQ.

Architecture Prerequisites for the MSMQ-MQSeries Bridge

The MSMQ-MQSeries bridge has a number of architectural prerequisites that must be in place before installation. One of the main prerequisites and dependencies is an installation of Microsoft Active Directory directory service. The MSMQ-MQSeries bridge picks up messages from queues defined in a foreign site (in Active Directory) and delivers them to a nominated queue on the WebSphere MQ server. Working the other way, the bridge picks up messages from a nominated WebSphere MQ queue and delivers them to a public MSMQ queue. The use of foreign sites and public queues generates this dependency on an Active Directory installation.

To ensure that the setup and operation of the bridge is correctly described in this chapter, we'll use the environment shown in Figure 10-1.

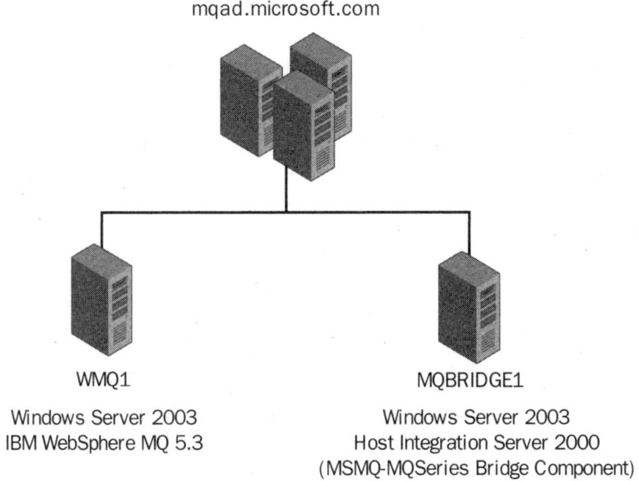

Figure 10-1 Example environment required to run the MSMQ-MQSeries bridge sample.

The figure shows an instance of Active Directory and two servers. In this example, the Active Directory Domain Name System (DNS) name is mqad.microsoft.com. (Its NetBIOS name is MQAD.) The requirements of the two servers in this example setup are listed in Table 10-1; these names will change depending on the details of your actual setup.

Table 10-1 Server Requirements

Server Name	Function	Operating System
MQBRIDGE1	The machine that will run the MSMQ-MQSeries bridge. This machine should be a domain controller (DC) for Active Directory.	Microsoft Windows Server 2003
WMQ1	The machine that will run the instance of WebSphere MQ.	Microsoft Windows Server 2003

In Table 10-1, *MQBRIDGE1* is nominated as a domain controller. This is because we'll use only two machines to show this sample. One of the features of MSMQ 3.0 is that it can participate in Active Directory MSMQ routing without being installed on a domain controller. (In a production environment, this would be the recommended approach.)

If you want to follow the samples and setup in this chapter, you should use the server layout described in Table 10-1. Feel free to use different names for the servers, but remember to replace the machine names as you work through the installation wherever appropriate. The two servers should be in the same Active Directory forest to ensure that authentication between them works correctly. Although it's possible to install both the MSMQ-MQSeries bridge and WebSphere MQ on the same machine, it's not recommended.

> **Note** To follow the sample, it's highly recommended that you perform this installation with a staging or development implementation of Active Directory. We'll install and configure MSMQ Routing Support, which will make modifications to the Active Directory tree. Thus, this setup should be thoroughly tested before deploying in a production environment.

To run this sample, configure the servers and instance of Active Directory as discussed earlier in this section. For additional information on planning and designing an Active Directory installation, see *http://www.microsoft.com/windowsserver2003/technologies/activedirectory/default.mspx*. Once this is complete, you can start installing the software required for the bridge.

Installing the Software Required for the MSMQ-MQSeries Bridge

Our first task is to ensure that all the software required for the bridge is correctly installed and configured. The server that will run the bridge requires MSMQ (with Active Directory and Routing Support) as well as the client portion of the WebSphere MQ 5.3 installation.

Installing MSMQ with Active Directory and Routing Support

To start, log on to the machine that will run the bridge (named *MQBRIDGE1* in our example setup). Open the Add Or Remove Programs control panel, and select the Add/Remove Windows Components option.

In the list of components displayed, select Application Server; then select Message Queuing. A number of options will be displayed, as shown in Figure 10-2. If some of the options have already been selected, you should clear these options first and run through the wizard once to uninstall any previous implementation.

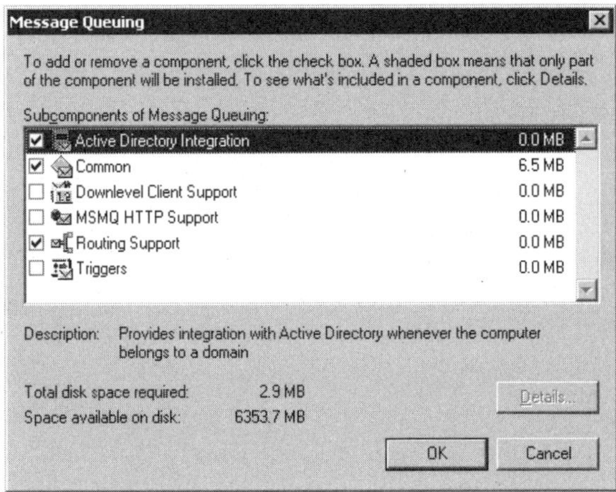

Figure 10-2 Installing the required MSMQ components for the bridge.

The installation of MSMQ requires the Active Directory Integration, Common, and Routing Support components. Once these are selected, click OK and continue through the wizard. If during this installation process you're prompted to serve local user accounts and MSMQ 1.0 clients, select the option to not change the security context.

After the wizard has completed, MSMQ with Active Directory and Routing Support will be installed.

Installing WebSphere MQ Client Components on MQBRIDGE1

As mentioned previously, the WebSphere MQ client software needs to be installed on the bridge. This is required because the MSMQ-MQSeries bridge application makes calls to the WebSphere MQ server by using the MQ client APIs.

On the server nominated to run the bridge (*MQBRIDGE1*), follow the installation of WebSphere MQ as outlined in Chapter 9, and select all options apart from the server component. This is shown in Figure 10-3.

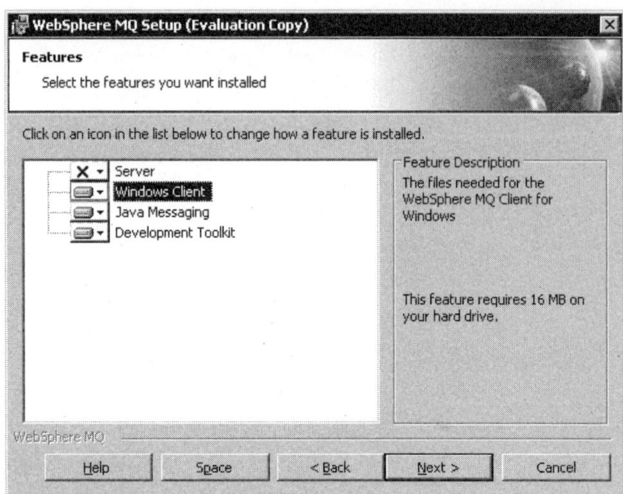

Figure 10-3 Installing the required WebSphere MQ client component for the bridge.

This installation will provide all the required WebSphere MQ components for the bridge and the required Java libraries for running the sample code at the end of the chapter.

Installing Host Integration Server 2000

The final installation step is to install the bridge software. To start the installation, launch the Host Integration Server 2000 installer and enter the CD key details. Unless you want other Host Integration Server 2000 options to be installed, you need only select the MSMQ-MQSeries bridge as shown in Figure 10-4.

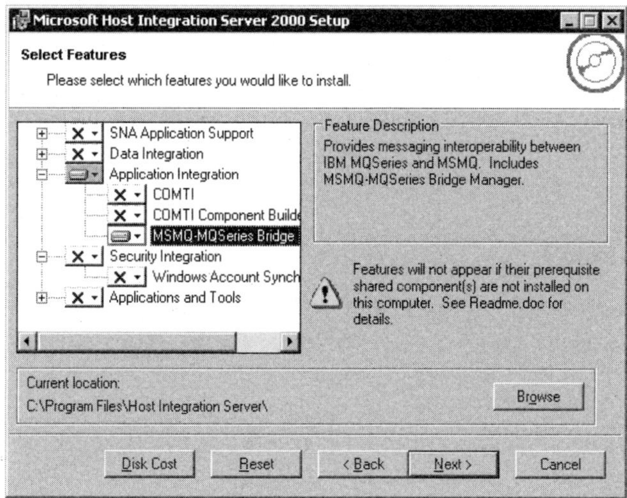

Figure 10-4 Installing the required Host Integration Server 2000 components—the bridge itself.

Click Next to continue through the wizard. In the account section, enter the details for an account in Active Directory that will be used to run the Host Integration Server 2000 Services. For this sample, this can be your logged-on account. Complete the wizard, and the required components will be installed.

Installing Host Integration Server 2000 SP1

After the installation has completed, if you're using the commercial version of Host Integration Server 2000 (as opposed to the evaluation version), it's recommended that you install Service Pack 1 (SP1) for Host Integration Server 2000. This fixes a number of known issues with the bridge and can be downloaded from *http://www.microsoft.com/hiserver/downloads/sp1/default.asp.*

After SP1 has completed, the installation of Host Integration Server 2000 is complete.

Installing WebSphere MQ 5.3 on WMQ1

If you haven't already, install WebSphere MQ 5.3 on the server that will manage the WebSphere MQ queues (*WMQ1*). Again, the installation instructions for the evaluation copy of this product can be found in Chapter 9. You should ensure that all the options are selected by using a custom installation. In addition to installing the software, create a new queue manager named STQM (which stands for STock Queue Manager and is also discussed in Chapter 9) and be sure to select Make This The Default Queue Manager. At this point, however, you don't need to create any local queues.

As you've no doubt noticed, the sample uses WebSphere MQ 5.3 on Windows Server 2003. At the time of this writing, IBM hasn't officially announced support for WebSphere 5.3 on this operating system (because the operating system has just been released). Although tests performed for this book's samples didn't turn up any issues, you should consult the latest IBM documentation if you plan to deploy to this server configuration in production.

Configuring Active Directory for MSMQ to WebSphere MQ Communication

Now that the required software is installed, let's configure the required components for Active Directory. This includes configuring a local and a foreign site (each representing different ends of the bridge), setting up security, and creating the required queues to allow the bridge to function correctly.

Setting Up Sites and MSMQ Routing Support

A clean Active Directory will have knowledge of the machines within—but will have no concept that the machine running WebSphere MQ (*WMQ1*) is part of a separate, connected network (known as a CN). In this section, you'll create a new site (known as a *foreign site*), which will contain the server and queues represented by the WebSphere MQ installation.

> **Note** If you've worked with MSMQ before, you know that the term *CN* was used with version 1.0 of the product, was dropped after the release of 2.0, and was replaced by Active Directory Sites and MSMQ Routing Links. The MSMQ-MQSeries bridge still uses the term, however, because it was designed during the MSMQ 1.0 and Microsoft Windows NT 4.0 era.

To create this new site, open the Active Directory Sites And Services administration tool on a server whose role is a domain controller. This sample will use the machine installed with Host Integration Server 2000 (*MQBRIDGE1*). This tool can be found in Program Files/Administrative Tools. In this tool, if you don't see a folder named Services in the left-hand side of the window, highlight the Active Directory Sites And Services tree root and select the Show Services Node option from the View menu.

Under the Services folder, right-click the MsmqServices subfolder and select New Foreign Site. Enter the name for the foreign site that describes the CN where the WebSphere MQ server resides. For this example, the foreign site name that will be used is **WMQ_CN**, as shown in Figure 10-5.

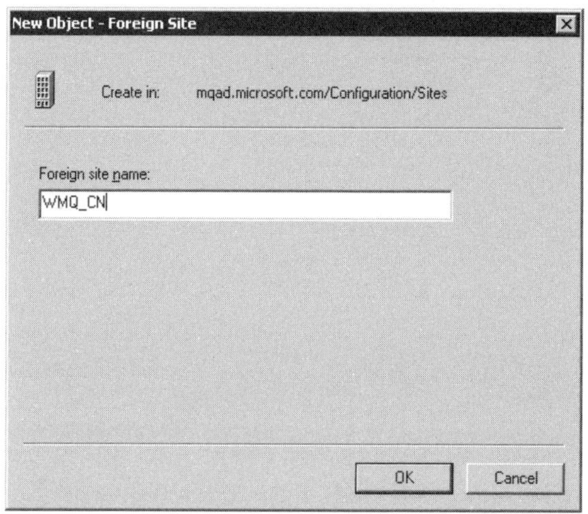

Figure 10-5 Creating the new foreign site in Active Directory.

Click OK to create this foreign site. Now that you have the site defined, let's define a reference to the WebSphere MQ queue manager that will reside in that site.

Right-click the MsmqServices folder again, and this time select New Foreign Computer. For the computer name, enter the queue manager name of the WebSphere MQ server. If you followed the setup discussed earlier in this chapter, this name will be STQM, as shown in Figure 10-6. In this same dialog box, ensure that the foreign site matches the one you just created (WMQ_CN), and click OK to create the new foreign computer.

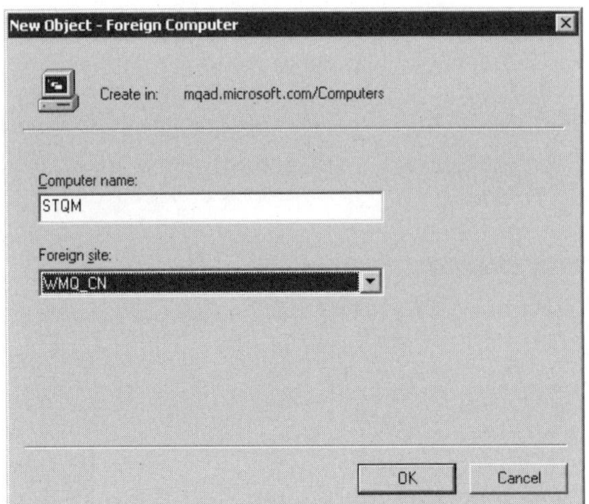

Figure 10-6 Creating the new foreign computer—a reference to the WebSphere queue manager.

> **Note** Although the dialog box shown in Figure 10-6 states Computer Name, this entry must be the queue manager name for the WebSphere MQ server and not the host name of the machine. Also, the case of this name (and the queues that we'll create later in the section) must match the case used on the WebSphere MQ server. Queues residing on WebSphere MQ are case sensitive.

Now that you have the foreign site and computer created, you need to set the security accordingly. We'll configure the foreign site so that the bridge process has permission to open the queue.

In the Active Directory Sites And Services tool, expand the Sites folder. Right-click the foreign site (WMQ_CN in our sample) and select the Properties option. Select the Security tab. Select Everyone and give permission to open the connector queue, as shown in Figure 10-7. Then click OK to save the security changes.

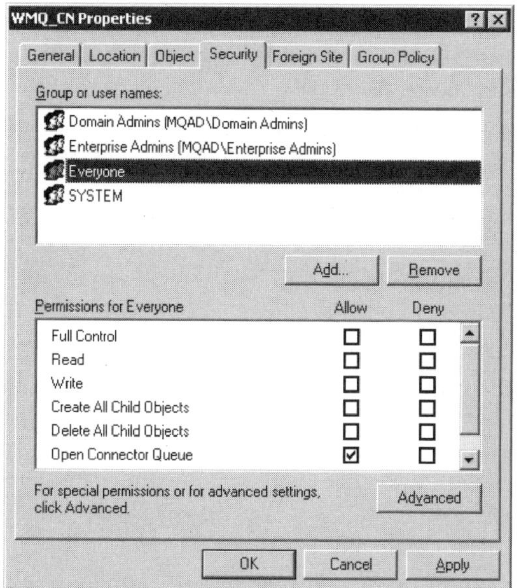

Figure 10-7 Correctly setting the security to allow the bridge to open the connector queue.

Now that you have the foreign site and computer configured for the WebSphere MQ server, let's set up an MSMQ Routing Link between the default Active Directory site and this new foreign site. Return to the MsmqServices Service in the administration tool, right-click MsmqServices, and select New/MSMQ Routing Link.

In the dialog box that's presented, set Site 1 to be the foreign site that contains the WebSphere MQ installation (in our example, this is WMQ_CN). Set Site 2 to be the local site, as shown in Figure 10-8. For the routing cost, enter a value of **1**.

Your local site (shown in Site 2) might have a different name from the one shown in Figure 10-8. In a production environment, it's good practice to change this default site name to a name that's more meaningful. Once these settings are configured, click OK.

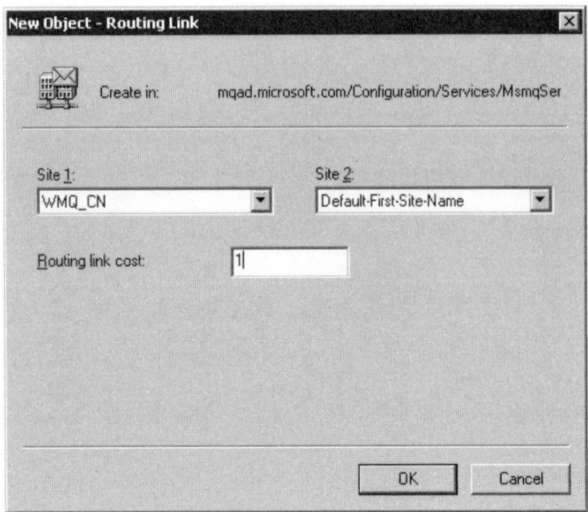

Figure 10-8 Configuring the MSMQ routing link in Active Directory.

Once the routing link has been created, right-click the new MSMQ Routing Link entry that's been created. This entry will be listed in the right-hand side of the administration tool. Select the Properties option. From here, you'll specify which machine will act as a site gate for this routing link.

Within this dialog box, select the Site Gates tab. Add the local server to the list of site gates, as shown in Figure 10-9. (In our example, the local server is *MQBRIDGE1*; the name of your server will be displayed in the Available Servers window.) Click OK to close this dialog box.

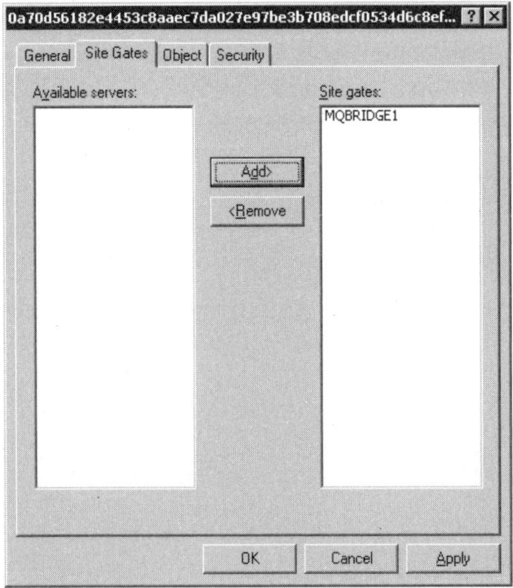

Figure 10-9 Configuring the site gates in Active Directory.

The configuration of the Active Directory Sites And Services tool is now complete. You may close the administration tool.

The final setup step is to add the bridge server itself to the foreign site that was created—so that it's a member of both the local site in Active Directory and the site created for the WebSphere MQ installation. This is performed with the Active Directory Users And Computers tool from the Administrative Tools program group.

Open the tool, and from the View menu, select Users, Groups, And Computers As Containers. Also select the Advanced Features option.

Because the bridge (*MQBRIDGE1*) is a domain controller in our sample, you should open the Domain Controllers folder. If the bridge is not a domain controller, it will be listed under the Computers folder. Locate the server and expand it so that the msmq object underneath is shown. (If you can't expand your computer, you need to select Users, Groups, And Computers as containers from the View menu.) Right-click this msmq object, and select Properties. (If the msmq item isn't visible within your computer's container, select Advanced Features from the View menu.) Click the Sites tab and add the foreign site (WMQ_CN) to the list of sites on the local machine, as shown in Figure 10-10.

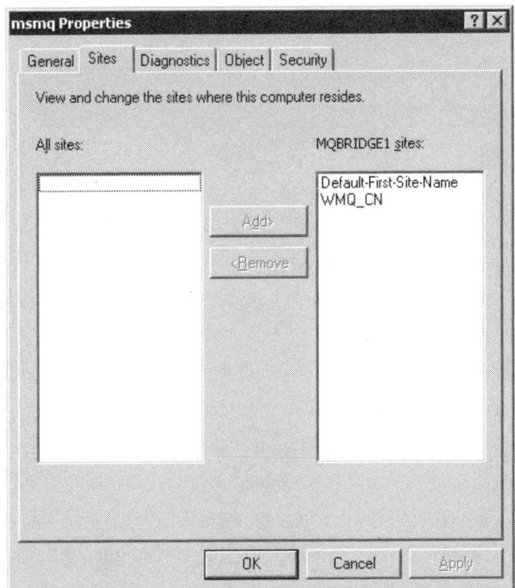

Figure 10-10 Adding the foreign site to the MSMQ-MQSeries bridge.

Click OK to save the changes. The Active Directory sites and routing support is now complete. By performing these steps, you've configured a new foreign site and computer, which represent the network and queue manager of the

WebSphere MQ installation. You've set up the security and configured some of the local site settings so that the bridge can communicate with the WebSphere MQ queue manager. Now it's time to create some queues.

Configuring the Queues

To enable the bridge to forward messages between MSMQ and WebSphere MQ, you need to create a total of four queues. Two of these queues will be for MSMQ, and two will be for WebSphere MQ. Figure 10-11 shows a logical representation of these queues and how they relate to each other within the setup of the bridge.

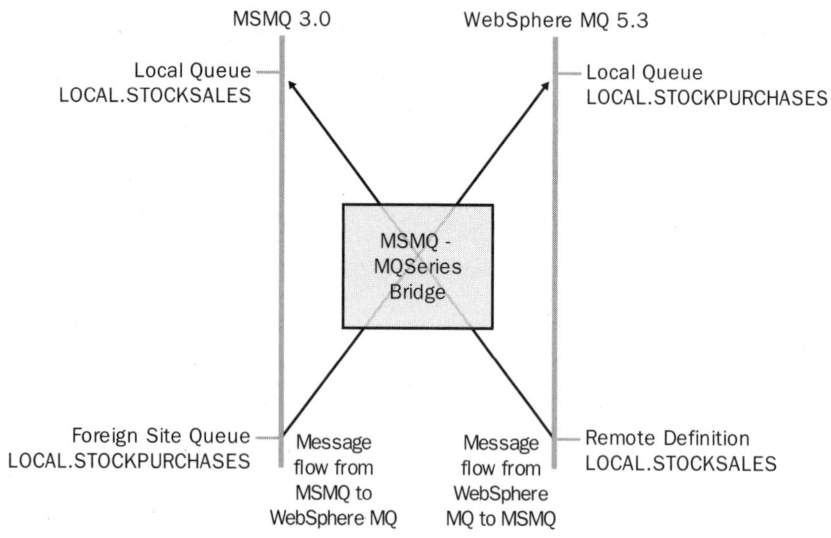

Figure 10-11 Logical representation of how the queues will be configured.

As Figure 10-11 illustrates, either MSMQ or WebSphere MQ will be designated as local and used by the bridge as a delivery point for new messages. The other product will be designated as remote and used to represent the queue on the other platform. With MSMQ, the remote queue is configured as part of the foreign site. With WebSphere MQ, the remote queue is created as a remote definition in the queue manager.

Creating the MSMQ Queues

In the Active Directory Users And Computers tool, right-click the msmq object under the MSMQ-MQSeries bridge computer. Select New/MSMQ Queue. Enter the name of the queue. This will be **LOCAL.STOCKSALES**, as shown in Figure 10-12.

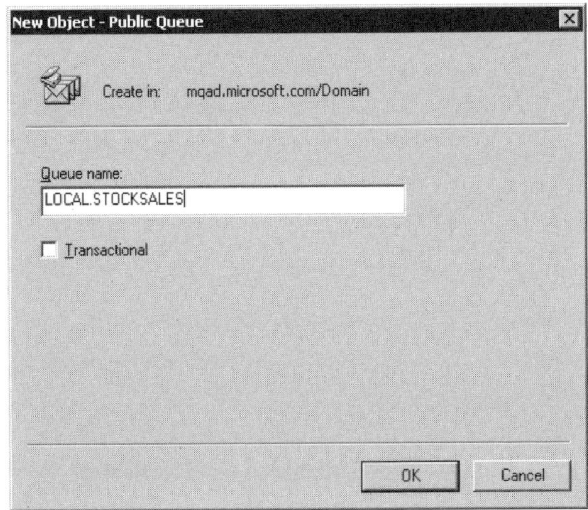

Figure 10-12 Creating the local stock sales sample queue in MSMQ.

For these samples, ensure that the queue isn't marked as transactional, as shown in Figure 10-12.

> **More Info** We won't cover transactional queues across the bridge in this chapter, but this is something that the MSMQ-MQSeries bridge can support. For more information, I recommend consulting the documentation that accompanies Host Integration Server 2000.

Click OK to create this queue. You now need to create a reference to the queue that will be local to the WebSphere MQ server. Within the Computers folder, expand the foreign computer that was created (STQM)—this will have the same name as the queue manager. Again, right-click the msmq object. Create a queue named **LOCAL.STOCKPURCHASES**.

After the two queues have been created, the Active Directory setup so far should look similar to Figure 10-13.

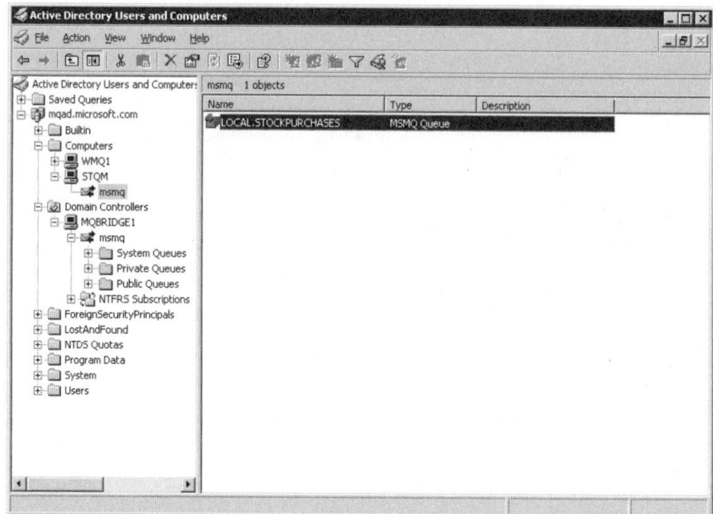

Figure 10-13 The Active Directory Users And Computers administration tool, showing the foreign site queue.

This concludes the configuration required for Active Directory. From here, you can configure the bridge and the WebSphere MQ server and can start sending some test messages.

Configuring the MSMQ-MQSeries Bridge

All configuration of the MSMQ-MQSeries bridge is performed using the MSMQ-MQSeries Bridge Manager. To launch the Bridge Manager, from the Start menu, select Programs\Host Integration Server\Application Integration\MSMQ-MQSeries Bridge Manager.

When opened, this will show the service that resides on the local machine, as depicted in Figure 10-14.

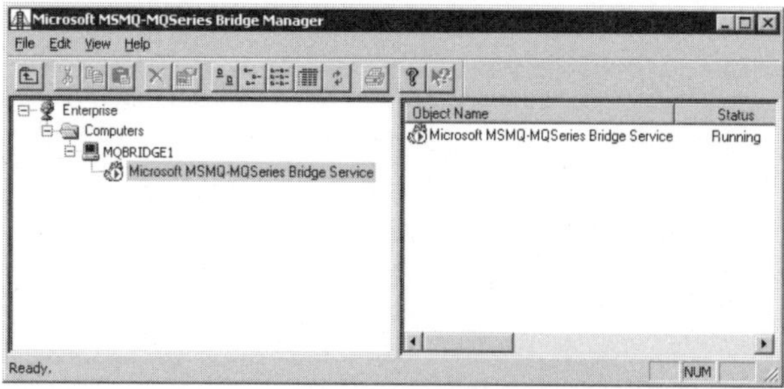

Figure 10-14 Using the MSMQ-MQSeries Bridge Manager.

The first step in the MSMQ-MQSeries Bridge Manager is to define an MQI channel to the WebSphere MQ server. This is the main TCP/IP channel that will be used to send messages to and read messages from the remote queues.

To do this, right-click the Bridge Service and select Properties. Within the Properties dialog box, select MQI Channels and click the Add button. In the Channel Properties window, configure the following settings. Figure 10-15 shows the dialog box you'll see as you make these configurations.

- **Channel name: CHANNEL.MQBRIDGE** The naming of this channel is flexible, but for the samples this should be CHANNEL.MQBRIDGE for consistency. This object will be created as an incoming server channel on the WebSphere MQ server.
- **Queue manager: STQM** This setting must match both the name of the queue manager running on the WebSphere MQ machine and the name of the foreign computer that was created in Active Directory in the previous section.

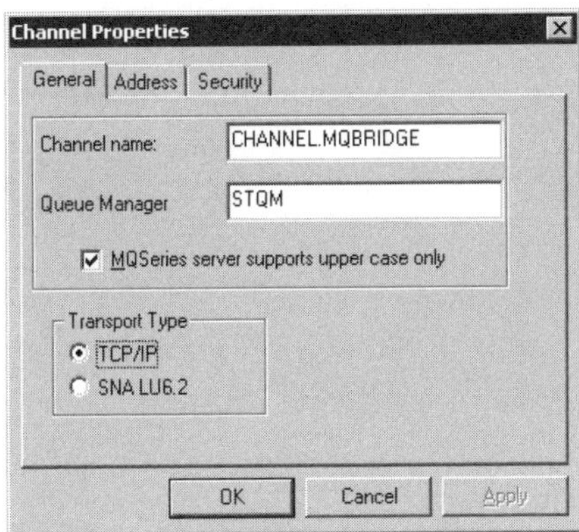

Figure 10-15 Defining the channel properties for the connection to the WebSphere MQ server.

Leave the MQSeries Server Supports Upper Case Only option checked, and set the transport to TCP/IP. (This does not apply to the evaluation version of Host Integration Server 2000.)

Click the Address tab. There, enter the host name of the WebSphere MQ server (*WMQ1* in the example setup; your server name may be different) and the port number (1414 is the default value), as shown in Figure 10-16.

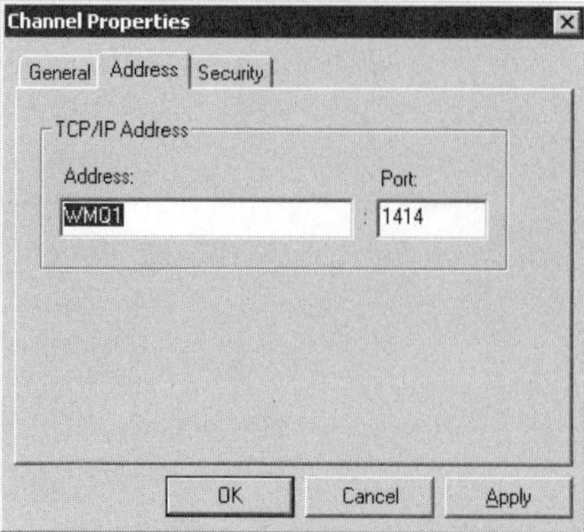

Figure 10-16 Correctly setting the address details for the WebSphere MQ server.

You can double-check the port number by going to the WebSphere MQ server and looking at the properties of the queue manager. The port number shown in Figure 10-16 is the default value for WebSphere MQ and will have been chosen if the setup instructions outlined in Chapter 9 were used.

Finally, in the Security tab, the MCAUSER field can be left blank. This is used for sending security information between machines that aren't part of the same domain. (For example, WebSphere MQ could be running on a UNIX server that can't be part of Active Directory.)

Click OK on the open dialog boxes to save the channel information and return to the main window of the bridge manager. We'll now set up the definition for the remote CN within the bridge manager tool.

Right-click the Bridge Service and select New/CN. Select the CN that matches the name of the foreign site created in the previous step (WMQ_CN).

In the CN Properties dialog box, select the MQSeries QM Name (STQM) and ensure that the ReplyTo QMNAME is the name of your MQBridge server, as shown in Figure 10-17.

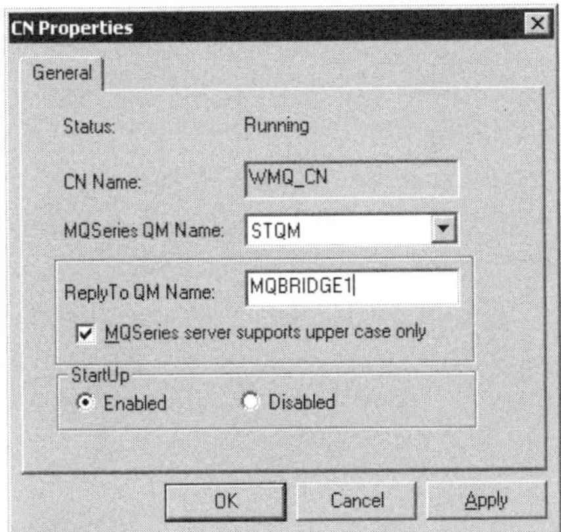

Figure 10-17 Creating and configuring the CN properties for the bridge.

Again, leave the MQSeries Server Supports Upper Case Only check box enabled, and ensure that the startup option is set to Enabled. (Again, this doesn't apply to the evaluation version.)

Click OK to save the settings. Return to the Bridge Manager window, and expand the new CN that's been created. Underneath the WMQ_CN are four message pipes (MSMQ->MQS, MQS->MSMQ, and two transactional representations), which are shown in Figure 10-18.

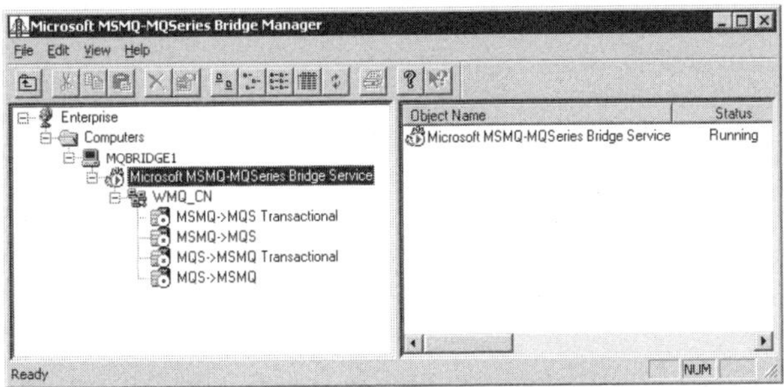

Figure 10-18 A view of the four message pipes within the MSMQ-MQSeries Bridge Manager.

These pipes are used for controlling the flow of messages to and from the MSMQ and MQSeries queues. Because the samples in this chapter won't show transactional delivery, you can right-click each of the transactional pipes, select Properties, and set the StartUp flag to Disabled.

The configuration for the MSMQ-MQSeries bridge is now complete. Next you need to export the configuration from the bridge. This is used to set up the channels and some of the configuration on the WebSphere MQ server.

Exporting the Configuration

You also use the MSMQ-MQSeries Bridge Manager to export the configuration and create the scripts required to configure WebSphere MQ. To export the configuration, right-click the Bridge Service. Select the Export Server Definitions option. Place the definition file in a directory that will be easily accessible.

Repeat the process, but this time select the Export Client Definitions option instead. Save this file to the same directory. In the directory that was chosen, these two files should now appear:

```
ClientDf.txt
STQM.txt
```

Copy these files to the server running WebSphere MQ. For this sample, we'll copy the file to the C:\TEMP directory of the WebSphere MQ machine.

Configuring the WebSphere MQ Server

Connect to the machine running WebSphere MQ Server. From a command prompt on this machine, navigate to the bin directory of the WebSphere MQ installation (normally C:\Program Files\IBM\Websphere MQ\bin).

From this directory, enter the following two commands. (Change the location of the scripts accordingly if you didn't copy to the C:\TEMP directory.)

```
runmqsc < c:\temp\STQM.txt
runmqsc < c:\temp\ClientDf.txt
```

After each of the scripts has completed, check the output displayed onscreen for any errors. A successful script will terminate with the following output:

```
No commands have a syntax error.
All valid MQSC commands were processed.
```

Once the import has completed, open the WebSphere MQ Explorer. Notice that additional objects have been created in the Queues folder under the default queue manager, STQM, as shown in Figure 10-19.

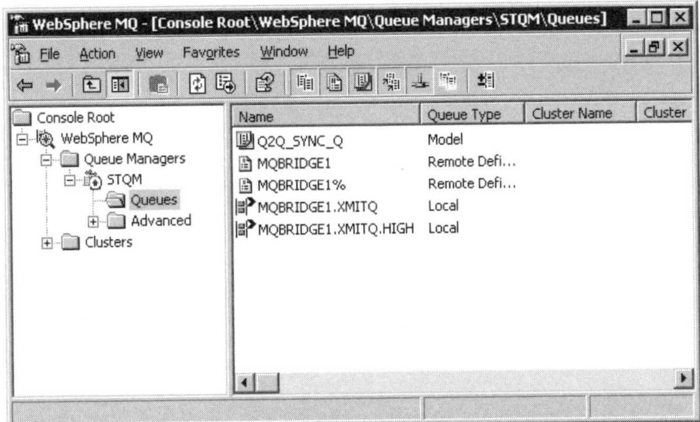

Figure 10-19 The objects created by importing the scripts on the WebSphere MQ server.

By default, the script creates five objects. (Note that the actual names will vary depending on the name of the bridge server machine.) *MQBRIDGE1*.XMITQ and *MQBRIDGE1*.XMITQ.HIGH are the transmission queues used to hold messages that will be picked up by the MSMQ-MQSeries bridge and forwarded to the appropriate MSMQ queue. (*MQBRIDGE1*.XMITQ.HIGH is the nontransactional transmission queue.) The next two objects, *MQBRIDGE1* and *MQBRIDGE1%*, are two remote definition managers to these transmission queues. (*MQBRIDGE1%* is the nontransaction remote definition.) And finally, Q2Q_SYNC_Q is a model used for keeping all the channels in synchronization.

Creating the Queues in WebSphere MQ

Create a new local queue named **LOCAL.STOCKPURCHASES**. To create a new queue, right-click the Queues folder and select New/Local Queue. This queue is local to the WebSphere MQ server and will be populated by incoming messages from the MSMQ-MQSeries bridge.

If a local queue is already defined for LOCAL.STOCKSALES, delete it. (We did use such a local queue in the samples in Chapter 9, so you might have to delete that local queue now.)

Right-click the Queues folder again and select New/Remote Queue Definition. As the menu option implies, this queue is a remote definition, which is a WebSphere MQ representation of the MSMQ queue. For the queue, enter the information shown in the following list, as shown in Figure 10-20:

- Queue name: **LOCAL.STOCKSALES**
- Remote queue name: **LOCAL.STOCKSALES**
- Remote queue manager name: ***BRIDGE_NAME*%**
- Transmission queue name: ***BRIDGE_NAME*.XMITQ.HIGH**

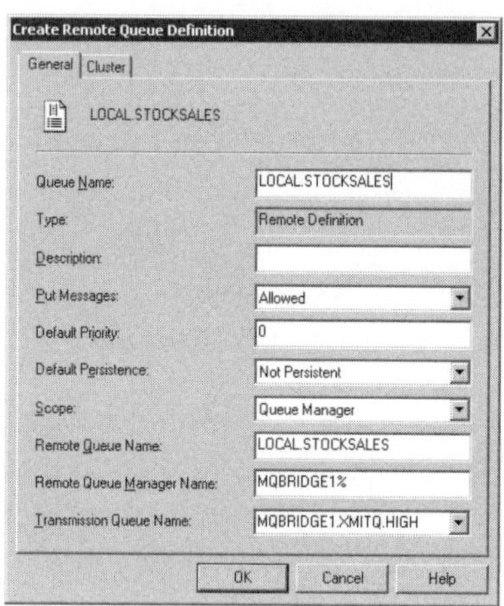

Figure 10-20 Creating the local stock sales remote definition on the WebSphere MQ server.

In the remote queue manager name and transmission queue name, replace *BRIDGE_NAME* with the host name of your bridge. In our sample, these will become *MQBRIDGE1%* and *MQBRIDGE1*.XMITQ.HIGH, respectively. You can also select the transmission queue name by selecting this option from the drop-down list.

Note that we're using the nontransactional channels for both the remote queue manager names and transmission queue names. Click OK to define the queue.

Exporting the Client Channel Table File

The final configuration step for the WebSphere MQ server is to export a channel table file from the WebSphere MQ server to the MSMQ-MQSeries bridge. This step is required because it allows the MSMQ-MQSeries bridge to interrogate the channels and queues that have been defined. If at any point in the future the WebSphere MQ configuration changes, it's a good idea to reexport this file.

To export this file, navigate to the C:\Program Files\IBM\Websphere MQ\Qmgrs\STQM\@ipcc directory on the WebSphere MQ server. This directory should contain a file named AMQCLCHL.TAB. This file needs to be copied to the MSMQ-MQSeries bridge.

Copy this file to a directory that's easily accessible on the MSMQ-MQSeries bridge. For this sample, I've copied the file to the C:\TEMP directory on the bridge machine.

The WebSphere MQ portion of the setup is now completed.

Completing the Configuration of the MSMQ-MQSeries Bridge

The final configuration step is to set up two environment variables that are used to locate the TAB file that was copied from the WebSphere MQ machine. On the bridge, if your file was copied to the C:\TEMP directory, I recommend copying it to the installation of the WebSphere MQ client on this machine (C:\Program Files\IBM\Websphere MQ). Next, right-click My Computer, select Properties, select the Advanced tab, and click the Environment Variables button. In the System Variables section, create two new variables, as shown in Table 10-2.

Table 10-2 System Variables Required for the MSMQ-MQSeries Bridge

Variable	Value
MQCHLLIB	**C:\Program Files\IBM\Websphere MQ**
MQCHLTAB	**AMQCLCHL.TAB**

Click OK to save the new variables and then click OK on the remaining dialog boxes. Close all command prompt windows that are open. (This ensures that all the environment variables are reset.)

Open a new command prompt window and type the following command, exactly as shown:

```
DIR "%MQCHLLIB%"\%MQCHLTAB%
```

The result of this should be the TAB file, located in the correct directory. If you receive a File Not Found error, recheck the location of the file and those environment variables. These two environment variables are crucial for the bridge to work.

Testing the MSMQ-MQSeries Bridge Setup

A number of test tools are supplied with the MSMQ-MQSeries bridge. These tools help validate the setup of the bridge and are run from the command line. You'll use these tools to first validate the MSMQ to WebSphere MQ bridging options, and then to validate the reverse.

Testing MSMQ to WebSphere MQ Connectivity

To test while still within a command prompt on the bridge server, run the following command:

```
MQSRRECV STQM LOCAL.STOCKPURCHASES
```

This tool actively listens to incoming queue messages on the WebSphere MQ server. The parameters specify the name of the queue manager and the local queue name. This tool and the others you'll use for testing in this section can be found in the C:\Program Files\Host Integration Server\System directory, in case this directory isn't on the System *PATH*.

If successful, the following message should be displayed:

```
Use <CTL-C> to stop !
```

If you don't receive this message, check that the channel definitions and scripts have been configured as outlined in this chapter. Also, ensure that the WebSphere MQ server is up and running and that the queue manager has been started.

If this is successful, open the MSMQ-MQSeries Bridge Manager. If not already running, start the service by right-clicking the Bridge Service and selecting Start. Do the same for the CN (WMQ_CN) site. Ensure that the two message pipes (MQS->MSMQ and MSMQ->MQS) are started. This is indicated with a green "play button" icon next to the service, as shown in Figure 10-21.

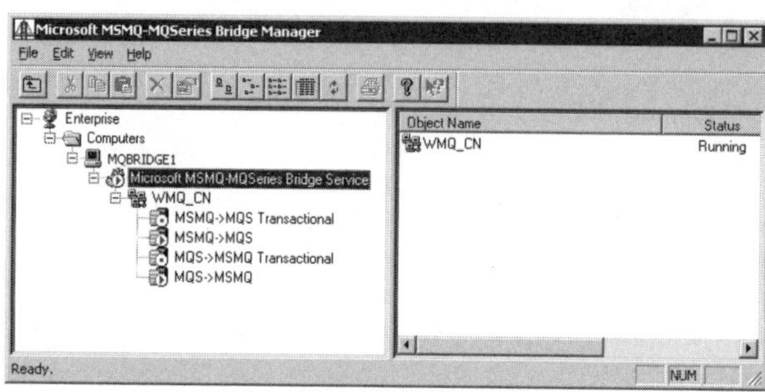

Figure 10-21 The two message pipes running within the MSMQ-MQSeries Bridge Manager.

Now that the test tool is listening for incoming messages on the queue, open another command prompt window. From there, type the following command:

```
MSMQSEND STQM\LOCAL.STOCKPURCHASES
```

This will send 10 test messages with the same name to the MSMQ queue. The following should be displayed in this window. (Note that the time information will be different.)

```
Test Message 0 - 20:18:02
Test Message 1 - 20:18:02
Test Message 2 - 20:18:02
Test Message 3 - 20:18:02
Test Message 4 - 20:18:02
Test Message 5 - 20:18:02
Test Message 6 - 20:18:02
Test Message 7 - 20:18:02
Test Message 8 - 20:18:02
Test Message 9 - 20:18:02
```

Now switch to the other command prompt window running the MQSR-RECV command. If the bridge was able to successfully route these messages, this same text will appear in this window too.

Testing WebSphere MQ to MSMQ Connectivity

To reverse the test (sending from WebSphere MQ to MSMQ), perform the following steps. Stop the MQSRRECV command by pressing CTRL+C. In this window, type the following command, replacing *MQBRIDGE1* with the name of your bridge server:

```
MSMQRECV MQBRIDGE1\LOCAL.STOCKSALES
```

This will enable your machine to listen to the incoming MSMQ queue. Now switch to the other command prompt window (used to send the messages earlier) and type:

```
MQSRSEND STQM STQM LOCAL.STOCKSALES
```

If all is successful, the test should now display messages that have been transferred the other way, such as these:

```
Test Message 0 - 20:23:15
Test Message 1 - 20:23:15
Test Message 2 - 20:23:15
Test Message 3 - 20:23:15
Test Message 4 - 20:23:15
Test Message 5 - 20:23:15
Test Message 6 - 20:23:15
Test Message 7 - 20:23:15
Test Message 8 - 20:23:15
Test Message 9 - 20:23:15
```

If the tests are unsuccessful, revisit the setup instructions to validate that you performed them correctly. The MSMQ-MQSeries bridge contains a tracing tool that can be used to debug messages that aren't correctly sent between the two queuing products and writes numerous events to the Event Log. Tracing can be enabled by using the Trace Initiator and Trace Viewer, two tools in the Applications And Tools folder of the Host Integration Server 2000 Programs Group.

If these tests are successful, congratulations are in order! The bridge is now fully configured to route messages. Before proceeding, stop the MSMQRECV process by pressing CTRL+C in the appropriate command prompt window.

Testing the Bridge with Previous Code Samples

To further show how the MSMQ-MQSeries bridge works, you can take the code samples shown in Chapters 8 and 9 and apply them to this setup. This will show how a client using the Microsoft .NET Messaging namespace (*System.Messaging*) and a client using IBM's libraries for Java can be used to exchange messages.

The sample code to show this can be found in the C:\Interoperability\Samples\Resource\MSMQBridge directory. This directory contains two subdirectories, dotNET and Java.

In the .NET client, notice how the queues are configured by using the queues available in Active Directory. (Also, note that you'll have to modify the code to replace all instances of example server names with the names of the servers in your actual setup.)

```
MessageQueue purchasesMQ
    = new MessageQueue(@"STQM\LOCAL.STOCKPURCHASES");
MessageQueue salesMQ
    = new MessageQueue(@"MQBRIDGE1\LOCAL.STOCKSALES");
```

Because this code references queues in Active Directory, the client machine that runs this sample should also reside within Active Directory. To facilitate this, these tests can be run on the bridge.

For the Java client, a number of properties are configured to reference the queue on the *WMQ1* server, as shown here. (Again, you'll need to change this name to the corresponding server name in your setup.)

```
String hostName = "WMQ1";
int port = 1414;
String channel = "SYSTEM.DEF.SVRCONN";

String qmName = "STQM";
```

```
String purchasesQName = "LOCAL.STOCKPURCHASES";
String salesQName = "LOCAL.STOCKSALES";

Hashtable props = new Hashtable();
props.put(MQC.HOST_NAME_PROPERTY,hostName);
props.put(MQC.PORT_PROPERTY,new Integer(port));
props.put(MQC.CHANNEL_PROPERTY,channel);
```

If you're accessing the queue remotely (and not running the sample code on the WebSphere MQ box), ensure that the WebSphere MQ client is installed on the client machine.

Build and run the .NET client sample code. Enter **nant** at a command prompt within the dotNET subdirectory to build the sample, and enter **client** to run it. Upon running, the .NET client will display the following:

```
Test message has been placed on the purchases queue.
This should be bridged to Websphere MQ
```

The .NET client places a message on the local purchases queue, which uses MSMQ and will then pause. The MSMQ-MQSeries bridge delivers this message to the corresponding queue on the WebSphere MQ server. Now run the Java client in a separate command prompt window. Enter **ant run** at a command prompt within the Java subdirectory to build and run the Java client. If successful, you should notice a number of operations.

> **Note** When running the sample code, if an error is generated with reason code 2009 (or if the Java client hangs when opening the connection to the queue), create a system environment variable named *MQNOREMPOOL* on the client and set the value to 1. This is a known TCP channel bug with JDK 1.4.1 and the WebSphere MQ client.

First, the Java client places a new message on the local sales queue, which uses WebSphere MQ:

```
Test message has been placed on the sales queue.
This should be bridged to MSMQ
```

The MSMQ-MQSeries bridge will take this message and deliver it to the corresponding MSMQ queue.

Next, the Java client picks up the message that has been delivered by the bridge from the .NET client:

```
Message delivered by MSMQ-MQSeries Bridge:
<?xml version="1.0"?>
<string>
    This is a test purchase, sent using a .NET System.Messaging client!
</string>
```

Notice how the message is encapsulated in an XML document. We'll get to the reasoning behind this shortly.

Before we do, switch back to the command prompt window that's running the .NET client. You should observe that the message that was sent by the Java client has been picked up (by the bridge moving it from the WebSphere MQ queue to MSMQ):

```
Message delivered by MSMQ-MQSeries Bridge:
This is a test sale, sent using a Websphere MQ client!
```

As shown, the test sale sent by the Java client was successfully received.

So, why the XML? Recall that in Chapter 8 you saw how the *System.Messaging* namespace was used by a .NET client to send a message to an instance of MSMQ. You might remember how messages sent to an MSMQ queue can be formatted either with an XML formatter or a binary formatter—similar to the formatting options available in Microsoft .NET Remoting.

With this example, we also must choose one of these options to send the message across the MSMQ-MQSeries bridge. Because there's no binary formatter on the Java 2 platform that's compatible—see Chapter 3, "Exchanging Data Between .NET and Java," for more details—the XML formatter is used. By specifying this formatter, the text string message that the .NET client sends is serialized into an XML document, which is the result displayed when the Java client reads the message.

For returning a message in an equivalent XML format, the Java client uses the following line:

```
msg.writeString("<?xml version=\"1.0\"?><string>This is a test sale,"
    +"sent using a Websphere MQ client!</string>");
```

As you can see, the string message is simply contained within an XML document.

Although this is fine for our test string message, in a production environment you'll want to avoid constructing your own XML documents in strings. One way for the Java client to create messages that the .NET client can understand is to use the XML serialization techniques, as discussed in Chapter 3. Because the .NET client is using the *XmlSerializer* classes to construct messages, the XML classes within the GLUE toolkit allow the messages to be deserialized to objects that the Java platform can understand. When sending messages back to the .NET client, the same libraries can be used to construct an XML document in the correct format.

Summary

In Chapters 8 and 9, you saw alternatives for connecting Java clients to MSMQ and for connecting .NET clients to WebSphere MQ. Both these chapters pointed out that although connectivity is possible, the alternatives discussed don't really offer a true message queue experience. The XML Web service wrapper for MSMQ lacks reliability and transactional support, and .NET can access only a subset of the WebSphere MQ classes.

The MSMQ-MQSeries bridge that ships with Host Integration Server offers a viable alternative to these two approaches. Using this bridge allows clients to use their native message queuing implementations (*System.Messaging* for .NET, and the IBM Java libraries for WebSphere MQ), which guarantees reliability and transactional message queue qualities.

If you have an existing investment in Active Directory, want to perform message transfer between MSMQ and WebSphere MQ queues, and need a supported product, the MSMQ-MQSeries bridge might be a good fit for you.

The bridge does have some drawbacks, however, which can affect implementation. First, it's dependent on an Active Directory installation, which is a consideration for J2EE-only environments. For this purpose, this chapter presented the steps required to configure the directory correctly. In addition, the bridge lacks the ability to process any messages while they're in transit. To understand when this might be important, imagine requiring that only messages meeting certain criteria are transferred, or requiring that the message schema must be changed as it flows between queues. The sample showed a great example of this, where the .NET client uses an XML structure to create messages, while the Java client is expecting a raw stream of bytes. The transformation of the message was the responsibility of the Java client and something that the bridge could not do automatically.

Now also imagine a requirement to communicate with other message-based systems (for example, queuing products other than WebSphere MQ or host-based systems). At this point, we're talking about a very different solution. To address some of these requirements, we'll look at a product named Microsoft BizTalk Server in the next chapter. We'll also summarize the four chapters on asynchronous interoperability to review what you've learned.

11

Asynchronous Interoperability, Part 4: BizTalk Server

In the last three chapters, you saw a variety of methods to perform asynchronous interoperability between the .NET and Java platforms. These included Java clients that access Microsoft Message Queuing (MSMQ), .NET clients that access WebSphere MQ, and the configuration of a bridge between the two queues.

In this chapter, we'll take a slightly different approach and look at how Microsoft BizTalk Server can be used not only to provide asynchronous messaging interoperability, but also to add significant orchestration functionality for messages that travel among various XML Web services. For those who haven't used the product, Microsoft BizTalk Server is Microsoft's integration server that combines core messaging capabilities with *orchestration* (or business-process) authoring, execution, and management. In general, this tends to encompass three areas:

- **Enterprise application integration** Available for use with BizTalk Server is a very rich set of adapters used for connecting multiple applications and services throughout the enterprise. Some of these adapters are shipped with the product; others are available for download or purchase. The functions of these adapters range from transferring files by using FTP to connecting to Enterprise Resource Planning (ERP) systems such as SAP.

- **Automation of business processes** BizTalk Server uses the concept of orchestration to create processes and schedules that can predictably control both enterprise applications and integration with partners and customers. To achieve this, BizTalk Server ships with an orchestration designer (providing a graphical view of business processes) and an orchestration engine (which allows orchestrations to be deployed independently of the design environment).
- **Deployment of applications** Using a technique known as SEED, it's possible to create integration solutions that can be deployed easily and effectively to both remote locations and business partners over the Internet.

Be aware that this isn't a book on BizTalk Server. Although you'll see some of the fundamentals of the product in this chapter, the BizTalk Server product provides a vast range of functionality. To cover all this functionality could fill up an entire book. This chapter will target the elements of BizTalk Server that are relevant to .NET and J2EE interoperability. This includes how a BizTalk Server orchestration can be used to predictably call and manage a number of Web services, regardless of the technology stack they're based upon.

> **More Info** For additional information on BizTalk Server, consult the Microsoft product page at *http://www.microsoft.com/biztalk/*.

Introducing BizTalk Server 2004 Beta 1

Although BizTalk Server 2002 is currently available as a supported product, the writing of this chapter coincides with the release of the first public beta of BizTalk Server 2004. Because this beta release has additional support for the functionality that this chapter will demonstrate, the sample code will use this newer version.

Note that the instructions for installing and configuring the product as well as the sample code in this chapter are based on this beta version of the product. Because things will likely change between this beta release and the final version, you should always consult and use the latest documentation and installation instructions.

Prerequisites for BizTalk Server 2004 Beta 1

Beta 1 of BizTalk Server 2004 has some dependencies that must be present before installing the product. These include the following:

- An accessible installation of Microsoft SQL Server 2000 Enterprise, Standard, or Developer Edition (installed with Service Pack 3 or higher)
- SQL Server Analysis Services (also installed with Service Pack 3)
- Microsoft Visual Studio .NET 2003 for both the development and deployment environment

> **Tip** It's always a good idea to refer to the full installation documentation that comes with the product for a complete list of prerequisites.

Microsoft SQL Server is used as the primary database for storing all of the Services configuration and deployment information for BizTalk Server. Visual Studio .NET 2003 houses the BizTalk Server design tools, including the Schema Editor, Mapper, Orchestration Designer, and BizTalk Explorer.

Before installing BizTalk Server 2004 Beta 1, you need to install the applications mentioned in the previous list. For the purpose of the sample in this chapter, it's assumed that these installations are on the same machine and that this machine is running Microsoft Windows Server 2003.

Installing BizTalk Server 2004 Beta 1

With the prerequisites fulfilled, to start the installation, launch the BizTalk Server 2004 Beta 1 Setup Wizard, and click the Install option on the welcome screen. After entering the product serial number and completing the license agreement page, select a complete installation of the product. By default, this will install the product to the C:\Program Files\Microsoft BizTalk Server 2004 directory. If you don't have Microsoft Windows SharePoint Services 2.0 installed on your machine, you might receive a warning indicating that Business Activity Services will not be installed. You can ignore this warning because this isn't a feature that we'll use when working with the sample code.

After installation has completed, the BizTalk Server 2004 Configuration Wizard will be launched. This allows you to configure how the product will run and to specify where databases required by the product will reside.

When the wizard starts, you'll be prompted to specify whether you want to create a new BizTalk Server group or join an existing one, and whether this server will hold the master secret key for the Enterprise Single Sign-On (SSO) features. For the purpose of running the sample code in this chapter, create a new BizTalk Server group and hold the key on the local machine, as shown in Figure 11-1.

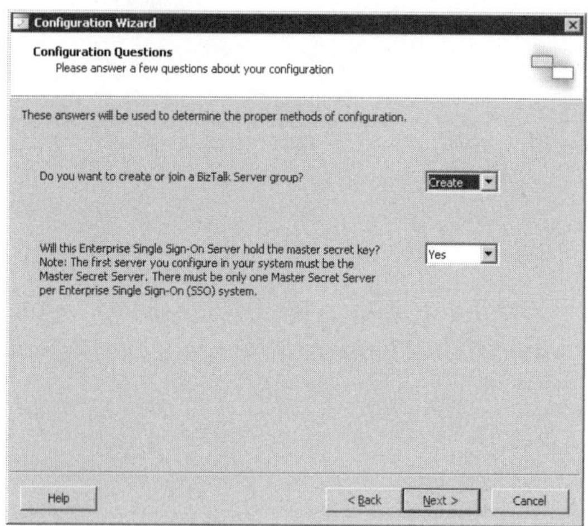

Figure 11-1 Starting the BizTalk Server 2004 Configuration Wizard.

In the next stage of the wizard, review the credentials configuration, as shown in Figure 11-2. This configuration should be prepopulated and shouldn't need changing. Ensure that an administrative account is designated for the SSO Administrator(s). If a prepopulated value needs to be changed, click the Edit button and enter a valid account.

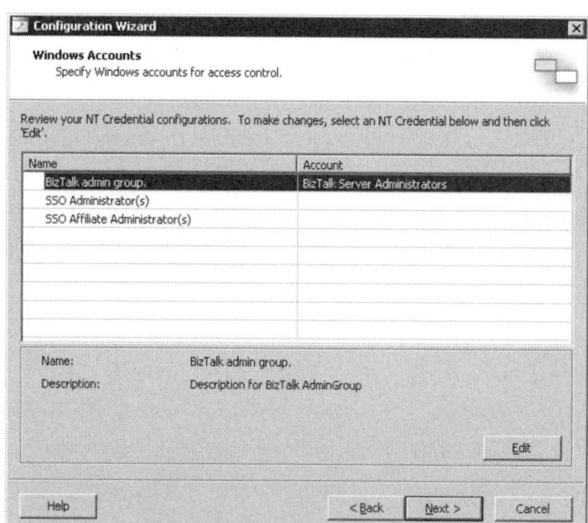

Figure 11-2 Setting the Windows accounts for access control.

Accept the defaults for the next two screens within the wizard. These set the BAM Query Web service URL and the machine name for the BizTalk SSO Server—neither of which will be used in our sample code.

The next screen shows the SQL Server setup and configuration that will be used for the BizTalk Server databases, as shown in Figure 11-3.

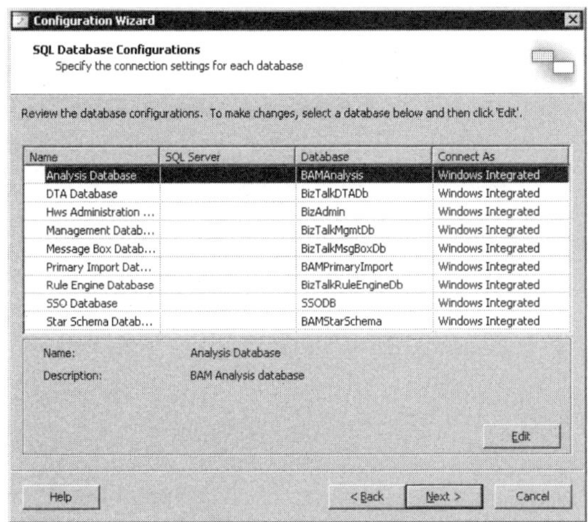

Figure 11-3 Specifying the database locations for BizTalk Server.

By default, the configuration wizard will detect the installation and connection type for SQL Server on the local machine. If this isn't automatically completed, or if the database will reside in a different location, you should click the Edit button to make changes as appropriate.

The next screen in the wizard requires credentials for the BizTalk Server services, as shown in Figure 11-4.

Configuration Wizard
NT Service Configurations
Enter the accounts for each NT service
Review your NT Service configurations. To make changes, select an NT Service below and then click 'Edit'.
Name | Log On As
BAM query web service user.
Enterprise Single Sign-On Service
Hws Web Service User
Rule Engine Update Service
Name: BAM query web service user.
Description: This account will be used by the BAM query web service to access system resources and services.
Edit
Help
< Back
Next >
Cancel

Figure 11-4 Defining the Microsoft Windows NT Service configurations.

Click the Edit button for one of these services and enter valid credentials as appropriate for your machine. Entering the credentials for one of the services will populate the remaining three.

Click the Next button within the BizTalk Messaging screen (again, we won't use this component in this chapter) and confirm the summary of items to configure. The configuration wizard will now set up BizTalk Server 2004 according to your settings.

After the configuration wizard has completed, the Host Creation Wizard will be launched. This wizard is used to set up the host-specific settings for the machine that will run BizTalk Server 2004. Within this wizard, choose not to configure the Analysis Server by clearing the check box, as shown in Figure 11-5.

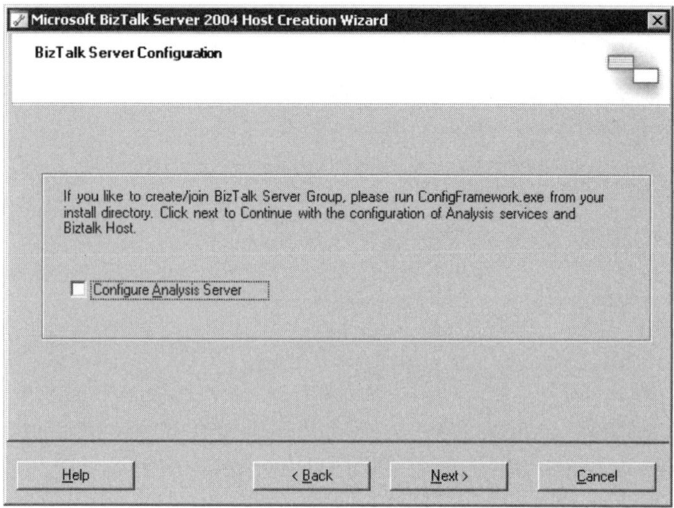

Figure 11-5 Launching the Host Creation Wizard.

In the next screen of the Host Creation Wizard, use a host name of BizTalkServerApplication for the host. The name of the BizTalk Host Users Group will reference one created on the server, as shown in Figure 11-6.

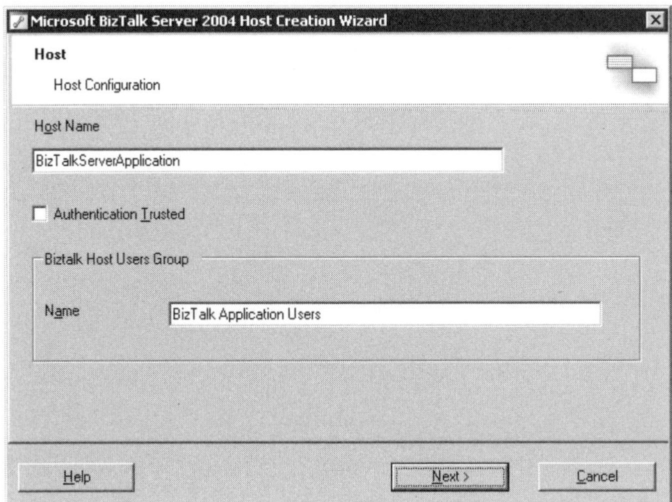

Figure 11-6 Setting the host name and user group settings.

Enter a valid username and password for the host in the next wizard screen. This is the username and password that will be used to run the Windows service for the instance of BizTalk Server. If you enter an account with administrative privileges, you'll receive a security warning indicating that a less-privileged account is recommended. As with the other security recommendations made throughout this book, the samples will work with an administrative account, but you should think carefully about such security implications if you're deploying BizTalk Server 2004 in a production environment.

Continuing through the wizard, enter a name and group for the BizTalk Isolated Host. The isolated host is used for applications that need access to the BizTalk Server databases in a controlled way. For the samples in this chapter, you can accept the default host name and group, as shown in Figure 11-7.

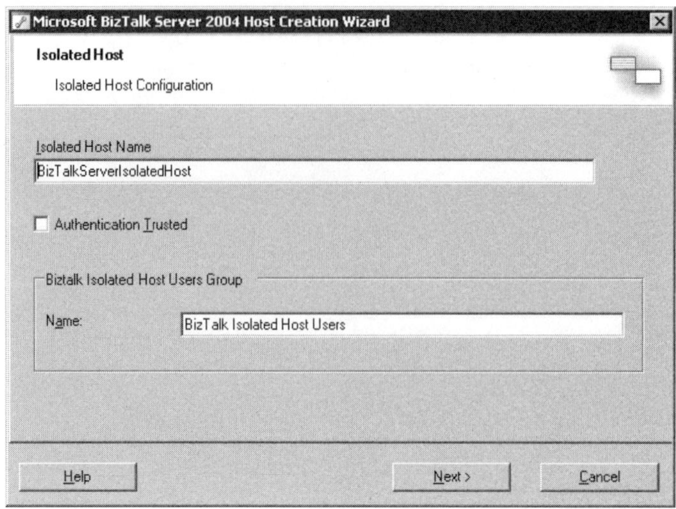

Figure 11-7 Setting the isolated host name and user group settings.

On the wizard's next page, it isn't necessary to configure the HTTP/SOAP settings for the isolated host. Click Next again, and then click Finish to complete the Host Configuration Wizard.

After the wizard has completed, the setup of BizTalk Server 2004 is complete. Now let's build and test the sample code.

Sample Use Case and Code

Recall that in the series of examples shown in the previous three chapters, a message was sent asynchronously using clients in both .NET and Java. To expand on this and to highlight the functionality that BizTalk Server 2004 can provide, we'll continue using this asynchronous approach but will create a BizTalk Server orchestration based on a use case.

The use case shown in this section is based on the stock-trading examples used in previous chapters. The samples in this chapter will show how an order message submitted by a client can be processed by a BizTalk Server orchestration. The orchestration will execute decision logic to determine which external Web services to call to fulfill the order. A result message will be created at the conclusion of the business process and will be returned to the client. This overall flow can be seen in Figure 11-8.

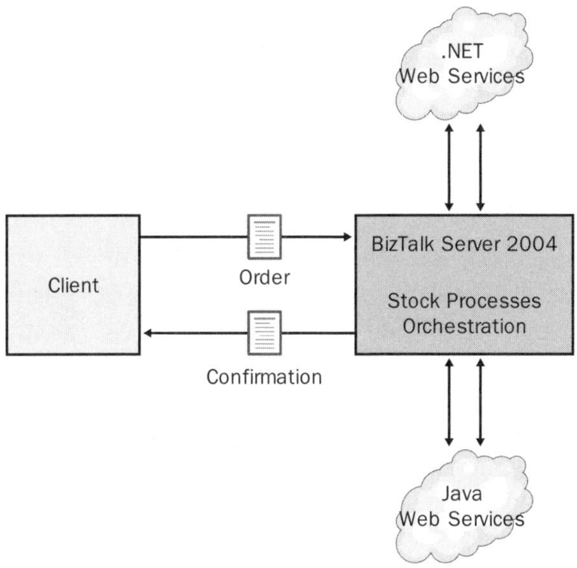

Figure 11-8 The sample stock processes orchestration running on BizTalk Server 2004.

To start, the order will be submitted from the client to BizTalk Server 2004 and will use the schema shown in Table 11-1.

Table 11-1 Schema for the Incoming Order

Field	Type	Description
Ticker	*String*	Used to identify the stock
Qty	*Integer*	Used to identify the quantity of shares
Action	*String*	Used to identify the action required (BUY or SELL)
Email	*String*	Used to identify the user

As an example of this schema in action, the following could be a valid order to purchase 1000 shares of the stock represented by the ticker WOOD:

```
<ns0:Order xmlns:ns0="http://StockProcesses.Order">
    <Ticker>WOOD</Ticker>
    <Qty>1000</Qty>
    <Action>BUY</Action>
    <Email>samples@microsoft.com</Email>
</ns0:Order>
```

As you can see, the order consists of a ticker symbol, a quantity, an action (BUY or SELL), and an e-mail address to identify the sender. Upon receiving the incoming message, the instance of BizTalk Server will start an orchestration. As mentioned earlier, an orchestration is a business process that coordinates message processing among various internal entities (such as a C# component) and external entities (such as a Web service).

The first step in the orchestration is the receipt of the order message. Next, the price for the stock is resolved by using a Web service that will return the current price based on the ticker symbol. After the price is returned, the total value of the order is calculated (by multiplying the stock price by the quantity requested). If the total value of the order is more than $250, the user will qualify for a smaller commission for this trade: $5.95. If the value is less than $250, the commission remains at the regular price of $19.95.

After the order commission is determined, the ticker symbol will be used to resolve a name for the company. This resolution will again be performed by calling a second Web service, passing it the ticker symbol, and returning a *String*. For example, if the ticker symbol WOOD is passed, the Web service will return a *String* containing *Woodgrove Bank* as the full name.

This resolved name, together with the current price and other details in the incoming order, will be used to construct a purchase or sale request that uses a schema, highlighted in Table 11-2. This request is the same as those shown in Chapter 5, "Connectivity with XML Web Services, Part 1," and Chapter 6, "Connectivity with XML Web Services, Part 2."

Table 11-2 Schema for the Request

Field	Type	Description
Ticker	*String*	Used to identify the stock
Name	*String*	Used to identify the stock
Price	*Double*	Offer price for the stock
Previous	*Double*	Used for output only
Volume	*Integer*	Used to specify quantity for incoming requests.

The action field within the incoming order will determine whether this request is sent to a Java Web service (to indicate that the user wants to sell stocks) or to the .NET Web service (to indicate a purchase). After the sale or purchase has been made, a confirmation message will be created and returned to the client. The schema for this final message is shown in Table 11-3.

Table 11-3 Schema for the Confirmation

Field	Type	Description
Ticker	*String*	Used to identify the stock
Message	*String*	Message to the user
Price	*Double*	Offer price for the stock
Qty	*Integer*	Number of shares
Name	*String*	Used to identify the stock
Commission	*Double*	Commission charged for this trade

This is an example of such a confirmation:

```
<ns0:Fulfillment xmlns:ns0="http://StockProcesses.UserResponse">
    <Ticker>WOOD</Ticker>
    <Message>Your order was fulfilled.
        An email has been sent to samples@microsoft.com</Message>
    <Price>14.45</Price>
    <Qty>1000</Qty>
    <Name>Woodgrove Bank</Name>
    <Commission>5.95</Commission>
</ns0:Fulfillment>
```

This typical confirmation message includes items from the original order, returned results from the Web services, and the calculated commission value. Once the confirmation is delivered to the client, the orchestration is considered complete.

Building the Web Services

To start building this Web service by using BizTalk Server 2004, you must first decide on a location and platform for the Web services. To demonstrate that BizTalk Server can call Web services written in both .NET and Java, we'll split the services between the two.

The Web services that provide stock quotes and allow the user to purchase stocks will be hosted by .NET, while the Web services that provide name resolution (finding out a company name from a stock ticker) and allow the user to sell stocks will be written in Java. Before we see the orchestration, we need to build and deploy these Web services. All of these Web services can be found in the C:\Interoperability\Samples\Resource\BizTalk\WebServices directory.

To build the .NET Web services, navigate to the dotNET subdirectory. Within this directory are the two subdirectories, BuyService and PriceService, which contain the required code for the two .NET Web services. For each of these services, use the provided NAnt script in each subdirectory to compile the code. Once compiled, launch the Microsoft Internet Information Services (IIS) administration tool by selecting the program from the Start/Programs/Administrative Tools menu. In the tool, expand the Web Sites folder and right-click Default Web Site. Select New/Virtual Directory to bring up the Virtual Directory Creation Wizard.

Enter the alias for the buy stocks Web service. For this sample, the alias must be **dotNETBuyWebService**, as shown in Figure 11-9.

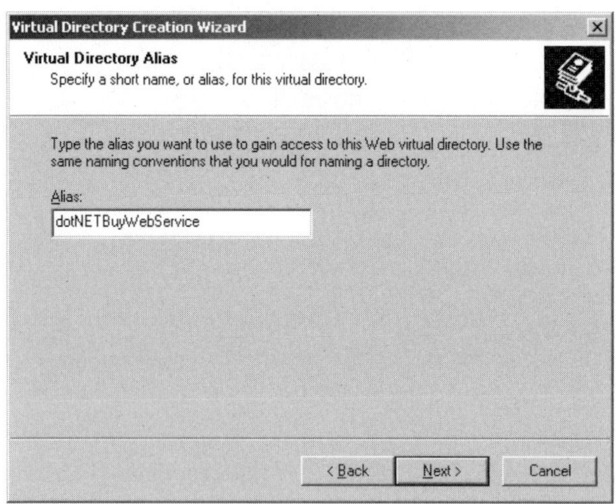

Figure 11-9 Creating the new virtual directory for the buy stocks Web service.

In the next part of the wizard, set the location of the virtual directory to **C:\Interoperability\Samples\Resource\BizTalk\WebServices\dotNET\BuyService**, as shown in Figure 11-10. Accept the defaults for the rest of the wizard to create this Web service.

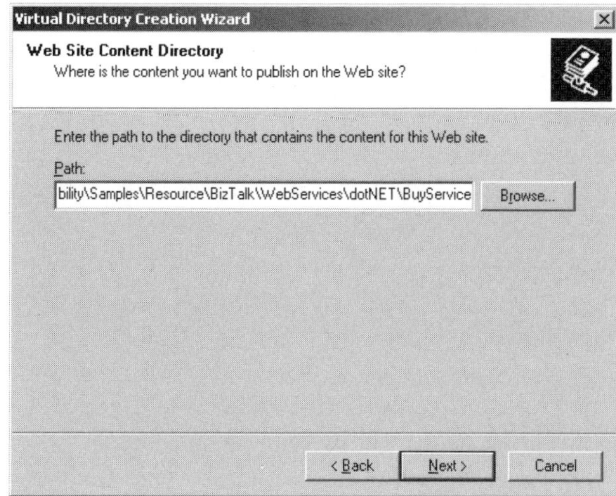

Figure 11-10 Specifying the location of the Web service files.

Repeat the process for the pricing Web service. For the sample to work correctly, the alias for the pricing Web service must be entered as **dotNETPriceService**, as shown in Figure 11-11.

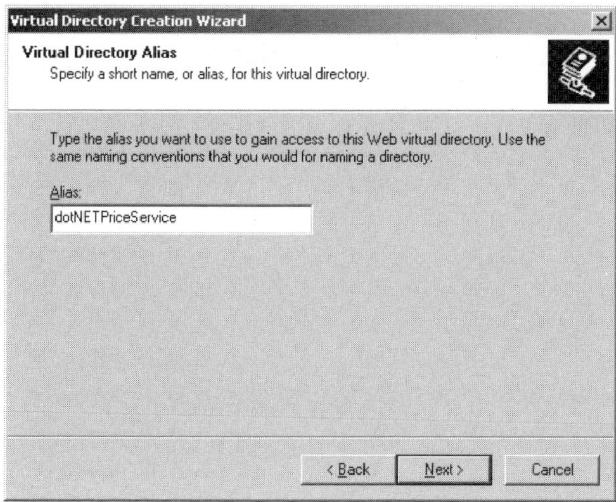

Figure 11-11 Creating the virtual directory for the .NET pricing Web service.

For the location of the pricing service, ensure that **C:\Interoperability\Samples\Resource\BizTalk\WebServices\dotNET\PriceService** is used.

Complete this wizard by accepting the default values, which concludes the setup of the two virtual directories required for the samples.

For the Java Web services, navigate to the C:\Interoperability\Samples\Resource\BizTalk\WebServices\Java directory. The two Web services (for the naming and selling of stocks) are located in this directory. To build and deploy these two Web services, execute the Ant script by using the run target within this directory. Entering **start ant run** at a command prompt within this directory will compile and publish the Web services by using a separate command prompt window. This will publish the Web services at *http://localhost:8004/JavaWebService/NamingService.wsdl* and *http://localhost:8004/JavaWebService/StockService.wsdl*, respectively.

If you followed the samples shown in Chapters 5 and 6, you might be wondering why the Web services used to buy and sell stocks are being redeployed. In this case, these Web services contain only the methods required for buying and selling the stocks—they don't contain the methods for retrieving recommendations.

Once both the .NET and Java Web services have been compiled and published, it's a good idea to validate that they have been deployed correctly. Navigating to the Web Services Description Language (WSDL) file for each of the Web services will confirm this.

The Stock Processes Orchestration: Step by Step

Now that the Web services are deployed, we can take a look at the BizTalk Server solution. Instead of creating the orchestration and related artifacts from scratch during this chapter, you can find the completed BizTalk Server 2004 solution in the C:\Interoperability\Samples\Resource\BizTalk\Project directory. The main solution file for the sample (StockProcesses.sln) should be opened with Microsoft Visual Studio .NET 2003. Note that it isn't possible to view the BizTalk Server orchestration or compile the project without first loading the solution into this integrated development environment (IDE).

Open the solution file, and display the ProcessOrder.odx file. This will show a graphical representation of the BizTalk Server orchestration, as displayed in Figure 11-12.

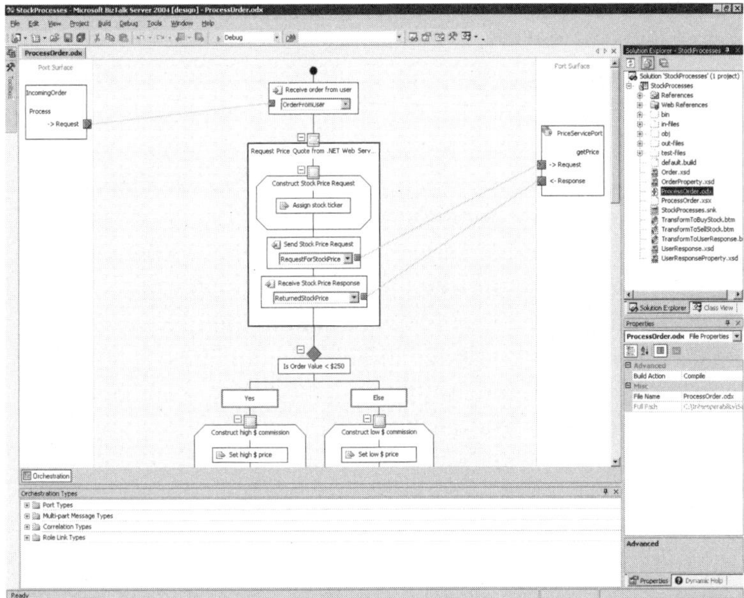

Figure 11-12 The orchestration designer, as shown in Visual Studio .NET 2003.

Let's now step through this orchestration to observe the tasks that will be executed. At the top left, the orchestration is activated based upon an incoming order. Notice how the *OrderFromUser* message is received at a "port" named *IncomingOrder* in a part of the orchestration design pane. This section of the design pane is known as the Port Surface and is shown in Figure 11-13. The Port Surface shows all the entry and exit points (ports) for messages flowing to and from the orchestration. Ports can define one-way or two-way (request-response) message flows.

Figure 11-13 The incoming order port within the orchestration.

We'll define endpoint information for this port as we deploy the orchestration, but for now imagine this port as a logical input point to the orchestration itself. As you can see here, the port delivers the incoming order message to a Receive shape in the orchestration.

How do we define the type for the incoming order? In BizTalk Server 2004, a message's type is defined either by an XML Schema Definition (XSD) document or a .NET class. We use XSD to define a message type here, similar to the way we used XSDs to define data types in Chapters 5 and 6. The XSD document for the incoming order is defined in the Order.xsd file. If you open this file within the BizTalk Server solution, the XSD is displayed in the BizTalk Server Schema Editor. Order.xsd defines *Ticker*, *Qty*, *Action*, and *Email* elements, similar to the schema shown earlier in the use case section.

This is the type of message that the client will be sending to the deployed orchestration. Let's return to the orchestration. Once the incoming order is received, a new message is created and a call is made to our first Web service.

The Construct Message shape shown in Figure 11-14 is used to create a new message that you'll send to the service that will return the current stock price. The *Assign stock ticker* message assignment contains the following code and is used to set the parameter of the request to the value of the ticker in the incoming order:

```
RequestForStockPrice.ticker = OrderFromUser.Ticker;
```

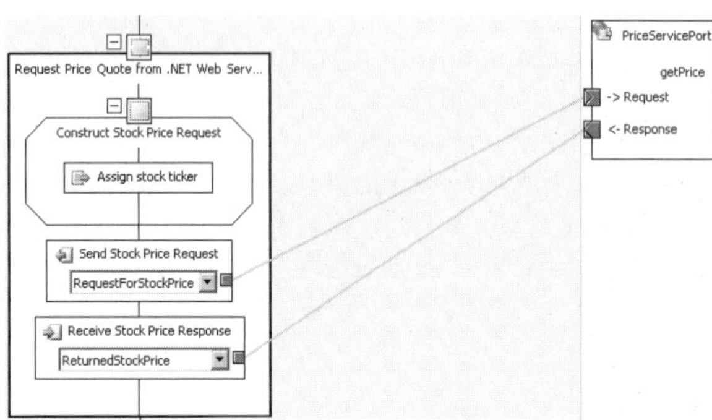

Figure 11-14 The outgoing port to the .NET pricing Web service.

After the message is constructed, a send/receive mechanism is used to call the.NET Web service. Notice how this Web service is represented as a second port in the orchestration.

The Web service port (*PriceServicePort*) was added to the BizTalk Server Port Surface simply by completing an Add Web Reference within the Visual Studio .NET 2003 BizTalk Server project. By simply pointing to the WSDL for the Web service, the BizTalk Server artifacts required to communicate with that service are automatically added to the project. Expanding the Web References folder in the Solution Explorer shows a list of Web services that have been added to the project this way, as shown in Figure 11-15.

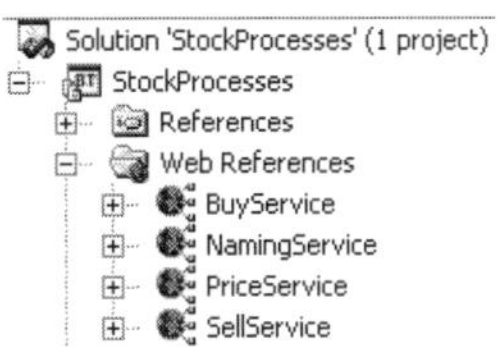

Figure 11-15 The list of Web references used by the BizTalk Server project.

As with the other examples used throughout the book, we could have also used the WSDL tool to define these Web proxy files. However, adding the reference to the Web service by using the IDE provides a natural way for BizTalk Server 2004 to create a port.

After the price has been returned for the stock, the next stage in our use case is to determine whether the total value of the order is greater than $250. If the order is less than this amount, the commission will be $19.95; if the order is more, the commission will be $5.95.

To facilitate this type of decision, BizTalk Server 2004 uses a Decision shape, which is used to conditionally branch based on a logical expression. Any number of conditional branches can be specified, but in this case, we effectively have an *if* branch and an *else* branch. This is shown in Figure 11-16.

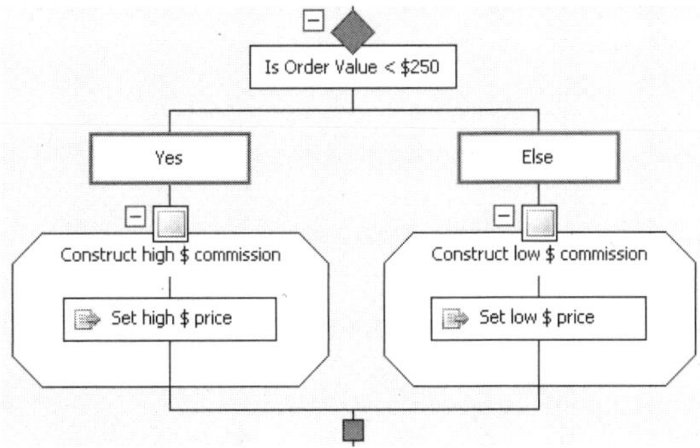

Figure 11-16 The Decision shape, used to branch based on the value of the order.

As shown, if the order is less than $250, a high commission rate message is constructed. If the order is greater than $250, a lower price is used instead. The conditional logic to determine whether the order value is above or below this limit can be found within the Decision shape. Double-clicking the Yes box will show the expression used to make this decision:

```
(ReturnedStockPrice.getPriceResult * OrderFromUser(Qty)) < 250
```

The expression shows how the result from the .NET pricing Web service is multiplied by the quantity supplied in the incoming order from the user. If this value is *true*, the orchestration continues through the high commission route—if not, the *else* branch is used instead. The value of the commission itself is stored in a BizTalk Server message named *Commission*, which is defined as a data type of *System.Double*.

You now have the price and commission for the trade. The next step in the orchestration is to resolve the name of the stock. This name is used to construct the purchase or sale request and is calculated in a way very similar to the way the price was calculated. This is shown in Figure 11-17.

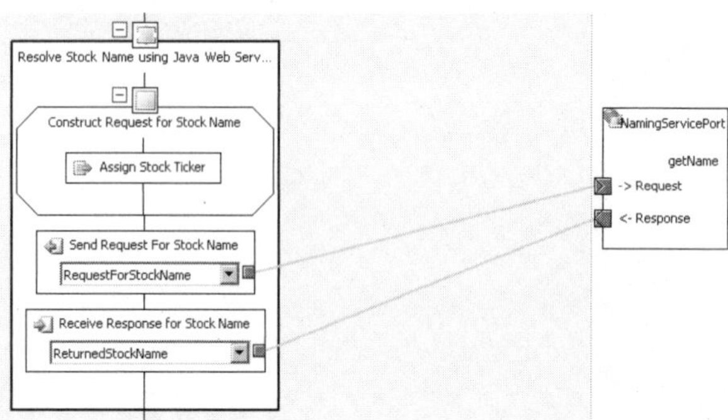

Figure 11-17 The call to the Java-based naming Web service.

Again, a message that defines the request for the name is constructed. The assignment takes the stock ticker from the order and uses that as the parameter to call the Web service. The Web service (shown as *NamingService-Port*) is based on a Web Reference that has been added to the BizTalk Server project and happens to be the first Java Web service to be called.

Once the name has been returned from this Web service, another Decision shape is used to determine whether the order is a purchase or sale. This will ultimately decide whether the .NET BuyStocks or Java SellStocks Web service is called to actually process the request.

As Figure 11-18 shows, the Decision shape determines whether the order is considered a purchase or sale. (The *OrderFromUser.Action* is tested to validate this.) Based on this decision, the orchestration follows one of two similar branches to process the request.

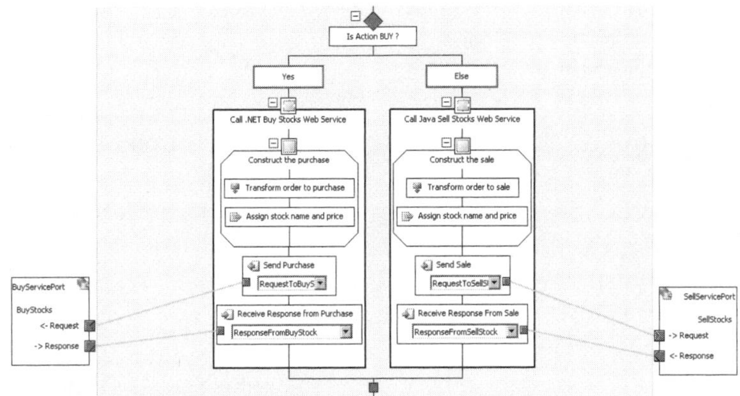

Figure 11-18 The Decision shape used to determine whether the process is a purchase or sale.

First, either a purchase or sale message is constructed. This is a two-part construction that first uses a *transform* and then a message assignment to set values of the request. A transform (often referred to as a *map*) within BizTalk Server 2004 is an artifact that describes how to map elements of one message type to the elements of a second message type. In this sample, two maps are required because the incoming order needs to be transformed at run time to either the purchase or the sale message. To see more closely how a transform works, open the TransformToBuyStock.btm file in the Solution Explorer.

This simple transformation, displayed in Figure 11-19, shows how the *Ticker* and *Qty* elements in the incoming order message are mapped directly to the *Ticker* and *Volume* elements, respectively, in the outgoing purchase message.

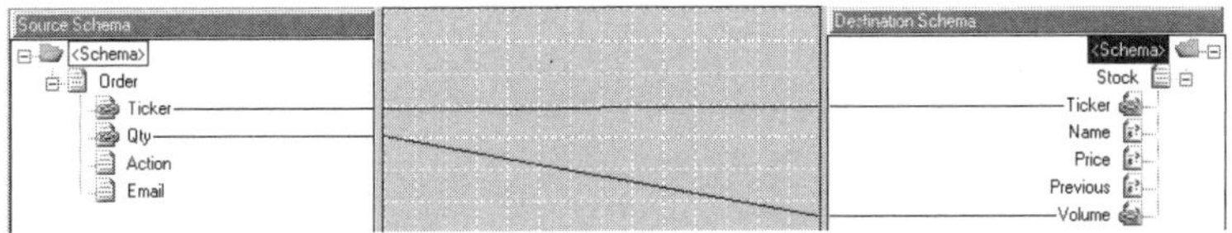

Figure 11-19 A transform showing the mapping between an order and outgoing request.

The BizTalk Mapper includes a rich and extensible palette of *functoids* that facilitate reusable and complex transformation logic. Prebuilt functoids support string manipulation, mathematical and logical functions, and data conversion. For example, a functoid could be used to adjust the *Qty* element by a fixed amount, or to pad the *Ticker* string field with 10 spaces.

Returning to the orchestration, the assignment to either the purchase or the sale message effectively sets the *Name* and *Price* for the request:

```
RequestToBuyStock.stockToBuy.Name
    = ReturnedStockName.getNameResult;
RequestToBuyStock.stockToBuy.Price
    =†(System.Single)ReturnedStockPrice.getPriceResult;
```

Recall how these fields are set based on the results from the .NET pricing and Java naming Web services.

After either the BuyStocks or SellStocks Web service is called, the confirmation message is finally constructed for the user. This is a message that indicates the original ticker value and quantity, the name and price of the stock (as resolved by the Web services), and the commission charged. The *Email* address is also used in the message to simulate a confirmation being sent.

You use a third transform and assignment, shown in Figure 11-20, to take the original incoming order and construct the confirmation. This confirmation is then sent to the outgoing port and will be based on the schema that was outlined in the use case.

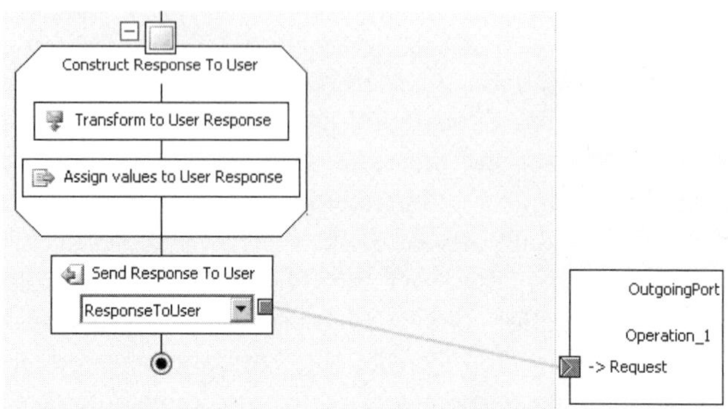

Figure 11-20 The final, late-bound outgoing port.

Within this orchestration, you've seen how the calls to the .NET and Java Web services are represented by ports that were defined by Web References added to the BizTalk Server project. You've also seen that the initial incoming and final outgoing operations are ports, but these are known as *logical*, or *late-bound*, ports. Endpoint information for these logical ports is defined outside the orchestration itself. This allows a compiled orchestration to be reused in a variety of deployment environments without having to be recompiled.

Let's now take a look at the steps required to define endpoint information for these logical ports and ultimately deploy this orchestration to the BizTalk Server.

Deploying the Orchestration

To compile the BizTalk Server 2004 project, select Build Solution from the Build menu. After building, you need to deploy the solution. There are two ways you can do this. Deployment can be performed by manually stepping through and creating the ports, or you can use a deployment script. Running the deployment manually will give you an insight into how late-bound ports are created in BizTalk Server 2004, but using the script will allow you to get the sample running in less time. Both of these methods are covered in this section.

For both the deployments, we'll use one-way FILE ports that send and receive XML message instances to and from well-defined folders in the file system. This gives us an easy, platform-neutral way of testing the orchestration with a number of permutations.

As mentioned previously, because these ports are late-bound, you're free to replace the FILE ports with any of the available port types. This might include combining the two separate one-way FILE ports into a single request-response Web service port. Alternatively, you could connect the orchestration to a running instance of either MSMQ or WebSphere MQ. We'll discuss some of these port options in the section on extending this sample.

Deploying Manually

To begin a manual deployment, select Deploy Solution from the Build menu. This will deploy the compiled orchestration to the local running instance of BizTalk Server 2004.

After the deployment has completed and while you're still within Visual Studio .NET, click the View menu and select BizTalk Explorer. This is a tool that shows the deployed assemblies, orchestrations, and ports. Expand the assemblies and orchestrations, as shown in Figure 11-21, to check that the project was deployed successfully.

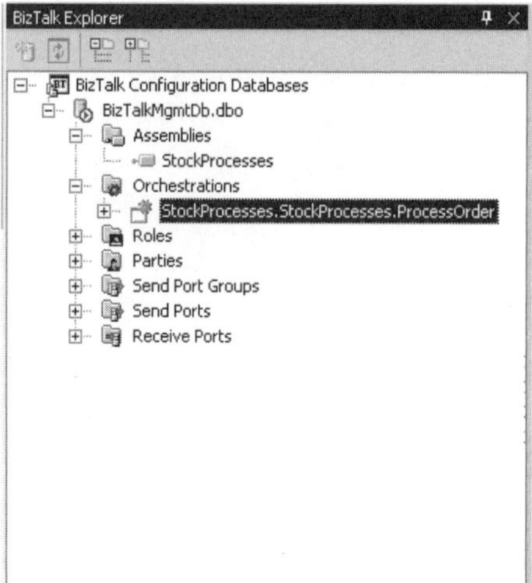

Figure 11-21 Viewing the BizTalk Explorer within Visual Studio .NET.

Before you start the orchestration, you must first create actual endpoint information for the late-bound incoming and outgoing ports. Recall that the incoming port is used to accept incoming orders and the outgoing port is used to return the confirmation.

Creating the late-bound incoming port To create the incoming port, right-click the Receive Ports folder within the BizTalk Explorer. Select the Add Receive Port option to create a new Receive Port.

For the type of port, select One-Way Port, as shown in Figure 11-22. Because we'll next define a file system location to represent the endpoint from which we receive incoming orders, this must be a one-way message flow. Click OK to confirm the type of Receive Port. In the property sheet that's displayed, change the name of the port to **IncomingOrderPort**, as shown in Figure 11-23.

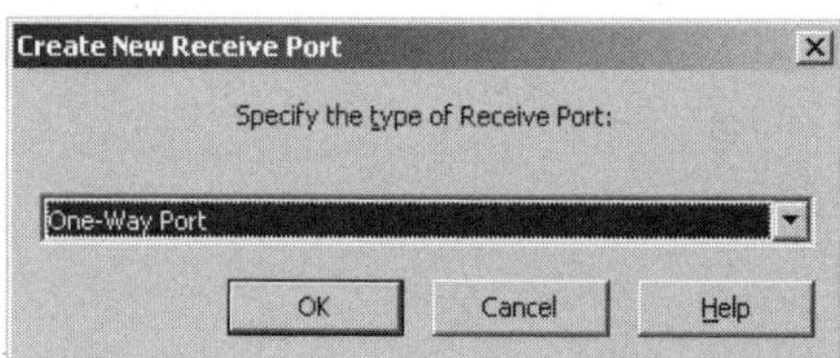

Figure 11-22 Adding a new incoming port.

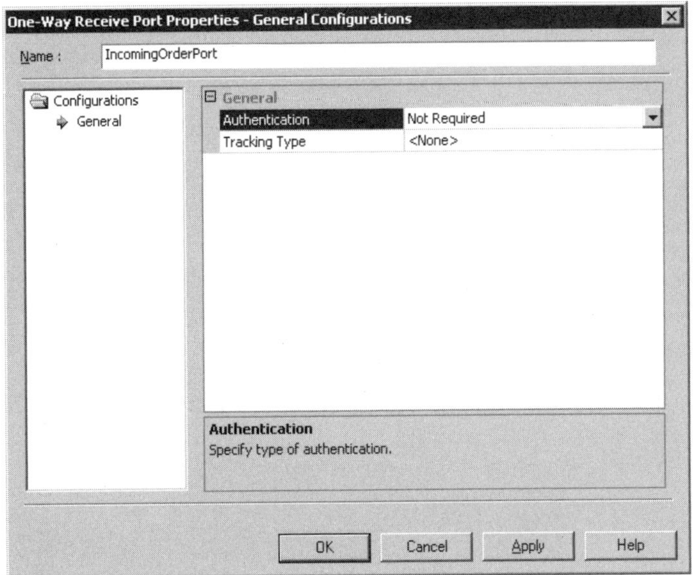

Figure 11-23 Configuring the details for the incoming port.

Click OK to create the port. You now need to create a location at which the port receives messages. This will specify the location and file types for the incoming orders. To do this, right-click the Receive Locations folder that appears under the newly defined port in BizTalk Explorer, and select Add Receive Location.

The Transport Type should be set to **FILE**. For the Address (URI), click the ellipsis button (…) that appears in this field. This will display a second dialog box that allows you to accurately specify the folder, as shown in Figure 11-24.

For the Receive Folder, enter the location of the in-files folder. The in-files folder is a subfolder of the BizTalk Server project itself and should be **C:\Interoperability\Samples\Resource\BizTalk\Project\in-files**. If you have installed the samples to a different location, you'll need to alter this folder to reflect your own settings.

For the file mask, enter ***.xml** and click OK to close this dialog box. This tells BizTalk Server that only files ending in .xml in this folder location should be picked up and delivered to the Receive Port defined previously.

Back on the property sheet, the Receive Handler should be set to **BizTalk-ServerApplication** and the Receive Pipeline should be set to **XMLReceive**. Once these settings are confirmed, as shown in Figure 11-25, click OK to save the Receive Location.

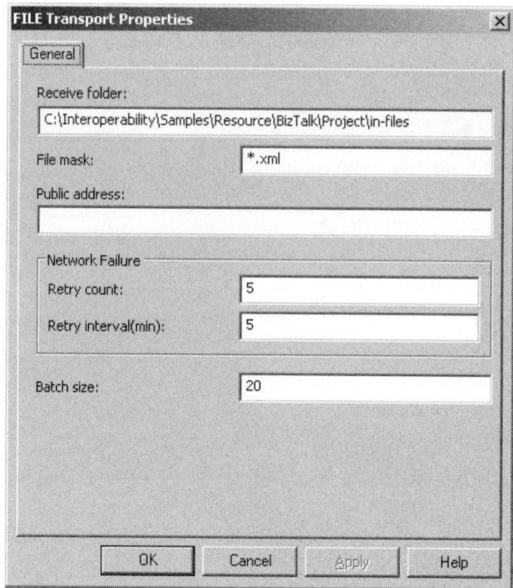

Figure 11-24 Setting the folder properties for the FILE transport.

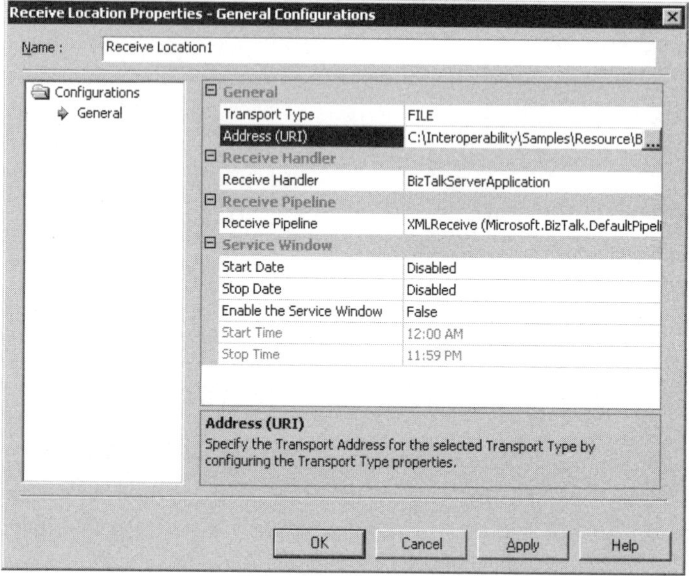

Figure 11-25 Configuring the details for the new Receive Location.

Creating the late-bound outgoing port You now need to create the outgoing port. This port will be very similar to the incoming one. But instead of receiving XML files in the in-files folder, this port will create XML files in the out-files folder of the project.

Within the BizTalk Explorer and the Visual Studio .NET IDE, right-click the Send Ports folder and select the Add Send Port option, as shown in Figure 11-26. As with the incoming port, this will be a (static) one-way type.

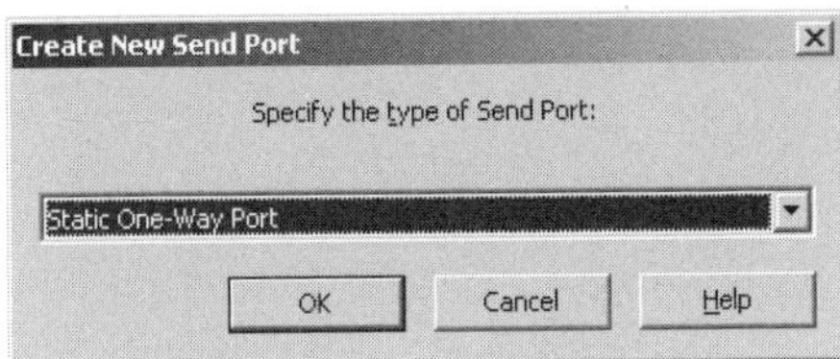

Figure 11-26 Creating a new send port.

Again, rename the port to something a little more meaningful—for this example, use **OutgoingPort**. Set the transport type to **FILE**, and again for the address, click the ellipsis button in the field.

In the dialog box that appears (see Figure 11-27), enter the destination folder to be the out-files folder of the sample project (**C:\Interoperability\Samples\Resource\BizTalk\Project\out-files**). Again, modify this path if the sample code hasn't been installed to the C:\Interoperability folder.

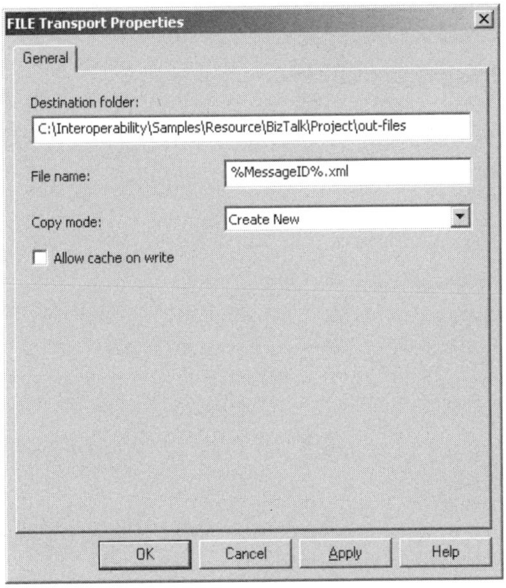

Figure 11-27 Configuring the destination for the FILE transport.

Ensure that the filename is set to **%MessageID%.xml**. This tells BizTalk Server to use a unique message identifier as the name of the output file saved onto the file system. This way, the orchestration can run more than once without overwriting the result message in the output folder. When you're done, click OK to close the File Transport Properties window.

Now expand the Send\General option in the properties window and set the Send Pipeline to **XMLTransmit**, as shown in Figure 11-28.

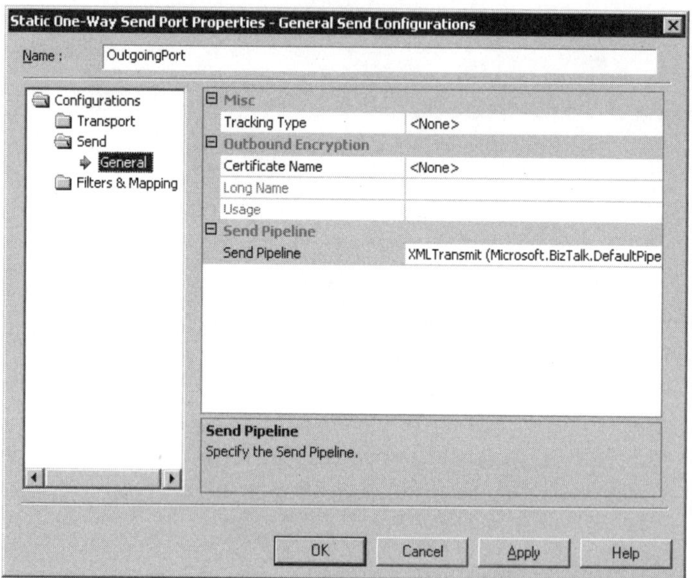

Figure 11-28 Completing the configuration of the outgoing port.

The properties for the outgoing port will now be properly configured, as shown in Figure 11-29.

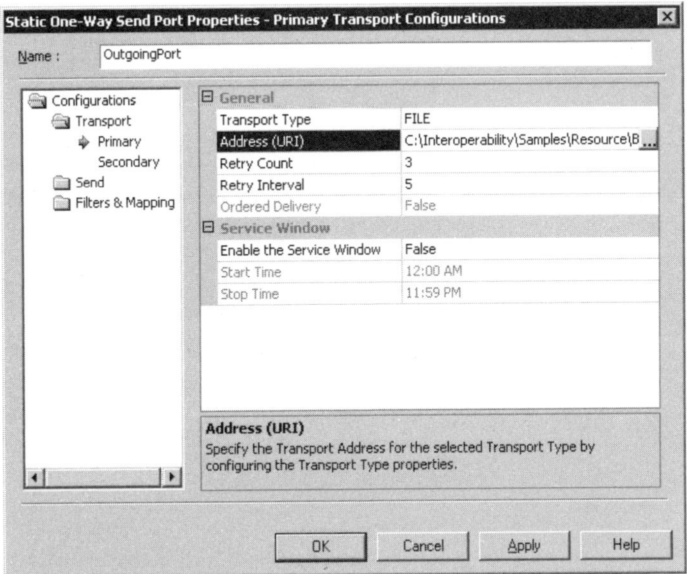

Figure 11-29 Setting the properties for the outgoing port.

Click OK. This will create the outgoing port. You're now ready to start and test the orchestration.

Deploying with a Script

In addition to the manual steps just described, deployment can be performed automatically with a script. The script is loaded and run by the BizTalk Deployment Wizard, which can be launched by selecting it from the Start\Program Files\BizTalk Server 2004 program group. If you've already followed the manual deployment, you can skip this section.

After the wizard has been launched, select the option Deploy BizTalk Assembly To Database, as shown in Figure 11-30. This option allows you to select the compiled BizTalk Server assembly and reference a binding file that will preconfigure the ports.

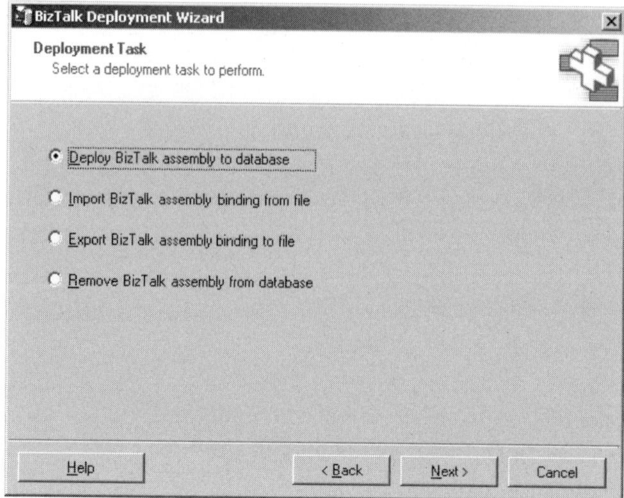

Figure 11-30 Launching the BizTalk Deployment Wizard and selecting an action.

In the next screen of the deployment wizard, select the machine that contains the BizTalk Server database, as shown in Figure 11-31. Ensure that the database points to the BizTalk Server Management Database, the default name for which is BizTalkMgmtDb. For these samples, I'll use the same machine.

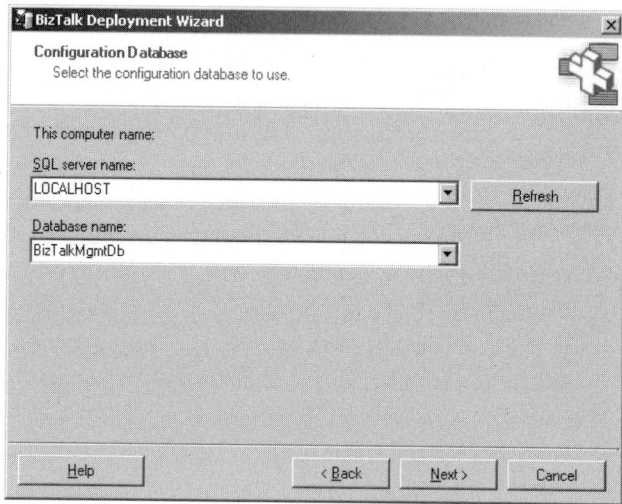

Figure 11-31 Selecting the BizTalk Server database to perform the deployment.

In the next screen in the wizard, you need to select the compiled BizTalk Server assembly (DLL file) and the script, as shown in Figure 11-32.

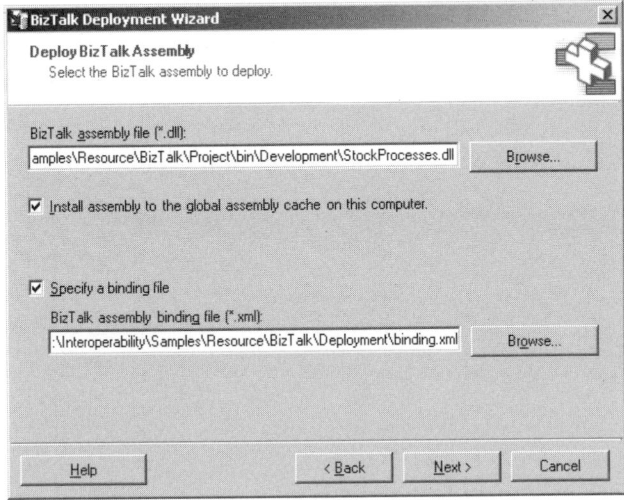

Figure 11-32 Specifying the location of the BizTalk Server assembly and bindings file.

For the DLL file, enter the following location:

C:\Interoperability\Samples\Resource\BizTalk\Project\bin\Development\StockProcesses.dll

For the binding file, use

C:\Interoperability\Samples\Resource\BizTalk\Deployment\binding.xml

This is the predefined deployment script for the sample code. Also ensure that the option to install the assembly into the global assembly cache (GAC) is selected. If you have installed the sample code to a directory other than C:\Interoperability, you should edit the binding.xml file and replace all occurrences of this with your installation path.

Once these values have been entered, finish the wizard to complete the deployment of the sample orchestration.

Starting the Orchestration

The final piece of the BizTalk Server project sample is to start the orchestration running. To start, if not already displayed within Visual Studio .NET, click the View menu and select BizTalk Explorer. Right-click the *StockProcesses.StockProcesses.ProcessOrder* orchestration in BizTalk Explorer (found in the Orchestrations folder), and select the Bind option. This is used to bind the orchestration to the ports that we've just created either manually or with the script. If you don't see this assembly, right-click the machine name in BizTalk Server Explorer and select Refresh.

In the Binding option, ensure that the *IncomingOrder* and *OutgoingPort* fields are set to the incoming and outgoing ports that were just created, as shown in Figure 11-33. Note that the Web service port binding is already established because the endpoint information was automatically created when the Web service references were added to the BizTalk Server project.

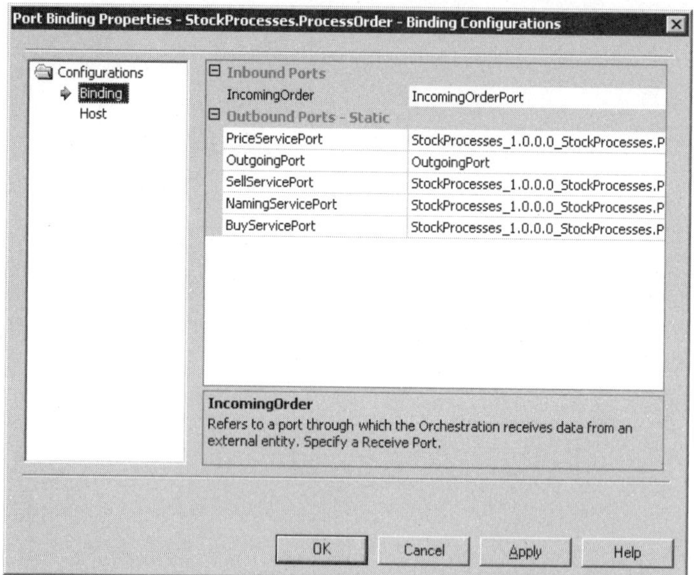

Figure 11-33 Checking the binding properties for the orchestration.

In the Host option, ensure that the host is set to **BizTalkServerApplication**, as shown in Figure 11-34.

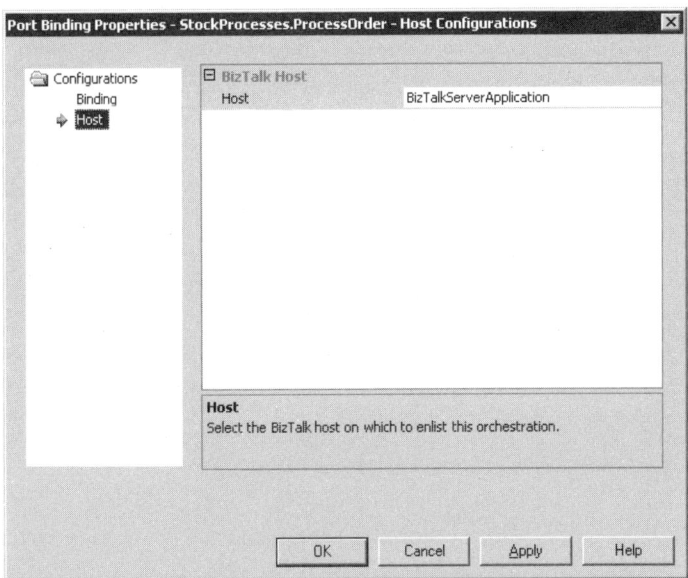

Figure 11-34 Checking the host properties for the orchestration.

Once configured, click the OK button. Now that the orchestration is fully bound to the ports, you start the orchestration and begin sending it messages. Right-click the StockProcess orchestration again, and select Start.

In the dialog box that appears (see Figure 11-35), select all the dependency options and click OK. This process will take a few seconds to start.

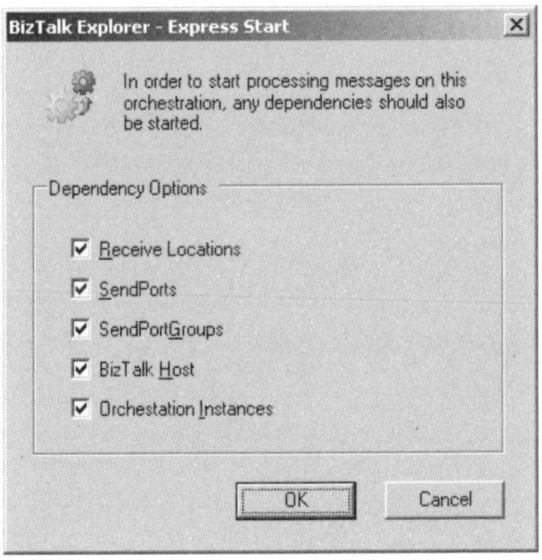

Figure 11-35 Selecting dependencies and starting the orchestration.

If the orchestration is running correctly, the color of the orchestration icon displayed in BizTalk Explorer should change and become more prominent. This means that the orchestration is ready to process messages.

Testing the Orchestration

To test the orchestration, we'll use some precreated sample order XML files. These files can be found in the C:\Interoperability\Samples\Resource\BizTalk\Project\test-files directory. This directory contains four files:

```
purchase-high-commission.xml
purchase-low-commission.xml
sale-high-commission.xml
sale-low-commission.xml
```

Each of the files is used to test various aspects of the orchestration. For example, purchase-low-commission.xml will be used to submit a purchase that should result in a low commission fee for the user. Likewise, sale-high-commission.xml shows a sale that will result in a high commission for the user.

Open the purchase-low-commission.xml file to examine the structure:

```
<ns0:Order xmlns:ns0="http://StockProcesses.Order">
    <Ticker>WOOD</Ticker>
    <Qty>1000</Qty>
    <Action>BUY</Action>
    <Email>samples@microsoft.com</Email>
</ns0:Order>
```

This is a relatively simple file that describes the incoming order for the BizTalk Server process. As covered earlier in the use case discussion, the order has a ticker (WOOD), a quantity of shares (1000), an action (BUY), and an e-mail address. If the orchestration works correctly, you should observe that this order triggers the .NET Web service to purchase a stock and has sufficient quantity to take the order of more than $250 (and result in a low commission).

Make sure that the Java naming and stock Web services are running in a command prompt window. To run the orchestration, from within Windows Explorer copy the purchase-low-commission.xml file from the test-files folder to the in-files folder. Do ensure that the file is copied and not moved (because BizTalk Server will eventually delete the incoming file once it's delivered to the orchestration).

If the orchestration can pick up this message, the file will disappear within a few seconds of being copied to this folder. If the file doesn't get picked up, check to see that the orchestration is running and check the Event Log to see whether there are any relevant warnings or errors.

Before we look at any output that was produced, let's validate that the Web services were called. Open the Event Log and check the Application Event Log. In here, with a date/time of when the orchestration was run, you should see a message that indicates that the pricing Web service was invoked by the orchestration and returned a value.

This confirms that the pricing Web service was correctly called. Next, you can check the Java Web service that performs the name lookup for the company. In the console window that's running the Java Web service, you should see a request for the name of the company that matches the Ticker, WOOD.

The Java Web service will return the name *Woodgrove Bank* for this ticker. Now switch to the Event Log. If the .NET BuyStocks Web service was able to successfully accept the request, a second entry should be logged in the Application Event Log.

As you should observe in the Event Log, the incoming .NET Web service successfully accepted the request to purchase stock from the BizTalk Server orchestration. Although this Web service writes to the Event Log, you can imagine how a real trade could be invoked in a production system.

Finally, let's view the output that was generated from the orchestration itself. Navigate to the C:\Interoperability\Samples\Resource\BizTalk\Project\out-files directory. This directory should contain an XML file that has a date/time that matches when the orchestration completed. The name of the file will be a unique ID. Open this file in Microsoft Internet Explorer or another XML editor.

You should see confirmation of the order itself, similar to the output shown in Figure 11-36.

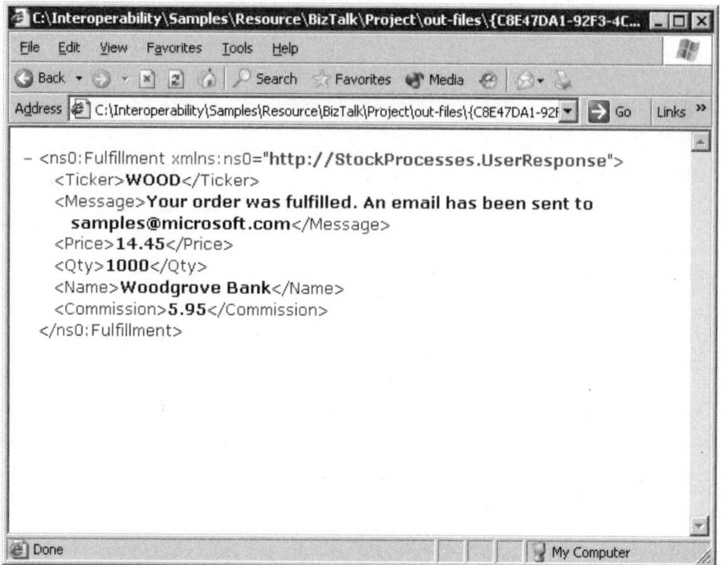

Figure 11-36 The final confirmation of the order generated by the orchestration.

In the XML file depicted, you can see that the order confirmation contains the ticker and a message to indicate that an e-mail was sent. (An e-mail message wasn't actually sent, but you can create a BizTalk Server Send Port that uses Simple Mail Transfer Protocol, or SMTP, to achieve this.) The price and name returned from the Web services are also displayed, as well as the commission that was calculated based on the value of the order ($14.45 x 1000 is indeed over $250).

Retest the orchestration by using the other XML orders in the test-files directory. For the Java Web services that are called by the orchestration, the output will be written the console window. For the .NET Web services, all output is written to the Application Event Log.

Extending the Sample

As you've seen, the sample used one-way FILE Receive and Send Ports to accept incoming orders represented as XML document instances, and to produce some output as well as an XML document. Although this works well with the sample code, chances are that in a production environment, ports that use other transport mechanisms will need to be employed. At the time of this writing, BizTalk Server 2004 is still in beta, meaning that many "adapters" that address this need are still in development. However, if you look at BizTalk Server 2002, you can see that there are more than 350 adapters (known in BizTalk Server 2002 as Application Integration Components, or AICs) available for selection. One of the AICs available today for BizTalk Server 2002 is used to connect to WebSphere MQ/MQSeries.

WebSphere MQ/MQSeries Support

Chapter 9, "Asynchronous Interoperability, Part 2: WebSphere MQ," and Chapter 10, "Asynchronous Interoperability, Part 3: Bridging with Host Integration Server," looked at how WebSphere MQ could be used to provide interoperability between clients and services in the .NET and Java programming environments. In these chapters, you saw how to use direct methods and the MSMQ-MQSeries bridge to achieve this.

With BizTalk Server 2002, you can use the MQSeries AIC to provide connectivity with WebSphere MQ (MQSeries). An equivalent adapter is planned for BizTalk Server 2004. The Microsoft BizTalk Adapter for MQSeries provides a port that will enable connection to an existing instance of WebSphere MQ.

If you were to expand on this example, you could see how instead of sending and receiving XML files to and from the file system, the MQSeries adapter could be used to receive the incoming order message from and place the outgoing confirmation message onto WebSphere MQ queues. This would then allow any external clients connected to these queues to send messages to or receive them from the BizTalk Server orchestration.

Inbound Web Services Support

Another interesting modification of the sample would be to expose the orchestration itself as a Web service. BizTalk Server provides a step-by-step wizard for publishing a compiled orchestration as a Web service. Note that this requires replacing the incoming and outgoing FILE ports with a single two-way SOAP port. Combined with the full suite of adapters, this offers a flexible and powerful way to connect the orchestration to external systems.

Exception Handling

One orchestration feature that wasn't shown in the sample was the handling of exceptions. You can effectively add a *catch exception* block to any set of orchestration shapes that are grouped into a scope. Scopes themselves can be nested. Within a Web services environment, where multiple Web services could potentially be called, such exception handling is an important consideration.

In the sample as written, if one Web service fails, the orchestration fails and the message is suspended. A more suitable approach would be to use the exception handling supported directly within the orchestration to provide some kind of corrective action if an error occurs. In a production environment, this could involve defaulting to a backup Web service, or if a more fatal exception occurs, having the ability to notify the user via e-mail to indicate that the order was unsuccessful. A more complex design could notify an external party of the problem and pause the orchestration until a notification to continue is supplied by that external party.

Enabling Transactions

Again, because this was a simple example designed to show orchestration of both .NET and Java Web services, it didn't cover transactions. Transaction support is a key feature of BizTalk Server orchestration. An atomic transaction in BizTalk Server is typically short-lived and is used to identify a portion of an orchestration that must exhibit these attributes: Atomicity, Consistency, Isolation, and Durability (ACID). Operations within an atomic transaction are guaranteed to complete successfully or are all rolled back in the event of an error during the lifetime of the transaction.

> **More Info** See Chapter 8, "Asynchronous Interoperability, Part 1: Introduction and MSMQ," for additional details on operations within an atomic transaction and for an example.

BizTalk Server also supports long-running transactions for cases in which traditional ACID transactions aren't possible or aren't desired. A long-running business process that might take many days or weeks to complete clearly can contain pieces that are atomic, but the process as a whole isn't normally expected or required to be ACID. Long-running transactions offer consistency and durability but are neither atomic nor isolated.

The real importance of long-running transactions is found in the concept of compensation. Every atomic and long-running transaction can be optionally associated with a *compensation block*. The purpose of a compensation block is to specify behavior that reverses (compensates for) the effects of an already-committed transaction. For example, the first part of a long-running business process might require inserting a new record into a database, sending an e-mail notification of this event, and committing these two operations as an atomic transaction. Three hours later an error might occur in the execution of a later part of the long-running business process. Unless such an error can be handled gracefully, the business process might need to compensate for the already-committed transaction. In this simple example, the compensation block for the atomic transaction can perhaps delete the previously inserted database record and send a second e-mail message notifying someone of this event.

Within the orchestration designer, a number of shapes can be grouped to identify such a transaction boundary that spans one or more processes. Obviously, if messages are being sent externally, the external port must offer some transactional support. For message queues, this can be achieved today. For Web services, I'm confident that in the near future, we'll see the new WS-Transaction specification that was briefly covered in Chapter 8 supported within the BizTalk Server framework model.

Asynchronous Interoperability: How to Decide

In this part of the book, you've seen a number of ways that asynchronous interoperability can be achieved between the .NET and J2EE platforms. This included creating a custom Web service wrapper for MSMQ, looking at the .NET SupportPac libraries supplied with WebSphere MQ, investigating how a Message Driven Enterprise JavaBean (MDB) can call a .NET Web service in a publish/subscribe model, implementing an MSMQ-MQSeries bridge to transfer messages between queues, and examining how BizTalk Server can orchestrate the flow of messages within a business process that uses Web services.

I'm often asked which method of asynchronous interoperability is most suited for a particular project or task. In general, the response tends to be driven by three goals:

- **Dependability** How reliable do you want the transfer of messages to be? How important is it if a message is lost? Do you need to perform transactions between one or more queues? If reliable messaging and transactions are key, wrapping the queuing API with a Web service won't suffice. With the implementation of reliable messaging and transactional specifications for Web services, this is starting to change, but for the time being this has to be an important consideration.
- **Maintainability and manageability** I always recommend looking at your existing infrastructure and accessing how maintainable or manageable interoperability will be. For example, if an organization has invested heavily in creating and deploying an MDB architecture, using the MDBs to call .NET Services via a Web service facade might be an attractive option. If such an investment hasn't been made, creating this infrastructure might add another layer of complexity to the problem.

- **Message transit** What do you want to do with the message? Is it acceptable just to take the raw byte representation of a message from one queue and deliver it to another, or are there some modifications that need to be made in transit? Likewise, should any logic be applied to the message as it's transferred between platforms? Answers to these questions determine whether the solution should be a natural bridge between two or more message queues, or whether a product such as BizTalk Server will offer a more comprehensive solution.

Regardless of the option that's best suited for your environment, I hope that the technology shown in these last four chapters has helped to demonstrate a number of permutations. Although point-to-point connectivity between .NET and J2EE is certainly a goal, asynchronous interoperability is often key to many successful enterprise applications.

Summary

This concludes this chapter on BizTalk Server 2004 and the four chapters on asynchronous interoperability. This chapter introduced and installed the product and walked you through a sample orchestration that sends and receives messages to and from external Web services. Hopefully, this chapter offered a good introduction to BizTalk Server 2004 and highlighted some of the features of the anticipated final product.

Part IV of the book, which starts with the next chapter, will explore the topic of advanced interoperability. The next chapter will cover interoperability at the presentation tier, what that means, and the potential benefits it can offer.

Part IV

Advanced Interoperability

- Interoperability
  - Samples
    - Advanced
      - Attachments
        - dotNET
        - Files
        - Java
      - Presentation
        - Authentication
        - dotNET
        - Java
        - JBoss
        - SQL
      - WS-Routing
        - dotNET
        - Java
      - WS-Security
        - Auth
        - Certs
        - Enc
    - Config
    - Data
    - Point
    - Resource
  - Tools

12

Presentation Tier Interoperability

In this first chapter of Part IV, "Advanced Interoperability," we'll cover a topic known as presentation-tier interoperability. To do so, we'll take the first scenario presented in Chapter 2, "Business Requirements for Interoperability," and explain the problem and a potential solution.

> **Note** In this chapter, the presentation is based on Microsoft ASP.NET for a Microsoft .NET application, and it's based on JavaServer Pages (JSP) for a Java application. In some cases, a presentation tier can also be thought of as an interface that runs on the client (for example, a smart client, Win32 application, or SWING/AWT-based application). For the purpose of this chapter, references to the presentation tier always mean the former, Web-based definition. For more information on both ASP.NET and JSP, refer to the "Creating Applications for the Web" section in Chapter 1, "Microsoft .NET and J2EE Fundamentals."

Some of the samples in this chapter refer to topics we've already covered in the book. This includes the serialization techniques discussed in Chapter 3, "Exchanging Data Between .NET and Java," and some of the shared database techniques presented in Chapter 7, "Creating a Shared Database." Although it's not necessary to read through these chapters, you might want to familiarize yourself with the relevant topics when running the sample code in this chapter.

What Is Presentation Tier Interoperability?

I'm asked this question a lot (usually after discussing the scenarios and boundaries presented in Chapter 2). Many of the chapters in this book have concentrated on interoperability with components that reside at the business tier. For example, in Part II, "Interoperability Technologies: Point to Point," you saw a number of components hosted by using a J2EE application server that were invoked from an ASP.NET page or a command-line client. You also saw this demonstrated the other way, with .NET components invoked from a JSP tier or Java client.

In most applications, the presentation tier is responsible for rendering and delivering content to the client. This content might be a number of HTML pages, images, and static controls. Some of the pages might also contain scripts (ASP.NET code-behind for .NET, and JSP for the Java platform). In general though, little "business processing" is done at the presentation tier. For example, heavy calculations and transactions are normally performed at tiers behind the presentation tier. This makes the concept of interoperability at the presentation tier more difficult to conceptualize and understand. Static pages—and even pages with script embedded—usually don't have the need or power to call other pages on a remote system. So why would we want to do this?

Requirements for Interoperating at the Presentation Tier

To start exploring the requirements for interoperability at the presentation tier and the benefits of doing so, let's revisit Chapter 2, where we covered the three common business requirements for interoperability. The first requirement involved replacing or extending an existing presentation tier. To illustrate this, the representation shown in Figure 12-1 was used.

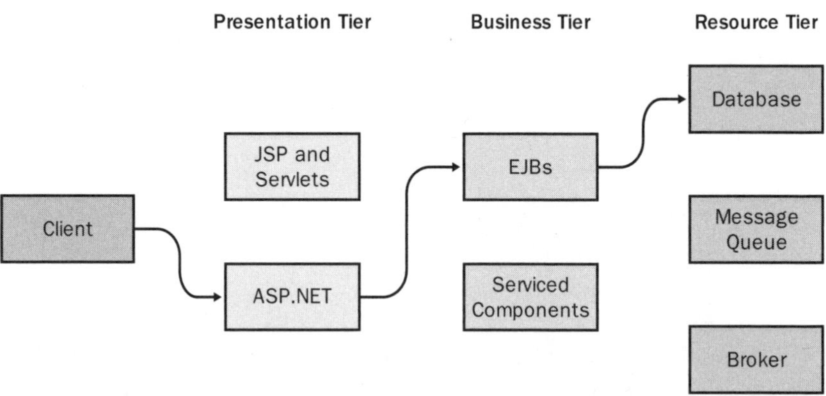

Figure 12-1 Replacing the J2EE presentation tier with ASP.NET.

As discussed in Chapter 2, this scenario shows how ASP.NET can be used to create a new presentation tier for an existing J2EE application. This model, combined with the requirement to provide interoperability between the presentation and business tiers, is perfectly valid, but it does assume that the entire presentation tier is hosted on one platform.

What about a scenario in which part of the presentation is based on a new ASP.NET implementation, yet part of the presentation still resides on the existing JSP and Servlet tier (or vice versa)? In this case, you might have an application flow that looks like Figure 12-2.

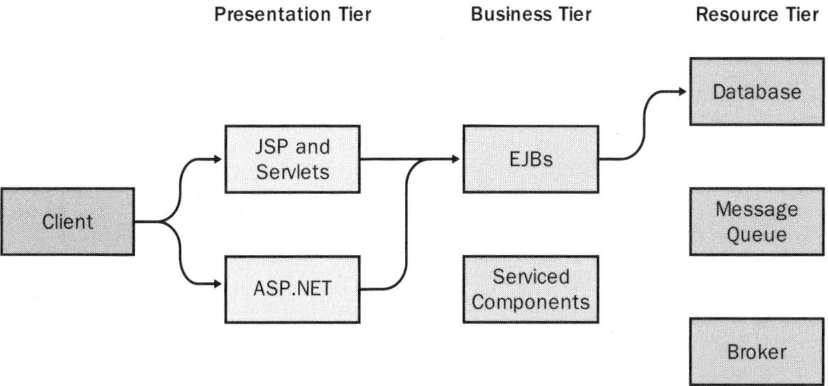

Figure 12-2 A presentation tier consisting of JSP, Servlets, and ASP.NET pages.

Here, a number of pages and/or controls are still served to the user via the existing technology (JSP and Servlets), whereas part of the application has been migrated to the new presentation tier (ASP.NET). To investigate this further, let's consider a fictitious but valid business requirement.

Woodgrove Bank is a large investment bank located on Wall Street. Free from corporate scandal, Woodgrove Bank operates a network of highly integrated applications and services for its trading floor. A lot of the bank's success with its existing system is based upon the introduction of a unified, Web-based portal. This particular portal delivers a user experience with separate Web components, many of which interact with each other and/or back-end systems. The layout for the bank's portal is shown in Figure 12-3.

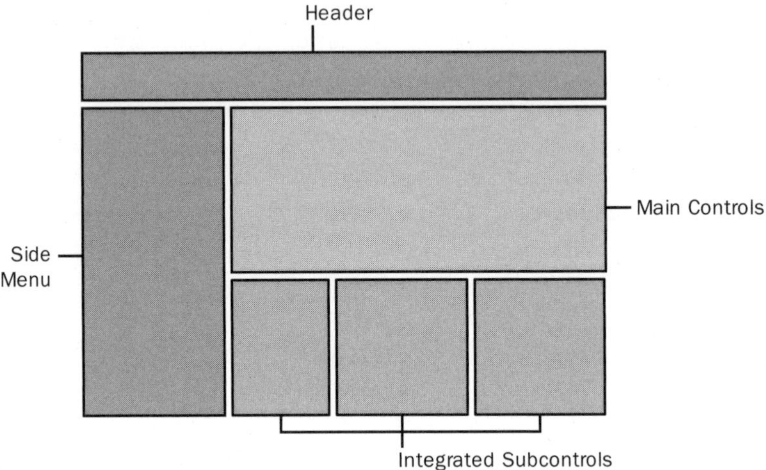

Figure 12-3 Layout of a Web portal consisting of many integrated parts.

The components within the portal (which are also known as *Web parts*) allow an investment banker to perform functions relative to his daily needs. For example, one Web part might show a summary of a particular banker's current trading portfolio. Another Web part might show the breakdown of a company that the banker is interested in, and another might show online news feeds about that particular company. This multiple–Web part interface isn't unique to the bank. Many of the more complex intranet and Internet sites in use today typically are built around a framework that consist of a number of integrated Web parts. To make the portal functional, each of the Web parts is integrated with the others to provide both a unified view of the application and a manageable way for the information services department to maintain the application. Each Web part can in theory be hosted and developed upon independently.

For this example, let's also suppose that the system has been in place for some time (and therefore is well proven) and is based upon a number of JSP and Servlets. For the upcoming financial year, the CTO has made a strategic decision to undertake and deploy a pilot application using .NET. Using ASP.NET, the CTO wants to create a new look and feel for the portal—displaying additional information and Web parts to create a more compelling user experience. During initial discussions about a new version of the portal based on ASP.NET, the CTO suggested a fundamental requirement to reuse existing Web parts that currently reside in the JSP/Servlet version of the application. A significant amount of development effort and time has already been invested in these JSP pages and Servlets, and the new .NET pilot application needs to seamlessly run side by side with this existing application to be accepted into production.

The integration required by this scenario might include the sharing of stock data, portfolios, and other trading recommendations among Web parts on these two different platforms. The ability of this new .NET application to *know the state of* and *interact with* the other components hosted by J2EE defines presentation-tier interoperability.

Challenges of Interoperating at the Presentation Tier

To continue with our example, let's assume that the investment bank's development team takes on the project with much enthusiasm. This is a great opportunity for the bank to embrace .NET, but to be accepted, .NET must be implemented in a way that's not considered a "rip and replace" of the existing system in production.

After reviewing the design of the new .NET application and based on using existing JSP Web parts in ASP.NET, the development team identifies two potential challenges for the new project:

- ASP.NET doesn't have access to session state used by the existing JSP and Servlets, and vice versa.
- No common authentication mechanism exists between ASP.NET and JSP.

Let's examine the first challenge for a moment: In the existing implementation, many of the Web parts within the portal rely on a technology known as *session state* to pass session-based data to and from other parts of the Web application. For example, when a user performs an action on one part of a Web page within the portal, the component may write a value into the session to indicate to other parts of the application that they should update themselves accordingly. A real-life example of this is a shopping cart for an online store. In many implementations, shopping cart data is created and maintained as online buyers select goods to purchase. This data is stored as one or more objects in the session.

Let's return to the investment bank scenario. A second example of the use of session data occurs when one of the components of a Web page within the portal asks the investment banker to select a company to display information for. This selection (and any other related information) can be saved to a session by one of the components of the Web page. When the page is refreshed, the other Web components within the portal will read the data stored within the session and alter their appearance accordingly.

> **Note** How does a session work for each platform? Both ASP.NET and version 2.0 of the Servlet API provide session functionality. A session gives users the ability to store and retrieve data for a particular Web session. This is achieved by associating every user of the application with a *System.Web.SessionState.HttpSessionState* object (for ASP.NET) and a *javax.servlet.http.HttpSession* object (for JSP). In most cases, the instance of the user's browser is tied with the session object by using a cookie. When the user first reaches a page on a Web server that supports sessions, a new Session ID is created. This Session ID is encrypted in some cases and is sent back to the user in the form of a cookie. When the user next browses to a page on the same Web site, the cookie is passed as part of the request and the session object for that user can be reactivated and accessed.

Using sessions involves taking some data that will be stored, serializing that data, and saving the value with the client's session for later use. Both the .NET and J2EE platforms store sessions by using different methods. In the Microsoft .NET Framework, the session object within ASP.NET serializes the object by using a proprietary serializer. This greatly increases the throughput for multiple accesses to the session object, but at the same time, it doesn't lend itself well to extending and working with the objects that have been stored. Sessions on the J2EE platform tend to depend on the vendor of the Servlet engine and/or application server. One vendor's implementation of the J2EE platform might store the session object differently from another vendor's platform. Writing an implementation for each vendor would be time-consuming. In addition, the .NET and J2EE implementations of session state don't lend themselves well to being accessed by other APIs—apart from the Web page making the call. If the session can't be accessed, components on one platform can't read and write session data on the other.

For the investment bank, the second challenge is that the existing application based on JSP requires the user to log in before she can access the data. This login process is done by using a user table in a database and then writing a cookie to the browser, thereby giving the user access for that session. Looking for an equivalent authentication mechanism in .NET, the IT group examines *Forms Authentication*, an authentication technology provided with ASP.NET. The group finds that Forms Authentication works using a process similar to their existing system in JSP, but the lookup, the format of the cookie sent to the browser, and the general operations are different.

In summary, if Web parts from each platform will be displayed in a unified way (via a single page) to the user, authentication can be an issue. Authentication will either have to be abandoned—clearly, not an option for the bank—or the user will be required to enter her credentials twice (once for the new .NET portal, and a second time for the collection of existing JSP components to be hosted). This is a classic example of a requirement for a Single Sign-On (SSO) at the presentation tier.

Avoiding a Disjoint User Experience

These fundamental challenges of session and authentication lead to what I refer to as a *disjoint user experience*. This isn't unique to interoperability between .NET and J2EE—in fact, it's common in new systems that involve rewrites of the user interface.

The problem with these systems is that the existing (or legacy) user interface has been in place for so long that replacing the entire framework in one step often isn't feasible or desirable. Because of these challenges with sessions and authentication, in many cases a new, second user interface is created. I've seen this scenario play out on a number of occasions where interoperability wasn't possible between two systems. When building a proof-of-concept project, the development team spends additional time creating a new experience that requires the user to work with a second interface in conjunction with the original. Unfortunately for the user, despite the effort that went into the project, this new user interface is disjointed (by being separate) from the original. The result can be that the user ends up rejecting the system (by not using it), and ultimately the project fails.

To help you overcome these challenges when interoperating between .NET and J2EE, this chapter will present sample code addressing shared session state and shared authentication among components and pages that are based on a mix of ASP.NET and JSP. This sample code is intended only to illustrate the concepts covered in this chapter and should be used only in conjunction with this chapter—these samples aren't production-ready implementations.

Shared Session State

Now that you better understand the problems associated with the .NET and Java platforms sharing session state, let's look at a sample implementation of a shared session. This sample illustrates how a stock portfolio (similar to the data types used in previous chapters) can be seamlessly passed between new session interfaces used by both ASP.NET and JSP.

The sample does require some installation and setup before proceeding. In addition to the prerequisites outlined in Chapter 1, this code relies on a local installation of Microsoft SQL Server 2000 and requires the Microsoft SQL Server Driver for JDBC to be installed. Installation of the JDBC driver was covered in Chapter 7.

The sample has three parts. First, a new database and series of tables are created in SQL Server. These tables are used to hold the session data that will be shared among the ASP.NET and JSP pages. Second, a new session API is installed for each platform. This new session API is used instead of the default to allow session objects to be written to the new database. Finally, an HTTP filter is used to create a registration process on each platform. This registration process joins an ASP.NET and JSP session running on a single machine, and it's used to correlate the shared session throughout the life cycle of the application.

Setting Up the Shared Session State Database

A precreated script is used to configure the new database that will run on SQL Server 2000. This scripts can be found in the C:\Interoperability\Samples\Advanced\Presentation\SQL directory.

To ensure that the sample runs correctly and to run this script, launch the Query Analyzer from the SQL Server Programs folder (Start\Programs\Microsoft SQL Server\Query Analyzer). Connect to the database by using either Windows Authentication or the sa password that you assigned when SQL Server was installed.

Open the script, dbscript.sql, in Query Analyzer, and press F5 (or select the Execute option from the Query menu) to run the script. This script will automatically create the database, tables, stored procedures, user accounts, and permissions required for the sample code to run correctly. Figure 12-4 shows the result.

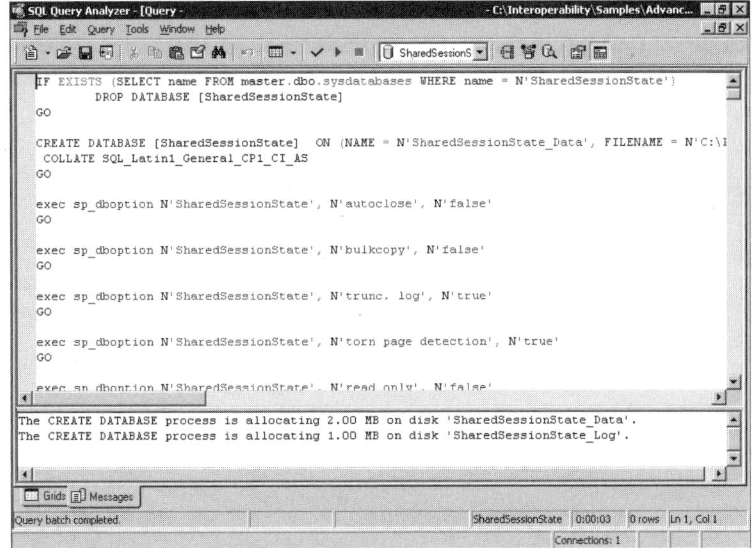

Figure 12-4 Using the Query Analyzer to configure the shared session state database.

This script creates a new database named SharedSessionState (which can be verified through SQL Server Enterprise Manager or the Query Analyzer tool). Upon successful creation of the database objects, the following message will be displayed in the Query Analyzer tool:

```
The CREATE DATABASE process is allocating 0.63 MB on disk 'SharedSessionState'.
The CREATE DATABASE process is allocating 0.49 MB on disk
    'SharedSessionState_log'.
Granted database access to 'testuser'.
'testuser' added to role 'db_owner'.
```

This script also creates a new SQL Server login named *testuser* (if it doesn't already exist—we used this same account in Chapter 7). The default password for this testuser account is *StrongPassword*. (The username and password can be easily modified if needed, but be sure to be consistent in both the SQL scripts and the sample code to prevent accidental logic errors.) This script will also assign the correct permissions to the newly created database so that the testuser account can correctly access the database.

This database is now set up and will act as the main repository for storing session information shared between the .NET and J2EE presentation tiers. You now need to install and configure the required components and sample code that will access this database. Before doing so, ensure that the MSSQLServer service is running and that the database can be accessed by using the testuser account. This can be done by closing and reopening Query Analyzer, logging in with the testuser credentials, and running *SELECT* statements against the SharedSessionState database. (For example, *SELECT * FROM OBJECT* should return zero rows.)

Installing the ASP.NET Sample Code

To install the sample code for ASP.NET, first navigate to the C:\Interoperability\Samples\Advanced\Presentation\dotNET directory. Within this directory are two subdirectories: Server and Web. The Server subdirectory contains the sample source code that will support a shared session. The Web subdirectory contains the source code for a test client. Despite their labels, the code in both subdirectories will run on the same machine in this sample.

Build the source in the Web subdirectory by typing **nant** at the command prompt. This will also build the source in the Server subdirectory. Once complete, you'll need a Microsoft Internet Information Services (IIS) virtual directory to host the pages. Launch the IIS Manager from Start/Programs/Administrative Tools/Internet Information Services. Expand the Local Computer and Web Sites folder, and right-click the Default Web Site icon. Select the New/Virtual Directory option from the submenu. Follow the Virtual Directory Creation Wizard to the second page, and enter **SharedSessionStateClient** as the alias for the Web site, as shown in Figure 12-5.

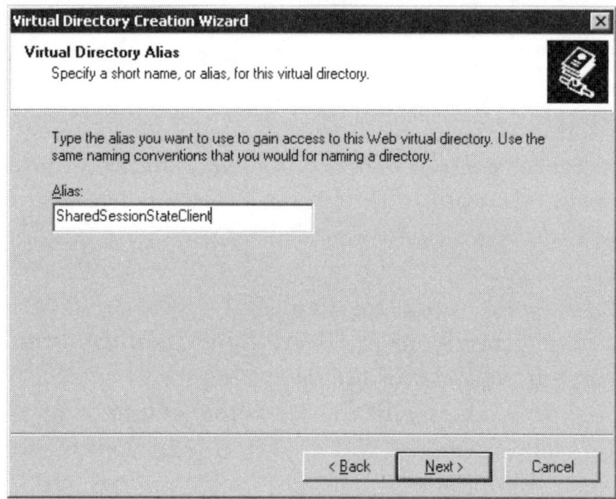

Figure 12-5 Creating a new virtual directory for the test client.

You must use this exact alias to ensure that the sample code works. Click the Next button to proceed. For the next step, enter (or use the Browse button to navigate to) the path of the virtual directory, **C:\Interoperability\Samples\Advanced\Presentation\dotNET\Web**, as shown in Figure 12-6.

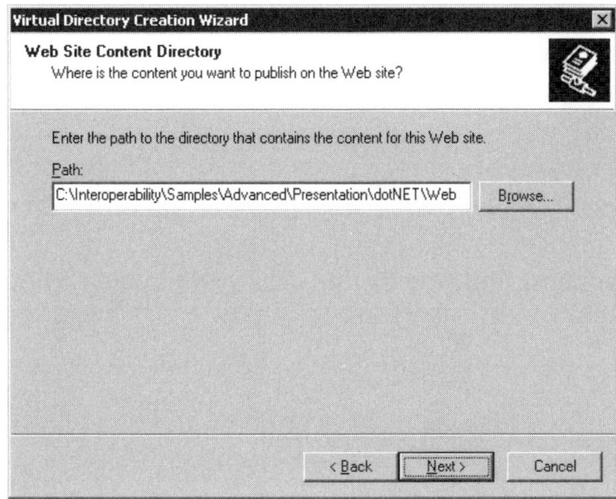

Figure 12-6 Specifying the directory for the shared session state test client.

Accept the defaults for the remainder of the wizard. The .NET implementation of the shared session code is complete, and a virtual directory now exists in IIS to host the test client. You now need to build and deploy the components that make up the Java side of the sample.

Installing the J2EE Sample Code

From the command prompt, navigate to the Java subdirectory (C:\Interoperability\Samples\Advanced\Presentation\Java). As with the .NET sample code, this directory contains a Server and a Web directory. These directories contain the source code for the shared session components and the Web sample application that will be used for the JSP and Servlet test client.

First, verify that JBoss is not running, and then, using Ant with the package target, build the sample code in the Web directory. Upon successful compilation, the same Ant script can be used to deploy the SharedSessionStateClient.war file to your local implementation of JBoss by using the deploy target. If you choose not to use JBoss, the Web Archive (WAR) file can be found in the Server\Deploy directory.

In addition to the sample code, a JDBC connection must be configured on the J2EE application server that will host the test JSP pages and Servlets. If you're using JBoss, you can automatically configure this by running the Ant script found in the C:\Interoperability\Samples\Advanced\Presentation\JBoss directory with the deploy target. This script copies a new MBean declaration (a JBoss managed bean) that configures JBoss to create a new JDBC connection. The script also ensures that the GLUE libraries are available in the lib directory of the JBoss installation.

If you're using an alternate J2EE Application Server, you'll need to consult the documentation that accompanies the product to set up this connection. The JDBC connection settings are shown in Table 12-1.

Table 12-1 Connection Settings for the JDBC Database Connection

Connection Setting	Value
JNDI name	*java:/MSSQLSSDS*
Connection URL	*jdbc:microsoft:sqlserver://localhost:1433;DatabaseName=SharedSessionState*
Driver class	*com.microsoft.jdbc.sqlserver.SQLServerDriver*
Username	*testuser*
Password	*StrongPassword*

Once the sample code, JDBC connection files, and libraries have been deployed, you should start your application server. If your application server generates a series of error messages, you might need to undeploy applications from previous chapters and then relaunch the application server.

Now let's test the deployment.

Testing the Deployment

Once all the required components are deployed, you can test the installation of the shared session state example by navigating to the URL *http://localhost:8080/SharedSessionStateClient/StockDisplay*, which Figure 12-7 shows.

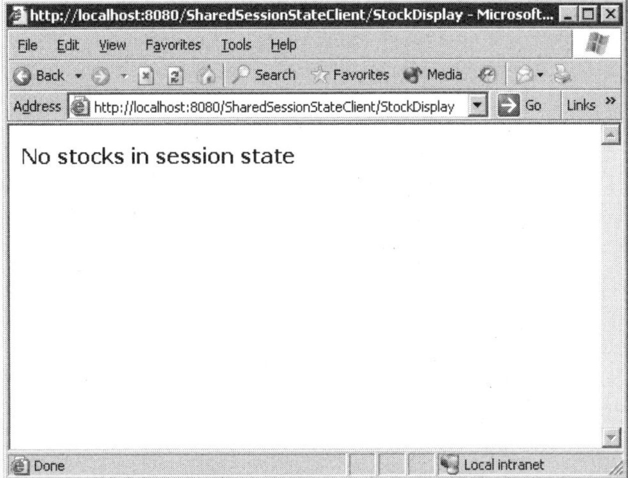

Figure 12-7 Viewing the Servlet standalone.

Calling this URL invokes a single Servlet named StockDisplay. When this Servlet executes, it reads two values from the session. The first value is a stock portfolio; the second value is an index to a single stock within the portfolio. When the Servlet is first run, neither of these values has been added to the session, so the page displays a "No stocks in session state" message.

To test the deployed shared session components, you can run this Servlet embedded within an ASP.NET page. To try this, in the same browser window, navigate to the URL *http://localhost/SharedSessionStateClient/StockDisplay.aspx*, shown in Figure 12-8.

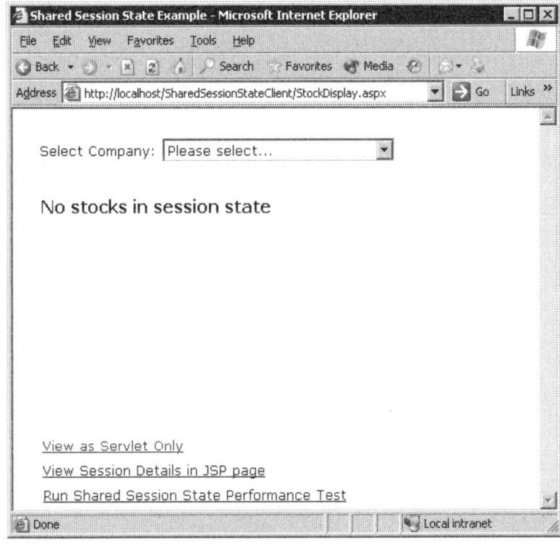

Figure 12-8 Viewing the Servlet, presented within an ASP.NET page.

The ASP.NET page shows a drop-down list of companies that can be selected. The component in the middle of the page should look familiar—it's the Servlet that's running on the J2EE application server. An ASP.NET control known as an *IFrame* (think of this as a browser window within a browser) is used to display the Servlet within the Web page. Select one of the companies from the drop-down list. When a new selection occurs, the Servlet is updated based on the company that's written to shared session state.

As displayed in Figure 12-9, the Servlet shows some sample stock information for the Northwind Traders company (Last, Previous Close, Change, and so on). Try selecting other companies from the drop-down list to test some of the other values.

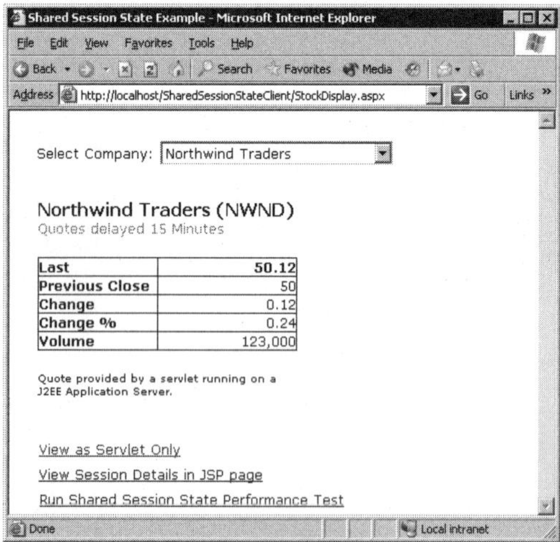

Figure 12-9 The Servlet displays additional information based on values in the shared session state for the Northwind Traders company.

Although on the surface this might seem like a simple example, the inner workings show shared session in action. When the ASP.NET page loads, the stock portfolio is written to shared session. As companies are selected from the drop-down list, an index value is written to the shared session, which is persisted in the database, and the page is reloaded. The Servlet that's presented through this ASP.NET page reads these values from the shared session to display the details of the selected stock (including performing a couple of simple calculations to show a change in stock price). Thus, the shared session state sample demonstrates the ability to read from and write to a session that can be shared among ASP.NET and JSP/Servlets.

To prove that the session remains with the Servlet outside the boundaries of the ASP.NET page, click the link that reads View As Servlet Only.

This link will display a Web page generated by the same Servlet that produced the Web page shown in Figure 12-7. However, the values in the session are no longer null; thus, the selected stock and its associated details are displayed by the Servlet, as shown in Figure 12-10.

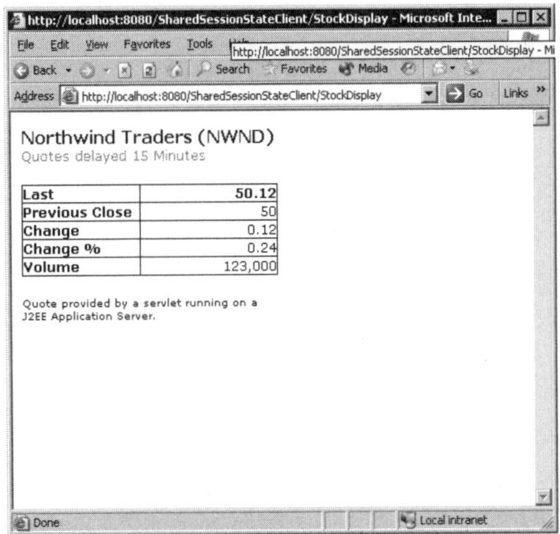

Figure 12-10 The Servlet running outside the ASP.NET page, but with the shared session context.

You can also interrogate the values stored in the shared session from within a JSP page. Return to the ASP.NET page (by pressing the Back button in the browser), and select the View Session Details In JSP Page option. A page similar to the one shown in Figure 12-11 will be displayed.

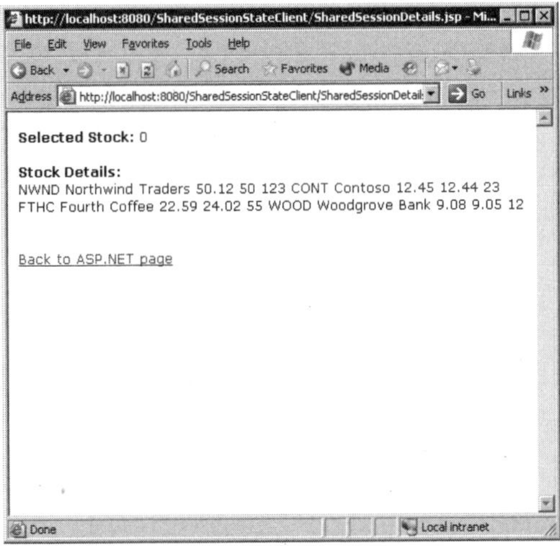

Figure 12-11 A JSP page that displays the values in shared session.

The JSP page displays the two objects stored in the shared session: the selected stock (this is a zero-based index) and the details of the stock portfolio that are held in the session.

What This Sample Shows

This example shows how you can store an object that can be shared among a number of JSP pages, Servlets, and ASP.NET pages. Using the serialization techniques described in Chapter 3 and the database access methods covered in Chapter 7, you can construct an object, store it in the shared session database, and update the object regardless of the platform that it's being accessed from.

To the user, this application looks as though it's being hosted using one platform only. However, the contents of the page actually originate from two platforms. The user shouldn't be aware that the page he's viewing is hosted by ASP.NET and has an *IFrame* that embeds a Servlet running on a different platform—potentially a different server. Nor should he be aware that the two platforms have the ability to read objects from and write objects to a shared session. This seamlessness is also aided if the new ASP.NET pages have been created with a similar look and feel.

The sample stock object shown in this section is merely an extension of the samples used in the previous chapters. The object could also be a shopping cart (allowing pages of an online store to be split between a J2EE and an ASP.NET solution), authentication credentials (allowing a user to log on to one platform and be authenticated when accessing pages on the next), or any other scenario in which presentation resources are spread across two distinct platforms but deliver a single user experience.

The advantages of this seamless user experience are also clear when dealing with a migration scenario. Suppose that an organization is migrating a J2EE-based application involving a large number of JSP pages to ASP.NET. This might be a full migration over an extended period of time or just a pilot for adopting ASP.NET for a particular business use case. Either way, the use of a shared session allows the ASP.NET tier to be "phased in" over a period of time. It might not be feasible to convert all the JSP pages to ASP.NET at once. (When you perform such a sweeping conversion, you might only be able to convert a few JSP pages at a time.) If the pages that *are* migrated need to access session state from the existing platform, using a shared session design similar to the one in this section's sample might be an approach you'll benefit from.

Viewing the Data Stored in SQL

To see the type of data being written to the database, you can use the SQL Server Query Analyzer to issue ISQL commands in order to view the tables that have been set up. This is the same tool that was used to run the scripts and configure the database.

After the test client has been run, you can use the analyzer tool to issue commands that will show the type of data being stored. Select the SharedSessionState database (from the drop-down list in the toolbar) and issue the following SQL command:

```
SELECT * FROM REGISTRATION
```

The output, shown in Figure 12-12, lists the number of registrations within the shared session database. (Your identification values will be different, but the overall format is the same.) At this point, you have only one registered session state. The table shows a unique *ID* that's been created for the shared session, the *ASPID* (the base Session ID that ASP.NET uses), the *JSPID* (the base Session ID that JSP uses), and the time that this session was last modified.

	ID	ASPID	JSPID	LastModified
1	5ED5E238-7620-4270-9BC1-170DCAAD3A56	u252za550...	2mk5763jv...	2003-07-21 16:25:20.890

Figure 12-12 Output from *SELECT * FROM REGISTRATION.*

To see what objects are associated with that session, you can perform the following SQL command:

```
SELECT * FROM OBJECT_LOOKUP
```

Figure 12-13 shows the registration-to-object relationships within the database. (Again, your ID values will be different.) Each entry in this table has a *REGISTRATIONID* and an *OBJECTID* to correlate the two.

	REGISTRATIONID	OBJECTID
1	5ED5E238-7620-4270-9BC1-170DCAAD3A56	D407C2A1-5F2B-4AC3-AFFD-39E08CD0FAE1
2	5ED5E238-7620-4270-9BC1-170DCAAD3A56	F8D87EB9-DFB0-4F53-988B-3CF1CEE56C95

Figure 12-13 Output from *SELECT * FROM OBJECT_LOOKUP.*

Finally, you can perform a lookup on the objects themselves by running a query against the *OBJECT* table:

```
SELECT * FROM OBJECT
```

In Figure 12-14, you can see the *OBJECTID*, the *OBJECTKEY* (the key that the object is referred to by either platform), the *OBJECT* itself (either a *String* value or the XML representation of the object after serialization), and the *TYPE*.

The *TYPE* isn't used specifically by the sample code, but it's useful for extending the example to handle multiple types of objects.

	ID	OBJECTKEY	OBJECT	TYPE
1	D407C2A1-5F2B-4AC3-AFFD-39E08CD0FAE1	myStocks	<?xml version="1.0"?> ...	String
2	F8D87EB9-DFB0-4F53-988B-3CF1CEE56C95	selectedStock	0	String

Figure 12-14 Output from *SELECT * FROM OBJECT.*

How the Sample Works

By now, you should have a good idea of how the sample runs and the type of data that's being stored underneath it. As mentioned at the start of this section, there are typically three steps for designing and creating a system that demonstrates shared session state between the .NET and J2EE platforms:

- Deciding where the shared data will live and how it will be managed
- Creating a shared session interface for ASP.NET and JSP/Servlets to access
- Creating a registration process for new shared sessions

Let's look at how these three steps are applied in the sample code.

Deciding Where to Store the Shared Session Data

As mentioned, both the .NET and J2EE platforms have a proprietary API for storing session state. Therefore, creating a system to read the existing session state each individual platform stores would be very difficult, if not impossible. You'd have to build interfaces to access the proprietary store and possibly versions of the code to run on each and every J2EE application server vendor. Thus, we have to concede that any session store that will allow session objects from .NET and J2EE to be persisted must be a custom implementation.

As you saw when setting up the sample code, a Microsoft SQL Server database is used as the store for all the shared session records. To enable this, a shared database was created that could be accessed by both the .NET and J2EE components. To facilitate this, we used a Data Access Object (DAO) pattern similar to the one shown in Chapter 7.

To store the session, the sample code uses three database tables and a number of stored procedures. Using a database to store a session isn't mandatory for enabling a solution to share sessions in this way—you could easily use another type of service. But using a database will help us utilize some of the concepts highlighted in earlier chapters of the book and will provide a manageable store for the session information. The database schema used is shown in Figure 12-15.

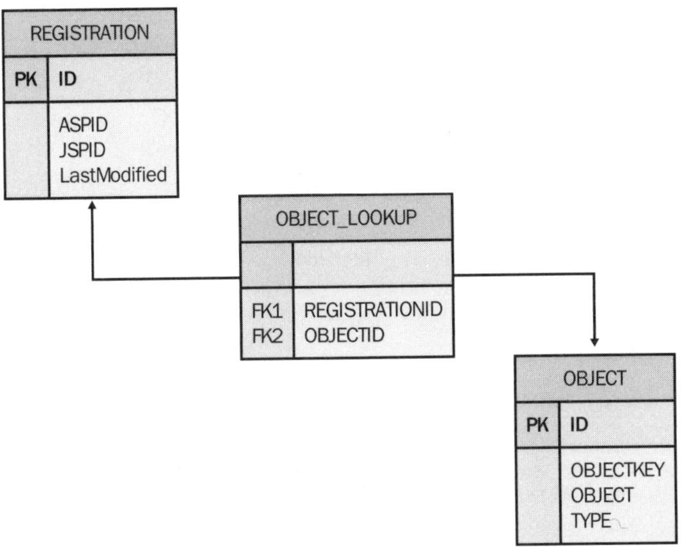

Figure 12-15 Database schema used for the shared session state database table.

The schema is quite simple. The *REGISTRATION* table is used to correlate different Session IDs from JSP and ASP.NET. A unique identifier is given for each pair, and a timestamp indicating the last time the record was accessed is also created for each record.

> **Note** A timestamp allows you to do some housekeeping for shared sessions that are no longer in use. One of the problems with sessions from browsers is that an application rarely knows when it has ended. (This problem affects both regular sessions and our shared session model.) Web sites might present users with a "logout" option, but frequently it's much more convenient (and therefore more likely) for users to just close the browser. The problem is that when a browser is closed, there's no way to notify the session that it has terminated. Because browsers are linked with these stateful sessions, you have to take a housekeeping approach and clean up unused sessions after a period of time. This section's example code keeps the timestamp up to date when objects are added or modified. This allows you to create housekeeping functionality at a later point in time.

Each shared session registration can store a number of objects. To facilitate a one-to-many relationship (one shared session to many objects stored within that session), a lookup table named *OBJECT_LOOKUP* is used. The lookup table maps registrations with objects in the *OBJECT* table. The objects that are stored here contain an object key, a value, and a type. The key is used the same way as it is in a regular session: as an index to uniquely identify objects stored per session. The value is a *string* type and is used to store the serialized XML representation of the object. The type is a placeholder for storing the type of the object that has been serialized to the table.

In addition to this database schema, a number of stored procedures have been created:

- ***Sp_CreateNewRegistration*** Creates a new registration for a shared session.
- ***Sp_DeleteRegistration*** Deletes a registration (shared session) along with any associated objects.
- ***Sp_AddObject*** Adds an object to shared session state. Also replaces an object in session state if an object with the same key exists.
- ***Sp_GetObject*** Retrieves an object from shared session state.
- ***Sp_DeleteObject*** Deletes an object from a registered session.
- ***Sp_DeleteObjects*** Deletes all objects from a registered session.
- ***Sp_GetRegistrationFromASP*** Returns the registration ID based on a passed ASP.NET Session ID.
- ***Sp_GetRegistrationFromJSP*** Returns the registration ID based on a passed JSP Session ID.
- ***Sp_UpdateTimestamp*** Used to update the timestamp for a registration when an object is added, modified, or removed.

The sample code uses stored procedures rather than using dynamic SQL (a number of SQL calls made from the middle tier to perform the same operation). By using stored procedures, we avoid having to write the database function code twice—once for each platform. To access these SQL stored procedures, two DAOs are used: one that uses ADO.NET, and one that uses the Microsoft SQL Server 2000 Driver for JDBC. These DAOs are respectively located in the DAO.cs and DAO.java files, found in the Server directories in the sample code. The connection strings for the DAOs are held in the web.config file for the ASP.NET implementation and in the JDBC connection properties (sharedsessiondb-service.xml in JBoss) for the J2EE implementation.

Creating a Shared Session API for ASP.NET and JSP/Servlets

Once the database is configured, the second task in creating the shared session sample is to create a shared session API for both ASP.NET and JSP/Servlets. This is an API for each of the presentation tiers that allows the two platforms to add and retrieve session objects from the database, as shown in Figure 12-16.

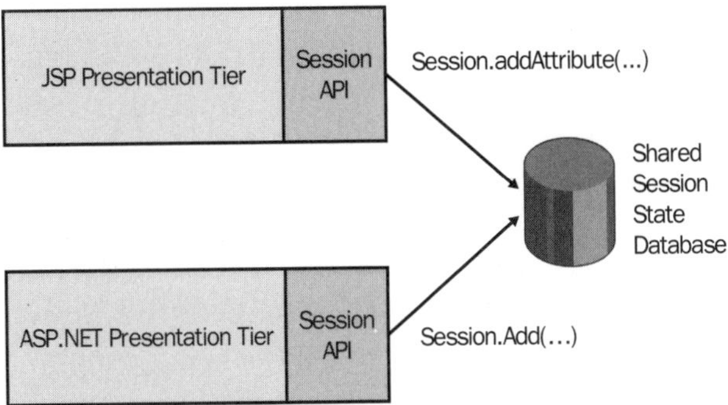

Figure 12-16 Using a shared session API for both the JSP and ASP.NET presentation tiers.

If you examine the native session components in both .NET and J2EE, you'll see that the two platforms handle their respective implementations of sessions by using a *Session* object. For example, to add an object using a regular session in ASP.NET, the following commands are used:

```
String tickerObject = "NWND";
Session.Add("ticker",tickerObject);
```

You can then refer to the saved *Session* object later in the same session by indexing it with the key that was used:

```
String ticker = (String)Session["ticker"];
```

Notice how the *Session* object returns types of value *System.Object*. To reconstruct the original value, you need to cast the *Session* object to the same type that it was saved to.

If you now look at the *Session* object used within J2EE (as part of the *javax.servlet.http* package in the Servlet API), you'll see that it works in a similar way to the .NET *Session* object. To add an object using the Servlet API, you can use this code:

```
String tickerObject = "NWND";
Session.setAttribute("ticker",tickerObject);
```

To refer to the saved object later in the session, use the *getAttribute* method in this way:

```
String ticker = (String)Session.getAttribute("ticker");
```

The sample code in this chapter loosely follows the functionality of these two APIs, creating a shared session object that can be used for data that needs to be accessed on both platforms. Because we've created similar functionality, you have the option—without having to make significant modifications to the majority of the method calls—of writing either to the native session state or to the custom shared implementation. This approach can also help when switching from existing implementations that use a regular session to this shared session concept.

The shared session API defines two new session objects that follow the functionality of the APIs described a moment ago. The two objects, *SharedSessionState.SharedSession* (for the ASP.NET tier) and *com.microsoft.samples.SharedSession* (for the JSP tier), can be found in the respective Server directories in the sample code.

Taking a closer look at these objects, you can see how they work. The *SharedSession* object for .NET declares two *private* variables. One is used to store the existing ASP.NET Session ID (used to pass to the database) and the implementation of the DAO itself. This code can be found in the SharedSession.cs (for ASP.NET) and SharedSession.java (for JSP) source files.

```
private String aspSessionID;
private DAO _dao = new DAO();

public SharedSession(String SessionID)
{
    aspSessionID = SessionID;
}
```

When the shared session interface is initialized, it's passed the Session ID for the existing ASP.NET session. The interface implements a subset of the methods typically found in the standard *Session* object. For this sample, we implement *Add*, *Remove*, *Clear*, *Abandon*, *SessionID*, and an index. These methods work by calling the respective DAO function calls, thereby passing the value of the current ASP.NET session:

```
public void Add(String name, String value)
{
    dao.AddObject(aspSessionID,name,value,"String");
}

public String this[String name]
{
```

```
    get
    {
        return _dao.GetObjectXML(aspSessionID,name);
    }
    set
    {
        dao.AddObject(aspSessionID,name,value,"String");
    }
}

public void Remove(String name)
{
    dao.DeleteObject(aspSessionID,name);
}

public void Abandon()
{
    dao.DeleteRegistration(aspSessionID);
}

public void Clear()
{
    dao.DeleteObjects(aspSessionID);
}

public String SessionID
{
    get
    {
        return _dao.GetRegistrationID(aspSessionID);
    }
}
```

Calling the shared session API from ASP.NET The Java class also contains a similar set of methods. You call this shared session API slightly differently, depending on whether you're using ASP.NET, a Servlet, or a JSP.

To enable an ASP.NET page to use the *SharedSession* object, the following line of code is inserted as a local declaration for each page or control that requires use of the shared session:

```
using SharedSessionState;
...
protected SharedSession SSession
    = new SharedSession(Session.SessionID);
```

In this declaration, you pass the existing *Session.SessionID* (from the original session that was created by ASP.NET) so that you can reference it against the database. To call the *SharedSession* object, the new *SSession* is then used:

```
SSession.Add("SelectedStock","2");
```

Calling the shared session API from a Servlet The Servlet implementation of the shared session API is very similar to the ASP.NET call. Again, a reference to the *SharedSession* object is created by using the following statements:

```
import com.microsoft.samples.SharedSession;
...
SharedSession SSession
    = new SharedSession(req.getSession().getId());
```

The shared session API again uses the *SSession* object, but this time, commands similar to the original Java *HttpSession* object are used to read and write values:

```
SSession.setAttribute("SelectedStock","3");
```

Calling the shared session API from a JSP Unlike Servlets, JSP pages by default automatically define an object that implements the *HttpSession* interface (named *session*) that can be called in a JSP scriptlet or scripting expression in any part of the page. This is demonstrated in the following command, where the default *session* object is automatically made available within a JSP scriptlet:

```
<% String value = session.getAttribute("myStocks"); %>
```

Our shared session state model, however, no longer needs the default *session* object (because we want our objects to be read from and written to the shared session store). To create an alternate reference to the shared session store, use the following declaration at the top of a JSP:

```
<%@ page session="false" import="com.microsoft.samples" %>
<% SharedSession session
    = new SharedSession(request.getSession().getId());%>
```

First the code instructs the JSP container to not provide support for the standard HTTP sessions, thereby preventing the inclusion of the default *session* object by setting the page directive's *session* attribute to *false*. Next the code defines a new *session* object for the shared store. Other calls within the JSP page use a similar set of calls to the original. For example:

```
<% out.write((String)session.getAttribute("selectedStock")); %>
```

The three methods just discussed showed you how the shared session API can be accessed from each of the presentation tiers. A final step remains to complete the shared session implementation. We need a process that "links" the ASP.NET session to the JSP session on an individual machine. The two presentation tiers need to know that both the ASP.NET and JSP sessions for a particular individual user are related—and cross-referenced—in order to pass objects by using the tables in the shared session database.

Creating a Registration Process

As discussed, each of the presentation tier implementations uses its own cookie or method to track the active session for each platform. This is fine for the individual platforms themselves, but we face a challenge when we need to synchronize these two approaches to create a shared session. For example, when I open a regular ASP.NET page, a new Session ID is created and stored as a nonpersistent cookie in the browser. Suppose I then navigate to a second page that's on a J2EE system. As I open this page, a new session is also created for me (this time a JSP Session ID). Again, this Session ID is stored on my machine in the form of a cookie, albeit a new and different cookie.

So how do we synchronize these sessions to create a single shared session? And how do we synchronize these two values with the shared session store in SQL Server? How does the system know that the ASP.NET page I called first needs to share session data with the JSP page I plan to call directly after it, or vice versa?

One option might be to look at the IP address of the calling machine: if the IP address matches for subsequent requests, you could associate the address with a shared session state. One problem with this approach is that some firewalls and proxy servers mask the IP address of clients, especially when using Network Address Translation (NAT). On the Internet, certain ISPs use this masking to hide the IP address of their dial-up clients. Therefore, all connections coming from a certain ISP might appear to come from a single IP address, which would invalidate this approach. The alternative demonstrated in the sample code is to use a registration process.

When you use a registration process, a call is made to the ASP.NET page, as shown in Figure 12-17. A filter (known in .NET as an *HttpModule*) is installed as part of the sample and intercepts the call.

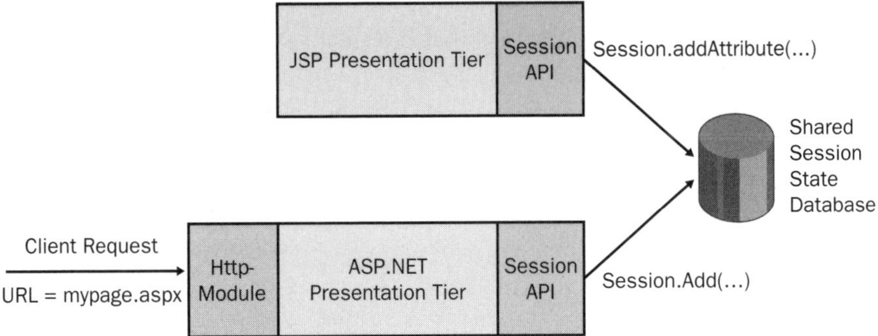

Figure 12-17 Incoming HTTP page request for the ASP.NET presentation tier.

The filter determines whether the call is a new ASP.NET session from the client. (You can find this out by looking at the real session object, which you still have access to.) The filter also determines that the user has requested mypage.aspx. If the call is a new session, the ASP.NET Session ID is retrieved from the ASP.NET page and a browser redirect to a nominated page on the J2EE server is performed. As part of the HTTP redirect, both the Session ID from the ASP.NET page and the URL of the original page that the user wanted to access are passed along as new request parameters. An example URL might be:

http://localhost:8080/SharedSessionStateClient/Register.jsp?aspid=1234&redir=http://localhost/SharedSessionStateClient/StockDisplay.aspx

This URL refers to a registration process on the JSP tier to perform a registration. It also passes the Session ID from the ASP.NET page and the page you should be redirected to once registration is complete. The call is then made to the Register.jsp page. A second filter (of type *javax.servlet.http.Filter*, this time on the J2EE server) intercepts the redirected call, as shown in Figure 12-18.

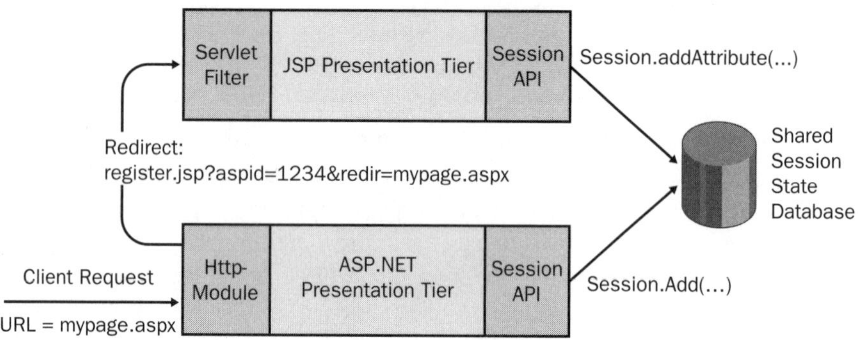

Figure 12-18 Incoming request is redirected to a registration JSP.

This filter determines that a registration request has been made from the ASP.NET page, collects the Session ID from the JSP session, and registers both the ASP.NET Session ID and the JSP Session ID with the shared session database. Figure 12-19 illustrates this.

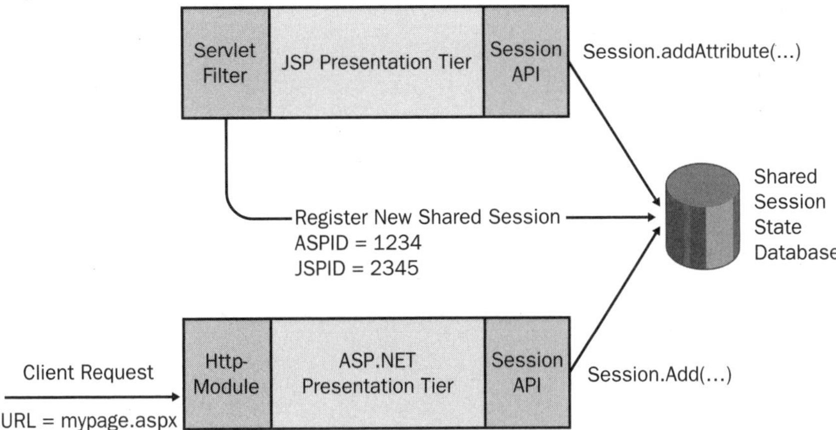

Figure 12-19 Intercepting Servlet filter creates a new session in the shared session database.

The browser is then redirected to the original ASP.NET page, and the original page is loaded for the user, as Figure 12-20 shows.

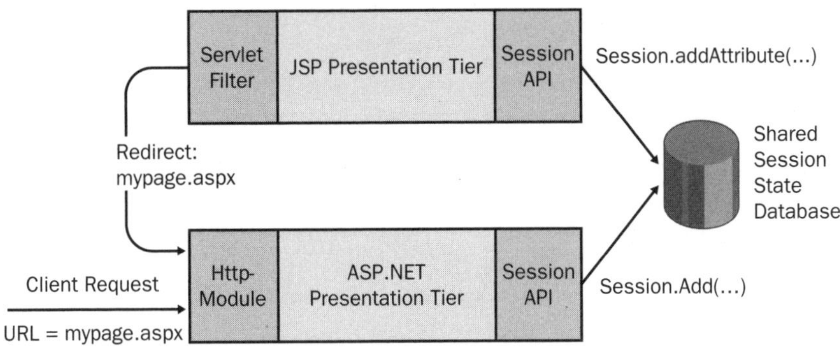

Figure 12-20 After registration, request is redirected to the original page.

Once this registration process is complete, subsequent calls to any of the presentation tiers (from the same browser session) are passed through without redirection, as shown in Figure 12-21. The shared session API uses the Session ID provided by the platform to cross-reference against the entry in the database.

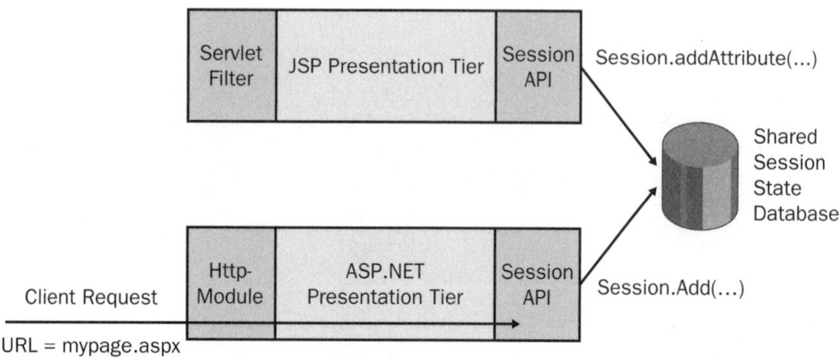

Figure 12-21 Once a shared session has been created, other requests are treated normally.

Such redirection clearly causes a performance hit. However, this redirection needs to happen only the first time a shared session is created. Regardless of which platform is used, future requests within the same session are passed with negligible performance impact.

This procedure also works in reverse. If the client first calls the presentation tier on the JSP server, a new JSP session state will be detected and a redirect to the ASP.NET page will be made, as highlighted in Figure 12-22. However, this redirect is made only if a shared session hasn't already been established.

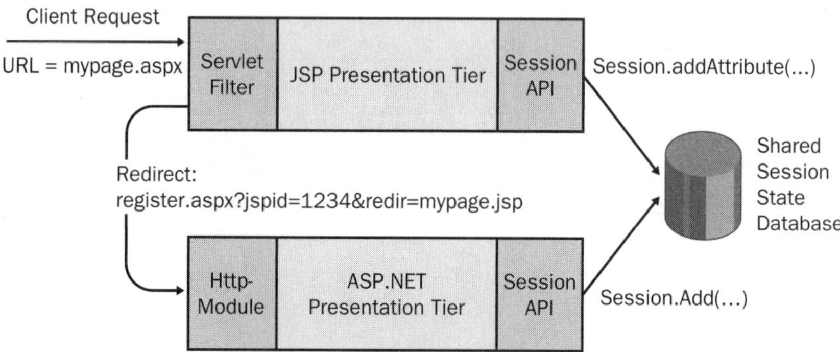

Figure 12-22 The registration process in the opposite direction.

The code for this redirection is implemented in SharedSessionFilter.cs on the ASP.NET tier and in SharedSessionFilter.java on the JSP tier. Both of the components work by matching the incoming URL to a registration page that must be present on both tiers. (For our sample code, this is Register.aspx on ASP.NET and Register.jsp for JSP.) The ASP.NET filter is configured via the web.config file, and the Servlet filter is configured by editing the J2EE deployment descriptor (web.xml). In the web.config file, which is located under the Web directory in the .NET sample, you can see the required declaration to load the *HttpModule*:

```
<httpModules>
    <add type
        ="SharedSessionState.SharedSessionFilter,SharedSessionState"
        name="SharedSessionState" />
</httpModules>
```

In addition, application keys have been added to configure the redirection to the J2EE tier:

```
<appSettings>
    <add key="IncomingRegistrationURL"
        value="/SharedSessionStateClient/Register.aspx"/>
    <add key="RedirectToURL" value=
        "http://localhost:8080/SharedSessionStateClient/Register.jsp"/>
</appSettings>
```

The filter uses the *IncomingRegistrationURL* key to determine that requests sent to the Register.aspx page are redirection requests from the J2EE tier. The filter will intercept these requests, examine the URL (because it contains the JSP Session ID and redirect data), and take appropriate action to register the shared session. The *RedirectToURL* key is used by the filter to determine the URL to redirect to if a regular request for a Web page is received but a shared session currently isn't established. Notice that the *http://localhost:8080* portion of the URL identifies the J2EE server running at this location.

The implementation for the J2EE version of the *SharedSessionStateFilter* works in a similar manner. The J2EE deployment descriptor, web.xml, contains the reference and parameters needed to perform the same operations in reverse:

```
<filter>
    <filter-name>Shared Session Filter</filter-name>
    <filter-class>
        com.microsoft.samples.SharedSessionFilter
    </filter-class>
    <init-param>
        <param-name>IncomingRegistrationURL</param-name>
        <param-value>
            /SharedSessionStateClient/Register.jsp
        </param-value>
    </init-param>
    <init-param>
        <param-name>RedirectToURL</param-name>
```

```
        <param-value>
            http://localhost/SharedSessionStateClient/Register.aspx
        </param-value>
    </init-param>
</filter>
```

As seen in this deployment descriptor, corresponding *IncomingRegistrationURL* and *RedirectToURL* parameters are supplied.

Interoperability Performance Test—Shared Session State

I've included a performance test for the shared session state sample code. The purpose of the test is show the time difference between writing to a regular session and writing to this chapter's custom shared session solution. (For the custom shared session solution, I have included two tests: a serialized and a nonserialized version.)

To run the performance test, click the Run Shared Session State Performance Test link toward the bottom of the StockDisplay.aspx page. This will take you to the performance test screen, shown in Figure 12-23.

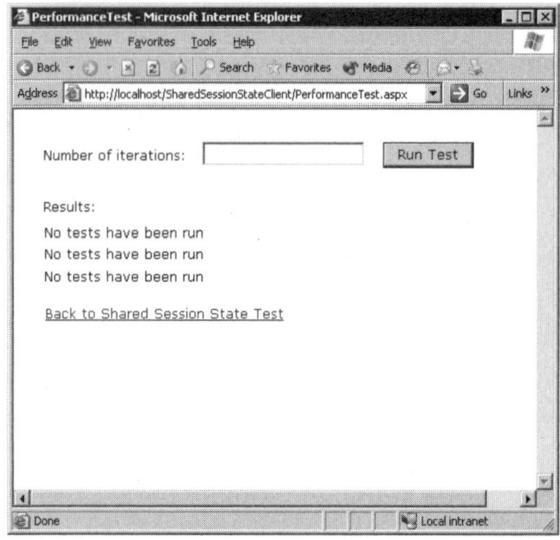

Figure 12-23 Running the shared session state performance test.

The test works by writing a stock portfolio to the platform-specific session and writing the same information to the new shared session. Running the test a number of times ensures a more accurate result. The test records show the time taken to read and write an object a number of times. When I ran the tests on my machine, I saw that serialization didn't seem to add that much time (maybe around 3 milliseconds [ms], which is in line with earlier test results in the book).

One thing that did stand out was the difference between writing to a regular session in ASP.NET and writing to the shared database implementation. Even when ASP.NET was configured to store its regular session information in SQL, it was still outperforming my sample solution by around 5 ms per call. My sample database code for persisting session information certainly wasn't written with optimization in mind, which brings up a valid point: when designing solutions that involve moving from a native platform technology to something that's more custom (to achieve interoperability), you must take into account the effort typically made to optimize and tune the native implementation. For any custom implementation to work well in production, a similar level of care must be taken to achieve the same results as the native implementation.

That said, you might find the results yielded by this example satisfactory for many applications. Despite the difference between the custom shared session solution and a native implementation, we've created a solution with an overhead of only a few milliseconds that enables interoperability at the presentation tier.

Shared Authentication

Shared authentication is the second area to address when dealing with interoperability at the presentation tier. Although some third-party implementations cover shared authentication and Single Sign-On, presentation-tier authentication on the whole tends to be specific to the platform. For example, if an organization selects a third-party implementation for handling Web authentication on the JSP tier, it typically will have to select the same implementation from the same vendor to achieve a similar level of authentication on the ASP.NET tier—and this doesn't guarantee that the authenticated session will work across both platforms. More often than not, in a heterogeneous environment, the user finds himself having to log in again when moving between ASP.NET and JSP pages.

When developing a custom solution, one way to achieve shared authentication is to extend the shared session component covered in the previous section. The shared session component provides a way to exchange authentication data between the two platforms' presentation tiers by using the shared session. But before we can do that, we need to agree on the method of authentication. We can use a Forms Authentication solution in ASP.NET to develop a custom solution.

> **Note** ASP.NET allows the developer to select one of three types of authentication for securing Web applications: Windows Authentication, Passport Authentication, and Forms Authentication. Forms Authentication allows you to apply page-level authentication to a Web application in ASP.NET and automatically redirects the user to a login page if certain credentials haven't been supplied. Once authenticated, the user is automatically redirected to the original page she requested. You configure Forms Authentication by modifying the web.config file for each Web application. Forms Authentication is flexible enough to secure individual pages, allowing you to set different permissions for each user.

To see this in action, let's enable Forms Authentication for both the .NET and Java platforms using the sample code. Returning to the previous example, open the web.config file in the .NET version of the shared session state test client. This can be found in the Web directory of the sample application (C:\Interoperability\Samples\Advanced\Presentation\dotNET\Web).

Within this file, locate the *<authorization>* section toward the end, uncomment the *<!--deny users="?"/ -->* line, and save the file. (To uncomment a line in XML, remove the leading [!--] and trailing [--] symbols. Doing so would make the previous line *<deny users="?"/>*.) After this change is made, save the file and close it. You don't need to rebuild the .NET solution because this file is automatically loaded at run time. A copy of how this file should look can be found in the C:\Interoperability\Samples\Advanced\Presentation\Authentication\dotNET\Web directory.

The authentication and authorization sections within the web.config file enable Forms Authentication security for the ASP.NET side of the sample application. To enable Forms Authentication on the J2EE tier, edit the web.xml file found in the Web\WEB-INF subdirectory of the Java directory. Locate the *FormsAuthenticationEnabled* parameter, and change the value from *false* to *true*:

```
<filter>
...
    </init-param>
    <init-param>
        <param-name>FormsAuthenticationEnabled</param-name>
        <param-value>true</param-value>
    </init-param>
</filter>
```

Again, for validation, a copy of how this web.xml file should look can be found in the C:\Interoperability\Samples\Advanced\Presentation\Authentication\Java\Web\WEB-XML directory. After changing this value and saving the file, rebuild the solution and redeploy to the J2EE server using the package and deploy targets, respectively. The forms authentication component for the J2EE tier is an additional piece of sample code that can be found in the SharedSessionFilter.java file.

Within a new instance of Microsoft Internet Explorer, open the ASP.NET shared session state sample that was shown in the previous section (*http://localhost/SharedSessionStateClient/StockDisplay.aspx*). You might notice that the shared session state registration still occurs. (If you're quick, you can see the redirect from ASP.NET to the Register.jsp page and back again.) This time, however, a login screen is displayed.

This login screen (login.aspx), shown in Figure 12-24, is an automatic redirect from the ASP.NET Forms Authentication service that you enabled by changing the web.config file earlier. For this example, the username and password have been hard-coded. (The username is testuser, and the password is StrongPassword.) Enter these and click the Login button. You'll be redirected to the original shared session state sample page as before. Figure 12-25 depicts this page.

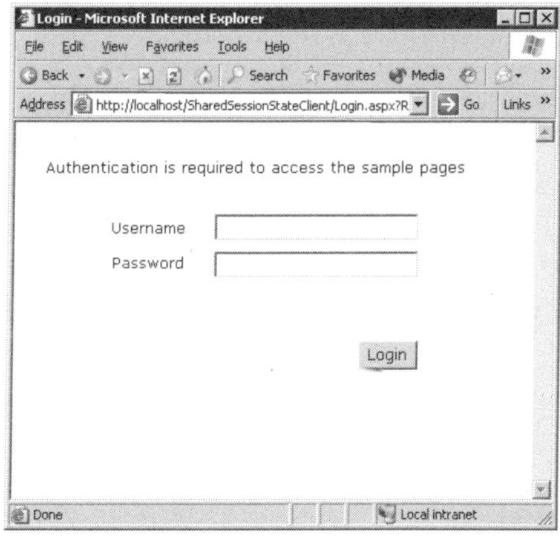

Figure 12-24 Using forms authentication to display a login.aspx page for ASP.NET.

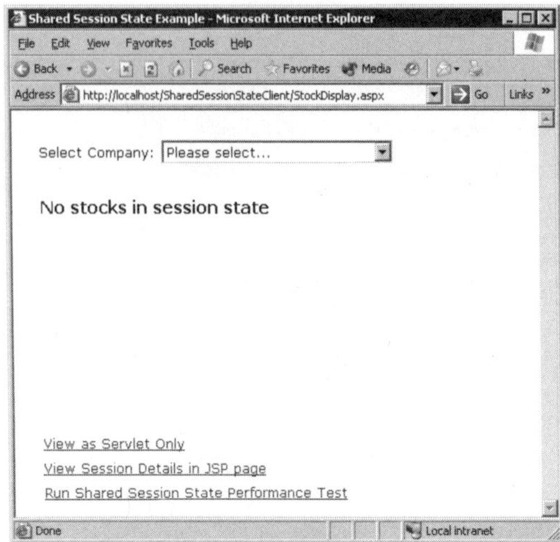

Figure 12-25 Authentication also applies for the Servlet hosted within the ASP.NET page.

You can also see how to protect both JSP and Servlets by using this same mechanism. By making the earlier change to the web.xml file, you protected the Servlet that's being hosted within the ASP.NET page. Because you've already logged in, you cannot detect this (because you aren't asked again for the Servlet authentication details). However, if you close the current Internet Explorer window so that the nonpersistent cookies holding the regular Session ID are no longer available, and if you instead use the *http://localhost:8080/SharedSessionStateClient/StockDisplay* URL to call up the Servlet running individually, you can detect this protection of the Servlet.

This Servlet is also protected by the Forms Authentication mechanism that we employed in ASP.NET. This mechanism will work for any JSP or Servlet that's hosted through this site.

Using Shared Authentication

This example shows how ASP.NET Forms Authentication, combined with the shared session concepts presented in the previous section, can be used to protect JSP and Servlets. This works whether the JSP and Servlets are hosted within an ASP.NET page or hosted individually on the J2EE application server.

This technique lends itself to a number of benefits when deploying applications. For example, organizations running both J2EE applications and introducing .NET applications in-house are likely to face the challenge of using two presentation solutions to authenticate incoming users (even if the store for holding the user credentials is the same). By using and extending the Forms Authentication technique shown here, a unified way of authenticating against the Web tier can be achieved—for both J2EE and .NET applications. This can enable users to navigate between pages hosted on a J2EE or .NET system and to authenticate themselves only once to perform this navigation.

How the Shared Authentication Solution Works

The shared authentication solution by no means fits all presentation-tier authentication issues. As with the shared session state example shown earlier in the chapter, this sample was written to show a potential solution for a very difficult interoperability problem. Taking this sample to the production stage would require additional development and a careful implementation strategy. That said, the underlying concepts for how the shared authentication sample works are similar to (and indeed based upon) the shared session mechanisms discussed earlier in this chapter.

The first configuration step to enable this shared authentication sample is to prevent the regular Forms Authentication mechanism from intercepting this Register.aspx file. If the Register.aspx file gets intercepted, this will interrupt and cause conflict in the shared session registration process. If this happens, our shared session will not be set up—and because we need the shared session to work in order to enable shared authentication, this results in a Catch-22! To stop Forms Authentication from trapping the Register.aspx file, security restrictions are removed from this file in the web.config file. This is done by placing the following section between the configuration elements in web.config for the ASP.NET tier:

```
<location path="Register.aspx">
    <system.web>
        <authorization>
            <allow users="*" />
        </authorization>
    </system.web>
</location>
```

To enable forms authentication to display a prompt when credentials aren't found, a login.aspx file is used. This login page was displayed the first time the sample was run. When the user clicks the Login button, the following code is executed:

```
if ((UserEdit.Text == "testuser") &&
    (PasswordEdit.Text == "StrongPassword"))
{
```

```
    SharedSession SSession = new SharedSession(Session.SessionID);
    SSession.Add("SharedAuthentication","true");
    SSession.Add("Username",UserEdit.Text);

    FormsAuthentication.RedirectFromLoginPage(UserEdit.Text,false);
}
```

First, the username and password are checked to see whether they're correct. (In a production system, these might be a found via a lookup to a database, Microsoft Active Directory directory service, or another Lightweight Directory Access Protocol directory.) For this example, however, we simply have the username and password hard-coded into the method. If they're valid, you write a token into the shared session, which allows the J2EE tier to confirm that this session has been authenticated.

You also write the username into the shared session by way of a simple token. This allows the J2EE tier to reference the username of the logged-in user. You could also include other information, which—as you can imagine—would require some kind of encryption if running in a production system. However, this technique has the potential to offer integration with some kind of authorization system to validate which parts of the application a user may access.

The code on the J2EE tier that reads when this value (token) exists in shared session and performs the redirection to the login page is located in the SharedSessionStateFilter.java class. The redirection that the code implements shows how the J2EE tier checks for the token in the shared session. If the token isn't present, a redirect to the login page is executed. The code that enables this follows:

```
String _formsLoginURI
    = filterConfig.getInitParameter("FormsAuthenticationLoginURL");
String _enabled
    = filterConfig.getInitParameter("FormsAuthenticationEnabled");

if (_enabled.equals("true"))
{
    try
    {
        DAO _dao = new DAO();
        String authenticated
            = _dao.getObjectXML(req.getSession().getId(),
                "SharedAuthentication");
        if (!(authenticated.equals("true")))
        {
            ((HttpServletResponse)response).sendRedirect(
                _formsLoginURI);
```

```
            }
        }
        catch (Exception e)
        {
            try
            {
                ((HttpServletResponse)response).sendRedirect(
                    _formsLoginURI+"?ReturnUrl="+sb.toString());
            }
            catch (Exception e2)
            {
                e2.printStackTrace();
            }
        }
    }
```

First, the filter reads two values from the web.xml file: the URL of the login.aspx page on the ASP.NET tier, and a value that indicates whether authentication will be checked for this session. Assuming that authentication will be checked, the filter performs a database lookup for the existing session to check whether an entry for *SharedAuthentication* exists with a value of *true*. If such a value doesn't exist (because it's not set to *true* or the key isn't present in the shared session), the user is redirected to the login URL in the web.xml file. The *?ReturnURL* request parameter is appended to the redirect so that when the user enters the correct username and password, he's redirected to the original page on the J2EE tier. If the value does exist (in other words, if this session has already been authenticated), processing passes through the filter code and the requested JSP or Servlet is processed normally.

Summary

Interoperability at the presentation tier is a complex problem to tackle and often requires a complex solution. To achieve a user experience that allows pages and components from both .NET and J2EE to be delivered via a consistent and common interface requires—in most cases—both a shared session and shared authentication. The sample code in this chapter introduced these concepts and offered the beginnings of possible solutions for them.

There's great scope for using this sample code to create more production-worthy solutions, tailored to your own requirements. One such expansion of the session state sample code could be to develop the serializer so that it can store and retrieve complex objects of any type (currently, it serializes only *Portfolio* objects). Using the type column in the database object table to store the value, the serializer could automatically detect the type of the object to allow multiple types to be stored for the same session.

This chapter concludes our discussion of interoperability at the presentation tier. The next three chapters will concentrate on the new XML Web services specifications. Up next, Chapter 13, "Web Services Interoperability, Part 1: Security," looks at the WS-Security standard. The goal of these three chapters is not only to cover the specification, but to show some of these standards in action, especially while bridging the gap between the .NET and Java platforms.

13

Web Services Interoperability, Part 1: Security

Toward the end of Chapter 8, "Asynchronous Interoperability, Part 1: Introduction and MSMQ," we introduced the new XML Web service specifications, formerly known as GXA (Global XML Web Services Architecture) and now more frequently referred to as WSA (Web Services Architecture). These specifications, which typically are prefixed with WS-, are designed to take Web services beyond just connecting endpoints together and instead detail how true application interoperability can be achieved.

In the next three chapters, we'll look at three of these new specifications, WS-Security, WS-Attachments (DIME), and WS-Routing. With each of these, we'll introduce the problem the specification is trying to solve and look at sample code that shows these specifications working between .NET and J2EE. To enable this functionality, we'll use Microsoft Web Services Enhancements (WSE) 1.0 and GLUE version 4.0.1.

In this chapter, we'll take the first of these specifications, WS-Security, present an overview of the specification, and then show sample code that uses WS-Security to create both authenticated and encrypted Web service requests between .NET and Java. Each sample will show both .NET and Java as a client and as a Web service.

The Need for WS-Security

Let's start by asking the question, "How do you secure a Web service?" In Chapter 6, "Connectivity with XML Web Services, Part 2," we introduced how authentication credentials could be applied to secure a Web service. By modifying the configuration settings in Internet Information Services (IIS) for .NET, or altering the security realm for the Java Web service, we were able to require clients accessing the service to provide authentication details.

When we are securing the Web service in this way, we are actually using transport-based security. In this case, we are relying on the security mechanisms provided by HTTP. Had we wanted to increase the security of the Web service by encrypting the transport itself, we could have used HTTPS (HTTP over Secure Sockets Layer, or SSL)—but again, HTTPS is a transport-specific solution.

When using either HTTP for authentication or HTTPS for encryption, there are generally two common flaws. First, transport-based security is point-to-point security. This means the connection is secure only from the point it is initiated to the point it is sent. This type of security is perfectly valid for the scenario shown in Figure 13-1.

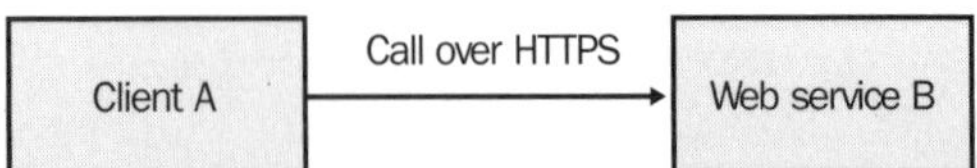

Figure 13-1 Point-to-point security using HTTPS (also applies to HTTP Authentication).

Let's imagine, however, that Service B is acting as a relay to Service C. Although security can be applied from A to B and from B to C as shown in Figure 13-2, we cannot ensure end-to-end security of the message as it travels from point A to point C. End-to-end security describes the safeguarding of the message from the originating point to the ultimate destination.

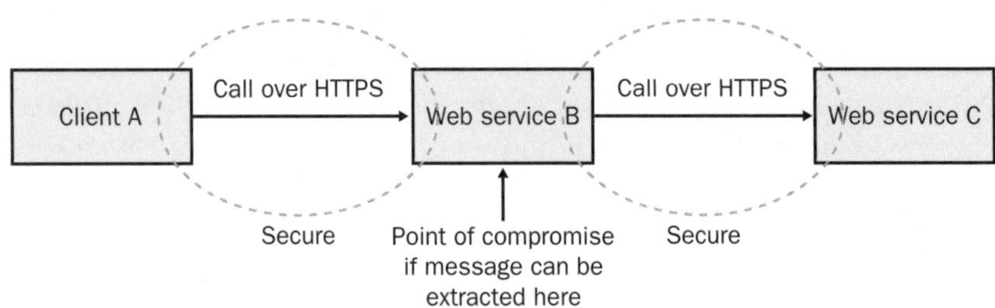

Figure 13-2 Point-to-point security using transport security and an intermediary.

If for some reason Service B is compromised, messages could be read by unauthorized users.

The second flaw is exposed when we try to move to another transport for Web services. As was mentioned in the introduction in Chapter 5, "Connectivity with XML Web Services, Part 1," Web services are designed to be decoupled from the underlying transport. This means that Web services have the potential for running on transports other than HTTP. Imagine the scenario shown in Figure 13-3, where a call is made via HTTP, yet the response is returned to the user as a Web service using SMTP.

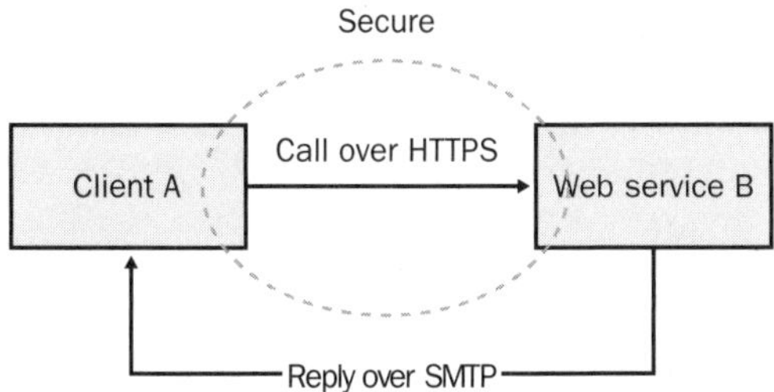

Figure 13-3 Point-to-point security showing secure and insecure transports.

In this case, we can secure the HTTPS channel to provide security, but there is little we can do to secure the message as it's sent over SMTP.

What is required is a security mechanism for Web services that works from end to end in solutions and is independent of the underlying transport. This requirement for Web services security is addressed by WS-Security.

WS-Security

Released in April 2002, a draft of the WS-Security specification was one of the first to be co-authored by IBM, Microsoft, and VeriSign. In general, the WS-Security specification aims to guarantee integrity and confidentiality of SOAP messages used in a Web services environment.

Although a number of security identifiers (known as tokens) can be used with WS-Security, the specification itself is designed to be extensible—allowing anyone to expand and introduce a customized token format. The specification also describes how to encode X.509 certificates, Kerberos tickets, and UsernameTokens as part of a message.

For authentication, implementations of the specification typically support an unsigned security token (such as a username and password token) or a signed security token (either an X.509 certificate or a Kerberos ticket). These authentication mechanisms are used in conjunction with claims. A *claim* is a statement that a client makes (for example, a name, privilege, or capability).

For encryption, the specification leverages the XML Encryption standard. Three elements of the XML Encryption standard (*xenc:ReferenceList*, *xenc:EncryptedKey*, and *xenc:EncryptedData*) can be used within the WS-Security header. The specification itself, and some extended samples, can be found at: *http://msdn.microsoft.com/webservices/building/wse/default.aspx?pull=/library/en-us/dnglobspec/html/ws-security.asp*.

Web Services Enhancements (WSE)

The first Microsoft implementation showing WS-Security and other new specifications is named Web Services Enhancements (WSE). WSE aims to show how these new specifications can be implemented for Microsoft technology and how Microsoft technology is a great proving ground for the specifications themselves.

In the next three chapters, we'll use Microsoft WSE 1.0 and show how the product works. For each area shown, we'll demonstrate how we can use WSE and the professional features in GLUE version 4.0.1 to apply these specifications in solutions that require interoperability between .NET and J2EE.

Downloading and Installing Microsoft WSE

Microsoft WSE 1.0 can be downloaded from *http://msdn.microsoft.com/webservices*. At the time of this writing, the latest version is WSE 1.0 Service Pack 1 (SP1), which is what we'll use throughout these three chapters.

When installing Microsoft WSE for the samples in this chapter, select a complete installation. After installation, the program files and samples that accompany the WSE can be found in the C:\Program Files\Microsoft WSE directory.

To use WSE in your own applications, you might also want to download the WSE Settings Tool for Visual Studio .NET. This can also be found on the *http://msdn.microsoft.com/webservices* site. This tool includes a means for controlling how Web service proxy files are created, and for ensuring that these files contain the correct references to the WSE libraries.

Now that we have the required software, let's take a look at the sample code to demonstrate WS-Security between .NET and Java.

Sample Code

The sample code in this chapter highlights using WS-Security between .NET and Java to show both authentication and encryption. For the authentication sample, the code will show how a Web service will accept a request only if the request is signed with a valid X.509 certificate. In the encryption sample, although the Web service request will be made over HTTP (a nonsecure transport), the sample will demonstrate how the contents of the actual request are encrypted. This encryption will be based on a symmetric key.

Authentication Using WS-Security

The first part of the WS-Security sample will show authentication between two clients (one a .NET client and the other a Java client) and two Web services (again, one in .NET and one in Java). The .NET client and service will use WSE, whereas the Java client and service will use GLUE.

The sample works by applying WS-Security headers to the client Web service requests, based on an X.509 certificate. The Web services will allow methods to be called only if they are made by a client with a correctly formed request that has been signed by such a certificate.

To get the sample running, we first must configure the Web services and set up the authentication mechanisms.

Configuring the .NET Web Service

The first task is to set up the .NET Web service. Taking our stock-trading theme from previous chapters forward, this Web service will return a recommendation for the top stock of the day. To ensure that this information is accessed only by authenticated clients, the Web service will be protected by using WS-Security.

The Web service itself can be found in the C:\Interoperability\Samples\Advanced\WS-Security\Auth\dotNET\WebService directory. Navigate to this directory and build the sample code using the provided NAnt script by entering **nant** at the command prompt. As with the previous .NET Web service samples shown in this book, we need to create a virtual directory to host this Web service.

To do this, launch IIS from the Start\Program Files\Administrative Tools program group. Expand through to the Default Web Site option, right-click, and select New\Virtual Directory. For the virtual directory alias, type **dotNETAuthWebService**, as shown in Figure 13-4.

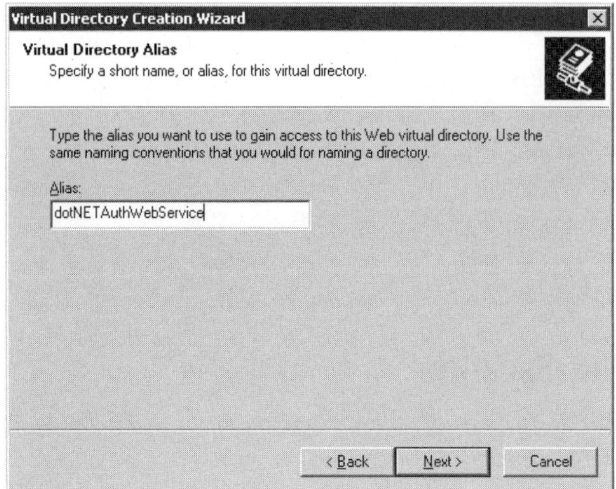

Figure 13-4 Creating the .NET WS-Security Authentication virtual directory.

Although this can be changed later, this exact name is important for the WS-Security authentication sample to run correctly. Click the Next button, and set the directory to **C:\Interoperability\Samples\Advanced\WS-Security\Auth\dotNET\WebService**, as shown in Figure 13-5.

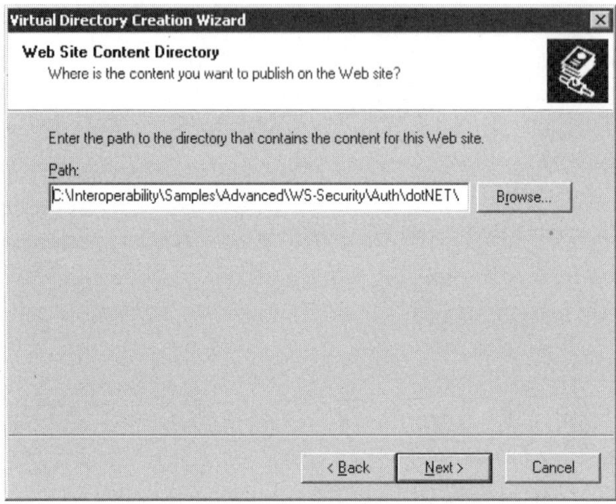

Figure 13-5 Setting the path for the virtual directory.

Click the Next button, and accept the defaults for the remaining pages to complete the wizard. The secure .NET Web service is now set up. We can verify this by browsing to *http://localhost/dotNETAuthWebService/StockService.asmx*.

If the Web service has been successfully deployed, the operations screen, as shown in Figure 13-6, will be displayed.

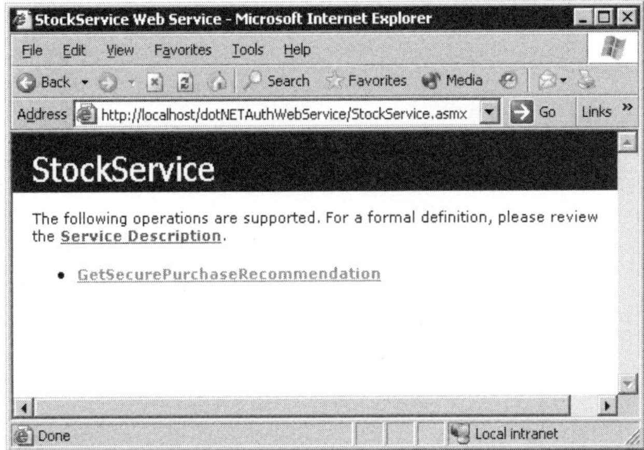

Figure 13-6 Validating the secure purchase recommendation operation.

As you can see, the StockService exposes a single method named *GetSecurePurchaseRecommendation*. Although we can see this method by using this interface, we cannot call it from the browser. If you try this, an exception will be thrown indicating that only SOAP requests are allowed to make such calls.

```
System.ApplicationException: Only SOAP requests are permitted.
```

If you get a Web page indicating that the page cannot be displayed (HTTP 500—Internal Server error) in Microsoft Internet Explorer, ensure that the Show Friendly HTTP Error Messages setting is disabled in the options within the browser itself, as shown in Figure 13-7.

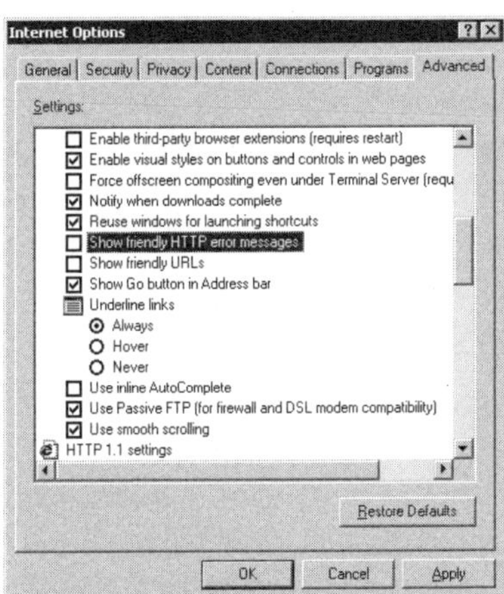

Figure 13-7 Disabling the Show Friendly HTTP Error Messages setting in Internet Explorer.

The .NET Web service is now configured. Using GLUE, we will now configure the equivalent Web service in Java.

Configuring the Java Web Service

The Java Web service can be found in the C:\Interoperability\Samples\Advanced\WS-Security\Auth\Java\WebService directory. As with previous examples, publishing the Web service itself is performed by using the Ant script in this directory to build and run the sample. To do this, type **start ant run** at a command prompt in this directory.

Once published, the WSDL of the Web service is available at *http://localhost:8004/JavaWSSWebService/StockService.wsdl.* As can be seen in the WSDL document, the Web service exposes a method named *GetSecureSaleRecommendation*, the opposite of the one exposed by the .NET Web service.

Setting Up Certificates

The two Web services required for the sample are now set up. Before we can build and run the clients that are going to call these Web services, we must first create some X.509 certificates.

> **More Info** X.509 is a certificate standard based on previous X.500 directories and is used to authenticate identities on the Internet. Certificates are issued by CAs (Certificate Authorities), of which there are a number of trusted roots (VeriSign, Thawte, and so on). A certificate itself consists of a public key and relates to a private key normally held in a separate location—a technique known as *asymmetric encryption.* When a certificate is sent over a network it will consist of the public key, and the private key will be retained by the sender. For encryption, the public key will be used to encrypt and the private will be used to decrypt. For authentication, the private key will be used to encrypt a hash of the message and the public key will be used to decrypt the hash to validate the signature. For more information on cryptography and algorithms used in asymmetric encryption, I recommend *Applied Cryptography: Protocols, Algorithms, and Source Code in C, Second Edition* by Bruce Schneier (John Wiley & Sons, 1995).

Creating the Windows X.509 certificate The certificate will be used to digitally sign the Web service request. For the purposes of these samples, we'll create two test certificates by using tools supplied with both the .NET Framework and the J2SE (Java 2 Standard Edition). To allow these certificates to work, we'll turn off some security guards within the sample. In a production system, you can imagine how these certificates would be issued and controlled by a central or third-party CA.

Navigate to the C:\Interoperability\Samples\Advanced\WS-Security\Certs directory. This is the directory where the certificate will be created. To create the Windows X.509 certificate, we will use a tool named MakeCert.exe. This tool can normally be found in the Framework SDK directory (for example, C:\Program Files\Microsoft Visual Studio .NET 2003\SDK\v1.1\bin); the latest edition can also be installed with the Platform SDK. If you haven't already, you should add this directory to the system *PATH* (or use a Visual Studio .NET 2003 command prompt) to allow it to be run from the sample directory. Use the following command to create the certificate:

```
makecert -n "CN=Simon Guest, OU=Authors, O=Microsoft Press,
L=Redmond, ST=WA, C=US" -ss my dotNETClient.cer
```

This command will create an appropriate test certificate that can be used with the sample code. The CN (common name) details are optional for this tool, and they can be adjusted to reflect your own settings within this sample.

Creating the Java certificate To create the Java certificate, a tool named keytool.exe is used. This tool can be found in the bin directory of your J2SE installation, and again it should be made accessible from the sample directory.

This tool works a bit differently from the MakeCert tool in .NET, as it stores all certificates and keys in a single file. (The .NET tool creates an individual file for each certificate.) To create the certificate and set up this store, use the following command:

```
keytool -keystore keystore.db -genkey -alias JavaClient -keyalg rsa
```

This command will create a new key store (named keystore.db) and generate a new key (certificate) named JavaClient that will be used for signing requests. When running this command, you'll be prompted for a password for the key store itself. Enter **StrongPassword**—this password will also be used in the sample code.

```
Enter keystore password:  StrongPassword
```

After the key store is set up, you'll need to provide some information about the certificate itself. This will include your name, organizational unit (department), organization, and location—similar to the information that was passed to MakeCert.exe on the command line. Enter these details as they apply to you—this information is not specific to the sample. For my details, the following information was used:

```
What is your first and last name?
  [Unknown]:  Simon Guest
What is the name of your organizational unit?
  [Unknown]:  Authors
What is the name of your organization?
  [Unknown]:  Microsoft Press
What is the name of your City or Locality?
  [Unknown]:  Redmond
What is the name of your State or Province?
  [Unknown]:  WA
What is the two-letter country code for this unit?
[Unknown]:  US
```

At the end of the details, you'll be prompted to confirm the certificate details (enter **yes** for this) and press Return to acknowledge that the password to access this certificate will be the same as the one to access the key store itself.

```
Is CN=Simon Guest, OU=Authors, O=Microsoft Press, L=Redmond, ST=WA, C=US correc
t?
  [no]:  yes

Enter key password for <JavaClient>
        (RETURN if same as keystore password):
```

If all steps were completed successfully, you will have two files in the C:\Interoperability\Samples\Advanced\WS-Security\Certs directory: the Windows certificate (dotNETClient.cer) and the Java certificate stored in keystore.db.

Running the .NET Client

Now that we have the two Web services configured and have created suitable X.509 test certificates, let's build and run the client code in the C:\Interoperability\Samples\Advanced\WS-Security\Auth\dotNET\Client directory. The first thing that the client requires is a certificate to use to sign the request. This is selected through a simple dialog box, shown in Figure 13-8, that lists all personal certificates in the Windows key store.

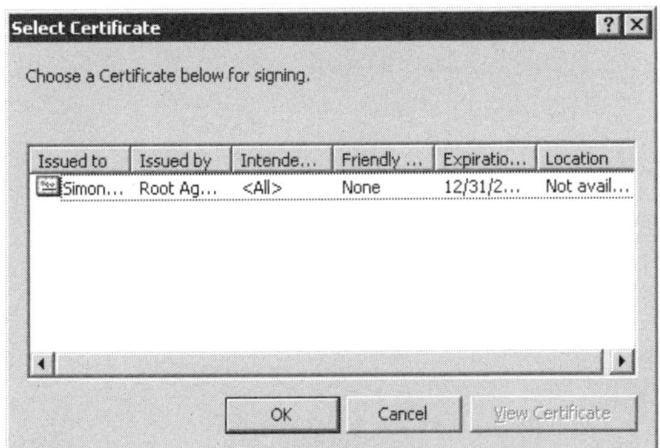

Figure 13-8 Selecting a certificate to sign the Web services request.

Select the certificate that was created in the previous section. Use the View Certificate option to verify the details of the certificate. Click OK to continue. The client will now display the details for the selected certificate (your details will vary depending on what you entered during the certificate creation earlier):

```
Key Name : C=US, S=WA, L=Redmond, O=Microsoft Press, OU=Authors, CN=Simon Guest

Key ID of Certificate selected : zVEz4a8D/vVPjnlOYCSPm1p+O8w=
```

Using this certificate, the client now makes a request to both the .NET (WSE) and Java (GLUE) Web services, signing the requests as appropriate. The .NET (WSE) Web service returns a recommended stock:

```
Calling the WSE Service...
Secure stock recommendation from the WSE Service:
Ticker: ASKI
Name: Alpine Ski
Price: 32.45
Previous: 32.09
Volume: 45
```

The Java (GLUE) Web service returns a similar result:

```
Calling the GLUE Service...
Secure stock recommendation from the GLUE Service:
Ticker: TRRE
Name: Trey Research
Price: 9.35
Previous: 9.48
Volume: 93
```

Running the Java Client

The Java client makes the same authenticated calls to the .NET and Java Web services and works in much the same way. The client, located in the C:\Interoperability\Samples\Advanced\WS-Security\Auth\Java\Client directory, produces the following output after it is built and run:

```
Calling the WSE Service...
Secure stock recommendation from the WSE Service:
Ticker: ASKI
Name: Alpine Ski
Price: 32.45
Previous: 32.09
Volume: 45

Calling the GLUE Service...
Secure stock recommendation from the GLUE Service:
Ticker: TRRE
Name: Trey Research
Price: 9.35
Previous: 9.48
Volume: 93
```

Tracing the Output

So far we have seen how both the .NET and Java client can use WS-Security to make an authenticated call to either a .NET or Java Web service. On the surface, however, this isn't apparent because when simply running the examples, the calls to the two services look like any other calls. With the exception of the calls being prompted for a certificate in the .NET client sample, there is little to indicate that these calls are being authenticated.

To prove that they are, we can check under the covers of the two client calls and observe the request and responses in their native SOAP format. One of the easiest ways to see the underlying call is to enable logging on the Java client. To do this, edit the Client.java file in the C:\Interoperability\Samples\Advanced\WS-Security\Auth\Java\Client directory and uncomment the following line:

```
electric.util.log.Log.startLogging("SOAP");
```

Rebuild and run the Java client. What you should now observe is that the SOAP messages sent to and from the Java client are now logged to the console.

The important element to observe in the call is the binary token itself. This is sent as part of the *<wsse:Security>* SOAP header:

```
<wsse:Security
    xmlns:wsse='http://schemas.xmlsoap.org/ws/2002/07/secext'>
    <wsse:BinarySecurityToken ValueType='wsse:X509v3'
```

```
        EncodingType='wsse:Base64Binary'
        xmlns:wsu='http://schemas.xmlsoap.org/ws/2002/07/utility'
        wsu:Id='electric-id-8575EC20-4536-59E5-2E49-41E5030EC2E6'>
MIICTjCCAbcCBD6uq/owDQYJKoZIhvcNAQEEBQAwbjELMAkGA1UEBhMCVVMxCzAJBgNVB
AgTAldBMRAwDgYDVQQHEwdSZWRtb25kMRgwFgYDVQQKEw9NaWNyb3NvZnQgUHJlc3MxED
AOBgNVBAsTB0F1dGhvcnMxFDASBgNVBAMTC1NpbW9uIEd1ZXN0MB4XDTAzMDQyOTE2NDQ
0MloXDTAzMDcyODE2NDQ0MlowbjELMAkGA1UEBhMCVVMxCzAJBgNVBAgTAldBMRAwDgYD
VQQHEwdSZWRtb25kMRgwFgYDVQQKEw9NaWNyb3NvZnQgUHJlc3MxEDAOBgNVBAsTB0F1d
GhvcnMxFDASBgNVBAMTC1NpbW9uIEd1ZXN0MIGfMA0GCSqGSIb3DQEBAQUAA4GNADCBiQ
KBgQChuZXZYPS+kVPsMc5Nl0x2TLrzede/ANP7KajAGC/lpYwRmaaBlzwQH1qC2wySi2g
taQ9af781FsQjvjFPeTeUBfyDrUG93HLwr3NL/mEXt9YnlYJW6HcqkM1OpG8kgQm+4Bv9
K5PrZF/FI43Hnq02/re983HgGsUcC46P3QVceQIDAQABMA0GCSqGSIb3DQEBBAUAA4GBA
HV4frsL6n5CC3a9X1Wlbp7IgMskFYMuIsGAaPkQd6nGQYoLy+IuHuXdoewi4ujBlstVvH
rnwPTr3gcloNGtw6Pt2wg6M6sFJQte0NfKt5ZCKNyP85ORaIrzaRFDHgeOtmzsdJbQuPU
+7C0ECKBKReEd6ZL0hFEv3aKcMu5imZRR
</wsse:BinarySecurityToken>
```

This is the binary representation of the public portion of the certificate itself (note that your version might differ from this). The actual signature of the Web service request comes slightly after this, in an element named *<SignatureValue>*:

```
<ds:SignatureValue>
YV9N+XtUJ4qRZseqK84KOSbiTotJqjtETXh7XOOadOzUk9Jl+WIPhUCKdTGPrlkdKr8jY
XfXhyrn0CTAKw1Dz46ARJ2OdT/8TriW6yB3uduPPwtRK+LK6ilgKEOMGCC/bzfy33Kxiv
rVDgMq4dVSWnDqivP0ZaILAKe2gZ04weE=
</ds:SignatureValue>
```

This element is a hashed value of the request itself, signed by the private key of the certificate. To compute whether the signature is valid, the service will use the public key to decrypt the hash value of the request, recalculate what should have been the hash value of the request, and compare the two. If they are the same, the signature and contents within are deemed valid.

In the response portion of the SOAP output, notice how the response does not contain any authentication—we could certainly do this by applying the same principles and mechanisms for the Web service itself. Notice also that the data returned back to the client is sent in as clear text:

```
<soap:Body
    soap:encodingStyle='http://schemas.xmlsoap.org/soap/encoding/'
    xmlns:soap='http://schemas.xmlsoap.org/soap/envelope/'>
    <n:GetSecureSaleRecommendationResponse xmlns:n='x'>
        <Result>
            <Ticker>TRRE</Ticker>
            <Name>Trey Research</Name>
            <Price>9.35</Price>
            <Previous>9.48</Previous>
            <Volume>93</Volume>
        </Result>
    </n:GetSecureSaleRecommendationResponse>
</soap:Body>
```

As we've seen in these message outputs, signing the message does not perform any encryption of the message data itself—it just acts as a mechanism to prove the details of the sender, which prevents spoofing. Both the request for data and the response are sent in plain XML. To ensure the privacy of this data, we need to use WS-Security to encrypt the message, a process we'll be looking at in the second half of this chapter.

Proving the Sample

We've seen in the previous section the type of SOAP headers that are created when using WS-Security on the client, but with this authentication example, how do we prove that the Web services cannot be called without the correct authentication mechanism? The easiest way to do this is to edit one of the clients and comment out the code that applies the WS-Security context. If we take the .NET client, for example, we can see how this is performed.

Navigate to the C:\Interoperability\Samples\Advanced\WS-Security\Auth\dotNET\Client directory, and edit the Client.cs file. Comment out the following lines in code:

```
wpReqContext.Security.Tokens.Add(token);
wpReqContext.Security.Elements.Add(new Signature(token));
```

Save the file, rebuild the sample, and rerun. Upon rerunning the sample, you will still get prompted for the X.509 certificate to use to sign the Web service request. Because these certificate details are not being added to the request (which is the result of them being commented out), you will see the following:

```
Calling the WSE Service...

Unhandled Exception: System.Web.Services.Protocols.SoapException: System.Web.Se
rvices.Protocols.SoapException:
The security information supplied was not valid.
    at dotNETAuthWebService.StockService.
        GetSecurePurchaseRecommendation()
    at System.Web.Services.Protocols.SoapHttpClientProtocol.
        ReadResponse(SoapClientMessage message, WebResponse response,
            Stream responseStream, Boolean asyncCall)
    at System.Web.Services.Protocols.SoapHttpClientProtocol.
        Invoke(String methodName, Object[] parameters)
    at WSEWebService.StockService.GetSecurePurchaseRecommendation()
    at Client.Client.Main(String[] args)
```

The preceding request was generated by the Web service itself. The Web service was expecting an authenticated request and instead received one that had not been signed. Logic within the Web service detected this, and the exception was thrown. This result can also be validated against the Java Web service by commenting out the relevant lines in the Java client.

How the Samples Work

The samples contain three key elements: the Web services containing the required configuration to allow WS-Security–style messages, the client files that contain the code for deciding which certificate to use, and the proxy files (which require some modification from their original state).

First, let's take a look at the .NET Web service. This can be found in the C:\Interoperability\Samples\Advanced\WS-Security\Auth\dotNET\WebService directory. The StockService.asmx.cs class file shows the *WebMethod* attribute for *GetSecurePurchaseRecommendation*:

```
[WebMethod]
public Stock GetSecurePurchaseRecommendation()
{
    SoapContext requestContext = HttpSoapContext.RequestContext;
    if (requestContext == null)
        throw new ApplicationException(
            "Only SOAP requests are permitted.");

    if ( !IsValid(requestContext) )
        {
            throw new SoapException(
                "The security information supplied was not valid.",
                new System.Xml.XmlQualifiedName("Bad.Security",
                "http://www.microsoft.com/interoperability/"
                +"dotNETWSSWebService"));
        }

    return Recommendations.Recommendation;
}
```

Notice how the Web method first checks for a valid *SoapContext* (a class from the WSE libraries) before returning the recommendation. Although this is in code within this method, you could also imagine how this could be applied to an *HttpModule* (a class that intercepts incoming HTTP calls) such that it applies to all methods or a group of methods.

The *IsValid* method within the Web service uses the *SoapContext* to check for a valid signature. At this point, we allow any calls to come through that have been signed by a valid X.509 certificate:

```
if (x509token != null)
{
    valid = true;
}
```

The Java Web service works in a slightly different way, but it follows the same principles. Just before the Web service is hosted, a new context is created to hold the WS-Security information. This context can be found in Server.java, located in the C:\Interoperability\Samples\Advanced\WS-Security\Auth\Java\WebService directory.

```
WSSContext wss = new WSSContext();
ProxyContext proxyContext = new ProxyContext();
proxyContext.setWSSContext(wss);
```

The *WSSContext* is configured by adding a new authenticator and signature guard.

```
WSSSignature signatureSpec
    = new WSSSignature(new ElementReference(
        "/soap:Envelope/soap:Body"));
wss.in.addAuthenticator(new X509NullAuthenticator());
wss.in.addGuard(new SignatureGuard(signatureSpec));
```

Notice how for the authenticator, an *X509NullAuthenticator* is used. This usage has an effect similar to the *IsValid* method in the .NET Web service in that this authenticator will allow any valid certificate to pass through. This approach is useful for demonstration purposes, but in production, the *X509Authenticator* class should be used. The *X509Authenticator* class relies on a preconfigured set of certificates that already exists in the key store. If an incoming request is signed by a certificate that is not in the key store, it is ultimately rejected.

Finally, the Web service is registered with the *publish* method.

```
Registry.publish("StockService", new StockService(), proxyContext);
```

This sample code sets up the Web services for both the .NET and Java Web service.

The client code follows a similar path, with additional instructions wrapping the existing calls to the Web services. First, references to the proxy files are created and two *SoapContext* objects are derived from each individual proxy. For the .NET client (Client.cs in the C:\Interoperability\Samples\Advanced\WS-Security\Auth\dotNET\Client directory), the code looks as follows:

```
WSEWebService.StockService wp = new WSEWebService.StockService();
GLUEWebService.StockService gp = new GLUEWebService.StockService();

SoapContext wpReqContext = wp.RequestSoapContext;
SoapContext gpReqContext = gp.RequestSoapContext;
```

As the *RequestSoapContext* method is not normally exposed by a Web service proxy, we'll look shortly at the additional steps to create this in the proxy file.

The next step is to ask the user for a certificate. We do this by using the same function as shown in the WSE 1.0 Quickstart samples (which were included as part of the WSE installation earlier). Given the ID of a certificate, we could have also used the following code instead:

```
X509SecurityToken token = GetSecurityToken("");
if (token == null)
    throw new ApplicationException("No key provided for signature.");
```

The *GetSecurityToken* method displays a small Windows Form that displays the list of certificates available in the Windows key store for the current user. When a certificate is selected, it's returned to the client as an *X509SecurityToken*.

The next step is to add this token to the *Tokens* and *Elements* class within the *Security* component of the *SoapContext* object. Doing this will both add the X.509 certificate details and cause the signature to be created that we observed earlier in the SOAP output. This is done for the call to both the .NET and Java Web services.

```
wpReqContext.Security.Tokens.Add(token);
wpReqContext.Security.Elements.Add(new Signature(token));

gpReqContext.Security.Tokens.Add(token);
gpReqContext.Security.Elements.Add(new Signature(token));
```

Finally, the calls to the two Web services are made—to the .NET Web service to get the recommendation for purchase, and to the Java Web service to get the recommendation for sale.

```
WSEWebService.Stock stock = wp.GetSecurePurchaseRecommendation();
. . .
GLUEWebService.Stock stock2 = gp.GetSecureSaleRecommendation();
```

As these clients are dealing with separate namespaces, we are using the *Stock* type from each (although technically, they relate to the same type).

Not surprisingly, the Java client works in a similar fashion, but it uses the appropriate calls from the GLUE libraries. The client (Client.java, which can be found in the C:\Interoperability\Samples\Advanced\WS-Security\Auth\Java\Client directory) starts by defining the URLs for both the .NET and Java Web services.

```
String wseURL
    = "http://localhost/dotNETWSSWebService/StockService.asmx?WSDL";
String glueURL
    = "http://localhost:8004/JavaWSSWebService/StockService.wsdl";
```

In previous examples, we have used a helper class to bind to the Web service. In this client, however, we need to create a context that holds the WS-Security information. As this context is not supported by any helper methods, we'll perform the binding in the client itself. In a production system, you could imagine how we could also use the agent-service pattern that was first shown in Chapter 6 to abstract these types of calls to a different class.

After the context has been created, the certificate used to sign the requests is loaded from the key store. Unlike with the .NET client, we have chosen to hard-code the location of the key store in the client source itself. The aliases and passwords used in this code to access the key store should equate to the ones used when the store was created.

```
ProxyContext proxyContext = new ProxyContext();

KeyStore keyStore = loadKeyStore("..\\..\\..\\Certs\\keystore.db",
    "StrongPassword");
PrivateKey privateKey = (PrivateKey) keyStore.getKey("JavaClient",
    "StrongPassword".toCharArray());
X509Certificate cert
    = (X509Certificate) keyStore.getCertificate("JavaClient");
```

After the certificate has been loaded, the signature is created and added to the *ProxyContext*.

```
WSSContext wss = new WSSContext();
proxyContext.setWSSContext(wss);

WSSSignature signatureSpec = new WSSSignature(
    new ElementReference("soap:Envelope/soap:Body"));
signatureSpec.setCertificate(cert);
signatureSpec.setPrivateKey(privateKey);
wss.out.addSignature(signatureSpec);
```

Notice how in this code the *setCertificate* and *addSignature* methods correspond with *Tokens.Add* and *Elements.Add* in the .NET sample.

Finally, the binding for each Web service is created, and the relevant stock-recommendation call is made.

```
WSEWebService.IStockServiceSoap wseService
    = (WSEWebService.IStockServiceSoap)Registry.bind(wseURL,
        WSEWebService.IStockServiceSoap.class,proxyContext);

GLUEWebService.IStockService glueService
    = (GLUEWebService.IStockService)Registry.bind(glueURL,
        GLUEWebService.IStockService.class,proxyContext);

WSEWebService.Stock stock
    = wseService.GetSecurePurchaseRecommendation();
GLUEWebService.Stock stock2
    = glueService.GetSecureSaleRecommendation();
```

The final piece for linking the client and Web service is the proxy file for each. Although the sample contains a proxy file that has been pregenerated, it's worth going through the steps required to create a proxy file to enable this authentication.

The proxy files for the .NET client can be found in the C:\Interoperability\Samples\Advanced\WS-Security\Auth\dotNET\Client directory. The two files are named WSEWebService.cs and GLUEWebService.cs. Both were generated with the WSDL.EXE tool that was used extensively throughout Chapter 6, but two slight modifications were made.

If you open one of these files, you'll notice that the *StockService* class inherits from *WebServicesClientProtocol* instead of *System.Web.Services.Protocols.SoapHttpClientProtocol.*

```
public class StockService : WebServicesClientProtocol
```

The *WebServicesClientProtocol* is actually part of the WSE libraries, and as a result, our second modification requires the library to be referenced within the class itself.

```
using Microsoft.Web.Services;
```

This inheritance allows the client to make the call to the *RequestSoapContext* method to add the X.509 token and sign the request. These modifications are required to use the WSE, and they can be made either by hand or with the WSE Settings Tool for Visual Studio .NET, which was mentioned earlier in this chapter.

For the Java client (Client.java in C:\Interoperability\Samples\Advanced\WS-Security\Auth\Java\Client), the proxy files for the two Web services are located in two subdirectories: GLUEWebService and WSEWebService. As the wsdl2java tool produces more than one file for each, this is a cleaner solution than having only one subdirectory. Although the proxy files do not need to be altered, the MAP files that are generated need to be placed in the same directory as the calling client. To enable this, the MAP files from the generated wsdl2java output were renamed to WSEWebService.map and GLUEWebService.map, respectively, and placed in the same directory as the client source. These MAP files differentiate among the *Stock* types exposed by each of the services.

Other Methods of Authentication

In this sample, we've seen how X.509 certificates were chosen to demonstrate authentication between the .NET and Java clients and Web services. Although the process is not shown in the sample code, in addition to authenticating with an X.509 certificate, both Microsoft WSE 1.0 and GLUE 4.0.1 support authentication with a Username/Password token or a binary security token. For more information, consult the product documentation for each.

Thinking About Authorization

This authentication sample using WS-Security has shown how either a .NET or Java Web service can be created to allow only authenticated requests from clients—requests that in this instance were signed with an X.509 certificate. What the example doesn't show is any authorization of the request once it has been accepted.

In a production solution, you would likely encounter a need to restrict both incoming requests that are not signed and incoming requests that are signed by a certificate that is not recognized. Performing this level of authorization will require additional work by both the .NET and Java Web services.

For the .NET Web service, achieving this level of authorization might involve expanding the *IsValid* method so that it checks the details of the certificate, or it might involve matching up the public parts of the certificate to a certificate stored in an Active Directory. For the Java Web service, this might involve restricting the certificates to the ones stored in the key store (by using the *X509Authenticator* class) or by using something more customized, where parts of the certificate are matched against a Java Authentication and Authorization Service (JAAS) realm.

Encryption Using WS-Security

We have now seen how WS-Security can be used to provide authentication between clients and Web services in both .NET and Java. While authentication enables the Web service to restrict access based on credentials, both the request and the response are sent in clear text. By examining the trace output of a message, anyone can see the data being passed.

A second area of the WS-Security specification allows both the request and the response to be encrypted. This encryption can be either based on a certificate (a public and private key mechanism) or use a symmetric key (a key that both the client and the Web service agree on).

In the sample code in the second half of this chapter, we'll assume the client wants to pass a credit card number to the recommendations stock service. While authentication allows the service to accept or deny the request by verifying the integrity of the data, encryption is required to ensure the privacy of the data that will be passed. To enable the sample to work, the method that's used for returning recommendations will accept a parameter of type *String*, which will be used for the credit card details.

Configuring the .NET Web Service

As with the authentication example, to show the samples in action we need to create a virtual directory to host the .NET Web service. The sample code used for the Web service can be found in the C:\Interoperability\Samples\Advanced\WS-Security\Enc\dotNET\WebService directory. Use the accompanying nant script to build the sample code in this directory.

To create the virtual directory using IIS, right-click the Default Web Site icon within the administration tool and select New/Virtual Directory. For the alias of the Web service, use **dotNETEncWebService**.

Set the path of the files correctly (**C:\Interoperability\Samples\Advanced\WS-Security\Enc\dotNET\WebService**) in the next stage of the wizard.

Accept the remaining default settings to create the virtual directory. Again, the publishing of the Web service can be validated by browsing to *http://localhost/dotNETEncWebService/StockService.asmx*. The method signature for the *GetSecurePurchaseRecommendation* should now require a *String* to represent a credit card, as shown in Figure 13-9.

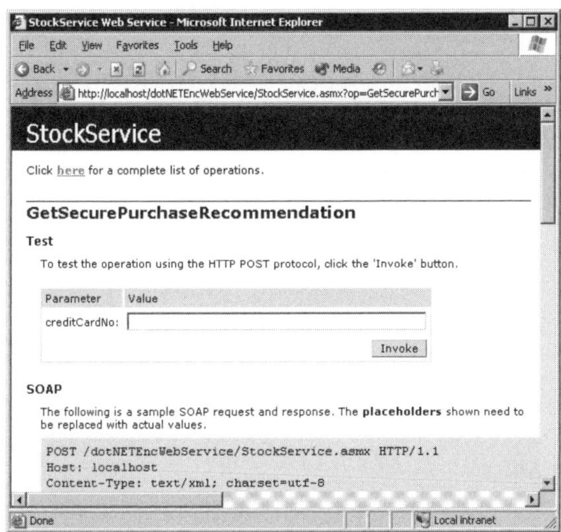

Figure 13-9 Validating the Web service with Internet Explorer.

The configuration of the .NET Web service is now complete.

Configuring the Java Web Service

The sample code for the Java Web service can be found in the C:\Interoperability\Samples\Advanced\WS-Security\Enc\Java\WebService directory. As with the previous authentication sample, build this code by using the supplied Ant script. The run target can be used with the Ant script to publish the Web service on *http://localhost:8004/JavaWSSWebService/StockService.wsdl*.

Both the .NET and Java Web services are published. Before we run the clients, let's first look at how the symmetric key is configured.

The Symmetric Key

You might recall that with the last authentication, sample certificates were created and used by both the .NET and Java clients to sign the Web service request. Although the WS-Security specification allows certificates for encrypting data, at the time of this writing, GLUE 4.0.1 doesn't support this. In this sample, we'll show how a symmetric key can be used instead. With symmetric-key cryptography, the same key is held by both the client and the service and is used to both encrypt and decrypt the data. In a production environment, symmetric keys are often distributed with the client and little additional setup is required. Additionally, the symmetric key can be negotiated at the time of connection. This is often referred to as a *handshake*.

The symmetric key that will be used in this sample is the same as the default key supplied with the Microsoft WSE 1.0 Quickstart samples, and it's currently hard-coded into each of the classes for the client.

> **Tip** When using WS-Security in a production environment, you would of course assign a key different than the one used in the samples here. You can assign a different key by creating a new key using the cryptography APIs in either .NET or Java. In addition, you should always store the symmetric key in a separate file that is loaded at run time by the client—and ideally, this file would be secured using a separate mechanism. These steps will help prevent malicious identity theft and spoofing and allow you to recycle the key without having to recompile any client code.

Running the Java Client

We'll first run the Java client to show the details of the message that is constructed. The sample code for the Java client can be found in the C:\Interoperability\Samples\Advanced\WS-Security\Enc\Java\Client directory. Ensure that both the .NET and Java Web services are running by testing the URLs through Internet Explorer, and build and run the sample client code using the provided Ant script.

If the client code is successfully run, you should see the following output:

```
Calling the WSE Service...
Secure stock recommendation from the WSE Service:
Ticker: ASKI
Name: Alpine Ski
Price: 32.45
Previous: 32.09
Volume: 45

Calling the GLUE Service...
Secure stock recommendation from the GLUE Service:
Ticker: TRRE
Name: Trey Research
Price: 9.35
Previous: 9.48
Volume: 93
```

The client has successfully constructed the Web service request to both the .NET and Java Web services, and both requests contain the encrypted credit card information. If you look at the running Java Web service, you should see that the credit card detail was successfully sent to the method.

```
Credit card details received: 1234 5678 9012 3456 (01/05)
```

Looking back at the Java *Client* class, you'll notice that this number and expiration date are hard-coded for sample purposes.

Again, as with the authentication sample, it's reassuring to check that the underlying communication was in fact secure. To do this, we can enable SOAP logging on the Java client. Open the Client.java file, and locate and uncomment the following line of code:

```
electric.util.log.Log.startLogging("SOAP");
```

Rebuild and rerun the Java client. The console window will now show the SOAP messages that are being sent to and received from the Web service.

Looking at the first message that was sent from the Java client to the .NET Web service, you can see that no credit card number was passed as part of the request. Instead, the SOAP message contains an element named *EncryptedData*.

```
<n3:EncryptedData
    xmlns:ds='http://www.w3.org/2000/09/xmldsig#'
    Id='electric-id-59E66E3D-ED83-8900-135B-F534FF089EAB'>
    <n3:EncryptionMethod
        Algorithm='http://www.w3.org/2001/04/xmlenc#tripledes-cbc'/>
    <ds:KeyInfo>
        <ds:KeyName>WSE Sample Symmetric Key</ds:KeyName>
    </ds:KeyInfo>
    <n3:CipherData>
        <n3:CipherValue>
```

```
AAAAAAAAAAAuIFS4iNzjpxPEihTVtlwbjL1QT5Ur/MdQGPutyfCwZ29YRk2GhpqKKsjsH
7c8j4KXCwa4P6gvIDzCyoOFXAegK9SwBU1FaG2UBW6OxceeUCjj06Y5Alw5IrIBU3phif
BkXTcdsWHzxsZP9138bcpHEpwY1/LhsU1iRG0k2WJ75HsuwZr4a+WJ3a/d2HjB9UMYf4N
ONVzMt5xzhzmvu89QLkSUb0/gNZDwprVTnK10iJ9izn5k8MpvtQX774mx1YYDS+l+WXEh
rMpfj5HHeV4z
        </n3:CipherValue>
    </n3:CipherData>
</n3:EncryptedData>
```

In this message, we can see three key bits of information. First, the *EncryptionMethod* element lists the algorithm that was used to encrypt the data. In this case, a Triple DES with CBC (Ciphertext Block Chaining) was used. The second element of interest is *KeyName*. This is a *String* field that is used to indicate to the Web service which key was used to encrypt the data. This allows both the client and Web service to distinguish between any number of keys shared between them. Finally, the *CipherValue* element contains the encrypted data itself.

When we look at the reply from the .NET Web service, we can see that the returned stock recommendation was not encrypted.

```
<GetSecurePurchaseRecommendationResult>
    <Ticker xmlns=
    'http://www.microsoft.com/interoperability/dotNETEncWebService'>
        ASKI</Ticker>
    <Name xmlns=
    'http://www.microsoft.com/interoperability/dotNETEncWebService'>
        Alpine Ski</Name>
    <Price xmlns=
    'http://www.microsoft.com/interoperability/dotNETEncWebService'>
        32.45</Price>
    <Previous xmlns=
    'http://www.microsoft.com/interoperability/dotNETEncWebService'>
        32.09</Previous>
    <Volume xmlns=
    'http://www.microsoft.com/interoperability/dotNETEncWebService'>
        45</Volume>
<GetSecurePurchaseRecommendationResult>
```

The preceding code shows us that the sample code encrypts the credit card details from the client to the Web service, but the response is sent in clear text. In the real world, you might be required to encrypt the data sent back to the client also. (Given that the information was paid for by a credit card, I would hope that it is worth encrypting!)

Encryption can certainly be applied to the response as well as to the request. The key observation here is that just because the request is encrypted it doesn't automatically mean the response is, too. This way of thinking is slightly different than in the HTTPS/SSL world, where once the secure link is established, both requests and responses are encrypted for the duration of the session.

Running the .NET Client

Before we look at how each client works, run the .NET client, the sample code for which can be found in the C:\Interoperability\Samples\Advanced\WS-Security\Enc\dotNET\Client directory. Use the accompanying NAnt script to build and run the sample code. You should see a result similar to that seen with the Java client.

How the Samples Work

First, each Web service must implement WS-Security. For the .NET Web service, this implementation is configured through the web.config file, which can be found in the directory of the Web service itself. Within the security elements of the web.config file is an entry that specifies the decryption provider:

```
<decryptionKeyProvider
    type="dotNETEncWebService.DecryptionKeyProvider,
          dotNETEncWebService"/>
```

As we can see, the provider refers to a class within the Web service itself. This class can be found in the StockService.asmx.cs file, and it overrides the *DecryptionKeyProvider* class method that specifies the key that will be used. As mentioned previously, this key is hard-coded in this class.

The Web method itself, *GetSecurePurchaseRecommendation*, does not need to make any calls to verify or decrypt the data. Verification is automatically handled by the WSE *HttpHandler* class.

```
[WebMethod]
public Stock GetSecurePurchaseRecommendation(String creditCardNo)
{
    SoapContext requestContext = HttpSoapContext.RequestContext;
    if (requestContext == null)
        throw new ApplicationException(
            "Only SOAP requests are permitted.");

    if (requestContext.Security.Elements.Count == 0)
        throw new ApplicationException(
            "No security information sent with request.");

    return Recommendations.Recommendation;
}
```

Two checks, however, are made within this method to ensure that only SOAP requests are allowed and that some security elements were supplied with the call. These checks allow the sample to reject calls made by clients who have not encrypted the data in the request.

For the Java Web service, the WS-Security properties are configured in the Server.java class. As with the previous Java examples, you can move these settings into a configuration file. Within the *Server* class, the configuration is performed in three stages. First, a new *BasicRealm* is created, with a principal that includes an account with the username and password that match the symmetric-key settings.

```
BasicRealm realm = new BasicRealm("test");
String userName = "WSE Sample Symmetric Key";
String password = "EE/uaFF5N3ZNJWUTR8DYe+0EbwaKQnso";
realm.addPrincipal(userName,password);
```

You can find additional information on realms in the "Web Services Authentication and Authorization" section in Chapter 6. Next, a WS-Security–specific context is created. This context will be used to set the encryption properties for the hosted Web service.

```
WSSContext wss = new WSSContext();
ServiceContext serviceContext = new ServiceContext();
serviceContext.setWSSContext(wss);
```

Finally, a new class of type *WSSEncryption* is created and configured with the symmetric-key settings. A guard is used to set up the WS-Security context and prevent nonencrypted requests from calling the Web service. In GLUE, a guard performs a role similar to that of a filter (in the Java Servlet API) or *HttpModule* (in .NET). The *EncryptionGuard* method intercepts the message before it reaches the Web service method. If the request is not encrypted based on a preconfigured set of parameters, it is rejected.

```
WSSEncryption encryptionSpec = new WSSEncryption();
ElementReference reference
    = new ElementReference("soap:Envelope/soap:Body/*");
encryptionSpec.setReference(reference);
encryptionSpec.setRealm(realm);
wss.in.addGuard(new EncryptionGuard(encryptionSpec));
```

The .NET and Java clients work in a way similar to the authentication examples shown in the first section. For the .NET client, the proxy file to the Web service is created and adjusted to include the WSE 1.0 references. After the SOAP context has been derived from the proxy, the symmetric key is added as a new security element to the call.

```
SoapContext wpReqContext = wp.RequestSoapContext;
SoapContext gpReqContext = gp.RequestSoapContext;

wpReqContext.Security.Elements.Add(new EncryptedData(key));
gpReqContext.Security.Elements.Add(new EncryptedData(key));
```

This key is obtained from *GetEncryptionKey* method in the client code. The data for the key is in the code for this sample and is used with the *SymmetricEncryptionKey* class to generate the symmetric key.

```
SymmetricEncryptionKey key
    = new SymmetricEncryptionKey(TripleDES.Create(), keyBytes);
```

The fictitious credit card number is then created and passed to the *GetSecurePurchaseRecommendation* method.

```
WSEWebService.Stock stock
    = wp.GetSecurePurchaseRecommendation(creditCardNo);
```

This method is used for both the .NET and Java Web services.

For the Java client, a similar approach is taken. A new *WSSContext* (WS-Security Context) is created for the call. The symmetric key is then added to the context with the following code:

```
byte[] secretKeyBytes = Base64.fromBase64(symmetricKey);
encryptionSpec.setSecretKeyBytes(secretKeyBytes);
wss.out.addEncryption(encryptionSpec);
```

After the Web service is bound, the client calls both the .NET and Java Web services.

```
WSEWebService.Stock stock
    = wseService.GetSecurePurchaseRecommendation(creditCardNo);

GLUEWebService.Stock stock2
    = gp.GetSecureSaleRecommendation(creditCardNo);
```

For both clients, the recommendation returned by each of the Web services is displayed to the console.

Summary

In this chapter, we have seen how WS-Security can be used in both .NET and Java to securely access Web services on either platform. In terms of interoperability, we've seen how a .NET client can sign and encrypt a request to a Java Web service—and vice versa—allowing a common method of Web services security regardless of the platform.

WS-Security is one of the most compelling specifications to be written. For the first time, the requirement for the transport to be responsible for the security of a message between a client and service has been removed. This change is highly significant because it allows the transport to be changed or replaced at any time without compromising the security of the overall system. I believe this will be one of the most widely adopted WS-* specifications.

This concludes our chapter on WS-Security. We'll continue looking at advanced interoperability with Web services in the next chapter by investigating how binary attachments can be exchanged between clients in both .NET and Java.

14

Web Services Interoperability, Part 2: Sending Binary Data

Up to this point in the book, the discussions and samples of interoperability using XML Web services have shown request/response style method calls. In our previous samples, we've seen clients in both .NET and Java ask for recommendations to buy and sell stocks and then for the Web service to reply with an appropriate value. These examples are fine for demonstrating data returning from a method, but sometimes an application has a requirement to send or receive binary data . Examples of binary data that an application might need to send or receive are a file (possibly even an executable file) from a Web site, an attachment to an e-mail (such as a document or file), and a collection of images (such as a photo album or collection of JPEG files). We need to provide a way for .NET and J2EE applications to use Web services to exchange these types of information. More importantly, we need to accomplish this in a platform-independent manner so that a Java client can receive a binary attachment from a .NET Web service, and vice versa.

In this chapter, we will explore the concepts of exchanging binary data using a Web service. We'll start by looking at a specification known as DIME (Direct Internet Message Encapsulation), and then examine how DIME can be implemented by using both Microsoft WSE (Web Services Enhancements) 1.0 Service Pack 1 and GLUE 4.0.1 (a product of The Mind Electric). The sample will show how to pass a document created in Microsoft Word between a Java

Web services client, a .NET Web service, and a .NET Web services client. After looking at this implementation, we'll briefly discuss other proposed specifications and ideas about where the industry is heading.

DIME and WS-Attachments

Direct Internet Message Encapsulation, as its name suggests, is a specification that covers a message format for sending binary data over the Internet. A link to the latest draft of the specification and additional information can be found at the following address: *http://msdn.microsoft.com/webservices/understanding/specs/default.aspx?pull=/library/en-us/dnglobspec/html/dimeindex.asp*.

A DIME message can be used to deliver a binary payload, as defined by the sending application. The DIME message can be contained in one or more records; each record has a payload length value that specifies the number of bytes in the payload. The type of the payload can also be defined (for example, a media type). Chunking allows the payload to be split, and an ID associated with a record allows it to be cross-referenced within the message.

So, given that it's been possible to send binary attachments over the Internet for years, why is DIME used for sending attachments via Web services instead of other formats? If you have worked with e-mail programs, you might have heard of the term MIME, which stands for Multipurpose Internet Message Encapsulation. This is the format used when sending attachments and documents with an e-mail message. An earlier specification of how attachments could be sent via Web services and SOAP, named SOAP messages with Attachments (SwA), was actually based on a SOAP message that used MIME to bind an attachment. This specification was coauthored by Microsoft and Hewlett Packard in December 2000.

The Microsoft DIME specification offers advantages over SwA in two major areas: enhanced performance and interoperability. DIME is more lightweight than MIME and doesn't require any encoding of the binary data. This in turn makes parsing quicker and memory allocation generally more efficient. DIME also has a simpler syntax than MIME—which makes it less flexible than MIME, but leads to better interoperability between parsers. For additional information on DIME vs. MIME, I recommend the following MSDN article: *http://msdn.microsoft.com/library/default.asp?url=/library/en-us/dnservice/html/service01152002.asp*.

DIME defines a mechanism by which arbitrary data can be delivered in a collection of formatted records, but to send this type of data over a Web service requires a link between the DIME data and the Web service itself. This link is provided by the WS-Attachments specification.

WS-Attachments defines a primary SOAP message part and secondary parts. As the previous MSDN article implies, you can think of this as a stack of paper attachments bound with a paper clip, with a memo on top. The memo, which equates to the primary SOAP message, contains the list of other attachments (secondary parts) in the stack of paper.

WS-Attachments indicates that the primary SOAP message part must be contained in the first record of an associated DIME payload. The primary SOAP message part is able to reference its secondary parts by using an *href* attribute. As with HTML, the *href* attribute can be used to reference an external URL. By using WS-Attachments this can also be the ID of a secondary part.

So, where does this leave us? The .NET and Java interoperability samples you'll see in this chapter use the DIME specification to pass an attachment between a .NET and Java client. As we look at future specifications toward the end of the chapter, you should be able to see how the specification can be used today and what could be in store for future applications.

Samples

As discussed in the introduction, the samples we are going to show will demonstrate a Java client taking a document created in Microsoft Word and sending it to a .NET-based Web service. When the Web service receives this document, it will be stored in a directory named Files. We'll then show how a .NET client can make a call to the Web service to request the document. This document flow is shown in Figure 14-1.

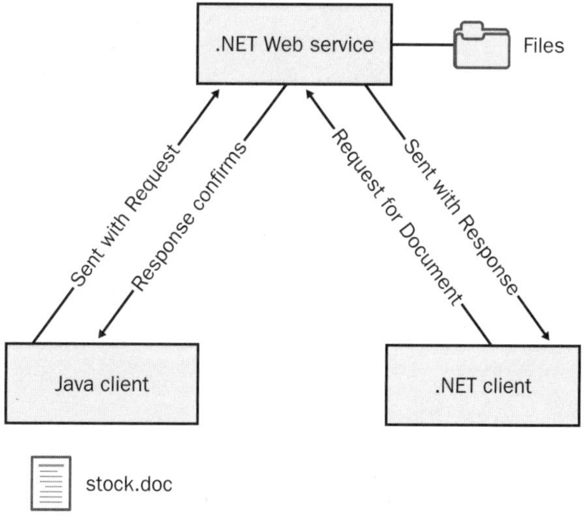

Figure 14-1 How the sample code is used to send attachments from a Java client to .NET.

All the attachment-related calls using .NET will be made with Microsoft WSE (Web Services Enhancements) 1.0. All the equivalent calls in Java will be performed using GLUE 4.0.1.

Downloading and Installing Microsoft WSE

This sample assumes that Microsoft WSE (Web Services Enhancements) 1.0 Service Pack 1 has been installed. This software package, available from *http://msdn.microsoft.com/webservices*, must be installed for the .NET client to compile correctly. Additional information about downloading and installing the product can be found in the "Downloading and Installing Microsoft WSE" section of Chapter 13, "Web Services Interoperability, Part 1: Security."

Setting Up the Document Web Service

The first task in showing the sample is to create the Web service itself. This Web service, based on .NET, will offer two methods:

```
String AddDocument(String documentName)
String GetDocument(String documentName)
```

The *AddDocument* method is used to send a binary attachment from a client to the Web service. The Web service will nominate a directory for storing the attachment. The *GetDocument* method works in reverse and returns an attachment to the client. Each method accepts a *String* that contains the filename of the document and returns a *String* to indicate whether the request was successful.

The sample code for the Web service can be found in the C:\Interoperability\Samples\Advanced\Attachments\dotNET\WebService directory. This sample code needs to be compiled using the supplied NAnt script, and a virtual directory needs to be created to host this .NET Web service.

To create the virtual directory, launch Internet Information Services (IIS) Manager from Start/Program Files/Administrative Tools. Within the IIS Manager, navigate through the Local Computer entry to find the Default Web Site. Right-click the Default Web Site entry, and select New/Virtual Directory. Within this wizard, set the alias of the directory to **dotNETDocService**, as shown in Figure 14-2.

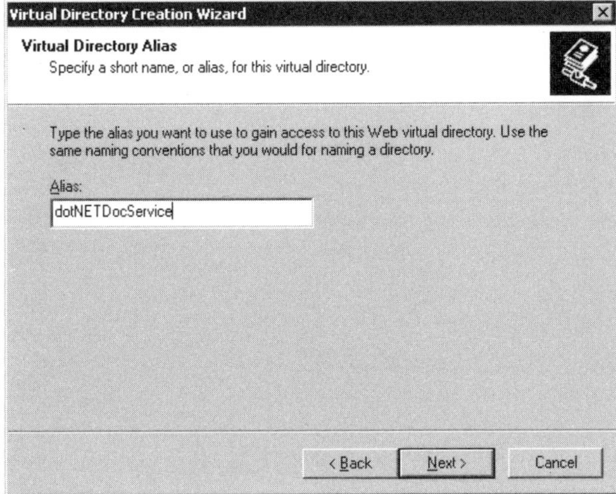

Figure 14-2 Creating the virtual directory required for the .NET Web service.

For the path, enter the location of the Web service, **C:\Interoperability\Samples\Advanced\Attachments\dotNET\WebService**, as shown in Figure 14-3.

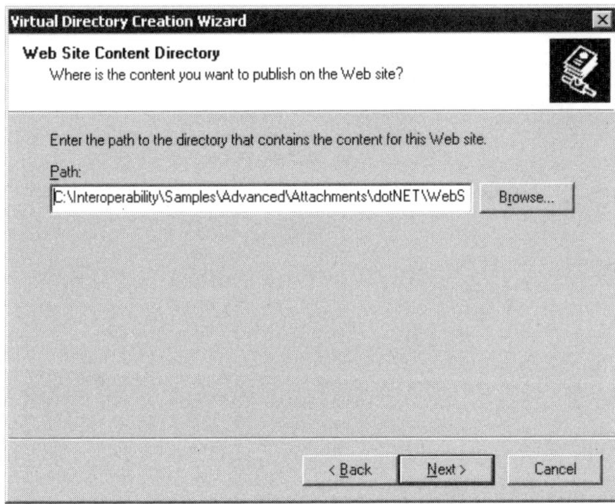

Figure 14-3 Specifying the directory for the .NET Web service.

Finish running the wizard to complete the setup of the virtual directory. When the Web service receives a request to add an attachment, the attachment will be automatically stored in the C:\Interoperability\Samples\Advanced\Attachments\Files directory. You should ensure that the account the Web service is running under (by default, ASPNET) has access to this directory. This check can be made by using Windows Explorer. Before you run the Java client, observe how the Files directory is empty.

Running the Java Client

In the sample, the Java client sends a Microsoft Word document to the Web service. This document is named *stock.doc*, and it can be found in the same directory as the Java client code, C:\Interoperability\Samples\Advanced\Attachments\Java\Client. If you have Microsoft Word installed, open the file now. If you do not have Microsoft Word installed, this file can also be opened using WordPad.

As shown in Figure 14-4, the Word document is simply a sample certificate of ownership—based on the stock trading samples we've been using throughout the book. This sample document can be used to demonstrate a scenario where certificates were generated using a J2EE application, forwarded to a .NET Web service, and then retrieved by a .NET client (which of course, with a .NET Add-In for Microsoft Office, could be Word itself).

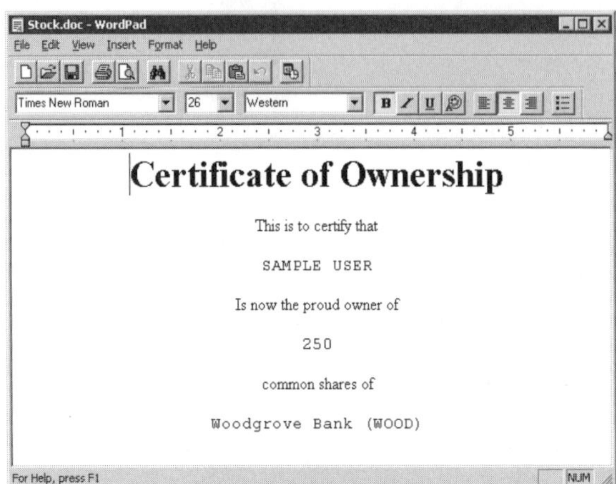

Figure 14-4 The Microsoft Word document that will be exchanged.

To show the client, navigate to the C:\Interoperability\Samples\Advanced\Attachments\Java\Client directory, and build and run the sample code using Ant with the run target. After the Word document has been sent to the Web service, the following message will be displayed:

```
Message from Web Service: stock.doc accepted.
```

The Web service has taken the file sent by the Java client and stored it in the Files directory (C:\Interoperability\Samples\Advanced\Attachments\Files). You can confirm this by using Windows Explorer to navigate to this location and reopening the file. The file doesn't get deleted from the Java client directory—this is like sending an attachment via e-mail.

The sending of this attachment was made possible by a number of underlying GLUE APIs that were used by the Java client. Examining the Client.java file in the Client subdirectory shows how this works.

First, the Word document is read into a *RandomAccessFile* by the client. This literally turns the file into a stream of UTF8-encoded bytes, which is required for forwarding it with the Web service call.

```
RandomAccessFile raf
    = new RandomAccessFile(FILE_PATH+"\\"+"stock.doc","r");

if( raf.length() > Integer.MAX_VALUE )
    throw new IOException("File too big to send");

byte[] buffer = new byte[(int)raf.length()];
raf.read(buffer);
```

Notice how this read is limited by the size of the buffer, defined by *Integer.MAX_VALUE*. (For a 16-bit integer, this is 64k.) This implicit buffer size currently limits the size of the files that can be sent, which is something that we will discuss after the sample code.

```
Context threadContext = Context.thread();
MIMEData attachment = new MIMEData(buffer,"application/msword");
threadContext.setProperty("unreferencedAttachments",attachment);
```

After we have the buffer containing the *byte* representation of the document, we use GLUE to build a new context and we use the *MIMEData* class to put the document into an *attachment* object. This *attachment* is set as a property of the client context.

> **Note** The class in GLUE to load the attachment is named *MIMEData* (instead of *DIMEData*, which you might have been expecting). This class has been named this way to allow backward compatibility. A setting in the GLUE global config.xml file can be switched to configure this class for either MIME or DIME. By default, and for our example, the *MIMEData* class is building a DIME attachment.

Finally, the Web service is bound, and a call to the *AddDocument* class is made.

```
String url
    = "http://localhost/dotNETDocService/DocumentService.asmx?WSDL";
IDocumentServiceSoap service
    = (IDocumentServiceSoap)Registry.bind(url,
        IDocumentServiceSoap.class);

String result = service.AddDocument("stock.doc");
```

The filename of the document is passed as a parameter of the method call. This parameter instructs the Web service what the name of the file should be when it is saved. The Web service itself will return a *String* indicating if the file was accepted.

Before we look at retrieving the Word document by using a .NET client, let's take a quick look at the *AddDocument* method itself. This method can be found in the DocumentService.asmx.cs, located in the C:\Interoperability\Samples\Advanced\Attachments\dotNET\WebService directory.

```
if (HttpSoapContext.RequestContext == null)
    throw new
        ApplicationException("Only SOAP requests are permitted.");

if (HttpSoapContext.RequestContext.Attachments.Count != 1)
{
    throw new
        ApplicationException("1 attachment required for this method."
        +HttpSoapContext.RequestContext.Attachments.Count
        +" were sent");
}
```

The first check for this method ensures that it is a true SOAP request (attachments cannot be forwarded using any other method), and that only one attachment is forwarded as part of the request. You'll notice that the WSE 1.0 class defines an array of attachments as part of the *HttpSoapContext* class.

After these items have been validated, a process is used that is the opposite of how the client attached the document. First the attachment is converted into a stream of bytes using the *BinaryReader* from the *System.IO* namespace.

```
BinaryReader br =
    new BinaryReader(HttpSoapContext.RequestContext.Attachments[0].Stream);
byte[] buffer = br.ReadBytes(Int32.Parse(
    br.BaseStream.Length.ToString()));
br.Close();
```

Once the attachment has been converted to a stream of bytes, a *FileStream* is used to write the file to disk.

```
System.IO.FileStream output
    = System.IO.File.Create(FILE_PATH+@"\"+documentName);
output.Write(buffer,0,buffer.Length);
output.Close();
```

Assuming this is successful, the return message is sent back to the client indicating that the file has been accepted.

Running the .NET Client

We've now seen how the Java client makes a request to the .NET Web service and how it attaches the Word document as an attachment to the call. Using similar methods, the Web service is able to convert the attachment back from a binary stream and write the file to disk.

The final piece of the sample is to show how a client in .NET can use the WSE libraries to make a call to the Web service and request the attachment. The sample code to show this can be found in the C:\Interoperability\Samples\Advanced\Attachments\dotNET\Client directory. Use the NAnt script to build and run the code in this directory. When run, the client will display the following:

```
Message from Web Service: Document Attached
File saved.
```

The first message is the *String* response, sent from the Web service when the *GetDocument* method was called. This message indicates the document was attached to the response. After the document is extracted and saved to disk, the client reports that the file is now saved. If you look in the Client directory, you should now be able to confirm this by observing that a stock.doc file has been created. The contents of this file can again be validated by opening the document in Microsoft Word.

This operation works in much the same way that the file upload task did. If we look at the Client.cs class, the first task the client performs is to call the *GetDocument* method of the .NET Web service.

```
DocumentService ds = new DocumentService();
Console.WriteLine("Message from Web Service: "
    +ds.GetDocument("stock.doc"));
```

This method (which can be viewed by again opening the DocumentService.asmx.cs class in the WebService subdirectory) starts by first checking that this is a SOAP request, and then it creates a reference to the existing response context.

```
if (HttpSoapContext.RequestContext == null)
    throw new
        ApplicationException("Only SOAP requests are permitted.");

SoapContext responseContext = HttpSoapContext.ResponseContext;
```

After this is done, the attachment is appended to the context by using the *DimeAttachment* class from the *Microsoft.Web.Services* namespace.

```
try
{
    DimeAttachment attachment
        = new DimeAttachment("application/msword",
        TypeFormatEnum.MediaType, FILE_PATH+@"\"+documentName);
    responseContext.Attachments.Add(attachment);
}
catch (System.IO.FileNotFoundException)
{
    throw new ApplicationException(documentName
        +" does not exist on the server.");
}
```

Notice how using the *DimeAttachment* class doesn't require the document to be converted into a stream of bytes, although this can still be done by using an overloaded constructor. If the file is not found (based on the file name that was passed to the method), an *ApplicationException* is raised. This exception will be received by the client as a *SoapFault*.

With the attachment complete, the Web service now returns the completion string.

```
return "Document Attached";
```

Getting back to the client, after the Web service call is made, the file is extracted from the context into a *byte* array by using the *BinaryReader* and the file is then saved to disk. This is exactly the same operation used by the Web service to add the document sent by the Java client.

```
BinaryReader br = new BinaryReader(
    ds.ResponseSoapContext.Attachments[0].Stream);
byte[] buffer
    = br.ReadBytes(Int32.Parse(br.BaseStream.Length.ToString()));
br.Close();

System.IO.FileStream output =
    System.IO.File.Create(FILE_PATH+@"\"+"stock.doc");
output.Write(buffer,0,buffer.Length);
output.Close();

Console.WriteLine("File saved.");
```

Finally, the client displays that the file is saved.

Two-Way File Operations

In this sample, we've seen how a Java client sends an attachment with a Web service request, and how a .NET client receives an attachment by making a corresponding request to the service. There is of course nothing to stop each client from both sending and receiving attachments to the Web service. For the .NET client, this can be achieved by using the *DimeAttachment* class, but in this case it will be used on the client. For the Java client, the Web service is bound and then the attachment is added to the context just before the actual method is called.

Extending the clients in this way offers a number of possibilities for using attachments in conjunction with Web services. For example, an extension of this sample could be to create a File Manager Web service, which could have the ability to upload, download, list, and display the properties of files via a Web service. Using the techniques in this chapter, the client for this Web service could be .NET, Java, or anything else that supports the DIME specification.

Looking Ahead—PASWA

To understand the degree to which technology for handling attachments is still a work in progress, we can look at other emerging specifications to see how the industry could evolve. DIME certainly doesn't come without problems—including the routing and security of DIME-based messages, both of which are difficult to handle within the existing specification.

One of the most recent specifications at the time of this writing is PASWA (Proposed Addendum to SOAP With Attachments). This specification, which is based on the original SOAP With Attachments specification, is coauthored by AT&T, BEA, Canon, Microsoft, SAP, and Tibco. Draft v0.61 of the specification can be found at: *http://www.gotdotnet.com/team/jeffsch/paswa/paswa61.html.* In short, this specification uses MIME and a superset of the original SwA headers to allow messages to be properly secured and handled by intermediaries, to ensure backwards compatibility with SwA/1.0 messages (which are in use today), and to provide an alternate message syntax for SOAP processors that do not understand the specification.

Summary

In this chapter, we've presented a high-level introduction to the DIME specification, including information on how it evolved and how it can be used to enable interoperability between .NET and Java—allowing binary attachments to be sent between the two. As we've seen in the previous sections, this technology is still evolving, and I expect a number of significant new specifications and changes based on the work currently underway. The samples shown in this chapter show some existing possibilities for sending and receiving attachments in a way that is agnostic—that is, in a way not dependent on the underlying platform or technology.

This concludes the topic of sending binary attachments via a Web service. In the next chapter, we'll be looking at the third area of advanced interoperability with Web services—how to perform routing with a mix of clients and Web services based on both .NET and Java.

15

Web Services Interoperability, Part 3: Routing

Routing, as a general concept, can be seen in many networks, applications, and services. For networks, routers are used to ensure that packets of data are correctly sent from one destination to another. Many routers are now considered "intelligent" because they will choose routes based on availability of systems and existing traffic. With regard to applications, e-mail is currently the most widely used routed application. If you have ever examined the path of an SMTP message, you might have had the opportunity to appreciate the complexity of the path.

Compared to routing for network devices and e-mail, routing for Web services is a new concept that has many of the same benefits—especially in a production environment. For example, if an organization wants to deploy multiple production Web services, they might have to consider how to load-balance the incoming requests. These days, load balancing can be performed with a network load balancer, but imagine a requirement where the route to the Web service was determined based on the content of the message. An organization might want to build a solution that exposes a single Web service that intercepts each message and then decides the route of the required Web service based on the content.

Throughout the book so far, Web services have been aligned with point-to-point interoperability, a term that was covered in Chapter 2, "Business Requirements for Interoperability." In this chapter, we'll look at how Web services can be expanded to include this routing capability. To do this, we'll cover a specification named WS-Routing and show a number of samples that are based on this specification and that use the .NET Framework and Java. We'll then discuss how this area is still evolving by looking at the shaping and reshaping of new specifications in this area.

WS-Routing

Similar to specifications we've looked at in the previous two chapters, WS-Routing is one of the more recent Web services specifications. In its simplest form, WS-Routing is designed to provide a stateless, SOAP-based protocol for routing messages asynchronously using a number of transports. The specification is written so that it is transport agnostic—meaning that WS-Routing can apply to SOAP messages sent via TCP, UDP, HTTP, or even SMTP.

The specification, which can be found at *http://msdn.microsoft.com/webservices/understanding/gxa/default.aspx?pull=/library/en-us/dnglobspec/html/ws-routing.asp*, was authored by Microsoft in October 2001 but was first published in May 2001 as SOAP-RP.

The specification states that the entire route (path) for a message as well as the reverse path (that is, the route the reply will need to take) can be described within the SOAP Header portion of a message. This path contains the Uniform Resource Identifiers (URIs) of the intermediaries that the message must follow to reach its destination. As an example, the following listing shows a route or path within a SOAP message:

```
<SOAP-ENV:Header>
    <wsrp:path xmlns:wsrp="http://schemas.xmlsoap.org/rp/">
        <wsrp:action>http://www.my.org/action</wsrp:action>
        <wsrp:to>http://www.my.org/d</wsrp:to>
        <wsrp:fwd>
            <wsrp:via>http://www.my.org/b</wsrp:via>
            <wsrp:via>http://www.my.org/c</wsrp:via>
        </wsrp:fwd>
        <wsrp:from>http://www.my.org/a</wsrp:from>
        <wsrp:id>uuid:A15E4356-36F1-4c49-9AB9-2E9A1AE346AF</wsrp:id>
    </wsrp:path>
</SOAP-ENV:Header>
```

The route is shown using the *<wsrp:to>*, *<wsrp:fwd>*, and *<wsrp:from>* details. These details indicate the final destination of the message (*http://www.my.org/d*), the route it should take (*http://www.my.org/b* to *http://www.my.org/c*), and the originator (*http://www.my.org/a*), respectively. The message also has an action. This is the SOAP action to perform once the destination is reached—in most cases, this will be the method that should be called.

This message will be passed through a series of intermediaries (also known as routers) as shown in Figure 15-1. The intermediaries will interrogate the path, make changes as applicable, and forward the message to the next destination. For example, using the message just shown, intermediary B might perform some action based on the message, as well as change the route to confirm that the next destination is C. The intermediaries also have the ability to change the action of the message, perhaps to specify an additional intermediary or to change the path completely.

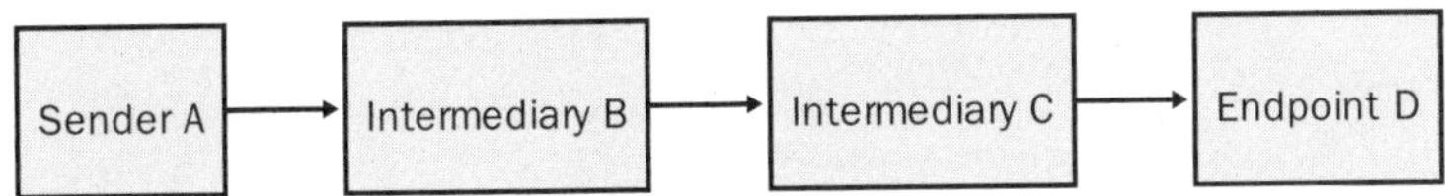

Figure 15-1 Message flow using sender, intermediaries, and an endpoint.

As all the messages are based on SOAP, which is platform independent, this example lends itself to being a great interoperability story. In theory, sender A could be based on Java, intermediary B could be on .NET, intermediary C could be a mainframe, and the endpoint D could be some kind of SOAP-aware mobile device.

In the scope of this chapter and by using the samples, I'll show a number of scenarios based on a client, router, and an endpoint. A combination of clients and Web services written in both Java and .NET will be used to show that WS-Routing can be used regardless of the underlying technology. To demonstrate these scenarios, we'll use the WS-Routing capabilities of Microsoft Web Services Enhancements (WSE) 1.0 and GLUE version 4.0.1 from The Mind Electric.

Downloading and Installing Microsoft WSE

This sample assumes that Microsoft WSE (Web Services Enhancements) 1.0 Service Pack 1 has been installed. This software can be downloaded from *http://msdn.microsoft.com/webservices* and must be installed for the .NET portions of the sample to compile correctly. Additional information about downloading and installing the product can be found in the "Downloading and Installing Microsoft WSE" section of Chapter 13, "Web Services Interoperability, Part 1: Security."

Sample Code

The sample code in this chapter will show how WS-Routing can be used to configure a routing path for both a .NET and Java client, both of which will be calling a .NET and Java Web service.

For the Web services, we'll use a stock-pricing example, similar to the one shown in Chapter 11, "Asynchronous Interoperability, Part 4: BizTalk Server." This Web service offers a single method to return the price of a stock based on a given symbol.

```
public double getPrice(String ticker)
```

For example, a client could pass a ticker symbol for "TREY", and the Web service would return the latest price (for example, 14.45).

To show the routing elements of the sample, we will configure and use an intermediary that will reside between the client and server portions of the sample. This setup is shown in Figure 15-2.

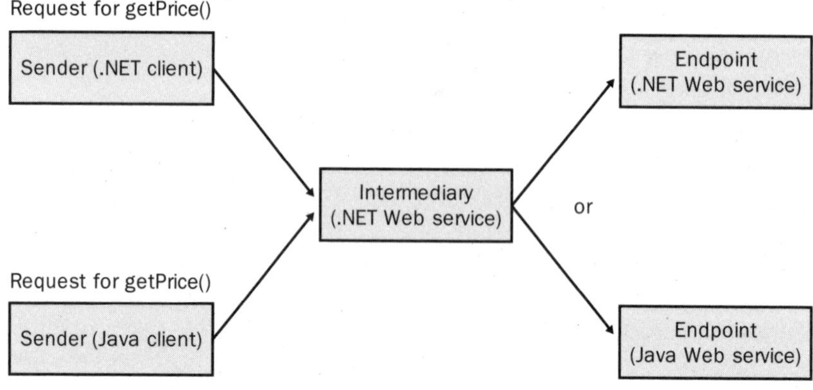

Figure 15-2 Message request and flow for sample code.

As we can see, both the .NET and Java clients will use the intermediary to reach either the .NET or Java Web service. (The Web service used will depend on the route taken.) The route will be configured by the client, and the intermediary itself will be hosted as a .NET Web service.

The return value (the price quote) will be passed back to the client by using a reverse route as shown in Figure 15-3.

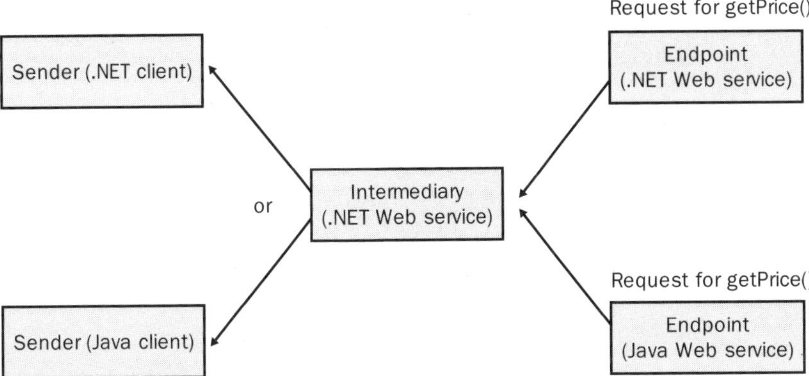

Figure 15-3 Message response and flow for sample code.

Setting Up the .NET Intermediary

The intermediary is configured as a .NET Web service and, as such, requires that a virtual directory be created. To create this virtual directory, launch Internet Information Services (IIS) Manager from the Start/Programs/Administrative Tools program group.

Within the administration tool, expand the tree and right-click the Default Web Site entry. Select New/Virtual Directory. For the alias of the virtual directory, enter **Router**. This alias is used by configuration files for both the .NET and Java clients. Click the Next button. For the directory, enter **C:\Interoperability\Samples\Advanced\WS-Routing\dotNET\Intermediary**. Click Next, and accept the rest of the defaults to complete the wizard.

The dotNET\Intermediary directory contains two files: Web.config and referralCache.config. Web.config is used to configure an *HttpHandler* that is going to process the routing request, shown in this section of the file:

```
<httpHandlers>
    <add verb="*" path="router.asmx"
        type="Microsoft.Web.Services.Routing.RoutingHandler,
              Microsoft.Web.Services, Version=1.0.0.0,
              Culture=neutral, PublicKeyToken=31bf3856ad364e35" />
</httpHandlers>
```

This means any request sent to *http://localhost/Router/router.asmx* will be processed by the *RoutingHandler* itself. As the handler deals only with SOAP requests, this can't be demonstrated through a browser.

The referralCache.config file isn't something we will be using in this sample, but it will be discussed in the "WS-Referral" section later in this chapter.

Once the virtual directory is created, the intermediary is ready to route messages.

Setting Up the .NET Web Service

To activate the .NET Web service, we will create a second virtual directory. Before creating this directory, compile the sample code in C:\Interoperability\Samples\Advanced\WS-Routing\dotNET\WebService. After this is done, use the same method shown in the previous section to create a virtual directory for this Web service. The alias of the virtual directory must be **dotNETPriceService**.

If you've run through the sample code outlined in Chapter 11, you might already have a virtual directory with this name. For this sample, you should delete the old virtual directory and re-create one using this new location. For the location of this virtual directory, use the folder containing the source (**C:\Interoperability\Samples\Advanced\WS-Routing\dotNET\WebService**).

Complete the steps in the wizard. After the virtual directory has been created, verify the Web service by browsing to *http://localhost/dotNETPriceService/PriceService.asmx*, as shown in Figure 15-4.

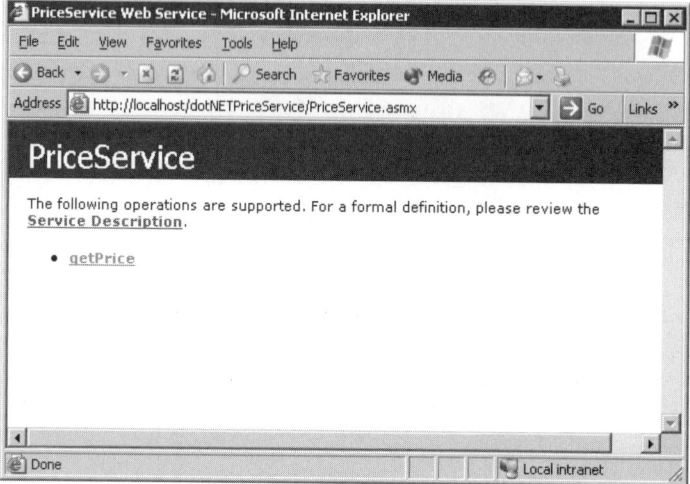

Figure 15-4 Testing the Pricing Web service by using Microsoft Internet Explorer.

To test the Web service, you can invoke the *getPrice* method by using the browser and specify a test parameter (WOOD, for example) to ensure that a valid value is returned.

Setting Up the Java Web Service

The Java Web service is a replica of the .NET Web service, offering stock prices based on the same list of ticker symbols. Using the same method and type names allows both the .NET and Java clients to easily "switch" between the two without using a separate proxy file.

To configure and run the Java Web service, navigate to the C:\Interoperability\Samples\Advanced\WS-Routing\Java\WebService directory. Use the Ant script to build and publish the Web service. The published Web Services Description Language (WSDL) can be verified at *http://localhost:8004/JavaPriceService/PriceService.wsdl.*

Running the .NET Client

We now have the two stock-price Web services configured, and we have an intermediary set up to correctly route messages. Let's now test them by using one of the clients.

The sample code for the .NET client can be found in the C:\Interoperability\Samples\Advanced\WS-Routing\dotNET\Client directory. We'll build the client, but before we run it, let's first look at how the code is going to work.

The proxy class used for both the .NET and Java Web service can be found in PriceService.cs. As with the other WSE clients in the previous two chapters, this class has been pregenerated using WSDL, the class now inherits from *WebServicesClientProtocol*, and a reference to the *Microsoft.Web.Services* namespace is included. Notice how the URL of the proxy is currently set to the .NET Pricing Web service. We'll be setting the URL and the route as part of the client, which will determine whether to keep the current .NET Web service reference or to use the Java Web service instead.

The client first creates a new reference to the Web service, as normal.

```
PriceService ps = new PriceService();
```

After this, the URL of the service is set. There are two options in the code—one for the Java Web service URL, and the other for the .NET Web service URL:

```
//ps.Url = "http://localhost:8004/JavaPriceService/PriceService";
ps.Url = "http://localhost/dotNETPriceService/PriceService.asmx";
```

As shown here, currently the URL is referencing the .NET Web service, with the reference to the Java Web service being commented out. This URL sets the end point of the route, and in this sample, it does not change during the lifetime of the call.

The route that the message will take will now be constructed. This is done by first obtaining the *SoapContext* of the Web service proxy request. With this context, we can then define a forward path (one that goes via the .NET intermediary) and ensure that the reverse path details are constructed when the message is routed.

```
SoapContext ctx = ps.RequestSoapContext;
ctx.Path.Fwd.Add(new Via(
    new Uri("http://localhost/Router/router.asmx")));
ctx.Path.Rev = new ViaCollection();
```

Finally, the call to the pricing Web service is made for a quote of a particular stock.

```
Console.WriteLine("Price of TREY = "+ps.getPrice("TREY"));
```

Build and run the sample code using the provided NAnt script. If all is successful, the price for the TREY stock will be returned.

```
Price of TREY = 9.35
```

To prove that routing really is working in this sample, we can enable tracing at the .NET intermediary. Doing this will show the messages being sent from the .NET client as they are handled by the router and forwarded to the .NET Web service.

Tracing is enabled on the .NET intermediary by modifying the Web.config file in the C:\Interoperability\Samples\Advanced\WS-Routing\dotNET\Intermediary directory. Within this configuration file is a line that enables/disables tracing:

```
<trace enabled="false" input="input.log" output="output.log"/>
```

Set the trace enabled setting to *true*, and rerun the sample code. This will create an input.log file for the messages received by the intermediary and an output.log file for those sent to the Web service.

> **Note** If after you run the sample the log files are not created, check the permissions of the dotNET\Intermediary directory. Ensure that the ASPNET account (or the account the .NET Web service is running under) has read and write permissions to this directory. You can double-check this by looking at entries generated in the application log.

In the input.log file, we can observe two messages, both wrapped in *<soap:Envelope>* elements. The first message is from the Web services client to the router.

In this first message, the *<wsrp:action>* field is the fully qualified name of the Web service method call. This is the request from the client.

```
<wsrp:action>
    http://www.microsoft.com/interoperability/ws-routing/getPrice
</wsrp:action>
```

Next, the *<wsrp:to>* element indicates the intended destination for the Web service call. In this case, it is an endpoint, which is the .NET PriceService Web service.

```
<wsrp:to>
    http://localhost/dotNETPriceService/PriceService.asmx
</wsrp:to>
```

The *<wsrp:fwd>* element contains the route, which for our code sample is the address of the intermediary:

```
<wsrp:fwd>
    <wsrp:via>http://localhost/Router/router.asmx</wsrp:via>
</wsrp:fwd>
```

Notice also how the *<wsrp:rev>* element is currently empty:

```
<wsrp:rev />
```

Because the message has not passed through any routers yet, no reverse path defined. The final part of the header is a timestamp. This contains a creation and expiration time. (The expiration time can be adjusted on the client.)

```
<wsu:Timestamp
    xmlns:wsu="http://schemas.xmlsoap.org/ws/2002/07/utility">
    <wsu:Created>2003-05-02T04:48:26Z</wsu:Created>
    <wsu:Expires>2003-05-02T04:53:26Z</wsu:Expires>
</wsu:Timestamp>
```

Now open the output.log file. In this log file, there are again two messages. The first message is the one the router constructed for the .NET Web service. Again, we have the timestamp as part of the header, but the router has included a *<wsu:Received>* element, which indicates where the message was received and the type of delay the message was subject to (between the client sending and the router receiving).

```
<wsu:Received
    Actor="http://localhost/Router/router.asmx"
    Delay="696">2003-05-02T04:48:26Z
</wsu:Received>
```

This delay is useful in multihop environments, as (with a little additional logic) routes for Web services could potentially be optimized based on network traffic or utilization.

For the route, we now see that the *<wsrp:to>* address remains the same, and this time there is no *<wsrp:fwd>* path.

```
<wsrp:to>
    http://localhost/dotNETPriceService/PriceService.asmx
</wsrp:to>
```

Because the end of the path has been reached, the message can now be sent directly to the Web service. We can observe, however, that the router has created (or added to) the reverse path.

```
<wsrp:rev>
  <wsrp:via>http://localhost/Router/router.asmx</wsrp:via>
</wsrp:rev>
```

The *<wsrp:via>* element means that once a reply is received from the Web service, it will be first passed back to the router (which then has to work out how to send it back to the originating client).

Let's go back to the input.log file. The second message (again, contained within the *<soap:Envelope>*) is the response that comes back from the .NET Web service. This message contains the *<getPriceResult>*, which is the price of the stock. Notice how there are no *<wsrp>* elements in this second message. Because this is a request/response type of call (using HTTP), the connection from the router to the Web service is never dropped. You can imagine, however, that in a solution based on a more asynchronous model this path would play a greater role.

Finally, let's return to the second message in the output.log file. This message is a forward of the result from the Web service, with a timestamp header to indicate the delay between the message being delivered to the Web service and a result being returned.

If you have reached this stage, congratulations! You have now sent and traced your first message using WS-Routing. Let's switch the path so that the .NET client now routes to the Java Web service. Doing so is easy, and it involves editing the Client.cs file in the dotNET\Client subdirectory.

Within this file, comment out the URL for the .NET Web service and uncomment the URL for the Java Web service. After doing this, the two URL lines should look as follows:

```
ps.Url = "http://localhost:8004/JavaPriceService/PriceService";
//ps.Url = "http://localhost/dotNETPriceService/PriceService.asmx";
```

Save this file, and rebuild the client. Also ensure that the Java Web service is running and is able to accept requests. Rerunning the client shows the same result, this time delivered from the Java Web service.

```
Price of TREY = 9.35
```

Examining the input.log and output.log files reveals a very similar trace to the .NET Web service, except now the Java Web service is being called.

Running the Java Client

Let's now take a look at the Java client. Looking at the main class (Client.java, which is found in C:\Interoperability\Samples\Advanced\WS-Routing\Java\Client), we can see that as with the .NET client, we have two instances of the URL:

```
String url
    = "http://localhost:8004/JavaPriceService/PriceService.wsdl";
//String url
//    = http://localhost/dotNETPriceService/PriceService.asmx?WSDL";
```

In this instance, the URL to the Java Web service is uncommented and will be used first.

To set the route for the client, a *ProxyContext* (*electric.glue.context.ProxyContext*) is used. The *ProxyContext* class specifies an *addForwardIntermediary* method, which sets the forwards as appropriate.

```
ProxyContext context = new ProxyContext();
context.addForwardIntermediary(
    "http://127.0.0.1/Router/router.asmx");
```

With this context, a new instance of the Web service proxy is then created, and the *getPrice* method is called to initiate the call.

```
IPriceService priceService
    = (IPriceService)Registry.bind(url,
        IPriceService.class,context);

double price = priceService.getPrice("WOOD");
System.out.println("Price of WOOD = "+price);
```

Build and run the sample using the provided Ant script. This time, using the GLUE libraries, the Java client will compose a Web service request to the Java Web service, but with the path containing the .NET intermediary. If you look at the recent entries in the input.log file generated by the router, you will observe the following:

```
<rp:to>http://localhost:8004/JavaPriceService/PriceService</rp:to>
<rp:fwd>
    <rp:via>http://127.0.0.1/Router/router.asmx</rp:via>
</rp:fwd>
```

As shown, the actual destination is the address of the Java Web service, yet the router remains as the .NET intermediary.

With the GLUE libraries, one useful logging feature is the ability to log the incoming or outgoing SOAP requests to the console. On either the Java Web service or client, this can be enabled by using the following line:

```
electric.util.log.Log.startLogging("SOAP");
```

Given that both the Web services used the same method and return the same results, logging Web service invocations can also be a neat way of finding out whether the result is coming back from the .NET or Java Web service.

Using the Same Proxy File

In both the .NET and Java client, you might have noticed that a single proxy file was used for both the .NET and Java Web services. On the client, doing this allows us to use `ps.URL = {…}` to easily switch between the two.

Ensure that both Web services are compliant to the Web Services Interoperability Organization (WS-I) basic profile by using document/literal-type encoding. For the .NET Web service, this will be the default. For the Java Web service, this is set manually in the WS-Routing example by adding a call to *context.setDocumentStyle* in the Publish.java file. By modifying the GLUE global config.xml file, this change can be applied to other projects.

Using the same Web services proxy file is something we haven't covered in previous chapters, but that's a topic very applicable to interoperability scenarios using WS-Routing. To enable using the same proxy file, I always recommend three steps:

1. **Use Doc/Literal for both Web services.**
2. **Agree on the target namespace and element names.** To share the same proxy file, the target namespace and element names within the WSDL must be the same. For the .NET Web service, the namespace is set using the *WebService* attribute at the start of the class. The element names automatically use the names of the parameters in the *WebMethods*. For the Java Web service, the namespace is set in the Publish.java file. The context is used to set the target namespace with the following line: `context.setProperty("targetNamespace","namespace")`

To ensure that the element names match the name of the parameters, the Web service must be run in debug mode. In the WS-Routing sample, this requirement is set in the Ant build.xml script.

3. **Allow considerations for more complex data types.** In the WS-Routing example, primitive types were used for the *getPrice* Web method. The method accepted a *String* and returned a *Double*—both values easily map to the equivalents in XSD. If you are looking to used a shared proxy file, consider the types of data exposed in the WSDL. Although both the .NET and Java type might have equivalents in XSD, their implementation is sometimes slightly different (and therefore would require a little manual intervention). A good example of this was with the *ArrayList*, as demonstrated in Chapter 5, "Connectivity with XML Web Services, Part 1." The *ArrayList* is returned by default with the .NET Web services, whereas an *.elements* field has to be called for the equivalent in GLUE.

WS-Referral

In the sample code, we've seen how WS-Routing can be used to specify a route from a Web services client to the service itself. One observation you might have made is that in all the examples, the route was always defined by the client. By configuring the SOAP context, both the .NET and Java client specified the address of the intermediary and the address of the destination (endpoint). Had the samples shown multiple intermediaries, these would have had to be included here also.

While having the client define the route works for the samples, you'll encounter a number of cases where the route is not always known. If we revisit the load-balancing example outlined at the start of this chapter, we'll see that it's likely the route to the final Web service is not going to be known by the client—instead, it will be determined by the intermediaries.

To enable a more dynamic approach for routing, there is a complimentary specification called WS-Referral. The specification, also created by Microsoft, and released at the same time as WS-Routing, outlines methods for inserting, deleting, and querying the routing entries in a SOAP router. The document itself, located at *http://msdn.microsoft.com/library/default.asp?url=/library/en-us/dnglobspec/html/ws-referral.asp*, shows the format that a SOAP router can use for implementing referrals.

For example, the route of the sample code, as shown in Figure 15-5, is currently determined by the client.

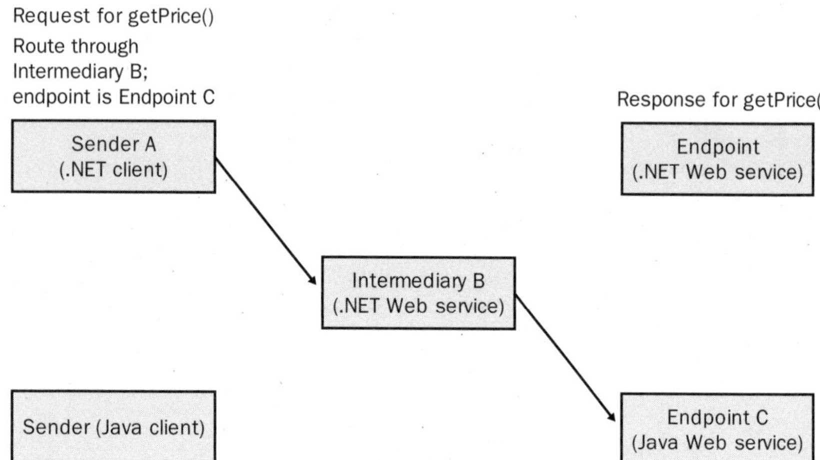

Figure 15-5 Current route used by the sample code.

With WS-Referral, the intermediary (B) uses a referral configuration file, which is used to match destinations with the next route or set of routes the message should take. This referral configuration might look similar to the following:

```
<r:ref xmlns:r="http://schemas.xmlsoap.org/ws/2001/10/referral">
    <r:for>
        <r:prefix>http://www.my.org/c</r:prefix>
    </r:for>
    <r:if/>
    <r:go>
        <r:via>http://www.another.org/route.asmx</r:via>
    </r:go>
    <r:refId>mailto:samples@microsoft.com</r:refId>
</r:ref>
```

Here, any request for the destination that matches the *<r:prefix>* element causes the router to add an additional path—to route the message through D first. Figure 15-6 shows how this would look as implemented with our sample.

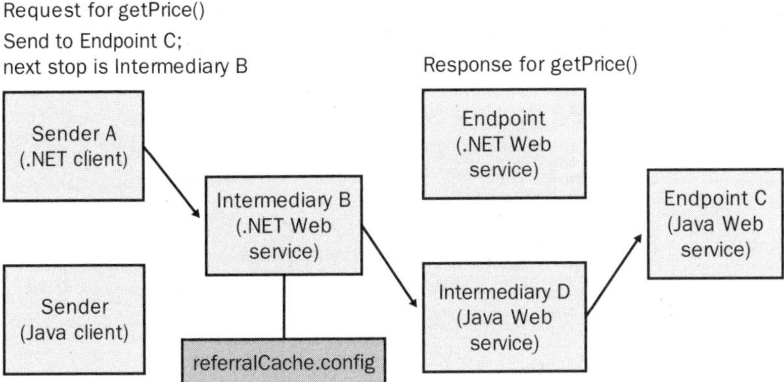

Figure 15-6 How WS-Referral can dynamically set the route by using the referralCache.config file.

Notice also that the client requires only the address of the destination (C) and the address of the first router (B). The client can be oblivious to any additional routes that might be inserted or deleted once the router has processed the message.

With the *<r:if />* statement in the referral, the router can determine the path based on a set of conditions. While these conditions are relatively open-ended, the WS-Referral specification does define two—a TTL (Time To Live) and an invalidation. The TTL can be particularly useful in a situation where certain messages had to reach the destination in a given timeframe.

The sample code itself does not show WS-Referral in action, but the directory of the .NET intermediary (C:\Interoperability\Samples\Advanced\WS-Routing\dotNET\Intermediary) does contain a sample referralCache.config file, which can be enabled by adjusting the Web.config file in the same directory. If you wish to do this, I would recommend first familiarizing yourself with the samples that ship with Microsoft WSE 1.0 to appreciate how WS-Referral is implemented.

WS-Addressing

A book showing the latest specifications wouldn't be complete if it wasn't out of date in some way or another, and this book is certainly no exception. While WS-Routing has been available since October 2001, and samples are available to show interoperability between .NET and Java, it is in the process of being deprecated by another specification. WS-Addressing is a specification that was released in March 2003 and was coauthored by BEA, IBM, and Microsoft. A copy of the released specification can be found at *http://msdn.microsoft.com/webservices/default.aspx?pull=/library/en-us/dnglobspec/html/ws-addressing.asp*.

WS-Addressing expands upon the WS-Routing and WS-Referral specifications by providing more support for faults and exceptions, a representation of the routing headers as an XML Information Set (Infoset), and additional security considerations that could not be addressed with the previous versions of the specifications. To include this security support, WS-Addressing has a dependency on WS-Policy. To achieve .NET and J2EE interoperability using WS-Addressing, you will ultimately need an implementation of WS-Policy for Java.

Summary

The goal of this chapter was to provide insight into routing for Web services, show what can be achieved today with a combination of .NET and Java services, and briefly discuss related specifications.

I find the implementation of routing for Web services to be an intriguing area. As Web services are increasingly used in conjunction with each other—as opposed to being used as standalone entities—I see routing as being a key part of enabling the technology. Routing and forwarding is something we can already see in the way HTML content is delivered through proxy servers and firewalls. As the adoption of Web services increases and a standard for routing emerges, I believe we will see similar support for Web services, too.

16

Interoperability Futures

In the previous 15 chapters, we covered a significant amount of content and a number of topics for achieving interoperability between .NET and Java. In this final chapter, I want to recap some of the lessons we have learned and the goals of the book, and take a look at how interoperability between .NET and Java could evolve.

Topics and Goals of the Book

Part I, "Getting Started," introduced some of the fundamentals of .NET and Java interoperability, including business requirements for interoperability and three common scenarios. In Part I, we also investigated data exchange between the two platforms. After defining the term *point-to-point interoperability*, in Part II, "Interoperability Technologies: Point to Point," we looked at two technologies that could immediately bridge the communication gap between .NET and Java. These technologies were .NET Remoting and XML Web services. For each technology, I showed a number of permutations of how interoperability could work—for example, how .NET Remoting could be used to expose both an Enterprise JavaBean (EJB) and a component hosted through Component Services, and how both .NET and Java clients could use Universal Description, Discovery, and Integration (UDDI) to locate Web services within an organization.

Part III, "Interoperability Technologies: Resource Tier," covered a broad range of interoperability topics related to the resource tier. After covering how to create a shared database, the remainder of Part III concentrated on asynchronous interoperability. A number of options were shown for connecting either a .NET or Java client to either Microsoft Message Queuing (MSMQ) or WebSphere MQ. Toward the end of Part III, we also saw how technologies such as the

MSMQ-MQSeries Bridge and BizTalk Server could both aid in bridging these message queues and provide additional value. And Part IV, "Advanced Interoperability," is focused on advanced interoperability. This part started with a discussion of the benefits of interoperability at the presentation tier—namely, sharing session state and authentication, with the samples showing examples of each. The last three chapters have focused on the latest specifications for Web services. For each of the areas—Security, Binary Attachments, and Routing—sample code was shown to demonstrate that although the specifications and ideas are relatively new, implementations can be achieved using the right tools and processes.

I have had three goals for each chapter and for this book as a whole: to thoroughly cover the topic, to maintain a neutral stance regarding .NET and Java, and to provide sample code.

Thoroughly Cover the Topic

I really wanted to show as many examples, requirements, and permutations of interoperability between .NET and Java as possible, and to do this in such a way that would provoke thought, and lead to a number of prototypes and, ultimately, implementations.

For the technical content, I wanted to make a distinction between point-to-point and resource-tier interoperability, and highlight them accordingly. Often papers and articles that explain interoperability cover only one of the topics (for example, how Web services can enable a particular interoperability scenario or how to connect .NET to a particular message-queuing product). I considered it important to give both fair coverage.

Maintain Neutrality Regarding .NET and Java

My second goal was to maintain a neutral stance throughout the book. There is a lot of debate in the industry about the pros and cons of .NET and Java. Developers in general tend to be a religious bunch, and organizations can also be guilty of following one vendor or standard when a mix can often pay dividends. (See the "Technology-Aligned Development" section in Chapter 2, "Business Requirements for Interoperability," for more details.)

What I've strived for is a balanced view of the two platforms. While I have my own opinions about which technology is more suitable for a particular task, the goal of the book has been to provide an impartial view of each technology and to show how interoperability between the two is possible.

One decision pertinent to this goal was the choice of the Web services vendor for the Java platform. When I was mapping out the content for the book and the areas that I wanted to show, it struck me that choosing the correct Web services stack for Java would be crucial for many of the chapters.

I had a number of options. I could have selected a particular J2EE Application Server vendor and used its Web services toolkit. This might have worked well for the application server in question, but I didn't want the book to alienate any readers who had chosen another. I could have also selected the open-source option, Apache Axis. The Axis stack could have worked given that it's independent of an application server, but I found the implementation too verbose for the samples and topics that I wanted to present. Also, at the time of this writing, it was unclear whether the toolkit supported the latest Web services specifications (for example, WS-Security, WS-Routing, and DIME).

This left me looking at third-party solutions. Out of the many products available, I chose to work with GLUE from The Mind Electric. (The technical reasons for this decision can be found in Chapter 5, "Connectivity with XML Web Services, Part 1.") In my opinion, GLUE takes an elegant approach with its implementation, and it follows a logic similar to a number of APIs also found in .NET. When we examined the code samples, you might have noticed how the flow, logic, and structure of the code of the two are very similar. This similarity offers many benefits for developers who work with both. In addition, The Mind Electric has a great underlying platform with Electric XML (which was used for the serialization examples in Chapter 3, "Exchanging Data Between .NET and Java") and appears to be very forward looking—most notably, by being one of the first vendors to adopt some of the latest Web services specifications shown in the previous three chapters.

Whatever Java Web services stack you select, I hope you find that many of the samples, lessons, and recommendations outlined in this book remain applicable.

Provide Sample Code

As you might have noticed, many chapters have been built around the sample code that ships on the accompanying CD. This approach comes from projects and presentations that I undertake, where I tend to be as pragmatic as possible.

I've sat through many presentations on the future and goals of Web services, industry standards, and new products. And while I really applaud all the efforts in these areas, I am naturally inquisitive to see how things work in code. My goal in this book, therefore, was to show as much working sample code as possible. Reading about how technology works is great, but taking examples and learning from them by running them in your own environment provides more benefit than reading alone.

Time for More?

As you look back through the chapters and review these goals, I hope you find that the book has shown that interoperability between .NET and Java today is certainly possible. If you've tried any of the sample code, you might well have seen small adjustments and recommendations that were necessary to get everything working.

I think this is very emblematic of the industry as it is today. Interoperability between .NET and Java is definitely a reality, but now and again small tweaks have to be implemented. As we move toward agreed-upon standards and more mature products, I think we'll all see a dramatic improvement in interoperability.

From a technology perspective, we've covered a lot of areas. There are a few topics that didn't get into the book (such as COM and Java interoperability), but generally we succeeded in covering a broad spectrum of scenarios and challenges.

So, given more time and space, what would have I included? I would have liked to have included a section on how all the different topics presented throughout the book can work together. In many presentations I make, I demonstrate how Microsoft Outlook can connect to a server-side Customer Relationship Management (CRM) system, which is based on J2EE. The CRM server-side application uses a combination of Entity and Session Enterprise JavaBeans (EJBs) for customer records. These EJBs are exposed via Web services by using GLUE, and WS-Security is applied to ensure that only certain records are available to authenticated Web services clients. The Microsoft Outlook client uses a .NET add-in, written in C#, and Microsoft WSE 1.0 to consume the exposed Java Web services. To connect to the CRM system, the user clicks a new contacts folder within his mailbox. This in turn prompts the user for a certificate, which is stored on a smart card. When the user provides a valid certificate, the EJBs are called across the Web services layer, and the records are returned and displayed as new contact items within Outlook.

This type of end-to-end interoperability—putting the pieces together that have been presented in this book—has the potential for creating very compelling solutions. Going back to the duck analogy that was used in the introduction of this book, I tried to show that the user experience is no different than it is when using Microsoft Outlook every day. When users use the add-in, they are typically unaware that the CRM is based on J2EE, how Web services are providing interoperability, or what methods were used to extract the data. Overall, I believe this is a key message to convey.

Predicting the Future

As I look at the current state of interoperability and the possibilities and opportunities that exist, a number of areas stand out as critical for enabling true interoperability within organizations. These areas are discussed in the following sections.

Acceptance and Agreement of Standards

Within the area of Web services, the acceptance and agreement of standards is currently ongoing and will likely continue to evolve at a fast pace. In the current market, we can already see widespread participation in the WS-I (Web Services Interoperability) organization. The success of these efforts will drive and promote more standards between more vendors, making interoperability between diverse products more of a reality.

I also welcome the coauthoring of these standards. Although a single vendor can easily announce new specifications, it's reassuring to hear proposals from a consortium of vendors. This type of cooperation not only helps the credibility of the specification, but typically also results in a multiplatform implementation and a quicker rate of adoption.

Vendor Adoption of Standards

As standards become accepted, we'll see tighter coupling with products and services from all vendors. For example, with many samples in this book, we have had to download toolkits, run command-line operations, and in some cases apply manual alterations and fixes to get the code working. Moving forward, I predict these toolkits will become simpler, more integrated, and possibly shipped with both the platform and application servers. The command-line operations will also be replaced by more IDE-aware tasks (for example, the ability to right-click a component, create a Web service, and apply WS-Security and WS-Routing by choosing settings from a dialog box).

Competition at the Implementation Level

A market that is driven by standards will see more and more competition at the implementation level. If solutions demand interoperability, creating and using a proprietary way of data exchange will no longer be an option. As this is the case, I believe vendors will start to compete more at the implementation level—making more robust platforms, more robust application servers, and slicker development environments to differentiate themselves.

Architecting Interoperability

The majority of development products today tend to be geared toward a single technology, be it .NET or Java. Typically an IDE will allow components from only one platform to be created. This paradigm has started to change—with many IDEs allowing external Web services to be referenced or multiple projects to be created based on different languages—but I wonder if at the architectural level this is enough. As a developer, I might want a more complete view of my application. For example, I might want to show the components that have been developed for .NET, the protocols I am using, and how this integrates with my Java/WebSphere MQ implementation.

One key element of this concept would be to support debugging between the two platforms, although I think that's a long way off. The ability to debug a component on .NET, for that component to call a Web service in Java, and for the debugger to attach to that process makes for an interesting set of possibilities.

Management, Operations, and Deployment

Management, operations, and deployment of interoperable solutions is something that needs addressing. Today, the ability to deploy an application that consists of multiple parts is difficult. Take those multiple parts and move them to different platforms, and the problems become exponentially difficult. Once the deployments are configured, you are faced with the question of how to manage the uptime of the application or service, version control, and upgrading of the components.

Within this area, I believe we'll see much more focus on Web services management in the near future. We are already seeing a number of companies creating offerings in this area, and I predict this will not only grow but will encompass the management of .NET and Java Web services in a single product.

Shift to Loosely Coupled Thinking

We've all read about how Web services enable loose coupling from a technology perspective, but I think building interoperable solutions requires a more loosely coupled approach from a thought perspective also. Although current technology allows for a loosely coupled approach, it's still possible to use it to unintentionally build a tightly coupled, RPC-based model.

We need to think more in terms of coarsely grained services within the enterprise—all of which interact with each other—and less about applications that merely fit a purpose or task. If companies adopt this services-based approach, the orchestration of those services will define very flexible and reusable applications.

With this goal, interoperability then becomes much more of an enabling technology, as opposed to something used solely to connect applications together.

Desktop Integration

Finally, many samples in the book have shown standalone clients or a Web-based experience for the user. As mentioned previously, I believe that integration with existing Microsoft Office–based components, operating system components, or both is something that is vastly underused and undervalued.

For example, with Microsoft Office I already have a proven, reliable interface for managing financial data (it's called Excel). Why not leverage the power of this application by using Web services and interoperability to connect with my server-side data. Granted, it might not be as exciting as creating something anew in ASP.NET or an alternative smart client technology. From my experiences of watching users understand and use—with little or no training—applications based on the concept of interoperability, I can attest to the amazing positive impact this type of desktop integration has.

Summary

With that, we've reached the end of the book. I hope the topics and goals of the book have been fulfilled, and to that end I've highlighted in this chapter some areas I see as pertinent to continuing the interoperability between .NET and Java.

In summary, I hope that every reader who foresees a requirement to build solutions that interoperate between .NET and Java benefits in some way from the content and samples we've covered.

Index

B

C

F

J

N

Q

R

T

U

V

W

Simon Guest

As a member of the Microsoft .NET Enterprise Architecture Team in Redmond, Washington, Simon specializes in enterprise interoperability and integration. This includes interoperability with J2EE applications, enterprise messaging, XML Web services interoperability, and end-to-end integration with desktop and smart client products.

In his tenure at Microsoft, Simon has worked on a wide variety of interoperability projects in the financial, medical, and telecommunications sectors and has been a frequent contributor to the Microsoft Developer Network (MSDN). Simon has also presented at numerous Strategic Architect Forums (SAFs); Partner Architect Summits; and Envision, MGB, and TechEd conferences.

Prior to joining Microsoft in 2001, Simon worked for an application service provider (ASP) in California and a leading systems integrator (SI) in London. Previously, Simon worked for a top-five law firm in London and as a systems analyst in semiconductor manufacturing.

Simon holds a Higher National Certificate (HNC) in Software Engineering from Plymouth College and a master's degree in IT Security from the University of Westminster (London).

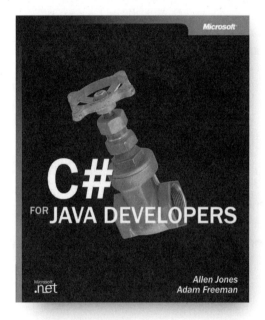

Proof of Purchase

Use this page as proof of purchase if participating in a promotion or rebate offer on this title. Proof of purchase must be used in conjunction with other proof(s) of payment such as your dated sales receipt—see offer details.

Microsoft® .NET and J2EE Interoperability Toolkit

0-7356-1922-0

____

CUSTOMER NAME

Microsoft Press, PO Box 97017, Redmond, WA 98073-9830